THE JOURNAL OF MEDIEVAL LATIN

THE JOURNAL OF MEDIEVAL LATIN

Editor
Greti Dinkova-Bruun, *Pontifical Institute of Mediaeval Studies*

Review Editor
Cillian O'Hogan, *University of Toronto*

Founding Editor

Michael W. Herren, *York University* and *University of Toronto*

Associate Editors

Alexander André	University of Toronto
Robert Getz	University of Toronto
Andrew Hicks	Cornell University
Bernice M. Kaczynski	McMaster University
John Magee	University of Toronto
Tristan Major	Qatar University
Jean Meyers	University of Montpellier
Stephen Pelle	University of Toronto
David Townsend	University of Toronto
Gernot Wieland	University of British Columbia

Advisory Board

Walter Berschin	University of Heidelberg
James P. Carley	York University
Paolo Chiesa	University of Milan
Michael Lapidge	Clare College Cambridge
Andy Orchard	Pembroke College Oxford
Danuta Shanzer	University of Vienna
Brian Stock	University of Toronto
Jan M. Ziolkowski	Harvard University

Publications of *The Journal of Medieval Latin*
General Editors: Michael W. Herren, Robert Getz, Alexander Andrée

The Journal of Medieval Latin is published annually by Brepols. For editorial policies and submission instructions, see the last page of the volume.

THE
JOURNAL
OF
MEDIEVAL LATIN

Volume 30
2020

BREPOLS

© 2020 BrepolsPublishers n.v. Turnhout, Belgium

All rights reserved. No part of this book may be reproduced, stored in a retrieval system, or transmitted, in any form or by any means, electronic, mechanical, photocopying, recording, or otherwise, without the prior permission of the publisher.

D/2020/0095/77
ISBN 978-2-503-58736-3
DOI 10.1484/J.JML.5.119951
Printed in the E.U. on acid-free paper.

Contents

- vii   Greti Dinkova-Bruun: *Thirty Years of The Journal of Medieval Latin*
- ix   In memoriam Édouard Jeauneau (1924–2019)
- xvii   In memoriam Richard Sharpe (1954–2020)
- xxiii   In memoriam Peter Dronke (1934–2020)

ARTICLES

1   EVAN WILSON
Stephen of Ripon's *Vita S. Wilfridi*: Genre, Political Theory and Historical Representation in the Early Middle Ages

41   BENJAMIN GARSTAD
Charlemagne's Failure of Charity in Ps. Turpin's *Chronicle* and Beyond

67   JASON O'RORKE
On the Date, Authorship, and Newly Discovered Old Irish Material in the *Ars Ambrosiana*

85   A.G. RIGG (†)
Clerical Concubines: Three Poems

147   DAVID A. TRAILL
Payen Bolotin's Targeting of the Tironensians and Cistercians in his *De Falsis Heremitis*

183   ISABELA GRIGORAȘ
Breuiarium Artis grammaticae Alcuini: Edition and Study

227   ÅSLAUG OMMUNDSEN
A New Manuscript Source for the Legend of Saint Clement in Denmark

257   JONATHAN RUBIN
The Manuscript Tradition of Burchard of Mount Sion's *Descriptio Terre Sancte*

287   ANDREW KRAEBEL
English Hebraism and Hermeneutic History: The Psalter Prologues and Epilogue of Henry Cossey, OFM

369   FRANCESCO STELLA
Latin Poetic Stories About Muhammad and Their Stylistic Network

REVIEW ESSAY

399 TRISTAN MAJOR
Editions of Texts for Teaching Medieval Latin: Martha Bayless, *Fifteen Medieval Latin Parodies*, Donka D. Markus, *Reading Medieval Latin with the Legend of Barlaam and Josaphat*, and Andrew Rabin and Liam Felsen, *The Disputatio puerorum: A Ninth-Century Monastic Instructional Text*

REVIEWS

411 V. ALICE TYRRELL. *Merovingian Letters and Letter Writers*. (Bronwen Neil and Catherine Rosbrook)

413 JOSHUA BYRON SMITH. *Walter Map and the Matter of Britain*. (Dylan Wilkerson)

416 VENETIA BRIDGES. *Medieval Narratives of Alexander the Great: Transnational Texts in England and France*. (Maureen Boulton)

419 SARAH B. LYNCH. *Elementary and Grammar Education in Late Medieval France*. (Hedwig Gwosdek)

422 PAULINA TARASKIN. *Reading Horace's Lyric: A Late Tenth-Century Annotated Manuscript from Bavaria (British Library, Harley 2724)*. (Sinéad O'Sullivan)

424 *Hugonis de Sancto Victore De Oratione Dominica; De Septem Donis Spiritus Sancti*, ed. Francesco Siri, CCCM 276. (David Foley)

429 INDEX OF MANUSCRIPTS, VOLUME 30

Cover Image: Toronto, Library of the Pontifical Institute of Mediaeval Studies, MS Bergendal 1 (a. 1329), fol. 1r. The codex contains the *Speculum sanctorale*, *Cronica imperatorum*, and *Cathologus summarum pontificum* of Bernard Gui, OP (1261/1262–1331). The historiated initial shows Bernard presenting the volume to Pope John XXII.

The editors wish to acknowledge the University of Toronto, the Pontifical Institute of Mediaeval Studies, and the Centre for Medieval Studies for their continuing support of *The Journal of Medieval Latin*.

Thirty Years of *The Journal of Medieval Latin*

Greti Dinkova-Bruun

This issue celebrates the thirtieth anniversary of the founding of *The Journal of Medieval Latin* by a group of Canadian scholars with the aim of fostering the study of medieval Latin language and literature. Since its inception in 1991, *JMLat* has appeared annually, reaching a steadily larger readership also through the contribution of our publisher Brepols which has played an important role in promoting the journal internationally. In its three decades, *JMLat* has published some 281 research articles (12 in French), 10 review essays, and 357 book reviews. In addition, it has included 23 obituaries of leading authorities in the field of medieval Latin studies, among them Bernhard Bischoff, Dag Norbert, Leonard E. Boyle, Vivien Law, Virginia Brown, Giovanni Orlandi, Claudio Leonardi, Paul Gerhardt Schmidt, Karsten Friis-Jensen, Paul Meyvaert, A.G. Rigg, and, most recently, Richard Sharpe. Among the journal's issues, volumes 17 and 18 (encompassing 54 articles in five languages) represent the Proceedings of the Fifth International Congress of Medieval Latin Studies ("Interpreting Latin Texts in the Middle Ages") held in Toronto in 2006. Each year, the journal also proudly publishes a revised version of the lecture given in memory of J.R. O'Donnell, a Basilian priest who was one of the founding members of the Pontifical Institute of Mediaeval Studies. The series, established in 1992, boasts a list of eminent speakers on a range of traditional and groundbreaking subjects.

The Journal of Medieval Latin is known for containing numerous, often extensive critical editions of medieval Latin poetry and prose across a variety of genres and styles, covering the entire span of the medieval period. The majority of these editions are *editiones principes*, while some are revised and improved versions of previously published texts. Many of the 83 Latin editions are accompanied by English translations, but the journal also contains free-standing translations, in prose and verse, of significant, unusual, or engaging texts. All editions and translations are accompanied by a detailed textual apparatus, a comprehensive accounting of sources, and commentary. A few articles contain editions of Old English, Greek, Hebrew, and medieval Czech texts and glosses.

In 1997, the journal established its publications series: the inaugural volume, Richard Sharpe's *A Handlist of the Latin Writers of Great Britain and Ireland before 1540*, has become an indispensable tool for all scholars working in Latin manuscript studies. Since then 13 further volumes have appeared, with the most recent in 2020.

Three editors have guided the journal over the decades. Founding editor Michael W. Herren (York University and University of Toronto) served as general editor for twenty years, from the first issue in 1991 through volume 20 in 2010. Gernot Wieland

(University of British Columbia) took over with volume 21 (2011) and continued as editor for six years, after which the responsibility was transferred to the present editor with volume 27 (2017). Under Gernot's leadership, the cover and typesetting of the journal changed, and each article was supplemented with an abstract in English for volumes 21–23 (2011–2013) and in English and French for volumes 24–26 (2014–2016). The present editor has continued the practice of providing bilingual abstracts, while refining the layout of the journal and in 2018 introducing an index of the manuscripts mentioned in each volume.

The work of the journal's general editors has been supported and enhanced by review editors Bernice Kaczynski (McMaster University) for the years 1991–2010, Greti Dinkova-Bruun (PIMS) for 2011–2016, Alexander Andrée (University of Toronto) for 2017–2019, and Cillian O'Hogan (University of Toronto) from 2020 onwards, as well as by a knowledgeable board of associate editors and a growing panel of peer reviewers. From its very first volume to its most recent, *JMLat* has been typeset by Ross Arthur (York University), whose expertise, dedication, and generosity the editorial board acknowledges with gratitude.

As *The Journal of Medieval Latin* enters its fourth decade, is seems fair to say that it has established itself as one among a handful of internationally leading journals for scholarly work on medieval Latin. Over the years, *JMLat* has matured and widened its reach, preserving its identity as a forum for traditional philological scholarship, while engaging with innovative trends in the humanities in general and medieval studies in particular. The editorial board continues to encourage submissions that expand the canon of medieval authors, texts, and genres, and hopes that its commitment to promoting and expanding the journal's mission will serve generations of scholars and students to come.[1]

---

[1] All volumes of the *JMLat* are available on Brepols Online, and volumes 1–24 (1991–2014) are also available on JSTOR. The editors can be contacted through the journal's official website: https://medievallatin.utoronto.ca/, where also the full lists of the O'Donnell lectures and the publications of the journal can be accessed.

In Memoriam Édouard Jeauneau (1924–2019)

In 1952 an aspiring French scholar and recently ordained priest, then only twenty-eight, made first contact with the Pontifical Institute of Mediaeval Studies (PIMS), which was to become his academic home and part-time residence twenty-three years later. Fr. Édouard Jeauneau (1924–2019) was then professeur de philosophie at the Grand-Séminaire de Chartres and was just embarking upon his first studies of the "School of Chartres," which would later be anthologized in his first essay collection, *"Lectio philosophorum": Recherches sur l'École de Chartres*.[1] The occasion for this first contact was, fittingly enough, Thierry of Chartres's *Heptateucon*, a compendium on the seven liberal arts that had been contained in MSS 497–498 of the Bibliothèque municipale de Chartres and was tragically destroyed on 26 May 1944 in a bombardment by the Allies. PIMS had procured a microfilm before the war, a copy of which was returned to Chartres in 1953 at Fr. Jeauneau's request (via Bishop Mgr Raoul-Octave-Marie-Jean Harscouët).[2] Fifty-five years later, in the lead essay of his third and final scholastic anthology – *"Tendenda vela": Excursions littéraires et digressions philosophiques à travers le Moyen Âge* – Fr. Jeauneau recounts this story as a personal aside in his remarks on the theme of *translatio studii*, which he had delivered as the 1994 Étienne Gilson Lecture at PIMS.[3] That initial contact and the *translatio studii* that it, too, represented – between *l'École de Chartres* ("created" by Alexandre Clerval in 1895) and "l'École de Toronto" (founded in 1929 by Étienne Gilson) – deeply shaped the trajectory of both the young French scholar and the eminent Canadian institution, in ways that neither could have anticipated in 1952.

Born in Coudray-au-Perche on 14 August 1924 to father Édouard, the village blacksmith, and mother Hélène (née Champdavoine), the young Jeauneau spent his early years in the *Pertica silva* or *Comté du Perche*, renowned for its Percheron draft horses, often shoed by Édouard senior, and its wonderful traditional cider, which Fr. Jeauneau delighted in offering to his academic visitors from across the world, though he preferred a gin and tonic. He pursued secondary education at nearby Nogent-le-Rotrou (1935–1941), in the shadow of the eleventh-century Château Saint-Jean, before continuing his studies in philosophy and theology in the longer shadow

---

[1] *"Lectio philosophorum": Recherches sur l'École de Chartres* (Amsterdam, 1973).

[2] Letter from Father George Flahiff to Mgr Raoul-Octave-Marie-Jean Harscouët, 30 January 1953: "Allow us to offer this film to Your Excellency and to beg You to accept it as a mark of our esteem for that noble Church of Chartres, which Thierry himself faithfully served, and of which Your Excellency is today the distinguished Chief representative."

[3] *Translatio studii: The Transmission of Learning, A Gilsonian Theme*, The Étienne Gilson Series 18 (Toronto, 1995), pp. 16–17; repr. in *"Tendenda vela": Excursions littéraires et digressions philosophiques à travers le Moyen Âge*, Instrumenta Patristica et Mediaevalia 47 (Turnhout, 2007).

of the Cathédrale Notre-Dame de Chartres at the Grand-Séminaire de Chartres, about seventy kilometers north-east of Coudray. He traveled much farther for advanced theological training at the Gregorian University in Rome (1945–1948) and was ordained a deacon in the Basilica di San Giovanni in Laterano at Rome on 21 December 1946 and a priest at the Cathedral of Chartres on 17 August 1947. Earlier that year (on 22 April), while still only a deacon, Jeauneau was invited by Mgr Harscouët, Bishop of Chartres, to accompany him at an audience with Pope Pius XII, during which the Pope himself encouraged the Bishop of Chartres to permit Dcn. Jeauneau to pursue a doctorate in theology.[4] Upon his return to France, he was appointed to teach scholastic philosophy at the Grand-Séminaire (1948–1958) before completing advanced degrees in medieval philosophy at Paris while Chercheur (1958–1974) at Le Centre national de la recherche scientifique (CNRS). In 1962 he attained a Diplômé de l'École pratique des hautes études, editing for his thesis the *Glosae super Platonem* by William of Conches, followed by a Doctorat de recherche (en histoire de la philosophie médiévale) in 1967 and a Doctorat ès lettres in 1973 at Paris Nanterre, during which time he turned his attention to Iohannis Scottus Eriugena, editing the *Homilia super "In principio erat Verbum"* and the *Commentarius in Euangelium Iohannis*.[5] In 1974 he was appointed Directeur de Recherche at CNRS (1974–1991) and received an invitation to join the Pontifical Institute of Mediaeval Studies, where (following a year as visiting fellow at Claire Hall, Cambridge) he became a Senior Fellow and Professor at the University of Toronto, thereafter dividing his time between Toronto, Paris, and Chartres (not to mention his summers in Greece).

Despite his globe-trotting academic career, Fr. Jeauneau never really left his family home in Coudray, located across the street from the village church, Saint-Pierre, where he was baptized on 17 August 1924 and in whose cemetery he was buried on 16 December 2019. Over the decades he transformed the family home into a fitting testament to his dual life as Professor and Priest. His father's blacksmith forge became a beautiful chapel, and a sculpture of Saint-Eloi (Sanctus Eligius), patron saint of metalworkers, still graces a niche on the exterior of the chapel to memorialize his father's profession. In 1992, he commissioned an octagonal stone well for the courtyard. Around its base is inscribed an elegiac couplet of his own composition:

---

[4] *La Fouine. La Revue de ceux qui ne se perdent pas de vue*, 6ᵉ année, no. 4 (juillet 1947), pp. 3–5.

[5] *Guillaume de Conches: Glosae super Platonem. Texte critique avec introduction, notes et tables*, Textes philosophique du Moyen Âge 13 (Paris, 1965); *Jean Scot: Homélie sur le prologue de Jean. Introduction, texte critique, traduction et notes*, Source chrétiennes 151 (Paris, 1969); *Jean Scot: Commentaire sur l'evangile de Jean. Introduction, texte critique, traduction, notes et index*, Sources chrétiennes 180 (Paris, 1972).

> diuinae ogdoadis sit fons munimine tutus
> > ut bibat inde nepos unde bibere patres
>
> May this spring be protected by the divine ogdoad,
> > so that the descendant may drink from the same source as his forefathers.

And another inscription, a lightly altered quotation from Virgil, *Ecl.* 4.28, honours his mother, née Champdavoine: "flauescet campus auenae" – "the field of oat will turn gold." In the back corners of the courtyard, flanking the well, he installed two small fountains inscribed with Proverbs 5.15, which balanced his respect for tradition with his own fiercely independent and innovative scholarly imagination: "bibe aquam de cisterna tua et fluenta putei tui" – "drink water out of thy own cistern and the streams of thy own well." And on a small grassy lawn above the courtyard he erected a monument to his love for classical antiquity, Platonism above all, with a stone *columna* inscribed with the prayer of Socrates, in both the original Greek (in a proper Ionic *scriptio continua*) and his own elegant French translation: "O mon cher Pan et vous autres, toutes tant que vous êtes, divinités de ce lieu accordez-moi la beauté intérieure quant aux biens extérieurs, faites en sorte que tout ce que j'en possède soit en harmonie avec mon intérieur" (*Phaedrus* 279B).

From his first arrival at PIMS in 1975 and long after he retired from teaching as Emeritus Fellow in 1989, Fr. Jeauneau was a regular presence around the campus of St. Michael's College during the fall semester (and often for several months in the spring). He loved routine: early mornings at his increasingly cluttered corner office in PIMS, at the top of the spiral staircase from the Shook Common Room; late morning work at his much neater carrel at the PIMS Library, just down the street on the fourth floor of the John M. Kelly Library; lunch (often with students) at the dining room of St. Mike's, where he nearly always began with the soup; a late afternoon nap, deadlines permitting; the occasional dinner at Jacques Bistro du Parc on Cumberland Street, just north of his room with the Basilian Fathers on St. Joseph's Street; and his treasured evening walks along Bloor Street, hands clasped quietly behind his back.

His carrel at PIMS library was his own blacksmith forge, and he led a school of eager apprentices (across many generations) who assisted in his scholarly endeavors. For more than twenty-five years that spanned a technological trajectory from Nota Bene, to Corel WordPerfect, to Classical Text Editor, he employed students from the Centre for Medieval Studies and postdoctoral scholars from PIMS with the support of the Social Sciences and Humanities Research Council of Canada, training them with a philological acuity and rigor matched by few. Initially each was only allowed to work under his watchful but gentle eye; however, if they worked with him long enough and earned his trust, he would allow them to work alone. But inevitably, upon return to the carrel, they would find their work printed, hand-corrected, and placed neatly on the desk with a kind note (usually in French) that work was not to proceed until corrections had been dutifully entered. In his Toronto workshop, he produced an impressive library of critical editions: Eriugena's Latin translation of the *Ambigua ad Iohannem* by Maximus the Confessor; his landmark five-volume edition of Eriugena's *Periphyseon*; a revised edition of William of Conches's *Glosae super Platonem*; a revised edition of Eriugena's *Homilia super "In principio erat Verbum" et Commentarius in Euangelium Iohannis*; and the (unfinished) *editio princeps* of William of Conches's *Glosulae super Priscianum*.[6]

Altogether, Fr. Jeauneau published twenty books – not counting the many revised editions and translations of his first, *La philosophie médiévale* (1963).[7] But he was al-

---

[6] *Maximi Confessoris Ambigua ad Iohannem iuxta Iohannis Scotti Eriugenae latinam interpretationem nunc primum edidit Eduardus Jeauneau*, in *Corpus Christianorum Series Graeca* 18 (Turnhout, 1988); *Iohannis Scotti seu Eriugenae Periphyson*, in *Corpus Christianorum Continuatio Mediaevalis* 161–165 (Turnhout, 1996–2003); *Guillelmi de Conchis Glosae super Platonem*, editionem nouam trium codicum nuper repertorum testimonio suffultam curauit Eduardus A. Jeauneau, in *Corpus Christianorum Continuatio Mediaevalis* 203 (Turnhout, 2006); *Iohannis Scotti seu Eriugenae Homilia super "In principio erat Verbum" et Commentarius in Euangelium Iohannis*, editiones nouas curauit Édouard A. Jeauneau, adiuuante Andrew J. Hicks, in *Corpus Christianorum Continuatio Mediaevalis* 166 (Turnhout, 2008).

[7] *La philosophie médiévale*, Collection "Que sais-je?" n° 1044 (Paris, 1963).

ways more at home in an essay than a book. In his first essay collection *"Lectio philosophorum"* (1973), he referred to the anthologized fruits of his initial labors with characteristic humility, offering the reader but "modestes essais ou simple articles."[8] These "modest essays or simple articles" inaugurated a career-long trajectory of meticulous archival work into the unpublished legacy of medieval Platonism. His personal, well-worn copy of J.H. Waszink's edition of Calcidus's Latin translation and commentary on Plato's *Timaeus* (17a–53c) is a remarkable diary of his dogged pursuit of Plato's medieval *Nachleben*. Alongside the 133 manuscripts of Calcidius's translation and/or commentary tabulated in Waszink's *Elenchus codicum*, Fr. Jeauneau patiently tallied the eighty-two he had autopsied *in situ* (more than Waszink himself); additional pasted-in leaves, marginal annotations, and penciled addenda to Waszink's *stemma codicum* record the various "manuscrits et extraits que j'ai découverts." The results of these discoveries occupied him in many essays.[9] His second collection of essays, *Études Érigéniennes* (1987), reflected his new preoccupation with Iohannis Scottus Eriugena;[10] it was awarded the 1990 Prix Victor Cousin by the Académie des sciences morales et politiques de l'Institut de France. His last, *"Tendenda Vela"* (2007), ranged widely across "sources bibliques," "sources patristiques," "sources profanes," and of course his perennial favourites, Jean Scot Érigène and l'École de Chartres. In recognition of these many scholarly contributions, he was elected Corresponding Fellow of the Medieval Academy of America (1990), an Honorary Member of the Royal Irish Academy (1991), a Corresponding Fellow of the British Academy (1992), and was the recipient of honorary doctorates from the University of Chicago (1996) and PIMS (2002). In 1996 he was appointed Chanoine titulaire de la cathédrale de Chartres.

In the sixty years between his first article on Thierry of Chartres (1954) and his last on Origen and Eriugena (2014),[11] Fr. Jeauneau wrote more than one hundred schol-

---

[8] *"Lectio philosophorum,"* p. xi.

[9] E.g., "Gloses sur le *Timée* et Commentaire du *Timée* dans deux manuscrits du Vatican," *Revue des études augustiniennes* 8 (1962), 365–73 (repr. in *"Lectio philosophorum"*); "Gloses marginales sur le *Timée* de Platon du manuscrit 226 de la Bibliothèque municipal d'Avranches," *Sacris Erudiri* 17 (1966), 71–89 (repr. in *"Lectio philosophorum"*); "Gloses sur le *Timée,* du manuscrit Digby 217 da la Bodléienne, à Oxford," *Sacris Erudiri* 17 (1966), 365–400 (repr. in *"Lectio philosophorum"*); and "Plato apud Bohemos," *Mediaeval Studies* 41 (1979), 161–214 (repr. in *"Tendenda vela"*).

[10] *Études érigéniennes* (Paris, 1987).

[11] "Un représentant du platonisme au douzième siècle: Maître Thierry de Chartres," *Mémoires de la Société archéologique d'Eure-et-Loir* 20 (1954–57), 1–12; "From Origen's *Periarchon* to Eriugena's *Periphyseon*," in *Eriugena and Creation: Proceedings of the Eleventh International Conference on Eriugenian Studies, Held in Honor of Édouard Jeauneau, Chicago, 9–12 November 2011*, ed. Willemien Otten and Michael I. Allen (Turnhout, 2014), pp. 139–82.

arly articles, homilies, and religious meditations.[12] A patient and imaginative exegete of Greek and Latin authors, and averse to dogmatic thinking (ecclesiastical and academic alike), Fr. Jeauneau was drawn to bold intellectuals who had "le goût du risque," as he once described Eriugena.[13] He spent his career following authors such as Gregory of Nyssa, Pseudo-Dionysius, Maximus the Confessor, Eriugena, Heiric of Auxerre, Bernard of Chartres, Thierry of Chartres, William of Conches, John of Salisbury, and many others into the high seas of theological and philosophical debate, from the bold Christianization of pre-Christian philosophy and myth in "L'usage de la notion d'*integumentum* à travers les gloses de Guillaume de Conches" to the Trinitarian complexities and Greek sympathies on display in "Érigène entre l'Ancienne et la Nouvelle Rome. Le *Filioque*."[14] It is no surprise that one of his favourite passages from Eriugena's *Periphyseon* (IV, 744A) urges *ratio* (reason) to set sail: "Tendenda uela nauigandumque…. cui (sc. rationi) delectabilius est in abditis diuini oceani fretibus uirtutem suam exercere, quam in planis apertisque otiosa quiescere, ubi uim suam non ualet aperire" – in his own translation: "Let us spread sails and set out to sea. … Indeed [reason] finds it sweeter to exercise her skill in the hidden straits of the Ocean of Divinity than idly to bask in the smooth and open waters, where she cannot display her power." Fr. Jeauneau saw in this passage the Irish love of traveling (*peregrinatio*), but could it be he was thinking of himself and his own *peregrinationes* when he further commented, in the conclusion to an essay on "The Neoplatonic Themes of *Processio* and *Reditus* in Eriugena": "The long wanderings of his *Periphyseon*, the ceaseless digressions which, like songs of Sirens, slow the return to the 'dear fatherland,' are, perhaps, not deprived of interest in a time when man is more and more aware of being a traveller"?[15]

Much as William of Conches had returned as *senex* (an old man) to work begun as *iuuenis* (a young man) – as William tells us in the prooemium to his revised commentary on Priscian's *Institutiones grammaticae*, yet another of Fr. Jeauneau's many manuscript discoveries – Fr. Jeauneau returned late in life to the object of his first studies, l'École de Chartres, and in 2009 he completed his last book, *Rethinking the*

---

[12] For a complete bibliography, see Paul Edward Dutton, "Édouard Jeauneau (1924–2019)," *Mediaeval Studies* 81 (2019), pp. xiii–xxxi.

[13] *La philosophie médiévale*, p. 36.

[14] "L'usage de la notion d'*integumentum* à travers les gloses de Guillaume de Conches," *Archives d'histoire doctrinale et littéraire du Moyen-Âge* 24 (1957), 35–100 (repr. in *"Lectio philosophorum"*); "Érigène entre l'Ancienne et la Nouvelle Rome. Le *Filioque*," in *Chemins de la pensée médiévale. Études offertes à Zénon Kaluza*, ed. Paul J.J.M. Bakker (Turnhout, 2002), pp. 289–321 (repr. in *"Tendenda vela"*).

[15] "The Neoplatonic Themes of *Processio* and *Reditus* in Eriugena," *Dionysius* 15 (1991), 28–29 (repr. in *"Tendenda vela"*).

School of Chartres (2009), a revision and expansion of *L'âge d'or des écoles de Chartres* (1995), translated by his francophone German Studies colleague Claude Paul Desmarais. It was a deeply personal endeavor. As he recounts in the Foreword:[16]

> From 1948 to 1958 I taught scholastic philosophy at the foot of the towers of the Cathedral of Chartres. Almost every day, and often several times a day, I would pass in front of the *Portail royal* (Royal Portal), which dates from the first half of the twelfth century. … Quite often I stopped in front of its right porch to contemplate the sculptures, found in the archivolts, which represent the seven Liberal Arts: Grammar, Rhetoric, Dialectic, Arithmetic, Geometry, Astronomy, and Music. These statues reminded me, naturally, how in a previous age the renowned schools of Chartres attracted students from the four corners of Europe. I wanted to learn more about these schools, and so I sought out the texts related to them, some printed and others – far more numerous – available only as manuscripts. So began my vocation as a medievalist.

And so, too, he concluded his career as a medievalist. Even after he was no longer able to travel between Chartres and Toronto, and had moved to St. Cheron in Chartres (fittingly down the street from the "Lycée Fulbert"), Fr. Jeauneau continued to work at the *editio princeps* of William of Conches's first and last work, the *Glosulae super Priscianum*, whose completion he has entrusted to the author of this memorial.

On 10 December 2019, Fr. Édouard Jeauneau died at l'Hôpital Louis Pasteur in Le Coudray, on the outskirts of Chartres. May he find what Eriugena offers as the end of *studium sapientiae* (the study of wisdom) – the return of all things to God – in the conclusion of the very passage Fr. Jeauneau so loved: "ad ueritatis contemplationem … frequenti literarum diuinarum laboriosoque studio ducente et adiuuante et cooperante, et ad hoc mouente diuina gratia, redeundo perueniat, perueniendo diligat, diligendo permaneat, permanendo quiescat" – "led, helped, and aided by his frequent and assiduous study of Divine Scripture, and moved to this by Divine Grace, may [Édouard Jeauneau] in his Return reach the contemplation of Truth, in reaching may he love it, in loving may he abide with it, and in abiding may he there find rest."

Andrew J. Hicks, Cornell University

---

[16] *Rethinking the School of Chartres*, translated from the French by Claude Paul Desmarais, Rethinking the Middle Ages 3 (Toronto, 2009), p. 11.

In Memoriam Richard Sharpe (1954 – 2020)

Richard Sharpe was Professor of Diplomatic at Oxford, and one of the world's outstanding authorities on the Latin literature of the British Isles, from the Roman occupation to 1600 and beyond. He was born on 17 February 1954 in York (his parents were both pharmacists) and was a student at St. Peter's School in York, where he received excellent training in Greek and Latin, and from where he won a Scholarship to read Classics at Trinity College, Cambridge. He came up in 1973 and took Part I of the Tripos in Classics in 1975; but at that point he decided to take Part II of his degree in Anglo-Saxon, Norse, and Celtic (ASNC). One of the factors in this change in academic direction was his familiarity with, and love of, the Western Isles of Scotland. While still a schoolboy he had spent many summers in these islands, particularly Raasay (a tiny island in the Inner Hebrides, between Skye and the mainland, with a present population of 160) and Iona (which lies off the southern tip of Mull), which housed a monastery founded by St. Columba in 597, and was one of the principal centres of Irish monasticism. At the time he switched to ASNC, the University Lecturer in Celtic History was Kathleen Hughes (1927–1977), who was a noted authority on the early Irish church and had some familiarity with the vast and largely uncharted sea of saints' Lives, in Latin and Irish, which were produced in Ireland during the Middle Ages.[1] Richard began his serious study of Hiberno-Latin hagiography while still an undergraduate, with the guidance of Kathleen Hughes. He took the ASNC Tripos in 1977, achieving the only First in that year, and then proceeded directly to doctoral research on Hiberno-Latin hagiography, for which his background in Classics had provided excellent training. In 1977, Richard also published his first book, a brief account (90 pp.) of the island of Raasay,[2] followed a year later by a second volume on Raasay, this time including documents pertaining to the history of settlement on the island.[3] His interest in the accurate presentation of documentary evidence, seen here in his very first publications, was to remain throughout his life.

---

[1] Her best-known work is *The Church in Early Irish Society* (London, 1966); she also published *Early Christian Ireland: Introduction to the Sources* (London, 1972), which contains on pp. 219–47 an introduction to Hiberno-Latin hagiography. This book is dedicated "To my undergraduates who have been my pupils and teachers," and Richard was certainly one of these. He was, however, unable to accept many of his teacher's interpretations of the administrative structure of the early Irish church, and his own essay, which confronted many of these interpretations, has become the defining account of this subject: "Some Problems Concerning the Organization of the Church in Early Medieval Ireland," *Peritia* 3 (1984), 230–70.

[2] *Raasay: A Study in Island History* (London, 1977).

[3] *Raasay: A Study in Island History. Documents and Sources, People and Places* (London, 1978; 2nd ed., 1982).

In the spring of 1977, at about the time he was taking his Tripos examinations in ASNC, Kathleen Hughes died suddenly of a heart attack, aged 50. By the time Richard began work on his PhD the following October, David Dumville had been appointed to replace Kathleen as the Department's Lecturer in Celtic History, and so David became Richard's thesis supervisor. Although in many ways the two were temperamentally very different, they shared a passion – one might even call it a mania – for comprehensive bibliographical control of the sources and scholarship on the medieval culture of the British Isles: the history, language and literatures of Scotland, Ireland, England, Wales, and Cornwall. Through this mutual commitment, they remained cordial colleagues,[4] though they made their separate ways across what was essentially the same field.

In the early years of his doctoral work Richard spent some time sorting out the almost unbelievably complex entanglements of the hagiography of St. Brigit,[5] but he soon settled on the problems presented by the compilation and transmission of the three major fourteenth-century collections of Hiberno-Latin saints' Lives, all compiled and written in Ireland: the *Salmanticensis* (45 *uitae*), the *Oxoniensis* (39 *uitae*), and the *Dublinensis* (28 *uitae*). His aim was to establish criteria which could be used to date the *uitae* in these late collections, and to identify any which could be dated to the hey-day of Hiberno-Latin hagiography (seventh to ninth centuries). This involved microscopic textual criticism of the nearly 100 *uitae* in question, combined with painstaking analysis of the aims of the compilers of the three collections. Such a large undertaking inevitably took longer than the three years which a UGC grant would support; in the end, the dissertation was not submitted and approved until 1987.[6] After some revision, it was published by the Clarendon Press as *Medieval Irish Saints' Lives: An Introduction to Vitae Sanctorum Hiberniae* (Oxford, 1991). The book is a landmark in the study of Hiberno-Latin hagiography: it contains a wealth of information about the history of research on this subject, principally by seventeenth-century Irish scholars, as well as a detailed analysis of the contents of the three collections. Perhaps most important, in the long run, is his convincing demonstration that a block of eight texts shared by the *Salmanticensis* and *Oxoniensis* collections could reasonably

---

[4] In 1996 the two of them conducted the oral examination of one of my PhD students. She referred to this examination ever afterwards as the "Sharpeville Massacre." (In spite of the severity of the examination the dissertation was approved – subject of course to typographical corrections demanded by these two fanatical proof-readers.)

[5] *Medieval Irish Saints' Lives* (cited below), p. 14, n. 44: "During 1977–9 I prepared a working text based on more than twenty manuscripts, but have not had the opportunity to complete the edition." The edition remained incomplete at the time of his death; for some indication of the problems involved in such an edition, see his "*Vitae S. Brigitae*: The Oldest Texts," *Peritia* 1 (1982), 81–106.

[6] *Medieval Irish Saints' Lives: A Study of the Three Irish Collections* (unpubl. Ph.D. Dissertation, University of Cambridge, 1987).

be assigned to the earliest period (seventh to ninth centuries) of hagiographic activity in Ireland. Unfortunately, no subsequent scholar has capitalized on this demonstration, and these eight *uitae* still await a modern critical edition.

After three years of state-supported doctoral research in Cambridge, followed by a year of continuing research as Senior Rouse Ball Student at Trinity College, Richard was in 1981 appointed Assistant Editor of the *Dictionary of Medieval Latin from British Sources.* The General Editor then was David Howlett, and at the time of Richard's appointment, the decision had been taken (by the British Academy, which was funding and overseeing production of the *Dictionary*) to move part of the dictionary staff from the Public Record Office in London to premises in the Bodleian Library in Oxford. So in 1981 Richard joined David Howlett in an office on the top floor of the Clarendon Building, adjacent to the Bodleian Library. By that time, two fascicules of the *Dictionary* had been published (*A–B*, 1975; *C*, 1981). While work proceeded on the letter *D*, Richard, with his characteristic energy, undertook to overhaul the list of British-Latin sources on which the *Dictionary* was based. Accordingly, when the third fascicule was published (*D–E*, 1986), it included a comprehensively revised bibliography of Latin sources (*D–E*, pp. xi–lxi: fifty densely-printed pages in two columns), to which Richard himself claimed to have contributed more than 700 items: a foretaste of bibliographical enterprises to come.

Meanwhile, in Dublin, the Royal Irish Academy was reviving its own projected *Dictionary of Medieval Latin from Celtic Sources.* Its principal lexicographers had left the project in 1980, and while plans were being made to appoint a permanent editor,[7] David Howlett and I were invited to join the editorial board of the RIA dictionary as advisers. It quickly became apparent that the working list of sources, on which the Celtic-Latin dictionary was to be based, was inadequate, and I was charged with the task of providing a revised list of sources. I was well aware that I lacked the expertise to cover the entire field of Celtic-Latin literature, so I asked Richard to help me, on the understanding that I would take responsibility for Roman Britain and Wales, while he would deal with Scotland and Ireland. Our collaboration resulted in the publication of *A Bibliography of Celtic-Latin Literature, 400–1200*, issued as the first Ancillary Publication of the Royal Irish Academy Dictionary of Medieval Latin from Celtic Sources (Dublin, 1985). This *Bibliography* lists some 1,300 texts and underpins the

---

[7] Dr. Anthony Harvey, a graduate of ASNC in Cambridge, was appointed to this post in 1985, and has remained its editor up to the present day.

Celtic-Latin Dictionary, still in progress,[8] as well as the Brepolis Database, *Archive of Celtic-Latin Literature*.[9]

Richard worked as Assistant Editor for *DMLBS* for nearly a decade, but it was always clear that the discipline of lexicography was too constricting for his huge intellectual ambitions. Accordingly, when Pierre Chaplais retired from his Oxford post as Reader in Diplomatic in 1989, Richard applied for the position, and, although he had no formal training in diplomatic (that is, the study of the physical nature, form, and language of charters and related legal instruments), he was successful in his application, so that in 1990 he became Reader in Diplomatic (subsequently promoted to Professor of Diplomatic in 1998, which post he still occupied at the time of his death), and, like Pierre Chaplais, became a Fellow of Wadham College from that date. His huge contribution to the field of diplomatic is represented by his on-line editions (with David X. Carpenter and others) of the 2,000 or so charters of William II (1087–1100) and Henry I (1100-35).[10] This project was incomplete at the time of his death, but will be continued by Richard's collaborators.

Also in 1990, Richard became involved in another huge project which would absorb much of his intellectual energies up until the time of his death: in that year he was appointed General Editor of the British Academy's *Corpus of British Medieval Library Catalogues*. At the time of his appointment, only one volume of a projected nineteen had been published; he himself oversaw the publication of Vols. 2–16 (that is, fifteen books bound in nineteen volumes), with Vols. 17–19 (and a revised edition of Vol. 1) still to come. In fact, "oversaw" is too light a word to describe the huge input of learning and acumen which Richard contributed to each and every volume. He himself was largely responsible for Vol. 4: *English Benedictine Libraries: The Shorter Catalogues*, published in 1996, with contributions from James P. Carley, Rodney M. Thomson and Andrew G. Watson. Library catalogues are an indispensable resource for our understanding of medieval culture and learning, but they are not of easy access to the uninitiated and unlearned, because all works composed in Latin (and, to a lesser degree, in Greek and Hebrew) acquired titles by which they were known in the Middle Ages, and which often differ substantially from the titles by which they are known to

---

[8] The first volume (of several) was published in 2005: *The Non-Classical Lexicon of Celtic Latinity*, I. *Letters A–H*, ed. A. Harvey and J. Power (Turnhout, 2005).

[9] The format which Richard and I devised for the *Bibliography of Celtic-Latin Literature*, whereby for each text we classified the bibliography as to General Bibliography, MSS, REF (references to alphanumerical compendia such as *BHL*), ED (editions), and COMM (studies), was subsequently adopted by C.A.L.M.A. (*Compendium Auctorum Latinorum Medii Aevi*, Florence, 2003–), founded at SISMEL in Florence by myself and Claudio Leonardi.

[10] These editions were posted in four separate "tranches" (as Richard called them), in 2013, 2014, 2016, and 2018 (see <https://actswilliam2henry1.wordpress.com/the-charters/>).

modern scholars. Sometimes these titles are straightforward: Augustine's *De ciuitate Dei* is usually recorded as such in library catalogues. But the editor (and user) of a library catalogue has also to know, for example, that 'Quintilian *de causis*' in fact refers to the "Major Declamations" of that author; or, among medieval authors, that the *Destructorium uitiorum* refers to a work by Alexander Carpenter (saec. XV), that the *Libellus de septem beatitudinibus* is part of Alexander of Canterbury's *Liber de dictis beati Anselmi* (saec. XII), or that *Corrogaciones Promethei* refers to an unprinted work by Alexander Nequam (saec. XII). Richard Sharpe carried much of this information in his head; but he realized that not all readers would do so, whereupon with his usual energy he set about to compile a "List of Identifications" to serve as a companion-piece to the *Corpus*. This "List of Identifications," compiled with the assistance of Lewis O. Ayres and David N. Bell, was first issued in 1993 (revised and amplified versions were issued in 1995 and 1999; the latest version, occupying more than 900 pages, is available on-line). Work on the *Corpus* and the "List of Identifications" led Richard to formulate entirely new views of how Medieval Latin texts should be described and cited; these views are set out in his *Titulus. Identifying Medieval Latin Texts. An Evidence-Based Approach* (Turnhout, 2003).

A product of the same vast energy and learning is *A Handlist of the Latin Writers of Great Britain and Ireland before 1540* (Turnhout, 1997, with "Additions and Corrections," 2001). This monumental work lists the compositions of some 2,300 named authors (providing references to manuscripts in cases where works are unpublished, to editions, and to bibliography relevant to defining the literary estate of a particular author). In a word, it is the fundamental tool for the study of all Latin literature composed in the British Isles before the Dissolution of the Monasteries. Anyone who has used this book can only marvel at how one person could have amassed, and then presented in so coherent and accessible a form, the vast amount of information which it contains.

Although these large bibliographical projects must have absorbed the large part of his intellectual energies, Richard still found time to produce a stream of books and articles. It is not possible to mention more than a few of these here (his personal bibliography runs to over 200 items, including more than forty book reviews), but mention must be made of his Penguin translation of *Adomnán of Iona: Life of St Columba* (1995), which makes accessible to a wide readership one of the principal Hiberno-Latin saints' Lives. The extensive notes (400+) provide the reader with (e.g.) valuable first-hand descriptions of the topography of Iona, and the organization of the monastic church in seventh-century Ireland. With John Blair Richard edited *Pastoral Care before the Parish* (Leicester, 1992), which includes his own essay on "Churches and Communities in Early Medieval Ireland" (pp. 81–109). With Alan Thacker he edited *Local Saints and Local Churches in the Early Medieval West* (Oxford, 2002), including his own essay on "Martyrs and Local Saints in Late Antique Britain" (pp. 75–154), which in my view contains the best discussion in print on the historical context of Gildas.

Richard had an abiding interest in Canterbury, in particular in the contract-hagiographer Goscelin, who ended a peripatetic career at St. Augustine's, Canterbury, at the beginning of the twelfth century.[11] His Canterbury interest extended to Goscelin's famous contemporary, Archbishop Anselm (1093–1109), who was the subject of Richard's 2007 O'Donnell Lecture in Toronto, subsequently printed as "Anselm as Author: Publishing in the Late Eleventh Century" in *The Journal of Medieval Latin* 19 (2009), 1–87. Another major work is his large monograph, in collaboration with Robert Easting, on medieval vision literature: *Peter of Cornwall's Book of Revelations*, published by the Pontifical Institute of Medieval Studies (Toronto, 2013).

In later years he turned his attention more and more to early modern Ireland and its scholars, which resulted in two large books printed by the Royal Irish Academy in Dublin: *Roderick O'Flaherty's Letters to William Molyneux, Edward Llwyd, and Samuel Molyneux, 1696–1709* (Dublin, 2013); and *Ciólista. Printing in the Irish Language 1571–1871. An Attempt at a Narrative Bibliography* (forthcoming; but available online at the RIA website). But Richard's abiding interest was always in the circulation of books and the establishment of libraries in medieval England, and this was the subject of his six Lyell Lectures, delivered in Oxford in Trinity Term, 2019: "Libraries and Books in Medieval England: The Role of Libraries in a Changing Book Economy."[12]

By means of his huge, indeed superhuman, energies, Richard Sharpe has put the study of the Medieval Latin Literature of the British Isles, from its beginnings to the Renaissance and beyond, on a permanent footing, and has thrown brilliant new light on countless authors and scholars previously unknown. Few scholars in this field have achieved as much, and all future students of the subject will be in his debt. Richard Sharpe was a Fellow of the British Academy, an Honorary Member of the Royal Irish Academy, and a Corresponding Fellow of the Medieval Academy of America. He died of a heart attack on 21 March 2020, aged 66.[13]

Michael Lapidge, Clare College, Cambridge

---

[11] See "Goscelin's St Augustine and St Mildreth: Hagiography and Liturgy in Context," *Journal of Theological Studies* 41 (1990), 502–16; "Words and Music by Goscelin of Canterbury," *Early Music* 19 (1991), 94–97; and (with Richard G. Eales), *Canterbury and the Norman Conquest* (London, 1995), including his own essay, "The Setting of St Augustine's Translation, 1091," pp. 1–13.

[12] Plans are underway for publishing these six lectures posthumously.

[13] I am grateful to Tessa Webber for information on Trinity College, Cambridge, and on the *Corpus of Medieval British Library Catalogues*.

In Memoriam Peter Dronke (1934–2020)

Composing an obituary can be daunting, even when its subject does not number among the world's premier and most prolific medievalists and Medieval Latinists.[1] First and foremost, the task means exercising pressure to transform the carbon of fresh grief into the diamond of enduring remembrance. Then, the medium demands taking stock of a lifetime's professional accomplishment, summing it up, and setting it into broader intellectual and cultural frames of reference. That is no mean feat when as a consequence dozens of books and hundreds of articles clamor for appraisal. As if the second challenge did not suffice to overwhelm, the genre cries out for the extra enhancement of bringing back the actuality of the deceased, in physique as well as character, while memory lingers – in the fleeting interval once the individual has shuffled off this mortal coil, but while a familiar scent hangs momentarily yet in the air and, if the ear strains, a faint echo of the speaker's voice still rings.

The competing presence and absence of the dearly departed are particularly poignant and painful when (please allow an awkward neologism) the necrologized and necrologist have been associated as dissertation director and writer. Astonishingly, the loanword *Doktorvater*, recognizable among academics, even if a trifle exotic, is nowhere to be detected in the all-comprehending vastness of the *Oxford English Dictionary*, but the borrowing from German captures a relationship that has manifested itself for centuries. To render the compound into the banal "doctoral adviser" overlooks all the humanness of an intimacy that approximates the cherished bond between parent and child. Full disclosure: we will ponder here my own "doctor father," whose other progeny in my immediate cohort included Charles Burnett (1951–), the late Peter Godman (1955–2018), and John Marenbon (1955–). This is plainly not to reel off all the entries that might have been penned in an entire official ledger.

The Germanness of the original noun suited Dronke well, since he was a German by birth, even if later a New Zealander by familial immigration and eventually a naturalized inhabitant of the United Kingdom (albeit by no reckoning an Englander who would have passed a fee-fi-fo-fum sniff test), but all along by his own measures European. At the end of the day, the bureaucratic categories carry small weight: he was a citizen of culture.

---

[1] To date, the following notices have appeared: Piero Boitani, "Dronke, medievista e latinista dell'amore," *Sole 24 Ore* (26 April 2020), p. v ("Letteratura: Il ricordo"); Sonia Gentili, "Dronke: L'immaginazione poetica del suo Medioevo liberato," *Il Manifesto* (3 May 2020), *Alias* (Sunday Section), p. 7; and Marina Warner, "Peter Dronke Obituary: Scholar of Medieval Latin who Shone Light on Hildegard of Bingen and Other Female Writers of the Middle Ages," *The Guardian* (UK), online, 14 May 2020.

Peter Dronke (formally, Ernst Peter Michael Dronke, though no one ever addressed him by any given name but the second) was born in Germany on 30 May 1934. The preceding year had been an *annus horribilis* for that nation. In 1933 Adolf Hitler (1889–1945) was appointed chancellor, suspended constitutional protections, inaugurated the Nazi state, founded the Dachau concentration camp, organized public book burnings, fixed a quota on Jews in public schools, initiated a countrywide boycott of Jewish-owned businesses, mandated sterilization of those with physical and mental disabilities, and prohibited reputed non-Aryans from working as journalists. Much more lay ahead, but already in Peter's year of birth Hitler commenced styling himself *Führer und Reichskanzler* ("Leader and Chancellor of the Reich"). We should need no reminding where this leader led.

Dronke's parents had held high stakes in the politics and culture of the Weimar Republic that preceded the regime that the dictator instituted. In 1931 his father, Adolf John Rudolf Dronke (d. 1982), a district court judge and musician, married his mother. Née Minnie Kronfeld (1904–1987), she was the youngest and sole female child of two Jews, the barrister Salomon Kronfeld and his wife Laura Liebmann. As an actress, Minnie employed the nom de théâtre Korten. Complicating matters, she took the baptismal name Maria-Magdalena upon converting to Catholicism in 1928 in Vienna. Eventually she became generally known as Maria Dronke.

In 1933 Peter's future mother, persecuted for her Semitic origins, had to abandon her vocation from one moment to the next. The couple shifted their base of operations from Hamburg to Cologne, where their son and his younger sister, Maria Gabrielle, from time to time also called Marei (with the married names of first Bollinger and later Webster, 1935–2012) had their start in life. The change of venue of course helped not a whit in altering the bigger picture. The inherited Jewishness persisted as an insuperable problem, one aggravated by the pair's profound antipathy to what became the Third Reich.

The situation in Germany deteriorated ever more ominously, with a new nadir reached on 9–10 November 1938, in the pogrom of Kristallnacht or "The Night of Broken Glass." In December Maria fled to England, while a few months later her husband and children with their nanny voyaged to rejoin her. From there the fivesome wended their way across the globe to New Zealand, much less distant from Antarctica than from Britannia, where they belonged to a total of 1,100 German-speaking emigrés who settled in the island country before 1940.[2] They disembarked on 2 August 1939. On September 1 World War II began with the invasion of Poland by the German Wehrmacht.

---

[2] Monica Tempian, "Negotiating Cultural Identity on the Stage: Maria Dronke, a German-Jewish Actor in New Zealand," *Shofar* 29/4 (2011), 46–66, at p. 46.

In their Pacific refuge, the immigrants had to construct an existence in an alien haven, a self-governing division of the British Empire where language and customs differed hugely from what they had encountered in Mitteleuropa. Jobs with decent pay were tough to find, more for John than Maria. Each parent eventually secured employment that drew upon past skills, but even then John no longer practiced as an attorney, let alone as a jurist, and Maria could not put food on the table as a full-time thespian. Still, she earned a respectable living in theater by training actors, directing performances, and staging solo poetry recitals. In the process, she turned to her advantage a light but attractive foreign accent.[3] Ultimately she constituted the principal source of income for her spouse and children. Since the terminology was not yet current, no talk of women's lib or feminism would have gone on in the household or elsewhere, but the family fulfilled a reality of higher revenue from the female than the male breadwinner that anticipated circumstances which in most economies would become even somewhat common only a half century later. The Dronkes personified first-wave feminism.

Maria Dronke possessed a beauty and flamboyance that would have made her stand out anywhere, but all the more so in the artistic isolation of what might have been deemed, fairly or not, a colonial backwater. Her most consequential and successful dramatic production in the early years is said to have been "Murder in the Cathedral," by T.S. Eliot (1888–1965). This choice holds interest for the twelfth-century theme, the assassination on 29 December 1170 of Archbishop Becket, canonized not much afterward as Saint Thomas, that the verse drama unfolded.[4] She put on the theater piece in Wellington's Old St. Paul's Cathedral in 1947. Another influence on her worth remarking is the Austrian director and producer Max Reinhardt (1873–1943). The centerpiece in his distinctive drama and filmmaking was repeated mass enactments of *The Miracle*, a medieval-style play by Karl Vollmöller (1878–1948). This spectacle contributed to her own conceptions of stagecraft.[5] Equally deserving of note, her one-woman recitations incorporated medieval lyrics.[6]

Not quite fifteen years after arriving in their new home, John and Maria Dronke's precocious son Peter obtained his bachelor's and master's from Victoria University of

---

[3] Tempian, "Negotiating Cultural Identity," pp. 61–62.

[4] Tempian, "Negotiating Cultural Identity," p. 60; and Peter Vere-Jones, "Maria Dronke," in *Out of the Shadow of War: The German Connection with New Zealand in the Twentieth Century*, ed. James N. Bade (Melbourne, 1998), pp. 113–117, at 113.

[5] Tempian, "Negotiating Cultural Identity," pp. 59–60.

[6] Ann Beaglehole, "Dronke, Minnie Maria," in *Dictionary of New Zealand Biography*, first published in 1998, Te Ara - the Encyclopedia of New Zealand, https://teara.govt.nz/en/biographies/4d19/dronke-minnie-maria

(accessed 7 June 2020).

Wellington, in 1953 and 1954, respectively. A bus accident left him with injuries that prevented him from participating in his interview for a Rhodes, but in 1955 he garnered a travelling scholarship from New Zealand that enabled him to immerse himself in English at Magdalen College. He received a second BA from Oxford with first-class honours in 1957. With funding from the Italian government he spent 1957–1958 in Rome, where he explored medieval philosophy and Dante with such luminaries as Bruno Nardi (1884–1968) and Tullio Gregory (1929–2019). Nardi became a fast friend.

In those days, the brightest young Englishmen were often assigned research fellowships directly after their first degrees and thus leapfrogged three or more years of doctoral studies. As a result, a reverse snobbism sometimes prevailed at Oxbridge in the second half of the twentieth century about not having proceeded to the PhD: being a mere mister could trump holding a doctorate. Peter Dronke never betrayed symptoms of caring one way or the other about honorifics. More important, he was also immune to the greybeard syndrome that preferred prolongation of graduate programs. Especially in the United States, where tarrying in higher education offered a means of dodging military conscription and therefore Vietnam, young and not-so-young scholars extended their programs years and even decades beyond what earlier generations had done. Not so the erstwhile New Zealander, who forwent the quest for supplementary credentials and hurtled ahead on the fast track as a research fellow at Merton College, Oxford, from 1958–1961.

In 1961 Dronke took up a lectureship in Medieval Latin at the University of Cambridge, which he held until 1979, and became a fellow (after retirement, emeritus fellow) of Clare Hall in 1964. He was awarded a personal readership in 1979, until being granted a personal professorship in Medieval Latin Literature in 1989 that he retained until retirement to emeritus status in 2001. Both such promotions were then exceedingly rare. At least during my stretch in the vicinity of the rivers Cam and Granta, his position was tucked into the Faculty of Modern and Medieval Languages. There it took a place among other such uncategorizable oddments (and the phrase is meant complimentarily) as Dutch, Modern Greek, and Hungarian. These dribs and drabs of European multiculturalism *avant la lettre* washed down into the linguistic catchment area charmingly named the Department of Other Languages.

In the Anglo-American orbit, Medieval Latin exists only precariously. Modern languages may benefit from the support of nation-states or immigrants who underwrite chairs so as to advertise and perpetuate their heritages. Classics, as an independent and venerable branch of interdisciplinary studies, frequently boasts endowments that reach back a century or more. But the Latin of the Middle Ages clings to life only by grace of recurrent community action by professors and students. Over the decades and now the centuries, every time the cause has been threatened with extinction, colleagues in the field and those affected in other neighbouring ones have rallied by banding together and arguing for the necessity of its continuance or resuscitation. Their audiences have been administrators needing to be disobliged of the conviction that "Some fields are just meant to die." The requisite resources may be lodged in Classics, History, English, or some other department, with teaching in many instances being done part-time by a medievalist whose main commitments are not in the disciplines of philology or palaeography and not even in the domain of Latin. All of this is to say that the marginality and instability of Medieval Latin at the University of Cambridge is anything but atypical.[7]

In an inaugural lecture given in 1990 to mark his appointment as Professor of Medieval Latin Literature, Peter Dronke acknowledged "two genial and generous-spirited scholars" as predecessors, Frederic James Edward Raby (1888–1966) and Frederick Brittain (1893–1969).[8] Raby, trained as a historian, was an independent scholar who never held an academic post, while Brittain came to Medieval Latin from Romance languages and literatures.[9] More to the point, Dronke's own professorship was created for him and evaporated when he ceased teaching. Just a quick question: Has a single slot for Medieval Latin ever been endowed in the English-speaking world? Philanthropists, step on up: better late than never.

My own contact with Peter Dronke started in 1977, when I turned up in Cambridge for the three years of Marshall-funded research and writing under his supervision that eventuated in my PhD. In the 1960s and 1970s the United States had witnessed a boom in medieval studies that had had a parallel in England, both phenomena probably propelled in part by the cult popularity of the seven-volume Narnia Chronicles by C.S. Lewis (1898–1963) and the fantasy novels *The Hobbit* and *The Lord of the Rings* by J.R.R. Tolkien (1892–1973), much as the nineteenth century had been marked by a medievalism stimulated potently by the wide-ranging fiction and erudition of the Brothers Grimm, Jacob (1785–1863) and Wilhelm (1786–1859), and the historical novels and verse of Sir Walter Scott (1771–1832).

By that juncture, I had been captivated by the scope and style of Dronke's two-volume *Medieval Latin and the Rise of European Love-Lyric* [=*MLERLL*], introductory

---

[7] Richard Sharpe and Alan Deyermond, "Latin," in *A Century of British Medieval Studies*, ed. Alan Deyermond (Oxford, 2007), pp. 353–62, at 357–59.

[8] *Hermes and the Sibyls: Continuations and Creations. Inaugural Lecture, Delivered 9 March 1990* (Cambridge, 1990), pp. 1–2.

[9] On the first, see Michael Lapidge, "Frederic James Edward Raby, 1888–1966," *Proceedings of the British Academy* 94 (1993–1996), 687–704. On the second, the best current information may well be https://collegecollections.jesus.cam.ac.uk/index.php/frederick-brittain (accessed 7 June 2020). For both as setting the stage for Dronke, see Michael Lapidge, "Medieval Latin Philology in the British Isles," in *La Filologia medievale e umanistica greca e latina nel secolo XX: Atti del congresso internazionale, Roma, Consiglio nazionale delle ricerche, Università La Sapienza, 11–15 dicembre 1989*, ed. Enrica Follieri, 2 vols. (Roma, 1993), 1:153–88, at 172–75.

The Medieval Lyric, and far-reaching *Poetic Individuality in the Middle Ages: New Departures in Poetry 1000–1150* (Oxford, 1970), all of which saw not only reprintings but also second and occasionally third editions. In these three instances I felt ensorceled by the verve of the writing (his elegant English translations never sound a false note) but even more by the vitality with which the author wove among languages, up and down the social register, and across geography and chronology. The unvarying traits were intense affection for literature and equally acute imagination in recreating the ambits of its composition and delivery. In *MLRELL* and *The Medieval Lyric,* Dronke established himself as one of the twentieth-century's leading experts in medieval lyric and Medieval Latin lyric, a reputation that he has maintained now two decades deep into the twenty-first century. Whereas many preceding interpreters had theorized that love lyric in particular originated in sun-drenched Provence near Arab-occupied Spain, he made the case that the form was widespread if not universal across time and space. In so doing, he uncovered roots that stretched back millennia. This argument was ineffably exciting: rather than being quarantined in a Latinate literary lazaretto, Latin-language love lyrics represented part of something far bigger.

Without having previously looked at any photograph of the prodigy responsible for these masterpieces or even chatted with anyone who had firsthand acquaintance of Peter, I rapped on the door of the Dronke house on Parker Street one evening in late September. My expectation, as an ingenuous twenty-year-old American newcomer to Cambridge, may have been to meet a elderly professor along the lines of the one in *The Lion, The Witch, and the Wardrobe.* Failing that, I may have been prepared for a Tolkienian Gandalf, tall and old with straggly white hair. Instead, the force of nature who threw open the door and greeted me could not have been further removed from debilitated donnishness or wizened warlockishness. On the contrary, he was in his mid forties, sporting a perturbingly purple shirt that was not only tieless but even unbuttoned halfway down, his skin bronzed from exposure to sun, a full head of dark hair undappled by grey, piercing eyes, a mouth ready to smile when inspiration struck, hands more disposed to gesture than those of many in his adoptive land, and an accent utterly his own.[10]

Adjectives to qualify what our ears hear may seem hopelessly limited when one person tries to describe another's voice. Dronke's made an identical impression regardless of the tongue he spoke – and among his numerous amazing gifts was his facility with spoken languages. At conferences he could switch seamlessly from English to German, German to French, French to Italian, Italian to Spanish, and back again. In all of them his vocal qualities sounded the same, fluent but oddly unnative or

---

[10] For an undated image of a slightly younger Dronke in similar apparel, see *Poetry and Philosophy in the Middle Ages: A Festschrift for Peter Dronke,* ed. John Marenbon (Leiden, 2001), p. ix.

at least idiosyncratic. This generalization holds for the content of his observations: he was *sui generis*.

A daily feature on Peter Dronke's parents that hit newsstands in the Antipodes the year before his father's death in 1982 singled out their exceptional mental vigor and curiosity.[11] As the article goes to show, he came naturally by the omnivorous energy and enthusiasm that he displayed for film and theater, concerts and museums, and poetry and philosophy – in sum, for culture. He ate it all up, like the seafoods or soft cheeses that he also adored, simultaneously gourmet and gourmand. In every direction he turned, but perhaps most of all in texts, he delighted in the unexpected, unprecedented, and unconventional.

Because Peter Dronke was much more concerned with learning and writing than with curating his online image, it can be hard to delineate his contours from the web. A man who submitted nothing but typed manuscripts to his publishers and never took to the personal computer, email, or other such deeply entrenched manifestations of the digital revolution, he experienced no impulse to create and manage a website on academia.edu or elsewhere, Facebook profile, Twitter feed, or presence on any of the other social media that twenty-first-century influencers and public intellectuals manipulate with aplomb. This is not to claim that distinctions and endorsements did not come his way, for they certainly did. He became a Fellow of the British Academy in 1984, a foreign member of the Royal Netherlands Academy of Arts and Sciences in 1997, and a corresponding Fellow of the Medieval Academy of America in 1999.

In 1959 Dronke met Ursula Brown (1920–2012), a fellow and tutor in English at Somerville College in Oxford from 1950 to 1961 (see *Oxford Dictionary of National Biography*). In 1960 they married, in 1961 moved to Cambridge, and in 1962 had their one child, Cressida. Ursula, her family name now Dronke, had a post in Munich in the early 1970s. In 1976 she was elected to the Vigfússon readership in Old Icelandic literature and antiquities, which she held in Oxford in tandem with a professorial fellowship at Linacre College. Her first book was an edition of the Old Norse *Þorgills saga* in 1952, but the lifelong heart of her research and writing would be her marvelous three-volume edition and translation, with commentary, of the Old Norse-Icelandic poems in the *Poetic Edda*. Because the two Dronkes were wedded intellectually as otherwise, the work effected by them both individually and collectively was coloured by their long partnership. Most concretely, they published fundamental articles in collaboration.

Peter Dronke has had admirers aplenty, but he instigated and craved no Dronkeism. He harboured no desire for anyone to be a card-carrying adherent of his approach, though he (and Ursula too) wanted his books and articles to be recognized

---

[11] Bryce Mason, "A Marriage That Has Been Golden," *Evening Post* (18 July 1981), p. 17, quoted in Tempian, "Negotiating Cultural Identity," p. 65.

and read. Rather than spinning grand theories, he pursued a multitude of passions relating to particular artists and works of arts, and he devised case-specific ways of articulating his insights. Similarly, he did not fuss about nomenclature for himself. He was not worried about being labeled a comparatist, feminist, humanist, philologist, or anything else of the kind. He was an eclectic.

If compelled to attach to him a single word ending in the suffix *-ist*, I would bracket him as an individualist. Recall that book first published in 1970 on *Poetic Individuality*. Dronke was drawn to Medieval Latin literature, which he esteemed as one of the world's major literatures and as one of Europe's less charted, because of its individuality – its "heights of individual artistic achievement" awaiting acknowledgment.[12] Yet to bandy about assertions, as has been done, of his membership in such an oxymoron as "the individualist school" is patently absurd.[13] His output bears scant resemblance to Robert Hanning's *The Individual in Twelfth-Century Romance* (New Haven, 1977) and Colin Morris's *The Discovery of the Individual, 1050–1200* (New York, 1972), beyond the superficial coincidence that both titles contain the constituent *individual*.

In Dronke, the concepts of individualism and individuality are closely allied with originality, which in turn connects with the notions of original genius, inspiration, and imagination.[14] All of these highlights remained fixtures in his oeuvre, as apparent from two volumes of his collected essays, one entitled *Sources of Inspiration: Studies in Literary Transformations, 400–1500* (Rome, 1997) and the other *Forms and Imaginings from Antiquity to the Fifteenth Century* (Rome, 2007), alongside a complex monograph on *Imagination in the Late Pagan and Early Christian World: The First Nine Centuries A.D.* (Florence, 2003).

At first blush these emphases may verge on being old hat, since they reach back all the way to the Romantics, if not beyond. But after World War II Medieval Latin studies had strong incentive to concentrate upon conventions and conventionality in medieval literature. As an expanse of scholarship, Medieval Studies has attracted over the years its fair share of systematizers who have sought to generate unified field theories that would explain everything. The Middle Ages resembles an element in the upper reaches of the periodic table, an atom that barely holds together, waiting to decompose. Confronted by such lability, some people ache to promote whatever one-size-fits-all solidity they can discover or concoct, while others rejoice in the fragile diversity of the enterprise. Dronke is to be subsumed among the latter.

---

[12] *Hermes and the Sibyls*, p. 2.

[13] Norman Cantor, *Inventing the Middle Ages* (New York, 1991), pp. 166, 198, 360–62, who with confident wrongness groups Dronke with Robert Hanning and Colin Morris and detects a lineage leading from Richard W. Southern.

[14] Haijo Westra, "Individuality, Originality and the Literary Criticism of Medieval Latin Texts," in *Poetry and Philosophy in the Middle Ages*, ed. Marenbon, pp. 281–92.

In the Cold War era the most powerful proponents for the centrality of Latin within medieval languages and literatures issued from within the guild of German-speaking Romance philologists, especially Ernst Robert Curtius (1886–1956) and Erich Auerbach (1892–1957). The first, not a Jewish émigré like Auerbach but an internal exile within a university in Hitler's Germany, propounded a view of European literature in which the Latin Middle Ages occupied center stage through commonplaces he designated *topoi*, which put a unifying imprint upon the welter of vernaculars. Dronke scrutinized Curtius more exactingly than he did Auerbach.[15] Yet although keenly respectful of the formalism that preceded him, the adoptive Englishman elected instead to affirm the capacity of the individual and personal to surpass the conformism of traditionalism. Not insignificantly, he proved himself more avid an aficionado of Curtius's term *excursus* than of the less centrifugal scaffolding for the rest of *European Literature and the Latin Middle Ages*.

If Dronke evinced any affinity for an approach that even in an unconventional way stressed conventionality, it may have been as embodied in the methodology and library of Aby Warburg (1866–1929). Charles Burnett, a PhD student of Dronke's, eventually became a professor at the institute in London named after the German-Jewish art historian. By and by, the two of them coorganized a colloquium there that led in due course to a coedited volume.[16] All of these happenstances are at once fortuitous and not at all so.

When the European Union materialized, Peter Dronke welcomed it. Ursula and he had long had one foot in the British Isles and another on the Continent, not solely from shuttling between their residence in Cambridge and their cottage in Brittany. His Europeanism had a Latin inflection: call it Europeanismus. He would not have embraced many previous political and imperial proclamations of Romanness, but all the same he aspired to being culturally a *civis Romanus*. At the core of *Romanitas* as he conceived of it lay his beloved Latin and the perception that without the ineffable riches of Latinity, the European Middle Ages and its vernacular literatures could make no sense. This perspective informed his succinct *Dante and Medieval Latin Traditions* (Cambridge, 1986), a slim study in which he had the brilliance to achieve the stunningly obvious by situating the greatest of Italian and medieval poets within the Latin Middle Ages.[17]

---

[15] Peter Dronke, "Curtius as Medievalist and Modernist," in *Times Literary Supplement*, 3 October 1980, pp. 1103–6; and *Poetic Individuality in the Middle Ages,* 2nd ed. (London, 1986), pp. xi–xix and 1–22.

[16] *Hildegard of Bingen: The Context of Her Thought and Art* (London, 1998).

[17] The book was, incidentally, only one stop in the long itinerary of his recurrent engagement with Dante. Further examples are hardly needed, but see Peter Dronke, *Dante's Second Love: The Originality and Contexts of the Convivio* (Exeter, 1997).

The drive to bridge the often misleading divide between Latin and vernacular was paramount in Dronke's writings for the first few decades, hence the aptness of the designation for one volume of his reprinted essays, *Latin and Vernacular Poets of the Middle Ages* (Aldershot, 1991). He sought to straddle various other supposed chasms, as between learned and popular or, in the name of another book, *Sacred and Profane Thought in the Early Middle Ages* (Florence, 2016). His application of such descriptors was not ironic, but at the same time it was not as naïve as had been for example Raby's triage between *Secular Latin Poetry* and *Christian Latin Poetry* in the titles of his surveys, which (somewhat sadly) have decades later still not been wholly displaced or replaced in English-language scholarship. Dronke relished taking hold of ostensible antitheses and demonstrating that they were not quite so opposite after all. This pleasure in dissolving dichotomies is likewise latent in the Carl Newell Jackson Lectures that he delivered at Harvard University, which he revised rapidly into *Verse with Prose from Petronius to Dante: The Art and Scope of the Mixed Form* (Cambridge, Mass., 1994). A keynote within this appreciation of Menippean satire is Boethius's *Consolation of Philosophy*.

At the beginning of my career, substantial attention was lavished upon twelfth-century stars such as Bernardus Silvestris and Alan of Lille, owing to the transcendent visions of their personification allegories and to the Chartrian Platonism with which these thinkers were allegedly linked. These texts had earlier elicited effort and praise from many intelligent people, such as Johan Huizinga (1872–1945), C.S. Lewis, and Ernst Robert Curtius – to stay silent about incisive medieval readers, such as Jean de Meun and Dante Alighieri. Now their ranks were joined by Brian Stock (1939–) and Winthrop Wetherbee (1938–), but eventually above all by Peter Dronke.

At first this development caught me unawares. Consider an understatement: graduate students, in their insecure and conflicted all-knowingness, can be judgmental. True to form, I had typecast my superviser rashly and wrongfully as exclusively belletristic. Sure, the front cover to his first volume of collected articles, what a German would put out under the heading of *Kleine Schriften,* proclaims its topic to be *The Medieval Poet and His World* (Rome, 1984). Yet on the whole, nothing could have been further from the truth than categorizing Dronke as purely literary when in contradistinction his corpus lists toward the heavily philosophical – and even more when it blends the literary and philosophical. First came *Fabula: Explorations in the Uses of Myth in Medieval Platonism* (Leiden, 1974) and next what would emerge as the standard working edition of Bernardus Silvestis's *Cosmographia* (Leiden, 1978). His second installment of collected essays, *Intellectuals and Poets in Medieval Europe* (Rome, 1992), though aptly entitled, could have had *Philosophers* swapped out for *Intellectuals:* it opens with "New Approaches to the School of Chartres" before segueing into "Bernard Silvestris, Natura, and Personification." Perhaps the most stupendous surprise was *A History of Twelfth-Century Western Philosophy* that Peter

Dronke edited (Cambridge, 1988). Twenty years later followed *The Spell of Calcidius: Platonic Images in the Medieval West* (Florence, 2008). John Marenbon astutely put his finger on the intersection between the two fields and its salience in the criticism of his dissertation director, mentor, and friend by publishing a collection called *Poetry and Philosophy in the Middle Ages: A Festschrift for Peter Dronke* (Leiden, 2001).[18] At a more advanced level, John distinguished, in Peter's perennial preoccupations, between poet-philosophers such as Eriugena and Peter Abelard, and philospher-poets, preeminent among whom would be Dante.[19]

Anglophone readers who are not determined bibliographers may miss other weighty contributions by Peter Dronke, such the five-volume Latin edition and Italian translation of John Scot Eriugena's *Periphyseon* that he oversaw (Rome, 2012–2017). In the same set of books will appear Peter's commentary and introduction to an edition of Boethius's *Consolation of Philosophy*. Just a few years ago, he attended the premiere in which the international ensemble for medieval music "Sequentia" performed and recorded the songs of Boethius as they would have been sung in the eleventh century.[20] Also posthumous will be, with help from John Marenbon, his edition of the *Problemata Heloissae* for the *Corpus Christianorum*.

The *Problemata* brings to mind Dronke's longstanding engrossment in Heloise and Peter Abelard. Here it warrants mention that he paid pioneering attention to the writings of women in the Middle Ages. His immensely impactful *Women Writers of the Middle Ages* (Cambridge, 1984) came out against the political backdrop of so-called second-wave feminism, which ran from the 1960s through the 1980s and advocated for equal rights for women. Whatever his values may have been from his own upbringing or from the atmosphere enveloping him at this later point in his life, ideological considerations do not radiate from the canon of his publications on female authors. Instead, once again his fascination with their personalities, styles, and words stands out. He has had his most positive effects in conjuring up some of the most remarkable personages of the Middle Ages, in fashions that make them step off the page as breathing, thinking, and feeling beings, women who had been largely ignored or unknown before he galvanized readers to picture them and even dream about them, Perpetua, Dhuoda, Hrotsvitha, and more.

Here too we can perceive without much exertion a consistent cluster of focuses. One is Hildegard of Bingen, to whom he devoted not just the longest chapter in that foundational work on women writers but also an appendix with a selection of texts by

---

[18] The fullest biography before his death was the introductory essay by John Marenbon, "Peter Dronke and Medieval Latin at Cambridge," in *Poetry & Philosophy in the Middle Ages*, ed. Marenbon, pp. 1–5.

[19] Marenbon, *Preface*, in *Poetry & Philosophy in the Middle Ages*, ed. Marenbon, p. x

[20] Sequentia, Dronke Nachruf: http://www.sequentia.org/images/Dronke_Nachruf.pdf (accessed 7 June 2020).

her. His engagement with the visionary spanned decades, leading among other things to seven CDs of her music that "Sequentia" launched into producing in 1982. This early collaboration, for which the groundwork was laid in correspondence one year earlier, led to at least a half dozen further recordings for which Peter Dronke supplied ever-meticulous texts and translations. In 1994 he inaugurated his ambitious but short-lived Cambridge Medieval Classics with his edition and English of *Nine Medieval Latin Plays*, one of which was Hildegard's *Ordo virtutum*. In 1998 came the volume coedited with Charles Burnett, entitled *Hildegard of Bingen: The Context of Her Thought and Art* (London, 1998). Dronke's philological commitment to the extraordinary German Benedictine had later resurgences when he edited for the *Corpus Christianorum Continuatio Mediaevalis* her *Liber divinorum operum* (Turnhout, 1996) and *Ordo virtutum* (Turnhout, 2007).

Scholars may deposit three sorts of *Nachlass*. One is the students who are shaped by their teachings, intellects, and charisma; another is the scholarship that outlives them, which in Medieval Latin studies continues mostly to radiate from printed books and articles; and the third comes from service to the profession. Though a few key names stand out here, I will rely on my successors to draw up full roll calls of certifiably Dronkean acolytes. Compiling a complete catalogue of his publications would make a worthy project for a generous soul. As for the third, I have touched upon many pieces of evidence that confirm a heartwarming love for our shared endeavour of Medieval Latin studies, counting his dual-language series with Cambridge University Press, even though it failed to survive. But the most memorable is the Third International Medieval Latin Congress in Cambridge in September 1998, roughly sixty papers from which saw the light in the *Publications of The Journal of Medieval Latin*.[21]

Our specialization has been on shaky ground all along—but as inhabitants of an earthquake zone, we know how to steady ourselves. Peter opened his inaugural lecture with a praise of Medieval Latin gleaned from *Lateinische Gedichte des X. und XI. Jahrhunderts*, a book Jacob Grimm co-authored in 1838. A round half century elapsed before 1888, when the legendary Ludwig Traube took up a chair devoted to the Latin language and literature of the Middle Ages. Fast forward not quite one and a half centuries: at this moment the area of study has the most vigour, in professorships and students, in Germany and the Romance-speaking countries, specially Italy, but it lives on too throughout Europe, the Americas and Asia, and here and there elsewhere. Worldwide, on all these continents people who once took courses and wrote dissertations with Peter Dronke remain active teachers and researchers.

---

[21] *Latin Culture in the Eleventh Century: Proceedings of the Third International Conference on Medieval Latin Studies Cambridge, 9–12 September 1998*, ed. Michael W. Herren, Christopher J. McDonough, and Ross G. Arthur, 2 vols. (Turnhout, 2001).

Peter Dronke (1934–2020)

It defies imagination, a cerebral and spiritual faculty he so valued, to accept that a creature of such creativity and dynamism should no longer be with us, but that is the new reality: Peter Dronke is gone. Despite a year-long decline and increasingly distressing frailness, he carried on, very much himself in mind and spirit. He toiled on until the end drew near, and his publications will be forthcoming for a while yet. Thanks to them, memories of him will last much longer. These thoughts would console him. At 2 a.m. on Sunday, 19 April 2020, he died of kidney failure in Cambridge at the age of 85. He leaves his daughter Cressida and two grandchildren by her, Gabriel and Lara. Although he was not a victim of COVID-19, Peter's demise punctuates in sad style for Medieval Latinists everywhere the saga of the pandemic, which has resulted in so many solitary deaths without the solace of memorial services.

Jan M. Ziolkowski, Harvard University

Stephen of Ripon's *Vita S. Wilfridi*: Genre, Political Theory and Historical Representation in the Early Middle Ages*

EVAN WILSON
University of California, Berkeley

Introduction

Stephen of Ripon's *Vita S. Wilfridi* (hereafter *VSW*), written ca. 712–714, can be described as an unusually "historical" saint's life in two senses: it both offers a surprising amount of historical detail and resembles, in some ways, a work of early medieval historiography.[1] Alan Thacker, for instance, remarks on the insertion of contemporary historical documents in the text, "according to the conventions of the day a feature of history rather than hagiography."[2] Walter Goffart, meanwhile, describes the *VSW* as "an outstanding biography" and "the nearest thing to a history of the English church until Bede."[3] Where scholars have noted such features, they have tended to interpret them as strategic elements of Stephen's polemical aims,[4] and the *VSW* has productively been read as part of a "pamphlet war" in early Northumbrian hagiography.[5]

---

* I am grateful to Katherine O'Brien O'Keeffe, Emily Thornbury, and Jacob Hobson for their generous feedback at multiple stages of the writing process. I also thank Mischa Park-Doob, the two anonymous readers of the journal, and Greti Dinkova-Bruun for their helpful questions and comments.

[1] *The Life of Bishop Wilfrid by Eddius Stephanus*, ed. Bertram Colgrave (Cambridge, 1927). For the date, see Clare Stancliffe, "Dating Wilfrid's Death and Stephen's *Life*," in *Wilfrid: Abbot, Bishop, Saint: Papers from the 1300th Anniversary Conferences*, ed. N.J. Higham (Donington, 2013), pp. 17–26. For an account of the *VSW*'s focus on historical detail in the context of Merovingian hagiography, see Paul Fouracre, "Merovingian History and Merovingian Hagiography," *Past and Present* 127 (1990), 3–38, at pp. 11–12.

[2] Alan Thacker, "Wilfrid, His Cult and His Biographer," in *Wilfrid: Abbot, Bishop, Saint*, ed. Higham, pp. 1–16, at 3.

[3] Walter Goffart, *The Narrators of Barbarian History (A.D. 550–800): Jordanes, Gregory of Tours, Bede, and Paul the Deacon* (Princeton, 1988), p. 281.

[4] See Thacker, "Wilfrid," p. 3; Goffart, *Narrators of Barbarian History*, p. 281; David Rollason, "Hagiography and Politics in Early Northumbria," in *Holy Men and Holy Women: Old English Prose Saints' Lives and Their Contexts*, ed. Paul E. Szarmach (Albany, 1996), pp. 95–114, at 104.

[5] Alan Thacker, "Lindisfarne and the Origins of the Cult of St Cuthbert," in *St Cuthbert, His Cult, and His Community to AD 1200*, ed. Gerald Bonner, David Rollason, and Clare Stancliffe (Woodbridge, 1989), pp. 103–22; Clare Stancliffe, "Disputed Episcopacy: Bede, Acca, and the Relationship Between

But the *VSW* can also be read as the product of a series of authorial choices that shed light on the status and uses of genres of historical writing in the early eighth century. Besides contemporary historical documents,[6] the *VSW* contains another passage with a distinctly historiographical flavor and which was apparently composed by Stephen himself: two battle narratives in chapters 19 and 20 which relate battles fought by King Ecgfrith of Northumbria against the Picts and Mercians in the 670s.[7] These battle narratives have been mentioned in passing by Goffart as an aspect of the unusually "historical" nature of the text and examined for what they reveal about Anglo-Saxon concepts of just warfare, but they have not been analyzed at any length.[8] Placed in the context of early medieval historical writing, however, they reveal a shift in the representation of political history that would have profound and long-lasting effects. Earlier saints' lives and histories tend to confine their representation of divine agency in battle to miracles, effectively preserving a distinction between sacred and political/military spheres of action. Stephen of Ripon, however, weaves divine agency and spiritual significance into the battle narrative itself by infusing his political and historical actors – Ecgfrith, Wilfrid, Northumbria, and their foes – with the language of biblical typology and ideal kingship. In doing so, he makes historical narrative into a more effective medium of political argument and propaganda. Most immediately, the innovative representation of battle in the *VSW* is the product of Stephen's hagiographical argument: that Wilfrid's position as bishop enabled Ecgfrith to enact ideal kingship, and Northumbria to enjoy national prosperity. On a more fundamental level, it rests on a distinctly Anglo-Saxon missionary paradigm that neatly aligns royal and ecclesiastical interests and that would be most famously enacted some fifteen or twenty years later in Bede's *Historia ecclesiastica gentis Anglorum* (hereafter

---

Stephen's *Life of St Wilfrid* and the Early Prose Lives of St Cuthbert," *Anglo-Saxon England* 41 (2012), 7–39.

[6] In *The Life of Bishop Wilfrid*, ed. Colgrave, they are: Wilfrid's petitions to Pope Agatho and Pope John VI (pp. 60–62, 104–6); the responses of Agatho and his synod (pp. 64–66); a letter from Theodore of Canterbury to Aethilred of Mercia (p. 88); Wilfrid's confession of faith at a Roman synod in 704 (pp. 112–14); and a letter from Pope John VI to Aethilred of Mercia and Aldfrith of Northumbria (pp. 116–20).

[7] *The Life of Bishop Wilfrid*, ed. Colgrave, pp. 40–42.

[8] Goffart, *Narrators of Barbarian History*, pp. 281, 288; Ben Snook, "Just War in Anglo-Saxon England: Transmission and Reception," in *War and Peace: Critical Issues in European Societies and Literature, 800–1800*, ed. Albrecht Classen and Nadia Margolis (Berlin, 2011), pp. 99–120, at 105–8. Snook argues that the battle narratives espouse a Ciceronian view of just warfare. However, since, as Snook notes, "there … is no particular reason to suppose that [Stephen of Ripon] had read Cicero," the significance of this finding is unclear (p. 116).

HE).[9] It would also go on to shape Carolingian political theology by way of the Anglo-Saxon mission to the Continent. Indeed, Carolingian histories offer the closest parallels to Stephen's manner of historical representation. By importing battle narratives and other historiographical conventions into his *Vita*, Stephen constructs Wilfrid as a figure within a public sphere of action traditionally associated with kings and other political figures. In the literary history illuminated by Stephen's act of generic experimentation, genre conventions thus serve as the building blocks of institutional identities. The traffic between *vitae* and *historiae*, I argue, ultimately allowed Stephen and others to construct a sacralised political sphere in historical narrative.

Early Medieval Genre and the Representation of Battle

Any discussion of the role of genre in shaping early medieval historical representation and political theory must first wrestle with the status of hagiography and historiography as genres. In recent decades, a number of scholars have questioned whether a boundary between these two "genres" makes sense for the early Middle Ages.[10] They have pointed out that early medieval authors did not use consistent terms of genre[11] and often combined political and ecclesiastical history in individual works.[12] Indeed, the notion of "hagiography" and "historiography" as genres concerning fundamentally different kinds of subject-matter collapses in the face of the self-conscious eclecticism of works such as Gregory of Tours' *Historiae* and Bede's *HE*. However, the problem

---

[9] Bede, *Historia ecclesiastica gentis Anglorum*, in *Beda: Storia degli Inglesi*, ed. Michael Lapidge, 2 vols. (Milan, 2008–2010).

[10] Felice Lifshitz, "Beyond Positivism and Genre: 'Hagiographical' Texts as Historical Narrative," *Viator* 25 (1994), 95–113, forcefully critiques the assumptions that underlie modern distinctions between "hagiography" and "historiography" for the Early Middle Ages and argues that "the concept of a genre of 'hagiography' is a historiographical construction and, ipso facto, an ideological tool ... [which] had no function in the ninth, tenth, and eleventh centuries and thus as a conceptual category did not exist" (p. 113). Guy Philippart, "L'Hagiographie comme littérature: Concept récent et nouveaux programmes?," *Revue des Sciences Humaines* 251 (1998), 11–39, traces the history of the term "hagiography" and concludes that it remains useful even though it embraces a number of literary genres. More recently, Anna Taylor, "Hagiography and Early Medieval History," *Religion Compass* 7 (2013), 1–14, reviews scholarship on the genres of hagiography and historiography over the preceding twenty years and argues, like Lifshitz, that "hagiography" imposes a false sense of unity on a diverse textual record.

[11] See Roger Ray, "Historiography," in *Medieval Latin: An Introduction and Bibliographical Guide*, ed. Frank A.C. Mantello and A.G. Rigg (Washington, DC, 1996), pp. 639–49, at 639.

[12] Gregory of Tours' *Historiae* is often cited in this regard: see Goffart, *Narrators of Barbarian History*, p. 245; Martin Heinzelmann, "Hagiographischer und historischer Diskurs bei Gregor von Tours?," in *Aevum inter utrumque: Mélanges offerts à Gabriel Sanders, professeur émérite à l'Université de Gand*, ed. Marc Van Uytfanghe and Roland Demeulenaere (The Hague, 1991), pp. 237–58, at 238–39. However, see below, pp. 17–18.

lies in the assumption that "genres" have to have mutually exclusive forms and objects of representation. Instead, genre may be usefully understood as a blueprint for composition that is in conversation with earlier models.[13] *Historiae* and *vitae*, in this view, offered two broad paradigms for the representation of history in the early Middle Ages. *Historia*'s eclecticism is precisely what makes it *historia*.[14] *Vitae*, on the other hand, are more formally restrictive and thematically unified; they aim to narrate exemplary lives.[15] Early medieval notions of history-writing were still influenced by the traditional focus of Greek and Roman history on politics and warfare,[16] and all works referred to as "histories" contain at least some material on these subjects.[17] *Vitae*, on the other hand, only tend to include references to political history insofar as their saintly subjects interact with that history. From the early days of the Church, textual representations of sanctity often emphasize the rejection of the political and social

---

[13] See Hans Robert Jauss, "Theory of Genres and Medieval Literature," in his *Toward an Aesthetics of Reception*, trans. Timothy Bahti, with an introduction by Paul de Man (Minneapolis, 1982), pp. 76–109, at 93–94: "Where there is no initially posited and described generic form, the establishing of a generic structure must be gained from the perception [*Anschauung*] of individual texts, in a continually renewed pre-conceiving [*Vorgriff*] of an expectable whole or regulative system."

[14] Christina S. Kraus, "Is *historia* a Genre? (With Notes on Caesar's First Landing in Britain, *Bellum Gallicum* 4.24–25)," in *Generic Interfaces in Latin Literature: Encounters, Interactions, and Transformations*, ed. Theodore D. Papanghelis, Stephen J. Harrison, and Stavros Frangoulidis (Berlin, 2013), pp. 417–32, at 422: "More than any other prose form except perhaps the novel, the portmanteau genre of *historia* delights in the genres with which it is affiliated and of which it is constituted. This inclusiveness is part of its self-image as genre, from the very beginning: This is not news."

[15] See Thomas D. Hill, "*Imago Dei*: Genre, Symbolism, and Anglo-Saxon Hagiography," in *Holy Men and Holy Women*, ed. Szarmach, pp. 35–50, at 36.

[16] Arnaldo Momigliano, *The Classical Foundations of Modern Historiography* (Berkeley, 1990), p. 59: "Thucydides saw to it that Herodotus did not prevail. In consequence history became a narration of political and military events, preference being given to the events of which the writer had been a witness. All the 'classic' historians after Herodotus – Thucydides, Xenophon, Ephorus, Polybius, Sallust, Livy, Tacitus – conformed to this pattern"; Roberto Nicolai, "The Place of History in the Ancient World," in *A Companion to Greek and Roman Historiography*, ed. John Marincola, 2 vols. (Malden, MA, 2007), 1:13–26, at 14: "[The] goal of an ancient historical account is never purely scientific and cognitive, but is always linked to creating paradigms, predominantly politico-militaristic or ethical ones."

[17] See Karl Ferdinand Werner, "Gott, Herrscher und Historiograph: Geschichtsschreiber als Interpret des Wirkens Gottes in der Welt und Ratgeber der Könige (4. bis 12. Jahrhundert)," in *Deus Qui Mutat Tempora: Menschen und Institutionen im Wandel des Mittelalters*, ed. Ernst-Dieter Hehl, Hubertus Seibert, and Franz Staab (Sigmaringen, 1987), pp. 1–31; and Karl Ferdinand Werner, "L'*Historia* et les rois," in *Religion et culture autour de l'an Mil: Royaume capétien et Lotharingie*, ed. Dominique Iogna-Prat and Jean-Charles Picard (Paris, 1990), pp. 135–43.

order by defiant, persecuted martyrs and ascetic monks and bishops.[18] This legacy, too, continued to shape early medieval hagiography, even as it came to deal with subjects who took a leading role in politics and engaged in violent political conflicts.[19] Martyrdom and the rejection of material luxury and secular status remained consistent themes of late Merovingian hagiography.[20]

By the time that Stephen of Ripon wrote the *VSW*, the battle narrative had come to be seen as the epitome of the political and military subject-matter of historiography. Herodotus,[21] Thucydides,[22] and Livy[23] all prioritize warfare in the prologues to their works. In these authors, warfare is not explicitly presented as the main subject of a work of history; rather, it can be seen as the prototypical example of a *res gesta*, the standard term for the sort of official, public event that histories were intended to

---

[18] On the influence of early martyr narratives on hagiography, see Andrew Louth, "Hagiography," in *The Cambridge History of Early Christian Literature*, ed. Frances Young, Lewis Ayres, and Andrew Louth, assisted by Augustine Casiday (Cambridge, 2007), pp. 358–61. Sulpicius Severus's *Vita S. Martini*, written ca. 396, created an influential model of an ascetic bishop who shunned worldly power. The text is edited by Karl Halm in *Sulpicii Severi libri qui supersunt*, CSEL 1 (Vienna, 1866), pp. 109–37. See Isabel Moreira, *Dreams, Visions, and Spiritual Authority in Merovingian Gaul* (Ithaca, NY, 2000), pp. 52–60.

[19] For discussions of the problem of late Merovingian sanctity, see František Graus, *Volk, Herrscher und Heiliger im Reich der Merowinger: Studien zur Hagiographie der Merowingerzeit* (Prague, 1965), pp. 353–90; Paul Fouracre and Richard Gerberding, *Late Merovingian France: History and Hagiography 640–720* (Manchester, 1996), pp. 43–52; and Jamie Kreiner, *The Social Life of Hagiography in the Merovingian Kingdom* (Cambridge, 2014), pp. 33–87.

[20] See below, pp. 25–26.

[21] Herodotus, *The Persian Wars, Volume I: Books 1–2*, trans. A.D. Godley, Loeb Classical Library 117 (Cambridge, MA, 1920), I.1, p. 3 (emphasis added): "What Herodotus the Halicarnassian has learnt by inquiry is here set forth: in order that so the memory of the past may not be blotted out from among men by time, and that great and marvellous deeds done by the Greeks and foreigners *and especially the reason why they warred against each other* may not lack renown."

[22] Thucydides, *History of the Peloponnesian War, Volume I: Books 1–2*, trans. C.F. Smith, Loeb Classical Library 108 (Cambridge, MA, 1919), I.i, p. 3 (emphasis added): "For this was the greatest movement that had ever stirred the Hellenes, extending also to some of the Barbarians, one might say even to a very large part of mankind. Indeed, as to the events of the period just preceding this, and those of a still earlier date, it was impossible to get clear information on account of lapse of time; but from evidence which … I find that I can trust, I think that they were not really great either *as regards the wars then waged* or in other particulars."

[23] Livy, *History of Rome, Volume I: Books 1–2*, trans. B.O. Foster, Loeb Classical Library 114 (Cambridge, MA, 1919), I.praef, pp. 5–7 (emphasis added): "Here are the questions to which I would have every reader give his close attention – what life and morals were like; through what men and by what policies, *in peace and in war*, empire was established and enlarged."

commemorate.[24] Augustine and Orosius made this prototypical status more explicit in the process of using classical historiography for new, polemical aims. For them, the focus of classical historians on warfare is evidence of the unremittingly violent nature of human history before the coming of Christianity. Warfare belongs to the sphere of the *civitas terrena*, not the *civitas Dei*, making it fallen and incomplete.[25] Some 150 years later, Gregory of Tours maintains this general view of warfare in his *Historiae*, contrasting it with holy miracles to reveal the polarised nature of morality in history:[26]

> Prosequentes ordinem temporum, mixte confusequae [sic] *tam virtutes sanctorum quam strages gentium* memoramus. Non enim inrationabiliter accipi puto, se *filicem beatorum vitam inter miserorum memoremus excidia*, cum idem non facilitas scripturis, sed temporum series praestitit ... Sic et Eusebius, Severus Hieronimusquae [sic] in chronicis atque Horosius *et bella regum et virtutes martyrum* pariter texuerunt.

> Following chronological order, I will record both *the miracles of the saints and the slaughters of nations* willy-nilly. For I do not think that it will seem irrational if I record *the happy life of the blessed amongst the disasters of the wretched*, since this is determined, not by the ease of the writer, but by the order of events ... In the same way, Eusebius, Severus, Jerome, and Orosius interwove *the wars of kings and the powers of the martyrs* in their chronicles.

Gregory develops a rhetorical contrast between *virtutes sanctorum, filicem beatorum vitam*, and *virtutes martyrum*, on the one hand, and *strages gentium, miserorum excidia*, and *bella regum* on the other, as two fundamentally distinct bodies of historical subject-matter. And though he declares his intention to bring together these facets of *historia*, he also suggests a potential contradiction between them, a distinction of both moral status and textual form.[27] It would have also been possible, he implies, to write a history containing only *bella regum* or *virtutes sanctorum*. A number of works from the seventh and early eighth centuries do just that, revising Gregory's *Historiae* to focus

---

[24] For classical Roman uses of *res gestae*, see Darryl W. Palmer, "Acts and the Historical Monograph," *Tyndale Bulletin* 43.2 (1992), 373–88, at pp. 380–81. For the role of prototype effects in classification, see George Lakoff, *Women, Fire, and Dangerous Things: What Categories Reveal About the Mind* (Chicago, 1987), pp. 40–46.

[25] For the primary sources, see *Sancti Aurelii Augustini: De Civitate Dei libri xxii*, ed. Emmanuel Hofmann, CSEL 40.1 and 40.2 (Vienna, 1899–1900); *Pauli Orosii Historiarum adversum paganos libri VII*, ed. Karl Zangemeister (Leipzig, 1889), V.iv, p. 146. See also R.A. Markus, *Saeculum: History and Society in the Theology of St Augustine* (Cambridge, 1970), pp. 22–71.

[26] *Gregorii episcopi Turonensis: Libri historiarum X*, ed. Bruno Krusch and Wilhelm Levison, MGH SS Rer. Mer. 1.1 (Hannover, 1885, repr. 1951), II.praef., p. 36 (emphasis added). All translations from this text are my own.

[27] Gregory often calls attention to the switch in subject-matter when he moves between political history and hagiographical episodes. On this fact and its implications for his practice as a historian, see Goffart, *Narrators of Barbarian History*, p. 154.

on political rather than ecclesiastical history.[28] A few of them also add continuations extending to their own time. One such work, the so-called *Chronicle of Fredegar*, includes a preface written sometime in the seventh century.[29] While it draws on prefaces from Jerome's translation of Eusebius's *Chronicon*,[30] it also includes an apparently original passage that sets out the subject-matter:[31]

> Trasactis [*sic*] namque Gregorii libri uolumine, temporum gesta que undique scripta potui repperire et mihi postea fuerunt cognita, *acta regum et bella gentium quae*

---

[28] On the manuscript tradition of Gregory's *Historiae*, see Pascale Bourgain and Martin Heinzelmann, "L'œuvre de Grégoire de Tours: La diffusion des manuscripts," in *Grégoire de Tours et l'espace gaulois: Actes du Congrès International Tours, 3–5 Novembre 1994*, ed. Nancy Gauthier and Henri Galinié (Tours, 1997), pp. 273–318. See also Walter Goffart, "From *Historiae* to *Historia Francorum* and Back Again: Aspects of the Textual History of Gregory of Tours," in *Religion, Culture, and Society in the Early Middle Ages: Studies in Honour of Richard E. Sullivan*, ed. Thomas F.X. Noble and John J. Contreni (Kalamazoo, MI, 1987), pp. 55–76, which argues that seventh-century redactors reworked Gregory's *Histories* into a political and ethnic history. Martin Heinzelmann notes the omission of almost every chapter of Gregory's work whose title refers to a cleric by name; see his *Gregory of Tours*, pp. 198–201. Helmut Reimitz has taken issue with Goffart and Heinzelmann's findings in his *History, Frankish Identity and the Framing of Western Ethnicity, 550–850* (Cambridge, 2015), arguing instead that the redactions of the *Histories* "released the text from the outdated spiritual topography it represented and the obsolete political constellation to which it was connected" (p. 158). However, the omission of ecclesiastical chapter-titles, along with the evidence of later Merovingian historiography, continues to support a view of secularization.

[29] *The Fourth Book of the Chronicle of Fredegar with Its Continuations*, ed. and trans. J.M. Wallace-Hadrill (London, 1960). The authorship and date of *Fredegar* remain difficult to pin down, but there is currently a rough consensus that the text was compiled by a single author working in Neustria or Burgundy, possibly ca. 660. See Walter Goffart, "The Fredegar Problem Reconsidered," *Speculum* 38.2 (1963), 206–41; Roger Collins, *Fredegar*, Authors of the Middle Ages 4 (Aldershot, 1996). The first three books of the work chiefly abridge and adapt earlier material, including the anonymous *Liber generationis*, the chronicles of Jerome and Hydatius, and Gregory's *Historiae*; see Goffart, "The Fredegar Problem Reconsidered," at pp. 209–16. The fourth book appears to be an original composition and more closely reflects the voice and priorities of its anonymous seventh-century author. Meanwhile, the entire *Chronicle* was revised and added to in the eighth century, possibly to coincide with the coronation of Pippin the Short in 751. I refer to the new annals of this version, extending from 724 to 751, as the *First Continuation of the Chronicle of Fredegar*. For the date and composition of this continuation, see Roger Collins, "Deception and Misrepresentation in Early Eighth Century Frankish Historiography: Two Case Studies," in *Karl Martell in seiner Zeit*, ed. Jörg Jarnut, Ulrich Nonn, and Michael Richter (Sigmaringen, 1994), pp. 227–47, at 241–46. For the annals, see *The Fourth Book of the Chronicle of Fredegar*, ed. and trans. Wallace-Hadrill, pp. 89–102.

[30] Justin Lake discusses the prologue, particularly the meaning of "Fredegar's" statements about his reuse of earlier historians, in his "Rethinking Fredegar's Prologue," *The Journal of Medieval Latin* 25 (2015), 1–27.

[31] *Fourth Book of the Chronicle of Fredegar*, ed. and trans. Wallace-Hadrill, praef., pp. 2–3 (emphasis added).

gesserunt, legendo simul et audiendo etim et uidendo cuncta que certeficatus [*sic*] cognoui huius libelli uolumine scribere non silui.

At the end of Gregory's work I did not fall silent but wrote on my own account the events of the times, which I could find written anywhere and which became known to me afterwards, [that is] *the deeds of kings and the wars of peoples which they waged*: everything, for which I could vouch, that I had learned through reading, hearing, or seeing.

The author appears to consider the "acta regum et bella gentium" the subject of a particular type of historical work. Battle narratives no longer hinted at pagan historiography; instead, they could now be loosely identified with the genre of historiography as a whole. Gone, too, is the negative moral valence attached to earthly warfare in Gregory and Orosius. Some fifteen years after the writing of the *VSW*, in about 727, an anonymous Frankish author made another use of a secularised version of Gregory's *Historiae*, adding a continuation up to his own time that focuses heavily on political and military history.[32] These handful of surviving Frankish histories from the period of the *VSW*, then, suggest an ongoing or even an increasing association between histories, kingship, and battle.

Contemporary saints' lives, on the other hand, almost never contain battle narratives except in the context of miracle stories. One of the most frequent kinds of saintly battle miracles, in fact, preempts battle itself by the power of prayer.[33] Other miracles tend to interrupt the ordinary course of battle. Bede's *Ecclesiastical History*, for instance, describes the Frankish bishop Germanus of Auxerre helping the Britons to defeat the pagan Picts and Saxons by shouting "Alleluia!" on the battlefield three times, which terrifies the pagans into fleeing and ends the battle then and there.[34] A number of *vitae* with Irish influences feature stories in which a saint miraculously knows that a battle is taking place elsewhere and weighs in on, or even influences, the outcome.[35] In two of these *vitae*, the saint is depicted as a reluctant interpreter of

---

[32] See Richard A. Gerberding, *The Rise of the Carolingians and the* Liber Historiae Francorum (Oxford, 1987), pp. 31–46.

[33] See *Vita S. Genovefae Virginis Parisiensis*, ed. Bruno Krusch, in *Passiones vitaeque sanctorum aevi Merovingici I*, MGH SS. Rer. Mer. 3 (Hanover, 1896), pp. 204–38, at 220. On the dating of this text to the Merovingian instead of the Carolingian period, as Krusch had argued, see Martin Heinzelmann, "Vita sanctae Genovefae: Recherches sur les critères de datation d'un texte hagiographique," in *Les vies anciennes de sainte Geneviève de Paris: Études critiques*, ed. Martin Heinzelmann and Joseph-Claude Poulin (Paris, 1986), pp. 1–111.

[34] Bede, *HE* i. 20, ed. Lapidge, 1:84, 86.

[35] See *Adomnán's Life of Columba* ed. Alan Orr Anderson and Marjorie Ogilvie Anderson (London, 1961), pp. 224–26; *Vitae S. Columbani abbatis discipulorumque eius libri duo auctore Iona* [hereafter *Vita S. Columbani*], ed. Bruno Krusch, in *Passiones vitaeque sanctorum aevi Merovingici*, MGH SS. Rer. Mer. 4

God's judgment in history. For instance, Cuthbert exclaims that a battle has just occurred and that "iudicatumque est iudicium de populis nostris bellantibus aduersum" – "a judgement has been handed down against our people in battle," then refuses to clarify the nature of his vision; Columbanus, on the other hand, receives a vision that a battle is currently taking place, then declares that it would be "foolish and impious" ("stultum ac religione alienum") to pray for the victory of one side, when God alone is the arbiter of history.[36] Adomnan's *Vita S. Columbae*, written in the early eighth century, differs from the *Vita S. Columbani* in claiming St. Columba's power and willingness to directly affect the outcome of the battle by prayer.[37] It cites a miracle in which Columba appears to Oswald, king of Northumbria, in a dream the night before a battle, ensuring his victory and conversion to Christianity.[38] While these *vitae* show an increasing engagement by the saint in warfare and consequently in political history, the battles narrated remain calamitous or far-off events that inspire miraculous intervention or prophetic knowledge. The battle narrative itself, consequently, is usually very brief and is contained within the framework of the miracle narrative. In almost every *vita*, the saint's intervention in a battle is a miraculous moment of contact between divine power and the *civitas terrena*. Even interpreting its significance calls for the prophetic powers of a Cuthbert or a Columbanus.

The same reluctance to interpret battle as a record of divine judgement obtains in pre-Wilfridian histories such as those by Gregory of Tours and "Fredegar." Gregory's battle narratives are typically straightforward and annalistic. Any moral or spiritual significance that they carry is conveyed through miracles or through events before or after battle, not in the details of the battle's progression.[39] For instance, Gregory tells the story of a conflict between three brothers for the control of the Thuringi, a civil war whose improbity Gregory makes clear by describing how one of them had an "uxor iniqua atque crudelis Amalaberga nomen [quae] inter hos fratres bellum civile dissimenat" – "a wicked and cruel wife named Amalaberga who stirred up civil war between these brothers."[40] This brother engages the military aid of King Theuderic of

---

(Hanover and Leipzig, 1902), pp. 1–156, at 105; *Two Lives of Saint Cuthbert*, ed. Bertram Colgrave (Cambridge, 1940), p. 122.

[36] *Two Lives of Saint Cuthbert*, ed. Colgrave, p. 122; *Vita S. Columbani*, ed. Krusch, p. 105. All translations of these texts are my own.

[37] *Adomnán's Life of Columba*, ed. Anderson and Anderson, I.i, p. 14.

[38] *Adomnán's Life of Columba*, ed. Anderson and Anderson, pp. 14–15.

[39] On the varying uses of narration and direct commentary in Gregory's *Historiae*, see Felix Thürlemann, *Der historische Diskurs bei Gregor von Tours: Topoi und Wirklichkeit* (Bern, 1974), pp. 73–112.

[40] *Libri Historiarum X*, ed. Krusch and Levison, III.iv, p. 100.

the Franks, and they defeat the forces of another brother. However, the wicked outcome of this wicked deed, the battle itself, is narrated in value-neutral terms:

> Ille autem gavisus, haec audiens, cum exercitu ad eum dirigit. Coniunctique simul fidem sibi invicem dantis, egressi sunt ad bellum. Confligentisque cum Baderico, exercitum eius adterunt ipsumque obtruncant gladio, et obtenta victoria, Theudoricus ad propria est reversus.
>
> Rejoicing upon hearing this, he proceeded towards him with an army. After pledging their loyalty to each other, they departed to battle. Fighting with Baderic, they crush his army and kill him with a sword, and having obtained victory, Theuderic returned to his own land.

Gregory only suggests the depravity of the victor by writing that he afterwards disdained to fulfill an agreement he had made with Theuderic to split the kingdom, causing a "great enmity" ("grandis inimicitia") to arise between the two men. By ending the chapter with the mention of this enmity, Gregory seems to be commenting ironically on the futility of the battle and the wickedness of its victors.[41] His annalistic style of narrating battle matches his disapproving reference to warfare as *strages gentium*, the epitome of the fallenness and incompleteness of human society. For Gregory, warfare belongs to the *civitas terrena*, and as such, does not ordinarily bear spiritual significance.

Gregory even preserves the distinction between political and sacred history in his narration of battles in which divine power plays a role. The most famous example is the battle with the Alamanni that serves as the occasion for Clovis's conversion to Christianity. Observing that the Franks were being routed, Clovis prays to Christ: "Te nunc invoco, tibi credere desidero, tantum ut eruar ab adversariis meis" – "I call upon you now, and I will believe in you, if only I may be delivered from my enemies."[42] Miraculously, "Cumque haec dicerit, Alamanni terga vertentes, in fugam labi coeperunt" – "As he said this, the Alamans turned their backs and began to flee," and the Alamanni surrender to Clovis."[43] Gregory does not state directly that God brought this victory to Clovis or portray the battle in explicitly moral terms; his locutions describing the Alamans' defeat, *terga vertere* and *fugam labi*, are standard ways that he – and historians before him – narrate retreat or flight in battle.[44] After Clovis converts

---

[41] As Goffart has argued, Gregory writes about the morally bankrupt events of human political history in a mode of satire; Goffart, *Narrators of Barbarian History*, pp. 197–203.

[42] *Libri historiarum X*, ed. Krusch and Levison, II.xxx, p. 75.

[43] *Libri historiarum X*, ed. Krusch and Levison, pp. 75–76.

[44] The expression "fugam labi" is found in *Historiarum adversum paganos libri VII*, ed. Zangemeister, V.iv, p. 146; Josephus, *Hegesippi qui dicitur Historiae Libri V, Pt. 1: Textum criticum continens*, ed. Vincentius Ussani (Leipzig, 1932), I.i, p. 33; and, not least, elsewhere in Gregory's *Libri historiarum X*, ed. Krusch and Levison, II.ii, p. 39; IV.xlii, p. 175. "Terga vertere" is also widely attested in ancient

to Christianity, he makes war on the forces of the Arian Visigothic king Alaric, offering Gregory the chance to stage warfare between believers and nonbelievers. Crucially, however, God's intervention on the Franks' behalf happens primarily through a series of miracles and signs before battle begins; the actual battle narrative is brief and unadorned. Clovis declares: "Eamus cum Dei adiutorium [sic], et superatis redegamus terram in ditione nostra" – "Let us go with God's help and, after defeating them, bring the territory back into our control," and the Franks benefit from a number of miracles on their way to battle, including a deer that guides them to a ford in a river and a ball of fire coming from the Church of St. Hilary.[45] Gregory even goes so far as to insert the phrase "Domino adiuvante" into the sentence describing Clovis's victory. However, this phrase is the only embellishment (indeed, the only such in all of the *Historiae*) of what is otherwise a straightforward battle narrative.[46] The marked separation between the progress of the battle and divine intervention supports Michael E. Moore's claim that, for Gregory, "the sphere of historical action was punctuated by the divine, rather than constantly guided by it."[47]

Battle narratives in later Merovingian histories show a continuity with Gregory's *Historiae*, suggesting that shifts in political thought and rhetoric were not instantly reflected in historiography; to some extent, genres offered distinct perspectives on kingship. Both *The Fourth Book of the Chronicle of Fredegar*, written or compiled ca. 660, and the *Liber historiae Francorum* (hereafter *LHF*), written ca. 726–727, continue to narrate battle primarily as an event of political history, not sacred history. Nonetheless, the era when these two texts were written has been shown to be a time when kingship was increasingly Christianised in Merovingian liturgy,[48] Church coun-

---

and early medieval historiography, including in Livy, *History of Rome, Volume I: Books 1–2*, I.xiv, p. 52; Caesar, *The Civil War*, ed. Cynthia Damon, Loeb Classical Library 39 (Harvard, 2016), I.xliii, p. 66; *Historiarum adversum paganos libri VII*, ed. Zangemeister, III.xvi, p. 82; and elsewhere in Gregory's *Libri historiarum X*, ed. Krusch and Levison, II.xix, p. 65; II.xxxvii, p. 87; IV.xlii, p. 175. See also Gen. 14.10 and Jos. 7.4.

[45] *Libri Historiarum X*, ed. Krusch and Levison, II.xxxvii, p. 85.

[46] *Libri Historiarum X*, ed. Krusch and Levison, II.xxxvii, 87: "Interea Chlodovechus rex cum Alarico rege Gothorum in campo Vogladense decimo ab urbe Pictava miliario convenit, et confligentibus his eminus, resistunt comminus illi. Cumque secundum consuetudinem Gothi terga vertissent, ipse rex Chlodovechus victuriam, Domino adiuvante, obtinuit" – "Meanwhile, King Clovis came togeher with King Alaric of the Goths in the field of Vouillé at the tenth milestone from Poitiers, and with the Goths fighting from a distance, the Franks attacked at close quarters. When the Goths, following their custom, turned their backs, King Clovis obtained victory, with the Lord helping."

[47] Michael E. Moore, *A Sacred Kingdom: Bishops and the Rise of Frankish Kingship, 300–850* (Washington, D.C., 2011), p. 109.

[48] See the *Missa pro principe*, in *The Bobbio Missal: A Gallican Mass-Book (MS. Paris. Lat. 13246)*, ed. E.A. Lowe, Henry Bradshaw Society 58 (London, 1920), pp. 151–53, at 151–52. For a discussion and translation of this mass and other Frankish liturgical texts for kings, see Mary Garrison, "The *Missa*

cil records,[49] and letters of advice to kings.[50] Two liturgical texts, the *Missa pro principe* and the Reichenau fragment, even contain prayers for kings that sacralize warfare by citing Old Testament precedent for God's intervention in battle.[51] While scholars have argued that Merovingian historiography also bears witness to this Christianization of kingship and political history, *Fredegar* and the *LHF* show the limits of this process.[52] Instead, the two texts show an increasing emphasis on military heroism and brutality. This typical battle narrative from *Fredegar* creates an impression of martial vigor through its annalistic, asyndetic series of active verb phrases:[53]

> Alamanni Transioranus *superant*, pluretate eorum gladio *trucedant* et *prosternunt*, maximam partem territurio Auenticense incendio *concremant*, plurum nomirum hominum exinde in captiuitate *duxerunt*.

> The Alamans *defeated* the Transjurans, *slaughtered* and *killed* a large number of them, *set fire to* great areas of the territory of the Avenches, and *took away* a host of prisoners to servitude.

The *LHF*, meanwhile, has a good amount of material that has been called "epic," and portrays some Merovingian kings as heroic warriors.[54] Explicit Christian elements,

---

pro principe in the Bobbio Missal," in *The Bobbio Missal: Liturgy and Religious Culture in Merovingian Gaul*, ed. Yitzhak Hen and Rob Meens (Cambridge, 2004), pp. 187–205. See also the Reichenau fragment, found in Karlsruhe, Badische Landesbibliothek, MS Aug. CCLIII, in "Prière," ed. Henri Leclercq, in *Dictionnaire d'Archéologie Chrétienne et de Liturgie*, ed. Fernand Cabrol and Henri Leclercq, with Henri Marrou, vol. 14.2: Portier-Rome (Paris, 1948), pp. 1767–75, at 1773.

[49] The preface to the canons from the Council of Clichy in 626–627 offers one of the first comparisons between a Frankish king and King David. See Eugen Ewig, "Zum Christlichen Köningsgedanken im Frühmittelalter," in his *Spätantikes und Fränkisches Gallien: Gesammelte Schriften (1952–1973)*, ed. Hartmut Atsma, 3 vols. (Munich, 1976), 1:3–71, at 17–18. The preface, and the canons, are printed in *Concilia Galliae a. 511–a. 695*, ed. Charles de Clercq, in CCSL 148A (Turnhout, 1963), pp. 290–97.

[50] In ca. 639, an unnamed bishop wrote to Clovis II urging him to to emulate David and Solomon, avoid drunkenness and wrath, and follow the advice of older, wiser counsellors. The letter is found in *Epistulae Aevi Merovingici*, ed. Wilhelm Gundlach, MGH Epp. III (Hannover, 1892), Ep. 15, pp. 457–60. See also Yitzhak Hen, "The Uses of the Bible and the Perception of Kingship in Merovingian Gaul," *Early Medieval Europe* 7 (1998), 277–90, at pp. 284–85.

[51] See above, n. 48. For a comparative table of all biblical references found in these two liturgical texts, among others, see Garrison, "The *Missa pro principe*," pp. 204–5.

[52] See Ewig, "Zum Christlichen Köningsgedanken," pp. 17–19; J.M. Wallace-Hadrill, "The Seventh Century," Chapter Three of his *Early Germanic Kingship in England and on the Continent: The Ford Lectures Delivered in the University of Oxford in Hilary Term 1970* (Oxford, 1971), pp. 47–71; and Hen, "Uses of the Bible."

[53] *Fourth Book of the Chronicle of Fredegar*, ed. and trans. Wallace-Hadrill, p. 30 (emphasis added).

[54] E.g., *Liber historiae Francorum*, ed. Bruno Krusch, in *Fredegarii et aliorum chronica. Vitae sanctorum*, MGH SS Rer. Mer. 2 (Hanover, 1888), pp. 215–328, at 304–6 (xxxvi) and 311–14 (xli). For discussion

however, are less prevalent in later Merovingian battle narratives than in Gregory's *Historiae*. There is one reference in *Fredegar* to a battle in which a Frankish army defeated the Gascons "Deo auxiliante" – "with God helping."[55] The author of the *LHF* seems to share Gregory of Tours' distaste for civil war, attributing a battle between two forces of *Franci* to the devil's instigation ("instigante diabulo").[56] However, he also fails to draw religious significance from Pippin II and Charles Martel's battles against the pagan Frisians.[57] Paul Fouracre plausibly explains this absence of explicit Christian material by suggesting that "sanctity has entered the grain of social and political life, and the miraculous requires less emphasis in the political narrative."[58] The development of a specifically political focus in historiography, traced in the rise of Frankish texts devoted to the *bella* or *gesta regum*, encourages the articulation of specifically political or military values such as martial heroism. However, it also entails a decline in the presence of explicitly Christian elements.

In the early eighth century, genre thus continued to structure differences in both the kinds of historical narratives contained in individual texts and the treatment of those narratives across the board. Battle narratives were strongly associated with "histories," which could include both hagiographical and political episodes, but which tended to maintain a distinction between the two. Saints' lives, meanwhile, only offered battle narratives in the context of miracles performed by the saint. The deep-rooted historical divide between sacred history and political/military history, one crystallised in Augustine's theory of the *civitas Dei* and the *civitas terrena*, went along with an annalistic, reportorial style of narrating battle. Where the battle narrative served as the paradigmatic illustration of political "business-as-usual" for early medieval historians, saints channeled an alternate source of power that disrupted the ordinary course of political and military history.

The Representation of Battle in the VSW

The battle narratives in the *Vita S. Wilfridi*, I now argue, stage a shift in both the place of political history in hagiography and the representation of that history. Unlike earlier *vitae*, the *VSW* offers battle narratives that are not marked by saintly miracles. Instead, the *VSW*'s battle narratives serve to illustrate how Wilfrid's occupation of the

---

of this material, see Gerberding, *The Rise of the Carolingians*, pp. 159–66; and Reimitz, *Framing of Western Identity*, pp. 251–58.

[55] *Fourth Book of the Chronicle of Fredegar*, ed. and trans. Wallace-Hadrill, xxi, p. 14.

[56] *Liber historiae Francorum*, ed. Krusch, pp. 215–328, at 325.

[57] *Liber historiae Francorum*, ed. Krusch, p. 326.

[58] Paul Fouracre, "The Origins of the Carolingian Attempt to Regulate the Cult of Saints," in *The Cult of Saints in Late Antiquity and the Early Middle Ages*, ed. James Howard-Johnston and Paul Antony Hayward (Oxford, 1999), pp. 143–65, at 150.

episcopacy of Northumbria shapes the kingdom's historical fortunes. Unlike earlier histories, Stephen embeds the progress of battle in a dense network of spiritual and moral signification, including biblical typology and the discourse of ideal kingship. Stephen's narrative style, which features the use of exact parallelism and antithesis along with lengthy modifying clauses, allows him to attach precise meaning to historical actors and events through the texture of the narrative itself and ultimately to represent battle as an event within a combined sacred-political sphere of action.

Stephen's battle narratives occur in a different narrative context from most early medieval battle narratives. Rather than simply recording the significant events of military history in a given year or under a given king, with at most a narrative link to prior or subsequent events, they are deployed to support a historical thesis: that Ecgfrith's fortunes as king depended on his relationship with Wilfrid as bishop of Northumbria.[59] They occur in a section of the *VSW* that serves as a résumé of Wilfrid's achievements as bishop: he heals two boys on the point of death, builds or restores two magnificent churches at York and Hexham, and helps Ecgfrith win two battles against foreign nations.[60] Within this section, the two battle narratives are set off by a passage that explicitly argues for the connection between Ecgfrith's good treatment of Wilfrid and the power and prosperity of Northumbria at this period:[61]

> In diebus autem illis Ecfrithus rex religiosus cum beatissima regina Aethiltrythae, cuius corpus vivens ante impollutum post mortem incorruptum manens adhuc demonstrat, simul in unum Wilfritho episcopo in omnibus oboedientes facti, pax et gaudium in populis et anni frugiferi victoriaeque in hostes, Deo adiuvante, subsecutae sunt. Sicut enim iuvenis Ioas rex Iuda, Ioada sacerdote magno vivente adhuc, Deo placuit et in hostes triumphavit; mortuo vero sacerdote, Deo displicuit et regnum minuit, ita, Ecfritho rege in concordia pontificis nostri vivente, secundum multorum testimonium

---

[59] This is true whether or not, as Martin Heinzelmann and Walter Goffart have argued, the Gregory's *Libri decem historiarum* make implicit arguments through the artful arrangement of episodes and scenes; see Goffart, *Narrators of Barbarian History*, pp. 153–68, and Heinzelmann, *Gregory of Tours*, pp. 94–152. For narrativity as a variable element of medieval historical sources, see Hayden White, "The Value of Narrativity in the Representation of Reality," Chaper One of his *The Content of the Form* (Baltimore, 1987), pp. 1–25. While I take issue with White's sweeping claims about early medieval historiography, his model of narrative and historical representation is useful. In his "Mixed Modes in Historical Narrative," in *Narrative and History in the Early Medieval West*, ed. Elizabeth M. Tyler and Ross Balzaretti (Turnhout, 2006), pp. 91–104, Joaquín Martínez Pizarro nuances White's terms and applies narrative analysis to the *Chronicle of Fredegar*, finding that it makes strategic use of the episodic form of late antique and early medieval historiography.

[60] *The Life of Bishop Wilfrid*, ed. Colgrave, pp. 32–46. See also Mark D. Laynesmith, "Stephen of Ripon and the Bible: Allegorical and Typological Interpretations of the *Life of St. Wilfrid*," *Early Medieval Europe* 9 (2000), 163–82, at p. 173.

[61] *The Life of Bishop Wilfrid*, ed. Colgrave, p. 40.

regnum undique per victorias triumphales augebatur; concordia vero inter eos sopita et regina supradicta ab eo separata et Deo dicata, triumphus in diebus regis desinit.

For in those days, [when] the pious King Ecgfrith with the most blessed Queen Aethilthryth –whose body, still remaining uncorrupted after death, shows that it was unstained before, while still alive – were both made obedient to Wilfrid in all things, [thus] peace and joy among the people, fruitful harvests, and victories against enemies followed with God's help. For just as the young King Joash of Judah, when the high priest Jehoiada was still alive, pleased God and triumphed over his enemies, but when the priest was dead, he displeased God and his kingdom diminished – so, according to the testimony of many, when King Ecgfrith lived in accord with our bishop, his kingdom expanded on all sides with triumphal victories, but when the accord between them had been broken and the aforesaid queen had separated from him and given herself to God, this triumph halted during the king's life.

The passage first makes an argument by strong implication: *after* (*and*, we can infer, *because*) Ecgfrith and Aethilthryth had been made obedient to Wilfrid, Northumbria enjoyed a series of boons, including peace, bountiful harvests, and victory over its enemies. Then, it offers an explicit thesis that connects cause and effect by way of an exemplum from 4 Regum and 2 Paralipomenon, the story of Joash and Jehoiada.[62] Just as Joash, king of Judah, prospered for as long as the high priest Jehoiada was still alive but then suffered a loss of power, so Ecgfrith prospered for as long as he allowed Wilfrid to be bishop of all Northumbria, but then experienced a reversal. Stephen's claim of a connection between national prosperity and righteous kingship ultimately goes back to the Old Testament covenant history from which he draws his exemplum. However, it is also mirrored in a contemporary source: his list of Northumbria's elements of prosperity is closely paralleled in a Hiberno-Latin treatise from the seventh century called *De xii abusivis saeculi*.[63] The ninth chapter of the treatise, on "the wicked king" ("rex iniquus"), lists both the elements of the king's justice and the national consequences of either upholding or failing to uphold that justice.[64] The benefits of just kingship include: "pax populorum ... tutamen patriae ... gaudium hominum ... terrae fecunditas" – "peace among the peoples ... the protection of the homeland ... the joy of men ... the fecundity of the earth."[65] This more specific list of boons is not found in Stephen's biblical source, and it suggests that he may have been influenced by contemporary discourse on ideal kingship.

However, Stephen also embellishes his biblical exemplum to make it better reflect his understanding of battle as the primary engine of political power and the prototypi-

---

[62] 4 Reg. 12; 2 Par. 24.

[63] *Pseudo-Cyprianus De xii abusivis saeculi*, ed. Siegmund Hellmann, Texte und Untersuchungen zur Geschichte der altchristlichen Literatur (Leipzig, 1909).

[64] *De xii abusivis saeculi*, ed. Hellmann, pp. 51–53.

[65] *De xii abusivis saeculi*, ed. Hellmann, p. 53.

cal narrative of political history. Unlike the two accounts of Joash's reign found in the Old Testament, Stephen claims that Joash "in hostes triumphavit" – "triumphed over his enemies," during the initial, happy period of his reign when Jehoiada was still living."[66] The biblical passages only mention that Joash repaired the Temple in Jerusalem during Jehoiada's lifetime; that he later turned his back on God and the Arameans invaded Judah; and that he eventually died at the hands of his rebellious subjects in retribution for his execution of Zacharias, Jehoiada's son.[67] Stephen's decision to make battle the primary form of narrative evidence for Wilfrid's influence on Northumbrian history suggests that he was thinking in terms of contemporary historiography, which, as I note above, was often identified with the battle narrative.[68] It also reflects the more programmatic nature of *De xii abusivis saeculi*, which spells out the connection between ideal kingship and "the protection of the homeland" ("tutamen patriae").[69]

Chapters 19 and 20 of the *VSW* go on to offer a miniature history of Ecgfrith's reign, with battle as the primary catalyst of change. The first battle, Stephen claims, occurred when Ecgfrith was "in primis annis eius tenero adhuc regno" – "in the first years of his reign, with the kingdom still weak," while the second battle narrative opens with a description of Ecgfrith ruling confidently.[70] The conjunction of the two battle narratives and Ecgfrith's apparent rise in power after the first implies that the first victory *caused* this rise: Wilfrid did not just help Northumbria win the battle, he also altered its relative standing. To illustrate Ecgfrith's progress in biblical terms, Stephen compares him to Judas Maccabeus in the first battle and King David immediately before the second.[71] Not only does this show an evolution from a rebel leader to a powerful king, it also makes the Northumbrians' victory in the first battle seem both righteous and miraculous, the defeat of a more powerful foreign enemy by a small rebel force.[72] Stephen's biblical frame of reference supports his focus on the history of Ecgfrith's reign, just as it did in his opening exemplum of Joash and Jehoiada.

Stephen's intertwined use of kingship and biblical history as frames of historical interpretation represents something new in early medieval historical writing. Explicit typological reference is not a prominent feature in the histories that predate the *VSW*.

---

[66] *The Life of Bishop Wilfrid*, ed. Colgrave, p. 40.

[67] See above, n. 62. Cf. Stephen's claim that King Aldfrith died because he spurned Wilfrid; *The Life of Bishop Wilfrid*, ed. Colgrave, p. 126.

[68] See above, pp. 5–8.

[69] *De xii abusivis saeculi*, ed. Hellmann, p. 53.

[70] *The Life of Bishop Wilfrid*, ed. Colgrave, pp. 40, 42.

[71] *The Life of Bishop Wilfrid*, ed. Colgrave, pp. 40, 42.

[72] See 1 Macc. 4.1–35.

On the rare occasions when Gregory of Tours makes use of explicit typology, he does so to emphasise a particular element of a situation or a person's character, not to model the pattern of their life. He famously refers to Chilperic as "the Nero and Herod of our day" ("Nero nostri temporis et Herodis") and compares Clothar and his son Chramn to David and Absolom as they are going into battle against each other.[73] Both references bring out a quality of the person so designated – Chilperic's persecution of his people and of the Church, and Clothar and Chramn's tragic interfamilial conflict – but they are not applied to the larger patterns of their lives or careers. Martin Heinzelmann has detected a comparison between Clovis and David in Book Two of the *Historiae*,[74] but if this comparison exists, it is implicit: nowhere is Clovis referred to as *sicut David* or a *novus David*. Gregory's debt to Orosius for his model of history, I would argue, leads him to interpret history in terms of broad patterns, not precise parallels.[75] The prefaces to his second and third books, which Heinzelmann uses as evidence for Gregory's deep interest in typology and kingship, are about patterns of universal history, not about kingship *per se*. The former simply claims that good and bad things – holy religion and calamity – happen at the same time, justifying their close conjunction in a historical narrative. This may even be seen as a response to Orosius's method in the *Historiarum adversus paganos*, which is focused on contrasting a happy present with an unhappy past.[76] The preface to Book Three, meanwhile, demonstrates the connection between one's fortunes and one's confession of belief in the Holy Trinity, extending the argument of Deuteronomistic History.[77] Kings, saints, and patriarchs are brought together in his series of exempla, which contrast pairs of contemporaries instead of comparing biblical history and the present day. Gregory is, of course, deeply interested in the Bible in his work, but he does not see it as offering a series of precise correspondences to present-day history. Rather, his biblical style and biblical ambitions – his beginning, for instance, with Adam and Eve, and his citation of the historical books of the Old Testament – suggest

---

[73] *Libri historiarum X*, ed. Krusch and Levison, VI.xlvi, p. 319; IV.xx, p. 153.

[74] Martin Heinzelmann, *Gregory of Tours: History and Society in the Sixth Century*, trans. Christopher Carroll (Cambridge, 2001), pp. 123–27.

[75] Heinzelmann, *Gregory of Tours*, p. 8.

[76] Gregory, admittedly, cites Orosius as a precedent for combining "bella regum et virtutes martyrum pariter" in *Libri historiarum X*, ed. Krusch and Levison, II.praef, p. 36. However, see also *Historiarum adversum paganos libri VII*, ed. Zangemeister, I, prologue, p. 4: "iure ab initio hominis per bona malaque alternantia, exerceri hunc mundum sentit quisquis per se atque in se humanum genus uidet" – "whoever beholds the human race through himself and in himself senses that this world has been controlled by alternating periods of good and evil since the creation of man."

[77] *Libri historiarum X*, ed. Krusch and Levison, III.praef., pp. 96–97.

that he views his own work as a sort of continuation of the Bible.[78] Clovis, Chilperic, and Guntram are merely the latest chapters in a history that stretches back to Creation. The *LHF*, which postdates the *VSW* by about fifteen years, has been argued by Helmut Reimitz to depict Frankish warfare in Old-Testament terms, but once again, this depends on an implicit comparison instead of a narrative "in an exegetical mode."[79]

This difference between writing in a biblical style and using the Bible as a series of interpretive exempla points to what makes Stephen's battle narratives unique. They are not merely written in a biblical style; rather, they embellish a terse battle narrative with the language of ideal kingship and biblical typology. Their use of explicit typology accords with their context in a *vita*, even if the application to political history is new.[80] The Bible offers Stephen a pattern for understanding Ecgfrith's battles against first the Picts and then the Mercians, but his style brings out the spiritual meaning of history far more explicitly than biblical battle narratives. Like Gregory's battle narratives, the battle narratives of the Old Testament make clear the role of God in directing history, but they narrate battle straightforwardly, without explicit moral interpretation. The kings or military leaders of both sides are flat characters who simply enact covenant history. Before going into battle against an invading army from Moab and Ammon, for example, King Josaphat is told by one of his men (2 Par. 20.15): "Haec dicit Dominus vobis: Nolite timere, nec paveatis hanc multitudinem; non est enim vestra pugna, sed Dei" – "Thus saith the Lord to you: Fear you not, and be not dismayed at this multitude, for the battle is not yours, but God's." During the battle itself, the Lord "vertit ... insidias [filiorum Ammon] in semetipsos" – "[T]he Lord turned their ambushments upon themselves," handing victory to the Judaeans (2 Par. 20.22). Even in battles where God is not attributed with such a direct role in the fighting, the victory of the *populus Dei* is narrated simply as a military victory. On their tour of righteous conquest in the Book of Numbers, the Israelites fight Sehon of the Amorrhites and Og of Basan in short order, with the Lord handing each army over

---

[78] See Goffart, *Narrators of Barbarian History*, p. 149: "The model for Gregory's kind of eloquence could hardly have come from elsewhere than the Bible. Bonnet, Antin, and others have shown the effect of scriptural studies on his prose, but great as that influence was, the biblical cast of his writings has more than a literary basis ... He is more notable for emulating the substantive contents of the Bible than for imitating its *sermo humilis* ... The revealed Word, by His deeds in the here and now, gave voice to Gregory's tonguelessness, and contemporary Gaul, portrayed without art, corroborated the letter of revelation."

[79] Reimitz, *History, Frankish Identity*, pp. 258–63, at 259.

[80] On explicit biblical reference in Merovingian hagiography, see Marc van Uytfanghe, *Stylisation biblique et condition humaine dans l'hagiographie mérovingienne (600–750)*, Verhandelingen van de Koninklijke Academie voor Wetenschappen, Letteren en Schone Kunsten van België – Klasse der Letteren 120 (Brussels, 1987), pp. 17–60.

to them for destruction. The entire narrative of the battle with Sehon reads (Num. 21.23–24):

> Qui concedere noluit ut transiret Israel per fines suos: quin potius exercitu congregato, egressus est obviam in desertum, et venit in Iasa, pugnavitque contra eum. A quo percussus est in ore gladii, et possessa est terra eius ab Arnon usque Ieboc, et filios Ammon.

> And he would not grant that Israel should pass by his borders; but rather gathering an army, went forth to meet them in the desert, and came to Jasa, and fought against them. And he was slain by them with the edge of the sword, and they possessed his land from the Arnon unto the Jeboc, and to the confines of the children of Ammon.

The brevity of the narrative fits with the lack of interest in the character of Israel or its leaders: they are simply achieving the victory that God has granted them.

Stephen's battle narratives, on the other hand, communicate the moral meaning of every historical actor and action in the process of narrating the battle itself. Their commitment to a moral and religious interpretation of battle lends an ideological charge to both the historical plot and the stylistic texture of the narrative. Each battle is described as defensive, making Ecgfrith the righteous respondent to an evil act of provocation. The Picts precipitate the first battle when they "feroci animo subiectionum Saxonum despiciebant et iugum servitutis proicere a se minabant" – "with a savage spirit despised their subjection to the Saxons and threatened to throw the yoke of servitude from themselves."[81] This description echoes Psalm 2.2–3, in which King David laments that his enemies "convenerunt in unum adversus Dominum et adversus christum eius" – "met together, against the Lord and against his Christ," saying: "Disrumpamus vincula eorum et *proiciamus* a nobis *iugum* ipsorum" – "Let us break their bonds asunder and let us *cast away* their *yoke* from us." Ecgfrith and Northumbria are thus analogous to King David and the ancient Israelites, making their enemies the enemies of "Dominus et christus eius." Stephen immediately goes on to compare the Picts and other northern peoples to ants "in aestate de tumulis verrentes [qui] aggerem contra domum cadentem muniebant" – "pouring from their mounds in summer who built an earthwork to shore up their falling house."[82] Whatever action this refers to,[83] Stephen presents it as requiring a swift and righteous response by Ecgfrith. To make clear the moral significance of that response and the moral status of Ecgfrith himself, Stephen embellishes the subject of the sentence, "rex Ecgfrithus," with two pairs of modifying phrases:[84]

---

[81] *The Life of Bishop Wilfrid*, ed. Colgrave, p. 40.

[82] *The Life of Bishop Wilfrid*, ed. Colgrave, p. 40.

[83] It is possible that the Picts tried to build a defensive wall on the Northumbrian border.

[84] *The Life of Bishop Wilfrid*, ed. Colgrave, p. 40.

> Nam, quo audito, rex Ecgfrithus, humilis in populis suis, magnanimus in hostes, statim equitatui exercitu praeparato, tarda molimina nesciens, sicut Iudas Machabeus in Deum confidens.
>
> Hearing this, King Ecgfrith, humble among his peoples, generous towards his enemies, having immediately prepared a horse-troop, not knowing slow preparations, trusting in God like Judas Maccabeus.

First, Ecgfrith is described with two corresponding adjectival phrases, "humilis in populis suis" and "magnanimus in hostes," which correspond precisely in each part: *humilis* contrasts with *magnanimus*, and *populis suis* with *hostes*. The precision of this contrast suggests that Ecgfrith treats both his own people and his enemies in the correct way, pointing to a standard of ideal behaviour. The two present participial phrases, "tarda molimina nesciens" and "sicut Iudas Machabeus in Deum confidens," also suggest ideal behavior; besides the typological reference, discussed above, "tarda molimina nesciens" echoes a phrase applied to the Holy Spirit by, first, Ambrose, and later the author of the anonymous *Vita S. Cuthberti*.[85] The subject *rex Ecgfrithus* governs the entire battle narrative, which continues immediately after *confidens*:[86]

> parva manu populi Dei contra inormem et supra invisibilem hostem cum Beornheth audaci subregulo invasit stragemque immensam populi subruit, duo flumina cadaveribus mortuorum replentes, ita, quod mirum dictu est, ut supra siccis pedibus ambulantes, fugientium turbam occidentes persequebantur et in servitutem redacti, populi usque ad diem occisionis regis captivitatis iugo subiecti iacebant.
>
> with a small band of people of God and with the brave sub-king Beornhaeth rushed on the vast and moreover invisible enemy and brought about a huge slaughter of that people, filling two rivers with the bodies of the dead, such that, marvelous to relate, walking on [them] with dry feet, they gave chase, massacring the crowd of those fleeing, and, returned to servitude, those tribes that lay under the yoke of captivity up until the day of the king's death.

Stephen contrasts the "parva manu populi Dei" with the "inormem et supra invisibilem hostem:" one is small, the other large; one is "the people of God," the other "invisible," creating a sense of magic and possibly of witchcraft. The destruction was so great, Stephen tells us, that the Northumbrian army was able to cross two rivers "with dry feet" by walking on the corpses of the Picts, which only made it easier to hunt down and kill those who were fleeing.[87] Stephen seems to revel in the brutality of

---

[85] See Stancliffe, "Disputed episcopacy," p. 13, n. 26. Stancliffe points out the incongruity of the allusion. I would add that the context of the phrase in the anonymous *Vita S. Cuthberti* is immediately before the chapter describing Ecgfrith's death, an especially likely place for Stephen to be consulting when writing about Ecgfrith.

[86] *The Life of Bishop Wilfrid*, ed. Colgrave, pp. 40–42.

[87] *The Life of Bishop Wilfrid*, ed. Colgrave, p. 42.

this battle, glossing over tactics entirely and summarizing it as a *stragem*, a slaughter: Gregory of Tours had once, in a morally horrified tone, used this term as a shorthand for the unholy acts of political history.[88] As a sign of how far Stephen's conception of battle is from Gregory's, this *stragem* is depicted triumphally as the result of Ecgfrith's ideal actions as king.

While the first battle narrative is heavily inflected with biblical language and typology, the second one uses an identical narrative framework to support a miniature *speculum regis*, revealing the operation of ideal and unideal kingship in divinely controlled political history. Stephen opens on Ecgfrith enjoying greater power than before and fulfilling the role of King David in contemporary history:[89]

> Deinde post hanc victoriam rex Ecgfrithus cum pontifice Dei iustus et sanctus regensque populos et validus sicut David in contritione hostium, humilis tamen in conspectu Dei apparens et colla tumentium populorum et ferocium regum, audacior a Deo factus, confringens, semper in omnibus Deo gratias agebat.
>
> Then, after this victory, King Ecgfrith, ruling the people with God's minister, just and holy, and appearing strong like David in destroying his enemies, humble, however, in God's sight, and crushing the necks of pride-swollen peoples and savage kings, made bolder by God, always in everything gave thanks to God.

As in the last chapter, the modifiers do much of the work of interpretation. Ecgfrith is described in a series of three participial phrases covering the actions of ideal kingship, governed by *regens*, *apparens*, and *confringens*. The first tells us, significantly, that Ecgfrith was ruling Northumbria with Wilfrid, hinting at the source of this ideal status. The second draws the same kind of contrast seen in the last battle narrative: if Ecgfrith there was "humilis in populis suis, magnanimus in hostes," he is now "validus sicut David in contritione hostium, humilis tamen in conspectu Dei apparens." He acts just as a king should, Stephen implies: fierce towards his enemies, who are presumably also God's enemies, and humble in the sight of God. Finally, the last term emphasises Ecgfrith's ferocity towards his enemies by describing him as "crushing the necks of pride-swollen peoples and savage kings, made bolder by God." This series of participial phrases connoting the actions of ideal kingship forms part of an early medieval Latin *topos* with parallels in Gregory of Tours' *Decem libri historiarum* and the *Vita S. Audoini*.[90] A comparison of these attestations shows that Stephen's use of the *topos* is more similar to that found in the *Vita S. Audoini*, which also emphasises power and violence. Describing Dagobert I, the anonymous author writes: "Qui licet

---

[88] See above, p. 6.

[89] *The Life of Bishop Wilfrid*, ed. Colgrave, p. 42.

[90] See *Libri Historiarum X*, ed. Krusch and Levison, III.xxv, p. 123; *Vita Audoini episcopi Rotomagensis*, ed. Wilhelm Levison, in *Passiones vitaeque sanctorum aevi Merovingici*, ed. Bruno Krusch and Wilhelm Levison, MGH SS Rer. Mer. 5 (Hannover and Leipzig, 1910), pp. 536–67, at 555.

sceptra regalia tenens, ut leo fervidus subditorum colla deprimens, gentius feritate vallante fortitudine triumphavit" – "And he, holding the royal sceptre as a raging lion oppressing the necks of his servants, bravely triumphed by containing the ferocity of [foreign] peoples."[91] The phrase "subditorum colla deprimens," in particular, echoes the *VSW*'s "colla tumentiorum populorum et ferocium regum ... confringens." However, Stephen's wording and concept have a more direct parallel in Cassiodorus's *Institutiones*, which notes that St. Jerome "modo *humilibus* suauiter blanditur, modo *superborum colla confringit*" – "at times he sweetly flatters the *humble*, at times he *breaks the necks of the proud*."[92] As with the phrase "tarda molimina nesciens," originally referring to the Holy Spirit,[93] Stephen has literalised a spiritual or metaphorical action to show how Ecgfrith enacts sacred kingship under Wilfrid's guidance.

The battle narrative itself develops a contrast between Ecgfrith and Wulfhere of Mercia as examples of righteous and wicked kings, mapping an abstract argument onto historical agents and the multiple stages of a historical event. As in the passages already discussed, Stephen interweaves his historical narrative with moral and psychological commentary, combining the forward motion of the narrative with a static rhetorical contrast between Wulfhere and Ecgfrith.[94]

> Nam Wlfharius, rex Merciorum, superbo animo et insatiabili corde omnes australes populos adversus regnum nostrum concitans, non tam ad bellandum quam ad redigendum sub tributo servili animo, non regente Deo, proponebat. Ecgfrithus vero rex Derorum et Bernicorum, animo rigido, mente fideli, consilio senum patriam custodire, ecclesias Dei defendere, episcopo docente, in Deum confisus, sicut Barach et Dabora, cum parili manu hostem superbum invadens, Deo adiuvante, cum parvo exercitu prostravit et, occisis innumeris, regem fugavit regnumque eius sub tributo distribuit, et eo postea quacumque ex causa moriente, plenius aliquod spatium pacifice imperavit.

> For Wulfhere, king of the Mercians, with a proud mind and an insatiable heart inciting all the southern tribes against our kingdom, intended not to make war but to make [us] pay tribute with a servile spirit, with God not guiding him. Ecgfrith, however, king of the Deirans and Bernicians, with a stern spirit and faithful mind, trusting in God to guard the country with the advice of his councillors and to defend God's Church, with the bishop [i.e. Wilfrid] instructing him, just as Barach and Debora, rushing on the proud enemy with a small band, God aiding him, laid them low with a small army and,

---

[91] *Vita Audoini episcopi Rotomagensis*, ed. Levison, p. 555. Translation is from Fouracre and Gerberding, *Late Merovingian France*, p. 154. Fouracre and Gerberding also note that "this sentence is a small *speculum regis*" (nn. 143 and 144).

[92] Cassiodorus, *Institutiones* I.xxi.1, in *Cassiodor: Institutiones divinarum et saecularium litterarum*, ed. Wolfgang Bürsgens, 2 vols. (Freiburg, 2003), 1:232 (emphasis added; translation is my own).

[93] See above, n. 85.

[94] *The Life of Bishop Wilfrid*, ed. Colgrave, p. 42.

having killed countless men, put the king to flight and placed his kingdom under tribute, and since he [i.e. Wulfhere] soon died for some reason, peacefully ruled a larger area.

Stephen uses the same plot as in the last battle narrative: a foreign enemy is acting against Northumbrian interests and, implicitly, divine law, requiring a swift and brutal response. This time, that enemy is another king, allowing Stephen to emphasise Ecgfrith's ideal behavior by contrast. Where Wulfhere of Mercia acts from a "superbo animo et insatiabili corde ... non regente Deo," Ecgfrith has an "animo rigido" and "mente fideli" and relies on both God and Wilfrid, God's representative. Ecgfrith and Wulfhere thus come to stand in for good and evil kingship as a whole, making the battle into a historical exemplum. Another thing suggests that these two battles have become far more than individual events; in the last chapter, the Picts "congrega[verunt] undique de utribus et folliculis aquilonis *innumeras gentes*" – "brought together *innumerable peoples* from all the nooks and crannies of the north," whereas Wulfhere now "*omnes australes populos* ... concita[vit]" – "called together *all the southern peoples*."[95] Just as Wulfhere and Ecgfrith represent types of kings, Northumbria's foes stand in for all of the peoples of Great Britain. As an ideal king, Ecgfrith's power thus has no bounds.

Stephen's style reaches its apogee in the sentence describing Ecgfrith's righteous response to Wulfhere's provocation, modifying "Ecgfrithus," the subject of the sentence, with six clauses before reaching the main verb. To establish Ecgfrith's ideal behavior, Stephen incorporates the language of the *speculum regis* into the battle narrative. Stephen's list of Ecgfrith's ideal actions and intentions echoes the list of actions that constitute the "king's justice" in *De xii abusivis saeculi*:

Iustitia uero regis est ... *ecclesias defendere* ... **senes** et sapientes et sobrios **consiliarios**. habere ... patriam fortiter et iuste contra adversarios defendere, per omnia in Deo confidere.[96]	Ecgfrithus vero ... **consilio senum** patriam custodire, *ecclesias* Dei *defendere*, episcopo docente, in Deum confisus.[97]
The justice of the king is ... to defend the churches ... to have old, wise, and serious men as councillors ... to defend the nation bravely and justly against enemies, to trust in God in all things.	Ecgfrith, however ... trusting in God, with his bishop guiding him, to guard the country with a council of elders and to defend God's churches.

---

[95] *The Life of Bishop Wilfrid*, ed. Colgrave, pp. 40, 42 (emphasis added). I follow Colgrave in rendering "utribus et folliculis" as "nooks and crannies": its literal meaning is something like "wine-skins and bladders." See *DMLBS*, "uter" (1) and "folliculus," online, *http://clt.brepolis.net/dmlbs/Default.aspx*, accessed May 18, 2016.

[96] *De xii abusivis saeculi*, ed. Hellmann, pp. 51–52.

[97] *Life of Bishop Wilfrid*, ed. Colgrave, p. 42.

The correspondence suggests that Stephen has relied on this list, or one like it, but also adapted it to the needs of narrative: two of its elements ("senes ... consiliarios habere" and "per omnia in Deo confidere") are rendered in other grammatical forms that allow them to describe the action of an ideal king at a particular moment in history rather than a list of ideal attributes. It is difficult to tell quite how these clauses fit together; though "in Deum confisus" might govern the infinitive phrases, and Colgrave translates it that way, it could also point ahead to the description of Ecgfrith's military response, and the infinitive phrases could be governed by "episcopo docente" instead. Given the difficulty and length of this sentence, Colgrave found it expedient to divide it into two shorter sentences in his translation, making *confisus* the main verb of the first. As in the last battle narrative and many of the battle narratives from *The Chronicle of Fredegar*, the sequence of active verbs ("prostravit ... fugavit ... distribuit ... imperavit") moves through the stages of victory and emphasises the agency of the victors.[98] After the two sides have been so thoroughly characterised in ideological terms, this triumphant victory is a foregone conclusion.

The battle narratives in the *VSW*, then, incorporate sacred and political history in a manner atypical of earlier battle narratives in both hagiography and historiography. Unlike nearly every battle narrative in earlier saints' lives and many in histories, they contain no miracles. There is no prophecy of the battle's outcome, no miraculous sign before or during the battle, no prayer at a crucial moment. They treat Old Testament history as a series of exempla that illustrate the power and spiritual status of kings, bishops, and peoples. Rather than piercing the scene of military history with a miracle, divine power radiates through the actors and events in that history, producing a style in which subjects and actions are glossed with ideologically charged qualifying phrases. Ecgfrith and the Northumbrians go into battle already imbued with the spiritual status that will make them victors. The sort of battle narratives found in *The Chronicle of Fredegar*, with their annalistic manner of portraying military heroism and brutality, offer the framework for a stylistic sacralisation of political history. As a genre that analyses the patterns of individual lives against a larger backdrop of sanctity and biblical typology, hagiography offers Stephen the tools with which to carry out this shift in historical representation.

---

[98] "Prostrare" and "fugare" appear together in at least two other texts from around the time of the *VSW*. See the *Liber Historiae Francorum*, ed. Krusch, xxx, p. 289 (emphasis added): "Chunos *prostravit* atque devicit et in ore gladii eos *fugabit*" – "He *laid low* the Huns and defeated them and *put* them *to flight* on the edge of the sword." Bede seems to draw on the language of historiography when he compares death to the return of a victorious army to its native land in his early commentary *In Epistolas Septem Catholicas*: "sicut positis in expeditione *fugato* hoste vel *prostrato* ad patriam redire" – "just as those on expedition return to the homeland after *putting* the enemy *to flight* and *laying it low*." See his *In epistolam II Petri*, in *Bedae Venerabilis Opera, Pars II: Opera Exegetica*, ed. David Hurst, CCSL 121 (Turnhout, 1953), pp. 261–83, at 265–66 (emphasis added).

Political Theory and Genre in the VSW

Stephen's decision to include battle narratives in the *VSW* and his representation of those battles are conditioned by his models of episcopal sanctity and the relationship between episcopal and royal power. Kingship is an abiding concern of the *VSW*, and these battle narratives serve to illustrate Wilfrid's role as a source of divine power for both kings and kingdoms. That process differs from the late Merovingian *vitae* often compared with the *VSW*; it is channeled through Wilfrid's occupation of the episcopacy, not his personal sanctity. Drawing on a specifically Anglo-Saxon model of mission, Stephen portrays bishop and king as the joint rulers of a Christian kingdom, the two poles of a sacralised sphere of public action that is not simply "punctuated by the divine," but "constantly guided by it."[99] The battles narrated in the *VSW*, then, become episodes of missionary warfare that expand both Ecgfrith's kingdom and Wilfrid's "kingdom of churches."[100] Finally, Stephen's conception of the close connection between episcopal and royal power underpins his act of generic borrowing. The association of *vitae* and *historiae* with different sources of authority meant that generic experimentation offered means of constructing new and useful kinds of textual identities for both episcopal biographers and royal propagandists in the eighth century.

The model of episcopal sanctity that underlies these two battle narratives differs even from that found in the Frankish hagiography which has been seen as offering a compelling context for Stephen's depiction of Wilfrid. While it has only been shown to rely directly on one other *vita*, the anonymous *Vita S. Cuthberti*,[101] the *VSW* also deploys a model of episcopal sanctity that appears to be indebted to a number of seventh-century Frankish *vitae*:[102] the saint as the powerful but embattled victim of secular authority, often as a martyr.[103] Stephen even explicitly flags this affiliation with an episode in which Wilfrid is nearly martyred alongside his early mentor, Aunemundus

---

[99] Moore, *A Sacred Kingdom*, 109.

[100] See below, pp. 30–31.

[101] See Rosalind C. Love, "The Sources of the *Vita S. Wilfridi*," 1997, *Fontes Anglo-Saxonici: World Wide Web Register*, http://fontes.english.ox.ac.uk/, accessed Jan. 2017.

[102] These *vitae* include: the *Vita Audoini episcopi Rotomagensis*, ed. Levison, pp. 536–67; the *Passio Leudegarii I*, ed. Bruno Krusch, in *Passiones vitaeque sanctorum aevi Merovingici*, ed. Krusch and Levison, MGH SS Rer. Mer. 5 (Hannover and Leipzig, 1910), pp. 282–322; the *Passio Praejecti episcopi et martyri Arverni*, ed. Bruno Krusch, in *Passiones vitaeque sanctorum aevi Merovingici*, ed. Krusch and Levison, pp. 212–48; and the *Acta S. Aunemundi alias Dalfini episcopi*, ed. Pierre Perrier, *AASS* Sept. (Antwerp, 1760), 7:744–46. All of these texts are translated in Fouracre and Gerberding, *Late Merovingian France*, pp. 98–329.

[103] William Trent Foley, *Images of Sanctity in Eddius Stephanus' Life of Bishop Wilfrid, an Early English Saint's Life* (Lewiston, NY, 1992), pp. 71–105; Simon Coates, "The Role of Bishops in the Early Anglo-Saxon Church: A Reassessment," *History* 81 (1996), 177–96.

of Lyon.[104] Martyrdom is, of course, a controlling paradigm for Christian sanctity from the early Church onward, and it experienced a resurgence in popularity during a contentious period in late Merovingian Francia.[105] Indeed, the embattled tone of the *VSW* and the unabashed power of its subject somewhat resemble a handful of late Merovingian saints' lives. But while a Frankish model of episcopacy may underlie some aspects of Stephen's representation of Wilfrid, the section of the *VSW* that includes the battle narratives bespeaks a far different model of the relationship between episcopal power and sanctity and royal power. These two chapters function as exempla of the ideal relationship between bishop and king in the theatre of military and political history. In both their style and their explicit typology, they make a strong argument for the importance of a close partnership between these two figures in their institutional roles. In the second battle narrative, for instance, Ecgfrith is "cum pontifice Dei ... regens" and acting with his "episcopo docente," and the two form a partnership "sicut Barach et Dabbora,"[106] alluding to an episode from the book of Judges 4.6 in which it was significantly the religious authority, Debbora, who incited the military leader Barac to fight the Amalekites after receiving a vision that the Israelites would triumph. While he may be persecuted by kings and queens at other points in the text, Wilfrid emerges in chapters 19 and 20 as a co-ruler of Ecgfrith and a guarantor of national prosperity. These roles represent an innovation over both the ascetic bishop model inhabited by Martin of Tours and Cuthbert, among others, *and* the model of the powerful and persecuted bishop inhabited by figures such as Aunemundus, Praejectus and Audoin of Rouen. Wilfrid's holy power as bishop is rooted in his office, not just in his personal sanctity.[107] Stephen does not merely permit Wilfrid's political power to be represented, or use it to explain how Wilfrid acquired powerful enemies; he theorizes it as a means of channeling divine power to Ecgfrith and to Northumbria as a whole.

The emphasis on Wilfrid's close connection to Ecgfrith in the battle narratives is underpinned by a much larger preoccupation in the *VSW* with the importance of Wilfrid as bishop in enacting ideal Christian kingship. Wilfrid interacts with some twenty kings and queens from nine kingdoms, often with a marked degree of intimacy.[108] Five

---

[104] *The Life of Bishop Wilfrid*, ed. Colgrave, pp. 12, 14. See also Janet L. Nelson, "Queens as Jezebels: The Careers of Brunhild and Balthild in Merovingian History," in *Medieval Women: Essays Dedicated and Presented to Professor Rosalind M.T. Hill*, ed. Derek Baker (Oxford, 1978), pp. 31–77, at 65–67; Fouracre and Gerberding, *Late Merovingian France*, pp. 172–76.

[105] See above, n. 19.

[106] *The Life of Bishop Wilfrid*, ed. Colgrave, p. 42.

[107] Foley, *Images of Sanctity*, pp. 107–25.

[108] In *The Life of Bishop Wilfrid*, ed. Colgrave, they are: **Northumbria**: Eanfled (p. 6), Oswiu (pp. 20, 22), Ecgfrith (pp. 40, 42, 48), Iurminburg (p. 48), Aethilthryth (pp. 40, 44), Alhfrith (pp. 14, 16),

kings are described as Wilfrid's *amici*;[109] two are installed on the throne through his maneuvering;[110] and two more protect him from his enemies on the Continent.[111] On the other hand, six kings and queens are afflicted, lose their power, or die through mistreatment of Wilfrid.[112] Stories abound in *vitae*, of course, in which powerful figures are punished by God for spurning or mistreating the saint.[113] What sets the *VSW* apart from these *vitae*, however, is its stress on Wilfrid's active political participation in the kingdom, his role as kingmaker and co-ruler. The most fascinating moment of the *VSW* for early medieval historians, the material on Wilfrid and Dagobert II of Austrasia, also functions as an exemplum about the role of powerful bishops in royal succession and rule.[114] Stephen claims that Wilfrid played a key part in restoring Dagobert to the throne in ca. 675 after a period of exile in Ireland. Dagobert is later overthrown and killed in a coup led by powerful figures in his kingdom, and when Wilfrid stops in Austrasia on his way back to England from Rome, he is confronted by the leaders of the rebellion for his part in putting Dagobert on the throne. His response is dense with intertextual resonances that frame his participation in biblical terms and in the contemporary language of ideal kingship:[115]

Aelfwini (pp. 36, 50), Aldfrith (pp. 90, 92, 94, 96, 98, 124, 126, 128, 130), Eadwulf (p. 128), Osred (p. 128); **Mercia**: Wulfhere (pp. 30, 32), Aethilred (pp. 80, 88, 90, 100, 124); **Wessex**: Centwini (p. 80), Ceadwalla (p. 84); **Kent**: Ercenberht (p. 8); **Sussex**: Aethilwalh (p. 82); **Neustria**: Baldhild (p. 14); **Austrasia**: Dagobert (pp. 54, 68); **Frisia**: Aldgisl (p. 52); **Italy**: Perctarit (pp. 54, 56).

[109] In *The Life of Bishop Wilfrid*, ed. Colgrave, they are: Eorcenberht, king of Kent (p. 8); Alhfrith, king of Northumbria (p. 16); Wulfhere, king of Mercia (pp. 30, 32); Aethilwalh, king of Northumbria (p. 82); Ceadwalla, king of Wessex (p. 84); Aethilred, king of Mercia (pp. 88, 90, 92, 124). On the pragmatic nature of *amicitia* between powerful men in early medieval Europe, see Gerd Althoff, *Family, Friends, and Followers: Political and Social Bonds in Medieval Europe*, trans. Christopher Carroll (Cambridge, 2004).

[110] In *The Life of Bishop Wilfrid*, ed. Colgrave, they are: Dagobert II of Austrasia (p. 54) and Ceadwalla of Wessex (p. 84).

[111] In *The Life of Bishop Wilfrid*, ed. Colgrave, they are: Aldgisl of Frisia (pp. 52, 54) and Perctarit of Italy (pp. 54, 56).

[112] In *The Life of Bishop Wilfrid*, ed. Colgrave, they are: Wulfhere of Mercia (p. 42); Ecgfrith of Northumbria (pp. 40, 50, 70); Iurminburg of Northumbria (p. 70); Aelfwini of Northumbria (p. 50); Aldfrith of Northumbria (pp. 124, 126, 128, 130); Eadwulf of Northumbria (p. 128).

[113] See, for example, *Vitae S. Columbani*, ed. Krusch, p. 88; *Passio Leudegarii I*, ed. Krusch, pp. 319–20; Muirchú, *Vita S. Patricii*, in *The Patrician Texts in the Book of Armagh*, ed. Ludwig Bieler (Dublin, 1979), pp. 64, 90; John Kitchen, *Saints' Lives and the Rhetoric of Gender: Male and Female in Merovingian Hagiography* (Oxford, 1998), pp. 34–46.

[114] *The Life of Bishop Wilfrid*, ed. Colgrave, pp. 66, 68. The episode is discussed by Paul Fouracre in "Forgetting and Remembering Dagobert II: The English Connection," in *Frankland: The Franks and the World of the Early Middle Ages*, ed. Fouracre and David Ganz (Manchester, 2008), pp. 70–89.

[115] *The Life of Bishop Wilfrid*, ed. Colgrave, p. 68.

> Veritatem dico in Christo Iesu et per sanctum Petrum apostolum non mentior, quod talem virum exulantem et in peregrinatione degentem secundum praeceptum Dei populo Israhelitico, qui accola fuit in terra aliena, auxiliatus enutrivi et exaltavi in bonum et non in malum vestrum, ut aedificator urbium, consolator civium, consiliator senum, defensor Dei ecclesiarum in nomine Domini secundum eius promissum esset.
>
> I tell the truth in Jesus Christ, and on the holy apostle Peter I do not lie, that according to the God's commandment to the Israelites, who were living in a strange land, I helped and nourished this man living in exile and itinerancy and raised him up to do good and not for your harm, so that he would be a builder of cities, a consoler of the people, a counselor of the aged, and a defender of God's churches in the name of the Lord, according to his [i.e. Dagobert's] promise.

Wilfrid claims to follow "the Lord's commandment to the Israelites, who resided in a strange land" – an allusion to the speech of self-defense offered in the Book of Acts by Stephen, the first Christian martyr.[116] If the allusion establishes Wilfrid as a potential martyr, it also establishes a parallel between Wilfrid's own situation of exile and Dagobert's. The same kind of personal identification with a king is repeated in Wilfrid's interaction with Perctarit of Italy.[117] Wilfrid's "I nourished and raised [him] up" ("enutrivi et exaltavi") compares his situation with Dagobert to the Lord's complaint about the Israelites in Isaiah 1.2: "Filios enutrivi, et exaltavi; ipsi autem spreverunt me" – "I have brought up children, and exalted them, but they have despised me." Just as the Israelites have turned their back on God and His commandments, Stephen implies, Wilfrid has raised up Dagobert to be king, but Dagobert has reneged on the promise (or even "oath") which he made to Wilfrid, namely, to be "a builder of cities, a consoler of the people, a counselor of the aged, and a defender of God's churches in the name of the Lord."[118] Once again, Stephen offers a list of ideal kingly actions or

---

[116] See Acts 7.6: "Locutus est autem Deus quia erit semen eius accola in terra aliena et servituti eos subicient et male tractabunt eos annis quadringentis" – "And God said to him: That his seed should sojourn in a strange country, and that they should bring them under bondage, and treat them evil four hundred years." For the "commandment" issued by God, see perhaps, Lev. 19.33–34: "Si habitaverit advena in terra vestra, et moratus fuerit inter vos, non exprobretis ei: sed sit inter vos quasi indigena, et diligetis eum quasi vosmetipsos: fuistis enim et vos advenae in terra Aegypti. Ego Dominus Deus vester" – "If a stranger dwell in your land, and abide among you, do not upbraid him, but let him be among you as one of the same country; and you shall love him as yourselves, for you were strangers in the land of Egypt. I am the Lord your God." For the importance of the Book of Acts to Stephen's conception of the *VSW*, see Laynesmith, "Stephen of Ripon and the Bible," p. 178; and Mark D. Laynesmith, "Anti-Jewish Rhetoric in the *Life of Wilfrid*," in *Wilfrid: Abbot, Bishop, Saint*, ed. Nicholas J. Higham (Donnington, 2013), pp. 67–79.

[117] *The Life of Bishop Wilfrid*, ed. Colgrave, pp. 54–56. It is worth observing that the first mention of Dagobert and the episode with Perctarit both occur in chapter 28: Stephen links the two kings together as uniquely fit for consoling Wilfrid because of their shared experience of exile.

[118] *The Life of Bishop Wilfrid*, ed. Colgrave, p. 68.

roles, and the items of the list closely resemble those applied to Ecgfrith in chapter 20: "consilio senum patriam custodire, ecclesias Dei defendere...in Deum confisus" – "to guard the country with a council of elders and to defend God's churches, trusting in God."[119] This time, however, the form of the list – a series of agentive nouns with genitive objects – is tantalizingly reminiscent of the earliest-known coronation text, a prayer called *Prospice omnipotens Deus* that occurs in the Sacramentary of Angoulême, from ca. 800:[120]

> Tribue ei, omnipotens Deus, ut sit fortissimus *protector patriae* et *consolatur* [sic] *ecclesiarum* atque cenubiorum sanctorum maxima cum pietate regalis munificentiae. Atque ut sit *fortissimus regum, triumphator hostium ad opprimendas rebelles et paganas nationes.*[121]

> Grant him, Almighty God, that he may be the strongest *protector of the country* and *consoler of the churches* and the holy monasteries with the greatest devotion of royal munificence. And that he may be the *strongest of kings, a victor over our enemies when putting down rebellions or pagan nations.*

While it remains true that we have "no evidence of any coronation ritual for the Merovingians,"[122] Wilfrid's mention of a *promissum* made to him as bishop on Dagobert's accession, along with the content and form of the promise, suggests that the *VSW* might offer one of the earliest witnesses to a Frankish royal coronation ritual.[123] Whether or not the episode is historically accurate, it indicates the *VSW*'s interest in the mutually constitutive roles of king and bishop. Just as Wilfrid's position as bishop

---

[119] *The Life of Bishop Wilfrid*, ed. Colgrave, p. 42.

[120] *Ordines Coronationis Franciae: Texts and Ordines for the Coronation of Frankish and French Kings and Queens in the Middle Ages*, ed. Richard A. Jackson, 2 vols. (Philadelphia, 1995), 1:55.

[121] *Ordines Coronationis Franciae*, ed. Jackson, 1:58 (emphasis added).

[122] Janet Nelson, "The Lord's Anointed and the People's Choice: Carolingian Royal Ritual," in *Rituals of Royalty: Power and Ceremonial in Traditional Societies*, ed. David Cannadine and Simon Price (Cambridge, 1987), pp. 137–80, at 140. In an earlier piece, however, "Inauguration Rituals," in *Early Medieval Kingship*, ed. Paul N. Sawyer and Ian N. Wood (Leeds, 1979), pp. 50–71, Nelson is more sanguine about the possibilities of a Merovingian coronation oath: "The regal benedictions that survive in late eighth- and ninth-century manuscripts for use 'when the king is elevated into the kingdom' seem to me to be of Merovingian origin" (p. 53).

[123] This passage is discussed in the context of Merovingian royal oaths in Reinhard Schneider, *Königswahl und Königserhebung im Frühmittelalter: Untersuchungen zur Herrschaftsnachfolge bei den Langobarden und Merowingern* (Stuttgart, 1972), pp. 169–72. Schneider notes, on p. 171, n. 596: "Verbalsubstantive auf *–tor* bzw. *–or* werden ziemlich häufig in der Sprache von Eiden und Promissionen verwendet ... Er begegnet schon in der Zeit Chlodwigs und als *defensor ecclesiae* in der Spätantike." He adduces two earlier mentions of oaths made by the Merovingian kings Charibert I and Childeric – oaths which, however, do not employ endings in *–tor* or *–or.*

depends on the support of kings, the power, legitimacy, and success of those kings depends on their relationship with Wilfrid.

The text immediately following the two battle narratives frames these battles as events in both political and ecclesiastical history by noting that they led to the simultaneous expansion of Ecgfrith's kingdom and Wilfrid's "kingdom of churches."[124]

> Sicut ergo Ecgfritho rege religiosissimo regnum ad aquilonem et austrum per triumphos augebatur, ita beatae memoriae Wilfritho episcopo ad austrum super Saxones et ad aquilonem super Brittones et Scottos Pictosque regnum ecclesiarum multiplicabatur.
>
> Just as the most pious King Ecgfrith expanded his kingdom to the north and south through triumphant victories, so Bishop Wilfrid of blessed memory multiplied the kingdom of churches to the South over the Saxons and to the north over the Britons, the Irish, and the Picts.

The battles just narrated, Stephen implies, result in the expansion of both Ecgfrith's *and* Wilfrid's kingdoms. Much like the second sentence of chapter 19, which linked Joash and Jehoiada's situation in Judea to Ecgfrith and Wilfrid's in Northumbria, this sentence uses rhetorical parallelism to argue for a historical parallel: the linked historical fates of Ecgfrith and Wilfrid as, effectively, secular and ecclesiastical co-rulers. The phrase "regnum ecclesiarum," apparently a coinage of Stephen's, has often been misunderstood as referring to Wilfrid's far-flung network of monastic foundations, one that crossed kingdom boundaries.[125] The context, however, makes clear that it must refer to Wilfrid's diocese.[126] Ecgfrith's *regnum* and Wilfrid's *regnum ecclesiarum* are one and the same territory, and both *regna* are expanded by the conquests "over the Britons, the Irish, and the Picts" that the two previous chapters have just described.[127] Indeed, chapter 21 goes on to detail how Wilfrid successfully fulfilled his "ecclesiastical duties" ("ecclesiastica officia"), sketching a portrait of Wilfrid in his full spiritual and temporal glory as Bishop of Northumbria. Stephen's description of Wilfrid's diocese as a *regnum ecclesiarum* echoes a number of early Irish sources that describe St. Patrick's domain of episcopal and abbatial authority as a *regnum*, though Stephen is unique in explicitly framing Wilfrid's kingdom as the ecclesiastical ana-

---

[124] *The Life of Bishop Wilfrid*, ed. Colgrave, p. 42.

[125] See, for example, John Blair, *The Church in Anglo-Saxon Society* (Oxford, 2005), p. 97; Rollason, "Hagiography and Politics in Early Northumbria," pp. 103–4; and Sarah Foot, "Wilfrid's Monastic Empire," in *Wilfrid: Abbot, Bishop, Saint*, ed. Higham, pp. 27–39, at 33–34.

[126] See Goffart, *Narrators of Barbarian History*, p. 287, n. 233.

[127] *The Life of Bishop Wilfrid*, ed. Colgrave, p. 42.

logue to Ecgfrith's secular one.[128] Stephen's image of corresponding *regna* relies on a broader correspondence between ecclesiastical and political spheres of action and suggests that the battles narrated in chapters 19 and 20 exist within both spheres at once.

The battles narrated in chapters 19 and 20 are, in effect, episodes of missionary warfare that expand both the kingdom of Northumbria and the territory of the orthodox Church.[129] Territorial conquest is also associated with Wilfrid's diocese in Stephen's story of the dedication ceremony of the church at Ripon. Wilfrid, he writes, stood at the altar and read out a list of the "loca sancta in diversis regionibus quae clerus Bryttanus, aciem gladii hostilis manu gentis nostrae fugiens, deseruit" – "the holy places in various regions which the British clergy, fleeing the edge of the hostile sword [wielded by] an army of our own people, deserted."[130] Wilfrid's litany of sites conquered from the Britons and their heretical *clerus* turns military history into liturgical performance. That scene of performance is analogous to Stephen's injection of the language of moral and spiritual interpretation into his battle narratives, which writes the battles as events within sacred history.

The *VSW* is famously preoccupied with orthodoxy, and it tends to associate orthodoxy or heterodoxy with ethnicity.[131] At one point, Stephen refers to "the Britons and the Irish" as *quattuordecimanni*, Christians who either choose to celebrate Easter at the same time as the Jewish Passover or who simply allow this to happen because of their method of dating Easter.[132] As Mark Laynesmith argues, the term "functioned ... as code [in the *VSW*] for those supporters of an old regime, those types of Jews or Judaizers, who were denying the fullness of a new revelation."[133] The Britons, Picts, and Irish, then, are both ethnically other and religiously heterodox. As such, even if the battle against the Picts narrated in chapter 19 does not have a missionary aim, it has a missionary outcome, and the equation of the political Other with the religious Other sets the terms of the conflict. The religious status of Mercia at this point is less

---

[128] See Wendy Davies, "Clerics as Rulers: Some Implications of the Terminology of Ecclesiastical Authority in Early Medieval Ireland," in *Latin and the Vernacular in Early Medieval Britain*, ed. Nicholas Brooks (Leicester, 1982), pp. 81–97, at 83–84; *Patrician Texts*, ed. Bieler, pp. 86, 126, 174.

[129] The term "missionary warfare," meaning warfare suffused with the rhetoric of Christian mission, is Michael E. Moore's; see his *A Sacred Kingdom*, pp. 7, 203–42.

[130] *The Life of Bishop Wilfrid*, ed. Colgrave, p. 36.

[131] There is a rich body of scholarship on this topic, including Clare Stancliffe, *Bede, Wilfrid, and the Irish*, Jarrow Lecture 2003 (Jarrow, 2003); Stanliffe, "Disputed episcopacy"; Laynesmith, "Stephen of Ripon and the Bible"; T. M. Charles-Edward, "Wilfrid and the Celts," in *Wilfrid: Abbot, Bishop, Saint*, ed. Higham, pp. 143–60.

[132] See Laynesmith, "Anti-Jewish Rhetoric in the *Life of Wilfrid*," pp. 68–69.

[133] See Laynesmith, "Anti-Jewish Rhetoric in the *Life of Wilfrid*," p. 69.

clear, but it may have been colored by an incident of episcopal regime-change similar to Wilfrid's own eventual deposition from his post. Winfrith replaced Chad in ca. 672 as Bishop of Mercia, but he was deposed by Archbishop Theodore because of "some act of disobedience"[134] sometime after the Synod of Hertford in 673 – a fate not dissimilar from Wilfrid's, and one that may have sprung from similar causes.[135] If Winfrith had already been deposed by the time of Mercia's battle with Northumbria, then Stephen may have blamed the deposition on Wulfhere, just as he blames Wilfrid's deposition on Iurminburg and Ecgfrith more than on Theodore.[136] A sense of mutual sympathy and shared experience between Wilfrid and Winfrith is suggested by the fact that Stephen inserts an episode about Winfrith immediately after the chapter in which he describes Wilfrid's deposition. The episode describes Winfrith – "driven from Litchfield" ("de Licitfelda expulsus") just as Wilfrid has recently been "driven from his seat" ("de sede sua expulso") – being mistaken for Wilfrid by Wilfrid's enemies and robbed.[137] Stephen's focus on ideal and unideal kingship in the Mercian battle narrative may have had a more particular meaning for contemporary readers familiar with the history of Wulfhere and Winfrith and able to understand the specific causes of Wulfhere's surprisingly negative depiction in this chapter.[138]

Stephen's construction of episcopal and royal power and sanctity reflects the paradigm of mission that had shaped the Anglo-Saxon Church from its beginnings and

---

[134] Bede, *HE* iv. 6, ed. Lapidge, 2:196, 198: "Non multo post haec elapso tempore, offensus a Vynfrido Merciorum episcopo per meritum cuiusdam inoboedientiae, Theodorus archiepiscopus deposuit eum de episcopatu post annos accepti episcopatus non multos" – "Not long after this [i.e. the Council of Hertford], having been offended by Winfrith, bishop of the Mercians, due to some act of disobedience, Archbishop Theodore deposed him from his episcopate not many years after he had accepted it." All translations from this text are my own.

[135] Some have suggested that Winfrith was deposed because he resisted Theodore's plan to divide large sees such as those based at York and Litchfield into smaller ones; see *The Life of Bishop Wilfrid*, ed. Colgrave, p. 169; C. John Godfrey, *The Church in Anglo-Saxon England* (Cambridge, 1962), p. 133. However, see the Right Rev. George F. Browne, *Theodore and Wilfrith: Lectures Delivered in St. Paul's in December 1896* (London, 1897), 122: "It has been suggested that Winfrid was deposed because he withstood Theodore's wish to subdivide the great Mercian bishopric; but if that had been so, it was surely a very lame conclusion to put one sole bishop in his place."

[136] *The Life of Bishop Wilfrid*, ed. Colgrave, pp. 48–49. On the role of kings in Anglo-Saxon episcopal elections, see Catherine Cubitt, "Wilfrid's 'Usurping Bishops': Episcopal Elections in Anglo-Saxon England, *c.* 600–*c.* 800," *Northern History* 25 (1989), 18–38, at p. 34.

[137] *The Life of Bishop Wilfrid*, ed. Colgrave, p. 50.

[138] Wulfhere is referred to as a "most kind-hearted king" ("regem mitissimum") and as Wilfrid's "most faithful friend" ("fidelissimo amico") several chapters earlier. See *The Life of Bishop Wilfrid*, ed. Colgrave, pp. 30, 32.

that, by Stephen's time, had in turn spawned a mission to the Continent.[139] Bede's *HE* is both the primary witness to this history and the most influential text to use Christianization as a historiographical paradigm.[140] Like the *VSW*, the *HE* emphasises the importance of bishops and the Church to kings and the fortunes of their kingdoms in history.[141] One episode makes explicit the logic of the battle narratives in the *VSW*. Coenwalh, king of Wessex had replaced Agilbert, coincidentally Wilfrid's patron, with a bishop named Wine, but in time deposed him too for an unspecified reason. Wessex subsequently experienced a number of defeats in battle. Finally, Bede writes, Coenwalh "intellexitque quod etiam tunc destituta pontifice prouincia recte pariter diuino fuerit destituta praesidio" – "realised that his kingdom, deprived of a bishop, was also justly deprived of God's favour."[142] Other battle narratives in the *HE* serve the needs of Bede's narrative of conversion by showing how kings who embrace Christianity are victorious in battle.[143] Some twenty years before the *HE*, Stephen locates Wilfrid in a missionary history of the Anglo-Saxon Church as an apostle to the pagan South Saxons in the 680s.[144] Indeed, Walter Goffart has compellingly argued that the *VSW* furnished Bede with both a model and a foil for his own historiographical project.[145] However, while Bede frames the relationship between bishop, king, and battle much

---

[139] The historiography of mission in the Anglo-Saxon Church is immense. The most influential text is Bede, *HE*, ed. Lapidge. For the history of the Anglo-Saxon mission to the Continent, William Levison, *England and the Continent in the Eighth Century: The Ford Lectures Delivered in the University of Oxford in the Hilary Term, 1943* (Oxford, 1946), remains indispensable. For a history of the concept of universal mission in the period leading up to Bede, see Wolfgang H. Fritze, "Universalis gentium confessio: Fromeln, Träger und Wege universalmissionarischen Denkens im 7. Jahrhundert," ed. Karl Hauck (Berlin, 1969), pp. 78–130. On the development of mission as a historical theme in Anglo-Saxon and continental texts of the eighth century, see Ian Wood, *The Missionary Life: Saints and the Evangelisation of Europe, 400–1050* (Harlow, 2001), pp. 42–142.

[140] As Ian Wood notes in *The Missionary Life*, p. 25: "[Despite] the model provided by Acts [of the Apostles], the notion of writing histories which concentrate primarily on mission has only been intermittently pursued."

[141] Wood, *The Missionary Life*, p. 44: "Bede showed that mission could become a dominant strand in a narrative ... In order to describe the Christianisation of the English kingdoms as a coherent whole, Bede turned the history of mission into a political narrative: missionaries go to kings, convert them, and they then Christianise their subjects: moreover, if they are powerful kings, they use Christianity to spread their hegemony, and force subordinate kings to convert." See also Catherine Cubitt, "St. Wilfrid: A Man for His Times," in *Wilfrid: Abbot, Bishop, Saint*, ed. Higham, pp. 311–30, at 312: "From Bede's *History*, one learns that bishops were intimately involved with the king and were closely identified with the kingdom."

[142] Bede, *HE* iii.7, ed. Lapidge, 2:40.

[143] In Bede, *HE*, ed. Lapidge, they are found in 1:218, 220 (*HE* ix.7) and 2:110, 112 (*HE* xxiv.1–2).

[144] *The Life of Bishop Wilfrid*, ed. Colgrave, pp. 80, 82, 84.

[145] Goffart, *Narrators of Barbarian History*, pp. 281, 306–24.

as Stephen does, his own battle narratives lack the syntactic density and ideological charge of Stephen's; Bede's tone is less polemical than Stephen's, and his method of argumentation is more implicit.

A closer parallel to the style of Stephen's battle narratives can be found in the propagandistic histories produced after the Carolingian accession in 751. The earliest such text is the *First Continuation of the Chronicle of Fredegar*, probably commissioned by Duke Childebrand to coincide with the crowning of his nephew Pippin the Younger in 751.[146] Pippin's father Charles Martel is variously described in the text as "excellent warrior" ("egregius bellator"), "shrewdest man" ("sagacissimus vir"), "excellent man" ("vir egregius"), and "Charles, the dauntless, mighty warrior" ("bellator insignis Carlus intrepidus"); his victories invariably occur with God's help.[147] This sentence, for example, would not be out of place in the *VSW*:[148]

> Deuicto aduersarium agmine, Christo in omnibus praesule et caput salutis uictorie, salubriter remeauit [*scil.* Carlus] in regionem suam in terra Francorum solium principatus sui.
>
> Having defeated his enemies' forces with the help of Christ, who is the head of salvation and victory in all things, [Charles] safely returned to his domain and the seat of his principate in the land of the Franks.

The continuator even makes explicit the logic that drives the battle narratives in the *VSW*, in which the evil behavior of one's enemies makes battle necessary:[149]

> Eodem anno Saxones more consueto fidem quam germano suo promiserant mentire conati sunt. Qua de causa adento exercitu eos praeuenire conpulsus est [*scil.* Pippinus].
>
> In that same year, the Saxons, in their usual way, tried to break the agreement they had made with his [i.e. Pippin's] brother. For this reason, Pippin was forced to raise an army to prevent them.

The *Annales regni Francorum* and the *Annales Mettenses priores*, from the early ninth century, are even more overtly encomiastic and, unlike the continuations of the *Chronicle of Fredegar*, rely on hagiographical style and biblical typology.[150] The *Annales Mettenses priores* open on a moment of Carolingian glory: Pippin II assumes the

---

[146] See above, n. 29.

[147] *Fourth Book of the Chronicle of Fredegar*, ed. and trans. Wallace-Hadrill, pp. 91, 93, 94.

[148] *Fourth Book of the Chronicle of Fredegar*, ed. and trans. Wallace-Hadrill, p. 95.

[149] *Fourth Book of the Chronicle of Fredegar*, ed. and trans. Wallace-Hadrill, p. 101.

[150] *Annales regni Francorum inde ab a. 741 usque ad 829*, ed. Georg Heinrich Pertz, MGH SS rer. Germ. 6 (Hannover, 1895); *Annales Mettenses priores*, ed. Bernhard von Simson, MGH SS rer. Germ. 10 (Hannover and Leipzig, 1905).

principatum, an ambiguous term, of the East Franks in 687.[151] This assumption of authority is enabled by divinely-sanctioned victories over both enemies of the Franks and the man responsible for killing his father:[152]

> Pippinus filius Ansegisili ... post plurima prelia magnosque triumphos a Deo sibi concessos orientalium Francorum glorioso genitori feliciter succedens suscepit principatum ... Principium tamen insignis victoriae et perpetuae laudis cumulus extat, quod adhuc in pueritiae flore positus indebitam gloriosi genitoris sui necem auxilio divine virtutis inestimabili prosperitate ultus est. Auctorem enim infandi facinoris, alienis deliciis affluentem, subita irruptione interimens, puerili quidem manu, sed heroica ferocitate prostravit, haud aliter quam ut de David legitur, quod Domino gubernante immanem Goliam puerili ictu proprio gladio vita capiteque spoliavit.

> Pippin, son of ... Ansegisel, happily succeeding his glorious father, took up the leadership of the eastern Franks after many battles and great triumphs given to him by God ... The leadership, however, stands as the crown of his famous victory and lasting praise because while still in the flower of youth and in inestimable good fortune he avenged the unjust death of his glorious father with the aid of divine power. He brought low the perpetrator of this unspeakable crime, a man awash with foreign pleasures, killing him with a surprise attack by his youthful hand, yet with heroic ferocity. This is not unlike what is read concerning David, who, with the Lord guiding him and with his youthful blow, deprived the immense Goliath of his life and head with his [Goliath's] own sword.

The mention of God-granted victory and the comparison to King David are reminiscent of the *Vita S. Wilfridi*. So is the style, which strings together short participial and adjectival clauses into grandiose, encomiastic sentences. Both authors cast their ideal rulers in a heroic light by emphasising the outsized and improbable nature of their victories. Just as Stephen noted that, in the battle against the Picts, Ecgfrith was "in primis annis eius tenero adhuc regno," the author of the *Annales Mettenses priores* emphasises the marvel of Pippin's revenge by noting that he was "adhuc in pueritiae flore positus."[153] The pair of contrasting phrases "puerili quidem manu, sed heroica ferocitate" also recalls a common technique of chapters 19 and 20 of the *VSW*.[154] We have no evidence for the direct influence of the *VSW* on the *Annales Mettenses priores*. At the very least, Stephen and the author of the *Annales* shared the belief that God operates in history through the agency of ideal rulers. Both also drew on the

---

[151] *Annales Mettenses priores*, ed. von Simson, pp. 1–2. See also the introduction to and translation of this text in Fouracre and Gerberding, *Late Merovingian France*, pp. 330–70.

[152] Fouracre and Gerberding, *Late Merovingian France*, p. 350.

[153] See above, n. 70.

[154] See, for example, above, p. 20. Fouracre and Gerberding note that the *Annals'* "treament of [Pippin II] often resembles the way in which hagiographers portrayed their saintly subjects": in their *Late Merovingian France*, p. 334.

grammatical and stylistic tools of Latin – in particular, its ability to qualify and thus attach meaning to every part of a sentence – to show how God had operated through specific rulers at specific moments in history. In their generic crossings between royal history and the lives of saints, the *VSW* and the *Annales Mettenses priores* testify to the resources that hagiography offered theorists and chroniclers of ideal Christian rulership in the early Middle Ages. Indeed, hagiography would go on to shape the nascent genre of royal biography from its Carolingian (new) beginnings onwards.[155]

The Anglo-Saxon mission to the Continent indirectly links the *Vita S. Wilfridi* to the Carolingian histories of the 750s and beyond. Stephen takes care to indicate Wilfrid's founding role in a mission that, by the time of the *VSW*'s composition, had been underway in Frisia for some twenty years. He writes that Wilfrid preached to the pagan Frisians in the winter of 678–679: "et primum ibi secundum apostolum fundamentum fidei posuit, quod adhuc superaedificat filius eius, Inhripis nutritus, gratia Dei Wilbrordus episcopus" – "And, in accordance with [the nature of] an apostle, he first laid the foundation of faith there [i.e. Frisia], which his son Willibrord, educated at Ripon, bishop by the grace of God, is still building on."[156] Not only did Wilfrid "lay the foundation of the faith" and of the Continental mission, but he could be claimed as the spiritual father of Willibrord, the first significant member of the mission, who had spent part of his youth at Ripon.[157] What is more, Willibrord served as Bishop of Frisia under Pippin II, the Carolingian ancestor memorialised so grandly in the *Annales Mettenses priores*, and later under Charles Martel. In this role, he served as a vital arm of support for the extension of the territorial base of Pippinid power.[158] This alliance between a missionary Church and a political dynasty would ultimately shape Carolingian political strategy and ideology, leading to a newly prominent rhetoric of universal mission and biblical kingship.[159] If Willibrord or his circle had written a

---

[155] See David Ganz, "Einhard's Charlemagne: The Characterisation of Greatness," in *Charlemagne: Empire and Society*, ed. Joanna Story (Manchester and New York, 2005), pp. 38–52, at 41–44; David Ganz, "Humour as History in Notker's *Gesta Karoli Magni*," in *Monks, Nuns and Friars in Medieval Society*, ed. Edward B. King, Jacqueline T. Schaefer, and William B. Wadley (Sewanee, TN, 1989), pp. 171–83; and Karen DeMent Youmans, "Asser's *Life of Alfred* and the Rhetoric of Hagiography," *Mediaevalia* 22 (1999), 291–305.

[156] *The Life of Bishop Wilfrid*, ed. Colgrave, p. 52.

[157] On Willibrord's career, see Levison, *England and the Continent in the Eighth Century*, pp. 53–69.

[158] See Richard A. Gerberding, "716: A Crucial Year for Charles Martel," in *Karl Martell in seiner Zeit*, ed. Jörg Jarnut, Ulrich Nonn, and Michael Richter (Sigmaringen, 1994), pp. 205–16.

[159] On Carolingian political theology, see Walter Ullmann, *The Carolingian Renaissance and the Idea of Kingship: The Birkbeck Lectures 1968–1969* (London, 1969), pp. 43–71; Ewig, "Zum Christlichen Königsgedanken im Frühmittelalter," pp. 39–71; Janet L. Nelson, "Kingship and Empire in the Carolingian World," in *Carolingian Culture: Emulation and Innovation*, ed. Rosamond McKitterick (Cambridge, 1994), pp. 52–87; and Moore, *A Sacred Kingdom*, pp. 203–327.

history of Pippin's campaigns in Frisia, it might have resembled Stephen's contemporaneous narrative of Northumbrian conquests in the 670s or the *First Continuation of the Chronicle of Fredegar* some forty years later. The fact that the Pippinids appear to have waited until their eventual accession to sponsor the production of historiography squares with the general notion, described above, that historiography was properly a genre about kings. As the Carolingian dynasty, they would build on this generic association by using historiography as a tool of dynastic legitimation.[160]

Stephen of Ripon, too, knew what he was doing when he used historiographical conventions in his founder's *vita*. His authorial choices could not help but resonate in a larger field in which generic conventions had specific social and ideological associations. In this light, his decision to include historiographical conventions is not simply a functional move that lays out evidence for his hagiographical argument. Rather, it makes an implicit literary-theoretical argument for Wilfrid's status as a public figure, a fitting subject for a work with elements of both hagiography and historiography. Deploying these conventions in a saint's life entails rethinking the way that genres of historical writing map onto episcopal and royal identities. The historical documents and battle narratives in the *VSW* do not just support Stephen's polemical account; they also function as textual monuments that inscribe Wilfrid into the public record.[161] Just as hagiography would later help to shape the depiction of ideal kingship, historiographical conventions allowed Stephen to construct a useful saintly and episcopal identity: a bishop who was the king's ecclesiastical double and who could use his office to channel God's favor to the entire kingdom.

Conclusion

The drift of the *VSW* towards historiography thus mirrors, in a curious way, the eventual drift of Carolingian royal history towards hagiography. There is no evidence that the *VSW* was read on the Continent in the eighth century, so we cannot posit direct influence.[162] Instead, it stands as the bellwether of a much larger process of literary and ideological change that made sanctity available to political actors, institutions, and bodies. No longer do the *bella regum* and the *virtutes martyrum* simply coexist within the roomy structure of providential history; they now depend on each other for their

---

[160] On the use of historiography as propaganda under the Carolingians, see, for example, Yitzhak Hen, "The Annals of Metz and the Merovingian Past," in *The Uses of the Past in the Early Middle Ages*, ed. Yitzhak Hen and Matthew Innes (Cambridge, 2004), pp. 175–90; Rosamond McKitterick, "Political Ideology in Carolingian Historiography," in the same volume, pp. 162–74; Collins, "Deception and Misrepresentation," p. 246.

[161] On *monumenta* and written history in Livy, see Christina S. Kraus and A.J. Woodman, *Latin Historians* (Cambridge, 1997), p. 55.

[162] Fouracre, "Forgetting and Remembering Dagobert II," pp. 88–89.

mutual fulfillment. God works in the sphere of political history through Wilfrid's ecclesiastical office, which he has earned through his sanctity. Stephen enacts this model of political sanctity in the very fabric of his battle narratives, which constantly alternate between the surface of history and the moral and typological meaning revealed by that surface. Both the political theology and the narrative style would have been alien to Gregory of Tours, writing only a century before him. Finally, Stephen's use of the battle narrative speaks to the complex interrelationship between hagiography and historiography in the early Middle Ages. Each genre offered something distinct to the would-be propagandist or hagiographer (or, in Stephen's case, to the rare individual who filled both roles). As the genre of official public memory, historiography allowed Stephen to portray Wilfrid as a public figure. As a genre dedicated to showing how sanctity works in the world, however, hagiography also made Christian political propaganda possible. By combining elements of both genres in texts that nonetheless remained identifiable as either *vitae* or *historiae*, eighth-century authors such as Stephen of Ripon managed to reimagine the relationship between sanctity and the political sphere within the space of historical narrative.

ABSTRACT

This article argues that the battle narratives in Stephen of Ripon's *Vita S. Wilfridi* (*VSW*) intervene in and illuminate the connected histories of genre, political theory, and historical representation in the early Middle Ages. As I demonstrate, battle narratives are ubiquitous in early medieval "histories," but only tend to occur in saints' lives in the context of miracle stories. Moreover, the manner of representing battle in both genres preserves a distinction between political and religious spheres of action. However, the battle narratives in the *VSW* contain no miracles; instead, they argue that Wilfrid's sanctity as bishop was transferred to King Ecgfrith and Northumbria as actors on the stage of political history. To carry out this argument, Stephen intersperses his battle narratives with discourses of ideal kingship and biblical typology. The model of sanctity he thus deploys, and the theory of closely coordinated royal and ecclesiastical power that underpins it, reflect a missionary ideology that would later be enacted in Bede's *Historia ecclesiastica* and in histories from the Carolingian period. Stephen's novel use of the battle narrative suggests that the boundary between *vitae* and *historiae* was both permeable and productive; it enabled him and others to construct a sacralised political sphere in historical narrative.

Résumé

Cet article avance que les récits de bataille dans la *Vita S. Wilfridi* (*VSW*) d'Étienne de Ripon contribuent et jettent une lumière sur l'histoire interreliée du genre littéraire, de la théorique politique et de la représentation historique au haut Moyen Âge. Comme je le démontre, les récits de bataille sont omniprésents dans les « histoires » du haut Moyen Âge, mais dans les vies de saints, elles ont seulement tendance à apparaître dans le contexte de récits miraculeux. Qui plus est, la façon de représenter les scènes de bataille dans ces deux genres littéraires maintient une distinction entre deux sphères d'action, l'une politique et l'autre religieuse. Cependant, les récits de bataille dans la *VSW* ne contiennent pas de miracles; elles font plutôt valoir que la sainteté de Wilfrid en tant qu'évêque s'est transférée au roi Ecgfrith et à la Northumbrie en tant qu'acteurs sur la scène de l'histoire politique. Afin de d'étayer cet argument, Étienne entremêle ses récits de bataille de références à la royauté idéale et à la typologie biblique. Le modèle de sainteté qu'il met de l'avant ainsi que la théorie sous-tendant ce même modèle, alliant étroitement pouvoirs royal et épiscopal, se font l'écho d'une idéologie missionnaire qui serait plus tard mise en pratique par l'*Historia ecclesiastica* de Bède et les histoires de l'époque carolingienne. La vision innovatrice que démontre l'emploi des récits de bataille par Étienne laisse entendre que la frontière entre *vitae* et *historiae* était à la fois perméable et productive; elle permettait à des auteurs comme Stéphane de construire une sphère politique sacralisée au sein d'un récit historique.

Evan Wilson
University of California, Berkeley
e.r.wilson@berkeley.edu

Charlemagne's Failure of Charity in Ps. Turpin's *Chronicle* and Beyond[*]

Benjamin Garstad
MacEwan University

The *Chronicle* of ps. Turpin purports to be an eyewitness account of Charlemagne's Spanish campaigns and the Battle of Roncesvalles in 778. It is, in fact, an anonymous composition of the first half of the twelfth century, roughly contemporary with the first written versions of the *Chanson de Roland* and dependent on the same legendary material as the *chansons de geste*.[1] The *Chronicle* has never achieved the prominence in the study of medieval Latin that the *Chanson de Roland* has long enjoyed in the study of Old French, nor in the undergraduate curriculum, for that matter, certainly because the *Chronicle* lacks the primacy of the *Chanson* in the history of the language and perhaps because it seems that ps. Turpin's cannot be offered as a characteristic example of the medieval chronicle. But the Middle Ages took the *Chronicle* as one of the chief sources on the Matter of France, there were numerous copies of the Latin text in different forms, and versions of ps. Turpin appeared in several vernacular languages.[2]

---

[*] I would like to thank Kevin Solez, who organized the venue at which a preliminary version of this paper was presented, the second annual meeting of the RAVEN Research Group in June 2017.

[1] See André de Mandach, *Naissance et développement de la Chanson de geste en Europe, I: La Geste de Charlemagne et de Roland* (Geneva, 1961), pp. 21–145; and Santiago López Martínez-Moras, "Carlomagno y la tradición oral: De Notker Balbulus a los primeros textos épicos," in *El Pseudo-Turpín, Lazo entre el Culto Jacobeo y el Culto de Carlomagno: Actas del VI Congreso Internacional de Estudios Jacobeos*, ed. Klaus Herbers (Santiago de Compostela, 2003), pp. 45–82.

[2] See Adalbert Hämel, "Los manuscritos latinos del falso Turpino," in *Estudios dedicados a Menendez Pidal*, 7 vols. (Madrid, 1953), 4:67–85; de Mandach, *Naissance et développement*, pp. 220–83, 364–98; Ian Short, "The *Pseudo-Turpin Chronicle*: Some Unnoticed Versions and their Sources," *Medium Ævum* 38 (1969), 1–22; Ian Short, "A Study in Carolingian Legend and its Persistence in Latin Historiography (XII–XVI Centuries)," *Mittellateinisches Jahrbuch* 7 (1972), 127–52; Susan E. Farrier, *The Medieval Charlemagne Legend: An Annotated Bibliography* (New York and London, 1993), pp. 56–68; Gabrielle M. Spiegel, *Romancing the Past: The Rise of Vernacular Prose Historiography in Thirteenth-Century France* (Berkeley, 1993), pp. 69–98; Amy G. Remensnyder, *Remembering Kings Past: Monastic Foundation Legends in Medieval Southern France* (Ithaca, 1995), pp. 150–52; Paolo Caucci von Saucken, "El "sueño de Carlomagno" en Italia: La *Entrée d'Espagne*," in *El Pseudo-Turpín*, ed. Herbers, pp. 347–52; Humberto Baquero Moreno, "El Pseudo-Turpín y Portugal" in *El Pseudo-Turpín*, ed. Herbers, pp. 353–58; Volker Honemann, "El Pseudo-Turpín y la literatura alemana de la Edad Media" in *El Pseudo-Turpín*, ed. Herbers, pp. 359–71; Jan van Herwaarden, "La *Crónica de Turpín* en los Países

Even Ariosto facetiously cited Turpin as his principal source throughout the *Orlando Furioso*.[3]

Recent years have seen important steps toward a more widespread appreciation of the *Chronicle* of ps. Turpin, particularly the appearance of Kevin Poole's 2014 English translation of that early version of the text which constitutes Book Four of the *Liber Sancti Jacobi* or *Codex Calixtinus*.[4] Ps. Turpin, nevertheless, continues to be judged in terms of his tortured Latin grammar and syntax, the inconsistencies of his narrative, and the nonsensical details found in his story.[5] Without challenging the validity of any

---

Bajos" in *El Pseudo-Turpín*, ed. Herbers, pp. 373–76; Robert Morrissey, *Charlemagne and France: A Thousand Years of Mythology*, trans. Catherine Tihanyi (Notre Dame, 2003), pp. 51–57; Matthias M. Tischler, "Tatmensch oder Heidenapostel: Die Bilder Karls des Großen bei Einhart und im Pseudo-Turpin," in *Jakobus und Karl der Große: Von Einhards Karlsvita zum Pseudo-Turpin*, ed. Karl Herbers (Tübingen, 2003), pp. 1–37, at 7–14; Jace Stuckey, "Charlemagne as Crusader? Memory, Propaganda, and the Many Uses of Charlemagne's Legendary Expedition to Spain," in *The Legend of Charlemagne in the Middle Ages: Power, Faith, and Crusade*, ed. Matthew Gabriele and Jace Stuckey (Basingstoke, 2008), pp. 137–52, at 140–43; Anne Latowsky, "Charlemagne as Pilgrim? Requests for Relics in the *Descriptio qualiter* and the *Voyage of Charlemagne*," in *The Legend of Charlemagne*, ed. Gabriele and Stuckey, pp. 153–67, at 154–55; Santiago López Martínez-Morás, "Le Pseudo-Turpin en Espagne," *Cahiers de recherches médiévales et humanistes* 25 (2013), 471–94; Miguel Dolan Gómez, "*Rex Parvus* or *Rex Nobilis*? Charlemagne and the Politics of History (and Crusading) in Thirteenth-Century Iberia," in *The Charlemagne Legend in Medieval Latin Texts*, ed. William J. Purkis and Matthew Gabriele (Woodbridge, 2016), pp. 92–114, at 94–97, 107, 112–13; Jace Stuckey, "The Twelfth-Century *Vita Karoli* and the Making of a Royal Saint," in *The Charlemagne Legend*, ed. Purkis and Gabriele, pp. 33–58, at 50–53; James B. Williams, "'For the Honour of the Blessed Virgin': The History and Legacy of Charles's Devotion to Mary in the *Gesta Karoli Magni ad Carcassonam et Narbonam*," in *The Charlemagne Legend*, ed. Purkis and Gabriele, pp. 148–80, at 157–58, 176–77.

[3] Ludovico Ariosto, *Orlando Furioso* 13.40, 18.10, 175, 23.38, 62, 24.44, 26.23, 28.2, 29.56, 30.49, 31.79, 33.85, 34.86, 38.10, 40.81, 44.23.

[4] Kevin R. Poole, *The Chronicle of Pseudo-Turpin: Book IV of the* Liber Sancti Jacobi (Codex Calixtinus) (New York, 2014). His excellent introduction sets the *Chronicle* of ps. Turpin in the context of the *Codex Calixtinus* and the ecclesiastical history and literature of twelfth-century Spain; see also Manuel C. Díaz y Díaz, "La posición del Pseudo-Turpín en el *Liber Sancti Jacobi*," in *El Pseudo-Turpín*, ed. Herbers, pp. 99–111. Poole's translation supersedes at long last that of Thomas Rodd, *History of Charles the Great and Orlando, Ascribed to Archbishop Turpin: Translated from the Latin in Spanheim's Lives of Ecclesiastical Writers* (London, 1812). Rodd's translation enjoyed some popularity on account of its inclusion in the *Medieval Tales* volume of Morley's Universal Library; *Medieval Tales*, ed. H. Morley, in Morley's Universal Library, vol. 18 (London, 1884).

[5] Christopher Hohler, "A Note on *Jacobus*," *Journal of the Warburg and Courtauld Institutes* 35 (1972), 31–80, went so far as to maintain the proposition that the errors in the *Codex Calixtinus* are altogether intentional and that the text was used as a teaching tool by an itinerant Latin master, who would have his students identify and correct the mistakes in everything from Latin grammar to Biblical references. Hohler's defence of his thesis is very erudite, but this is hardly the only explanation for what sloppy material we find in the text, not least in ps. Turpin's *Chronicle*. Poole's notes to his translation are also

of these criticisms, I would like to draw attention here to one of the strengths of the *Chronicle*. This is the emphasis that ps. Turpin places on Charlemagne's failure to adequately provide for the poor at his table, which prevents the conversion of the Saracens and the cessation of the Spanish War, and ultimately results in the death of Roland. In terms of composition, the stress on this incident provides a coherence by showing how the principal events of the work are consequent on this incident and recalling provision for the poor in the conclusion of the work. This episode also provides Charlemagne's Muslim enemies with a motive for their intransigent resistance, which is not found in, for instance, the *Chanson de Roland*. Charlemagne's failing also makes for a more subtle and sympathetic treatment of the encounter between paladins and paynim than that found in the *Chanson* and creates an opportunity for sharp social criticism aimed not at the heathen enemy, but at Christendom itself. Having outsiders and infidels give voice to such censure of Christian society also seems to have been one of the enduring influences of this passage.

According to ps. Turpin, after Charlemagne's initial conquest of Spain at the behest of St. James and his return to Gaul, the country was reconquered by the African king Aigolande and all the Christians massacred.[6] Charlemagne led his armies back to Spain and after many battles he and Aigolande agreed to put their religious dispute to the arbitrament of arms; a series of fights between representatives of the two sides is arranged and the losers are to concede the superiority of the creed of the winning side.[7] The Christians are triumphant in this trial by combat and Aigolande agrees to be baptized along with his people. When Aigolande comes the next morning to receive baptism, he finds Charlemagne sitting down to breakfast with his court. Charlemagne explains who are the variously garbed clerics at his table, bishops and priests, monks and canons. But Aigolande notices another group of diners at the meal:[8]

---

peppered rather heavily with strictures of ps. Turpin's slips in regard to consistency, reasoning, and geography.

[6] Ps. Turpin, *Chron.* 6, ed. Paul Gerhard Schmidt, *Karolellus atque Pseudo-Turpini Historia Karoli Magni et Rotholandi*, (Stuttgart and Leipzig, 1996), p. 26.

[7] Ps. Turpin, *Chron.* 12, ed. Schmidt, *Karolellus atque Pseudo-Turpini Historia*, pp. 52–60.

[8] I have employed one of the most recently published texts of the *Chronicle* of ps. Turpin, ed. Schmidt, *Karolellus atque Pseudo-Turpini Historia*, which is compiled from previous editions and appears opposite the definitive edition of the Latin verse paraphrase of the *Chronicle*, the *Karolellus*, but have checked Schmidt's text against the following editions and noted only the most significant variations: Cyril Meredith-Jones, *Historia Karoli Magni et Rotholandi ou Chronique du Pseudo-Turpin, Textes revus et publiés d'après 49 manuscrits* (Paris, 1936); Hamilton Martin Smyser, *The Pseudo-Turpin, Edited from Bibliothèque Nationale, Fonds Latin, MS. 17656, with an annotated synopsis* (Cambridge, MA, 1937); Adalbert Hämel, *Der Pseudo-Turpin von Compostela: Aus dem Nachlaß herausgegeben von André de Mandach*, Sitzungsberichte der bayerischen Akademie der Wissenschaften, philosophisch-historische Klasse, Jahrgang 1965, 1 (Munich, 1965); Hans-Wilhelm Klein, *Die Chronik von Karl dem Grossen und*

Interea videns Aygolandus in quadam parte tredecim pauperes miserrimo habitu indutos, ad terram resedentes, sine mensa et lintheaminibus commedentes, parvo cibo et potu utentes, interrogavit, cuiusmodi homines essent. At ipse Karolus ait: "Hec est gens Dei, nuncii domini nostri Ihesu Christi, quos sub numero duodecim apostolorum Domini unumquemque diem ex more pascimus." Tunc Aygolandus respondit: "Hii, qui circa te resident, fideles[9] sunt et tui sunt, et feliciter commedunt et bibunt et induuntur; illi vero, quos Dei tui omnino esse dicis et nuncios eius esse asseris, cur fame pereunt et male vestiuntur et longe proiciuntur a te et male tractantur? Male domino suo servit, qui sic nuncios eius turpiter recipit. Magnam verecundiam facit domino[10] suo, qui eius famulis ita servit; legem tuam, quam dicebas esse bonam, nunc ostendis falsam." Et accepta ab eo licencia scandalizatus[11] rediit ad suos et baptizari renuens mandavit ei die crastina bellum.[12]

Meanwhile Aigolande saw in a certain spot thirteen poor men, dressed in the most pitiful clothing, sitting on the ground, eating without table and linens, making do with a little bit of food and drink, and he asked what sort of men these were. And Charlemagne said: "This is the people of God, the messengers of our Lord Jesus Christ, whom according to custom we feed each and every day to the number of the twelve disciples of the Lord." Then Aigolande replied: "These who sit around you are your own faithful servants and they sumptuously eat and drink and are clothed; those indeed, whom you say belong altogether to your God and whom you declare to be his messengers, why are they perishing of hunger and poorly clothed and thrust a long way from you and are badly treated? He serves his lord poorly, who thus vilely receives his messengers. He does a great insult to his lord, who thus treats his servants; your law, which you were saying is good, you now show to be false." And taking his leave of him he returned of-

---

Roland: Der lateinische Pseudo-Turpin *in den Handschriften aus Aachen und Andernach* (Munich, 1986); Klaus Herbers and Manuel Santos Noia, *Liber Sancti Iacobi: Codex Calixtinus* (Santiago de Compostela, 1998), Ps. Turpin = Liber 4, pp. 193–229.

[9] Most editions, including Meredith-Jones, *Chronique du Pseudo-Turpin*, p. 139; Smyser, *The Pseudo-Turpin*, p. 72; Hämel, *Der Pseudo-Turpin von Compostela*, p. 58; Klein, *Die Chronik von Karl dem Grossen und Roland*, p. 66; and Herbers and Noia, *Liber Sancti Iacobi*, p. 209, have *felices* instead of Schmidt's *fideles*, but *felices* seems to reduplicate *feliciter*, while *fideles* emphasizes that those who receive fortunate treatment are Charlemagne's own loyal servants.

[10] The *Codex Calixtinus* and the Aachen and Andernach texts have *Deo* in place of *domino*: Meredith-Jones, *Chronique du Pseudo-Turpin*, p. 139; Hämel, *Der Pseudo-Turpin von Compostela*, p. 58; Klein, *Die Chronik von Karl dem Grossen und Roland*, p. 66; and Herbers and Noia, *Liber Sancti Iacobi*, p. 209. This makes it clear that Aigolande understands Charlemagne's conduct to be a disservice to God but interrupts the not insignificant analogy whereby Charlemagne's duty to God is understood in terms of a liegeman's obligations to his lord.

[11] Most editions omit *scandalizatus*: Meredith-Jones, *Chronique du Pseudo-Turpin*, p. 139; Smyser, *The Pseudo-Turpin*, p. 72; Hämel, *Der Pseudo-Turpin von Compostela*, p. 58; Klein, *Die Chronik von Karl dem Grossen und Roland*, p. 66; and Herbers and Noia, *Liber Sancti Iacobi*, p. 209. The word, however, is a helpful indication of the sentiments and reaction of Aigolande.

[12] Ps. Turpin, *Chron.* 13, ed. Schmidt, *Karolellus atque Pseudo-Turpini Historia*, p. 62. All translations, unless otherwise noted, are my own.

fended to his own people and refusing to be baptized he offered him battle the next day.

The passage continues with a lesson on Charlemagne's mistake and the obligation of all Christians to tend to the poor. On account of Aigolande's disgusted refusal to be baptized, however, the war continues and although Aigolande himself is shortly killed in battle the war proves disastrous for Charlemagne's army. No such incident is found in the *Chanson de Roland*, but it is far more than a curiosity introduced into the work of ps. Turpin, but rather one of the central and unifying elements of the *Chronicle*.

Immediately after the departure of Aigolande, Charlemagne tries to make amends by supplying all of the poor in his army with food and clothing ("tunc ... omnes pauperes, quos in exercitu invenit, diligenter procuravit et optime induit, cibum et potum honorifice illis ex more prebuit"), but the concern with taking care of those in need is by no means isolated to this one passage in the *Chronicle*.[13] Ps. Turpin's verse epitaph for Roland notes that he was "the bread of the needy, bountiful to the poor, lavish to guests" ("panis egentum, / Largus pauperibus, prodigus hospitibus").[14] And Charlemagne is said to have lauded Roland not only as a great warrior for the faith, but also as "the staff of orphans and widows, the food and refreshment of poor and rich alike" ("baculus orphanorum et viduarum, cibus et refectio tam pauperum quam divitum").[15] Among the other memorial endowments that he made for the sake of Roland and his companions, Charlemagne is supposed to have fed and clothed thirty paupers every year on the anniversary of their martyrdom ("die passionis eorumque annuatim trigenta pauperes cunctis vestibus necessariis induerent cibariisque reficerent").[16] And for the repose of the souls of the dead Charlemagne is said to have given twelve thousand ounces of silver and as many talents of gold to the needy of Arles, near which many of the casualties were buried ("pro quorum animabus uncias duodecim milia argenteas totidemque talenta aurea Karolus apud Arelaten egenis dedit").[17]

As Smyser pointed out some time ago, ps. Turpin's account of the contentions of Charlemagne and Aigolande is based in no small measure upon earlier anecdotes concerning Charlemagne's conflicts with a more historically verifiable, and more genuinely pagan, enemy, the Saxons.[18] According to the older *Life of Queen Mathilda*, written sometime between 996 and 1002, Charlemagne and the Saxon king Widukind

---

[13] Ps. Turpin, *Chron.* 13, ed. Schmidt, *Karolellus atque Pseudo-Turpini Historia*, p. 64.

[14] Ps. Turpin, *Chron.* 24, ed. Schmidt, *Karolellus atque Pseudo-Turpini Historia*, p. 150.

[15] Ps. Turpin, *Chron.* 25, ed. Schmidt, *Karolellus atque Pseudo-Turpini Historia*, p. 156.

[16] Ps. Turpin, *Chron.* 29, ed. Schmidt, *Karolellus atque Pseudo-Turpini Historia*, p. 172.

[17] Ps. Turpin, *Chron.* 30, ed. Schmidt, *Karolellus atque Pseudo-Turpini Historia*, p. 174. This donation seems to have been reduplicated in chapter 29 in regard to the needy in the vicinity of Blaye.

[18] Smyser, *The Pseudo-Turpin*, pp. 29–31.

agreed to settle their dispute on the basis of a single combat between themselves; since the Lord was moved by the tears of the Christians ("Dominus lacrimis pulsatus christianorum"), the victory went to his faithful warrior ("fideli suo bellatori").[19] But the *Chronicle* of ps. Turpin does not modify this source merely by having numerous champions fight on behalf of the rival kings; it also changes the outcome. While the *Life of Mathilda* has Widukind submit to baptism and turn from being a persecutor of the Church to a worshipper of the true God and a patron of the Christian religious, Charlemagne's neglect of the poor prevents any such conversion on the part of Aigolande. Charlemagne goes from being the champion of his cause and the reason for its victory to becoming a stumbling block to pagans who would convert and the reason for the disasters that befall the Christian armies. This reworking of an important

[19] *Vita Mahthildis reginae antiquior* 1–2, ed. Rudolph Koepke, MGH SS 10 (Hanover, 1852), p. 576: "Illo autem tempore Karolus Magnus arcem tenens inperii, vir christianissimus, armis strenuus, lege eruditus, totusque in fide catholicus, et erga Dei cultores benivolus ac devotus, contra eundum Widikindum bella cum exercitu iniit, defendendae causa fidei, ut semper contra paganos solebat. Cumque simul convenissent, utrisque placuit principibus, ut ipsi singuli invicem dimicaturi consurgerent, et cui sors victoriam contulisset, ipsi totus exercitus sine dubio pareret. Quibus congressis ac diu multumque concertantibus, tandem Dominus lacrimis pulsatus christianorum, fideli suo bellatori de hoste concessit triumphum, ut fides meruit. Tunc tanta mentis mutatio Widikindi invasit pertinaciam, ut se voluntarius cum familia sua omnique paganorum exercitu tam potestati regis quam fidei submitteret catholicae, quem inperator benigne suscipiens, baptizari fecit a sancto Bonifacio episcopo, ipse eum levans de sacro fonte. Ille vero relicto errore credulus ad agnitionem veritatis poenitendo sponte pervenit, et sicut prius persecutor destructorque, pertinax fuit ecclesiae, deinde christianissimus ecclesiarum et Dei extitit cultor, ita ut ipse singulas totis viribus studendo construeret cellulas, quas plurimis sanctorum reliquiis nec non ceteris perfectas relinquebat utilitatibus, quarum una multis adhuc nota remanet Aggerinensis dicta, et eadem quae modo retulimus adhuc aliqua ibidem supersunt" – "At that time, however, Charlemagne held the dignity of empire, a most Christian man, doughty in arms, learned in law, and altogether Catholic in faith, and kindly and devoted toward the worshippers of God, he embarked with his army on a war with this same Widukind, for the sake of defending the faith, as it was always his custom to oppose pagans. And when they met together it pleased both princes that they themselves alone should stand up to fight each other, and him upon whom chance should bestow the victory the whole army should obey without hesitation. After they had come together and struggled greatly for a long time, at length the Lord was moved by the tears of the Christians and granted a triumph over the enemy to His faithful warrior, as his faith deserved. Then such a great change of mind overcame the stubbornness of Widukind that he voluntarily submitted himself with his own family and the whole army of pagans as much to the power of the king as to the Catholic faith. The Emperor kindly took him in and caused him to be baptized by St. Boniface, the bishop, though he himself lifted him from the holy font. Indeed, abandoning error and devoted with a penitent will he arrived at a knowledge of the truth, and just as he was previously a stubborn persecutor and destroyer of the Church, he subsequently arose as the most Christian upholder of churches and worshipper of God, so much so that he himself striving with all his powers built many individual monk's cells [*or* chapels], which he left finished with many relics of the saints and not a few revenues besides, of which one known to many to this day endures, called Enger, and likewise the others, which we have just mentioned, remain there to the present day."

model highlights the distinct interests and intentions of the author who wrote under the name of Turpin and how much weight his narrative put upon the scene in which Aigolande is repelled by Charlemagne's lack of charity.

Widukind is also Charlemagne's counterpart in a story that provides a model for and goes to the heart of the concern of the modified narrative in ps. Turpin's *Chronicle*. This anecdote is found in Peter Damian's (1007–1072) epistle on almsgiving, a letter to Mainard, bishop of Urbino (1056–1088), datable to the summer of 1064. After complaining of those rich men who dine at high tables ("excelsae mensae") covered with embroidered tablecloths ("mantelibus acu variante depictis"), while the poor men they entertain eat off their own laps amidst a pack of dogs, Peter Damian tells a story related to him by the duke and margrave Godfrey of Lorraine:

> quoniam Karolus imperator quindecim vicibus cum rege Saxonum, qui gentilitatis adhuc detinebatur errore, bellum commisit, quindecies perdidit, tribus vero consertis postmodum proeliis Karolus superavit, eumque postremo captum victor optinuit. Aliquando sane dum Karolus idem excelsa, ut assolet, inthronizatus arce discumberet, pauperes vero, quos alebat, solotenus ignobiliter resideret, rex qui remota procul ab imperatore mensa prandebat, talia per nuntium legata direxit: Dum vester, inquit, Christus sese perhibeat in pauperibus recipi, qua fronte persuadetis nostra sibi colla submitti, quem vos ita despicitis, eique nullam honoris reverentiam exhibetis? Ad quod imperator corde compunctus erubuit, et ex ore gentilis hominis evangelicam prodire sententiam vehementer expavit. Ait enim Dominus: *Quod uni ex minimis meis fecistis, mihi fecistis*. Laetatus ergo est rex, dum a tali correptus est, utpote qui necdum fidei rudimenta perceperat, iam fidei fructum, misericordiae scilicet opera, praedicabat.[20]

> When the emperor Charles joined battle fifteen times with the king of the Saxons, who was still enmeshed in the error of paganism, he lost fifteen times; but in three battles fought afterward Charles prevailed, and at last, as the victor, he took him prisoner. One time when this very same Charles was sitting down to dine enthroned upon an elevated dais, as was his custom, while the poor whom he fed were sitting on the ground in a lowly situation, the king, who was eating at a table removed some distance from the emperor, sent the following words by a messenger: "Inasmuch as your Christ," he said, "declared that he was to be received in the poor, by what impudence do you urge us to submit to him, whom you thus despise, and to whom you show no respect or honour?" At which the emperor was stung at heart and blushed and he was struck with fear[21] that

---

[20] Peter Damian, *Epist.* 110, ed. Kurt Reindel, *Die Briefe des Petrus Damiani*, MGH, Epp. 2, Die Briefe der deutschen Kaiserzeit 4, 4 vols. (Munich, 1983–1993), 3:243–44. This letter is printed in the older, but perhaps more accessible *Patrologia Latina*, not amongst the letters of Peter Damian, but as one of his *opuscula* (Number 9), entitled *De eleemosyna*; this passage is found at PL 145:220D–221B. Compare Owen J. Blum, *Peter Damian, Letters 91–120*, The Fathers of the Church, Mediaeval Continuation 5 (Washington, DC, 1998), p. 245.

[21] Charlemagne's two reactions to the rebuke of Widukind seem inconsistent, but "he was struck with fear" or "was greatly afraid" is what *expavit* (from *expavesco*) must mean, although Blum translates it as

the Gospel verdict should proceed powerfully from the mouth of a heathen man. For the Lord said: *What you have done to the least of mine, you have done to me.*[22] So the king[23] was glad that he had been corrected by even such a man, seeing that while he had not yet grasped the rudiments of the faith, he was already preaching the fruit of faith, to be sure, the works of mercy.

In Peter Damian's account it is a pagan who takes Charlemagne to task for not heeding the Gospel injunction to look after the needy and warns him that this presents an impediment to his conversion. All this is taken over by ps. Turpin. But while it is enough for Peter Damian that Charlemagne should be pleased to receive the reproof of even a pagan who could recognize the fruits of a faith he did not yet possess, ps. Turpin works out the terrible consequences of Charlemagne's failure in charity, not by implication, but through an involved narrative, which would not have proceeded to cataclysm if Charlemagne had done nothing to earn the censure of a defeated pagan ruler.

The crucial importance of the incident of Charlemagne and the beggars and Aigolande's rebuke was not lost on those responsible for later versions of ps. Turpin's *Chronicle*. It is regularly found in subsequent redactions and in vernacular translations.[24] A comprehensive survey would be tedious, but we may offer a couple of salient examples. The *Agulandus þattr*, which constitutes the fourth and easily the longest part of the *Karlamagnús saga*, the Old Norse rendition of the Matter of France that was translated, compiled, and revised over the course of the thirteenth and fourteenth centuries, and is based largely on the *Chronicle* of ps. Turpin and the French *Chanson d'Aspremont*, not only includes this episode, but the B-redactor of the *Karlamagnús saga* also elaborates upon it, putting into the mouth of Charlemagne a rebuttal of Aigolande's charges.[25] Charlemagne responds that it is in accord with a "godly arrange-

---

"marveled." Perhaps Charlemagne's gladness ("laetatus ergo est") is supposed to imply time for some reflection after his initial shock.

[22] A paraphrase of Matt. 25.40.

[23] Heretofore, *imperator* has been used to refer to Charlemagne, and *rex* to the Saxon king, Widukind, but in this instance the *rex* must be Charlemagne; a slip, no doubt.

[24] See Marianne Ailes, "Tolerated Otherness: The 'Unconverted' Saracen in the *Chansons de geste*," in *Languages of Love and Hate: Conflict, Communication, and Identity in the Medieval Mediterranean*, ed. Sarah Lambert and Helen Nicholson (Turnhout, 2012), pp. 3–19, at 12–14.

[25] *Karlamagnús saga* 4.18, ed. Bjarni Vilhjálmsson, *Karlamagnús saga og kappa hans*, 3 vols. (Reykjavík, 1954), 2:296–99. This passage is translated in Constance B. Hieatt, *Karlamagnús saga: The Saga of Charlemagne and His Heroes*, 3 vols. (Toronto, 1975), 2:113–16. For the date of the *Karlamagnús saga*, see Eyvind Fjeld Halvorsen, *The Norse Version of the Chanson de Roland* (Copenhagen, 1959), pp. 75–76. See also Peter G. Foote, *The Pseudo-Turpin Chronicle in Iceland: A Contribution to the Study of the Karlamagnús Saga* (London, 1959); and Vicente Almazán, "Carlomagno y el Pseudo-Turpín en las lenguas escandinavas," in *El Pseudo-Turpín*, ed. Herbers, pp. 377–81.

ment" (*guðleg skipan*) that the poor are provided with no more than the bare necessities of life and not luxuries, otherwise they would cease to be poor and so share in the humility of Christ and his disciples (this rather unsatisfying defence is undercut by the retention of the *Chronicle*'s note that Charlemagne amended his treatment of the poor after Aigolande's departure). *Turpines Story*, the Middle English translation of the ps. Turpin *Chronicle*, without any remarkable expansion includes this same story, rendering into homely phrases the story of how it came about that Aigolande "toke his leue of Charlis, gretly disklawnder how vngodely Charlis tretide Goddis messengeris."[26]

Recognition of the importance of the episode could also be signalled by its omission. The *Vita Karoli Magni* was commissioned by Frederick Barbarossa sometime between 1171 and 1184 and intended to promote the canonization of Charlemagne by the Anti-Pope Paschal III in 1165; it borrows much from ps. Turpin to embellish its subject, but makes no mention of his failure to provide for the beggars or Aigolande's disgust, rather presenting him as a model of almsgiving.[27] In their own way the monks of the abbey of St. Denis, often taken to have been custodians of the manuscript tradition of the *Chronicle* and avid proponents of the sainthood of Charlemagne, acknowledged the extent to which the passage under examination presented the king in a negative light and undermined his reputation for sanctity by quietly excising it from some of the versions of ps. Turpin they produced. The earliest text of ps. Turpin associated with St. Denis, included in a miscellany of works that seem to derive from the abbey, includes several of the initial chapters of the *Chronicle*, but omits the story of Aigolande coming for baptism and then withdrawing.[28] The *De sanctitate Karoli*, a work from the later twelfth century that may have been based on the version of ps. Turpin in this miscellany, also leaves this episode out.[29]

Helinand of Froidmont, likewise, in an account of Charlemagne's Spanish wars taken in all essentials from ps. Turpin, relates the series of encounters that comprise the first trial by combat with their attendant miracles in great detail, but omits Aigolande's determination to receive baptism and subsequent recantation as a conclu-

---

[26] *Turpines Story* ch. 16, ed. Stephen H.A. Shepherd, *Turpines Story: A Middle English Translation of the Pseudo-Turpin Chronicle* (Oxford, 2004), pp. 20–21. See Stephen H.A. Shepherd, "The Middle English *Pseudo-Turpin Chronicle*," *Medium Ævum* 65 (1996), 19–34.

[27] Gerhard Rauschen, *Die Legende Karls des Grossen im 11. und 12. Jahrhundert* (Leipzig, 1890), pp. 84–85.

[28] Elizabeth A.R. Brown, "Saint-Denis and the Turpin Legend," in *The* Codex Calixtinus *and the Shrine of St. James*, ed. John Williams and Alison Stones (Tübingen, 1992), pp. 51–88, at 54–56.

[29] Brown, "Saint-Denis and the Turpin-Legend," p. 56.

sion to the course of events.[30] Rather, he has Aigolande precipitously withdraw before the arrival of Charlemagne's reinforcements from Italy and the king return to France, and this is the end of the war in Spain.[31] So intent does Helinand seem to be to preserve the glory and virtue of Charlemagne unalloyed that he even leaves out the battle of Roncesvalles and the death of Roland, unless the note on the pestilential winter that followed the close of Charlemagne's Spanish war is intended as a veiled reference to these events.[32] Helinand does, however, convey a passage from Einhard that lauds Charlemagne's unbounded generosity to the needy and peerless almsgiving (see below), which offers a very different picture than would have resulted from the inclusion of ps. Turpin's story of the conversation between Aigolande and Charlemagne.[33]

On the whole, though, Helinand's expurgated and manipulated version of ps. Turpin must be seen as something of an aberration. Alberic of Trois-Fontaines counts both Helinand and ps. Turpin among his sources and expands upon the passages from Helinand with material taken directly from ps. Turpin; he mentions, albeit very briefly, the incident at Charlemagne's breakfast table and the battle of Roncesvalles.[34] Vincent of Beauvais, who does occasionally rely on Helinand for the reign of Charlemagne, also had access to a complete text of ps. Turpin and included from it accounts of the scandal of Charlemagne's treatment of the beggars and the battle of Roncesvalles in his *Speculum historiale*.[35] Nevertheless, the omissions perpetrated by

---

[30] PL 212:850D–851C. The excerpts from ps. Turpin begin at 838C, Turpin's narration of Charlemagne's acquisition of Spain commences at 847C, and after an interruption the material resumes at 850B.

[31] PL 212:851C: "Altera die venerunt Carolo in auxilium quatuor marquisii de locis Italiae, cum quatuor millibus virorum bellatorum. Quod ut Aigolandus agnovit, in fugam versus est: tunc Carolus cum suis exercitibus remeavit in Galliam" – "The next day four marcher lords came to the aid of Charles from the lands of Italy, with four thousand warlike men. So, when Aigolande learned of it he turned to flight; then Charles returned to Gaul with his armies."

[32] PL 212:851C: "Hiems mollissima et pestilens fuit." This follows immediately on the passage quoted in the previous note.

[33] PL 212:837D.

[34] Alberic of Trois-Fontaines, *Chronicle*: Annis 805–806, ed. Paul Scheffer-Boichorst, *Chronica Albrici monachi Trium Fontium, a monacho Novi Hoiensis interpolata*, MGH SS 23 (Hannover, 1874), p. 724.3–5: "Postea venit Aygolandus per conductum videre Karolum, qui videns ordines ducum, clericorum et monachorum in convivio Karoli, tandem de 13 pauperibus, quos seorsum vidit, scandalum sumpsit et baptizari rennuit" – "Afterward Aigolande came under safe conduct to see Charles, and when he saw the ranks of dukes, clergymen, and monks at Charles's banquet, and then the thirteen poor men, and noticed they were apart, he took umbrage and refused to be baptized." Compare with pp. 724.39–725.21.

[35] Vincent of Beauvais, *Spec. hist.* 24.14–22; *Vincentii Burgundi, ex Ordine Praedicatorum Venerabilis Episcopi Bellovacensis Speculum Quadruplex sive Speculum Maius. Opera et studio Theologorum*

the monks of St. Denis and Helinand constitute a recognition of the critical importance of the episode of Aigolande's offence to the characterization of Charlemagne, as well as the negative tendency of that characterization.

Other chroniclers, less interested in safeguarding the reputation of Charlemagne, had no qualms about including the story of the altercation at the king's breakfast table in their material from ps. Turpin.[36] Ranulph Higden, who as a Briton will have had rather less invested in the figure of Charlemagne than Helinand, worked the story of Aigolande's reaction to the treatment of the beggars into his *Polychronicon*, ostensibly as an indication of the French king's character, especially his willingness to repent when convicted of error, but perhaps also for the sake of the lesson it has to offer on the stern obligations and high expectations of charity.[37] This passage was duly rendered into English by John Trevisa in his translation of the *Polychronicon*, but Trevisa's hierarchical sensibilities blinded him to the narrative and rhetorical force of Aigolande's rebuke and he censured the Saracen king as a "lewed goost" who spoke out of turn, misled by the devil, and could not see that men ought to be served according to their estate.[38]

Benedictinorum Collegii Vedastini in alma Academia Duacensi, 4 vols. (Douai, 1624; repr. Graz, 1964), 4:967–70. See Short, "The *Pseudo-Turpin Chronicle*," pp. 10–12; Joachim Ehlers, "El Pseudo-Turpín en las grandes Chroniques de France," in *El Pseudo-Turpín*, ed. Herbers, pp. 285–96, at 290–91.

[36] Shepherd, *Turpines Story*, pp. xxxiii–xxxv.

[37] Ranulph Higden, *Polychronicon* 5.26; *Polychronicon Ranulphi Higden Monachi Cestrensis, together with the English Translations of John Trevisa and of an Unknown Writer of the Fifteenth Century*, 9 vols., ed. Joseph Rawson Lumby (London, 1876), 6:250, 252: "Die quadam Aygolandus, fortis princeps Hispaniae, concessis mutuo treugis, ad Karolum baptismi causa venit. Cumque videret commensales Karoli pretiosis indutos, delicatis vesci, et [e] regione tresdecim pauperes dejectos ad terram cum vili victu et sine mensa sedere, quaesivit quinam essent illi. Cui dictum est; 'Hi tresdecim Dei sunt nuncii, et pro nobis orant, numerumque Christi et discipulorum ejus repraesentant.' Cui Aygolandus: 'Ut video, lex vestra non est aequa, quae nuncios domini sic permittit tractari; et male domino servit qui ejus ministros sic recipit.' Et sic scandalizatus contempto baptismo ad suos recessit. Sed Karolus ex hoc emendatus magis pauperes honoravit" – "On a certain day Aigolande, the mighty prince of Spain, mutual pledges having been struck, came to Charles for the sake of baptism. And when he saw the table companions of Charles, clothed in finery and eating delicacies, as well as the thirteen poor men from the region, cast down on the ground with cheap food and without a table to sit at, he asked what men they might be. It was said to him, 'These thirteen are the messengers of God, and they pray for us, and they represent the number of Christ and His disciples.' To which Aigolande said, 'As I see it, your law is not just, which permits the messengers of the Lord to be treated thus; and he serves the lord poorly, who thus receives his messengers.' And thus scandalized he despised baptism and withdrew to his own people. But Charles, chastened by this, treated the paupers with greater honour."

[38] John Trevisa, *Translacion of Ranulphus of Chestre's Bookes of Cronykes* 5.26, ed. Lumby, *Polychronicon Ranulphi Higden*, p. 253: "Aigolandus was lewed goost, and lewedliche i-meved as þe devel hym tauȝte, and blende hym þat he kouþe nouȝt i-knowe þat men schulde be i-served as here astaat axeþ" –

Still in Britain, moreover, we may observe this incident of Charlemagne and the beggars being abstracted from its narrative context altogether in order to serve the didactic purposes of homiletics.[39] In two different sermons from about 1376–1377 Thomas Brinton, the Bishop of Rochester, cited this story from the *Chronicle*. In one he endeavoured to teach that the rich and the poor ought to serve one another so that they might be as one (Ps. 49.2, Vulg. 48.3).[40] In the other he sought to demonstrate that the feet of Christ, anointed, washed, and kissed by Mary Magdalene, might be mystically understood as the poor, who like the feet, the lowest of the members of the body are often offended and bruised, so that we kiss the feet of Christ with the Magdalene whenever we reach out to the poor with mercy and friendship, and it is a great scandal to the infidels when we do the opposite; Brinton ends this passage by citing the verse from the Epistle of James (2.26), "faith without works is dead," that ps. Turpin himself brings up in order to explicate the lesson of this episode.[41] Brinton himself may have derived his knowledge of the story of Charlemagne and the beggars not directly from the *Chronicle*, but rather from the widely read collection of sermon material by his contemporary and fellow Englishman, John Bromyard (d. ca. 1390), the *Summa praedicantium*, in which the account of Charlemagne and the paupers appears under the heading of *Eleemosyna* ("Almsgiving").[42] For Bromyard the story shows that the uncharitable sin twice, first by offending the infidels and condemning

"Aigolande was an uncouth scoundrel and ignorantly moved as the devil prompted him and blinded him so that he could not know that men should be treated as their state requires."

[39] See Shepherd, *Turpines Story*, pp. xxxiv–xxxv.

[40] Thomas Brinton, 'Simul in vnum diues et pauper' (Sermon 44); *The Sermons of Thomas Brinton, Bishop of Rochester (1373–1389)*, 2 vols., ed. Mary Aquinas Devlin, Camden Society, Third Series, 1:85–86 (London, 1954), 1:194–200, esp. 196. This sermon is translated in Jeanne Krochalis and Edward Peters, *The World of Piers Plowman* (Philadelphia, 1975), pp. 115–24.

[41] Thomas Brinton, "De Sancta Maria Magdalena" (Sermon 77), ed. Devlin, *Sermons of Thomas Brinton*, 2:351 (the sermon as a whole is printed over pp. 349–53): "Mystice pedes Christi sunt pauperes, quia sicut pedes infimi inter membra sepius offenduntur, sicut pauperes fame, siti, nuditate, et ceteris mundi aduersitatibus sepius colliduntur. Tociens igitur Christi pedes cum Magdalena deuote osculamur quociens pauperes familiariter et misericorditer attrectamus. Cuius contrarium est ipsis infidelibus scandalum satis magnum. Hoc claret ex gestis Karoli magni ... " – "Allegorically the feet of Christ are the poor, since just as the feet as the lowest among the members are more often hit, so the poor are more often struck by hunger, thirst, nakedness, and the rest of the adversities of the world. Therefore, we devoutly kiss the feet of Christ with the Magdalene as often as we treat the poor with familiarity and mercy. The opposite of this is a very great scandal even to the infidels. This is clear from the deeds of Charlemagne ... "

[42] Bromyard's aid for preachers may have enjoyed considerable popularity in its day, but has since fallen into desuetude; in consequence, its last printing was John Bromyard, *Summa praedicantium* (Venice: Domenico Nicolino, 1586). The account of Charlemagne's failure in charity occurs in vol. 1, pp. 229–30 of the Venice edition.

them to spiritual death, and then by denying the needy what they require for survival and killing them bodily.[43] A stark lesson indeed to derive from the deeds of Charlemagne! It may also be thought that William Langland's image in *Piers Plowman* of the thief who received salvation on the cross sharing the heavenly banquet as a beggar on the bare ground, not seated at the board with the saints and martyrs, may owe something to our story from ps. Turpin.[44]

His treatment of the poor seems to be the one and only failing imputed by ps. Turpin to Charlemagne, who is otherwise presented as a paragon of virtue.[45] There is no apparent warrant in the most prominent sources on Charlemagne for attaching this fault to him.[46] On the contrary, according to Einhard, perhaps the most widely read biographer of Charlemagne in the Middle Ages and one almost certainly known to the author of ps. Turpin's *Chronicle*,[47]

> Circa pauperes sustentandos et gratuitam liberalitatem, quam Graeci eleimosynam vocant, devotissimus, ut qui non in patria solum et in suo regno id facere curaverit, verum trans maria, in Syriam et Aegyptum atque Africam, Hierosolymis, Alexandriae, atque Carthagini, ubi christianos in paupertate vivere conpererat, penuriae illorum

---

[43] John Bromyard, *Summa praedicantium*, "Eleemosyna" cap. 3, p. 230: "tales immisericordes dupliciter peccant, primo, quia infideles (ut dictum est) scandalizant, et in spirituali morte detinent, secundo, quia illos, a quibus talia subtrahunt subsidia, corporaliter occidunt" – "Such unmerciful people sin twice, first, because they scandalize the infidels and keep them confined in spiritual death, second, because they bodily kill those from whom they withdraw such aid."

[44] William Langland, *Piers Plowman passus* 12, pp. 198–205; see Shepherd, *Turpines Story*, pp. xxxv–xxxvi.

[45] So while Spiegel, *Romancing the Past*, p. 83, may be right to say that the weaknesses and faults, such as Charlemagne's indecision, that propel the action of the *Chanson de Roland* have been erased from – or perhaps better to say never make their appearance in – ps. Turpin, it is a bit of a misleading overstatement to say that in the *Chronicle* "both king and aristocracy are treated in wholly homologous terms, in an epic celebration of a unitary, deproblematized world, where Charlemagne becomes the ideal knight and Roland is presented in language borrowed from the moral conspectus of royal virtues."

[46] A negative tradition that imputed vice to Charlemagne did come into being, perhaps shortly after his death, and – despite the suggestion that it was effectively stifled within no more than two decades by the appearance of Einhard's *Vita* – endured for some time, but it tended to depict his failings as sexual in nature; see Thomas F.X. Noble, "Greatness Contested and Confirmed: The Raw Materials of the Charlemagne Legend," in *The Legend of Charlemagne*, ed. Gabriele and Stuckey, pp. 3–21; Paul Edward Dutton, "KAROLVS MAGNVS or KAROLVS FELIX: The Making of Charlemagne's Reputation and Legend," in *The Legend of Charlemagne*, ed. Gabriele and Stuckey, pp. 23–37; Andrew J. Romig, "Charlemagne the Sinner: Charles the Great as Avatar of the Modern in Petrarch's *Familiares* 1.4," in *The Charlemagne Legend*, ed. Purkis and Gabriele, pp. 181–201. It seems unlikely that the characterization of Charlemagne we find in ps. Turpin is derived from this tradition.

[47] On Einhard's *Vita Karoli* generally, see Matthias M. Tischler, *Einharts* Vita Karoli*: Studien zur Entstehung, Überlieferung und Rezeption* (Hannover, 2001). On some of the relations between Einhard's biography and ps. Turpin's *Chronicle*, see Tischler, "Tatmensch oder Heidenapostel," pp. 1–37.

conpatiens pecuniam mittere solebat, ob hoc maxime transmarinorum regum amicitias expetens ut christianis sub eorum dominatu degentibus refrigerium aliquod ac relevatio proveniret.[48]

He was most devout when it came to supporting the poor and the spontaneous open-handedness, which the Greeks call almsgiving, so that he took care to do this not only in his fatherland and in his own kingdom, but also across the seas, to Syria and Egypt and Africa, in Jerusalem, Alexandria, and Carthage, wherever he should learn that Christians lived in poverty, having compassion on their penury, he was in the habit of sending them money. It was for this reason especially that he sought out the friendship of kings across the sea, so that some solace and relief might come about for those Christians living under their rule.

As in ps. Turpin's account, concern for the poor is both a measure of kings and a matter that comes up in regard to Charlemagne's relations with foreign potentates, but Einhard gives a very different impression of Charlemagne.[49] Notker the Stammerer, in his miscellany of clerical foibles and the Emperor's rough and ready discipline, has Charlemagne reprove a spendthrift bishop in terms drawn from the same passage in Matthew's Gospel that is so important to ps. Turpin:[50] "Vos patres et provisores nostri episcopi, pauperibus, immo Christo in ipsis ministrare, non inanibus rebus inhiare debuistis" – "You, our bishops, as fathers and providers ought to minister to the poor, indeed to Christ in them, not gape at vain things." This exhortation also calls for a correct estimation of charity on the one hand and worldly frippery on the other, but, of course, it is Charlemagne giving, not receiving, the reprimand in this case. Such an interest in charity was not without precedent in the chronicles of the Frankish kings, but did not always redound to the king's credit; the Fredegar chronicler, for instance, maintains that Dagobert I (623–638/9) might have attained the kingdom of heaven if he had been more generous in giving alms.[51] Charlemagne's earnest concern for the poor, as conveyed by the biographers who wrote after his death, is also evident in his own statutes, which were perhaps the inspiration for these aspects of the *Lives*. The *Admonitio generalis*, promulgated in 789, for instance, encouraged the maintenance of hospices to accommodate foreign travelers, pilgrims, and the poor, as called for by the *Rule* of St. Benedict (ch. 53), and justifies this injunction with reference to the same

---

[48] Einhard, *Vita Caroli* 27, ed. Louis Halphen, *Éginhard, Vie de Charlemagne*, 3rd ed. (Paris, 1947), p. 78.

[49] See Johannes Fried, *Charlemagne*, trans. Peter Lewis (Cambridge, MA, 2016), p. 29.

[50] Notker, *De Carolo Magno* 1.16; ed. Georg Heinrich Pertz, MGH SS 2 (Hanover, 1829), p. 737.

[51] Fredegar, *Chronicae* 4.60; ed. Bruno Krusch, MGH SS rer. Merov. 2 (Hanover, 1838), p. 151. See Andreas Fischer, "Rewriting History: Fredegar's Perspectives on the Mediterranean," in *Western Perspectives on the Mediterranean: Cultural Transfer in Late Antiquity and the Early Middle Ages*, ed. Andreas Fischer and Ian Wood (London, 2014), pp. 61–69.

passage from Matthew in which Christ identifies Himself with the needy that figures so prominently in the thirteenth chapter of ps. Turpin's *Chronicle*.[52]

If ps. Turpin introduces a fault to the character of Charlemagne, it is hardly an unforgivable one. At worst he is presented as being thoughtless in his disregard for the needs of the poor, and he is quick to mend his ways once his fault is pointed out. There is no suggestion that his failure of charity reveals some inherent parsimony or lack of love for his fellow men. Charlemagne remains a good man, albeit a flawed one. But the *Chronicle*'s introduction of faults to Charlemagne's character opens the door to a rather darker depiction of the emperor. In later twelfth- and early thirteenth-century *chansons de geste*, particularly the so-called "epics of revolt" such as the *Chevalerie Ogier*, *Doon de Mayence*, and *Renaut de Montauban*, we see an uglier side to Charlemagne, who provokes his vassals with vicious and brutal treatment and surrounds himself with villainous traitors.[53] The Charlemagne of these *chansons* seems to reflect how the barons of France saw the efforts of Philip Augustus (1180–1223) to assert royal authority at their expense. It may thus be suggested that the ps. Turpin *Chronicle* prepares the ground for the critique of royal conduct in the literary treatment of Charlemagne. Ps. Turpin, however, is not fundamentally concerned with kingship. While Robert Morrissey concedes that in the *Chronicle* Charlemagne compounds his "lack of moral exemplarity" by failing in regard to a royal virtue, namely largesse, he is surely right to see him as not so much an example of kingship for ps. Turpin, as a substitute for every one of the text's Christian readers:[54]

> Charlemagne represents the legitimacy of power, but he also represents each of us in our daily struggles and weaknesses. He is the very principle of the collectivity; thus the collectivity assumes the characteristics of a person, and is equipped with a psychology

---

[52] *Admonitio generalis* cap. 73; ed. Hubert Mordek, Klaus Zechiel-Eckes, and Michael Glatthaar, *Die Admonitio generalis Karls des Großen*, MGH Fontes iuris Germanici antiqui 16 (Hanover, 2012), pp. 226–28: "Omnibus. Et hoc nobis conpetens et venerabile videtur, ut hospites, peregrini et pauperes susceptiones regulares et canonicas per loca diversa habeant, quia ipse dominus dicturus erit in remuneratione magni diei: Hospes eram et suscepistis me. Et apostolus hospitalitatem laudans dixit: Per hanc quidam placuerunt deo angelis hospitio suscepti" – "To everyone. This also seems fitting and praiseworthy to us, that strangers, pilgrims, and paupers should have regular and canonical accommodation in guest-houses throughout various places, since the Lord Himself will say in the reckoning of the Last Day, 'I was a stranger, and ye took me in' [Matt. 25.36]. And the Apostle praises hospitality, saying, 'thereby some have pleased God, hospitably taking in angels' [Hebr. 13.2]." See Fried, *Charlemagne*, pp. 265–66, compare pp. 175, 433–34.

[53] Edward Peters, *The Shadow King: Rex Inutilis in Medieval Law and Literature, 751–1327* (New Haven, 1970), pp.104–14; Paul Aebischer, *Des annales carolingiennes à Doon de Mayence: Nouveau recueil d'études sur l'épique française médiévale* (Geneva, 1975); Wolfgang van Emden, "Kingship in the Old French Epic of Revolt," in *Kings and Kingship in Medieval Europe*, ed. Anne J. Duggan (London, 1993), pp. 305–50; and Morrissey, *Charlemagne and France*, pp. 76–78.

[54] Morrissey, *Charlemagne and France*, p. 55.

similar to that of an individual. Charlemagne's story, the story of his kingdom, is also the story of each one of us. The technique of analogy carries a moral lesson, but it is one that, at the same time, enables a greater internalization of the foundations and representations of political power.

Charlemagne is less a model for princes and more the Christian man writ large, the chief difference being that as a king his sins have vaster consequences.[55]

The fault of which the chief character of the *Chronicle* is guilty, moreover, is one which is notably absent from the tragic hero and the martyr of the piece. The supposed author himself, in summing up the character of Roland, calls him, as we have seen, "the bread of the needy, bountiful to the poor, lavish to guests" ("panis egentum, / Largus pauperibus, prodigus hospitibus").[56] And he has Charlemagne praise Roland as "the staff of orphans and widows, the food and refreshment of poor and rich alike" ("baculus orphanorum et viduarum, cibus et refectio tam pauperum quam divitum").[57] There seems to be an intentional contrast here, a point on which the paladin outdoes the king. It is not a case of Saul having slain his thousands and David his ten thousands, but of Roland remembering his obligations to the poor, whereas Charlemagne has, at least on occasion, forgotten them. In an effort at social criticism upon which I would like to expand later, the character of Charlemagne, who is certainly presented by ps. Turpin as the ruler of Christendom, is adjusted and reconstructed so that he can represent all Christians in their dereliction of pious duty and remind them to be assiduous in their charity to the poor.

His neglect of the needy may be the one fault attributed to Charlemagne in the *Chronicle*, but from the perspective of narrative and composition it is a critical failing. The consequences of Charlemagne's treatment of the poor and Aigolande's reaction to it are of the first importance in determining the success of Charlemagne's aims and bringing about the most salient events in the subsequent account. Implicit in St. James's commission to Charlemagne to liberate his country from the Saracens is the obligation to convert the Saracens to Christianity. The aim of converting Muslims was not merely a literary conceit in the twelfth century, but a very real goal of Christian society, pursued through Crusader conquests and missionary preaching, and so the ps. Turpin *Chronicle* constitutes something of a reflection on the failure, or

---

[55] Dominique Boutet, "Charlemagne dans la littérature des XIIe et XIIIe siècles," *Travaux de Littérature* 18 (2005), 19–31, esp. p. 23, points out that while Charlemagne is very much a mirror for princes in the literature derived from it, in the ps. Turpin *Chronicle* itself his place as the "grand homme" is contested, particularly with St. James.

[56] Ps. Turpin, *Chron.* 24, ed. Schmidt, *Karolellus atque Pseudo-Turpini Historia*, p. 150.

[57] Ps. Turpin, *Chron.* 25, ed. Schmidt, *Karolellus atque Pseudo-Turpini Historia*, p. 156.

at least the difficulty, of these efforts.[58] For the most part we see this objective carried out according to the brutal method familiar to the time of the Crusades, with the conquered being given the stark alternative between conversion and the sword.[59] Charlemagne and Aigolande agree on trial by combat as a somewhat more civilized way to decide the issue, but the results of the trial by combat, which are supposed to prove the superiority of Christianity, are contradicted and undermined by Charlemagne's conduct. And so the king's manifest neglect of the poor overturns the victory won by his knights and prevents the conversion of the Saracens, who had promised to be baptized in light of the outcome of the trial by combat. The war in Spain is being fought to determine who will have the mastery, the Christians or the Saracens, and with Aigolande's disgusted response to Charlemagne's treatment of the poor and his rejection of the results of the trial by combat, the conflict is prolonged. The suffering and death that arise from the subsequent fighting might have been avoided or mitigated if the war had concluded with the conversion of Aigolande, and Charlemagne must bear some responsibility for it all. Ultimately, Roland and his rearguard are slain because the war is prolonged, and so the climax of the whole *Chronicle*, the martyrdom of Roland, takes place on account of Charlemagne's failure to treat the poor properly.

A concern for the poor is vital to the composition of the *Chronicle* not only inasmuch as its neglect brings about the primary action of the piece, but also because its remembrance allows for a satisfying conclusion to the narrative. Charlemagne's bad treatment of the poor may have caused the protraction of the war in the first place, and in consequence the massacre of Roland and his troops, but he seems to atone for this in the memorial endowments he makes at the burial of the dead of Roncesvalles, which include generous provision for the poor. Every year on the anniversary of their demise Charlemagne fed and clothed thirty paupers ("die passionis eorumque annuatim trigenta pauperes cunctis vestibus necessariis induerent cibariisque reficerent").[60] And for the repose of the souls of the dead he also gave an impressive amount of money, twelve thousand ounces of silver and as many talents of gold, to the indigent

---

[58] See Benjamin Z. Kedar, *Crusade and Mission: European Approaches toward the Muslims* (Princeton, 1984).

[59] Ps. Turpin, *Chron.* 2, ed. Schmidt, *Karolellus atque Pseudo-Turpini Historia*, p. 16: "Sarracenos vero, qui baptizari voluerunt, ad vitam reservavit, et qui renuerunt, gladio trucidavit" – "Indeed, he kept alive the Saracens who wished to be baptized, and those who refused, he slew with the sword." On the willingness of the *Chronicle*'s author to assent to physical compulsion as a last resort in the conflict between Christianity and Islam, see Matthias M. Tischler, "Modes of Literary Behaviour in Christian-Islamic Encounters in the Iberian Peninsula: *Pseudo-Turpin* versus Peter the Venerable," in *Languages of Love and Hate*, ed. Lambert and Nicholson, pp. 201–21, at 210–11. See also Kedar, *Crusade and Mission*, pp. 69, 111–12, 185.

[60] Ps. Turpin, *Chron.* 29, ed. Schmidt, *Karolellus atque Pseudo-Turpini Historia*, p. 172.

in the city of Arles ("pro quorum animabus uncias duodecim milia argenteas totidemque talenta aurea Karolus apud Arelaten egenis dedit").[61] These provisions for the poor, after all is said and done, do not merely make up for a deficiency at the outset and show Charlemagne compensating for an earlier failure. They are also an example of the tragic delay in the exhibition of virtue until it is too late to do any good to preserve the life and well-being of the protagonist, which is characteristic of heroic epic.[62]

The incident at Charlemagne's breakfast table offers not only a narrative coherence to the composition as a whole, but also a plausible motivation to the antagonists. The *Chanson de Roland* opens with the council of the Saracen king Marsille of Saragossa, who bewails the depredations of Charlemagne's invading army and his inability to resist him.[63] The Saracens' intention of defending their homeland is understandable, might even elicit some sympathy, but the plot they hatch does not reflect so well on them. At the advice of Blancandrin, they plan to send to Charlemagne tribute and hostages, as well as promises to convert to Christianity, in order to get him to quit the country, but their promises are from the outset insincere and they would rather see their sons beheaded than follow Charlemagne to receive baptism. The *Chanson* offers no explanation for the intransigence of the Saracens, except perhaps their determination to retain their sovereignty and their innate wickedness.[64] Ps. Turpin paints the Saracens with a rather more sympathetic brush. There is nothing to suggest that Aigolande is not perfectly sincere in his willingness to abide by the results of the trial by combat; indeed, he is apparently determined to receive baptism until he witnesses the contradiction between the claims of the Christians and their conduct. The Saracens resist conversion and submission not because they are stiff-necked and perverse, but because the Christians have failed to make their actions measure up to their words. And if it is not some irredeemable stubbornness in them that prevents the conversion of the heathen, it lies within the power of the Christian community to amend the failure that has proved a stumbling block to them. This transfer of responsibility is one of the messages which ps. Turpin endeavours to convey.

Quite apart from the literary virtue of creating sympathetic, or at least understandable, antagonists, Aigolande's reaction to Charlemagne's neglect of the

---

[61] Ps. Turpin, *Chron.* 30, ed. Schmidt, *Karolellus atque Pseudo-Turpini Historia*, p. 174; compare chapter 29.

[62] In the *Iliad*, for example, at the funeral games of Patroclus, Achilles and Agamemnon display all of the deference and forbearance, which, if they had given some evidence of these virtues during their initial contention over Chryseis and Briseis, might have prevented Patroclus from dying in the first place and Achilles from committing himself to the fate of perishing at Troy.

[63] *Chanson de Roland*, laisses 1–7 (verses 1–95).

[64] *Chanson de Roland*, laisses 3–5 (verses 45–46, 59–61, 70).

poor might betray a knowledge of the realities of Muslim teaching and practice. Ps. Turpin indulges in the popular conceit that the Saracens were idolaters, but does not maintain it by any means as consistently as does the *Chanson de Roland*.[65] Rather, Aigolande identifies Muhammed as a prophet of God, not as a god of the Saracens, as he appears in the *Chanson*.[66] And in his lengthy religious debate with Roland, the Saracen giant Ferragus insists upon a strict monotheism, rather than idolatry, and raises the sorts of objections to Christian doctrine that might be expected of a pious Muslim.[67] Aigolande's particular sensitivity to the treatment of the poor might suggest some awareness of the importance of almsgiving (*zakāh*) amongst the religious obligations or "acts of devotion" (*'ibādāt*) incumbent upon an observant Muslim. Our scant and scattered sources suggest that a few western authors had some notion of the place of charity and almsgiving in Islam, but that it remained vague and imprecise.[68] In the medieval West, however, Muslim almsgiving must have been seen not so much as evidence of pious virtue in those regarded as enemies and strangers, as an incitement to Christians not to be outdone by the heathen in regard to charity.

The emphasis on charity to the poor in the encounter between the Saracen and the Christian kings need not necessarily have depended on some acquaintance with Muslim teaching and practice; it is equally consistent with certain stereotypes current in the Middle Ages about the Muslim faith and its founder. Muhammed was commonly depicted in medieval polemics as something of a lecher who propounded the novel teachings of his heretical sect in order to satisfy his enormous appetites, and the promises of the Islamic religion as principally intended to satisfy physical, especially sexual,

---

[65] On the idolatry imputed to the Saracens in western sources, see Norman Daniel, *The Arabs and Mediaeval Europe*, 2nd ed. (London and New York, 1979), pp. 95–98, 134, 238–41; Norman Daniel, *Heroes and Saracens: An Interpretation of the* Chansons de Geste (Edinburgh, 1984), pp. 121–78; Kedar, *Crusade and Mission*, pp. 87–89; Michael Camille, *The Gothic Idol: Ideology and Image-Making in Medieval Art* (Cambridge, 1989), pp. 129–64; Jean Flori, "La caricature de l'Islam dans l'Occident medieval: Origine et signification de quelques stéréotypes concernant l'Islam," *Aevum* 66 (1992), 245–56; Norman Daniel, *Islam and the West: The Making of an Image*, 2nd ed. (Oxford, 1993), pp. 338–43; John V. Tolan, "Muslims as Pagan Idolaters in Chronicles of the First Crusade," in *Western Views of Islam in Medieval and Early Modern Europe: Perception of Other*, ed. David R. Blanks and Michael Frassetto (New York, 1999), pp. 97–117; John V. Tolan, *Saracens: Islam in the Medieval European Imagination* (New York, 2002), pp. 105–34; and Suzanne Conklin Akbari, *Idols in the East: European Representations of Islam and the Orient, 1100–1450* (Ithaca, 2009), pp. 200–47.

[66] Ps. Turpin, *Chron.* 12. See José Mª. Díaz Fernández, "El diálogo cristiano-musulmán en el Pseudo-Turpín," in *El Pseudo-Turpín*, ed. Herbers, pp. 167–75.

[67] Ps. Turpin, *Chron.* 17, ed. Schmidt, *Karolellus atque Pseudo-Turpini Historia*, pp. 76–96. On this contrived Christian-Muslim dialogue in the *Chronicle*, see Tischler, "Modes of Literary Behaviour," pp. 203–4 and 208–11.

[68] See Kedar, *Crusade and Mission*, pp. 85–96; and Daniel, *Islam and the West*, pp. 248–50.

rather than spiritual longings.[69] As Roger Bacon put it, the law of the Saracens, "which is altogether voluptuous and lascivious" ("quae est tota voluptuosa et venerea"), comes about when Jupiter is in conjunction with Venus.[70] But if sensuality was supposed to be the characteristic vice of Muslims, their correspondingly characteristic virtue seems to be presented as generosity, which might be construed as just as physical or material – that is, unspiritual – as sensuality. And so Saladin, among the most famous Saracens in the medieval world, came to be known for his liberality amongst other virtues, and in later Italian literature was reputed to be a paragon of generosity and munificence.[71] The depiction of Islam as a sensuous religion is little in evidence in the *Chronicle* of ps. Turpin, but the heat of Aigolande's reaction to Charlemagne's niggardliness could still be taken as a sign of the concern for generosity and open-handedness, which is supposed to be characteristic of Muslims. As such, it could further be taken to contribute to ps. Turpin's subtly positive, or at least even-handed, depiction of Charlemagne's enemies.

Charlemagne's failure to properly succour the poor and his upbraiding by Aigolande introduce one of the homiletic excursus that distinguish the *Chronicle* of ps. Turpin:[72]

> Hinc animadvertendum, quam magnam culpam Christianus quilibet adquirit, qui Christi pauperibus studiose non servit. Si Karolus regem baptizandum[73] perdidit eo, quod pauperes male tractavit, quid erit de illis in extremi examinis die, qui male pauperes tractaverunt? Quomodo audient vocem dominicam terribilem dicentem: *Discedite a me, maledicti, in ignem eternum,* quia *esurivi et non dedistis michi manducare,* et cetera? Considerandum, quia lex Domini et fides eius in Christiano parum valet, nisi operibus adimpleatur apostolo affirmante, qui ait: *Sicut corpus mortuum est sine anima, ita fides sine operibus* bonis *mortua est* in semetipsa.

---

[69] See Daniel, *The Arabs and Mediaeval Europe*, pp. 42–43, 193, and 237–38; Daniel, *Heroes and Saracens*, pp. 69–78; Daniel, *Islam and the West*, pp. 158–85, 351–53; Tolan, *Saracens*, pp. 135–69; and Akbari, *Idols in the East*, pp. 248–79.

[70] Roger Bacon, *Opus Maius* 4.16, ed. John Henry Bridges, *The 'Opus Majus of Roger Bacon*, 2 vols. (London, 1897–1900; repr. Frankfurt am Main, 1964), 1:256; compare Robert Belle Burke, trans., *The Opus Majus of Roger Bacon*, 2 vols. (Philadelphia, 1928), 1:278–89.

[71] Giovanni Boccaccio, *Decameron* i.3.18, x.9.4, 39, 55, 59, 74–87, 92; Dante Alighieri, *Il convivio* iv.11.14. See Daniel, *The Arabs and Mediaeval Europe*, pp. 187–90; John V. Tolan, *Sons of Ishmael: Muslims through European Eyes in the Middle Ages* (Gainesville, 2008), pp. 79–100; and Akbari, *Idols in the East*, pp. 266–68.

[72] Ps. Turpin, *Chron.* 13, ed. Schmidt, *Karolellus atque Pseudo-Turpini Historia*, p. 64.

[73] After "regem baptizandum" most editions add "et gentem suam"; see Meredith-Jones, *Chronique du Pseudo-Turpin*, p. 139; Smyser, *The Pseudo-Turpin*, p. 72; Hämel, *Der Pseudo-Turpin von Compostela*, p. 58; Klein, *Die Chronik von Karl dem Grossen und Roland*, p. 66; and Herbers and Noia, *Liber Sancti Iacobi*, p. 209. This broadens the unfortunate implications of Charlemagne's misconduct.

From this it might be realized how great a fault any Christian incurs, who does not diligently serve the paupers of Christ. If Charlemagne lost the opportunity to have the king baptized because he treated the poor badly, what will it be like on the day of the Last Judgement for those who have treated the poor badly? How will they bear to hear the terrible voice of the Lord saying: *Depart from me, ye cursed, into everlasting fire, because I was an hungred, and ye gave me no meat* [Matt. 25.41–42], and the rest? It ought to be borne in mind that the law of the Lord and his faith avails very little in the Christian unless it be fulfilled with deeds, as the Apostle affirms, who says: *For as the body without the spirit is dead, so faith without* good *works is dead* in the selfsame way [James 2.26.].

Gabrielle Spiegel speaks of ps. Turpin's "awkward mix of epic narrative and clerical sermonizing," but to allow the – to us – incongruous combination and especially its homiletic element to grate is to miss the purposes, both edifying and literary, the homiletic intrusions were quite intelligently intended to serve.[74] On the one hand, I can only assume that conveying the lessons contained in these brief sermons is one of the intentions of the *Chronicle*. The work as a whole is unabashedly didactic. On the other hand, these digressions contribute to the development of the character of the narrator and supposed author, Archbishop Turpin of Rheims, which takes shape as that of a learned prelate given to assuming a tone more pastoral than sanctimonious. And this character is a consistent one, with a steady concern for almsgiving and the poor. The account of Aigolande taking offence is anticipated by the vivid story of one of Charlemagne's knights, who in anticipation of his eminent death asked a kinsman of his to sell his horse and distribute the proceeds to the clergy and the poor ("clericis et egenis"), but the kinsman spent the money from the sale on himself instead; the dead man appeared to his kinsman in a dream, predicting that he would forthwith take his place amidst the torments of Tartarus, and indeed he was soon snatched away by demons and his mangled body found four days journey away.[75] The Archbishop leaves his readers in no doubt about the terrible consequences of neglecting the poor for the sake of self-indulgence. In any case, the lesson of the sermon is reinforced by the exchange between Charlemagne and Aigolande. It is Charlemagne himself who identifies the poor as the messengers of the Lord, a designation that is made clear with the quotation from the twenty-fifth chapter of the Gospel of Matthew in the little homily. And Aigolande insists that Charlemagne's treatment of the poor is unworthy of the emissaries of any lord who might deserve his fealty.

Aigolande's rebuke of Charlemagne is not altogether surprising in the context of an encounter between the Christians and their Muslim enemies. The *Apocalypse* of ps. Methodius, one of the earliest Christian literary treatments of the rise of the Islamic Empire and its challenge to the "Kingdom of the Christians" and one of the most widely read works of the Middle Ages, does not so much dwell upon the atroci-

---

[74] Spiegel, *Romancing the Past*, p. 69.

[75] Ps. Turpin, *Chron.* 7, ed. Schmidt, *Karolellus atque Pseudo-Turpini Historia*, pp. 28–30.

ties perpetrated by the "Ishmaelites" as upon the sins of the Christians, which bring about their defeat and subjection. The Arab invasions are characterized as a "castigatio" – "chastisement" and the just judgement of God.

> Et erit adventus eorum castigatio sine misericordia et praehibunt eis super terra quattuor iste plage, id est: interitus et perditio, corruptio quoque et desolatio.
>
> Dicit enim Deus ad Israel per Moysen: "Non quia diligit vos dominus Deus, introducit vos in terram promissiones, ut herediteminini eam, sed propter peccata inhabitantium in eam." Sic etenim filios Ismahel, non quod eos diligat dominus Deus, dabit eis potentiam hanc, ut obteneant terram christianorum, sed propter peccatum et iniquitatem, quae ab eis committitur. Similia eis non sunt facta, sed neque fiunt in omnebus [*sic*] generationibus.[76]

And their arrival will be a chastisement without mercy and these four blows will go before them over the earth, that is, death and destruction, and ruin and desolation.

For God says to Israel through Moses, "Not because the Lord God loves you does he bring you into the Land of Promise, that you should inherit it, but because of the sins of those who dwell in it" [see Deut. 9.4–6]. Just so with the sons of Ishmael, it is not because the Lord God loves them will he give them this power that they should conquer the land of the Christians, but because of the sin and lawlessness, which are committed by them. For nothing like these things has been done nor will be done in all generations.

The text goes on to specifically itemize the climactic sinfulness of the Christians, particularly in regard to sexual perversion, in consequence of which God delivered them into the hands of the outsiders. The ground is prepared in the *Apocalypse* for ps. Turpin to take an encounter between Christians and Muslims as an opportunity for judgemental introspection and censure of the Christians, rather than vitriolic denigration of the Islamic Other.[77] Even if Charlemagne does not suffer defeat at the hands of Aigolande, he still receives a sharp tongue-lashing as chastisement on behalf of the Christian community.

Nor is Aigolande the last Muslim observer to be made to take the Christians to task for their failure to look after the poor. Indeed, this device of introducing an outside critic, and especially one from the Muslim world, seems to have been seen as a particularly effective method of engaging in unsparing introspection in the medieval West. The author of *The Book of John Mandeville*, for example, relates a private interview with the Sultan of Babylon, in which he asks his visitor how the Christians con-

---

[76] Ps. Methodius, *Apoc.* 11.4–5, ed. Benjamin Garstad, *Apocalypse of Pseudo-Methodius. An Alexandrian World Chronicle* (Cambridge, MA, 2012), pp. 110–13.

[77] The derivation from the *Apocalypse* of other aspects of the legendary material on Charlemagne and Roland is discussed by Matthew Gabriele, *An Empire of Memory: The Legend of Charlemagne, the Franks, and Jerusalem before the First Crusade* (Oxford, 2011), pp. 116–17.

Charlemagne's Failure of Charity 63

duct themselves in their own country.[78] When his guest replies, "Well enough, by the grace of God" ("bien, Dieu Graciez"), the Sultan flatly denies it. The Sultan points to, among other faults in their society, the hypocrisy of the Christians, especially in regard to giving to the poor: "They should be simple, humble, honest, and charitable, as was Christ, in whom they believe. But they are decidedly otherwise and altogether inclined to evil-doing" ("Ils deussent estre simples et humbles et veritables et almoigners si come fust Jhesu en qy ils croient. Mes ils sont tout a revers et tout enclins a malfaire").[79] It turns out that the Sultan knows of what he speaks, since he sends out spies disguised as merchants who travel throughout Christendom and report back to him what they observe there. And like the contention of Charlemagne and Aigolande, the Sultan's observation of the Christians' lack of charity is pertinent to the political conflict between the Saracens and the Christians. The Sultan informs "Sir John" that God has permitted the Saracens to conquer the lands of the Christians not because of the strength of the Saracens, but because of the evil living and disobedience of the Christians, and that when the Christians turn to a devout service of God, they will be invincible.[80]

As the vistas of European geography later expanded the heathen outsider continued to serve as a mouthpiece to shame Christian society for its failure to live up to its own high ideals, though his colours might be changed somewhat. At the turn of the eighteenth century the Baron de Lahontan prepared a stinging critique of contemporary French manners and customs in the form of a dialogue between himself and Adario, a Huron chief whom he is attempting to civilize, convert to Christianity, and turn into a good Frenchman.[81] Adario proves a shrewd and unflappable observer of the weaknesses and hypocrisies of French society and makes the arguments Lahontan purports to offer him seem trite and ill considered. Charity and provision for the poor are amongst the many topics he raises in pointing out the failings of the French. Adario protests that he could not possibly become a Frenchman since he could not bear to see the needy suffering and perishing without handing over to them all that he had.[82] And he points out that the Huron are careful to distribute the produce of their

---

[78] John Mandeville, *The Book of the Marvels of the World* 15, ed. Christiane Deluz, *Jean de Mandeville, Le Livre des Merveilles du Monde*, Sources d'histoire médiévale 31 (Paris, 2000), pp. 278–80.

[79] John Mandeville, *Book of Marvels* 15, ed. Deluz, *Jean de Mandeville*, p. 279.

[80] John Mandeville, *Book of Marvels* 15, ed. Deluz, *Jean de Mandeville*, p. 279.

[81] See Olive Patricia Dickason, *The Myth of the Noble Savage and the Beginnings of French Colonialism in the Americas* (Edmonton, 1984), p. 193; and Réal Ouellet, "Adario: Le Sauvage philosophe de Lahontan," *Québec français* 142 (2006), 57–60.

[82] Lahontan, *Dialogues avec un sauvage* suivi de Gueudeville-Lahontan, *Conversations de l'auteur avec Adario, sauvage distingué*, ed. Réal Ouellet (Montréal, 2010), p. 135: "Comment verrois-je languir les Nécessiteux, sans leur donner tout ce qui seroit à moy?" Compare Baron de Lahontan, *New Voyages to North-America*, ed. Reuben Gold Thwaites, 2 vols. (Chicago, 1905), 2:584–85.

hunting and their farming to those who are without in order to ensure that they can provide for their families.[83] When Adario can see so much wrong with the French way of life and how often and how far the French fall short of their own ideals, it is hardly surprising that the best efforts of Lahontan and the Jesuits to convert the Huron prove unavailing. As in the dispute between Charlemagne and Aigolande, this encounter with the Other shifts the focus of attention from the outsider to one's own society and reminds the Christians that they must set their house in order if they should ever hope to achieve their goal of converting the heathen.

If we wish to move beyond a critical stance that derides the *Chronicle* of ps. Turpin for the bad Latinity and sloppy logic it is supposed to display, the episode of Charlemagne's neglect of the paupers and Aigolande's response to it, easily one of the most redeeming passages in the *Chronicle*, is an excellent place to start. From a literary point of view, it exhibits a thoroughgoing competence, if not artfulness. This incident provides an overall cohesion to the composition as a whole, provoking at the outset the major action of the piece and being recalled at its conclusion. Here ps. Turpin depicts not the monstrous paynim of the *chansons de geste*, but an understandable, perhaps even sympathetic, antagonist and provides him with a sensible motivation for his opposition to the virtuous aims of the protagonist. And the protagonist, in turn, is painted in revealingly human colours, rather than the albescent glare of sanctity, with foibles and failings that produce disastrous results for himself and those around him – a fatal flaw in Aristotelian terms. This episode is also used to develop the character of the narrator, Archbishop Turpin, who seizes it as an opportunity to admonish his flock, not to make war on the unbelievers, but admirably insisting on the demands of Christian charity. It furthermore reveals a certain amount of moral instruction to be one of the purposes of the *Chronicle* itself, showing the author to be no less able in this didactic regard as well. Ps. Turpin proves particularly adept at delivering a lesson on the Christian's duty to the poor that might have been quite tedious. He stingingly sets his rebuke in the mouth of an outsider and a heathen – it may be moving "to see oursels as ithers see us," but it is rarely comfortable – and lays stress on the concrete, rather than abstract, and unforeseen consequences of a failure to succour the poor. The effectiveness of this teaching method is seen in its widespread influence and imitation, though the Other who takes Christendom to task for its shortcomings assumes many and varied guises.

---

[83] Lahontan, *Dialogues*, ed. Ouellet, *Conversations*, p. 136: "Y a-t-il des Hurons qui aïent jamais refusé à quelque autre sa chasse, ou sa pêche, ou toute ou en partie? Ne cotizons nous pas entre toute la Nation les Castors de nos Chasses, pour suppléer à ceux qui n'en ont pu prendre suffisamment pour acheter les marchandises dont ils ont besoin? N'en usons-nous pas de même de nos bleds d'Inde, envers ceux dont les champs n'ont sçeu raporter des moissons sufisantes pour la nourriture de leurs familles?" Compare Lahontan, *New Voyages*, ed. Thwaites, 2:586.

Abstract

The *Chronicle* of ps. Turpin is disparaged for its compositional failings, but it has its strengths too. These are exemplified by the episode in which the pagan king Aigolande upbraids Charlemagne for neglecting to provide for the paupers he sustains as well as the clergymen of his court. On account of Charlemagne's oversight Aigolande refuses baptism and continues the war that eventually results in Roland's death. This episode serves many purposes; it provides coherence to the narrative, motivation and sympathetic humanity to the antagonists of the piece, depth and fallibility to the character of Charlemagne, substance to the character of Turpin himself, and a punch to a moral lesson the *Chronicle* attempts to deliver. Its importance was recognized in the ps. Turpin tradition, and the remarkably subtle and effective device of turning the criticisms of a heathen on the faults of Christian society was adapted and repeated for centuries.

Résumé

La *Chronique* du Ps. Turpin a souvent été critiquée en raison de ses défauts de compositions, mais elle comporte également des qualités. Celles-ci sont mises en évidence par l'épisode dans lequel le roi païen Aigolande semonce Charlemagne, l'accusant d'avoir négligé de subvenir aux besoins des pauvres sous sa protection ainsi qu'à ceux des hommes d'Églises de sa cour. Au nom de la négligence de Charlemagne, Aigolande refuse le baptême et continue la guerre qui mènera éventuellement à la mort de Roland. Cet épisode remplit plusieurs fonctions : il donne une cohérence au récit, des motifs et une humanité aux antagonistes du récit, une profondeur et une certaine faillibilité à la figure de Charlemagne, de la substance au personnage de Turpin lui-même et finalement, de la force à la leçon morale que la *Chronique* tente de transmettre. L'importance de cet épisode a été reconnue par la tradition du Ps. Turpin, et la technique remarquablement subtile et efficace de diriger les critiques d'un païen contre les fautes de la société chrétienne a été adaptée et émulée pendant des siècles.

Benjamin Garstad
MacEwan University
GarstadB@macewan.ca

On the Date, Authorship, and Newly Discovered Old Irish Material in the *Ars Ambrosiana*

JASON O'RORKE
National University of Ireland, Galway

Introduction

The *Ars Ambrosiana* is an anonymous commentary on Donatus's *Ars maior* preserved in a single manuscript – Milan, Biblioteca Ambrosiana, MS L 22 sup., fols. 1r–145v, dated to the third quarter of the ninth century.[1] Scholars generally agree that it was compiled at the monastery of Bobbio,[2] on the basis that the manuscript has a

---

* I am greatly indebted to Prof. Michael Clarke, Dr. Sarah Corrigan, and Dr. Máirín McCarron for reading and providing constructive feedback on this article. I am also very grateful to Dr. Jacopo Bisagni and two anonymous reviewers for the journal, who made valuable suggestions that improved the clarity and precision of some of the Latin translations. All remaining errors are, of course, my own. It should also be noted that when no explicit reference is provided, the translation is my own.

[1] The standard edition is *Ars Ambrosiana*, ed. Bengt Löfstedt, CCSL 133C (Turnhout, 1982). For a description of the commentary and a list of references, see James F. Kenney, *The Sources for the Early History of Ireland: Ecclesiastical*, 2nd ed. (Dublin, 1968), p. 362; Vivien Law, *The Insular Latin Grammarians*, Studies in Celtic History 3 (Suffolk, 1982), pp. 93–97; Donnchadh Ó Corráin, *Clavis litterarum Hibernensium: Medieval Irish Books and Texts 400–1600*, 3 vols. (Turnhout, 2017), 2:644–645, no. 504; and James E.G. Zetzel, *Critics, Compilers and Commentators: An Introduction to Roman Philology 200 BCE–800 CE* (Oxford, 2018), pp. 357–58. For a discussion of the manuscript and its date, see Charles H. Beeson, "The Palimpsests of Bobbio," *Studi e testi* 126 (1946), 162–84, at p. 179; Bernhard Bischoff, *Katalog der festländischen Handschriften des neuten Jahrhunderts (mit Ausnahme der wisigotischen)*, 4 vols. (Wiesbaden, 1998–2017), 2:162, no. 2641; and Paolo Collura, *Studi paleografici. La Precarolina e la Carolina a Bobbio*, Fontes Ambrosiani 22 (Milan, 1943), pp. 140–42. The manuscript has also been dated to the tenth century, see Max Manitius, *Geschichte der lateinischen Literatur des Mittelalters*, 3 vols. (Munich, 1911–1931), 1:519–21, at p. 519; and Remigio Sabbadini, "Spogli Ambrosiani latini," *Studi italiani di filologia classica* 11 (1903), 165–388, at p. 166.

[2] On the localisation of the commentary at Bobbio, see Beeson, "The Palimpsests of Bobbio," p. 179; Law, *Insular Latin Grammarians*, p. 97, Löfstedt, *Ars Ambrosiana*, p. vii; Manitius, *Geschichte*, 1:520; Michael Richter, *Bobbio in the Early Middles Ages. The Abiding Legacy of Columbanus* (Dublin 2008), pp. 148–50, 185; and Sabbadini, "Spogli Ambrosiani latini," p. 168. Prior to the publication of the critical edition, it was suggested that the commentary may have been compiled in Ireland (see below for the evidence), see Sabbadini, "Spogli Ambrosiani latini," p. 168; and Louis Holtz, *Donat et la tradition de l'enseignement grammatical: Étude sur l'Ars Donati et sa diffusion (ive–ixe siècle) et édition critique*, 2nd ed. (Paris, 2010), p. 271. Subsequently, Holtz became more convinced that it originated in Bobbio. See Louis Holtz, "Les grammairiens hiberno-latins étaient-ils des anglo-saxons?," *Peritia* 2

Columbanus *ex libris*, verses added on a flyleaf in a ninth-century hand detailing that the manuscript was gifted to the monastery of Bobbio by Boniprandus,[3] and the fact that almost all the sources that the compiler of the *Ars* used can be identified in Bobbio's tenth-century catalogue,[4] or survive in a manuscript of Bobbio provenance.[5] But who compiled it and when?

Authorship of the Ars Ambrosiana: *A Seventh-Century Irish Scholar*

Up to the early 1980s, scholars like Remigio Sabbadini,[6] Charles Beeson,[7] Bernhard Bischoff,[8] Louis Holtz,[9] and Bengt Löfstedt[10] argued that its compiler was Irish primarily on the basis of a single, corrupt Old Irish gloss embedded in the main body of the text:[11] "doindarbethacha no co·mbetis agaldemathacha" – "with reference to

---

(1983), 170–84, at pp. 174–77. More recently, Louise Visser has suggested that it may have been composed in a "Northern Italian location outside Bobbio such as Verona" and later was brought to Bobbio. However, she did not adduce new evidence in support of this hypothesis; she merely speculated. Therefore, her hypothesis should remain *sub iudice* until new evidence is brought forward. See Louise Visser, "Heritage and Innovation in the Grammatical Analysis of Latin: The *Ars Ambrosiana* Commentary (6th/7th century) on Donatus (ca. 350 A.D.)," *Historiographica Linguistica* 38/1–2 (2011), 5–36, at p. 9.

[3] On the date of the script, see Bischoff, *Katalog*, 2:162, no. 2641; and Collura, *La Precarolina*, p. 142. Others dated the script to the eleventh century, see Sabbadini, "Spogli Ambrosiani latini," p. 166; Manitius, *Geschichte*, 1:519; and Law, *Insular Latin Grammarians*, p. 94.

[4] For editions of the medieval catalogue of Bobbio, see Gustav Becker, *Catalogi Bibliothecarum Antiqui* (Bonn, 1885), pp. 64–73; and Michele Tosi, "Il governo abbaziale di Gerberto a Bobbio," in *Gerberto: Scienza, storia e mito. Atti del* Gerberti Symposium *(Bobbio 25–27 luglio 1983)*, Archivum Bobiense Studia II, ed. Michele Tosi (Bobbio, 1985), pp. 71–234. The diplomatic edition spans pp. 198–214.

[5] On the sources used by the anonymous compiler, see Law, *Insular Latin Grammarians*, pp. 94–96; and Löfstedt, "Zu den Quellen des hibernolateinischen Donatkommentars im Cod. Ambrosianus L 22 sup.," *Studi Medievali* 21 (1980), 301–20. On the observation that the Bobbio catalogue contains many of the sources used by the compiler, see Beeson, "The Palimpsests of Bobbio," p. 179; and Manitius, *Geschichte*, 1:520.

[6] Sabbadini, "Spogli Ambrosiani latini," p. 168.

[7] Beeson, "The Palimpsests of Bobbio," p. 179.

[8] Bernhard Bischoff, "Il monachesimo irlandese nei suoi rapporti col continente," in *Il monachesimo nell'alto medioevo e la formazione della civiltà occidentale*, Settimane 4 (Spoleto, 1957), pp. 121–38; repr. in Bernhard Bischoff, *Mittelalterliche Studien: Ausgewählte Aufsätze zur Schriftkunde und Literaturgeschichte*, 3 vols. (Stuttgart, 1966–81), 1:195–205, at p. 198.

[9] Holtz, *Donat*, p. 271.

[10] Löfstedt, *Ars Ambrosiana*, p. vii.

[11] Löfstedt also identified a small number of orthographical features in the commentary that he argued were characteristic of a Hiberno-Latin author. Several are found commonly in Medieval Latinity (e.g. *ss* for *s*), but some appear to be quite unique to Hiberno-Latin (e.g. *Alaxander* for *Alexander* influenced by

driving or, as it were, things that name."[12] The Irish phrase is glossing the lemma *appellativa* ("common nouns") and indicates that the author of the gloss was uncertain whether the noun *appellativum* is a derivative of the verb *appellare* ("to name") or *appellere* ("to drive"). Rudolf Thurneysen dated the gloss to before 700 on the basis that it preserves early orthographical norms representing the sounds /b/, /d/ and /g/ in the medial and final position by the letters *b*, *d* and *g* instead of *p*, *t*, and *c* (*agaldemathacha*).[13] Scholars like Bischoff[14], Holtz[15] and Löfstedt[16] thus dated the commentary to before 700.[17]

Old Irish *Alaxandair*). See Löfstedt, *Ars Ambrosiana*, p. viii. At the very least, the presence of Hiberno-Latin orthography suggests that an Irish hand was involved in the transmission of the commentary, or that the compiler used an Irish source. For detailed discussions of Hiberno-Latin orthography, see Bengt Löfstedt, *Der Hibernolateinische Grammatiker Malsachanus* (Uppsala, 1965), pp. 86–107; Bengt Löfstedt, "Some Linguistic Remarks on Hiberno-Latin," *Studia Hibernica* 19 (1979), 161–69; Michael Herren, "Hiberno-Latin Philology: The State of the Question," in *Insular Latin Studies: Papers on Latin Texts and Manuscripts of the British Isles: 550–1066*, ed. Michael Herren (Toronto, 1981), pp. 1–22; Michael Herren, "Sprachliche Eigentümlichkeiten in den hibernolateinischen Texten des 7. und 8. Jahrhunderts," in *Die Iren und Europa im früheren Mittelalter*, ed. Heinz Löwe (Stuttgart, 1982), pp. 425–33; repr. in Michael Herren, *Latin Letters in Early Christian Ireland* (Aldershot, 1996), ch. 11; and Jean-Michel Picard, "The Schaffhausen Adomnán: A Unique Witness to Hiberno-Latin," *Peritia* 1 (1982), 216–49.

[12] *Ars Ambrosiana*, p. 11.11–12. The manuscript reads *do inter bēthoha l commodes āgal demathācha*. See Milan, Bibl. Ambrosiana, MS L 22 sup., fol. 8r. I would like to express my gratitude to Dr. Pádraic Moran for a stimulating discussion about this gloss.

[13] Thurneysen reconstructed and dated the gloss in a letter sent to Bischoff in 1940. The letter was published by Löfstedt as part of the introduction to his critical edition. See Löfstedt, *Ars Ambrosiana*, xvii. For a discussion of early Irish orthographical norms, see Damian McManus, *A Guide to Ogam* (Maynooth, 1991), pp. 44–45. Ó Cróinín identified additional evidence that may support an early dating for the gloss, specifically horizontal strokes above it distinguishing it as a non-Latin phrase. He argued that these strokes were primarily used by the earliest Irish glossators, since later glossators generally differentiated non-Latin words and phrases by the critical sign the apex. See Dáibhí Ó Cróinín, "The Earliest Old Irish Glosses," in *Mittelalterliche volkssprachige Glossen. Internationale Fachkonferenz des Zentrums für Mittelalterstudien der Otto-Friedrich-Universität Bamberg, 2. Bis 4. August 1999*, ed. Rolf Bergmann, Elvira Glaser, and Claudine Moulin-Frankhänel (Heidelberg, 2001), pp. 7–31, at 12.

[14] Bischoff, "Il Monachesimo," p. 198.

[15] Holtz, *Donat*, p. 271.

[16] Löfstedt, *Ars Ambrosiana*, p. vii.

[17] Sabbadini and Manitius dated the commentary to the ninth century. See Sabbadini, "Spogli Ambrosiani latini," pp. 165–68; and Manitius, *Geschichte*, 1:521. Richter suggested that the commentary may be dated to the eighth century. He argued that the compiler may have been educated in the seventh century and learned the Old Irish orthographical norms of that time. Thereafter, in the early eighth century, he compiled the commentary and used the same orthographical norms he learned as a child, even though they were no longer in general use. There is nothing inherently flawed with the

Evidence for Irish Authorship

This hypothesis went largely unchallenged[18] until 1982 when Vivien Law published her monograph *The Insular Latin Grammarians*, in which she suggested that the compiler of the commentary may not have been the author of the Old Irish gloss. He may have copied the gloss from an Irish source and integrated it into his commentary.[19] Law also proposed that an Irish scholar may have added the gloss to a version of the commentary, and thereafter a different scribe may have inserted it into the main body of the commentary as he was making a copy of it.[20] Although Law never made it clear which of the two hypotheses she considered to be more plausible, it is evident that she was sceptical of the prevailing theory that attributed the commentary to an Irish scholar. She declared that "one Irish gloss does not prove a grammar to be Irish"[21] and ultimately concluded on the basis of the sources used that the commentary may have originated in the Mediterranean (possibly in Bobbio), but that nothing more specific can be established on its authorship.[22] She also dated the commentary to the sixth[23] or seventh century, with the Old Irish gloss providing the *terminus ante quem*, i.e. 700.[24]

In 1985 (in a review of *The Insular Latin Grammarians*) Löfstedt[25] reaffirmed his position, namely that the compiler of the *Ars Ambrosiana* was Irish, and announced

---

logic of this argument, although it is very speculative. As far as I can tell, he appears to favour the later dating so he may attribute the commentary to Cummian, the Irish bishop who retired to Bobbio in the first half of the eighth century. See Richter, *Bobbio*, pp. 150, 185. For historical background on the life of Bishop Cummian, see pp. 89–94.

[18] Prior to Law, only Manitius, as far as I am aware, was hesitant to ascribe the commentary to an Irishman. He designated the commentary accordingly: "Irischer (?) Donatkommentar im Ambros. L.22 sup.;" see Manitius, *Geschichte*, 1:519.

[19] Law, *Insular Latin Grammarians*, p. 97, n. 73.

[20] Law, *Insular Latin Grammarians*, pp. 94, 97.

[21] Law, *Insular Latin Grammarians*, p. 93–94.

[22] Law, *Insular Latin Grammarians*, pp. 94–97.

[23] If the commentary originated at Bobbio, a sixth century date cannot be accepted, since the monastery was founded in the early seventh century by the Irish monk Columbanus. Her hypothesis can only be defended if we assume that she was not entirely certain that the commentary was a product of the Columbanian foundation and was composed elsewhere. In any event, Law subsequently was convinced that the commentary was compiled at the monastery; see Vivien Law, "The Transmission of Early Medieval Elementary Grammars: A Case Study in Explanation," in *Formative Stages of Classical Traditions: Latin Texts from Antiquity to the Renaissance*, ed. Oronzo Pecere and Michael D. Reeve (Spoleto, 1995), 239–61, at p. 241.

[24] Law, *Insular Latin Grammarians*, p. 97.

[25] Bengt Löfstedt, "Review of Vivien Law's *The Insular Latin Grammarians*," *Mittellateinisches Jahrbuch* 20 (1985), 261–63, at p. 261.

that Bischoff had discovered a second Old Irish gloss (*abacc* "dwarf")[26] embedded in the commentary that displayed a long horizontal stroke above it marking it out as a non-Latin word.[27] The relevant passage is as follows (*Ars Ambrosiana*, p. 48.334–37):

> Nomen in o vero, ut Scipio, Iuno, papirio "avis," quae per morem loquendi papirio dicitur; proprie enim papirio homo minimus, id est abac:[28] parvus est "qui crescit," papirio "qui numquam crescit."

> [There is] in fact a noun [ending] in o such as *Scipio, Iuno*, and *papirio*, [that is] a bird which is so called *papirio* by a habit of speaking. But strictly speaking *papirio* is a very small man, that is *abac* "dwarf": a small man is one who grows; *papirio* is one who never grows.

The compiler tells us that *papirio* (Classical Latin *papilio* – "butterfly") is generally used to signify *avis* "bird," although it should be used to mean *homo minimus* – "very small man," that is *abac* – "dwarf." This passage is striking because the Latin word for "dwarf" is not *papirio* but *pomilio* (Classical Latin *pumilio*) or *nanus*, which raises an important question: How did the Old Irish word *abacc* come to be a synonym of *papirio*? Before I explain how this passage may have taken shape, let us first look at the relevant part of Donatus's *Ars maior*:[29]

> Nomen in o vocalem desinens nominativo casu numero singulari aut masculinum est, ut Scipio, aut femininum, ut Iuno, aut commune, ut pomilio, [papilio].

> There is a masculine noun ending in the vowel o in the nominative singular like *Scipio*, a feminine like *Iuno*, and a common like *pomilio* "dwarf" and *papilio* "butterfly."

Following Holtz's edition, I have placed *papilio* in brackets indicating that not all manuscripts preserve this reading. However, the lemma was undoubtedly transmitted in many manuscripts that are no longer extant, as it is juxtaposed with *pomilio/pumilio* in extant commentaries on Donatus's *Artes*. Below I have cited from two commen-

---

[26] On *abacc*, see *eDIL: Electronic Dictionary of the Irish Language*, ed. Gregory Toner, Máire Ní Mhaonaigh, Sharon Arbuthnot, Marie-Luise Theuerkauf, and Dagmar Wodtko (www.dil.ie 2019), *s.v. abacc*, Accessed on 10 September 2019; Joseph Vendryes, Édouard Bachallery, and Pierre-Yves Lambert, *Lexique étymologique de l'Irlandais ancien*, 7 vols. (Paris, 1959–1996), 1:*s.v. abacc*; Jacopo Bisagni, "*Leprechaun*: A New Etymology," *Cambrian Medieval Celtic Studies* 64 (2012), 47–84, at pp. 63–84; Eric P. Hamp, "Varia 26: Early Irish abacc," *Études celtiques* 24 (1987), 185.

[27] Dáibhí Ó Cróinín, "The Earliest Old Irish Glosses," p. 12.

[28] The manuscript reads *ahāc*. See Milan, Bibl. Ambrosiana, L 22 sup., fol. 37r. Löfstedt could not make sense of the reading and chose NANOC, the Greek word for "dwarf". His choice was based on a suggestion made by Mary Charlotte Lane in her unpublished thesis which I have been unable to consult. See Mary Charlotte Lane, "A Study of the *Commentarium Ambrosianum in Donati Artem Maiorem*" (Ph.D. diss., University of Chicago, 1941). Bischoff deciphered the reading after the critical edition appeared in print.

[29] Donatus, *Ars maior*, p. 622.4–6, ed. in Holtz, *Donat*, pp. 603–74.

taries on Donatus, the ninth-century *Ars Laureshamensis* and a thirteenth-century compilation attributed to Sedulius Scottus containing material that goes back to the ninth century.[30]

> Pomilio dicitur parvus homo; papirio autem genus avis est, quae maxime abundat florentibus maluis et gignere solet de stercore suo vermiculos.[31]

> *Pomilio* is said to be a small man; *papirio*, however, is a kind of bird that is very abundant when mallows bloom and is accustomed to beget [its] larvae from its dung.

> Hic et haec pomilio dicitur "nanus homo," "nana mulier"; pomilio dicitur "vetulus vetula" – Papilio uero genus avis est, quae maxime abundat florentibus malvis et gignere solet de stercore suo vermiculos.[32]

> *Pomilio* is said to be a small man or woman; *pomilio* is said to be an old man or woman. *Papilio* is in fact a kind of bird that is very abundant when mallows bloom and is accustomed to beget [its] larvae from its dung.

The two commentators preserve the lemmata *papilio/papirio* and *pomilio/pumilio* in parallel and define them as a kind of bird and a person short in stature (i.e. a dwarf) respectively. When we compare these passages to the *Ars Ambrosiana*, it is evident that the meanings of *pomilio/pumilio* and *papirio/papilio* have been conflated. The common scribal error of homeoteleuton occasioned by parablepsis may explain how this occurred. I hypothesise that there existed a commentary on Donatus which included the following passage: "Papirio est avis; pomilio est homo minimus qui numquam crescit." A scribe copied this passage but, since the *papirio* and *pomilio* look rather similar, he made an error during transcription; instead of copying *pomilio*, he transcribed *papirio* a second time, resulting in the passage: "Papirio est avis; papirio est homo minimus qui numquam crescit." This was copied numerous times and probably circulated in several manuscripts, until eventually the compiler of the *Ars Ambrosiana* incorporated a version of it and added the gloss *abacc*, or copied a version that already contained the gloss. Although this reconstruction is speculative, it serves as one plausible way of explaining the development of this rather difficult passage.

To return to the main point, does the identification of a second gloss prove that the compiler was Irish? The short answer is "no." The problem is that the presence of two embedded glosses (as opposed to one) does not disprove Law's hypotheses. The

---

[30] For a comprehensive discussion of the two commentaries, see Louis Holtz, "Sur trois commentaires irlandais de l'Art *majeur* de Donat au IXᵉ siècle," *Revue d'histoire des textes* 2 (1972), 45–72; and Michael Haslam, "On the Sedulius Commentary on Donatus' Ars Maior," *Revue d'histoire des textes* 18 (1989), 243–56.

[31] *Ars Laureshamensis*, ed. Bengt Löfstedt, CCCM 40A (Turnhout, 1977), p. 40.60–62.

[32] Sedulius Scottus, *In Donati artem maiorem*, ed. Bengt Löfstedt, CCCM 40B (Turnhout, 1977), p. 128.60–63.

compiler may have derived the two glosses from an Irish source, or an Irish scholar may have added the glosses to a pre-existing version of the *Ars Ambrosiana*, and thereafter the commentary may have been copied by a different scribe, who inserted the glosses into the main body of the text. Since the evidence as it stands can be interpreted in at least three different ways, the question of attribution will continue to be a matter of dispute until new evidence comes to light.[33]

A Newly Discovered Bilingual Latin-Old Irish Etymology

Recently, I discovered evidence that may settle this dispute, specifically a passage that appears to contain a bilingual Latin–Old Irish etymology of the word *centaurus*. The passage reads as follows (*Ars Ambrosiana*, p. 42.143–47):

> Centaurus, ut aiunt, nomen viri est, a quo navis appellata est. Aliter: "Centaurus" conpositum, hoc est "caput tauri." Et per metaforam navi hoc nomen inpositum est per similitudinem non propriam rostri pro latitudine; navis enim, quae centaurus dicta, formam capitis tauri habuit.

> *Centaurus*, as some say, is the name of a man, after which a ship was named. Alternatively, *centaurus* [is] a compound, that is head of a bull. This name was bestowed on a ship as a metaphor, through a similarity that does not relate to the width of the [ship's] beak. For the ship which was called *centaurus* was shaped like the head of a bull.

The compiler comments on the lemma *centaurus* which does not refer to the mythical creature made of human and horse parts, but to a ship owned by Sergestus, one of Aeneas's Trojan comrades, in the *Aeneid* (Virgil, *Aen.* 5.120–220). He tells us that *centaurus* is a compound meaning *caput tauri* – "head of a bull," and that the noun was applied to a ship that was "shaped like the head of a bull" ("formam capitis tauri habuit"). The etymology is striking because it is not attested anywhere else and is entirely different from the standard etymology transmitted by Isidore[34] and Servius Auc-

---

[33] Most scholars accept that the commentary is probably Irish. See Dáibhí Ó Cróinín, *Early Medieval Ireland 400–1200*, 2nd ed. (London, 2017), p. 211; Ó Corráin, *Clavis*, 2:644–45, no. 504; Richter, *Bobbio*, p. 185; Pádraig Breatnach, "Review of Bengt Löfstedt's Edition of *Ars Ambrosiana*," *Peritia* 6–7 (1987–88), 327–28; Rijcklof Hofman, "The Irish Tradition of Priscian," in *Manuscripts and Tradition of Grammatical Texts from Antiquity to the Renaissance: Proceedings of a Conference Held at Erice, 16–23 October 1997*, 2 vols., ed. Mario De Nonno, Paolo De Paolis, and Louis Holtz (2000, Cassino), pp. 257–87, at 271; and Zetzel, *Critics*, pp. 357–58. Since Law, only Louise Visser, as far as I am aware, has questioned the Irish hypothesis; see Louise Visser, "Heritage and Innovation," p. 7.

[34] *Isidori Hispalensis Episcopi Etymologiarum sive Originum Libri XX*, 2 vols., ed. Wallace M. Lindsay (Oxford, 1911), 14.4.12: "Thessalia patria Achillis et origo Lapitharum fuit, de quibus fertur quod hi primo equos frenis domuerunt, unde et Centauri dicti sunt" – "Thessaly was the birthplace of Achilles and the original home of the Lapiths, of whom it is said that they were the first to break horses to the bit, whence they were also called Centaurs." See *The Etymologies of Isidore of Seville*, trans. Stephen A. Barney, Wendy J. Lewis, Jennifer A. Beach, and Oliver Berghof (Cambridge, 2006), p. 290. For a

tus.[35] The word *caput* is an exegetical gloss explaining the meaning of the first part of the compound *cen*, which appears to be the Old Irish word for "head."[36] The author of the passage seems to have been ignorant as to the meaning of *centaurus* and used his own vernacular (*cenn* – "head") as well as Latin (*taurus* – "bull") in an attempt to explain it.[37]

After presenting the etymology, the compiler attempts an explanation, although as we shall see he appears to misunderstand it entirely (*Ars Ambrosiana*, p. 42.149–52):

> Plerique mirantur nomen quod est caput in tantum corruptum esse, ut nihil remanserit nisi c in conpositione; non minus mirentur nihil remansisse in nomine tibicen a verbo cano nisi c.
>
> Many are astonished that the noun *caput* "head" is so corrupted that nothing has survived in the compound formation except for "c." [Just as] they are as astonished that

---

discussion of ancient etymologies and accounts of the centaur, see Minerva Alganza Roldán, Julian Barr, and Greta Hawes, "The Reception History of Palaephatus 1 (On the Centaurs) in Ancient and Byzantine texts," *Polymnia* 3 (2017), 187–235.

[35] *Servii Grammatici qui feruntur in Vergilii Carmina Commentarii*, 3 vols., ed. Georg Thilo and Hermann Hagen (Leipzig, 1878–1881), 3:285–86 (*ad Georg.* 3.115): "Pelethronium oppidum est Thessaliae, ubi primum domandorum equorum repertus est usus. Nam cum quidam Thessalus rex, bubus oestro exagitatis, satellites suos ad eos revocandos ire iussisset illique cursu non sufficerent, ascenderunt equos et eorum velocitate boves secuti, eos stimulis ad tecta revocarunt. Sed hi visi, aut cum irent velociter, aut cum eorum equi circa flumen Peneon potarent capitibus inclinatis, locum fabulae dederunt, ut Centauri esse crederentur, qui dicti sunt Centauri ἀπὸ τοῦ κεντᾶν τοὺς ταύρους" – "Pelethronium is a town in Thessaly where the practice of domesticating horses was first invented. For when his bulls were stirred up by a gadfly, a certain Thessalian king ordered his subjects to go and retrieve them. Since they were not fast enough on foot, they mounted horses and with the aid of the horses' speed, tracked the bulls and brought them back home using goads. But the sight gave rise to a topic for myth – whether because they moved so quickly, or because the horses inclined their heads as they drank from the river Peneus – and they were believed to be Centaurs, the name coming from the Greek ἀπὸ τοῦ κεντᾶν τοὺς ταύρους 'to pierce the bulls.'" See Minerva A. Roldán et al., "The Reception History of Palaephatus," p. 203.

[36] *eDIL*, s.v. *cenn*. It should also be mentioned that *cen* is a preposition in Old Irish meaning "apart from" or "without"; however, taking it as a preposition does not adequately explain the etymology. See *eDil*, s.v. *cen*.

[37] Many similar etymologies are attested in Medieval Irish language glossaries. For example, see *De origine scoticae linguae (or O'Mulconry's Glossary). An Early Irish Linguistic Tract with a Related Glossary, Irsan*, ed. Pádraic Moran, CCCM Lexica Latina Medii Aevi 7 (Turnhout, 2019). In this glossary certain Old Irish words are identified as compound forms containing both Latin and Old Irish elements. For a discussion of these words, see p. 42 of Moran's edition and study. For background on Medieval Irish glossaries, see Paul Russell, "The Sounds of a Silence: The Growth of Cormac's Glossary," *Cambrian Medieval Celtic Studies* 15 (1988), 1–30; Paul Russell, "Dúil Dromma Cetta and Cormac's Glossary," *Études celtiques* 32 (1996), 147–74; Paul Russell, "Read it in a Glossary: Glossaries and Learned Discourse in Medieval Ireland," *Kathleen Hughes Memorial Lectures* 6 (Cambridge, 2008).

nothing has survived from the verb *cano* "I sing" in the noun *tibicen* "flautist" except for "c."

The compiler does not recognise that the element *cen* is being interpreted as an Old Irish word and instead suggests that *cen* is a corrupt form of *caput*. In fact, he tells us that the noun *caput* has become so thoroughly corrupted that the only surviving trace of it is the letter c. He is hypothesising that there was once a Latin word **caput-taurus*, which no longer exists, because extensive corruption has given rise to the form *centaurus*. The compiler then compares *centaurus* to *tibicen* "flautist," a noun ending in the syllable *cen*. *Tibicen* is formed from the verb *cano* "I sing," although it too is corrupted and is no longer entirely visible; all that remains is the letter c. In this case, he is hypothesising that there existed a noun **tibicano*, but extensive corruption has given rise to the form *tibicen*. The reason for comparing the two nouns is evident: both represent results of linguistic corruption and both incorporate the syllable *cen*. The compiler seems to be implying that the presence of *cen* in these words is a sign that corruption has occurred, although he does not state this explicitly.

Reconstructing and Dating a Lost Irish Source

If what I have argued carries conviction, then the most important inference is that the compiler did not understand the etymology and therefore cannot possibly have been Irish. That said, he did attempt an interpretation indicating that he used a source that already included the etymology. This source was almost certainly composed by an Irish scholar, as the following passages excerpted from the *Ars Ambrosiana* will confirm (p. 8.72):

> "Roma" Grecum "sublimitas" interpretatur.
>
> *Roma*, the Greek word, translates as *sublimity*.

Löfstedt emended this passage. The manuscript does not read *grecum* but *genus*.[38] Pádraig Breatnach pointed out that this error probably arose as a result of an inability to decipher Insular minuscule.[39] As is well known, continental scribes often confused Insular "r" with "s."[40] In this case, the Irish source probably contained the abbreviation

---

[38] See Milan, Bibl. Ambrosiana, L 22 sup., fol. 6r.

[39] Breatnach, "Review," p. 328.

[40] Wallace M. Lindsay, *Palaeographia Latina*, 6 parts (Oxford, 1922–1929), 1:43; Löfstedt, *Der Hibernolateinische*, p. 33; Gerard MacGinty, *Pauca problemata de enigmatibus ex tomis canonicis. Praefatio – De Pentateucho Moysi*, CCCM 173 (Turnhout, 2000), p. xix; Jane Stevenson, *The Laterculus Malalianus and the School of Archbishop Theodore*, Cambridge Studies in Anglo-Saxon England 14 (Cambridge, 1995), p. 113.

"gr" (*grecum*), but the compiler read it as "gs" and expanded it as *genus*.[41] Perhaps a similar confusion also explains the following peculiar passage about analogy (*Ars Ambrosiana*, p. 73.610–12):

> Analogia est similium inter se loquellarum observatio. "Analogia" Grece, proportio Latine dicitur vel propositio, quia proponitur certum ad [ad] intellegendum incertum.
>
> *Analogia* "analogy" is the observance of agreement between similar words. Analogy in Greek is named either *proportio* "regular relation" or *propositio* in Latin, because a form that is certain is placed next to an uncertain one for the purposes of interpretation.

In the passage two Latin translations of the Greek term *analogia* are provided, *proportio* and *propositio*. The former is the correct translation whereas the latter is not,[42] and seems to have arisen as a result of misreading an insular "r" as a ligature "si" (propor-tio → proposi tio). Considering that the hook of the Insular "r" is very pronounced and often extends down towards the baseline as though it is forming a ligature with a letter "i," it is easy to understand how a Continental scribe not well-versed in Insular minuscule might have made this error. The peculiar reading generated required explanation. The compiler tells us that *propositio* is a synonym of *analogia* because it involves a form that is certain being placed (*proponere*) next to one that is uncertain. Here the compiler has cleverly reworked the definition of analogy transmitted in Isidore's *Etymologiae*, 1.28.1 (trans. Barney et al., *Etymologies*, 54):

> Analogia Graece, Latine similium conparatio sive proportio nominatur. Cuius haec vis est ut, quod dubium est, ad aliquid simile, quod non est dubium, referatur, et incerta certis probentur.
>
> The Greek term *analogia* "analogy" is called in Latin the comparison or *proportio* "regular relation" of similar forms. Its force is that something doubtful is compared to a similar thing that is not doubtful, and uncertain forms are tested against forms that are certain.

As we can see, he has replaced the verb *probare* with *proponere* to justify why the term *propositio* is an appropriate synonym of *analogia*.

The presence of errors is not the only means of demonstrating that source was Irish. Several passages in the *Ars Ambrosiana* are quite distinct and find parallels only in other Irish treatises. The following passage concerned with the etymology of *feria* "weekday" is one such example (*Ars Ambrosiana*, p. 50.60–61):

---

[41] On the abbreviations "gr" (meaning *graecum*) and "gs" (meaning *genus*), see Wallace M. Lindsay, *Notae Latinae: An Account of Abbreviation in Latin MSS of the Early Minuscule Period (c. 700–850)* (Cambridge, 1915), pp. 91–92, 427.

[42] On the Greek and Latin terminology of analogy, see Francesca Schironi, "Ἀναλογία, analogia, proportio, ratio: Loan words, Calques, and Reinterpretations of a Greek Technical Word," in *Bilinguisme et terminologie grammaticale Gréco-Latine*, Orbis Supplementa 27, ed. Louis Basset, Frédérique Biville, Pierre Swiggers, and Alfons Wouters (Leuven, 2007), pp. 321–38.

Feriae autem dictae quasi fariae vel a fiendo, eo quod factae sunt dicendo *fiat lux*.

Feriae "weekdays" are so called as if from *faria* "words" or from *fiendo* "being made," because they were made by saying *fiat lux* – "let there be light."

The derivation of *feria* from *faria* or *fando* is quite common in medieval sources and ultimately can be traced back to Isidore (passage cited below);[43] the derivation from *fiendo* by contrast is extremely rare. In fact, I have only found the two etymologies preserved in parallel in Irish or Irish-influenced *computistica*. Compare, for example, the etymology of *feria* in the so-called *Munich Computus* composed in Ireland in the eighth century.

Feria a fando dicta est, vel a fiendo, dicente Domino: Fiat lux et facta est lux.[44]

Feria "weekday" was so called from *fando* "speaking," or from *fiendo* "being made," as the Lord said: "Let there be light" and there was light.

These passages as well as the other three containing Irish vernacular material cited above suggest strongly that the compiler of the *Ars Ambrosiana* used an Irish grammatical source. But is it possible to date this newly identified source? If we assume for the sake of argument that all the vernacular glosses preserved in the *Ars Ambrosiana* originated in a single Irish source as opposed to being derived from several (although we cannot be certain of this), then the gloss "doindarbethacha no co·mbetis agaldemathacha" provides us with a *terminus ante quem* of 700 because, as

---

[43] Isidore, *De rerum natura*, 3.1.4–6, ed. and transl. in Jacques Fontaine, *Traité de la nature: Introduction, texte critique, traduction et notes*, Série Moyen Âge et Temps Modernes 39, 2nd ed. (Paris, 2002), pp. 164–335. This etymology of *feria* is also attested in the following texts: *Anonymus ad Cuimnanum*, ed. Bernhard Bischoff and Bengt Löfstedt, CCSL 133D, (Turnhout, 1992), p. 57.52; *Commentum Einsidlense in Donati artem maiorem*, Grammatici Latini 8, ed. Hermann Hagen (Leipzig, 1870), pp. 219–74, at 241.14; *De ratione conputandi*, ed. Dáibhí. Ó Cróinín, (Toronto, 1988), p. 135.10; Muretach, *In Donati artem maiorem*, ed. Louis Holtz, CCCM 40 (Turnhout, 1977), p. 90.30; and Sedulius Scottus, *Commentum in Donati artem maiorem*, p. 133.51.

[44] *Munich Computus*, 11.2–3, ed. and transl. Immo Warntjes, in *The Munich Computus: Text and Translation. Irish Computistics between Isidore of Seville and the Venerable Bede and Its Reception in Carolingian Times* (Stuttgart, 2010), pp. 2–317. The two etymologies are also attested in unedited Irish and Irish influenced computistical texts and glosses. See Angers, Bibliothèque municipale, MS 477 (saec. IXex., Brittany), fol. 19r; and Einsiedeln, Stiftsbibliothek, MS 321 (saec. IX$^{2/3}$, Lake Constance region or Strasbourg), p. 92. The derivation from *fiendo* is found also in Laon, Bibliothèque municipale, MS 422 (saec. IX$^{1/4}$, Northern Francia), fol. 45r. On the Irish influenced computistical materials in Angers 477, see Warntjes, *The Munich Computus*, pp. civ–cv. For a discussion of the Irish *computus* in Einsiedeln 321, see Jacopo Bisagni and Immo Warntjes, "The Early Old Irish Material in the Newly Discovered Computus Einsidlensis (c. AD700)," *Ériu* 58 (2008), 77–105. On the Irish *computus* in the Laon 422, see Jacopo Bisagni, "La litterature computistique irlandaise dans la Bretagne du haut Moyen Âge: Nouvelles découvertes et nouvelles perspectives," *Britannia Monastica* 20 (2019), 241–85, at pp. 264–70.

we have already mentioned, it can be dated quite precisely on linguistic grounds (see above, pp. 68–69). A *terminus post quem* can be assigned on the basis of the etymology of *feria* cited above. I suggested that this passage was derived from the Irish source, but it ultimately depends on Isidore's *De rerum natura* 3.1.4–6, which was composed in the second decade of the seventh century:[45]

> Feria quoque a fando dicta quasi faria, eo quod in creatione mundi per singulos dies dixit Deus fiat; item quia dies sabbati ab initio feriatus habetur.
>
> *Feria* "weekday" takes its name from the verb *fari* "to speak" as if it were pronounced *faria*, because in the creation of the world God said "let it be made" on each separate day, and also because the day of the Sabbath is considered to have been a holiday from the beginning.[46]

If the Irish source was compiled in Ireland and later brought to Bobbio, it can be dated to the second half of the seventh century, as it is generally accepted that the works of Isidore arrived in Ireland after 650. A narrower date range may be assigned, if Marina Smyth is correct that the works of Isidore only reached Ireland in the final decades of the seventh century.[47] This slightly later dating is also compatible with a hypothesis positing that an Irish scholar compiled the source at Bobbio, since, according to Alessandro Zironi and Veronika von Büren, the works of Isidore were circulating in Northern Italy from the end of the seventh century.[48]

---

[45] Fontaine, *Traité de la nature*, p. 1.

[46] *Isidore of Seville. On the Nature of Things*, trans. Calvin B. Kendall and Faith Wallis (Liverpool, 2016), p. 115.

[47] For the traditional view that the works of Isidore were transmitted to Ireland in the middle of the seventh century, see Michael Herren, "On the Earliest Irish Acquaintance with Isidore of Seville," in *Visigothic Spain: New Approaches*, ed. Edward James (Oxford, 1980), pp. 243–50; repr. in Michael Herren, *Latin Letters in Early Christian Ireland* (Aldershot, 1996), ch. 3; Jocelyn Hillgarth, "Ireland and Spain in the Seventh Century," *Peritia* 3 (1984), 1–16; and Dáibhí Ó Cróinín, "A Seventh-Century Irish computus from the Circle of Cummianus," *Proceedings of the Royal Irish Academy* 82C (1982), 405–30, at pp. 423–24; repr. in D. Ó Cróinín, *Early Irish History and Chronology* (Dublin, 2003), pp. 99–130, at 122–23. For a critique of this view and arguments in favour of dating the arrival of Isidore's treatises later to the end of seventh century, see Marina Smyth, "Isidorian Texts in Seventh-Century Ireland," in *Isidore of Seville and His Reception in the Early Middle Ages. Transmitting and Transforming Knowledge*, ed. Andrew Fear and Jamie Wood (Amsterdam, 2016), pp. 111–30. For a critique of the arguments made by Ó Cróinín, "A Seventh-Century Irish computus," see Marina Smyth, "Isidore of Seville and Early Irish Cosmography," *Cambrian Medieval Celtic Studies* 14 (1987), 69–102, at pp. 94–101; Immo Warntjes, "A Newly Discovered Prologue of AD 699 to the Easter Table of Victorius of Aquitaine in an Unknown Sirmond Manuscript," *Peritia* 21 (2010), 255–84, at p. 257; and Warntjes, *The Munich Computus*, pp. xxviii–xxix.

[48] Veronika Von Büren, "La place du manuscrit Ambr. L 99 sup. dans la transmission des *Étymologies* d'Isidore de Séville," in *Nuove ricerche su codici in scrittura latina dell'Ambrosiana. Atti del convegno Milano, 6–7 ottobre 2005*, ed. Mirella Ferrari and Marco Navoni (Milan, 2007), pp. 25–44; and

Authorship of the Ars Ambrosiana: An Italian Scholar at Bobbio

Let us summarise the argument so far. The compiler of the *Ars Ambrosiana* was not Irish but used an Irish grammatical source that was probably compiled in the second half of the seventh century. Who then compiled the commentary and when? Louise Visser has suggested that the compiler was from Italy, a reasonable hypothesis considering that it is generally accepted that the commentary originated in Bobbio. She observed that the compiler's language appears to be "of a vulgar or spoken nature compatible with the way Stotz[49] describes the Latin of Early Medieval Italy," although she cautioned that her findings were preliminary and should remain *sub iudice* until a systematic linguistic study is carried out.[50] I should add that there is one flaw with the methodology she used. Medieval grammars are compilations of sources woven together by compilers who generally repeat the words of their sources verbatim. How can we ever be certain that we are analysing the language of the compiler and not the language of his sources? For the methodology to work, we would first have to identify "original" passages, but the problem is medieval grammarians are not known for their originality and even when so-called original passages are identified, later it is often found that they too derive from older sources. For this reason, an analysis of the compiler's language may not help us address the question of authorship.

The Date of the Ars Ambrosiana

Let us now turn to the matter of dating. We can assign the commentary a secure *terminus ante quem* of the third quarter of the ninth century on the basis of the manuscript and a *terminus post quem* of the middle of seventh century on the basis of the lost Irish source. But can we date the commentary more precisely? In an instructive article published in 1992, Law examined the revival of the study of dialectic during the Carolingian *Renovatio* and the affect the revival had on the development of grammatical thought.[51] Dialectic was the art of discerning truth from falsehood and was concerned

---

Alessandro Zironi, *Il monastero longobardo di Bobbio. Crocevia di uomini, manoscritti e culture* (Spoleto, 2004), pp. 53–56.

[49] Peter Stotz, *Handbuch zur lateinischen Sprache des Mittelalters*, 5 vols. (Munich, 1996–2004), 1:93–98.

[50] Visser, "Heritage and Innovation," p. 10.

[51] Vivien Law, "Carolingian Grammarians and Theoretical Innovation," in *Diversions of Galway. Papers on the History of Linguistics from ICHoLS 5*, Studies in the History of the Language Sciences 68, ed. Anders Ahlqvist (Amsterdam, 1992), pp. 27–37; repr. in Vivien Law, *Grammar and Grammarians in the Early Middle Ages* (London, 1997), pp. 154–63. See also Vivien Law, "The Study of Grammar under the Carolingians," in *Carolingian Culture: Emulation and Innovation*, ed. Rosamond McKitterick (Cambridge, 1994), pp. 88–110, at pp. 97–99; repr. in Law, *Grammar and Grammarians*, pp. 129–53, at pp. 138–40.

primarily with the formulation of sound arguments. The discipline was studied throughout antiquity up until the sixth century, but by the seventh century it went into somewhat of a decline, possibly because scholars were not entirely certain how to integrate it into the new Christian educational curriculum emerging during this period. From the beginning of the ninth century an interest in the discipline can be detected again in the Carolingian world. During this period manuscripts containing seminal works of dialectic, including Boethius's translations of, and commentaries on, Porphyry's *Isagoge* and Aristotle's *De interpretatione*, as well as a Latin translation of Aristotle's *Categories* entitled *Categoriae decem*, were copied widely in *scriptoria* across Europe. These treatises provided scholars with a comprehensive introduction to dialectic and ignited a profound interest in the discipline that would persist throughout the Carolingian period and beyond.[52]

The influence of dialectic can also be detected in the grammatical treatises compiled during the ninth century.[53] From 800 onwards Carolingian grammarians increasingly borrowed terminology, categories and concepts from the discipline and integrated them into their grammatical writings. Most notably, they incorporated and adapted a systematic classification of definition derived from the writings of Marius Victorinus,[54] Cassiodorus,[55] and Isidore,[56] who listed fifteen categories of definition, including *substantialis* "substantial," *notio* "notional," *qualitas* "qualitative," *descriptio* "descriptive," *ad verbum* "substitutional," *differentia* "distinction," *translatio* "metaphor," *per privantiam contarii eius* "the negation of the opposite," *imaginatio* "formal," *veluti* "by example," *per indigentiam pleni ex eodem genere* "omission of the whole in the same genus," *laus* "praise," *proportio* "analogy," *ad aliquid* "relational," and *ratio rei* "causational." Carolingian grammarians modified the classification so that it could be applied in the context of grammar, typically reducing the number of categories to six and adding new ones not attested in their Late Antique sources.

---

[52] On the revival of dialectic in the Carolingian period, see John Marenbon, *From the Circle of Alcuin to the School of Auxerre: Logic, Philosophy and Theology in the Early Middle Ages* (Cambridge, 1981).

[53] On grammar and dialectic, see Anneli Luhtala, "Grammar and Dialectic: A Topical Issue in the Ninth Century," in *Johannes Scottus Eriugena. The Bible and Hermeneutics. Proceedings of the Ninth International Colloquium of the Society for the Promotion of Eriugenian Studies Held at Leuven and Louvain-la-Neuve, June 7–10, 1995*, ed. Gerd van Riel, Carlos Steel, and James J. McEvoy (Leuven, 1996), pp. 279–301.

[54] Marius Victorinus, *De definitionibus*, ed. Thomas Stangl, in *Tulliana et Mario-Victoriniana* (Munich, 1888), p. 32.18–33.

[55] Cassiodorus, *Institutiones divinarum et saecularium litterarum*, ed. Roger A.B. Mynors (Oxford, 1937), 2.3.14.5–15.

[56] Isidore, *Etymologiae*, 2.29.2–16.

Definitionis autem genera secundum grammaticos sunt vi: prima substantialis, ut "nomen est pars orationis cum casu"; secunda soni, ut nomen dictum est quasi notamen; tertia specialis, ut "corpus aut rem proprie communiterue significans"; quarta accidentalis, ut "nomini accidunt vi"; quinta numeralis, ut "partes orationis sunt viii"; sexta ethimologiae, ut homo dictus est ab humo et humus ab humore.[57]

There are six types of definition according to the grammarians. The first pertains to substance, e.g. a noun is a part of speech with case. The second pertains to sound, e.g. the noun is so called as if a denoter. The third pertains to specific characteristics, e.g. signifying a body or an abstraction and either proper or common. The fourth pertains to its accidents, e.g. the noun has six accidents. The fifth pertains to number, e.g. there are eight parts of speech. The sixth pertains to etymology, e.g. *homo* "man" is so called from *humus* "earth," and *humus* from *humor* "moisture."

This sophisticated six-fold categorisation of definition is not attested in the *Ars Ambrosiana* or indeed in other early medieval grammars datable before the beginning of the ninth century, including the *Ars Asporii*,[58] *Ars Tatuini*,[59] *Ars Bonifacii*,[60] *Ars Bernensis*,[61] *Epistolae* and *Epitomae* of Virgilius Maro Grammaticus,[62] *Quae sunt quae*,[63] and *Anonymus ad Cuimnanum*.[64] This suggests that the *Ars Ambrosiana* was compiled

---

[57] *Ars Laureshamensis*, p. 10.14–21. See also Clemens Scottus, *Ars Grammatica*, ed. Joannes Tolkiehn (Leipzig, 1928), p. 25.20–26; Donatus Ortigraphus, *Ars Grammatica*, ed. John Chittenden, CCCM 40D (Turnhout, 1982), p. 66.29–39; *Liber de verbo: E codice Parisiensi 7491*, ed. Cécile Conduché, CCCM 40E (Turnhout, 2018), p. 172.30–32; and Sedulius Scottus, *Commentum in Donati artem maiorem*, ed. Bengt Löfstedt, CCCM 40B (Turnhout, 1977), p. 64.16–20.

[58] *Ars Asporii*, ed. Heinrich Keil and Hermann Hagen, Grammatici Latini 8 (Leipzig, 1870), pp. 39–61. On the date of the text, see Holtz, *Donat*, pp. 272–74; and Law, *Insular Latin grammarians*, pp. 35–41.

[59] Tatwine, *Ars Grammatica*, ed. Maria De Marco, in *Tatuini Opera Omnia*, 2 vols., ed. Maria de Marco and François Glorie, CCSL 133 (Turnhout, 1968), 1:1–93. On the date of this text, see Law, *Insular Latin Grammarians*, pp. 64–67.

[60] Boniface, *Ars Grammatica*, ed. George J. Gebauer and Bengt Löfstedt, CCSL 133B (Turnhout, 1980). On the date of this text, see Law, *Insular Latin Grammarians*, pp. 77–80.

[61] *Ars Bernensis*, ed. Heinrich Keil and Hermann Hagen, Grammatici Latini 8 (Leipzig, 1870), pp. 62–142. On the date and authorship of the text, see Louis Holtz, "L'*Ars Bernensis*, essai de localisation et de datation," in *Aquitaine and Ireland in the Middle Ages*, ed. Jean-Michel Picard (Dublin, 1995), pp. 111–26.

[62] Virgilius Maro Grammaticus, *Omnia Opera*, ed. Bengt Löfstedt (Leipzig, 2003). For a comprehensive discussion of this enigmatic scholar, see Michael Herren, "Some New Light on the Life of Virgilius Maro Grammaticus," *Proceedings of the Royal Irish Academy* 79C (1979), pp. 27–71. See also Law, *Insular Latin Grammarians*, pp. 42–52.

[63] *Quae sunt quae*, ed. Luigi Munzi, in *Multiplex Latinitas. Testi grammaticali latini dell'Alto Medioevo* (Naples, 2004), pp. 17–38. On the date of this text, see Law, *Insular Latin Grammarians*, pp. 85–87; and Munzi, *Multiplex Latinitas*, pp. 9–14.

[64] On the date, authorship and localisation of the commentary, see Bischoff and Löfstedt, *Anonymus ad Cuimnanum*, pp. vii–xxiii; Marco De Nonno, "Note all'editio princeps dell'Anonymus ad Cuimnanum,"

prior to the year 800 before there was a renewed interest in the systematic study of dialectic. For this reason, I date the commentary between 650 – the earliest possible date for the Irish source – and 800.

Conclusion

To conclude I will make additional observations about the newly identified Irish source. Its identification raises an important question: Was it available to other compilers? Evidence suggests that it was also consulted by the compilers of the *Anonymus ad Cuimnanum* and the *Ars Bernensis*, two Hiberno-Latin grammars that modern scholars have dated to the late seventh or early eighth century and localised at Bobbio. These grammars (especially the *Anonymus ad Cuimnanum*) display close affinities with the *Ars Ambrosiana*.[65] Notable similarities include the use of the term *propositio* for *porportio*, a usage that appears to be particular to the *Ars Ambrosiana* (pp. 70.528, 73.611) and *Anonymus ad Cuimnanum* (pp. 73.262, 74.270, 121.80, 121.82). Further research may reveal that the Irish source was copied by an (Italian) scribe at Bobbio, who made an error during transcription and established the faulty reading *propositio*. The compilers of the *Ars Ambrosiana* and *Anonymus ad Cuimnanum* may have consulted this copy of the Irish source and incorporated the faulty reading *propositio* into their commentaries. Another similarity between the three grammars is the striking passage that we discussed above concerning the word *papirio* "butterfly." We will recall that the compiler of the *Ars Ambrosiana* (p. 48. 334–38) defined it as *avis* "bird" or "homo minimus, id est abac ... qui numquam crescit" – "an extremely small man, that is a dwarf ... [a man] who never grows." The compilers of the *Ars Bernensis* (p. 110.7) and the *Anonymus ad Cuimnanum* (p. 52.261–62),[66] by contrast, defined it as "avis qui numquam crescit" – "a bird who never grows." As we can see, the latter two compilers preserve a more "correct" definition, insofar as they recognise that term *papirio* should only denote a kind of flying creature, although they modified it by adding the phrase "qui numquam crescit," which originally was associated with the definition of dwarf. The following steps may explain how this definition was formed. The compilers of the *Anonymus ad Cuimnanum* and *Ars Bernensis* relied on the Irish source which contained precisely the same passage that we find in the *Ars Ambrosiana* or something very close to it: "*papirio avis, quae per morem loquendi papirio dicitur; proprie enim papirio homo minimus, id est abac: parvus est qui crescit, papirio qui numquam

---

Latomus 55/3 (1996), 638–53; and María Adelaida Andrés Sanz, "Sobre el lugar de origen del *Anonymus ad Cuimnanum*: Notas a partir del estudio de una de sus fuentes (Isidoro, *De differentiis* 2)," *Euphrosyne* 25 (1997), 435–42.

[65] Holtz has already noted the close affinity between the *Ars Ambrosiana* and *the Anonymus ad Cuimnanum* and suggested that they may share a common Irish source. See Holtz, *Donat*, p. 291.

[66] The *Anonymus ad Cuimnanum* preserves a slightly different reading: "avis que numquam crescit."

crescit." They were aware that the term *papirio* did not mean "dwarf" and therefore did not copy that part of the passage. However, they preserved the phrase "qui numquam crescit" and applied it to *papirio* meaning *avis* "bird", possibly because it aptly described the particular type of *avis* – a butterfly which completes its life cycle once it emerges from its chrysalis (and therefore does not grow). The evidence presented here does not prove that the three compilers used the same Irish source; more evidence is required before this hypothesis can be substantiated. But if it turns out that I am correct, we will know far more about the nature of the relationship between three Latin grammars composed at the monastery of Bobbio in the Pre-Carolingian period.[67]

Abstract

The *Ars Ambrosiana* is an anonymous commentary on Donatus's *Ars maior* transmitted in Milan, Biblioteca Ambrosiana, MS L 22 sup. (saec. IX$^{3/4}$, Bobbio), fols. 1r–145v. Modern scholars generally agree that it was compiled by an Irish scholar at Bobbio in the seventh century. The article argues contrary to the consensus that the compiler was not Irish. New evidence is presented in favour of the hypothesis, specifically an Old Irish textual element embedded in the grammar, which the compiler attempted to explain but misunderstood entirely. The most logical conclusion is that the compiler was a Continental scholar who used an Irish grammatical source, from which he derived the Old Irish material. The article also identifies passages that may have originated in the Irish source and uses evidence contained within them to establish an approximate date of composition. Finally, the article proposes a new criterion for dating the *Ars Ambrosiana* and argues for a composition date between 650 and 800.

Résumé

L'*Ars Ambrosiana* est un commentaire anonyme sur l'*Ars maior* de Donat, transmis par le biais de Milan, Biblioteca Ambrosiana, MS L 22, sup. (saec. IX¾, Bobbio), fols. 1r–145v. De nos jours les chercheurs s'entendent généralement pour affirmer que l'œuvre a été compilée par un érudit irlandais à Bobbio au cours du VIIe siècle. Cet article va à l'encontre du consensus scientifique et soutient que le compilateur n'était pas irlandais. Il présente de nouvelles preuves pour démontrer cette hypothèse, en particulier un élément textuel en vieil irlandais inclus dans la grammaire, que le compilateur a tenté d'expliquer mais qu'il a tout à fait mal compris. La conclusion la plus logique s'avère donc que le compilateur aurait été un érudit originaire du Continent, ayant employé une source grammaticale irlandaise, de laquelle il aurait dérivé quelque matière en vieil irlandais. Cet article identifie également des passages qui auraient pu provenir de la source irlandaise et utilise des indices fournis par ces mêmes passages pour établir une date de composition approximative. En dernier lieu, l'article propose

---

[67] I am currently writing an article discussing the relationship between these grammatical treatises.

un nouveau critère pour la datation de l'*Ars Ambrosiana* et avance une date de composition se situant entre 650 et 800.

Jason O'Rorke
National University of Ireland, Galway
jason.ororke@nuigalway.ie

Clerical Concubines: Three Poems*

A.G. Rigg (†)
University of Toronto

Introduction

The three poems edited and translated here concern the celibacy of the clergy, which had been an issue for the Western church since the Council of Nicaea in 325. Frequent attempts had been made to enforce it: in 1179 Pope Alexander III and in 1215 Pope Innocent III vigorously tried to ban wives or concubines for all those in holy orders.[1] The three poems, *Nouus Rumor Anglie* (NR), *Prisciani Regula* (PR), and *Clerus et Presbiteri* (CP) were first published in modern times by Thomas Wright in 1841,[2] who did not know the fullest version of NR; an edition of PR and CP (truncated with a translation into French) was also made by Olga Dobiache-Rojdesvenski in 1931.[3] Otherwise, there have been brief discussions by Lehmann,[4]

---

* Editor's Note: George Rigg completed a first draft of this article in January 2014 and submitted it for consideration to *The Journal of Medieval Latin*. Gernot Wieland, who was editor at the time, sent his preliminary comments back to George in July of the same year. George continued to work on the introduction and the verse translations in 2015 and had a revised version of the article ready in early 2016 when Gernot had already stepped down as editor. The project remained in this intermediate stage at George's death in January 2019. His original copy, written on his legendary typewriter, was found by his widow Jennifer among his papers and given to me, as per George's wishes. I converted the text into electronic form, completed some of the references, and tidied up the edition, but the final result is still very much representative of George's authorial version. George seems to have wanted to submit this work to *Books and Bookmen in Early Modern Britain*, the Festschrift for James Carley published in 2018 by the Pontifical Institute of Mediaeval Studies, but his health was already failing. It is a privilege to present to the scholarly community this final contribution by George.

[1] See *Decrees of the Ecumenical Councils*, vol. 1: Nicaea I – Lateran V, ed. Norman P. Tanner (Georgetown, 1990). See below, pp. 87, 90–91.

[2] Thomas Wright, *The Latin Poems Commonly Attributed to Walter Mapes* (London, 1841), pp. 171–82 (pp. 171–73: *De concubinis sacerdotum* = *Prisciani regula*; pp. 174–79: *Consultatio sacerdotum* = *Clerus et presbiteri*; and pp. 180–82: *De conuocatione sacerdotum* = *Nouus rumor Anglie*). For PR, Wright used **Ht** and Flacius Illyricus, *Varia doctorum piorumque virorum de corrupto Ecclesiae statu poemata* (Basel, 1557), pp. 236–38; for NR he used used **Vt** and **Tx**.

[3] Olga Dobiache-Rojdesvensky, *Les poésies des Goliards* (Paris, 1931), pp. 127–30 (*Prisciani regula*) and 130–39 (*Clerus et presbiteri*, extracts).

[4] Paul Lehmann, *Die Parodie im Mittelalter*, 2nd ed. (Stuttgart, 1963).

Walther,[5] and Ziolkowski.[6] This neglect may be due to the tendency for histories of Medieval Latin to end with the twelfth century, and perhaps to a feeling that such poems were parochial and not worthy of much attention.

For the sake of clarity I have chosen to refer to the poems by their first lines rather than by the titles given by Wright (*De convocatione sacerdotum*, *Consultatio sacerdotum*, and *De concubinis sacerdotum*) which do not help to distinguish the poems and are unlikely to be authorial. The *Nouus Rumor* (NR) is called in **T** *Consilium* (perhaps for *Concilium*) *sacerdotum* at its opening in stanza 7 and its end at stanza 36.4. In **Bd** it is called *Examinacio sacerdotum propter concubinas*, **Tx** calls it *Quedam conuocacio sacerdotis*, and **Vt** *De concilio quodam circa matrimonium clericorum*. *Prisciani regula* (PR) is called by Flacius *Rhythmi de sacerdotali coniugio* and in his preface "in sacerdotalis coniugii favorem."[7] **Ho** calls it *Allegacio cuiusdam presbiteri*.

The Poems: Setting

All three poems are written in quatrains of the regular Goliardic line (7pp + 6p, rhyming *aaaa*); the *Clerus et Presbyteri*, as the notes indicate, is frequently deficient in the rhythms and length of lines. The topic in all three is the opposition of the clergy to attempts to ban clerical marriage or concubinage; if any satire is intended, it is directed not so much at the pope or the corrupt church (as Flacius seems to have hoped judging from the title of his edition), but at the clergy who have only one thing on their minds, i.e. sex. The themes are similar in all the poems, but their narratives and structures vary widely.

The *Nouus Rumor*, in its longest version (**Bd**), reports a rumour that spread through England commanding all priests and clergy to assemble, and they realize that it must concern their concubines. They have little confidence in their delegate and fix on a date (specifically in **Tx**, a Friday) and they assemble in a big meadow. They take their turns to speak (stanzas 9–39), concluding with a chaplain (stanzas 37–47 only in **Bd**). There is uproar and everyone leaves. A day is fixed for the obligatory meeting (stanzas 42–46). The pope takes his seat and addresses them, ending by saying that married priests are excommunicated. They are dumbfounded (**Bd** ends at stanza 47.3).

The *Prisciani regula* has no setting to explain the occasion of the protest, and there is no structure for the order of speakers: many of the stanzas are unconnected to each other. There may be the trace of an original structure in stanza 6, which begins "Ita

---

[5] Hans Walther, *Das Streitgedicht in der lateinischen Literatur des Mittelalters*, 2nd ed., with additions by Paul G. Schmidt (Hildesheim, 1984), p. 143.

[6] Jan Ziolkowski, *Alan of Lille's Grammar of Sex* (Cambridge, Mass., 1985), pp. 68–69.

[7] See above, n. 2.

quidam presbiter"; this "certain priest" appears to speak the whole of stanzas 6–19 along with the conclusion, which is a prayer implying a victory for the "married" clergy.

The *Clerus et presbyteri* also lacks a setting for the debate, but it does have a narrative structure for the clergy to present their case. Unlike NR (in the **Bd** version), CP has an ending that shows the clergy winning the argument. Stanza 1: Clergy and priests sit sadly in the chapterhouse, worried that the *praesul* wants to remove their maids. Stanzas 2–5: The dean and the "doctor" speak about the threat; stanzas 6–10: an argument follows between an old man and the chanter, which is interrupted by the cellarer, causing general amusement; stanzas 11–13: these are followed by a scholar, a builder, and a canon; stanzas 14–15: the rotation comes round to priests, the first one skilled in canon law; stanzas 16–36: each speaker takes his turn up to the twentieth (at stanza 36); stanzas 37–44: a monk concludes the series, giving biblical precedents and arguing that the pope has approved of the declension of *sacerdos* in the feminine; thus all priests will be able to have multiple female companions.

Personnel

Decrees against wives or concubines were addressed to bishops, priests, or any of the clergy (Nicaea, 325); to priests, deacons, and subdeacons (First Lateran, 1123); to those in the rank of subdeacon and above (Second Lateran, 1139) and to clerics in holy orders (Third Lateran, 1179). The poems reflect these categories. NR mentions *clerici*, *presbiteri*, *sacerdotes*), and at stanza 24.3 the audience is addressed as *decani* and *presbiteri*. PR also refers to only *presbiteri* and *clerici*, and the final speaker says that he has spoken *pro clericis* and *pro presbiteris* and asks them to pray for him. CP, however, shows a different picture: the speakers of stanzas 2–13 seem more appropriate to a religious community, including *capituli doctor et praelatus* (stanza 4.1), followed by a *senior* (stanza 6.1), *cantor* (stanza 7.1), *cellarius* (stanza 9.1), *scholasticus* (stanza 11.1), *structuarius* (stanza 12.1), and *canonicus* (stanza 13.1). At this point the rotation comes to priests, apparently implying (though surely wrongly and thus perhaps indicating a separate origin for the list) that the earlier list had not included any priests. The terms for this group vary slightly and have correspondences with the matching stanzas in NR. After stanzas 14–15, most are called *presbiteri*, but some roles are specified or different terms are used, e.g. *vicarius* (stanza 17.1), *sacrificus* (stanza 22), and *pauper commodista* (stanza 32, an assistant priest). The concluding speaker (stanza 37, perhaps responsible for all the remaining stanzas) is a *monachus praedicator* (presumably a monk/preacher rather than a Dominican friar). His last inclusive stanza lists all the religious who will now be able to have multiple concubines: *clerici*, *monachi*, *canonici*, *decani*, and *praelati* (stanza 44). The large range of terms and offices in CP may simply be a way of varying an otherwise tedious list of *presbiteri*.

When the clerics defend their women, they have different names for them. One is personal (*Malota*; NR, stanza 13.4). Often simple pronouns are used (*mea, nostra*, etc.) or more general nouns, e.g. *puella, mulier, femina*, and the morally neutral *socia* (CP, stanza 26.3) and acceptable *uxor* (NR, stanzas 20.4 and 34.4) and *coniux* (NR, stanzas 28.2, 30.4, 31.4). Although probably disapproving when the pope uses it in 45.4, *concubina* seems to have no moral overtones (NR, stanzas 12.2, 24.2 and 4, 27.4; or CP, stanzas 15.2, 21.3, 30.3, 44.1). Interestingly, CP, but not NR or PR, uses a range of words from domestic service to describe the concubines: *famula* (stanzas 3.1, 4.4, 6.3, 13.4, 29.4, 31.3, 32.4), *ancillula* (stanza 1.3), *coqua* (stanzas 8.2, 9.4, 17.4, 21.2, 28.1). At CP, stanza 31.3–4, it seems that one *famula* is worth three pretty *scorta*.

The principal target of the clerics' outrage is the pope, but only PR specifies Innocent III (1198–1216). In NR he is referred to throughout as *papa* (stanza 1.4, etc.) or *dominus papa* (stanzas 10.3, 15.2). Sometimes the legate is given as an alternative (stanzas 10.3, 29.3, 41.2); he is not given any other title. In PR the author of the clerics' concerns is *presul* (stanzas 1.4, 10.3), but also *pontifex* (stanza 2.1); he is addressed as *Romane pontifex* in stanza 7.3 and referred to by name as *Innocencius* in stanza 8.1. In CP, however, he is hardly ever referred do as *papa* except at stanzas 42.1 and 43.1, where he is specified as the person who established the legal precedent they need. Otherwise he is *praesul* (stanzas 1.3, 8.4, etc.), *pontifex* (stanzas 2.3, 27.2), or *praelatus* (stanzas 6.3, 19.2, 21.2, 44.3). The author of CP may have intended the words to mean "bishop," perhaps indicating a diocesan bishop. Where NR and CP "share" a stanza, we get CP *praeses* for *domini pape* (stanza 3.3) and *praelatus* for *dominus papa uel legatus* (stanza 21.2) and *pontifex* for *papa* (stanza 27.2). The charge that the pope fathered a son on his sister (CP, stanza 42.4) may be a grammatical joke.

The papal legate is mentioned (not by name) several times in NR (stanzas 6.4, 9.3, 10.3, etc.), frequently paired with the pope (*papa uel legatus*) and *legatus* is in rhyme position four times. He is mentioned only once in CP (stanza 3.3, in rhyming position in a stanza closely related to NR, stanza 10). Only once (NR, stanza 6.1) is the legate given a separate function, i.e. of fining those who fail to attend the meeting. He is probably anonymous because the poets did not know his identity, or because they were reluctant to offend him, or because finding suitable rhymes for his name might have been too difficult. The most likely candidate in 1215 is Pandulf, later bishop of Norwich, though Durand, a Templar, was one of the negotiators between the pope and King John in 1211. Also, in Rome a settlement was reached between King John and the pope (resigning England and Ireland to papal suzerainty), which was ratified by Nicholas, cardinal bishop of Tusculum, also a legate. Doubtless, a papal legate (never mentioned in PR) would have had some role in spreading the pope's wishes to major churches and abbeys.

Content and Structure

This is not the place (nor the poem) to look for serious theological arguments about clerical celibacy. For the most part, in NR and CP the individual speakers simply assert that they will not give up their girls (e.g. NR, stanzas 13.3–4, 22.3–4, etc.); others defy the pope by stating that these are "old" ideas (CP, stanza 20.2; compare also the proverb cited at NR, stanza 17), or that this is an out-of-date concept (NR, stanza 19.3–4). The ban on wives, they argue, is unjust, as sexual activity is natural (PR, stanzas 6, 9, 15, 16, 18) and we were born from men and their wives (NR, stanza 16.3–4). Men need women (CP, stanza 12.2–3) and only angels are chaste (CP, stanza 5). A sterile field is useless, and anyone who does not like ploughing is crazy. Many speakers have medical needs (NR, stanza 27.3–4 = CP, stanza 30.3–4), and warm blood requires warmth of flesh (NR, stanza 20 = CP, stanza 24 and NR, stanza 28.3–4). The Pope should realize that all priests live immorally (NR, stanza 21; CP, stanza 35). If priests lack wives for themselves, they will go after the wives, daughters, and nieces of others (PR, stanzas 3, 14). Conjugal sex also keeps one from unnatural sin, as in NR, stanza 33.3–4, and implicitly PR, stanza 1. Biblical stories supply many examples: Abraham and Sara (NR, stanza 38), Solomon and David (NR, stanza 39), Zacharias (CP, stanza 38 = PR, stanza 11), St. Paul (PR, stanza 12). The Virgin Mary likes faithful servants (CP, stanza 36), and Christ was crucified for the sake of women (CP, stanza 37). In CP the sixth priest says that if he is condemned with his concubine, only he is guilty (CP, stanza 21 = NR, stanza 15). The seventh claims that if he is forced to abstain from his wife, the pope ought to pay compensation (CP, stanza 22).

The three poems vary in their structures. NR and CP are narrative, with a sequence of speakers; CP is very careful in the order of speaking (using ordinal numbers), but NR goes astray at stanza 20, ascribed to *alter*, where CP has the correct *undecimus*. PR, however, does not keep to a formal order of speaking, but its stanza 6, beginning "Ita quidam presbiter," may betray a tradition in which they spoke in turn. The narrative styles of NR and CP lend themselves to addition and digression: in NR speakers interrupt each other, and the assembly and its bustle are described in some detail (stanzas 1–9, 12, 24, 16, 25). In CP the digressions are frequently comic: in stanzas 6–10 an older cleric says that he is weak for battle but will still be fine. The chanter rebukes him for not thinking of others who are being deprived of their fun. The old man is confused and blushes, and changes his statement to say that he will not set aside his cook but will conceal her for a while "for laymen's sake and to beguile the *praesul*." At this the cellarer says that he would like to exchange his one-eyed whore for the old man's cook. Then everyone laughs at the cellarer's cunning in wanting to get rid of his own woman in favour of the old man's pretty girl. As I have already stated, these poems are comic and entertaining. If satire is intended, it is not against the papacy or traditional morality, but against the clerics themselves, who have only one thing on their minds, that is, sex. There are jokes aplenty, of which the neatest is the play on the word *declinare* in its senses of grammatical declension of a noun and the laying down of a woman for intercourse; this is used not only to rebuke the pope for bad grammar in abolishing the feminine gender of *sacerdos* (PR, stanza 1), but also to infer that his approval of the feminine declension of *sacerdos* in the approval of a candidate for the priesthood (CP, stanza 42) means that he thus approves of the sexual activities of the clergy. Some of the jokes found their way into the vernacular: the bawdy use of *quoniam* (PR, stanza 7.1–2) appears in Chaucer's *Wife of Bath's* Prologue (Canterbury Tales D 607–608: "And trewely, as myne housbondes tolde me, | I had the beste *quoniam* mighte be),[8] and the expression "diuina faciat ulcio me cecum" (NR, stanza 14.3–4) reappears as Cockney slang in the nineteenth century, namely "Gorblimey" ("God blind me").[9]

Place and Date of Composition

In the NR it is quite clear that the setting is England; it begins with a rumour spreading through *Anglie partes* (stanza 1.1) and the chaplain in stanza 33.2 says he was born in England. Also, stanza 35.3 alludes to the end of the Interdict and England's subjection to the papacy, when the pope is reported as having taken English *redditus*, i.e. income. The absence of these allusions from PR and CP is probably insignificant, as there is normally no need to specify to your audience where you are writing. All manuscripts of the NR are English, and all but two of PR (the two printed versions **F** and **Bp**), whose origins are unknown.

As the poems (and parts of them) may have been written at different times, it is impossible to be precise about the date of composition. Celibacy had been enjoined on those in holy orders (*in clero*) since the First Nicaean Council (325) and reaffirmed frequently and progressively more adamantly, as in First Lateran (1123), par. 7: "presbyteris, diaconibus vel subdiaconibus concubinarum et uxorum contubernia penitus interdicimus et aliarum mulierum cohabitationem." This was strengthened further by Pope Alexander III in 1179 in the Third Lateran, par. 11. As Lehmann noted, Gerald of Wales in the *Gemma Ecclesiastica* (ca. 1197),[10] while stating that a priest could not be absolved from a vow of celibacy except by a general council, also stressed his opposition to celibacy, mentioning that clerical marriage was

---

[8] *The Works of Geoffrey Chaucer*, ed. Walter W. Skeat, *The Canterbury Tales*, 2nd ed. (Oxford, 1900).

[9] *The Supplement to the Oxford English Dictionary* (Oxford, 1987) and Eric Partridge, *The Penguin Dictionary of Historical Slang* (Harmondsworth, 1972, first published in 1937) both say it is nineteenth century, mainly Cockney.

[10] Gerald of Wales, *Gemma Ecclesiastica*, Dist. II, ch. 6 (London, 1861–1891), Rolls Series 21/2:187–91.

not originally forbidden and was still practised in the Greek church. The issue was clearly very hot by the time of the Fourth Lateran (1215). Moreover, Pope Innocent III made clear his intentions to enforce the prohibition, and several local English councils were active in promoting celibacy in the early thirteenth century, as seen in Roger of Hoveden's *Chronica*[11] and Benedict of Peterborough's *Gesta Henrici secundi*.[12]

Lehmann favoured a date around 1200 for the poems, but there are some pointers to IV Lateran itself for at least parts of the poems: 1) the last part of NR (in **Bd** only, written in the first half of the fifteenth century, a section of the poem unknown to Lehmann[13]) says that the pope's sermon was on the Faith and the Trinity (NR, stanza 45.1–2). This corresponds exactly to IV Lateran, ch. 1, and does not seem to be in any other conciliar account; 2) **Ht** (saec. xiv, early) of the PR has four stanzas (2–5) which are not in any other manuscript and which do not contribute to the celibacy debate: PR, stanza 4, concerns Bacchus, i.e. the evils of drinking, which is the subject of IV Lateran, ch. 15: "a crapula et ebrietate omnes clerici diligenter abstineant," which is not, as far as I can see, in any other papal rebuke. It is, however, in several English ordinances, such as the Statutes of Canterbury (1213–1214), written under Stephen Langton, in which clerics are told not to visit taverns or to engage in public drinking where lewd songs are sung. Even if a date of 1215 is not certain for the composition of the poem, it is fairly safe to say that 16 July 1216 (when Innocent III died) is the *terminus ad quem*, unless PR, stanza 7.4, is a very tasteless joke: "Ne in tanto crimine moriaris, cave." Also relevant to the date is an allusion to the settlement of the Interdict in 1213, when Gervase of Canterbury states in his *Chronaca*: "Johannes rex Angliae dedit Romanae ecclesiae, non nomine tributi sed munificenciae, redditum de Anglia et Hibernia, de Anglia DCC marcarum, de Hibernia CCC."[14] This seems to be alluded to at NR, stanza 35.3: "Papa tollit redditus et res diuinorum."[15]

---

[11] Roger of Hoveden, *Chronica*, IV (London, 1871), Rolls Series 51:134.

[12] Benedict of Peterborough, *Gesta Henrici secundi* (London, 1867), Rolls Series 49/2:234.

[13] Lehmann used Wright's edition which is based only on manuscripts **Vt** and **Tx**.

[14] Gervase of Canterbury, *Chronaca* (London, 1879–1890), Rolls Series 73/2:108.

[15] The allusion in CP, stanza 15, to a Clementine is a distraction; if it refers to a decree in the collection of Pope Clement V (1264–1314), known as *liber septimus*, it must be dated to after 1317, when the decree was incorporated after Clement's death. It could conceivably refer to the Clementine literature, fabulous material related about St. Clement, first bishop of Rome, ca. 90 A.D., which includes in the "Recognitiones" a repudiation of celibacy; it could also be the name of the speaker's girl-friend ("you know this Clementine of mine") like Malota in NR, stanza 13.4. Most likely, as Lehmann suggests, it refers to the first-century Pope Clement I, whose decrees are now called pseudo-Isidorean "canones per Clementem papam prolati." They are collected in PL 130.

Transmission of the Texts

There is no adequate criterion for authenticity that would help to establish a clear picture of the transmission of the texts. The only thing that is sure, in all versions, is the maintenance of the rhymes (or at least the rhyming syllables); the regularity of the Goliardic stanza and line (4: 7pp + 6p; *aaaa*) is maintained throughout NR and PR, but in CP fails in over 25% of the poem, as the notes show. Even variation among individual manuscripts of each poem rarely betrays an obvious error and never indicates a textual relationship. For example, there is no clear evidence for where the NR poem actually ends, and thus whether the conclusive **Bd** text is the original (and all the others witnesses simply deficient) or **Bd** made up a new ending to fill the gaps in the other manuscripts. The absence of any mention of England in CP and the different terms for the concubines between CP and other texts reveals nothing about the "real," i.e. original, texts. First we need to clarify the main characteristics of the three poems.

Lehmann writes: "Sie (i.e. the three poems) … gehen vielleicht alle auf eine Satire zurück,"[16] and Dobiache-Rojdesvensky states even more confidently: "il est certain qu'un seul texte, qui remonte au XIIe siècle, se trouve à la base de tous."[17] It is fair to state that neither scholar had access to the fuller range of manuscripts listed by Walther's *Initia*,[18] but all three poems are quite separate entities, with different shapes, different openings, and different conclusions. PR, which follows no particular order in the arguments, ends with an appeal to the audience to pray for him and his sweetheart; CP cites the pope's acceptance of a candidate for the priesthood because he was able correctly to decline *sacerdos* in the masculine, feminine, and neuter: as the pope has the power to loose and bind, all of them will now be free to have as many wives as they want. On the other hand, the conclusion of NR (in **Bd** alone) describes the historically accurate decision that all married priests are *ipso facto* excommunicated, to the great dismay of all the clerics. In CP the names for the architect of their problems ("pope" in NR and CP) is variously "bishop," rarely "pope." In CP the female companion (commonly wife, companion, etc. in NR and PR) is often a term for a serving girl (*ancilla, coqua*). Independence of minor variants is evident in NR and PR even in individual manuscripts where the words are not confirmed by rhyme. The order of stanzas varies from one manuscript to another (see

---

[16] Lehmann, *Die Parodie*, p. 112.

[17] Dobiache-Rojdesvensky, *Les poésies des Goliards*, p. 121.

[18] Hans Walther, *Initia carminum ac versuum medii aevi posterioris latinorum*, 2nd ed. (Göttingen, 1969), nos. 762, 5014, 14460, 16022, 19433, 20322, 20325.

charts of the manuscripts of NR and PR).[19] That is, scribes/adaptors have freedom to introduce new ideas at will, subject only to the rhymes, which are always maintained.

Despite this "licence to invent" and the clear separation of NR, PR, and CP as distinct poems, there are contra-indications of some relationship between them. These are the sharing of stanzas between NR and CP and between PR and CP, and are presumably what Dobiache-Rojdesvensky refers to when she writes: "Leur parenté foncière se révèle dans l'identité de strophes entières."[20] There are two groups: 1) between NR, stanzas 9–27 and CP, stanzas 2–30, in which the two poems share fourteen stanzas, as shown in the "Summary Chart of Correspondences" below (p. 94), that is, they share at least the rhyme (either the rhyming word or rhyme-syllable) and sometimes the same words and sense; and 2) between PR, stanza 11 (= CP, stanza 38) and PR, stanza 15 (= CP, stanza 40). There is also a resemblance between PR, stanza 1 and CP, stanza 42. Group (1) falls in the section of NR which is represented only by **Bd** and **T** (as **Tx** ends at stanza 19 and **Vt** had ended before stanza 30). It is impossible to know how this happened, but it seems very likely that NR preceded CP: stanza 24 in NR reads

> In has uoces irruit alter repentinas:
> "Concubine gremio psallo matutinas.
> Decani (or Romani), presbiteri, propter breues minas
> Vultis vos dimittere vestras concubinas?"

The corresponding stanza in CP (28) reads:

> Protulit tredecimus: "Coquas repentinas
> Nolumus dimittere propter breues minas.
> Fideles in omnibus nostras concubinas,
> Quae mane pectore pulsant matutinas."

The variant in NR, stanza 24.3 (**T**) "the threats of the Roman priest" makes sense, even if it sounds Protestant, but the CP version is nonsense, unless "hasty cooks" has a meaning that is unknown to me.[21] Most probably, the CP reviser simply constructed a new stanza from the rhymes that he remembered. If so, it illustrates that rhyme, rather than sense, was dominant in the transmission of the poem: it was the rhymes that fixed it in the memories of its reciters and transmitters, and sometimes led them astray. The two stanzas (2) shared by PR and CP contain the key to the whole argument of the poem and were therefore more likely to have been remembered.

---

[19] See below, pp. 98–99 and 119.

[20] Dobiache-Rojdesvensky, *Les poesies des Goliards*, p. 121.

[21] It is conceivable that *repentinas* could be construed with "propter breues minas" – "because of unexpected short threats," but this is unlike how the verses normally work.

Summary Chart of Correspondences

This chart uses the order of the present edition; for orders in different manuscripts of NR and PR, see charts on pp. 98–99 and 119.

NR	CP	PR
1	1	1°
2	2°	2
3	3	3
4	4	4
5	5	5
6	6	6
7	7	7
8	8	8
9°	9	9
10	10	10
11°	11	11°
12°	12	12
13°	13	13
14	14	14
15°	15	15°
16	16°	16
17	17	17
18	18°	18
19	19	(**D**)
20°	20°	19
21	21°	
22	22	
23	23	
24	24°	
25	25	
26	26	
27°	27	
28	28	
29	29	
30	30°	
31	31	
32	32	
33	33	
34	34	
35	35	
36	36	
37	37	
38	38°	
39	39	
40	40°	
41	41	
42	42°	
43	43	
44	44	
45.1–3		

The freedom of individual manuscripts to change the words (while maintaining the rhymes) is seen everywhere in NR and PR.[22] For example, NR, stanza 2.3: seua **Bd**, fera **Tx**, noua **Vt**; NR, stanza 7.2: plus quam centum **TTx**, tria plusquam **Bd**, plusquam decem **Vt**; NR, stanza 12.3: Et quam modo teneo **VtT**: Vnam michi teneo **Bd**, Et quas mecum tenui **Tx**. See also further examples in textual apparatus for minor differences at NR, stanzas 13.4, 14.1, 15.2, 16.2, 18.2, 19.4, 26.3, 27.2, 27.4, 28.2, 28.4, 32.4, 35.4, 36.4. At stanza 24.3 the difference between **Bd**'s vocative "Decani, presbiteri" and **T**'s genitive "Romani presbiteri" affects the sense considerably. In PR the variant readings often offer radically different senses: see notes to PR, stanzas 8.3 (**HoHt**), 10.2 (**Ho**), 10.3 (**Ht**), 11.2 (**BpF**), and also 6.4; 7.1; 9.3. No pattern emerges among these variants; any of them could be the result of an individual's preference. Much the same absence of a pattern is seen in the shared stanzas of CP and individual manuscripts of NR: e.g. 2.4: metuo CP: timet **TxVt**, timens **Bd**; 3.4 damnati CP, **BdVt**, grauati **T**; note also the change from second person plural (NR) to first person plural (CP). There are many others.

Similarly, there is wide divergence among the number and order of stanzas in each manuscript of the poems. NR (extant in four manuscripts) has seventeen stanzas in **Tx**, seventeen (not the same) in **Vt**, thirty in **T**, and forty-seven in **Bd** (with its entirely unexpected conclusion). Stanza 4 is in **Tx** alone, stanza 6 in **Vt** alone, **T** lacks stanzas 1–6, **Tx** lacks stanza 10; also **Tx** ends at stanza 19, **Vt** at 18, and **T** at 36. In PR, extant in five witnesses (**Ho, Ht, D**, and the almost identical **BpF**), there are eight stanzas in **Ho**, fourteen in **Ht**, fourteen (not the same) in **D**, and thirteen in **BpF**. PR starts at PR, stanza 1 in **Ht** and **BpF**, but at stanza 6 in **DHo**. It ends at stanza 11 in **Ho**, 17 in **Ht**, 19 in **D** (where it is written twice). **Ht** has extra stanzas: 2–5 (on topics unrelated to celibacy) and 17. There is no particular logic to any of these different orders.

More significant than variant readings and different stanza orders is (as mentioned above) the endings of the various versions of the poems. PR ends with a request that the speaker's grateful audience will say a prayer for him and his girlfriend. CP (after it parts company from NR (at stanza 30, after the shared stanzas) continues with the usual refusals to separate from their female, companions and then concludes in confidence of a verdict in their favour, now that the pope has approved the proper declension of "priest" in both masculine and feminine, and has himself produced a son from a daughter (probably a grammatical joke); now they may all have as many concubines as they like. NR, however, has as many endings as it has manuscripts: most, as we have seen above, end in mid-stream without a conclusion, except for **Bd**, which reports the gloomy but historically correct finale, the defrocking of all married

---

[22] For the freedom which some scribes treated their texts, see A.G. Rigg, *Gawain on Marriage (De coniuge non ducenda)* (Toronto, 1986), "Scribal Intervention and Wit," pp. 54–57.

clergy. Could this be the "original" conclusion? More likely, it was just another individual departure, one intended to provide a neat ending to what the other manuscripts had left unfinished (perhaps having simply no known version to follow or having forgotten what it was). Despite the late date of **Bd** (in this section, after 1439), it was probably composed at the time of the final decision of the Fourth Lateran in 1215 and remembered by its scribe, Dodsthorp, as a well-known song on a popular topic. On the other hand, it remains quite possible that **Bd** (despite its frequently careless copying and its late date) actually preserves the "original" poem.

There are two apparent anomalies in the stanza orders. Both NR and CP try to indicate the sequence of speakers by the use of ordinal numbers between NR, stanzas 11–27 and CP, stanzas 16–30. The order of CP agrees fairly closely with that of NR, as the chart shows:

Stanza and Speaker in NR	Stanza and Speaker in CP	Rhyme
11 alter presbiter	16 unus presbyter	-ali
	17 vicarius, secundus	-undus
12 alter consors	18 tertius	-entum
	19 quartus	-ato
13 quintus	20 quintus	-ita
14 quintus (continued)		-ecum
15 alter	21 sextus	-atus
16 septimus	22 septimus	-ere
17 alter	23 octaui	-entum (NR), -ata (CP)
18 nonus		-onus
19 decimus		-etus
20 alter	24 nonus	-orem
21 undecimus	25 decimus	-este
22 duodecimus	26 undecimus	-ectus
23 duodecimus (continued)	27 duodecimus	-ore
24 alter	28 tredecimus	-inas
25 capellanus	29 decimusquartus	-anus
26 capellanus (continued)		-ura
27 capellanus (continued)	30 quindecimus	-ina

The intrusion of the ubiquitous *alter* ("another," "the other," "the second") between *decimus* (NR, stanza 19) and *undecimus* (NR, stanza 21) disturbs an otherwise correct numerical sequence, one supported by CP. On the other hand, there is nothing to prove whether the CP order is original or the result of a desire of the CP's reviser to improve the text.

The second "anomaly" occurs at CP, stanza 34, which is not in NR or PR. It is hard to see why "this religious order of the *praesul*," if it refers to Innocent III's ban on concubines, is not injurious to the wives of citizens. The stanza would be better placed after CP, stanza 15, which alludes to the decree of the first-century Clement's order that a bishop or priest should not reject a wife on the grounds of their religion: the danger would consist in the perils of unmarried priests who might be a threat to other married couples. Once again, we have no way of confirming the misplacement.

Memorial Transmission

The preceding pages have stressed the importance of the rhymes and rhyming syllables, which seem to be immune from variation, even in stanzas that differ in meaning and content from their equivalent stanzas in other manuscripts: these rhymes appear to be constant in all versions of the poems, even the "shared" stanzas of NR and CP. This seems to be a sign of stability in a textually chaotic tradition. Sometimes the rhyming words themselves differ, but the rhyming syllables remain constant, even where the sense itself is strained, as in CP, stanza 28, which is almost nonsense beside its source NR, stanza 24 (see above, p. 93), as if the adaptor did not care about the sense, as long as the words ended in *-inas*. This seems to me to indicate memorial transmission: the scribe knew that they must rhyme in *-inas*, whatever the sense. The same thing occurs when children learn a hymn, filling in mental blanks with the right sound, regardless of sense. Conversely, there was considerable freedom in the non-rhyming positions, as is seen in the great variations described above (p. 95). It is as though, in the absence of rhymes the scribe was free to extemporize at will: he was not bound to a written and established text as a simple copyist was. The opportunities for the introduction of new ideas and even episodes (as in the comic scenes in CP between the old man and the others) were unlimited; similarly, PR was able to introduce four stanzas (2–5), which do not even touch on the theme of celibacy. Thus, the fixed rhymes made possible a greater flexibility in other areas.

Much the same – evidence for memorial transmission and greater freedom for additional ideas and jokes – is evident in the extremely popular *De coniuge non ducenda*,[23] another lighthearted poem which may have circulated in witty, imaginative, and totally irreverent places such as universities. The parallel may be in the back of buses of football teams, where parodies of hymns are common, just as they were in Medieval Latin.

---

[23] See above, n. 22.

Nouus Rumor Anglie

Manuscripts

Bd   Oxford, Bodleian Library, MS Bodley 851 (scribe Dodsthorp, after 1439), fols. 75va–76rb.[24]

Tx   London, British Library, MS Cotton Titus A.XX (ca. 1367–1400), fols. 167ra–167rb.[25]

T   Cambridge, Trinity College, MS O.2.45 (saec. XIII, after 1248), pp. 342–344.

Vt   London, British Library, MS Cotton Vitellius A.X. (after 1248, Lichfield, annals to 1325, material of 1454, mandate of Edward IV, 1466).

Bd contains stanzas 1–47.3 (lacks stanzas 4 and 6); **Tx** contains stanzas 1–19 (lacks stanzas 6 and 10); **T** contains stanzas 7–36; **Vt** contains stanzas 1–18.2 (lacks stanza 4).

Edition

Wright, *The Latin Poems Commonly Attributed to Walter Mapes*, pp. 180–82, from **Tx** and **Vt**.

Order of Stanzas

	Bd	**Tx**	**T**	**Vt**
1. Nouus rumor Anglie	1	1		1
2. Per uillas iuit	2	2		2
3. Cogitant presbiteri	3	3		3
4. Sexta dies domini		4		
5. Sacerdotes confluunt	4	5		4
6. Leue quid est dicere				5
7. Partibus ex omnibus	5	6	1	6
8. Locus ad quem uenerant	6	7	2	7
9. Posito silencio	7	8	3	8
10. Pro nostris uxoribus	8		4	9
11. Surgit alter presbiter	9	9	5	10
12. Alter consors irruit	10	10	6	11
13. Surgit quintus presbiter	12	11	7	12
14. Quicquid papa cogitat	11	12	8	13

---

[24] A.G. Rigg, "Medieval Latin Poetic Anthologies (II)," *Mediaeval Studies* 40 (1978), 387–407, at p. 391. This article was reprinted, with corrections, in *Piers Plowman. A Facsimile of the Z-Text in Bodleian Library, Oxford, MS Bodley 851*, ed. Charlotte Brewer and A.G. Rigg (Cambridge, 1994), pp. 25–42.

[25] A.G. Rigg, "Medieval Latin Poetic Anthologies (I)," *Mediaeval Studies* 39 (1977), 281–330, at p. 308.

15. Ex hinc loqui presbiter	13	13	9	14
16. Septimus hinc presbiter	14	14	10	15
17. Alter capur erigit	15	15	11	16
18. Papa noster arbiter	16	16	12	17.1–2
19. Decimus probabilis	17	17	13	
20. Alter ait ueterem	18		14	
21. Presbiter undecimus	19		15	
22. Ad hoc duodecimus	20		16	
23. Unusquisque loquitur	21		17	
24. In has uoces irruit	22		18	
25. Turbarum de medio	23		19	
26. Cogitare possumus	26		20	
27. Nam cum bibo siceram	24		21	
28. Oculis si dedero	25		22	
29. Vestris rationibus	27		23	
30. Postquam noui semitas	28		24	
31. Tractat fila Lachesis	29		25	
32. Cum dicatur Atropos	30		26	
33. Ne sint in ambiguo	31		27	
34. Verberare possumus	32		28	
35. Papa cum sit dominus	33		29	
36. Cuncta rerum genera	34		30	
37. Si fas esse dicere	35			
38. Vt uir sit cum femina	36			
39. Salomon rex sapiens	37			
40. Ex his clamor oritur	38			
41. Certus est presbiteris	39			
42. Quando pedes domini	40			
43. Papa sedet cathedra	41			
44. Tunc sub Christi baculo	42			
45. Tunc fatur apercius	43			
46. Concordat quas predicat	44			
47. Alter spectat alterum	45.1–3			

Nouus Rumor: *Revised Edition*

1. Nouus rumor Anglie partes peragrauit:
   Clericos presbiteros omnes excitauit
   Quos bonis ecclesie fortuna ditauit.
   Omnes ut citati sint – sic papa mandauit.

   BdTxVt. 1.1 Nouus rumor **BdTx**: Rumor nouus **Vt**; peragrauit **Bd**: pergirauit **Tx**, pererrauit **Vt**

2. Per uillas iuit rumor atque per castella,
   Domni pape baiulans mandata nouella.
   Nascitur presbiteris hinc seua procella:
   Quisque timet grauiter pro sua puella.

   BdTxVt. 2.1 iuit rumor **Bd**: unus rumor **Tx**, hic rumor it **Vt** ‖ 2.3 hinc seua **Bd**: hinc fera **Tx**, hec noua **Vt** ‖ 2.4 timet **TxVt**: timens **Bd**

3. Cogitant presbiteri super hoc mandato
   Et confidunt modicum de suo legato.
   Statuunt concilium die nominato,
   Tractent ut uelocius de uerbo prefato.

   BdTxVt. 3.2 Et **BdTx**: Nam **Vt**; suo **BdTx**: nostro **Vt** ‖ 3.3–4 **VtTx**: *trans.* **Bd** ‖ 3.4 Tractent ut **Tx**: Tractant ut **Bd**, Vt tractent **Vt**

4. Sexta dies domini confertur uenire –
   Heu dies miserie atque dies ire!
   Ad hanc quisque studeat sic se preuenire,
   Vt ad celi gloriam possit peruenire.

   Tx at foot of fol. 167r with a *caret* mark.

5. Sacerdotes confluunt atque capellani;
   Tendunt ad concilium iuuenes et cani.
   Qui non ibi uenerit cordis est uesani,
   Vel est boni nesciens, capitis uel uani.

   BdTxVt (**Bd** order of verses: 1342). 5.1 confluunt **TxVt**: profluunt **Bd** ‖ 5.2 ad **BdVt**: at **Tx**; concilium **BdVt**: consilium **Tx** ‖ 5.3 uenerit **Vt**: fuerit **Tx**, uenerat **Bd** ‖ 5.4 = **Tx**, Aut est boni nesciens capitis uel uani **Bd**, Vel est sensus nescius capitis uel uani **Vt**

6. Leue quid est dicere, set[1] non est leue scire:
   Cerneres presbiteros undique uenire.
   Nam si quis noluerit ad hoc consentire,
   Legatus in loculo uellet hunc punire.

   Vt.

English Translation

1. A rumour's spread through England's bounds
   That priests and clerks alike astounds:
   Those who with church's gifts are blest
   Are summoned at the Pope's behest.

2. Through towns and castles runs the shout,
   The Pope's new mandates bearing out.
   From these a storm now comes to pass:
   Each priest is worried for his lass.

3. This summons makes the priesthood meditate:
   They've little faith in their own delegate.[a]
   They call a council and they fix a day
   To talk about it all without delay.

4. Day Six[b] is now assigned for them to meet,
   A day, alas, of misery and grief.
   Each one should strive to hurry for this date
   To get to heaven's bliss and celebrate.

5. The priests and chaplains rush, the count untold.
   And hurry to the council, young and old.
   Whoever isn't there has lost his mind,
   Is empty-headed or lacks moral guide.

6. To speak is easy, but to know is not:
   From everywhere you'd see priests on the trot.
   If anyone the summons should decline,
   The legate would, in cash, impose a fine.

7. Partibus ex omnibus ruit hic et ille,
   Sacerdotes numero plus quam centum mille.
   Non tam spisse nubibus imbris cadunt stille,
   Nec uolant ab ignibus tam spisse scintille.

   BdTxTVt. 7.1 ex **BdTx**: ab **TVt**; ruit **BdTxT**: eunt **Vt** ‖ 7.2 plus quam centum **TxT**: tria plusquam **Bd**, plusquam decem **Vt** ‖ 7.3 imbris cadunt **TVt**: cadunt imbris **Bd**, imbris *corr. ex* imbres **Tx** ‖ 7.4 Nec **BdTVt**: Non **Tx**

8. Locus ad quem uenerant fuit grande pratum,
   Ad tale concilium forte destinatum.
   Collocant in ordine cetum congregatum.
   Nullus ibi laicus habet principatum!

   BdTxTVt. 8.1 fuit **BdTVt**: fuerit? **Tx** ‖ 8.3 = **Vt**: Collocante ordine cetum congregatum **Bd**, Calcatur in ordine totum congregatum **Tx**, Collocat in ordine cetum congregatum **T**

9. Posito silencio pax tranquilla datur.
   Surgit quidam ueterum primitus et fatur:
   "Fratres, nobis omnibus legatus minatur
   Et post minas metuo quod peius sequatur!

   BdTxTVt. 9.2 et fatur **BdTxVt**: affatur **T** ‖ 9.3 nobis **Bd?TVt**: uobis **Tx**; legatus **TxTVt**: legatum **Bd** ‖ 9.4 Et **BdTVt**: Sed **Tx**; metuo **BdTxT**: timeo **Vt**

10. "Pro nostris uxoribus sumus congregati.
    Videatis prouide quod sitis parati
    Ad mandatum domini pape uel legati
    Respondere grauiter, ne sitis dampnati!"

    BdTVt. 10.1 nostris **TVt**: uestris **Bd** ‖ 10.4 dampnati **BdVt**: grauati **T**

11. Surgit alter presbiter de cetu totali,
    Quem tangebat species generalis mali:
    "Vnam michi teneo sub lege uenali
    Quam nolo dimittere pro sermone tali."

    BdTxTVt. 11.1 alter **BdTVt**: quidam **Tx**; totali (unclear) **Vt** ‖ 11.3 michi **BdTVt**: mecum **Tx**; sub lege **BdTxT**: lege sub **Vt**

7. They rush from everywhere, both short and tall,
   More than a hundred thousand priests in all.
   So many drops of rain don't fall from clouds
   Nor sparks fly up from fires in such crowds.

8. A great big meadow was the place they met,
   For such a council happily well set.
   The gathering was organized with care:
   No layman holds a leading office there!

9. They call for silence; quiet peace ensues.
   An elder rises first, his case pursues:
   "The legate, brothers, threatens all of us,
   And after threats, I fear, will follow worse.

10. We're gathered here together for our wives:
    Take care to be prepared – upon your lives –
    To answer to the mandate of the Pope
    Or of his legate, lest you lose your hope."

11. From all the crowd another priest arose,
    Affected privately by public woes:
    "I have a woman by a legal sale;
    I won't release her for this kind of tale."

12. Alter consors irruit in hoc argumentum:
    "Ego forsan habui concubinas centum,
    Et quam modo teneo carnis ad fomentum
    Non uellem dimittere propter marcas centum."

    BdTxTVt. 12.1 irruit **BdTVt**: erigit **Tx** ‖ 12.2 forsan **TxTVt**: forte **Bd** ‖ 12.3 Et quam modo teneo **TVt**: Vnam michi teneo **Bd**, Et quas mecum tenui **Tx** ‖ 12.4 Non uellem dimittere **TVt**, Quam nolo dimittere **Bd**, Nollem has dimittere **Tx**

13. Surgit quintus presbiter et respondit ita:
    "Hec sunt noua friuola diu satis trita.
    Per reginam glorie que est polo sita,
    Non Malotam deseram, nisi priuer uita.

    BdTxTVt. 13.2 noua **TxTVt**: uerba **B**; diu satis **TxTVt**: satis diu **Bd** ‖ 13.3 polo **BdTVt**: in polo **Tx** ‖ 13.4 Malotam **TxT**: Magotam **Bd**: ...otam **Vt**; nisi priuer uita **Vt** (priuet **T**): donec priuor uita **Bd**, dum me durat uita **Tx**

14. Quicquid papa cogitat uel legatus secum,
    Expertes sunt penitus diuinarum precum,
    Et diuina faciat ulcio me cecum,
    Nisi mea dormiat quaqua nocte mecum!"

    BdTxTVt. 14.1 Quicquid **Bd**: Quid hic **TVt**, Quid hoc **Tx** ‖ 14.3 faciat **TxVt**: faciet **BdT**; cecum **TxTVt**: secum **Bd**
    (After 14.2 **Bd** has "Vultis uos dimittere uestras concubinas" (= 24.4) with mark for transposition.)

15. Ex hinc lequi presbiter alter est paratus:
    "Quid de me uult dominus papa uel legatus?
    Si cum meretricibus fuero mechatus,
    Cogor meos proprios portare reatus."

    BdTxTVt. 15.1 hinc **TxTVt**: hunc? **Bd** ‖ 15.2 Quid de me uult **TxT** (de *sup.l.* **Tx**): Quicquid de me **Bd**, Quid uult de me (unclear) **Vt** ‖ 15.3 meretricibus **BdTxVt**: mulieribus **T** ‖ 15.4 portare **BdTxVt**: partire **T**

16. Septimus hinc presbiter nequibat tacere;
    Dixit quod "Non opus est nobis hinc timere.
    Papa scit et alii qui nos precessere
    Quod nos ab uxoribus uiri genuere."

    BdTxTVt. 16.1 hinc **TxT**: hunc? **Bd**, hic **Vt**; nequibat **TxTVt**: nequiuit **Bd** ‖ 16.2 hinc **Tx**: hec **Bd**, hic **T**, hoc **Vt**; timere **BdTVt**: cauere **Tx**

12. Another rushed into the great debate:
    "I've had about a hundred as a mate.
    The one that I have now for carnal glow
    I wouldn't for a hundred marks let go!"

13. The fifth priest then stood up and thus replied:
    "These are but novelties, though often tried.
    By Heaven's Queen who's set up in the sky,
    I won't give Malotte up, unless I die.

14. Whatever Pope may think, or delegate,
    They have no sense of what God's prayers dictate:
    Now may God's vengeance take away my sight,
    Unless my girl sleeps with me every night."

15. Another priest is ready to debate:
    "What plan for me has Pope or delegate?
    If I should live with whores a life of shame,
    I'm forced myself to bear the weight of blame!"

16. A seventh pushy priest then took his turn
    And said: "There is no need for our concern.
    The Pope and all our predecessors know
    That from wives men begot us long ago."

17. Alter caput erigit, loquens ad conuentum:
    "Satis est terribile sequens argumentum.
    Vetus est prouerbium nostrorum parentum:
    Sacerdotis uxor est Sathane iumentum!"

    BdTxTVt.

18. "Papa noster arbiter est," dicebat nonus
    Presbiter, "et hominum pater et patronus.
    Sed hoc si permiserit, pastor esset bonus
    Quod sacerdos uiueret saltem ut colonus."

    BdTxT (**Vt** 18.1–2). 18.1 arbiter est **BdTVt**: est arbiter **Tx** ‖ 18.2 Presbiter et hominum **TxTVt**: sacerdotum omnium **Bd**; **Vt** ends here at foot of page. ‖ 18.3 pastor esset **TxT**: esset pastor **Bd** ‖ 18.4 saltem ut **TxT**: et saltem **Bd**

19. Decimus probabilis uir atque facetus.
    Inter omnes alios presbiter discretus:
    "Stuprum[2] prohibicio clericis est uetus.
    Tamen proles procreat atque gignit fetus."

    BdTxT. 19.3 blank in **T**; clericis **Tx**: clericus **Bd**; est **Bd**: et **Tx** ‖ 19.4 Tamen proles **T**: Tamen plures **Bd**, Tantum prolem **Tx**; **Tx** ends at this point; stanza 4 is written at the foot of the column in **Tx**.

20. Alter ait: "Veterem non dimittam morem;
    Dedit michi calidum natura cruorem.
    Oportet me uiuere carnis per teporem.
    Nolo derelinquere pro nummis uxorem."

    BdT. 20.3 carnis per **T**: per carnis **Bd** ‖ 20.4 derelinquere **T**: dimittere **Bd**; pro nummis **Bd**: perimens **T**

21. Presbiter undecimus loquitur modeste,
    Tamen uerba talia suscepit moleste:
    "Si papa considerat cuncta manifeste,
    A quo uel a quibus hic uiuitur honeste?"

    BdT. 21.2 Tamen **Bd**: Tantum **T**; suscepit moleste **T**: suscipit modeste **Bd** ‖ 21.3 Si papa **T**: Supra **Bd** ‖ 21.4 = **T**; Hic cum meretricibus uiuit inhoneste **Bd**

22. Ad hoc duodecimus presbiter erectus,
    Artibus uenereis potens et perfectus:
    "Nunquam sine coniuge noster erit lectus,
    Donec me decrepitum faciet senectus.

    BdT. 22.1 Ad hoc **Bd**: Adhuc **T** ‖ 22.2 uenereis **T**: in orneris **Bd**; potens **T**: prudens **Bd** ‖ 22.4 faciet **Bd**: faciat **T**

17. Another raised his voice for all to hear:
    "The consequence is something we should fear.
    Our parents had a dated sentiment,
    That wives of priests are Satan's instrument."

18. "The Pope's our arbiter," the ninth said then,
    "The father and the patron of all men.
    But he'd good shepherd be, if he would give
    That priests should live at least as farmers live."

19. A witty man that one could trust was tenth,
    A priest outstanding for his commonsense:
    "For clerics whoring long has been taboo.
    But it produces kids and breeds them too."

20. Another[c] said: "I will not change my ways:
    From birth I've been warm-blooded all my days.
    My flesh needs constant heat to save my life:
    I won't for any cash give up my wife."

21. Eleventh spoke a priest of manner mild.
    But arguments like this made him quite wild:
    "Now if the Pope weighs everything, he'll see
    How many – even one – lives honestly!"

22. The twelfth priest then continued on his feet.
    In arts of love a mighty man, complete:
    "At no time without wife will be my bed,
    Until old age unmans me, nearly dead!

23. Vnusquisque loquitur nostrum suo more.
    Si nos papa terreat minis uel terrore,
    Respondebo breuiter, sicut sedet ore:
    Carnis est in fulmine[3] qui caret uxore."

    BdT. 23.1 suo **Bd**: sine **T** ‖ 23.2 terrore **Bd**: pauore **T** ‖ 23.3 Respondebo **T**: Respondendo **Bd**; sicut **Bd**: uelut **T**; sedet ore **T**: credet ore **B**

24. In has uoces irruit alter repentinas:
    "Concubine gremio psallo matutinas.
    Decani, presbiteri, propter breues minas
    Vultis uos dimittere uestras concubinas?"

    BdT. 24.2 gremio smudged in **Bd**; psalla? **Bd** ‖ 24.3 Decani (two words) **Bd**: Romani **T** ‖ 24.4 In **T** and **Bd**, *uos* and *uestras* could be *nos* and *nostras*, but in **Bd** there is a clear correction to *uos* and *uestras*.

25. Turbarum de medio surgit capellanus,
    Disputanti similis pretendendo manus:
    "Ager est inutilis, sterilis et uanus;
    Qui non amat uomerem[4] plus est quam uesanus.

    BdT. 25.1 de **T**: in **Bd** ‖ 25.2 Disputanti **Bd**: Disputandi **T** ‖ 25.4 uomerem **T**: feminam **Bd**

26. Cogitare possumus atque loqui plura:
    Tempora presentia sunt atque futura.
    Sed cum tango candida mulieris crura,
    Oportet quod faciat ius suum natura.

    BdT. 26.2 futura **T**: fitura **Bd** ‖ 26.3 mulieris **T**: concubine **Bd** ‖ 26.4 = **T**; Conuenit ut faciat insultus natura **Bd**

27. Nam cum bibo siceram uel fortasse uina
    Et me sompnus capiat hora uespertina,
    Ne michi deficiat carnis medicina,
    Oportet quod dormiat mecum concubina.

    BdT. 27.1 Nam **T**: Aut **Bd**; siceram **T**: siseram **Bd** ‖ 27.2 uespertina **Bd**: matutina **T** ‖ 27.4 dormiat **T**: iaceat **Bd**

28. Oculis si dedero sompnum uel palebris,
    Iacens sine coniuge noctis in tenebris,
    Caro passionibus me circumdat crebris.
    Tremens ac si frigida me uexasset febris.

    BdT. 28.2 sine **T**: cum **Bd**; noctis **Bd**: nocte **T** ‖ 28.3 circumdat **Bd**: tutundat **T**

23. Each one of us is speaking in his way.
    Though Pope with threats and fear may cause dismay,
    My answer is – as I'm about to say –
    That wifeless men will have a stormy day."

24.[d] Another bursts into these great alarms:
    "I sing my matins in my sweetheart's arms.
    You deans and priests, for threats not worth a dime[e]
    Do you want now to fire your concubines?"[f]

25. From out the crowds a chaplain then arose;
    He stretched his hands and struck a teacher's pose:
    "A barren field is useless and in vain:
    Who does not love to plough is quite insane!

26. We have the power to think (and more to tell).
    There's present time and future time as well.
    But when I touch my darling's shiny thighs,
    Then nature must her power exercise![g]

27. For when I drink of cider, maybe wine.
    And sleep takes hold of me at evening time,[h]
    Lest I should lack my fleshly medicine,
    I must have by my side my concubine.

28. If I lie wifeless in the dark at night
    And let my eyes or lids in sleep shut tight,
    Then frequent sickly shivering takes hold,
    As if I'd had a fever from a cold.

29. Vestris rationibus bene sum placatus;
    Ad carnis officium fuit homo natus.
    Quicquid dicat dominus papa uel legatus,
    Vxor nostra dormiet iuxta nostrum latus.

    BdT. 29.1 bene **Bd**: leue **T** ‖ 29.4 = **T**; Nostra nostrum dormiet uxor iuxta latus **Bd**

30. Postquam noui semitas que ducunt ad polum,
    Non ego secutus sum zelum[5] neque dolum,
    Sed dum michi baiulat mea Cloto colum,
    Lectum sine coniuge non tenebo solum.

    BdT. 30.2 zelum *scripsi*: zelus **T**, zelus over dolus canc. **Bd**, zelum canc. before dolum **Bd** ‖ 30.3 Cloto **T**, clota **Bd**

31. Tractat fila Lachesis pollice uexato
    Et feruenter disputant Socrates et Plato,
    Sed dum michi spiritus spirat in palato,
    Nostra mecum dormiet coniux in grabato.

    BdT. 31.1 Tractat **T**: Trahit **Bd**; Lachesis **T**; lachisis **Bd** ‖ 31.2 feruenter **T**: frequenter **Bd**; disputant **Bd**: disputat **T**; Socrates **T**: sacrates **Bd** ‖ 31.4 mecum **T**: nostro **Bd**

32. Cum dicatur Atropos ab "a" quod est "sine",
    Rumpens uite stamina languentis in fine,
    Non me pape poterunt sic terrere mine
    Quin michi sint quatuor et tres concubine.

    BdT. 32.1 Cum **Bd**: Dum **T**; Atropos **Bd**: antropos **T** ‖ 32.2 Rumpens **T**: Rupens **Bd**; stamina **T**: famina **Bd** ‖ 32.4 michi sint quatuor **T**: tresdecim michi sint **Bd**

33. Ne sint in ambiguo uota mee mentis,
    Natus sum in partibus Anglicane gentis.
    Natura cuiuslibet est uiri uiuentis
    Iungi cum uxoribus et non cum iumentis.[6]

    BdT. 33.2 Natus **Bd**: Fatus **T**; in **Bd**: de **T**

34. Verberare possumus aera loquelis
    Sed, per ipsum Dominum qui regnat in celis,
    Ante festa uenient Sancti Michaelis
    Ter, quam mea deserat uxor me fidelis.

    BdT. 34.1 loquelis **T**: cum loquelis **Bd** ‖ 34.3 Ante **T**: Quando **Bd** ‖ 34.4 quam ... me **T**: ludam ne deserat me coniux **Bd**

29. By your fine reasoning I'm quite refreshed,
    For human kind was born to serve the flesh.
    Whatever pope or legate may decide,
    My wife will sleep with me close by my side.

30. Since I have learned the roads to ecstasy,[i]
    I haven't swindled or shown jealousy.
    As long as Clotho spins for me her thread,[j]
    I won't be wifeless, lonely in my bed.

31. Lachesis draws the threads with busy thumb
    And Socrates and Plato hem and hum,
    But while my breath is breathing in my head,
    My wife will sleep with me inside our bed.

32. Since Atropos from "a" ("without") derives
    And breaks the final threads of sick men's lives,
    No papal threats can hinder my design
    Of having three or four fine concubines.[k]

33. Lest there's any doubt at all as to my persuasion,
    I was born within the bounds of the English nation.
    For all virile living men this the proper course is
    To have sex with their own wives, not with cows or horses.

34. Though, beating air with words, we can debate,
    Yet, by the Lord of Heaven, I will state:
    St. Michael's feast will come three times before
    My faithful wife will leave me at my door![l]

35. Papa, cum sit dominus et pastor uirorum.
    Nimis est contrarius turbe clericorum:
    Papa tollit redditus et res diuinorum
    Et suarum, quod plus est, solamen uxorum.

   BdT. 35.3 Papa tollit **Bd**: Aufert prauos **T**; diuinorum **Bd**: dominorum **T** ‖ 35.4 suarum ... uxorum **Bd**: suorum ... uirorum **T**

36. Cuncta rerum genera tendunt ad naturam;
    Creatura similem querit creaturam.
    Ergo si cum coniuge facio mixturam,
    Non transcendo debitam in hac re mensuram.

   BdT. 36.2 querit **Bd**: gignit **T** ‖ 36.3 = **T**: Nemo sine coniuge faci(e)t mixturam **Bd** (fac^t) ‖ 36.4 Non transcendo debitam **T**: Non transcendit presbiter **Bd**; **T** ends at this point; Expl. consilium sacerdotum.

37. Si fas esset dicere uel fateri uerum,
    Papa nimis officit in subiectum clerum.
    Multorum qui uidimus tempora dierum,
    Cur nunc nobis denegat cetum mulierum?

   Bd. 37.3 uidimus *scripsi*: uidumus **Bd**

38. Vt uir sit[7] cum femina, ut est consuetus,
    Vt dat testimonium testamentum uetus,
    Abraham cum Sarray uixit preter metus.
    Cur tunc contempnendi sunt mulierum cetus?

   Bd. 38.1 sit *scripsi*: sic **Bd**

39. Salamon rex sapiens et Dauid propheta,
    Vterque cum Domini fuerit atleta,
    Cognouerunt celica diuina secreta,
    Nec est illis societas[8] mulierum spreta!"

   Bd.

40. Ex his clamor oritur et strepit tumultus;
    Quisque putat sapiens esse quasi stultus.[9]
    Frangitur silencium et fit sermo multus;
    Sic decedunt pariter paruus et adultus.

   Bd.

35. The Pope is shepherd of his flock, their lord,
    But he is hostile to the clerkly horde.
    He takes away the clergy's property and tithes[m]
    And, what is worse, the solace of their wives!

36. To nature's law all kinds of thing incline;
    Each creature seeks[n] for one of its own kind,
    So if I should co-mingle with my mate,
    I don't in this due measure violate.

37. If it were right to speak the truth out loud,
    The Pope's a hindrance to his clerkly crowd.
    A multitude of days has passed us by:
    Why does he grudge us women's company?

38. As man with woman, as he used to do,
    And as the ancient Testament holds true,
    Did Abram live with Sarah, unsurprised.
    So why is women's company despised?

39. Wise Solomon and prophet David[o] too –
    Both kings and warriors of God – these two
    Knew secrets of the heavens up above,
    But they did not reject a woman's love."

40. From these a clamour and a shout arise:
    To play a kind of fool now think the wise!
    The silence breaks and many tales are told.
    They all depart together, young and old.

41. Certus est presbiteris dies nominatus,[10]
    Vt prefixit dominus papa uel legatus.
    Hic est omnis Anglie clerus congregatus,[11]
    Siue sponte siue non – sic est obligatus.

    Bd.

42. Quando pedes domini pape consedere,
    De longinquis partibus quotquot aduenere
    Argumenta uaria sibi parauere,
    Quilibet pro qualibet sua respondere.

    Bd. 42.3 parauere *scripsi*: parauerere **Bd**

43. Papa sedet cathedra sullimi suffultus,
    Sed respersos oculos et sullimes uultus
    Spiratiem congerit hauriens tumultus,
    Nullus ibi loquitur: demptus est tumultus.[12]

    Bd.

44. Tunc sub Christi baculo contulit sermonem,
    Faciens de clericis inquisicionem,
    Horum tangens grauiter conuersacionem,
    Grauem minans omnibus castigacionem.

    Bd.

45. Tunc fatur apercius rebus in diuinis
    De tractatu fidei et personis trinis,
    Sed[13] semper inter cetera eius fuit finis
    De laciuis[14] clericis et de concubinis.

    Bd.

46. Concordat quas predicat res amor irati,
    Addens hanc parabolam apte predicati,
    Quod omnes presbiteri qui sunt uxorati
    Sunt a sanctis omnibus excommunicati.

    Bd.

47. Alter spectat alterum et[15] male sunt loquuti,
    Caput inter genua tenent deuoluti,
    Et qui prius fuerant artibus inbuti

    Bd ends here at the foot of the column but there was certainly room for one more line. Fol. 76v contains the conclusion of the Execution of Archbishop Scrope which began on fol. 74va.

41. For all the priests is named a certain date
    Determined by the Pope or delegate.
    Here all the English clergy congregate,
    Both willingly and not, as is their fate.

42. Now when the papal feet had settled down,
    Then all who had assembled from around
    Began their arguments to formulate,
    Each one and all to answer for their mate.

43. The Pope sits on a lofty throne on high;
    He checks the scattered looks, the haughty eye.
    He draws his breath and discord unifies.
    Now no one speaks and uproar's pacified.

44. Beneath Christ's staff upon his speech he works
    And frames an inquisition of the clerks.
    He touches on their conduct with concern
    And threatens everyone, his visage stern.

45. He speaks more openly of things divine,
    The topic of the faith, the godhead trine,
    But most of all his sermon he confines
    To clergy's lechery and concubines.[p]

46. The zealot's love unites what he has preached
    And adds a coda suited to his speech,[q]
    That everyone of priestly rank who'd wived
    Should be of all the sacraments deprived.

47. Each stares at other, cursing without cease;
    They bend and hold their head between their knees,
    And those who'd been before in arts imbued ... (incomplete).

Notes to the Edition

[1] Present in **Vt** only, *set* is hypermetrical and could be omitted.

[2] I have seen no other example of *prohibicio* meaning *res prohibita*, and emendation to *stupri* would be easy, but the linguistic development is possible.

[3] *carnis ... in fulmine*: it is tempting to emend to *turbine*, but Isidore, *Etym.* XIII.ix.1–2 gives sufficient hints of "storm" for *fulmen*.

[4] For *uomer* as the male sexual organ, see Lucretius, *De rerum nat.* 4.1263–1277, at 1273. An echo of such a rare poet would be surprising, and the metaphor may have been in popular use.

[5] *zelum*: it is surprising that both **Bd** and **T** get the gender of *zelus* wrong (it is usually masculine, even in the Medieval Latin dictionaries such as Balbi's *Catholicon*).

[6] Cf. Ex. 22.19: "Qui coierit cum iumento, morte moriatur."

[7] The emendation *sit* for *sic* seems likely, but the line would fit better after 38.3.

[8] Unless *societas* can be scanned as a trisyllable, we would perhaps read *his* for *illis*.

[9] Cf. I Cor. 3.18.

[10] Cf. NR 3.3–4.

[11] Cf. NR 6.3–4.

[12] The overall sense is that the pope quells the uproar, but there are difficulties in 43.2 (why accusative?), and 43.3 (*spiratiem*, *congerit*, and *hauriens*). It might be best to emend *sedet* to *sedat* and *sic* for *sed* in 43.2: "the Pope, supported on a high seat, *quietens* the scattered looks and haughty faces; drawing in his breath, he gathers together the tumults." Possibly *congerit* is for *conquirit* in its medieval sense of "conquers". The repetition of *tumultus* in 3–4 is suspicious.

[13] Omission of *sed* would ease the rhythm.

[14] *laciuis = lasciuis*.

[15] This *et* is hypermetric and should be omitted.

Notes to the Translation

[a] The is probably Pandulf Masca, papal legate during the Interdict and later bishop of Norwich.

[b] *Sexta dies*, i.e. Friday, a fast day, is found only in **Tx**. See Walter of Wimborne, *De Palpone* 38.3–4 (of truth-tellers at court), in *The Poems of Walter of Wimborne*, ed. A.G. Rigg (Toronto, 1978), p. 45:

> qui uera loquitur et serit seria
> grauis est aulicis ut sexta feria.

[c] *Alter ait*: on the problem caused by *alter*, see Introduction pp. 89, 96.

[d] For a different version, see CP 28. The significance of the two versions, see Introduction, p. 93.

[e] I have translated the text of **Bd**, but **T**'s "For Roman priest's brief threats" is also possible.

[f] **T**'s *nos* and *nostras* would give equally good sense.

[g] In **Bd**: "that nature should make assaults."

[h] Either *uespertina* (**Bd** and CP) or *matutina* (**T**) would be possible.

[i] "ecstasy," literally "heaven" (*polum*) but it probably means the religious life.

[j] The three Fates are given in their traditional order, as in Isidore, *Etym.* VIII.xi.93: "Parcas κατ' ἀντίφρασιν appellatas, quod minime parcant. Quas tres esse voluerunt: unam, quae vitam hominis ordiatur; alteram quae contexat; tertiam, quae rumpat."

[k] I see nothing to choose between "four and three" (**T**) and "thirteen and three" (**Bd**).

[l] **Bd** seems to mean: "May I play three times, lest my wife leave me."

[m] The meaning of **T** ("he takes away wrongful rents and the property of lords") is unclear. **Bd** seems to refer to England's subjection to the papacy in the settlement at the end of the Interdict (see Introduction, p. 91).

[n] **T**'s *gignit* makes little sense in context.

[o] For David, see also CP 39.

[p] The account of the pope's speech matches the beginnings of the Fourth Lateran: i.e. the Faith and Trinity, and then the lascivious clergy.

[q] Literally, "the love of the angry man harmonizes the things that he preaches, fittingly adding this parabola of what he has preached." *predicati* may have a logical sense, "predicate."

Prisciani Regula

Manuscripts

D Oxford, Bodleian Library, MS Digby 166, fols. 109v–110v (Part VIII.C, saec. XV).[26]

Ho London, British Library, MS Harley 200, fol. 144r (saec. XV).

Ht London, British Library, MS Harley 3724, fols. 51r–52r (saec. XIV*in*., Irish?). The text has been cancelled by heavy hatching but is quite clear.

The last page of **D** is badly damaged. Fols. 109v–110r contain **D**'s stanzas 1–10; the outer top corner of fol. 110 is missing and the remainder is in most places hardly legible, though much of stanza 13 (= stanza 8) and stanza 14 are easily reconstructed. The illegible stanza (11?) may be either stanza 16 or stanza 17 in my edition. To put it differently, the space on fol. 110v would accommodate four stanzas, of which only stanza 13 (= stanza 8) and stanza 19 are clear.

Early Printed Editions

F Flacius Illyricus, *Varia doctorum piorumque virorum de corrupto Ecclesiae statu poemata* (Basel, 1557), pp. 236–38.

Bp Bale ex Pullano, in John Bale, *Scriptorum Illustrium maioris Brytanniae … Catalogus* (Basel, 1557), pp. 262–63, sent to Bale by John Pullan.

Bp and **F** differ only slightly (at 1.2; 6.1; 11.2; 13.1): Pullan, a fervent Protestant, was in Geneva for most of 1554–1558 (DNB) and it is likely that while he was there, he made his copy from Flacius's text, which was printed in 1557.

Editions

Wright, *The Latin Poems Commonly Attributed to Walter Mapes*, pp. 171–73, from **Ht** and **F**.

Dobiache-Rojdesvensky, *Les poésies des Goliards*, pp. 127–30, from **F**. Dobiache-Rojdesvensky knew of **D** but says that it was inaccessible to her.

---

[26] A.G. Rigg, "Medieval Latin Poetic Anthologies (III)," *Mediaeval Studies* 41 (1979), 468–505, at p. 487 (Part VIIIC).

Order of Stanzas

	Ht	**D**	**Ho**	**Bp**	**F**
1. Prisciani regula	1			1	1
2. Quid facis, O pontifex	2				
3. Quid agant presbiteri	3				
4. Notus in deliciis	4				
5. Si quis uelit pauperem	5				
6. Ita quidam presbiter	6	1	1	2	2
7. O quam dolor anxius	7	2	2	3	3
8. Non est Innocentius	8	3	3	4	4
9. Nonne de militibus	10	4	6	7	7
10. Gignere nos precipit	11	5	7	5	5
11. Zacharias habuit	9	6	8	9	9
12. Paulus celos rapitur		7	4	10	10
13. Propter hec et alia		8 (13)	5	11	11
14. Proximorum femina		9		12	12
15. Dedit enim Dominus	12	10		6	6
16. Si fortasse memor es	13	11(?)			
17. Olim quando Dominus	14				
18. Nobis adhuc precipit		12		8	8
19. Ecce iam pro clericis		13 (8)		13	13

Prisciani Regula: *Revised Edition*

1. Prisciani regula penitus quassatur:
   Sacerdos per *hic* et *hec* olim declinatur,
   Sed per *hic* solummodo nunc articulatur,
   Cum per nostrum presulem *hec* amoueatur.

   HtBpF. 1.2. olim **BpF**, iam iam **Ht**; declinatur **HtBp**: declinabatur **F**

2. Quid facis, O pontifex, unam adimendo?
   Sed tu crimen cumulas, plures largiendo!
   Minus malum crederem unam permittendo
   Parcere sic aliis, nephas minuendo.[1]

   Ht.

3. Quid agant presbiteri propriis carentes?
   Alienas uiolant clanculo molentes,[2]
   Nullis pro coniugiis feminis parcentes,
   Penam uel infamiam nichil metuentes.

   Ht.

4. Notus in deliciis Bachus est pincerna,
   Dissolutus, ebrius Venerisque uerna.
   Esse posset aliis quomodo lucerna,
   Nisi ad interitum dampna per eterna?

   Ht.

5. Si quis uelit pauperem bene castigare,
   Non oportet aliud quam inpauperare.
   Cum cogantur inopes multum laborare,
   Cogitabunt aliud quam luxuriare!

   Ht.

6. Ita quidam presbiter cepit allegare:
   "Peccat criminaliter qui uult separare
   Quos Deus coniunxerat, feminam a mare,
   Vnde dignum duximus omnes appellare."[3]

   HtDHoBpF. 6.1 Ita quidam **HtDBp**: Ita quidem **F**, Quidam ita **Ho** ‖ 6.3 Quos **HtHo**: Quod **DBpF**, coniunxerat *illeg.* **D**; feminam **DHoBpF**: feminas **Ht**; a mare **Ho**: amare **HtDBpF** ‖ 6.4 = **D**: Vna statim volumus omnes appellare **Ht**, Tales dignum duximus fures appellare **BpF**

English Translation

1.[a] The rule of Priscian is undermined,
For *priest* till now by *he* and *she* declined,
But henceforth will decline in only *he*,
Since *she* is to be dropped by pope's decree.

2.[b] Removing *one*, o Pope, what's in your mind?[c]
By granting more, you multiply the crime!
There'd be less harm in letting one remain
And sparing others, thus reducing blame.

3. What would priests do, if they should lack their mate?
They'll others' wives grind fine and violate!
They'll spare no women (as their substitute)
And fear no penalty or disrepute.

4. In pleasures Bacchus,[d] famously, pours wine –
Drunk, dissolute, a slave at Venus's shrine.
How could he light the others on their way
Except to death, eternally astray?

5.[e] If someone wishes to chastise the poor,
It's better to impoverish them more.
If poor men have to toil in misery,
They'll have their thoughts on more than lechery!

6.[f] Then thus a priest began his case to state:
"They're criminal, who want to separate
What God has joined – a woman and her mate.
Against such people we should remonstrate!"

7. O quam dolor anxius, o quam ualde graue
   Nobis est dimittere quoniam[4] suaue!
   O Romane pontifex, statuisti praue:
   Ne in tanto crimine moriaris, caue!

   HtDHoBpF. 7.10 quam ualde graue **D**: quam dampnum graue **HoHt**, quam tormentum graue **BpF** ‖ 7.2 Nobis est **HtDBpF**: Est nobis **Ho** ‖ 7.3 O **DHoBpF**: Hoc **Ht**; statuisti **HtDBpF**: tu fecisti **Ho**

8. Non est Innocentius, ymmo nocens uere,
   Qui quod facto docuit,[5] uerbo uult delere.
   Et quod olim iuuenis uoluit habere,
   Modo uetus pontifex studet prohibere.

   HtDHoBpF. 8.2. Qui quod facto docuit **HoBpF**, Qui quod deus docuit **Ht**, Nam quod olim decuit **D**; uerbo uult delere **HoBpF**, studet abolere **Ht**, modo uult delere **D** ‖ 8.3 Et quod olim iuuenis **DBpF**: Et quod omnis iuuenis **Ho**, Iussit iehim dominus **Ht**; uoluit habere **DBpF**: semper uult habere **Ho**, feminis herere **Ht** ‖ 8.4 Modo uetus pontifex **DHoBpF**: Sed hoc noster pontifex **Ht**; studet prohibere **DHoBpF**: iussit prohibere **Ht**

9. Nonne de militibus milites procedunt
   Et reges a regibus qui sibi succedunt?
   Per locum a simili[6] omnes iura ledunt,
   Clericos qui gignere crimen esse credunt.

   HtHoBpF (**D** damaged). 9.1 Nonne **HtDBpF**: Nam **Ho** ‖ 9.3 Per locum a simili **HtDBpF**: Exemplis similibus **Ho**; omnes iura ledunt *illeg*. **D** ‖ 9.4 Clericos qui gignere (**D**)**HtBpF**: Gignere qui clericis **Ho**; esse credunt *illeg*. **D**

10. Gignere nos precipit uetus testamentum;[7]
    Vbi nouum prohibet nusquam est inuentum.
    Presul, qui contrarium donat documentum,
    Nullum necessarium his dat argumentum.

    HtHoBpF (**D** damaged). 10.1 precipit (**D**)**HtBpF**: admonet **Ho**; testamentum *illeg*. **D** ‖ 10.2 Vbi nouum prohibet **Ht**: Nouum quod non retinet **BpF**, Et illud quod renuit **Ho**, Quod id nouum ren ... **D**; nusquam est inuentum **HtBpF** (*illeg*. **D**) ‖ 10.3 Presul qui contrarium donat documentum **HoBpF** (**D** Presul qui co ...): A modernis datum est istud documentum **Ht** ‖ 10.4 = **BpF**: Nullum ... **D**, Nullum necessarium dabit argumentum **Ho**, Id (*or* Ad) quod nullum racio prebet argumentum **Ht**

7. O what anxiety and heavy loss
   For us to go without our sweet "because"!
   O Roman pontiff, your decree's awry:
   Beware lest in such error you should die![g]

8. He isn't "Innocent," but harms indeed,
   Who wants to cancel what he taught by deed!
   And what he wanted once in his young days[h]
   As Pope he seeks to outlaw now he's grey![i]

9. Don't soldiers come from soldiers by descent
   And kings from kings, a similar event?
   In such a way the law they overset
   Who think it wrong for clerics to beget!

10. The Ancient Testament bids us beget.
    And that the New dissents is not found yet.[j]
    The prelate now proclaims the contrary:[k]
    He's no support in logic I can see![l]

11.[8] Zacharias habuit prolem et uxorem
Inter natos hominum omnibus maiorem;
Baptizauit etenim mundi saluatorem.
Pereat qui teneat nouum hunc errorem!

HtHoBpF (**D** damaged). 11.1 Zacharias habuit prolem ... em **D** ‖ 11.2 = **Ho**: Nec prole quem genuit memini maiorem **Ht**, Per uirum quem genuit adeptus honorem **BpF**, In mundo non ... meliorem **D** ‖ 11.3 etenim **HoHtBp**: etiam **DF**; mundi **HoHtBp**: nostrum **BpF**

12. Paulus celos rapitur ad superiores,
Vbi multas didicit res secretiores.[9]
Tandem ad nos rediens instruensque mores,
"Suas," inquit, "habeat quilibet uxores."[10]

HoBpF (**D** damaged). 12.1 capit(?) ... superiores **D** ‖ 12.2 multas **HoBpF**: multa **D**; didicit ... ecreciores **D** ‖ 12.3 Tandem ad nos **DHo**: Ad nos tandem **BpF**; rediens **BpF**: ueniens **Ho**, ...iit **D**; mores **HoBpF**: ... es **D** ‖ 12.4 quilibet **HoBpF**: ...uilt **D**

13. Propter hec et alia dogmata doctorum
Reor esse melius et magis decorum:
Quisque suam habeat et non proximorum,
Ne incurrat odium uel iram eorum.

HoBpF (**D** damaged). 13.1 Propter hec et **HoBp**: Propter hoc et **F**, Ob hec et ob **D**; ...ata **D** ‖ 13.2 Reor **DBpF**: Videtur **Ho**; magis: ...is **D** ‖ 13.3 Quisque **DBpF**: Vt quisque **Ho**; suam **HoBpF**: suas **D**

Where this stanza is repeated in **D** (five stanzas later) it reads: ... et alia dogmata doctorum | ... esse melius et magis decorum, | ...isque suam habeat et non proximorum. | Ne incurrat odium uel iram eorum.

14. Proximorum feminas, filias et neptes
Violare nephas est, quasi nil deceptes.
Vere tuam habeas et in hac delectes,
Vt sic diem ultimum tucius exspectes.

DBpF. 14.1 femina(.) **D** ‖ 14.2 est **BpF**: ...t **D**; quasi **DF**: quare **Bp** ‖ 14.3 habea(.) **D** ‖ 14.4 Vt sic diem **D**: Diem ut sic **BpF**

15.[11] Dedit enim Dominus malediccionem
Viro qui non fecerat generacionem.
Ergo tibi consulo per hanc racionem:
Generes ut habeas benediccionem.

HtDBpF. 15.1 = **DBpF**: Dedit deus Israel **Ht**; dominu(.) **D** ‖ 15.2 fecerat **Ht**: ...c'at **D**, fecerit **BpF** ‖ 15.3 = **DBpF**: Nullam quidem faciens hic excepcionem **Ht** ‖ 15.4 Generes **HtD**: Gignere **BpF** (cf. CP 40 Vt generent quo habeant benedictionem).

11. Zacharias had both a wife and son
    Than whom there nowhere was a greater one;[m]
    His son baptized the saviour of mankind.
    To death this novel view should be consigned!

12. Saint Paul was snatched above, up to the skies,
    And there he learned much hidden lore and wise.
    At last he came to us, instructing lives:
    "Now everyone," he said, "should have their wives."

13. For these and other teachings of the wise
    It seems more fitting and more well advised
    That each should have his own – not others' – mate,
    Lest he incur their anger and their hate.

14. It's wrong to rape a neighbour's wife or niece
    Or daughter, as it were without deceit.[n]
    But have your own, for with her you may play
    And in more safety wait your final day.

15. The Lord proclaimed a curse on anyone
    Who hadn't made a generation,
    So, by this reasoning, I'd say: "Take heed:
    To get a blessing, propagate your seed!"

16. Si fortasse memor es istius diei
    In quo fabricauerant uitulum Iudei,[12]
    Leui dedit infulam et progeniei.
    Ergo qui non generant omnes erunt rei.

    Ht. 16.4 generant *scripsi*: gignerant **Ht**

17. Olim quando Dominus ylem informauit,
    Vtriusque generis animal creauit,[13]
    Neutri uero generi nullum uegetauit;
    Quod debemus gignere satis intimauit.

    Ht ends here: Explicit.

18. Nobis adhuc precipit Vetus Testamentum,
    Quod nostrae iam legis est uerax fundamentum,
    Vt mares et feminae sciant instrumentum
    Tale per quod habeant prolis incrementum.

    BpF (**D** illegible, probably rhyming in -entum: 18.4 ... prolis incrementum).

19. Ecce iam pro clericis multum allegaui,
    Necnon pro presbiteris plura comprobaui.
    Pater Noster nunc pro me, quoniam peccaui,
    Quisque dicat presbiter cum sua suaui!

    DBpF. 19.2 plura comprobaui **Bp**: multa comprobaui **F**, multaque probaui **D** ‖ 19.4 Quisque dicat **D**: Dicat quisque **BpF**.

Notes to the Edition

[1] Wright's *nuptas muniendo* makes excellent sense, but I see *nep* and possibly *h* in the photo of the MS. *minuendo* and *muniendo*, of course, would be indistinguishable in most scripts.

[2] For the sexual sense *molentes*, see Lewis and Short s. *molo* II, e.g. Ausonius, *Epigr.* 71.7 (Roger P.H. Green, *The Works of Ausonius* (Oxford 1991), p. 85): "Deglubit, fellat, molitur per utramque cauernam."

[3] **HtHo** use *appello* in the legal sense "accuse," whereas in **BpF** it takes a predicative accusative, "call them thieves."

[4] *quoniam*: Dobiache-Rojdesvensky, *Les poésies des Goliards*, p. 127, n. 1, proposes to emend *quoniam suaue* to *quod est tam suaue*, but the word is doubtless the euphemism for the female sexual organ; see Introduction, p. 90.

16. You may perhaps recall that day of old
    When those Judeans built a calf of gold.
    And Levi gave a headdress to his line?
    Thus all who don't beget commit a crime!

17. When once the Lord shaped matter, he then next
    Created animals of either sex;
    To neither kind did he some life deny
    And thus made clear we should multiply!

18. The true foundation of our law today –
    The Ancient Testament – still now does say
    That males and females ought to know the means
    By which they may now multiply their genes.

19. For clerics I've made many arguments;
    For priests also my speech much proof presents.
    Now let each priest, together with his friend,
    For me say *Pater Noster*, since I've sinned!

----

[5] This may refer to CP, stanza 42.4: "Ex sorore filium ipse procreauit," which may be an unrecorded piece of curial gossip or another grammatical joke, if the Pope, while teaching Latin grammar, declined first *soror* and then *filius*.

[6] *locum a simili*: i.e. by the rhetorical trope "from a similar case," what we would call analogy. Cf. *Ad Herennium* IV.xlv, xlviii, 59–61.

[7] Gen. 1.22; 8.17; 9.1, etc.

[8] Lc. 1–2.

[9] II Cor. 12.2–4.

[10] I Cor. 7.2: "Propter fornicationem autem unusquisque suam uxorem habeat."

[11] Gen. 38.1–10 (Onan); cf. Lev. 15.

[12] Ex. 32.1–8; cf. Gen. 29.34 (where the *infula* is not mentioned). There is no connection between Aaron and the golden calf and Levi (from whose family Aaron was descended).

[13] Gen. 1.27.

Notes to the Translation

[a] At first reading this stanza seems to be lamenting the prohibition of female priests, but in the late Middle Ages this seems more than unlikely. It refers, in fact, to the ban on clerical wives and concubines, as shown by Dobiache-Rojdesvensky, *Les poésies des Goliards*, pp. 120–21 and (very fully) by Jan Ziolkowski, *Alan of Lille's Grammar of Sex* (Cambridge, Mass., 1985), pp. 68–69: it is a pun on *declinare* in the grammatical sense of "decline' and the literal "lay down" or "lie down beside." The joke is used again in CP 42, where the pope approves of someone who declines *sacerdos* in masculine and feminine and is consequently admitted to the priesthood.

[b] Stanzas 2–5 are only in **Ht** and do not seem to deal directly with the theme of clerical celibacy.

[c] This seems to interpret the papal ban as "excluding one" (and thus encouraging promiscuity), perhaps from a sentence like "clericis non licet unam concubinam habere."

[d] The evils of Bacchus (i.e. drunkenness) are denounced in Fourth Lateran, ch. 15: "de arcenda ebrietate clericorum," but are also found in earlier (1213–1214) sources, such as Stephen Langton's *Statutes of Canterbury*, in *Councils and Synods with Other Documents Relating to the English Church*, II A.D. 1205–1313, ed. Frederick M. Powicke and Christopher R. Cheney (Oxford, 1964), p. 26, where the anticoncubine rule is followed immediately by par. 7 which states that clerics are not to visit taverns or indulge in public drinking where lewd songs were sung.

Clerus et Presbiteri

Early Printed Edition

> Flacius Illyricus, *Varia doctorum piorumque virorum de corrupto Ecclesiae statu poemata* (Basel, 1557), pp. 371–77. I have retained the humanistic spellings but revised the punctuation according to modern usage.

Editions

> Wright, *The Latin Poems Commonly Attributed to Walter Mapes*, pp. 174–79, with only one error (*famularum* for *famulorum* in stanza 36.4).
> Dobiache-Rojdesvensky, *Les poésies des Goliards*, pp. 130–39 (stanzas 1–18 and 30–45).

[e] The poet of **Ht** seems to have digressed into the topic of lechery among the poor.

[f] In **D** and **Ho** this is the first stanza of the poem and goes straight into the topic of clerical marriage. It could be an extract from another branch of the poems, or it could indicate that it is already part of a continuous sequence of speakers.

[g] As Innocent III did in fact die in 1216, a year after Fourth Lateran, this may provide a *terminus ad quem* for this poem, unless the author was being very tactless.

[h] **Ho**: "What's sought by all when they are young and gay." **Ht**: "For God bade us by women close to stay" (Wright misread the line as "Iussit enim Dominus feminas habere").

[i] For *uetus* **Ht** has *noster*: "Our Pope seeks to deprive us of today."

[j] **Ho**: "Its converse hasn't been discovered yet."

[k] **Ht**: "The modern teaching is the contrary."

[l] **Ht** may have *Id quod* or *Ad quod*, "with regards to which (teaching) reason has no argument," i.e. which reason does not support.

[m] **BpF** "Through whom great honour in the world he won."

[n] *quasi nil deceptes*: "As though you were not deceiving." I have no idea what this means in context.

Clerus et Presbiteri: *Revised Edition*

1. Clerus et presbyteri nuper consedere
   Tristes in capitulo simul et dixere:
   "Nostras uult ancillulas Praesul remouere.
   Quid debemus super hoc ergo respondere?"

2. Quaestio proposita rite commendatur.
   Decanus collegii primus sic praefatur:
   "Fratres, nobis omnibus Pontifex minatur,
   Postque minas metuo ne poena sequatur.

3. Cum igitur[1] propter famulas simus aggrauati,
   Videamus prouidi quo simus parati,
   Ad mandatum Praesidis nostri uel legati
   Respondere fortiter, uel sumus damnati."

4. Incipit capituli Doctor et praelatus,
   Vir in iure canonico[2] bene[3] fundatus:
   "Grauis hic est questionis, Domini,[4] status:
   Remouere famulas non leuis est tractatus.[5]

5. Non humana dirimit lex et praelatura
   Quod inter se fragilis copulat natura.
   Vitae castae regula nimium est dura:
   Vita sola angelica est pura."[6]

6. Hinc est gradu senior tremulo sic fatus:
   "Ego credo, Domini, quod sum fascinatus.
   Vult remouere famulam meam[7] Praelatus;
   Impotens ut praelio, ero contentatus."

7. Audit Cantor callidus, ergo[8] sonat cum clamore:
   "Quid si uos supponere[9] non estis[10] in ualore,
   Vultis ergo reliquos priuare hoc[11] uigore?"
   Confusus est senior magno cum rubore.

English Translation

1. Just now the clergy and the priests convened;
   They sat in chapter sadly and they keened.
   "Our girls the bishop wants to put away,
   So on this subject what should we now say?"

2. The question here proposed is now agreed;
   The college dean was first his case to plead:
   "The pontiff, brothers, threatens all of us
   And after threats, I fear, will follow worse.

3. So since we have been troubled for our maids,
   Let's thoughtfully take care to be prepared
   To answer to the mandate of our Pope
   Or of his legate, or we'll have no hope."

4. Then came the chapter's teacher, speaking first,
   A man in canon law quite fully versed:
   "The status of the question, lords, is grave.
   It will be no light thing to sack our slaves!

5. What fragile nature has linked by her art
   Can't be by man or prelates pulled apart.
   Chaste life is much too heavy to endure,
   For only angels lead a life that's pure."

6. An elder spoke next, with unsteady stance:
   "I'm sure, my lords, that I have been entranced.
   The prelate wants to take my concubine:
   I'm weak for battle, but I'll still be fine."[a]

7. A crafty chanter heard and gave a shout:
   So what, if you're too weak to put it out?
   Would you deprive the others of their game?"
   The elder was confused and blushed with shame.

8. Ergo suum uotum sic caepit emendare:
   "Nolo, Cantor domine, coquam alienare.[12]
   Ad tempus ob laicos placet occultare,
   Vt possimus Praesulis iussis obuiare."

9. Ait Cellarius:[13] "Non potest hoc transire;
   Me regit una bestia – sinerem salire,
   Sed meretrix monocula renuit abire;[14]
   Cum senioris coqua cuperem cambire."

10. Tunc in consistorio omnes corrisere:
    "En noster cellarius non est stultus uere,
    Quod pro cute pessima, quam nequit consilere,[15]
    Senioris lepidam cogitat habere!"

11. Increpat Scholasticus: "Pulchras remouere
    Non est res ridicula, dico uobis uere.
    Si uult Dominus noster, potest prohibere,
    Sed ego per animam non possum abstinere."[16]

12. Hinc Structuarius longa cum structura:[17]
    "Homo," inquit, "fragilis ut est creatura,
    Nequit absque foemina esse atque cura:
    Scio, mihi minime fallit haec scriptura."

13. Vltimus Canonicus sic argumentatur:
    "Vir ad impossibile nullus obligatur.
    Clero pudicitia, scitis, quod non datur;
    Retinere famulas ergo concludatur."

14. Venit ad presbyteros ordo circularis.
    Primus in urbe fuit olim curialis
    Atque[18] in iure Canonum tritus et uocalis;
    Huius ergo allegatio erat talis:[19]

15. "Credo quod hanc, Domini, nostis Clementinam:
    Omnis debet clericus habere concubinam.[20]
    Hoc dixit, qui coronam gerit auro trinam:[21]
    Hanc igitur retinere[22] decet disciplinam."

8. He then began to take another look:
   "Sir chanter, I won't put aside my cook.
   For laymen's sake I'll hide her for a while,
   So that we can the pontiff's rules beguile."

9. The cellarer said: "This can't carry on.
   A beast is ruling me – let her begone!
   The one-eyed whore says she won't be replaced.
   I'd like the elder's cook to take her place!"

10. Then in the chapter everybody laughed:
    "In truth, our cellarer is not so daft:
    For some cheap flesh that he can't hush in bed,
    He'd like the elder's pretty girl instead!"

11. "To lose our beauties," then a scholar pressed,
    "To tell the truth, is not a cause of jest;
    If our lord[b] wishes to, he can restrain.
    But, by my soul, I can't myself abstain!"

12. A builder said, himself in structure tall:
    "A man's a creature and thus prone to fall,
    He can't live without women, he needs care –
    I know – for me this teaching is quite fair."

13. Then finally a canon thus declaimed:
    "To what's impossible no man's constrained.
    For chastity, you know, clerks were not made,
    So let's conclude that each should keep his maid."

14. The rota came to priests, just as it ought;[c]
    The first had once in town been at the court,[d]
    Well-versed in canon law and eloquent,
    And this, as follows, was his argument:

15. "You know, my lords, Pope Clement's legal line:
    Each cleric ought to keep his concubine,
    For he who wears a triple crown of gold
    Said this. We should this rule retain and hold."

16. Surgens unus presbyter turba de totali,
    Quem tangebat species generalis mali:
    "Vnam," dixit, "teneo amore legali,
    Quam nolo dimittere pro lege tali."[23]

17. Loquitur Vicarius, ordine secundus,
    Qui natura uir minime[24] fuit facundus:
    "Sermo meus erit[25] breuis et rotundus:
    Non ego possum[26] uiuere sine coqua mundus."

18. Tertius sic retulit, loquens ad Conuentum:
    "Ego quondam habui concubinas centum.
    Et nunc unam teneo charam ad complementum:[27]
    Aegrius hanc dimitto quam auri talentum."

19. Quartus ait presbyter animo irato:
    "Vah, quid est loquendum[28] de nostro Praelato?
    Vult quod meam deseram pro suo mandato;
    Ego nunquam deseram etiam[29] pro Deo beato."

20. Inde quintus ordine respondebat ita:
    "Ista noua friuola sunt iam satis trita.
    Per reginam gloriae, quae est caelo sita:
    Meam nunquam deseram in praesenti uita."

21. Sextus est loquendo sic effatus:[30]
    "Quid de mea facere coqua uult Praelatus?
    Quod si cum concubina fuero damnatus,
    Ego tantum proprios portabo reatus."

22. Septimus sacrificus nequibat tacere:
    "Non opus est," dicens, "hoc nobis timere.[31]
    Qui nos ab uxoribus iubet abstinere,
    Debet in redditibus plura prouidere."

23. Octaui presbyteri uox est sic formata:
    "Eia, mea foemina fuit decorata
    Vt retrorsus habeat membra deaurata
    Et a me sic tanto magis sit amata."[32]

16. From all this crowd another priest arose,
    Afflicted privately by public woes:
    "I have a woman in a legal bliss,
    Whom I won't give up for a law like this."

17. A vicar spoke – in order he was next;
    In public speaking he was not the best:
    "My speech will be not only brief but round:
    Without my cook my life will not be sound."

18. A third addressed the group and spoke his mind:
    "I used to have a hundred concubines.
    I now have just one girl to fill my life;
    I'd sooner lose my gold than lose my wife."

19. The fourth priest spoke and he was very cross:
    "What should we say about our bishop-boss?
    Am I to leave my wife just at his nod?
    I won't leave her, no not for blessed God!"

20. The fifth in sequence then replied like this:
    "They're quite well known, these new frivolities.[e]
    By Mary, Queen of Glory up above,
    In all my life I won't give up my love!"

21. The sixth then spoke – another line he took:
    "What is the prelate planning for my cook?
    If I'm condemned beside my concubine,
    The sins I'll carry will be only mine!"

22. The seventh priest[f] could not his tongue restrain:
    "For us," he said, "in fear there is no gain.
    He who from wives proposes abstinence
    Should make us more provision from our rents."[g]

23. The eighth priest then performed his speech out loud:
    "With looks my woman has been well endowed,
    So that her limbs are decked with gold behind
    And she a greater love from me can find."

24. Nonus ait: "Veterem non dimitto morem;
    Dedit mihi calidum natura cruorem;
    Oportet me uiuere carnis per laborem.
    Nolo propter animam linquere uxorem."

25. Decimus hinc senior loquitur modeste
    Quod antea sumpserat in corde moleste:
    "Si fateri debeo uerum manifeste,
    Nullus potest uiuere clericus honeste."

    25.2 antea *scripsi*: ante se **F**

26. Ad haec est undecimus presbyter erectus,
    Artibus rhetoricis plenus et perfectus:
    "Nunquam sine socia meus erit lectus,
    Donec me decrepitum fecerit senectus."

    26. Order of verses: 1324 **F**

27. Duodecimus clamat magno cum clamore:
    "Non me Pontifex terret minis et pauore,
    Sed[33] ego nummos prebeam pro Dei amore,
    Vt in pace maneam chara cum uxore."

28. Protulit tredecimus: "Coquas repentinas
    Nolumus dimittere propter breues minas,
    Fideles in omnibus nostras concubinas,
    Quae mane pectore[34] pulsant matutinas."

29. Inde decimus quartus unus Capellanus
    Disputando iratas praetendebat manus:
    "Actus est inutilis, friuolus et uanus:
    Qui non amat famulam, non est mente sanus."

30. Dixit quindecimus:[35] "Quando bibo uina
    Et me somnus recipit hora uespertina,
    Tunc ut mecum dormiet uolo concubina,
    Ne mihi deficiat carnis medicina."

24. The ninth priest said: "I will not change my ways:
    From birth I've been warm-blooded all my days.
    My flesh needs constant work to save my life;
    I won't, to save my soul, give up my wife!"

25. The tenth, an elder, spoke quite modestly
    Of what he had resented bitterly:
    "If I should state the truth quite openly:
    No cleric can live on in chastity!"

26. Eleventh spoke a priest upon his feet –
    In arts of rhetoric perfected and complete:
    "At no time without wife will be my bed,
    Until old age disarms me, nearly dead."

27.[h] The twelfth one with a mighty roar cries out:
    "I'm not upset by pontiff's threat or shout,
    But, by the love of God, I'd give much gold
    My dearest wife in peace to have and hold."

28.[i] The thirteenth argued: "I will not dismiss
    For short-lived threats, my hasty cooks of bliss,
    My concubines who, faithful in the rest,
    In morning beat out matins on my breast."

29. A chaplain spoke, the fourteenth in the list,
    And as he argued shook an angry fist:
    "The act[j] is useless, frivolous and vain:
    Who has no maid to love is quite insane."

30. The fifteenth said: "Whenever I drink wine
    And sleep takes hold of me at evening time,
    I then want in my bed my concubine,
    Lest I should lack my fleshly medicine."

31. Doctus sedecimus[36] in philosophia,
    "Omne quare," ait,[37] "habet suum quia:
    Si mihi[38] mea famula tollitur e uia,
    Extra uolo alere scorta pulchra tria."

32. Septimus et decimus, pauper commodista,
    Pectore de toto[39] prorsus dixit ista:
    "Ego non sum, Domini, diues sophista;[40]
    Non possum[41] famulam alere e cista."

33. Decimus octauus,[42] uentre ualde crassus,
    Omnibus in medio dixit, uerum fassus:
    "Certe meus socius fuit diu lassus;
    Propter pudicitiam non multa sum passus."

34. Nonus ait decimus: "Dicam hic sub rosa:
    Totus hic ad literam textus est cum glosa.
    Iussio Praesulis[43] haec religiosa
    Non erit uxoribus ciuium damnosa."

35. Addidit ulterius: "Sitis memor horum:
    Si uetare Praesul uult specialem thorum,
    Cernet totum breui[44] plenum esse chorum
    Ordine sacrorum adulterorum."[45]

36. Hinc est uox uigesimi prece terminata:
    "Sancta Maria uirgo, nostra aduocata,
    Iuua nos, ne Praesulis lex sit durata;[46]
    Est tibi deuotio famulorum grata."

37. Tandem[47] conclusit Monachus ita Praedicator:
    "Quis scit, an hoc hominum cupiat creator,
    Vt sacerdos mulierum desinat esse amator,[48]
    Pro quibus est positus in cruce Saluator.

38. Zacharias habuit prolem et uxorem,
    Quae Iohannem genuit, filium maiorem,
    Praedicentem totius mundi redemptorem.
    Non credo quod peccat,[49] seruans istum morem.

31. The sixteenth, learned in philosophy,
    Said: "There's a cause for every question 'Why?'.
    If I and my young serving maid should part,
    I'll elsewhere need to cultivate three tarts!"

32. The seventeenth, a poor assistant priest.
    Spoke then and all his inner thoughts released:
    "My lords, I'm no philosopher, I'm poor –
    From my small purse I can't maintain a whore."

33. The eighteenth priest – his belly was not small –
    Proclaimed the truth while speaking to them all:
    "My colleague certainly has long been tired;
    By being chaste I've not been sorely tried!"[k]

34. The nineteenth said: "I'll say this 'under rose':[l]
    The text is literal, but with its gloze.[m]
    The bishop's order, catholic in sense,
    Will not do harm to wives of citizens."[n]

35. He then went on: "Remember this instead:
    If bishop's wish forbids our special bed,[o]
    Our choir is wholly full, as he'll soon see,
    Of holy men steeped in adultery."

36. The twentieth then ended with a prayer:
    "Saint Mary, maid, our advocate up there,
    Please help us now: let not this law endure.
    You're pleased by serving men whose love is pure!"[p]

37. And then a monk concluded, preaching thus:
    "Who knows if God wills this (for He made us),
    That priests should not be lovers of their wives,
    For whom our Saviour once was crucified?

38. Zacharias had both a wife and son;
    His wife produced a greater child, named John,
    Who prophesied the one that ransomed us.
    He didn't sin, I think, behaving thus.

39. Dauid rex sanctissimus, frigidus senecta,
    Lusit cum iuuencula, quae fuit electa.
    Quae res in[50] Propheta non fuit suspecta,
    Nobis peccatoribus facile est recta.

40.[51] Dedit enim Dominus maledictionem
    Viro qui non fecerit generationem.
    Ergo cunctis consulo per hanc rationem,
    Vt generent[52] quo habeant benedictionem.

41. Canis semel rapiens carnem ad macellum
    A furto non abstinet nec timet cultellum;
    Sic nocturnum clericus suetus[53] ad duellum
    Non curat Praesulis[54] minas nec flagellum.

42. Coram tota curia Papa declarauit
    Sacerdotem, qui hic et haec et hoc declinauit,[55]
    Omnem non generantem excommunicauit.
    Ex sorore filium ipse procreauit.

43. Quod Papa concesserat, quis potest uetare?
    Cuncta potest soluere solus et ligare.[56]
    Laborare rusticos, milites pugnare
    Iussit, at praecipue clericos amare.

44. Habebimus clerici duas concubinas.
    Monachi, Canonici, totidem uel trinas,
    Decani, Praelati[57] quatuor uel quinas:
    Sic tandem leges implebimus diuinas!"[58]

39. Most holy David,[q] king, was old, like ice,
    But sported with a girl beyond all price.
    What in a prophet was quite free from blame
    For us poor sinners easily lacks shame.

40. The Lord proclaimed a curse on anyone
    Who hadn't made a generation.
    So by this reasoning I'd say: 'Take heed;
    To get a blessing, propagate your seed!'

41. A dog that goes to market for a steak
    Does not dread knife, or fear his loot to take.
    The clerk who's used to wrestling in the night
    Does not at bishop's threats or whip take fright!

42.[r] Before his curia the Pope acclaimed
    Him priest who *he* and *she* and *it* declined.
    He cursed all those who do not generate,
    And from a sister did a son create![s]

43. What Pope has granted, who can now deny?
    Alone he has the power to loose and tie.
    That peasants toll and soldiers fight, he bade,
    But most of all that clerks should love, he said.

44. We clergy now will have two concubines,
    And likewise monks and canons, or three times,
    And deans and prelates four, or even quine,
    And thus we will fulfil the laws divine!"

Notes to the Edition

Most of the notes here are on meter: the "improvements" are not intended as serious conjectures but as indications of how easily the poet could have made the lines scan properly.

[1] Two syllables long. Perhaps *nos* for *igitur*.

[2] One syllable long. Perhaps *canonum* for *canonico* (cf. 14.3 below).

[3] One syllable short. Perhaps *bene est* for *bene*.

[4] Uneven rhythm. Perhaps *Domini questionis* for *questionis Domini*.

[5] Second half of line one syllable long.

[6] The scansion of the entire line is problematic. Perhaps: "Vita solis angelis est omnino pura."

[7] One syllable short. Perhaps *meam nunc* for *meam*.

[8] One syllable long. Perhaps omit *ergo*.

[9] *supponere*: apparently in an obscene sense (cf. "get it up").

[10] One syllable long. Perhaps *es* for *estis*.

[11] One syllable long. Perhaps omit *hoc*.

[12] One syllable long. Perhaps treat *i* in *alienare* as a semi-vowel.

[13] Uneven rhythm. Perhaps read *Cellarius ait* for *Ait Cellarius*.

[14] The first half-lines of both lines 2 and 3 are one syllable too long: perhaps a metrical licence.

[15] One syllable long and *consilere* is not a word. Perhaps read *cillere* (lengthening the *e*) "put into motion, arouse," translating: "whom he can't rouse in bed." The present translation "hush" assumes that *consilere* = *silere* with an active sense.

[16] Second half of line one syllable long.

[17] First half of line one syllable short.

[18] One syllable long. Perhaps *Et* for *Atque*.

[19] Perhaps re-order: "Huius allegatio erat ergo talis."

[20] *Clementinam*: a decretal, ascribed in the text to the first century Pope Clement ("per Clementem Papam prolati"), identified, almost certainly correctly, by Lehmann as Canon 6, which said that a bishop or priest should not reject their wife on the grounds of religion: "episcopus aut presbyter uxorem propriam nequaquam sub obtentu religionis abiiciat. Si vero reiiecerit, excommunicetur, sed et si perseveraverit, deiiciatur," PL 130:15C. Second half of line 15.2 one syllable long.

[21] *coronam trinam*: i.e. the Pope's emblem.

[22] One syllable long. Perhaps *Hanc tenere igitur* for *Hanc igitur retinere*.

[23] Second half of line one syllable short. See NR, stanza 11.4 *pro sermone tali* rather than *pro lege tali*.

[24] Perhaps *minime uir* for *uir minime*.

[25] One syllable short. Perhaps *erit nunc* for *erit*.

[26] One syllable long. Perhaps *potero* for *ego possum*.

[27] Second half of line one syllable long.

[28] One syllable long. Perhaps *loquendum nunc* for *loquendum*.

[29] Three syllables long. Perhaps omit *etiam*.

[30] Second half of line three syllables short.

[31] First half of line one syllable short. NR, stanza 16.2 ("nobis hinc timere"), would fit.

[32] First half of line one syllable short.

[33] One syllable long. Perhaps omit *Sed*.

[34] One syllable short. Perhaps read *Quae in meo pectore* for *Quae mane pectore*.

[35] First half of line one syllable short. Add *Tunc* or similar.

[36] First half of line one syllable short. Probably read *sextus decimus* (cf. stanza 32.1).

[37] One syllable short. Perhaps *ait is* for *ait*.

[38] One syllable long. Perhaps *mi* for *mihi*.

[39] First half of line one syllable short. Perhaps add *tunc* or similar.

[40] Second half of line one syllable short. Perhaps add *uel* before *sophista*.

[41] One syllable short. Perhaps *potero* for *possum*. The line answers CP, stanza 31.4.

[42] First half of line one syllable short. Perhaps add *et* after *decimus*.

[43] First half of line one syllable short. Perhaps add *nam* after *iussio*.

[44] One syllable short. Perhaps *breuiter* for *breui*.

[45] Each half line lacks a syllable. The speaker is perhaps implying a new religious order "Sacri Adulteri" which would be against the ban in Fourth Lateran on new religious orders.

[46] Second half of line one syllable short. Perhaps add *haec* before *lex*.

[47] One syllable long. Perhaps *Tunc* for *Tandem*.

[48] The line has three syllable too many, but emendation is difficult, as we need an antecedent for *quibus*.

[49] One syllable short. Perhaps *peccauit* for *peccat*.

[50] First half of line one syllable short. Perhaps add *tunc* after *res*.

[51] Gen. 38.1–10 (Onan); cf. Lev. 1.15.

[52] One syllable long. Perhaps *gignant* for *generent*.

⁵³ *suetus* is scanned with *su* semiconsonantal.

⁵⁴ First half of line one syllable short. Perhaps *is curat* or similar.

⁵⁵ The line will scan if *et* is omitted: "qui hic, haec et hoc declinauit" but betrays his own lack of grammar, as *sacerdos* is never neuter.

⁵⁶ Matt. 16.19.

⁵⁷ First half of line one syllable short. Perhaps add *et* after *Decani*.

⁵⁸ The whole line lacks one syllable. Perhaps read: "Sic tandem implebimus nos leges diuinas."

Notes to the Translation

ᵃ "As being weak for battle, I will be contented," i.e. as I am too feeble for sex, I won't mind. Compare the reply of the chanter in stanza 7.

ᵇ Is *dominus* here God or the pope?

ᶜ On the sequence of speakers, see Introduction, p. 24.

ᵈ *curialis*: perhaps referring to his status (courtier) or his disposition (courteous).

ᵉ This line may allude to the number of anticoncubine decrees.

ᶠ *sacrificus*: "mass-priest."

ᵍ See note to NR, stanza 35.3.

ʰ See NR, stanza 23, with widely differing sense.

ⁱ See NR, stanza 24. On the priority of NR before CP, see Introduction, p. 93.

ʲ *Actus* probably refers to masturbation.

ᵏ That is, "chastity has not been a problem for me (as I have not practised it.)"

ˡ *sub rosa*: for the phrase, see A.G. Rigg, "*Sub rosa*: A Confidential Note," *Notes and Queries* 58 (2011), 367–68.

ᵐ That is, the order needs to be explained away by sophistry.

ⁿ This seems to refer to the decree ascribed to Clement I; see above, note 20 to edition and Introduction, p. 91).

ᵒ "special bed" suggests a clerical privilege.

ᵖ The sense seems to be that just as the Virgin is pleased by the devotion of her servants, so she should be by men who serve women. Wright's *famularun* may be a simple slip or an emendation. For *famula* in the sense of concubine, cf. CP, stanza 32.4.

ᑫ David: cf. NR, stanza 39 (Solomon and David).

ʳ The stanza uses the declension of *sacerdos* differently from PR, stanza 1. Here there is a real examination on Latinity, which the candidate passes successfully and is admitted to the priesthood by declining *sacerdos* in both masculine and feminine: the present speaker (i.e. the monk) takes *declino* in a sexual sense ("lay down") and infers the Pope's approval of clerical heterosexuality.

[s] This may reflect a piece of gossip, but it is also possible that the Latin examination also required the declension of *soror* and *filius*, which is also misinterpreted. For examples of clerical Latin examinations, see John Shinners and William J. Dohar, *Pastors and the Care of Souls in Medieval England* (Notre Dame, 1998), pp. 48, 61–62, nos. 28 and 34; and also *The Register of Eudes of Rouen*, trans. Sidney M. Brown with notes by Jeremiah F. O'Sullivan (New York, 1964), on May 30, 1253 (pp. 174–75). I am indebted to Prof. Joe Goering for these references.

Abstract

This article presents a new edition and the first English translation of three satirical poems that address the issue of the celibacy of the clergy. The poems, *Nouus Rumor Anglie*, *Prisciani Regula*, and *Clerus et Presbiteri*, were first published in modern times by Thomas Wright in 1841. The three texts are written in quatrains of regular Goliardic verse and the topic in all is the opposition of the clergy to attempts to ban clerical marriage or concubinage. Even though the themes in the three poems are similar, their narratives and structures vary widely. It is impossible to be precise about the date of composition, but the first half of the thirteenth century can be postulated. There is a very strong connection to England which is probably where the poems were written.

Résumé

Cet article offre une nouvelle édition et la première traduction anglaise de trois poèmes satiriques portant sur le célibat du clergé. Les poèmes, *Nouus Rumor Anglie*, *Prisciani Regula*, et *Clerus et Presbiteri*, ont été publiés pour la première fois à l'époque contemporaine par Thomas Wright en 1841. Ces trois textes ont été composés en quatrains de la forme régulière goliardique et tous traitent le sujet de l'opposition du clergé face aux tentatives de prohiber le mariage des clercs ou le concubinage. Bien que les thèmes abordés par les trois poèmes soient similaires, les récits qu'ils relatent et la structure qui les définit varient grandement. Il est impossible d'être précis quant à la date de composition de ces textes, mais on peut avancer comme hypothèse la première moitié du XIIIe siècle. On trouve également dans ces œuvres un lien fort avec l'Angleterre, lieu où elles ont probablement été rédigées.

A.G. Rigg (†)
University of Toronto

Payen Bolotin's Targeting of the Tironensians and the Cistercians in his *De Falsis Heremitis**

DAVID A. TRAILL
University of California, Davis (emeritus)

Introduction

The late eleventh and early twelfth centuries witnessed a great upheaval in the monastic world of Europe. Many had become dissatisfied with traditional Benedictine monasticism as it had developed under the leadership of Cluny. There seems to have been a widespread yearning for a more eremitical form of life, away from the distractions and corrupting influence of towns.[1] This led to the burgeoning, especially in France, of a wide range of eremitical orders, of which the most important was that of the Cistercians. The groundbreaking work of Constance Berman provides a new perspective on the swift rise of the Cistercians in this period, prompting a general reassessment of their early growth.[2] As part of this reassessment, primary texts need to be re-examined to see if conventional views have led to misinterpretation. Saint Bernard's famous *Apologia* (1125–1126) ushered in a series of satirical attacks on Cluniac practices that deviated from the Benedictine Rule and corresponding responses from the Benedictines.[3] Payen Bolotin's satirical *De Falsis Heremitis,* written in the unusual metre of rhyming adonics (three units, each consisting of a dactyl plus trochee or

---

*I would like to express my indebtedness to the two anonymous readers of an earlier version of this study for saving me from a number of embarrassing errors and suggesting a considerable number of significant improvements and to Greti Dinkova-Bruun for further suggestions for refining the arrangement of the article.

[1] For a good account of the crisis, see Jean Leclercq, "The Monastic Crisis of the Eleventh and Twelfth Centuries," in *Cluniac Monasticism in the Central Middle Ages,* ed. Noreen Hunt (London, 1971), pp. 217–37. Leclercq includes a short discussion of Payen's poem at pp. 226–31.

[2] Constance H. Berman, *The Cistercian Evolution* (Philadelphia, 2000); on the importance of this study, see John Van Engen's review in *Speculum* 79 (2004), 452–55.

[3] See André Wilmart, "Une riposte de l'ancien monachisme au manifeste de Saint Bernard," *Revue bénédictine* 46 (1934), 296–344, for a listing with brief summaries. Wilmart begins the series with Bernard's 1120 letter to Robert of Châtillon and the response of Peter the Venerable. Mention is made (pp. 304–5) of the excerpts from Payen's poem printed in *Histoire littéraire de la France,* 46 vols. (Paris, 1835), 18:808–16, but not to Meyer's edition (see below, n. 4). Wilmart's list is updated by Jean Leclercq in his "Nouvelle réponse de l'ancien monachisme aux critiques des Cisterciens," *Revue bénédictine* 67 (1957), 77–94.

spondee, per line) and found only in a single Paris manuscript, appears to be one of the earliest responses on the Benedictine side, though it was written by a canon of Chartres rather than a Benedictine monk.[4] The poem was written in 1130, for lines 195–200 refer to a "new development in religious life thirty-two years earlier," which led monks and would-be monks to a widespread turning away from the Benedictine order.[5] It is generally accepted that this "new development" refers to the events in 1098, when Robert of Molesme left the abbey of Molesme with about twenty others and founded a new monastery at Cîteaux that would observe a stricter observance of the Benedictine Rule than had become customary. This marks the beginning of the Cistercians whose rapid growth was to dominate the monastic scene in Europe throughout the twelfth century. The event came to be regarded as a turning-point in a larger reformist movement that embraced the rise of such orders as the Grandmontines, Tironensians, Premonstratensians (canons regular), Community of Fontevraud, Congregation of Savigny, and others. Payen's poem represents an attack on one or more of these eremitical orders, whose monks, he argues, lead lives that, so far from being eremitical, allow them to wander around towns and to focus on accumulating wealth. It is unclear, however, which of the eremitical orders he is actually condemning. Wilhelm Meyer argues that the entire array of new eremitical orders is under attack, and the Cistercians above all; he further maintains, on the basis of line

---

[4] The manuscript, Paris, Bibliothèque nationale de France, MS lat. 8433 (saec. XIII), fol. 112r–114v, hereafter referred to as **P**, is accessible on line at https://gallica.bnf.fr/ark:/12148/btv1b9066189x/f113). The Latin text has been edited and discussed by Wilhelm Meyer, "Zwei Gedichte zur Geschichte des Cistercienser Ordens," *Nachrichten des königlichen Gesellschaft der Wissenschaften zu Göttingen, Philologisch-Historishe Klasse* (1908), 377–95; and by Jean Leclercq, "Le poème de Payen Bolotin contre les faux ermites," *Revue bénédictine* 68 (1958), 52–86. The first full translation of the text (into Portuguese) is in Gabriel de Carvalho Godoy Castanho's 2007 University of São Paulo dissertaion, which accompanies Leclercq's Latin text (with a few improvements from Meyer), https://www.teses.usp.br/teses/disponiveis/8/8138/tde-07082007-151100/publico/TESE_GABRIEL_C_GODOY_CASTANHO.pdf. This was followed by Castanho's article, "O texto polêmico ou a polêmica do texto: Eremitismo, literatura e sociedade na Chartres do século xii," *Revista Signum* 12/2 (2011), 100–22; the English abstract reads in part: "Our aim is to join historical, literary and codicological methodologies in order to explain the principles of the argumentative process in which the poet built the social image of the false hermit." The Paris manuscript contains the following works (Payen's poem is item 6): 1. Anonymi carmina de rebus ad Christianam religionem spectantibus: praemittitur fragmentum synonymorum Magistri Matthaei Vindocinensis; 2. Alcuini praefatio in vitam S. Richarii presbyteri; 3. Sermones Gaufridi Babionis; 4. Anonymi tractatus de duodecim articulis fidei; 5. Bernardi Morlanensis liber de contemptu mundi; 6. Poetarum variorum satyrae sine nomine; 7. Vita sanctae Mariae Aegyptiae authore Hildeberto, Cenomanensi Episcopo. Most of the works seem to come from the west and northwest of France. Items 5–7 are all satirical.

[5] The phrase "thirty-two years earlier" dates the writing of lines 195–200 to 1130; presumably, the poem was finished in that year or shortly thereafter. Leclercq, "Le Poème," p. 57, concludes that the poem was finished a few years before 1135.

26, that the Tironensians must also be targeted.[6] Leclercq agrees that all eremitical orders are criticized, but avoids singling out any order as a specific target.[7] I agree with Meyer against Leclercq in arguing that, while the author does seem hostile to all the new eremitical orders, he blames the Cistercians and their charismatic leader, Bernard, in particular, for the seismic shift away from the Benedictines towards these eremitical forms of religious life. In addition, I will argue that Payen is particularly provoked, to a considerably greater degree than Meyer seems to suggest, by the comparatively nearby and financially very successful Tironensians. Much of the time, however, it is unclear whether he is thinking collectively of the eremitical orders or of one unidentified order in particular, and this is probably a deliberate tactic.

The Author

The manuscript identifies the author of the poem as Paganus Bolotinus. We know nothing about him except that Orderic Vitalis, who comments approvingly on the poem, refers to him as a canon of Chartres.[8] Paganus turns out to have been a common name in the region around Chartres, for Leclercq reports that no fewer than eighty-five *personnages* in the cartulary of St. Père de Chartres are called Paganus, none of whom has an added "Bolotinus," though not all names are given in full.[9] The popularity of the name Paganus and the tendency not to add further clarification make the task of identifying our poet very difficult. The most likely candidate Leclercq found to be a "Paganus qui et Belotinus," is a canon from 1106, who served as archdeacon from 1126. He was also known as "Paganus de Mongervilla," and was still around in 1137 and perhaps even later.[10]

Summary of the Poem's Contents

Monks who profess to be eremitical openly condemn avarice and are thought to be poor but are obsessed with gathering riches. They sometimes dress as Benedictines. However, instead of engaging in religious pursuits in the monastery, they roam city

---

[6] Meyer, "Zwei Gedichte," p. 384. Tiron is about 25 miles from Chartres. The nearest Cistercian monasteries in 1130 were about 40 miles from Chartres and much closer to Orleans.

[7] Leclercq, "Le poème," p. 73.

[8] Marjorie Chibnall, *The Ecclesiastical History of Orderic Vitalis*, 6 vols. (Oxford, 1969–1980), 4:312–13. Payen could have been a teacher at the Chartres school, as Alexandre Clerval, *Les écoles de Chartres* (Paris, 1895), p. 174, asserts, but this is not proved, for, as Richard W. Southern, *Medieval Humanism* (New York, 1970), p. 68, points out, the mere appellation *magister* without accompanying *scolae* is no proof of the status of teacher of a cathedral school.

[9] For a detailed discussion, see Leclercq, "Le poème," pp. 60–63; and Benjamin Guérard, *Cartulaire de l'abbaye de Saint-Père de Chartres*, 2 vols. (Paris, 1840), 2:789–90.

[10] Leclercq, "Le poème," pp. 62–63.

streets. This is a widespread plague, but our city is particularly hard-pressed by it. These monks accumulate wealth, hardly eating or spending anything (lines 1–30). They are not religious but wicked. Their habits are white, off-white, and grey, with grey considered the holiest. Though their dress may suggest hermits, they are in fact parasites. A monk, skilful in teaching both the simple and the sophisticated about his order, unabashedly exacts sexual favours. He has daily bouts of drunkenness, spurns the needy, and claims poverty for himself. He secretly charges the clergy with hypocrisy (lines 31–66). These monks are city-lovers, not hermits, and are either adulterers or sodomites. They deny the good works done by the clergy. A hermit monk claims that their rule alone leads to a blessed hereafter. He describes their austere way of life, contrasting it with the "epicurean" lifestyle of the clergy. He loves the smoky city because he can mingle with important people and be invited to much tastier meals than the forest provides (lines 67–90). His impressive tonsure is to deceive the simple into thinking him pious. Asked why he finds the company of the young so agreeable, he says that young men look for guidance and that the order's teaching shows them how to live holy lives. In this way he conceals his evil intentions, which he cannot control. He feels no shame over his disgraceful association with these young men (lines 91–110). With them he lives a disorderly life, protecting himself with his white habit and cowl. Peasants want to be dressed like him to safeguard their possessions. Though he is uneducated, the whole countryside flocks to him and applauds him. He acts as mediator between magnates and dines with the rich and powerful. Arriving early at church councils, he senses what is new, impresses bishops, eats little, drinks less, and makes dramatic shows of piety. Many are taken in and he is made a bishop. Once appointed, however, he amasses wealth and readily breaks agreements (lines 111–140). Abandoning sackcloth for linen, he now drinks Falernian wine, and rather than performing vigils he rides stallions over the fields. To hide his crimes, he hires other hypocrites. Our country is suffering from a plague of such men.

To punish us for our guilt a great false prophet has arisen with his disciples. The four horses of the Apocalypse (Rev. 6.1–8) are then described with the fourth, the pale horse, signaling the present, the time of this false prophet and his followers. The fires of hell await them. When Christ passes judgement, they will all go to hell. It is an evil time that has long been festering (lines 141–190). The evil has been reinvigorated, as Christ predicted. It started thirty-two years ago with the new development in religious life, when hermit monks criticized the Benedictines for failing to observe the Benedictine Rule, charging them with idleness and eating fish and fatty foods, but they do not understand the deprivation of the cloistered life or the benefits conferred by these "idle hours." Benedictines avoid delicacies as harmful to the soul (lines 191–220). Abstaining from attainable delicacies is a virtue not available to hermit monks who go after rich food that they do not have. Also, when food is scarce in the forest, they turn to townspeople to take pity on their attenuated limbs. Episcopal collusion with recruitment to eremitical orders has provoked widespread resentment among the populace thanks to the consequent depletion of forest resources (lines 221–248).

Hermit monks dine with the bishop, and diocesan matters are now handled by men in tunics. However, their pursuit of glory in this world and their enjoyment of habits of different colours is short-sighted. In the old days, monks all wore the same habit and focused on religious concerns rather than on the gifts from the powerful. In the forest they drank only water. Now they pursue the vanities of idleness or restlessly roam from one region to the next. They prefer city cuisine to the forest's offerings, for there the rich vie with one another to provide hermit monks with peppered fish and other expensive delicacies (lines 249–292). Hugh, bishop of Nevers, however, offered only plain food and water to visiting monks to avoid awakening in them a yearning for expensive food. He thereby contributed to their salvation. We judge people not by the garments they wear but by their religious devotion. Some hermit monks are devout and deserve our admiration, but others are not. The crowd adores them, as do the magnates. Our old ways are spurned, and everyone is rushing to become a hermit, but hermit monks are not unsullied. They teach one thing and do another. They pursue pleasure, praise, and money. They will not achieve joy in the afterlife, for what they seek is transitory (lines 293–338).

The Tironensians

The recent publication of Kathleen Thompson's excellent study of the Tironensians has put us in a much better position to evaluate whether Meyer was right to suggest that Payen might well have been targeting them.[11] After an extended discussion of a surprisingly large array of relevant sources, she turns her attention to the founder, Bernard of Tiron, who became abbot of St. Cyprien at Poitiers in 1100, but left the abbey shortly thereafter, either in protest against its being made subordinate to Cluny or forced out by Cluniac supporters.[12] He moved to the region of Chartres, where he was well received by the count of Perche, Rotrou II, and Ivo, bishop of Chartres.[13] Rotrou gave Bernard a substantial piece of his forested land as a place where Bernard and his followers might settle, and later, in 1114, Ivo appears to have been influential in persuading the Chartres chapter to add an adjoining piece of land owned by it.[14] The

---

[11] Kathleen Thompson, *The Monks of Tiron* (Cambridge, 2014).

[12] Thompson, *The Monks*, pp. 50 and 101–2. The date of his departure is unclear.

[13] Thompson. *The Monks*, p. 96.

[14] Thompson, *The Monks*, pp. 51–52.

monastery was founded in 1107.[15] Orderic Vitalis gives this account of the early days:[16]

> Here in a wooded spot called Tiron he built a monastery in honour of our holy Saviour. A multitude of the faithful of both orders[17] flocked to him there, and Father Bernard received in charity all who were eager for conversion to monastic life, instructing individuals to practise in the monastery the various crafts in which they were skilled. So, among the men who hastened to share his life were joiners and blacksmiths, sculptors and goldsmiths, painters and masons, vine-dressers and husbandmen, and skilled artificers of many kinds. They industriously carried out the tasks imposed on them by their superior and handed over for the common good whatever they earned.

Thompson notes that the Tironensians, who "seem to have been prepared to extend the title of monk very broadly," admitted artisans and their wives, recognizing both as monks, and that some of these artisans would need to live in an urban setting in order to ply their trades profitably so that there would be the expected earnings to hand over for the common good, as Orderic describes.[18] She then remarks: "The presence of this community of fellow-travelling artisans at Chartres is likely to have induced some of the satire of Payn Bolotin."[19] She also notes that the Tironensian monks "may well have resorted to animal skins and a habit that was 'remarkably similar to the very sheep from which it was made,'"[20] just as he is almost certainly thinking of them in line 26, when he complains about hermit monks roaming the streets of Chartres. The accumulation of wealth that is decried in the opening lines of the poem runs contrary to the ideals of the Tironensians and, apparently, to their practice under their founder, Bernard.[21] However, Bernard died in 1116 and after two short-lived abbots, the fourth abbot, the comparatively young William, who had a strong entrepreneurial bent, was installed in 1119.[22] It is important to bear in mind, accordingly, that in 1130, when

---

[15] Thompson, *The Monks*, p. 95.

[16] Translation from Marjorie Chibnall, ed., *The Ecclesiastical History of Orderic Vitalis*, 6 vols. (Oxford, 1969–1980), 4:331 (Latin on p. 330, where, in n. 1, Chibnall cites evidence for dating the founding of Tiron to 1107).

[17] Chibnall, *Ecclesiastical History*, 4:330, n. 2, suggests: "Probably clerks and laymen; but possibly secular clergy and monks."

[18] Thompson, *The Monks*, p. 138; and Chibnall, *Ecclesiastical History*, 4:330–31.

[19] Thompson, *The Monks*, p. 139.

[20] Thompson, *The Monks*, pp. 128–29. Accordingly, here Payen may be thinking of the Tironensian monks along with others. However, with the reference to the sheepskins in line 1 and wolf under them in line 11, he is probably thinking primarily of the Cistercians; see the last sentence in the section on the Cistercians below.

[21] On Bernard of Tiron's aversion to wealth, see Thompson, *The Monks*, pp. 21–22.

[22] Thompson, *The Monks*, pp. 131–32 and 135.

Payen was writing his poem, Bernard had been dead for fourteen years and that William had been abbot for at least ten years, during which time both the financial situation and the ethos of the monastery seem to have changed considerably.

Bishop Ivo had also died in 1116 and had been replaced by Geoffrey, who served from 1116 to 1149 and who was even more favourably disposed to the Tironensians than Ivo had been, and, as Thompson argues, seems to have "encouraged the Thibaudian comital family in their support of the Tironensian community."[23] The reader of the Tiron cartulary cannot help being impressed by the numerous gifts of land, churches, tithes, etc. that fill its pages from about 1115 onwards.[24] Besides gifts from the kings of France and England and the local nobility there are numerous gifts of land and properties from what appear to be fairly ordinary people.[25] Thompson astutely notes that the monks, who were recording the increase in their possessions in the cartulary, apparently felt the need to seek biblical authority to justify their departure from poverty, for "three preambles to acts in the Tiron cartulary, for example, refer to Christ's remark recorded at Luke 16.9: 'use worldly wealth to make friends for yourselves so that when it's gone, you will be welcomed into the eternal homes.'"[26] It is more than likely that others in the Chartres chapter shared Payen's antipathy to these upstart hermit monks who seemed to be so successful in winning for themselves donations that otherwise might well have gone to the chapter. By the late 1140s the Tironensians owned no fewer than 134 properties in France, mainly abbeys, priories, and churches, but also the rights to the bridge-tolls over a river and the rents of a castle and the tithe of a mint and eleven cross-Channel properties. These properties are listed in a document of Pope Eugenius III, dated 1147, confirming Tironensian ownership of them.[27]

Thompson also speaks of "the development of a Tironensian community" in the city of Chartres itself. As we have seen, Orderic Vitalis reports that a multitude flocked to see the Tironensian monks, who had recently arrived in the forest, and many were sufficiently impressed to choose to join them.[28] Many of these were artisans and although perhaps usefully employed at Tiron during the building of the monastery,

---

[23] Thompson, *The Monks*, pp. 136–37.

[24] Lucien Merlet, *Cartulaire de l'abbaye de la Sainte-Trinité de Tiron*, 2 vols. (Chartres, 1883).

[25] Henry I of England granted to the monks of Tiron land and or properties given them by others (Merlet, *Cartulaire*, 1:27–28, 29, 41), and Louis VI gave them some land at Saintry, west of Orleans (Merlet, *Cartulaire*, 1:18).

[26] Thompson, *The Monks*, pp. 134–35.

[27] See Thompson, *The Monks*, pp. 221–45, for the list; surprisingly, it appears to include no property in Chartres itself, though the cartulary contains a considerable number of documents detailing the acquisition and selling of properties in and near the town.

[28] Chibnall, *Ecclesiastical History*, pp. 330–31.

later chose to live in Chartres to earn money in order to make their contributions to the Tironensian community. The leader of the town monks from an uncertain date was Hubert Asinarius ("the donkey-man"), who appears frequently as a witness to documents in the cartulary.[29] After William became abbot of Tiron in 1119, there was a transaction whereby the abbot and monks of Tiron gave a certain Evard the houses they owned in the *forum* of Chartres in exchange for his house on the *Vicus fabrorum* ("Street of the craftsmen") "with all its appendages."[30] The transaction took place in the chapter-house of Tiron and Hubert Asinarius is named among the "secular" witnesses.[31] Evard's establishment seems to have been a large one; the "appendages" included a blacksmith's workshop, in which Evard retained the right to work until his death, and, given the street's name, probably other workshops among the "appendages." While perhaps an unlikely location for a traditional monastery, it could have provided very suitable accommodation for those artisans who had become Tironensian monks but who needed to work at their trades in an urban environment.

No doubt related to this development was the gift of Theobald IV, count of Blois 1102–1151, to the Tironensians which Merlet tentatively dates to 1121. The gift comprised six *servientes*, namely, a smith, a rope maker, a wine dealer, a fuller, a keeper of vineyards, and a baker.[32] Six additional bakers, not designated as *servientes*, were also included in the gift. That the *servientes* were to serve the Tironensians in Chartres, not in Tiron, is clear from the stipulation that in their case *pernoctatio* was not granted.[33] There was no such stipulation with regard to the six additional bakers, who presumably either lived in the town with their wives or would join the others in the Tironen-

---

[29] In a charter at Merlet, *Cartulaire*, 2:3, he is described as "Hubert Asinarius, prior of the Tironensian monks living in Chartres." At Merlet, *Cartulaire*, 1:195, n. 2, Merlet calls him "prieur de l'abbaye de Tiron á Chartres."

[30] Merlet, *Cartulaire*,1:44. The charter is merely dated 24 June, but William is mentioned as abbot; Merlet dates it 1119–1136.

[31] Presumably, *secularis*, when applied to a Tironensian monk, denotes a monk who "lives in the world," as opposed to those living in the monastery at Tiron itself.

[32] Merlet, *Cartulaire*, 1:64.

[33] The *servientes* were required to return to the count's household every night. This stipulation makes it clear that the gift was only of the service of the servants and that Theobald had not relinquished control of them. That the service of six servants was granted suggests that there was a substantial presence of Tironensian monks already living in Chartres and that the acquisition of Evard's house and "appendages" was probably an early move by Abbot William predating 1121. The six additional bakers, who were not *servientes*, but clearly in some sense dependent on the count, may have been his vassals. Presumably, they had expressed the desire to become Tironensian secular monks and live communally in Chartres while plying their trade. For the readiness with which the Tironensians were prepared to extend the status of monkhood, probably as "secular monks," compare the cases of William the mason and his wife and Gerard Ensaielana and his wife Amelina at Thompson, *The Monks*, p. 138.

sian establishment in Chartres. Besides providing the services appropriate to their trades, some of the *servientes* and, occasionally some of the additional bakers, participated in property transactions for the Tironensians, for their names appear as witnesses in the relevant documents. In this way they played a significant role for the Tironensians in building up what Thompson observes might today be described as a "property portfolio in the city: land was purchased, houses were leased, and property exchanged."[34]

The artisan monks living in Chartres and plying their various trades would, like most tradesmen, probably be dressed in tunics much of the time, and this would have distinguished them, in Payen's eyes, from "real monks." Naturally, it would be these artisan monks residing in Chartres, who would be seen most frequently in the town, provoking the indignation of Payen, who thought it hypocritical of "eremitical monks" to be seen roaming the town's streets (line 26). His indignation reaches its climax in lines 251–258, where he denounces what he sees as their outrageous behaviour, by applying to them the term *tunicati* in a clearly derogatory manner, complaining that they are now in charge of the diocese and deciding who should be awarded ecclesiastical offices. The contemptuous conclusion, "tunicati, non heremite," makes it clear that he is referring to Tironensian monks, not to those of any other order, for how could the Cistercians or the monks of any other of the new orders plausibly be expected to have any sway over Bishop Geoffrey, given their minimal and temporary presence in Chartres and the bishop's well-known admiration for the ever-present Tironensians? Besides, the reality was no doubt much more mundane. Presumably, from time to time the bishop would invite some of the town monks for a meal at the palace. If, shortly after such an event, an allocation of an ecclesiastical position was announced that was rather suprising, this would be seen in hostile quarters as adequate proof that the "care of the diocese" was in the hands of the *tunicati*.

The reference at lines 229–232 to hermit monks appealing to townspeople for the food they needed when supplies in the forest were inadequate appears to be a tendentious account of a very real and severe famine, accompanied by sickness that Orderic Vitalis reports was widespread in France for the years 1109–1111 and that was particularly severe in the areas around Chartres and Orleans.[35] The hagiographical *Vita Bernardi* records that the count of Nevers gave Bernard of Tiron a gold vase, the sale of which enabled Bernard to buy enough food from the townspeople for the community in Tiron to survive.[36] One might conclude therefore that Payen is thinking

---

[34] Thompson, *The Monks*, p. 137.

[35] Chibnall, *Ecclesiastical History*, 6:166–67.

[36] Geoffrey Grossus, *The Life of Blessed Bernard of Tiron*, ed. and trans. Ruth H. Cline (Washington, 2012), section 70.

here of the Tironensians. However, since in the immediately preceding lines Payen is clearly dealing with St. Bernard's criticisms of the Benedictines and at line 235 we seem to be hearing the words of one or more Cistercian recruiters, it seems best to imagine here that Payen is generalizing from what he saw as the Tironensians' dependence on Chartres, to depict all eremitical groups as having to resort to the nearest town for food in hard times.

The Cistercians

There are three clear indications that the Cistercians are also to be identified as targets in Payen's poem. The first of these occurs in lines 84, 91, and 111, where a monk is so characterised as to appear to have illicit motives for enjoying the company of young men and is revealed to be a Cistercian by his white habit. If Payen's scenario of a Cistercian frequently seen in the company of young men in or near Chartres (lines 97–112) has any basis in reality, then he was probably trying to recruit lay brothers (or *conversi*) to work on Cistercian granges rather than prompted by the motives implied by Payen. These lay brothers were for the most part recruited from among the young peasantry to work on, and even manage, the granges usually located at some distance from the monastery itself.[37] Of the six pre-1130 Cistercian foundations in western France listed by Leclercq the two closest to Chartres (both roughly equidistant from it at about forty miles as the crow flies) were l'Aumône in the diocese of Chartres (founded in 1121 in the Forest of Marchenoir) and La Cour Dieu (founded 1119 in Ingrammes) in the diocese of Orleans.[38] Either monastery, or both, could well be looking to recruit lay brothers in the neighborhood of Chartres after 1120.[39] We encounter one or more Cistercian recruiters giving their pitch to potential recruits at lines 235–248.[40] Neither Meyer nor Leclercq, however, makes any mention of lay

---

[37] Giles Constable, *The Reformation of the Twelfth Century* (Cambridge, 1996), p. 79, writes generally of lay brothers in the twelfth century: "The lay brothers were not monks, therefore, though they wore a religious habit and were considered members of the community. They may sometimes have been to a certain extent integrated with the monks and shared their liturgical life, but in the stricter orders they constituted a separate community beside that of the monks or lived apart or in small groups in granges. They were occupied principally with agricultural work, and both their status and the nature of their duties made them inferior to the choir monks who celebrated the holy offices."

[38] The foundation dates of these monasteries are those given at Leclercq, "Le Poème," p. 58.

[39] Both monasteries were much closer to Orleans (l'Aumône about 25 miles distant and La Cour Dieu, 12 miles), and it would be there they would go on more humdrum business rather than to Chartres, where Tironensians would certainly be much more frequently seen on the streets, especially with a number of artisan monks living there.

[40] The manuscript's reading *perdicionis* at line 235 is clearly wrong, as Meyer points out (p. 392), since a rhyming word cannot rhyme with itself. Neither Meyer nor Leclercq proposes an emendation, but Meyer suggests that a word like *dignitatis* is required. Meyer does not indicate where the direct speech

Payen Bolotin's Targeting of the Tironensians and the Cistercians 157

brothers in their comments on the passage and both give the impression that they think the recruiters are recruiting regular monks; this, however, seems highly improbable, for most who wished to become regular Cistercian monks would probably not be enticed into an organization that could be described as "laicalis forma videtur condicionis" – "similar to a lay organization."[41] Clearly, the people being recruited here are the lay brothers who did most of the hard physical labour. It would be the task of the lay brothers on the granges to make the land donated to the monastery suitable for agricultural exploitation, thereby provoking the hostility of the local peasantry (line 238), who witnessed the deforestation and the concomitant loss of forest resources on which their livelihood depended (lines 245–248). It makes sense for a recruiter of lay brothers to tell potential recruits that the organization he is asking them to join is "not one of high standing, rather its format resembles that of a lay organization" (lines 235–236) in order to reassure them that they are not being asked to join an elite organization, in which they would be expected to read and write.[42] The phrase "nullius ordo prelationis" can also be understood to mean "an order with no episcopal support," and it is this meaning that Payen then refutes in lines 237–238, for this was patently untrue, given that the Cistercian text, *Exordium Parvum*, prescribes that the Cistercians should recruit lay brothers only "with the permission of the bishop."[43]

The second indication occurs at lines 163–164, where Payen speaks contemptuously of the "great pseudo-prophet and the false coinage of his disciples." Meyer was right to see in this a scarcely veiled reference to Bernard of Clairvaux, the

---

begins and ends, while Leclercq confusingly makes all of lines 235–238 direct speech. The emendation, *prelationis*, rhymes, fits metrically, and is suitably ambiguous, since it can mean "preference," "high office," "office of a prelate," (*DMLBS*, praelatio 1 and 2) or "importance" (Albert Blaise, *Dictionnaire latin-français des auteurs chrétiens*, [Strasbourg, 1954], *praelatio*), with the different meanings providing natural transitions to lines 236 and 237. The scribal error is a classic example of dittography.

[41] Meyer, "Zwei Gedichte," p. 392, explains the reference to episcopal support (line 237) as reflecting the Cistercian rule that new monasteries could only be established with the support of the bishop, while Leclercq, "Le Poème," p. 52, merely comments in his summary of the poem that "ils se glorifient de leur austérité, du caractère laic de leur ordre" and offers no further elucidation of this passage elsewhere.

[42] It is not impossible that Payen is also thinking here of Tironensian recruiters, in which case they would be recruiting artisan monks.

[43] Jacques Dubois, "L'institution des convers au XIIe siècle," in his *Histoire monastique en France au XIIe siècle* (London, 1982), article VI, pp. 183–261, at 187: "Ils décidèrent qu'ils recevraient, avec la permission de leur évêque, des laïques convers portant la barbe, et qu'ils les traiteraient en tout comme eux-mêmes durant leur vie et à leur mort, à l'exception du monachat."

leading light in the rapid growth of the Cistercian movement, and his followers.[44] This leads Payen into a digression about the four horses of the Apocalypse (lines 165–192), and how the breaking of the fourth seal alludes to the false prophets of the day (line 168), while the emerging pale horse denotes "the hypocrites" (lines 173–174). The evil – "hec mala radix" – ushered in by the pale horse has long been festering underground and its release in our day, predicted by Christ, has infected contemporary thought and religion (lines 186–194). Immediately after this, we have the reference to the move to Cîteaux – "the new development in religion that occurred thirty-two years prior" (lines 195–196) – that led to attacks on the Benedictines. It is hard to see how Leclercq could have failed to see in this sequence of thought an obvious denunciation of Saint Bernard and the Cistercians.

The third indication is to be found in Payen's responses to some of the specific charges made against the Benedictines by Bernard in his *Apologia* regarding their mode of dress, alleged idleness, and eating of fish and fatty foods (lines 200–202).[45] While merely mentioning the criticisms about dress, Payen responds at some length to the charges about idleness and rich food in lines 205–218. That Payen was familiar with Bernard's *Apologia* and that his poem is a response to it is also indicated by the opening of the poem (lines 1 and 11), where the wolf in sheep's clothing theme seems deliberately chosen to contradict the opening of the *Apologia*, where Bernard insists that although Cistercians may be clad in sheepskins, the skins conceal no wolves.[46]

Conclusion

I agree with the view shared by both Meyer and Leclercq that in Payen's poem the entire eremitical movement is under attack.[47] This is clear from the opening section (lines 35–36) where he lists the varied habits of the Cistercians, Grandmontines, Tironensians, and the Congregation of Savigny against the black habit of the Benedictines, and also by his distinct reluctance most of the time to spell out clearly which eremitical orders he is talking about. However, it is clear that Meyer was right to see in the "great pseudoprophet" (line 163) an unmistakable reference to Bernard of Clair-

---

[44] Meyer, "Zwei Gedichte," p. 385. Remarkably, Leclercq, "Le poème," makes no mention of the "great pseudo-prophet" either in his summary of the poem (pp. 53–55) or in his discussion of it (pp. 56–77).

[45] *S. Bernardi Opera*, ed. Jean Leclercq and Henri M. Rochais, 9 vols. (Rome, 1957–1998), 3:81–108, at pp. 96–98 for laxity, idleness (*inertia* can mean both) and food, and pp. 101–2 for dress. For English translation, see *Cistercians and Cluniacs: St. Bernard's* Apologia *to Abbot William*, trans. Michael Casey (Kalamazoo, 1970), pp. 54–55, 55–56, and 59–60.

[46] See *S. Bernardi Opera*, 3:81.14–15; and Casey, *Cistercians*, p. 34.

[47] Meyer, "Zwei Gedichte," p. 384; Leclercq, "Le poème," p. 73.

vaux and equally clear that we should see in Payen's refutation of criticisms of the Benedictines (lines 197–222) his responses to Bernard's *Apologia*. Payen saw the Cistercians as the instigators of the eremitical movement and Bernard as its leading spokesman. Strikingly, Leclercq avoids any mention of the "great pseudoprophet" in his summary of the poem or anywhere else in his article. I also agree with Meyer that the Tironensians are a specific target too. However, I see them as a considerably more important target than Meyer seems to do. Given that they were the largest group of eremitical monks living close to Chartres and that a number of them, the artisan monks, lived and worked in the town itself, it is clear that their presence in Chartres and their success in winning donations from the nobility and ordinary people living in and around the town was a thorn in the flesh of Payen and probably of others in the chapter.

Editorial Method and Aims

The text is based on the single manuscript that preserves it (**P**). All deviations from **P**'s text are indicated in the *apparatus criticus* below the text, as are the corresponding readings of Meyer and Leclercq. However, to avoid unnecessary clutter, I have not recorded an initial blunder subsequently corrected by the scribe (or a later scribe), as, for example, at line 205, where the scribe initially wrote "decipientes decipiuntur" instead of "obicientes decipiuntur" and then corrected his error. I have gratefully adopted a number of emendations made by Meyer and Leclercq. One reader's suggested "emendation" (at line 180) proved, on closer inspection, to be **P**'s actual reading. I have added a few emendations of my own where **P**'s text made inappropriate or no sense. The translation, which I believe to be the first, is intended to make Payen's poem, which presents a revealing picture of some of the tensions prevailing among competing monastic orders and between the new eremitical orders and the secular clergy in the early twelfth century, accessible to a wider audience. I have sought to make the meaning of the Latin clear in idiomatic modern English rather than in English that closely imitates the syntax of the Latin.

Versus Pagani Bolotini de falsis heremitis qui uagando discurrunt: Revised Edition[1]

Ordinis expers, ordo nefandus, pellibus agni
Cum sit amictus, religiosus uult reputari,
Nec tamen actis religionem testificatur.
Horrea, penus, archa replentur; res cumulantur,
5   Multiplicantur, multiplicantes nec saturantur,
Nullaque prorsus cotidiani copia questus
Immoderatos pectoris eius temperat estus.
Plus et habundans, pauper habetur. Iam puto uerum
Quod perhibetur: non miseretur pectus auarum.
10 Da<m>pnat auaros, cum sit auarus. Cum sit amarus
Dulcia fatur, corde lupinus, uestibus agnus.
Sic simulator religionis: dum tunicatur,
Religioso uestibus atris assimilatur.
Sed sacra nobis esse uidetur pagina testis
15 Quod pia reddit uita beatum, non nigra uestis.
Iamque solutus menteque preceps ad leuitatem,
Claustra relinquens, sepe uagando circuit urbem.
Quique legendo siue docendo uerba salutis,
Fratribus intus commodus esset religiosis,
20 Hunc modo frustra detinet extra causa forensis.
Hec noua nostro pessima tabes fluxit ab euo,   fol. 112rb
Nostraque tali commaculantur tempora neuo,
Inque ruinas ecclesiarum tam maledictum
Tamque nociuum nostra dederunt secula ramnum.
25 Hec mala pestis iam prope totum polluit orbem,
Sed grauiori pondere nostram deprimit urbem.
Nobilitatem nullus honorat nec probitatem,
Nullaque morum gloria confert utilitatem.

11 Cf. Matt. 7.15

---

2 religiosus uult reputari *Traill* : uult reputari religiosus **P** *Meyer Leclercq* ‖ **4** cumulantur *Traill* : cumulate **P** *Meyer Leclercq* ‖ **5** multiplicantes *Meyer* : multiplicantis **P** : multiplicatis *Leclercq* ‖ **9** non miseretur pectus auarum *Traill* : pectus auarum non miseretur **P** *Meyer Leclercq* ‖ **10–11** cum sit amarus, / dulcia fatur *Traill* : dulcia fatur / cum sit amarus *Meyer Leclercq* dulcia fatur / cum sit auarus **P** ‖ **16** Iamque **P** *Meyer Leclercq* : Namque *sugg. Leclercq* ‖ **17** urbem **P** *Leclercq* : orbem *Meyer* ‖ **28** morum gloria *Leclercq* : morum gratia *Meyer* : mecum(?) gloria **P**

Verses by Payen Bolotin on False Hermits Who Wander and Gad About

An abominable order that is out of order wants to be regarded as religious because it is clad in lambskins, and yet its activities show no evidence of religious feeling.

Its granaries, larder, and strongbox are full; its wealth piles up and multiplies, and those doing the multiplying are still not satisfied, and absolutely no abundance of daily revenues quells the monstrous urgings of the order's heart.

While becoming even more abundantly rich, it is held to be poor. I now think it is true what they say: an avaricious heart knows no pity.
Though avaricious itself, the order condemns those who are avaricious {10}. Despite its harshness, it speaks gently. A wolf at heart, the order is a lamb in its clothing.
This is what one who lays claim to a religious calling does: when he dresses, he mimicks a real monk by wearing a black habit.
But the sacred page clearly provides us with testimony that it is a pious life that makes one blessed, not a black habit.
Let loose, and with his mind inclined to frivolity, he leaves the monastery and roams around the city time and again.
A monk who, by reading or teaching words of salvation, would benefit his religious brothers inside the monastery, is now pointlessly detained outside by some worldly issue {20}.
This new and awful pestilence is a product of our age, and our times are stained by this blemish; it is to the ruination of our Christian communities that our generation has bestowed such a cursed and noxious briar on them.

This foul plague has now infected practically the entire world but is crushing our city with a particularly oppressive burden.
Nobody honors nobility or rectitude and a reputation for morality does no one any good.

Qui sua seruant sunt et auari, uix comedentes;[2]
30 Qui coaceruant publica passim lucra sequentes.
Sint licet isti concubitores[3] atque <s>celesti
Tempore nostro religiosi sunt et honesti.
Iam quia finis temporis instet, ne dubitemus,
Cum tot oriri religionum monstra uidemus.
35 Candida nigris, nigra fit albis emula uestis,
Tertia mixtim texta uidetur sanctior istis;
Et quasi pannus religionem conferat ullam,
Sic fugit unus, quam tulit alter, ferre cucullam.
Hec quasi quedam recia nobis decipiendis
40 Insidiatrix hypocritarum turba tetendit,
Vt quasi tales intus honestos esse putemus,
Quos ita uiles exteriori ueste uidemus.
Tonsus ad aures usque supremas fronte patenti,
Cui nitet, ut nix, candida ceruix ore rubenti,
45 Tam sinuosa tamque rotunda ueste togatus,
Quique coturnis ore repandis est honeratus,
Bestia talis creditur artam ducere uitam,
Sed parasitum res probat istum, non heremitam.
Nam uagus omnes circuit urbes et regiones,
50 Dando nouarum reli<gi>onum traditiones,
Arte maligna decipiendo simpliciores,
Perque fauores exteriores ambit honores.
Si tamen illi clam subigendi copia detur,
Esse nefandi criminis actor non reueretur.
55 Quod nec honestas nullaque uirtus hunc comitatur.   fol. 112va
Ebrietates cotidiane testificantur.
Spernit egentes nec sua cuiquam par<ti>cipatur,
Cum satis illis pauperiorem se fateatur.
Clericus illi sordet, et ipsum dampnat et odit.
60 Sed, manifeste dum minus audet, clanculo rodit.
"Qualiter," inquit, "uiuere possit religiosus
Mollibus utens, rebus habundans, deliciosus?
Curue potestas traditur istis hec animarum,
Quos prope nullo tempore tangit cura suarum?

---

35 fit *Leclercq, sugg. Meyer* : sit **P** *Meyer* ‖ **63** curue **P** *Meyer* : carne *Leclercq*

They are men who guard closely what is theirs, and they are miserly, scarcely eating anything at all. They stockpile what belongs to the people and are everywhere in pursuit of gain {30}. Though these men sleep with others and are wicked, in today's world they are religious and honorable.

Let us be in no doubt that the end of time is at hand when we see so many monstrosities of religious life arising.

White habit vies with black and black habit with treated hides, while a third, of mingled color, is viewed as more holy than these two.[a] As if dress could confer any holiness, one avoids wearing a hooded habit that another has worn.[b]

A treacherous band of hypocrites has set these nets, as it were, to deceive us {40} into thinking that these men whom we see so vilely dressed outwardly are virtuous within.

A monk, tonsured down to the top of his ears and with an unruffled brow, whose neck gleams as white as snow beneath his rosy lips, and who is clad in such a round, enveloping garb and weighed down by high boots that curve back at the top – such a creature is believed to lead a life of constraint, but the facts prove that he is a parasite not a hermit.

He wanders around all the cities and regions dispensing the teaching of the new orders, {50} while deceiving the simple with pernicious skill, and courts worldly advancement by doing favors.

But should the opportunity for secretly screwing someone present itself, he unabashedly assumes the active role in an unspeakable crime.

That neither honor nor any virtue is to be found in his makeup, his daily bouts of drunkenness attest.

He spurns the needy and shares what he has with nobody, for he says he is significantly poorer than they are.

A cleric is foul in his eyes; he both condemns and hates him.

While he does not dare to malign him openly, he does so in private {60}.

"How," he asks, "can a man of religion live a life of luxury, flush with wealth, and pampered?

Or why is this power over souls given to those who are almost never concerned with the care of their own?

65 Insuper autem, quam bene uiuant, fine probatur,
　　Cum morituri se monacando tunc fateantur."
　　Hec agit in nos urbis amator, non heremita.
　　Sic fremit in nos non Heliseus, sed Gyezita.
　　Iudicat in nos quem sua dampnat pessima uita;
70 Nam uel adulter clam reperitur uel Sodomita.
　　Sed quod honestum laudeque dignum non dubitatur,
　　Subprimit illud, quod bona cleri nemo loquatur.
　　"Ordinis," inquit, "regula nostri sola tenetur;
　　Ipsa beate premia uite sola meretur.
75 Altior ista, sanctior ista nulla uidetur.
　　Qui uolet ergo saluificari nos imitetur.
　　Mane refectis pocula nobis dantur aquarum,
　　Cepa, legumen dona ministrant deliciarum,
　　Strata parantur fragmine culmi uel palearum,
80 Solaque nobis cognita fiunt lustra ferarum.
　　Clericus autem premia uite non habiturus
　　Carnibus utens uinaque sorbens est Epicurus."
　　Ista docendo nos inhonorat pseudopropheta,
　　Qui reputatur uestibus albis anachoreta.
85 Sed fateatur cur ita fumum diligit urbis
　　Seque potentum gaudeat interponere turbis:
　　"Curia, credo, dat mihi cenas uberiores
　　Atque Falerni nobilioris mille colores."
　　Dona potentum curia confert atque fauores,　　　　　　fol. 112vb
90 Nec sibi tales prebuit unquam silua sapores.
　　Dicat et istud ueste sub alba qua racione
　　Tam spaciose timpora cingit forma corone.
　　Hoc tamen ipsum nos manifeste scire fatemur,
　　Scilicet ut sic simpliciores deciperentur,
95 Vtque uidentes exteriorem simplicitatem,
　　Interiorem non pauitare<n>t impietatem.

68 4 Kings 5.1–27　∥　**80** lustra ferarum: Verg., *Georg.* 2.471

---

65 probatur *Meyer Leclercq* : probantur **P**　∥　**76** qui *Meyer Leclercq* : c' **P**　∥　**78** legumen **P** *Meyer* : tegumen *Leclercq*　∥　**85** diligit **P** *Meyer Leclercq* : diligat *sugg. Meyer*　∥　**86** seque *Meyer* : sed que **P** *Leclercq*　∥　**87** mihi *Leclercq* : michi **P** *Meyer* : sibi *sugg. Meyer*　∥　**90** sibi **P** *Meyer Leclercq* : mihi *sugg. Meyer*　∥　**92** tam *Meyer Leclercq* : nam **P**　∥　**94** deciperentur **P** *Leclercq* : deciperemur *Meyer*

Besides, how good there lives are is proved in the end, since they confess it by becoming monks only when on the brink of death."

It is a city-lover, not a hermit, who does this to us. It is not an Elisha who rages against us like this but a Gehazi.[c]

It is one who is damned by his own appalling life that passes judgement on us, for he is found to be a clandestine adulterer or sodomite {70}.

He suppresses what is unquestionably honorable and praiseworthy about us so that no one speaks of the clergy's good works.

"We observe only the rule of our order," he says. "By it alone is the reward of a blessed life earned.

No rule is held to be loftier than it, no rule more holy. Accordingly, anyone who wishes to win salvation should do as we do."

In the morning we are given cups of water for breakfast. They serve us onions and pulse as treats. Our beds are made of broken thatch or straw. We are becoming familiar with the lonely haunts of wild animals {80}.

The cleric who enjoys meat and downs wine is an Epicurus and not destined to enjoy the rewards of eternal life."

By spreading this doctrine, the false prophet, whose white habit make people think he is an anchorite, brings us into disrepute.

But let him explain why he is so fond of the smoke of the city and takes delight in mingling with crowds of important people:

"The court, I believe, offers me richer meals and a thousand varieties of the most distinguished Falernian wine."

The court bestows the gifts and favors of the powerful. The forest has never given him such tasty meals {90}.

He should also say why it is that along with his white habit there is such a far-reaching tonsure girding his temples.

However, we openly confess that we know why: namely, so that simpler souls may be deceived and when they see his outward simplicity, not fear an inner impiety.

Hoc tamen unum quero supremum: cur famulatus,
Quem sibi defert iunior etas, est ita gratus?
Nam generalem iam mouet istud suspicionem,
100 Cum uehementer ledere possit religionem.
"Iunior," inquit "quem leuiorem reddidit etas
Nos imitando uult leuitati ponere metas.
Laxa iuuentus, spiritualis nescia doni,
His documentis mancipat artus religioni,
105 Doctaque nostro uiuere sancte discipulatu
Postea, Christi f<er>uida perstat sub famulatu."
Sic inhonestus fallit honestos arte loquendi,
Sed latet intus praua uoluntas crimen agendi,
Cuius habenas dum bene nescit iam moderari,
110 Non pudet illum turpiter istis associari.
His comitatus uiuit oberrans ordine nullo,
Seque tuetur uestibus albis atque cucullo.
Rusticus omnis, quo sua possit salua tueri,
Veste sub alba religiosus querit haberi;
115 Sic decet istum talis amictus religionis,
Sicut asellum cum tegeretur pelle leonis.
Quem prius herbis pascere crudis silua solebat
Nec saciari posse secundo pane dolebat,
Iste potentum collateralis consiliator
120 Iuraque tractans fit quasi princeps et dominator.
Cum prius esset bestia simplex hic idiota,
Hinc modo currens obuia plaudit regio tota.
Deliciose fercula mense dum triplicantur,   fol.113ra
Dum melioris splendida uini pocula dantur,
125 Dum fauet illi curia, dum sic carus habetur,
Linquere siluas, ire per urbes dulce uidetur.
Conciliorum preuius hospes tempus odorat,
Vtque uideri uel noua possit scire laborat.
Dum quasi sanctum quilibet illum presul honorat,
130 Bubo diurnus cor tenebrosum ueste colorat.
Vina refutans, raro cibatur, raro saporat.

118 secundo pane: cf. Hor., *Ep.* 2.1.12

---

100 uehementer *Meyer Leclercq* : uehementur **P** ‖ **112** seque *Meyer Leclercq* : neque **P** ‖ **116** sicut *Meyer Leclercq* : s'icut **P** ‖ **122** hinc **P** *Leclercq* : huic *Meyer*

This one final question I ask: Why does the attention that the young pay him please him so much? This is now provoking widespread suspicion, since it can seriously damage a religious calling {100}.

"A young man," he says, "whose age has made him irresponsible, wants to put restraints on his frivolity by modeling himself on us.
Thanks to this teaching of ours, free-ranging youth, ignorant of the gift of spirituality, devote their energies to religion and, once taught to live in a holy manner by serving as our disciples, they subsequently stay on as fervent members in the service of Christ."
In this way an immoral man deceives the innocent with rhetorical skill but hidden within lurks a vile desire to commit a crime and since he cannot properly control the reins of his desire, he feels no shame in his disgraceful association with these young men {110}.
In the company of these youths he wanders around, living a life of complete disorder, protecting himself with his white habit and hood.
Every peasant wants to be regarded as a monk in a white habit with which to safeguard his possessions.
This religious garb suits him every bit as much as it suits an ass to be covered with a lion's skin.[d]
A man whom the forest previously used to feed with raw greens and who grieved that he could not fill himself with coarse bread, has become a neutral mediator between magnates and, by dealing with legal rights, has become something of a prince and ruler. {120}
Though this uneducated layman was previously a simple creature, it is for this reason that the entire region now comes running to meet and applaud him.
Now that the courses at his sumptuous meals are tripled, that gleaming goblets of excellent wine are provided, that the court favors him, and that he is so much loved, he finds it pleasant to leave the forest and walk through the towns.

First guest to arrive at the councils, he catches a whiff of the times and works hard so as to be able to appear knowledgeable even about new trends.
While every bishop honors him as if he were a saint, like an owl in the daytime he disguises his black heart with his habit {130}.
He refuses wine, rarely eats or tries a taste of anything.

Fletibus undans, per pauimentum stratus adorat.
Ista uidentes, insipientes decipiuntur,
Qui nouitatum precipitanter laude feruntur.
135 Tale sepulchrum sorde repletum dum uenerantur,
Ordine dignum pontificali uociferantur.
Sicque subintrans fur in honores ecclesiarum
Gaudet aceruis accumulandis diuiciarum
Perque rapinas iste manutus fit Briareus[4]
140 Pactaque frangens nec bene constans est quasi Protheus.
Namque prioris ponere querit uellera uite,
Vt neque uictus, sed neque uestes sint heremite.
Iamque perhorrens asperitates ciliciorum
Linea uestit leuia fratrum more suorum.
145 Quique cauebat uespere fontis sumere potum,
Nocte Falernum tercio poscit iam bene notum.
Qui uigilabat iam prope nona noctis ab hora
Nunc temulentus surgit ad himnos luce decora.
Quique miselli curuus aselli terga premebat,
150 Vix quoque plantas poplite flexo fune regebat,
Magnanimorum iam faleratus sessor equorum
Iam pede tenso plana perherrans currit agrorum.
Vtque suarum crimina celet spurciciarum,
Hic aliorum fit pater et dux ypocritarum.
155 Ecce per orbem multiplicata messe bonorum
Hic inimicus semina sparsit zizaniorum
Nostraque nobis ecce nouellas et ueteranas   fol.113rb
Misit Egyptus de tenebroso flumine ranas.
Flumina, fontes, stagna, paludes rana repleuit.
160 Iam super ipsas improba mensas scandere sueuit.
Hec super omnes pessima nobis plaga uidetur
Hancque reatus ultio nostri digna meretur.
Militat isto tempore magnus pseudopropheta
Atque suorum discipulorum falsa moneta.

135 Matt. 23.27 ‖ **156** Matt. 13.24 ‖ **158–159** Cf. Ex. 8.1–4

141 ponere **P** *Meyer* : poneri *Leclercq* ‖ **149** curuus *Meyer Leclercq* : currus **P** ‖ **152** perherrans **P** *Leclercq* : pererrans *Meyer* ‖ **156** hic *Traill* : h' **P** : hec *Meyer Leclercq* ‖ **159** stagna *Leclercq* : stangna **P** *Meyer*

Payen Bolotin's Targeting of the Tironensians and the Cistercians 169

Bathed in tears, he offers his worship lying prostrate on the paving-stones. Seeing this behavior, fools are deceived and are at once swept up with praise of the new practices.

While they venerate this tomb filled with filth,[e] they shout out that he deserves to be made a bishop.
Having in this way sneaked like a thief into the ecclesiastical hierarchy, he delights in piling up great masses of wealth, and with his plundering he becomes a many-handed Briareus[f] and in breaking agreements he proves as capricious as Proteus {140}.
He seeks to lay aside the sheepskins of his earlier life so that neither his food nor his clothes are those of a hermit.
Now horrified by the roughness of sack-cloth, he dresses in smooth linen after the fashion of his brothers.
He who shrank from taking a drink of water from a spring in the evening now calls at night for a third time for a famous vintage of Falernian.
He who kept vigil from about the ninth hour of the night now gets up in a drunken state for hymns in broad daylight.
He who, hunched down, sat on the back of a miserable little ass and could scarcely control its steps with a squeeze of his knee and a piece of rope {150}, now, in full ornamental gear, rides spirited steeds and, with a twitch of his foot, roams at high speed over level fields.
To hide the crimes of his foul ways he becomes the father and leader of other hypocrites.
See how, at a time when the harvest of good men has multiplied throughout the world, this enemy has sown the seeds of weeds and, behold, our Egypt has sent us young and old frogs up from its dark river![g]

Frogs have filled the rivers, springs, pools, and marshes. The brazen creature has become accustomed to leap up onto our very tables[h] {160}.
This seems to me the worst of all the plagues. Fitting requital for our guilt earns us this plague.
A great false prophet is campaigning at this time along with the false coinage of his disciples.

165 Nunc manifeste prospiciamus quid super ipsis
　　 Sacra Iohannis uerba prophetent Apocalipsis.
　　 Mystica quarti claustra sigilli dum reserantur,
　　 Temporis huius pseudoprophete significantur.
　　 Primus equorum uenerat albus, sacra nouorum
170 Tempore primo milia signans Christicolarum.
　　 Post rufus exit, tempora signans martiriorum.
　　 Post niger exit, tempora signans scismaticorum.
　　 Vltimus exit pallidus; hic est ypocritarum,
　　 Iusta suarum quos male ducit mors animarum.
175 Que quia semper presidet illis et dominatur,
　　 Restat ut ardens inferus illos iure sequatur;
　　 Inferus ardens penaque perpes hos comitatur.
　　 Ne locus ullus diffugiendi iam uideatur,
　　 Decolor hec gens iure notatur pallida uultu,
180 Interiori perdita morbo siue reatu.
　　 Mors quia semper corpora reddit pallida iure,
　　 Ferre uidetur preuia mortis signa future.
　　 Nec color ullus congruit illis apcius isto,
　　 Quos loca mortis pallida tollent iudice Christo.
185 Ipsa prophete pagina nobis testificatur,
　　 Hanc quia plagam tam diuturnam nemo sequatur.
　　 Hec mala radix ex Phariseis orta uidetur,
　　 Germine cuius centuplicato terra repletur.
　　 Primitus illi nulla nocendi causa patebat
190 Nam sub abisso tempore prisco tecta latebat.
　　 Sed modo uires illa resumens tota reuixit;　　　　　　　　fol. 113va
　　 Sicque futurum Christus in isto tempore dixit.
　　 Ipsa moderno tempore mentes dum uiciauit
　　 Nobilis ordo religionis degenerauit.
195 Nouimus omnes hanc nouitatem religionis:
　　 Prima duobus terque decenis uenit ab annis.
　　 Ordo nigrorum iam monachorum uilis habetur
　　 Sanctaque claustri uita quibusdam laxa uidetur
　　 Vt Benedicti regula sancti non reputetur,
200 Dum cibus istis formaque uestis dispar habetur.

166–173 Cf. Rev. 6.1–8

---

179 iure notatur pallida uultu *Traill* : pallida uultum iure notatur **P** : pallida uultu iure notatur *Meyer Leclercq*　‖　**180** siue **P** : sine *Meyer Leclercq*

Now let us examine clearly what the sacred words of the Apocalypse of John prophesy about them. When the mystical locks of the fourth seal are undone, today's false prophets are signified.

The first of the horses to come was white, signifying the holy thousands of new Christians in the earliest days {170}.
Then came a red horse, signifying the time of the martyrdoms, then came a black horse signifying the time of the schismatics.
Last came the pale horse; this is the time of the hypocrites, led astray by the merited death of their souls.
Because this death always rules and controls them, it remains inevitable that the fires of hell are duly in store for them; hell-fire and everlasting punishment dog them.

To ensure that there no longer appears any opportunity for escape, these people have lost their natural colour and are duly stigmatized by their pale faces, destroyed by an inner sickness or their guilt {180}.
Because Death always makes bodies duly pale, these people are seen to bear the anticipatory signs of their coming death.
No color is more suitable than this for those whom the pallid halls of death will win when Christ passes judgment.
The very words of the prophet testify to us that no horse follows this affliction that is so enduring.
This evil root seems to have its origin in the Pharisees; the earth is filled with its shoots multiplied a hundredfold.
At first there was no obvious reason for it to cause harm, for it lay hidden in an abyss, concealed over a long period of time {190}.
But now it has regained its strength and has completely come back to life. Christ said it would be so in our time.
It has corrupted minds in modern times and the noble orderliness of religious life has changed for the worse.
We are all aware of this new development in our religion. It began thirty-two years ago.
Since then the order of black monks is reviled and the holy life of the cloister seems to some people lax to the point that the rule of St. Benedict is not held in high esteem, since their food and their style of dress is held to be out of compliance {200}.

His heremite turpiter audent ponere crimen:
Ocia claustri, mandere pisces atque sagimen.
Hinc manifeste possumus horum noscere crimen:
Dum sibi querunt ex alieno crimine laudem.
205 Hec tamen illis obicientes decipiuntur,
Se quia claudi carcere claustri non paciuntur
Nec diuturnas asperitates experiuntur,
Quas bene norunt qui studiose claustra secuntur.
Religiosis ocia claustris nulla sinuntur,
210 Namque uel orant, uel sacra patrum scripta leguntur.
Hec, per amorem dum cor adurunt atque saginant,
Dulcia summi nectaris illis mella propinant.
Talia fluxas ocia curas mente repellunt.
Hec quoque sentes iam fruticantes inde reuellunt,
215 Carnis et hostes, celica semper qui speculantur.
Pinguibus escis aut preciosis non saciantur;
Quicquid in escis esse uidetur deliciosum,
Quando retractat[5] ad quod an<h>elant, est onerosum.
Experimentis nec retinentur deliciarum,
220 Hec animarum dampna uidentes esse suarum.
Fit monachorum gloria maior, dum potuerunt
Et tamen escis prorsus ab istis abstinuerunt.
Ast heremite deteriores inueniuntur,
Qui nec habentes, sed cupientes, ista secuntur.
225 Omnibus istis ingluuies est tanta ciborum, fol. 113vb
Vt manifeste sit deus ipsis uenter eorum.
Sicut auaros grandis aceruus diuiciarum,
Haut secus istos afficit esus deliciarum.
Si tamen illis arida pisces silua negauit,
230 Nec preciosi uina saporis cella parauit,
Vt cibus arens et labor artus extenuauit,
Gens noua sese ciuibus urbis notificauit.
Que noua spargens dogmata praue tradicionis
Miscuit intus triste uenenum perdicionis.
235 "Noster," ut aiunt, "nullius ordo prelationis,[6]
Sed laicalis forma uidetur condicionis."

206 se *Traill* : sed **P** *Meyer Leclercq* ‖ **218** retractat **P** : retractant *Meyer* Leclercq; anhelant *Traill* : hanelant **P** *Meyer Leclercq* ‖ **230** preciosi **P** *Meyer* : preciosa *Leclercq* ‖ **235** prelationis *Traill* : perdicionis **P** *Meyer Leclercq*

The hermit monks have the shameless audacity to charge the Benedictines with the following; idleness in the monastery and the eating of fish and food rich in fat.

From these accusations we can clearly recognize their offence: they seek praise for themselves by bringing charges against others.

However, by making these accusations against the Benedictines they are mistaken, because they do not allow themselves to be imprisoned in the cloister and do not experience the prolonged deprivations with which those who conscientiously follow the cloistered life are very familiar.

No idle hours are permitted in religiously observant monasteries. They either pray or read the holy works of the Fathers {210}.

While firing and nourishing their hearts with love, these preoccupations offer them the sweet honey of supreme nectar.

These "idle hours" drive transient cares from our minds; they also wrench out the brambles that are already fruiting, and those who are always contemplating heavenly matters are enemies of the flesh.

They do not stuff themselves with rich or expensive food. If there is something delicious in their food and that which they pant after disappears, that causes problems. They are not taken with experiencing delicacies for they see that they harm their souls {220}.

The greatest glory for monks occurs when they have been in a position to enjoy such food and yet have completely abstained from it.

Hermit monks are reckoned to be worse, for they go after food they do not have but long for.

They all have such an enormous appetite for food that their stomach is clearly a god to them.

As misers feel about huge piles of wealth, so hermit monks feel about eating delicacies.

If, however, a parched forest has denied them fish and their cellar has failed to provide them with the wine of an expensive vintage {230}, the newcomers have brought themselves to the attention of the townspeople once dry food and hard work have attenuated their limbs.

Spreading their new teaching formulated by a corrupt tradition, they have thrown the bitter poison of perdition into the mix.

"Our order," they say, "is not one of high standing;[g] rather, its form resembles that of a lay organization."

Quos nisi quedam pontificalis turba foueret,
Rusticus ordo talia nunquam bella moueret.
Sed quia pars hec utraque consors esse uidetur,
240 Iam duplicatum clericus hostem iure ueretur,
Qui simulatam dum foris offert religionem,
Ardet in omnem cor quasi fornax ambitionem.
Iste uorando quando per urbes transiit istas,
Pisce comesto non saturatus suxit aristas.
245 Obruta passim stirpitus omnis silua uidetur,
Vtque locustis sic heremitis terra repletur.
Nunc aper, ursus, caprea, ceruus non agitantur,
Cum neque silue quas coluerunt inueniantur.
Nunc heremitis pontificalis mensa repletur;
250 His comitatus religiosus presul habetur.
Per tunicatos pontificatus cura tenetur;
Ordine dignus uel reprobandus quisque uidetur.
Per tunicatos dantur honores ecclesiarum;
Vnde uidetur precipitari status earum.
255 Sed licet istos turba potentum sic ueneretur,
Tocius huius fructus honoris raro habetur.
Nam quasi fumus preterit huius gloria uite,
Quam male querunt hi tunicati, non heremite.
Sic et honores preripientes atque fauores   fol. 114ra
260 Vndique, gaudent ferre cucullas multicolores.
Dum monachorum sancta uigebat uita priorum,
Nulla cuculle sola fiebat mentio horum.[7]
Omnibus idem, non fuit ulli discolor usus,
Nec uariato uellere traxit stamina fusus.
265 Vrbis honores, dona potentum nullus amabat.
Quisque labori, fletibus, imnis inuigilabat.
Carcere silue quisque reclusum se coibebat,
Nec nisi fontem uespere tantum quisque bibebat.
Sed modo nostri semper in aula sunt heremite,
270 Desidiose uana sequentes ocia uite.

246 repletur *Meyer Leclercq* : repletis **P** ‖ **247** nunc *Meyer* : hunc **P** *Leclercq* ‖ **250** his *Leclercq* : hiis **P** *Meyer* ‖ **254** unde *Meyer Leclercq* : unde unde **P** ‖ **256** imnis *Meyer Leclercq* : ignis **P** ‖ **262** mentio horum *Traill* : mentio *orum sugg. Meyer* : mentitiorum **P** *Meyer Leclercq* ‖ **266** imnis *Meyer Leclercq* : ignis **P**

But if they were not supported by a crowd of bishops, peasants would never be stirring up these wars.

But because these two parties[h] seem to be working in tandem, the clergy is right to fear a two-fold enemy {240}, who outwardly maintains the pretence of a religious life but its heart burns within, like a furnace, with every ambition.

When the enemy has made its way through these cities, devouring food, not satisfied with the fish it has eaten, it has sucked on ears of wheat.[k]

The entire forest seems completely devastated, root and branch, and the land is filled with hermits like so many locusts.

Boar, bear, wild goat, and deer are no longer hunted, for even the woods they once inhabited are not to be found.

Now the bishop's table is filled with hermits; when accompanied by them a bishop is considered to be devout {250}.

The care of the diocese is in the hands of men in tunics; anyone, even a reprobate, is judged worthy of admission to the order.

Ecclesiastical positions are assigned by men in tunics. As a result, the standing of the churches is seen to be plummeting.

But although a group of high-ranking people revere them in this way, fruit from all this honor accorded them is rarely to be found.

The glory of this life mistakenly sought after by these men in tunics, who are not hermits, passes like smoke.

After snatching up high positions and favors on all sides, they take joy in wearing their "habits" of varied colors {260}.[l]

When the holy life of earlier monks was flourishing, not a single mention of their habit was made.

Everyone had the same; no one had a different-coloured habit nor did the spindle draw threads from a fleece differently dyed.

No one was attracted by high office in the town or the gifts of magnates. Everyone was intent on work, tears, and hymns.

Everyone confined himself to his prison in the woods, and no-one drank anything in the evening except only water from the spring.

But now our hermits are always at court pursuing the empty idleness of an indolent life {270}.

Nouimus istos uentris amicos atque ciborum,
Inrequietos, more uagantes achefalorum,[8]
Quosque uagando per regiones ire uidemus,
Non heremitas, sed tunicatos esse putemus.
275 Hos prius herbas reicientes atque legumen,
Iste culine nidor herilis traxit ad urbem.
Vtque sequentis uulnera fiunt causa doloris
Primaque culpe causa uidetur posterioris,
Sic tunicatis urbe receptis ista secuntur,
280 Quod modo ciues ypocritales esse feruntur.
Possit ut hospes religionis laude notari,
Omnibus istis officiose uult famulari.
Tunc piperati piscibus assis accumulantur,
Queque redundant nectare puro, pocula dantur.
285 Quicquid agatur rebus in istis immoderate,
Impius hospes computat actum pro pietate,
Sed super omnes, hec noua res est, esse gulosum
Et tamen ipsum uelle uideri religiosum.
Arte coquorum res preciose quando parantur,
290 Deliciosis, non heremitis, danda uidentur.
Non heremite prebeat hospes fercula, per que,
Si caro querit luxuriari, peccet uterque.
Vgo Niuernis religionis laude probatus,   fol.114rb
Ex heremita sumpsit honorem pontificatus.
295 Hunc heremite uisere multi sepe solebant
Auribus eius deposituri si quid habebant.
Hos bene clausos in penetrali semper habebat,
Nec nisi solis religiosis porta patebat.
His adaquati pocula uini conficiebat,
300 Nec precioso pascere quemquam pisce uolebat
Ne cibus ullum postea talis sollicitaret,
Dum sibi caules atque legumen silua pararet,
Vt nichil illic post nociturum discere possent
Preter id usu cotidiano quod didicissent.
305 Hec ut honestus, non ut auarus, prorsus agebat,
Namque saluti sic animarum proficiebat.

283 piperati *Meyer* : piperatis **P** *Leclercq* ‖ **300** pascere *Meyer* : parcere **P** *Leclercq* ‖
303 discere *Meyer* : dirè (i.e. dicere) **P** : dicere *Leclercq*

We know that they are friends of their stomachs and of food and that they are restless, wandering around like *acephali*;^m and when we see them wandering from one region to another, we should regard them not as hermits, but as men in tunics.
Rejecting herbs and legumes, they have been attracted to the city by that gleam of their master's kitchen.
Just as wounds become the cause of the ensuing pain and an earlier fault is viewed as the cause of the subsequent fault, so the reception of monks in tunics in a city has the consequence that its citizens are now called hypocritical {280}.

So that he can be singled out for praise for his religion, the host seeks to provide attentive service to all of these men.
Accordingly, peppered fish are heaped on roasted fish and they are given cups brimming with pure nectar.
Whatever in these matters might be done to excess the impious host reckons was done out of piety. But this is a new fashion, to outstrip everyone else in gluttony, while at the same time wishing to be seen, personally, as devout.

When expensive dishes are prepared by the skill of cooks, they seem appropriate offerings to the self-indulgent, not to hermits {290}.
A host should not provide a hermit with dishes such that if flesh seeks to indulge in them, both host and guest would sin.
After living as a hermit, Hugh of Nevers,^n lauded for his devotion, assumed the office of bishop.
Many hermits often went to see him to confide to his ears any concerns they had.

He always kept them strictly confined in an inner chamber and the door was open only to religious.
He made them cups of watered-down wine and refused to feed expensive fish to anyone {300} lest he be subsequently tormented by thoughts of this food (since it was kale and legumes that the forest offered them), to prevent them from learning of anything there that would harm them later, beyond what they had become familiar with from daily use.

It was certainly out of honorable not miserly motives that he did this, for in this way he contributed towards the salvation of their souls.

Omnibus ergo sic heremitis est miserendum,
Ne, quasi coruus, detineantur propter edendum.
Hoc heremitas tempore multos esse uidemus,
310 Nec tamen omnes religiosos esse fatemus,[9]
Non quia uestes exteriores uilificemus,
Sed quia gratam religionem mentis habemus.
Non reprobamus, sed ueneramur religiosos
Nec ueneramur, sed reprobamus luxuriosos.
315 Absit ut illos ore procaci dedecoremus,
Quos et honestos et quasi sanctos non dubitamus.
Vtilis arbor fructibus ipsis notificatur,
Sed sine fructu digna ruina iure crematur.
Iam sapientum deciperentur corda uirorum,
320 Sed probat illos et manifestat fructus eorum.
Non in acutis uua rubetis uindemiatur,
Spinaque ficus edere dulces nulla uidetur.
Hec sine fructu spina per orbem fructificauit.[10]
Iam rubus ad se cuncta trahendo nos lacerauit.
325 Spernitur omnis uita priorum, dum noua surgit,
Totus et orbis post heremitas esse cucurrit.
Municipales atque potentes hos uenerantur, fol. 114va
Vulgus adorat, iam quasi sancti concelebrantur.
Sed tamen horum uita uel actus discuciatur;
330 Non erit illis mentis honestas quanta putatur.
Sepe uidentur conlacrimari contribulatis;
Sed facit istud gracia lucri, non pietatis.
Scripta legentes, que didicerunt, non imitantur;
Recta docentes, que docuerunt, non operantur.
335 Fluxa uoluptas, laus popularis, grandia dona,
Hec erit illis ultima merces atque corona,
Non habituri que sicierunt gaudia sancti,
Dum perituri gaudia querunt emolumenti.

317–318 Matt. 7.17–19 ‖ **320–322** Cf. Matt. 7.16; Luke 6.44

308 ne *Traill, sugg. Meyer* : nec **P** *Meyer Leclercq*; detineantur *Traill* : detineatur **P** *Meyer Leclercq* ‖ **310** fatemus *Traill* : fatemur **P** *Meyer Leclercq* ‖ **318** fructu *Meyer Leclercq* : fructus **P** ‖ **326** esse **P** *Meyer Leclercq* : ecce *sugg. Meyer*

We should have similar compassion for all hermits to ensure that they are not held back like the raven because of what they ate.º

Today we see that there are many hermits and yet we do not say that all of them are devout {310}, not because we disparage their outer garments but because we have a favorable regard for religious devotion.

We do not revile but rather venerate people who are devout, and we do not venerate but rather revile the self-indulgent.

Far be it from us to discredit with insolent taunts those whom we do not doubt to be irreproachable and more or less saints.

A productive tree is known by its fruits but if it produces no fruit it deserves to be cut down and burned.

The hearts of wise men can at any time be deceived but their fruit proves and makes manifest their worth {320}.

Grapes are not harvested from prickly brambles and no thorn-bush is seen to produce sweet figs.

This fruitless thorn-bush has borne fruit throughout the world.ᵖ By drawing everything to itself the briar has now mangled us.

Our predecessors' entire way of life is spurned, as a new way arises and the entire world has rushed in pursuit of becoming hermits.

Town officials and magnates revere them, and the crowd adores them; they are now celebrated as if they were saints.

But still their way of life and what they do should be scrutinized. The integrity of their intentions will not prove as unsullied as is thought {330}.

They often seem to share in the sorrow of those who are troubled. But they do this for the sake of gain, not out of compassion.

After reading scripture they do not put into practice what they have learned. They teach what is right but do not do what they have taught.

Transient pleasure, the praise of the populace, and large donations – this will be their ultimate reward and their crown, for they are not destined to experience the joys that the saints thirsted after, since they seek the joys of a reward that is doomed to perish {338}.

Notes to the Edition

[1] The changes in lines 2, 4, 9, and 10–11 restore the end-rhymes (usually two-syllable, but often single-syllable) that are found consistently throughout **P**'s text except in these opening lines; the sole exception is at lines 39–40, where, nonetheless, there is almost a two-syllable rhyme. Presumably, the scribe initially thought the poem was in dactylic hexameters (which are metrically very similar but avoid end-rhymes) and "corrected" accordingly until he realized his mistake.

[2] The juxtaposition of *comedentes* with *auari* here suggests that Payen is also playing with the meaning "spending, squandering," as did Horace in *Epistles* 1.15.40-41.

[3] The only instance of *concubitor* in the Vulgate is at 1 Cor. 6.10: "masculorum concubitores."

[4] The *-eus* ending is scanned as a trochee (cf. *Heliseus*, line 68) but in *Protheus* (line 140) it is, as usual, a single syllable.

[5] For *retractare* in the intransitive sense see *DMLBS*, s.u. retractare 3.

[6] On *prelationis*, see Introduction, n. 40.

[7] Bede allows "h" to function as a consonant for metrical purposes; see his *De Arte Metrica*, in *Grammatici Latini* 7, ed. Heinrich Keil (Leipzig, 1874), pp. 227–60, at 230–31; so, the "o" of *mentio* is not elided; cf. the ending of line 256.

[8] The initial "a" in "achefalorum" is short by nature, here lengthened by the addition of "h".

[9] For active forms of *fateor*, see *MlWb*, s.u. fateor.

[10] *Fructificare* appears to be an invented equivalent to *fructicare* (cf. line 214) to fit the metre.

Notes to the Translation

[a] The Cistercians had white habits and the Benedictines black. The Tironensians, the Savigny monks, and Cistercian lay brotherss had grey habits. Some Grandmontines apparently wore oxhides; see Carole Hutchison, *The Hermit Monks of Grandmont* (Kalamazoo,1989), p. 113. When treated (tawed) these would be *alba* (DMLBS, *albus*, 2a).

[b] Only the Grandmontines rejected the hood; see Hutchison, *Hermit Monks*, pp. 114–15.

[c] Elisha refused money for curing Naaman of leprosy; his servant, Gehazi, devised a scheme to get the money for himself. When Elisha asked him where he had been, he lied and was promptly afflicted with leprosy (4 Kings 5.1–27).

[d] Aesop's fable tells how an ass who donned a lion's skin frightened other animals until it brayed.

ᵉ The reference is to Matthew 23.27, where Christ likens the scribes, Pharisees, and hypocrites to whitewashed tombs, which are beautiful on the outside, but are filled with bones and all kind of filth on the inside (cf. Payen's "sorde repletum").

ᶠ Briareus is a hundred-armed giant of Greek mythology. Proteus could transform himself at will into any creature.

ᵍ The weeds are sown in a wheat field by an enemy at Matthew 13.24. Egypt stands allegorically for our world when beset by plagues or disasters; see Cassiodorus, *Expositio in Psalterium*, Ps. 134/135, verse 9 (PL 70:964B). Presumably, the young and old frogs reflect the fact that both young and old are joining the hermit monks. Frogs are born from slimy mud (see Ovid, *Met.* 15.375–78), but our world, i.e. our "Egypt," produces not only young frogs, i.e. young novices, but also old ones, i.e. these adult "monks."

ʰ The leaping on to the tables presumably alludes disparagingly to the hermit monks turning up at Benedictine monasteries expecting hospitality as they travel on their way to join some new eremitical order.

ⁱ On the ambiguity here, see Introduction, n. 40.

ʲ Namely, the bishops and the eremitical orders.

ᵏ Presumably, sucking on wheat-ears was considered peasant behaviour and inappropriate for a "real monk."

ˡ It is unclear to what "cucullas multicolores" refers. I have assumed that it refers ironically to the more colourful dress now worn by a former hermit monk who has been appointed a bishop. Hugh of Nevers (line 293) is an example of a former hermit monk who became a bishop, but, oddly enough, Payen approves of him.

ᵐ In the fifth century a group broke away from the Christian Monophysites under the leadership of Peter Monge, maintaining they did not want a leader; they were given the name *Acephali* (Latinized Greek for "the headless ones"). In the Middle ages, the term was applied to monks, whose abbot or prior had died who were left leaderless.

ⁿ Hugh of Nevers was Hugh IV, bishop of Nevers 1111–1121. Leclercq, "Le Poème," p. 56, cites an act in the Nevers cartulary, whereby Hugh, a former hermit monk, assigns prebends to the canons of Nevers cathedral.

ᵒ The reference is to the raven sent out from the ark by Noah after forty days. When it did not return he sent out the dove, which, on its second mission, returned with a leaf in its beak. The Bible does not explain why the raven did not return. One explanation was that it fed on floating carcasses. This explanation is incorporated into Prudentius' poem, *Scenes from Sacred History*, 3.11 in: *The Poems of Prudentius,* tr. by Sister M. Clement Eagan vol. 2 (Washington, D.C., 2017) 180: "For the raven, held captive by gluttony, clung to foul bodies."

p Payen is probably here thinking primarily of the rapid Tironensian expansion, both in France and internationally (into England, Wales and Scotland), about which he would be well informed, rather than the Cistercian, which came somewhat later; see Thompson, *The Monks,* 156: "The Cistercians have a higher profile in the historical record … but their expansion was by no means as early or as spectacular as that of the Tironensians … ."

Abstract

Written in 1130, Payen's poem provides a vivid picture of the reaction of a canon of Chartres to the burgeoning eremitical orders of the twelfth century. After summarizing the poem, the article goes on to suggest that while the author avoids explicitly identifying which monastic orders he is criticizing, a thinly veiled reference to Bernard of Clairvaux at line 163 makes it clear that the Cistercians are principally to blame. However, it was the Tironensians who lived closest to Chartres and, now led by an entrepreneurial abbot, were successfully contending with the Chartres chapter for support from the bishop, the local aristocracy, and ordinary people, and it is now clear, thanks to Kathleen Thompson's excellent study of their order that they are also targeted and to a greater extent than she suggests. The article concludes with the Latin text and the first translation of the poem.

Résumé

Composé en 1130, le poème de Payen nous brosse un portrait saisissant de la réaction d'un chanoine de Chartres sur la naissance des ordres érémitiques du XIIe siècle. Cet article débute avec un résumé du poème. Il propose ensuite que, bien que Payen se garde d'identifier explicitement les ordres monastiques dont il fait la critique, une allusion peu subtile à Bernard de Clairvaux (au vers 163) démontre clairement que ce sont les Cisterciens qui font les frais des reproches de l'auteur. Pourtant, les Tironiens étaient ceux qui vivaient le plus proche de Chartres et qui, sous la direction d'un abbé entreprenant, rivalisaient avec bien du succès contre le chapitre de Chartres pour l'appui de l'évêque, des aristocrates de la région et du peuple. Il est désormais évident, grâce à l'excellente monographie de Kathleen Thompson sur les Tironiens, qu'ils sont eux aussi visés dans le poème, et ce même davantage que Thompson l'a suggéré. L'article se termine avec le texte latin du poème et sa toute première traduction en anglais.

David A. Traill
University of California, Davis (emeritus)
datraill@ucdavis.edu

Breuiarium Artis grammaticae Alcuini: Edition and Study[*]

ISABELA GRIGORAȘ
University of Fribourg / University of Bucharest

Introduction

This study is part of a wider project whose final aim is to produce a modern critical edition of Alcuin's *Ars grammatica*. Here, however, only the text transmitted in Vatican City, Biblioteca Apostolica Vaticana, MS Reg. lat. 251 (saec. IX^3, Reims?), fols. 38'r–52v, entitled *Breuiarium Artis grammaticae Alcuini*, is discussed and edited. I consider this work a unique text, which deserves to be treated separately, because it represents the only known abridged version of Alcuin's *Grammar*. For the edition presented below I have collated the text of MS Reg. lat. 251 (hereafter **V**₃), first, with the most recent printed edition of the *Ars grammatica* in PL 101, 854B–902B, and, second, with the text preserved in St. Gall, Stiftsbibliothek, MS 268 (saec. IX*in.*, Tours), pp. 19–165 (hereafter **S**₁), which is one of the oldest manuscripts of Alcuin's grammatical text.[1] I have collated the text of **V**₃ with those of PL and **S**₁ in order to comprehend the specificity of the *Breuiarium*, and in order to understand **V**₃ better where its text was corrupted. I have not discussed the possible archetype of the *Breuiarium* in the present study; this question will be dealt with in the introduction to the edition of the *Ars grammatica*.

---

[*] I would like to express my gratitude for the very useful suggestions and corrections that I received from Prof. Greti Dinkova-Bruun (Toronto) and from Prof. Adrian Papahagi (Cluj-Napoca) when writing this paper. I am also very thankful for all the invaluable observations and emendations made by Prof. Karin Schlapbach (Fribourg).

[1] See Ernst Tremp, "Alkuin und das Kloster St. Gallen," in *Alkuin von York und die geistige Grundlegung Europas. Akten der Tagung vom 30. September bis zum 2. Oktober 2004 in der Stiftsbibliothek St. Gallen*, ed. Ernst Tremp and Karl Schmuki (St. Gall, 2010), pp. 229–50, at 240, who considers this manuscript to be the oldest one in the tradition. After collating all the manuscripts of the *Ars grammatica*, I can state with certainty that **S**₁ is indeed one of the oldest codices, but it is difficult to argue that it is "the oldest" one, since there are several other manuscripts which can be dated to the early ninth century, similarly to **S**₁. What distinguishes **S**₁ among the other ninth-century manuscripts is the fact that it transmits only Alcuin's *Ars grammatica*, preceded by the introductory text *Disputatio de uera philosophia*.

The Context for the Ars grammatica *and Its* Breuiarium

The *Ars grammatica*[2] was most probably composed during Alcuin's abbacy at St. Martin of Tours, towards the end of his life.[3] By its content, the text is an elementary grammar that continued a tradition begun about one century earlier on the British Isles.[4] The elementary grammar, as defined by Vivien Law,[5] answered the needs of a different type of public than that to which the ancient grammarians had aimed their works and which did not require complete nominal and verbal paradigms. Alcuin himself, while compiling grammatical texts of Donatus, Priscian, Isidore, and others,[6] addressed his work to non-native Latin students with a Germanic or a Romance mother tongue, and many of whom were most likely from illiterate families. Thus, he tried to keep his *Grammar* short and appealing, but at the same time

---

[2] I have chosen the title proposed in *Clavis scriptorum Latinorum Medii Aevi. Auctores Galliae 735–987*, ed. Marie-Hélène Jullien et al., 3 vols., CCCM (Turnhout, 1999–2010), 2:21–23. Most of the manuscripts do not present titles for Alcuin's *Grammar*, and when they do, it is always a different one. In Munich, Bayerische Staatsbibliothek, clm 14823 (saec. XII, St. Emmeram in Regensburg), fol. 1v (one of the manuscripts where the *Ars grammatica* is preceded by the *Disputatio de uera philosophia* – see further below, n. 14), one can read: *Incipit gramatica Albini*. Five other manuscripts introduce Alcuin's grammatical text through a headline: Bern, Burgerbibliothek, MS 123 (saec. IX–X, Fleury), fol. 55v (*in margine*): *Expositio duorum discipulorum Albini in Donati Arte feliciter*; Paris, Bibliothèque nationale de France, MS lat. 8319 (saec. IX–X, Corbie), fol. 60r: *Alchuini opusculum quod uocatur ENKIPIΔION feliciter incipit*; St. Andrews, University of St. Andrews Library, MS 38904 (saec. XV, Northern Italy), (no foliation): *Albini grammatici et rethoris liber de octo partibus orationis*; Florence, Biblioteca Medicea Laurenziana, MS Ashburnham 876 (saec. XV, Florence?), fol. 76v: *Albini magistri dialogum de arte grammaticae lege feliciter*; Vatican City, Biblioteca Apostolica Vaticana, MS Urb. lat. 308 (saec. XVex., Central Italy), fol. 150v: *Schola Albini grammatici de grammatica et partibus orationis et eorum accidentibus per dialogum*. Moreover, all printed editions have so far published both the *Disputatio de uera philosophia* and the *Ars grammatica* under the title *Grammatica*. Other titles that scholars generally use for Alcuin's *Grammar* are mentioned in the *Clavis scriptorum Latinorum*, ed. Jullien et al., 2:21.

[3] Louis Holtz, "L'oeuvre grammaticale d'Alcuin dans le contexte de son temps," in *Alkuin von York und die geistige Grundlegung Europas*, ed. Tremp and Schmuki, pp. 129–49, at 131.

[4] Vivien Law, *Grammar and Grammarians in the Early Middle Ages* (London and New York, 1997), p. 77.

[5] "By the end of the seventh [century], a new kind of grammar, the elementary grammar designed not for native speakers but for foreigners ignorant of the language, had come into being; and it bore a marked resemblance to the more traditional type of teaching grammar in use today."; "Each section opens with a series of remarks … on the properties of that part of speech, generally based on Donatus but incorporating varying amounts of material from other ancient grammarians. The inflected parts of speech … are exemplified by a series of paradigms arranged by declension or conjugation, and by various systems within that." (Law, *Grammar and Grammarians*, pp. 75, 106).

[6] For further information regarding the *Ars grammatica*'s sources, see Louis Holtz, "Le dialogue de Franco et de Saxo," *Annales de Bretagne et des Pays de l'Ouest* 111–13 (2004), 133–45.

furnishing as much as possible all the necessary details and examples. Teaching Latin as a foreign language was not a new challenge and other teachers had already struggled with it, especially in the Anglo-Saxon milieu, where Alcuin received his education. From this point of view, Alcuin is far from being a pioneer. Still, he contributed to the development of grammatical studies in three important ways: 1) in the rediscovery and use of Priscian's *Institutiones grammaticae* (hereafter *IG*);[7] 2) in the introduction of dialectics into the grammatical discourse (these two aspects have already been considered by scholars such as Holtz,[8] Law,[9] and Irvine,[10] and will not be discussed here); and 3) in the unique fashion in which Alcuin rendered the grammatical text to his audience, which has not yet been thoroughly examined.[11]

Alcuin presents a fictional dialogue which can be read, to a certain extent, as a faithful portrait of a school situation;[12] the playful exchange of replies between the two

---

[7] Manuscripts that contained Priscian's *IG* were present in Southern Italy as early as the sixth century, and in the British Isles in the seventh. Therefore, Alcuin was not the first to read Priscian's work, but he was the first truly to understand it and to make use of it, by integrating the information on syntax (offered by Priscian in the last two books of the *IG*) in a grammatical text; see Louis Holtz, "Priscien dans la pédogogie d'Alcuin," in *Manuscripts and Tradition of Grammatical Texts from Antiquity to the Renaissance. Proceedings of a Conference Held at Erice, 16 – 23 October 1997, as the 11th Course of International School for the Study of Written Records*, ed. Mario De Nonno, Paolo De Paolis, and Louis Holtz, 2 vols. (Cassino, 2000), 1:289–326, at pp. 289–90, 301–2. This grammatical text, namely *Excerptiones super Priscianum* (whose edition is being prepared by Louis Holtz and Anne Grondeux for the CCCM), was clearly intended for more advanced students, since it does not refer to the books of *IG* that contain information on morphology, which was supposed to be known already by the initiated students; see Holtz, "Priscien dans la pédogogie d'Alcuin," p. 310. Thus, Alcuin wrote two different grammars, for two different groups of pupils: *Ars grammatica* for beginners and *Excerptiones* for advanced ones.

[8] Holtz, "Priscien dans la pédogogie d'Alcuin," pp. 289–326; Holtz, "Le dialogue de Franco et de Saxo," pp. 137–40.

[9] Law, *Grammar and Grammarians*, pp. 83, 86.

[10] Martin Irvine, *The Making of Textual Culture: 'Grammatica' and Literary Theory, 350–1100* (Cambridge, 1994), p. 321.

[11] Louis Holtz offers a look into this matter by underlining the uniqueness of Alcuin's dialogued *Grammar*: "Alcuin a tout fait pour donner de la vie à cette sorte de jeu, qualifié par les acteurs eux-mêmes de *lusus*, et il y est parvenu en donnant à chacun des deux partenaires une personnalité, ce qui fait de l'opuscule d'Alcuin un texte très différent des grammaires dialoguées entre le maître et l'élève que les écoles du haut Moyen Âge ont multipliées sur le modèle de l'*Ars minor* de Donat," in Holtz, "Le dialogue de Franco et de Saxo," p. 136. However, Holtz does not analyse thoroughly the students' conversation, which transmits more than simple grammatical information and whose playful aspect hides a very clever pedagogy.

[12] Carin Ruff observes the "element of literary realism" added "to a form that must draw as much from real-life classroom practice as from the conventions of the genre," and she considers the insertion of jokes into the student's dialogue as an innovation; see Carin Ruff, "'Desipere in loco': Style, Memory,

students, who compete for knowledge, is an excellent example of indirect pedagogy[13] and, at the same time, gives us some idea of how communication in Latin took place at the Palace School – two research questions that are definitely worth exploring.

Furthermore, the motivation and the goal of writing such a text are both obvious and unsurprising, having in mind the historical and cultural context provided by Charlemagne's politics. Alcuin's *Grammar* was intended to offer basic instruction in Latin, with the explicit purpose of serving the interests of the Church which was endangered by the clergy's lack of Latin literacy.[14] From this point of view, Alcuin's *Grammar* surpasses the status of "ars bene loquendi" and becomes also "ars bene credendi" (or even better, "ars fidem bene defendendi"). It is interesting, however, that Charlemagne's Minister of Education and of Religious Affairs, as some modern scholars have called Alcuin,[15] did not "Christianize" his *Grammar*, as for instance, Asper had done at the end of the sixth century, by introducing religious terms in the provided examples. On the contrary, Alcuin left his grammatical text as "classical" as it could be, while ensuring that he made one thing clear in his introductory text known as the *Disputatio de uera philosophia*, namely, that grammar (along with the other liberal arts) has a very important function for Christians, as it is the first step on the path towards perfect wisdom and thus an essential weapon in the battle to defend the true faith.

---

and the Teachable Moment," in *Verbal Encounters: Anglo-Saxon and Old Norse Studies for Roberta Frank*, ed. Antonina Harbus and Russell Poole (Toronto, 2005), pp. 91–103, at 92, 98. Nonetheless, Ruff analyses only two lines from the *Ars grammatica*, regarding the discussion on interjection.

[13] The use of the dialogue form and the competition for knowledge are not novelties for the medieval pedagogical texts. In this sense, Irina Dumitrescu argues that "dialogues were standard tools in Anglo-Saxon schools in England and on the continent," and that there was an "*agon* implicit in the educational dialogues so beloved by Anglo-Saxons"; see Irina Dumitrescu, *The Experience of Education in Anglo-Saxon Literature* (Cambridge – New York, 2018), p. 5. In my opinion, what makes *Ars grammatica* interesting and contributes to what I call "indirect pedagogy" is the personalities of the speakers, the type of humour, and the strategies that Alcuin uses to render the text instructive: he inserts in the dialogue of the two pupils examples of grammatical forms which had previously been presented as part of the theory, as well as quotations from classical authors. In this way, even what would seem to be just a frame for the technical part of the grammar, namely the interaction of the two students, is imbued with grammatical information.

[14] This purpose is not stated in the *Grammar* itself, but it emerges clearly from other texts. Firstly, it is expressed in Alcuin's *Disputatio de uera philosophia*, which is often taken as an introduction to the *Grammar* (but is actually an introduction to all seven liberal arts, among which the first is grammar); secondly, Charlemagne's legislation makes the point obvious through the capitulary *Admonitio generalis* and the *Epistola de litteris colendis* addressed to Abbot Baugulf of Fulda.

[15] See Donald Bullough, *Alcuin: Achievement and Reputation: Being Part of the Ford Lectures Delivered in Oxford in Hilary Term 1980* (Leiden – Boston, 2004), p. 12.

As far as the *Breuiarium* is concerned, it can be argued that it is part of a general tendency of compiling and abbreviating grammars that was ever growing in the Carolingian period. If grammatical codices copied in the Gallic region were very sparse by the mid-eighth century,[16] Alcuin's influence at the Carolingian court seems to have generated in the centuries to come "a whole industry of ... compilation,"[17] along with an increasing number of teachers and pupils. Through the experience of the educators and through the cultural background of the students, grammar texts of important *auctores* progressively acquired individual features that distinguished them from the original by simple glossing, compiling, abbreviating, or even rewriting. Thus, the fact that Alcuin's *Grammar* was abridged means that it was validated as "an object of interpretation and knowledge"[18] and integrated into and adapted for a certain school curriculum. It is left to us to understand which one.

Textual Tradition

Alcuin's *Grammar* became popular in the Frankish Empire shortly after his death. There are twenty-four known extant manuscripts transmitting the work, of which sixteen date to the ninth century, two to the tenth, one to the twelfth, and five to the fifteenth century.[19] With the exception of one lost manuscript formerly preserved in the United States,[20] all the other witnesses are currently kept in French, Italian, German, Swiss, and British libraries. As already mentioned, only V_3 contains the abridged version of the *Grammar*.[21]

---

[16] Louis Holtz, "La grammaire carolingienne," in *Histoire des idées linguistiques. Tome 2: Le développement de la grammaire occidentale*, Philosophie et langage, ed. Sylvain Auroux (Liège, 1992), pp. 96–106, at 96.

[17] Vivien Law, "La grammaire latine durant le haut Moyen Âge," in *Histoire des idées linguistiques*, ed. Auroux, pp. 83–95, at 92.

[18] Irvine, *The Making of Textual Culture*, p. 372.

[19] My assessment differs from the one of Jullien and Perelman (*Clavis scriptorum Latinorum*, pp. 21–23), according to whom there are twenty-three manuscripts of Alcuin's complete or partial text, of which seventeen are dated to the ninth century, one to the tenth, one to the twelfth, and four to the fifteenth century. Another fifteenth-century manuscript has recently been discovered at St. Andrews, University Library, MS 38904. However, manuscript catalogues and lists of books found in manuscripts provide hints that there were more copies of the text than we know today; see Irvine, *The Making of Textual Culture*, pp. 338–44.

[20] Washington, Hay-Adams House, MS 1054 (saec. XV, Italy), fols. 125r–190v.

[21] It might be of interest to mention that the twelfth-century manuscript, Munich, Bayerische Staatsbibliothek, clm 14823, fols. 7v–68v, contains a revised variant of Alcuin's *Grammar* in the sense that, besides numerous changes of word position and emendations, the scribe left out most of the verb paradigms by simply adding "et cetera ut in Donato habentur."

The *editio princeps* of Alcuin's *Ars grammatica* was produced by Henricus Canisius at the beginning of the seventeenth century (1604),[22] based on a single manuscript, our S_1. Shortly thereafter the text was republished twice, with no major changes: in 1605 by Helias Putschen, in a collection entitled *Grammaticae Latinae Auctores Antiqui*,[23] and in 1617 by André Duchesne, as part of Alcuin's *Opera*.[24] It took more than a century and a half for the text to be edited again, in 1777, in the more complete edition of Frobenius Forster, who used two additional manuscripts: Munich, Bayerische Staatsbibliothek, clm 6404 (saec. IX*ex.*, Freising), and Munich, clm 14823 (saec. XII, St. Emmeram in Regensburg).[25] The most recent edition was published by Migne in the second half of the nineteenth century, as part of the *Patrologia Latina*, vol. 101,[26] with no major emendations to the text published by Forster.

No critical edition or serious study of the *Breuiarium Artis grammaticae Alcuini* has been presented until now. The manuscript preserving the text, V_3, was most certainly copied in the ninth century in North-East France (see below, pp. 189–90, 192, for the origin and dating of the codex). It is unknown, however, when and where exactly the text itself was composed. It is likely that the *breuiator* was not the same person as the *copista*, and that the two were from different schools or even from different regions (see the discussion of orthography below, pp. 201–3). An interesting feature of the *Breuiarium Artis grammaticae Alcuini* is that the work is not a mere collection of snippets excerpted from the full *Grammar*. In fact, there are also fragments not belonging to Alcuin's text and which come from other known and unknown sources (more about this aspect is presented below, pp. 195–201).

Description of the Manuscript

1. General Aspects

V_3 is found in the Vatican Library and, as its shelf mark, Reg. lat. 251, indicates, the codex was one of the manuscripts forming the collection previously owned by Queen

---

[22] *Antiquae lectionis tomus V. bipartitus, in quo L. vetera monumenta nunquam visa pauculis exceptis, quorum catalogum versa pagina indicat*, ed. Henricus Canisius (Ingolstadt, 1604), pp. 988–1050.

[23] *Grammaticae Latinae Auctores Antiqui*, ed. Helias Putsch (Hanau, 1605), cols. 2075–2142.

[24] *B. Flacci Albini, sive Alchuuini abbatis Karoli Magni Regis, ac Imperatoris, magistri Opera quae hactenus reperiri potuerunt*, ed. Andrea Quercetanus (Paris, 1617), cols. 1255D–1320B.

[25] *Beati Flacci Albini seu Alcuini abbatis, Caroli Magni Regis ac Imperatoris, magistri Opera*, ed. Frobenius Forster (Regensburg, 1777), pp. 265–300. Forster also had access to Paris, Bibliothèque nationale de France, MS lat. 8319, but he seems not to have collated it.

[26] *B. Flacci Albini seu Alcuini, abbatis et Caroli Magni Imperatoris magistri, opera omnia juxta editionem illustrissimi et reverendissimi d. Frobenii, abbatis sancti Emmerami Ratisbonensis, novissime ad prelum revocata et variis monumentis aucta: tomus secundus*, in PL 101:849C–902B.

Christina of Sweden. It is a composite codex, comprising six codicological units, written on parchment, with the following structure: fol. i (paper) + 103 + i (paper). The quires are disposed as following: I$^{8+1\,(\text{at the beginning of the quire})}$ II–VI^8 VII^6 VIII–XIII.^{8}

The initial foliation, indicating 102 folios and written in ink, is incorrect. In fact, fol. 38 is numbered twice (38, 38a), so there are actually 103 folios. The first quire displays three foliations, subsequently reduced to a single one. The codex follows the rule of Gregory, with flesh side out (considering the first complete quire that starts with fol. 2), and ruling is generally made on the flesh side. The parchment is of medium quality – in view of their content, the manuscript's texts were supposed to be used quite often by teachers and clerics. None of the quires presents catchwords or signatures.

All codicological units seem to have been produced in the French area, although each of them was copied at a different time. While it is unknown when they were bound together (possibly before they entered Queen Christina's collection), it is certain that the manuscript has been restored several times and rebound at least two or three times.[27] Thus, **V**$_3$ has a modern binding, with a cover made of white artificial leather pasted on cardboard. On the back of the codex there is a red title label with the current shelfmark in golden letters (MS Reg. 251), along with the coat of arms of the Biblioteca Apostolica Vaticana (also stamped on the first leaves of the manuscript). On fol. 1r, "1403" has been struck through, and on fol. 2r, one can read "322" – both may be previous shelfmarks. Other distinctive signs are indicated by André Wilmart: "F. 2 in laevo angulo rubra crux notata est; ex quo constat codicem Antverpiae inter 'non Petavianos' computatum esse; re vera superior pars f. 2 non integerrima nunc est. At reginae proprius numerus f. 1 traditur: 1508."[28]

The first codicological unit comprises fol. 1rv, which most probably used to be a flyleaf and which transmits a fragment of the *Commentatio de Prisciani grammatici Institutionibus*, dating from the first half of the twelfth century.[29] The second and longest codicological unit comprises seventy leaves and will be discussed below, as it contains Alcuin's abridged *Grammar*. The third codicological unit is a quire containing grammatical excerpts from Remigius of Auxerre's *In Artem Donati minorem* (fols. 71r–74v), from Priscianus's *Institutiones* (fol. 75r), and an anonymous

---

[27] The most recent restoration was made at the very beginning of 2017, when the manuscript was also digitized and published online: http://digi.vatlib.it/view/MSS_Reg.lat.251.

[28] Andreas Wilmart, *Codices Reginenses Latini*, 2 vols. (Vatican City, 1945), 2:6.

[29] I dated the different codicological units of the manuscript taking into consideration both their palaeographic and codicological features. I also verified my opinions by comparing them with the information provided by Wilmart. Moreover, I completed the data that Wilmart offered regarding the works found in MS Reg. lat. 251 with titles that were not previously identified.

grammatical work about the eight parts of speech (fols. 75v–78v),[30] written by three different hands. It is possible to date the first half of the quire to the late eleventh century, due to the general aspect of the script, which is more compressed, with letters that tend to have sharper edges and a large number of abbreviations. The forks on the ascenders indicate a French scribe. However, the second half of the quire, where the letters are more rounded, seems to have been copied earlier; the wedges sometimes alternating with the forks are another sign of an early eleventh-century script.

The fourth codicological unit contains two works: Maurus Servius Honoratus's *De centum metris* (fols. 79r–83v) and an excerpt from Flavius Mallius Theodorus's *De metris* (fols. 83v–87r). The first text is *mutilus*; the upper right part of fols. 79–81 was destroyed and recently restored. This quire has a strange structure, since its last folio (fol. 87) seems to be part of the next gathering. Wilmart explains the situation of fols. 88–94 as follows: "Prius, ut videtur, quinio dispositus erat, qui nunc ita seruatur: x x 88 89 90 || 91 92 93 x 94."[31] I would date this Carolingian script to the tenth century: the words are clearly separated, there is punctuation, constant use of the Carolingian minuscule *a* and the ÷ abbreviation.

The fifth codicological unit is unrelated to grammar, as it contains a glossed fragment of *The Book of Revelation* (fols. 88r–92r), a Commentary on the Eucharist (fols. 92r–93r), and a fragment from the *De concordia praescientiae et praedestinationis necnon gratiae Dei cum libero arbitrio* by Anselm of Canterbury (fols. 93r–94v). This quire seems to have been copied during the eleventh or twelfth century, as it presents some Gothic features, such as the sharper edges of the letters, and the use of round *d*. In the lower margin of fol. 89r, one can read a line in French: *je suis troz minoz*,[32] written in a Gothic semi-cursive hand.

The last codicological unit, fols. 95r–102v, contains fragments from a *Commentarium in Satiras Horatii* that refers to the following *Satires*: 1.6, 1.7, 1.8, 1.9, 1.10, 2.1, 2.2, 2.3, 2.4. The text, *mutilus* both at the beginning and the end, was written in *littera gotica textualis media*, most probably in the first half of the thirteenth century.

2. Particular Aspects

The second codicological unit (which I will call V_3^b) of this composite manuscript is the most consistent and complete one. It contains the following works:

---

[30] Fol. 75v, inc. "Interrogatio de nomine: Quę pars? Responsio. Nomen. Interrogatio: Cuius qualitatis? Responsio: Apellatiuę." This abridged text about the eight parts of speech contains many definitions given by Donatus in his *Grammar*.

[31] Wilmart, *Codices Reginenses Latini*, 2:5.

[32] The meaning of these words cannot be ascertained.

1) fols. 2r–10v: Aldhelmus Schireburnensis, *Carmina ecclesiastica*.
2) fol. 10v: *De duodecim uirtutibus Herculis*.
3) fols. 10v–11r: *De Samsone fortissimo*.
4) fol. 11r: *De tribus mulieribus uictricibus atque ab eisdem de totisdem uiris interfectis*.
5) fols. 11v–13r: Gregorius Magnus, *Moralia in Iob*, 21.45 ("Gregorii de dutibus siue exercitibus uitiorum").
6) fol. 13r: Hieronymus: *In Abacuc prophetam*, 1.2.
7) fols. 13r–15r: Gaius Plinius Caecilius Secundus: *Epistulae*, 6.16.
8) fols. 15v–27v: Faltonia Betitia Proba, *Cento Vergilianus*.
9) fols. 27v–38'r: Maximus Victorinus, *De arte grammatica*.
10) fols. 38'r–52v: *Breuiarium Artis grammaticae Alcuini*.
11) fols. 53r–69r: *Coniugationes uerborum*.
12) fol. 69v: Martianus Capella: *De nuptiis Philologiae et Mercurii*, 3 (*De formatione litterarum*).

V_3^b is a compilation of texts intended for the study of *grammatica*, though not all works are grammatical ones. Irvine shows that this was a typical situation for the medieval canon of texts meant for the study of grammar: "The catalogues make clear that both grammatical *artes* and the corpus of classical and Christian Latin *auctores* belonged to *grammatica* as a unified *disciplina*."[33] In our case, an investigation of the codex would suggest four sections:[34] Christian poems (Aldhelm, followed by three anonymous and short medieval poems), moral prose (Gregory the Great and Jerome), Christian epic based on Vergilian hexametres (Proba), and grammatical texts. The choice of works in V_3^b suggests that this manuscript was copied for the use of monks or clerics, since it contains mostly Christian writings. The only classical text, that is, Pliny the Younger's Letter to Tacitus, in which he describes the death of his renowned uncle during the eruption of Vesuvius (fols. 13r–15r), is copied after a few lines from Jerome's *In Abacuc prophetam*, just as if it were part of Jerome's text. Furthermore, grammar was seemingly not meant to be practised on the pagan work of Virgil,[35] but on a very popular (at that time) Christian rewriting of his hexametres, Proba's *Cento Vergilianus*.[36]

---

[33] Irvine, *The Making of Textual Culture*, p. 338.

[34] The fragment from Capella's *De formatione litterarum* might have been copied from a feeling of *horror uacui*.

[35] Otherwise, recent research has proved that during the ninth and tenth centuries Christian readers had great interest in Virgil's works, which were intensively glossed; see Sinéad O'Sullivan, "Glossing Vergil and Pagan Learning in the Carolingian Age," *Speculum* 93/1 (2018), 132–65.

[36] The text has been recently edited in a Teubner edition: Faltonia Betitia Proba, *Cento Vergilianus*, ed. Alessia Fassina and Carlo M. Lucarini (Berlin – Boston, 2015).

As far as the grammatical texts are concerned, they also have their rationale. The first work (inc. "Ars quid est? Vnius cuiusque rei scientia," fol. 27v) is Maximus Victorinus's *De arte grammatica*.[37] The second grammatical text is the *Breuiarium Artis grammaticae Alcuini* (inc. "Cuius cause littere inuente sunt," fol. 38'r), the compendium under discussion here. The third text (inc. "Congugationes uerborum quot sunt," fol. 53r) is a popular type of medieval grammar that is made of verb paradigms;[38] about twenty verbs are exemplified here (but not all of them with complete paradigms). The choice of these three grammatical works points to the fact that those who learned grammar from V_3^b were most probably beginners in Latin.

From a codicological and palaeographical point of view, V_3^b is the oldest section of V_3. Rudolf Ehwald dates it to the tenth century and locates its production in the monastery of St. Benignus of Dijon.[39] Other scholars, such as Paola Francesca Moretti, date the manuscript to the eleventh century, which is clearly incorrect.[40] This date also appears in Bernhard Bischoff's *Katalog*, in which he mentions: "Ms. Reg. lat. 251 (Bl. 2–70) [(s. XI, Dijon, S. Bénigne). Aldhelmus, Carmina ecclesiastica; al.]."[41] However, I think that this information concerns not the date of the manuscript, but the place where it was found in the eleventh century, according to an ownership note on fol. 70v (see below, p. 194). Bischoff further affirms that fols. 2–70 were probably copied at Reims in the first half of the ninth century.

In my opinion, V_3^b has to be dated to the third quarter of the ninth century. The reasons for this dating can be outlined as follows: the *cc* Merovingian *a* is still used occasionally, but the Caroline *a* predominates; the *-us* abbreviation is still misused for *–ur* and there is no use of NT; there is punctuation and word separation, even though it is not consistent;[42] only *st* and *et* ligatures are used (invariably); and finally, *h* has the claw-like bow rarely going below the baseline, and there are no feet applied to minims.

---

[37] See Maximus Victorinus, *De arte grammatica*, ed. Heinrich Keil, *Scriptores artis metricae*, in *Grammatici Latini* 6 (Leipzig, 1874), pp. 187–205.

[38] See more about the "coniugationes uerborum" in Law, *Grammar and Grammarians*, p. 132.

[39] See Aldhelm, *Carmina ecclesiastica*, ed. Rudolf Ehwald, *Aldhelmi opera*, MGH AA 15 (Berlin, 1919), p. 10.

[40] Paola Francesca Moretti, "In margine a due testimoni del centone di Proba: Milano, Biblioteca Ambrosiana, D14 inf. e G111 inf.," *Segno e testo* 8 (2010), 285–312, at p. 304, n. 81; Paola Francesca Moretti, "Proba e la tradizione del testo di Virgilio. Qualche riflessione," *Acme. Annali della Facoltà di lettere e filosofia dell'Università degli studi di Milano* 61.1 (2008), 61–86, at p. 64, n. 15. Moretti seems to have adopted this particular dating from Schenkl; see Proba, *Cento*, ed. Carolus Schenkl, *Poetae Christiani minores Pars I*, CSEL 1 (Milan, Pisa, Naples, 1888), p. 520.

[41] Bernhard Bischoff, *Katalog der festländischen Handschriften des neunten Jahrhunderts*, 3 vols. (Wiesbaden, 1998–2014), 3:425.

[42] There are still examples of *scriptio continua*, and also many situations of incorrect word separation, which, however, could indicate that the copyist did not understand the text.

V_3^b shows a typical Carolingian layout and structure (1–1/0/0/J);[43] the *folia* (215 x 130 mm) are ruled by dry-point; the writing space (200 x 90 mm) mainly contains a single column of twenty-eight lines, even though the number of ruled lines can vary between twenty-seven and twenty-nine; only fol. 69v is written in two columns (both fols. 69 and 70 are ruled in two columns). On most of the leaves, the pricking is no longer visible. Comparing the description offered by Wilmart in the first half of the twentieth century and the present physical appearance of the codex, one can conclude that the margins have been trimmed recently, probably when the manuscript was last rebound, as the dimensions of the leaves are smaller than the ones indicated by Wilmart.[44] The height of the folios might have been about 220–225 mm: the inferior margin of fol. 38' still has a longer piece in the outer bottom corner.

The decorative program includes two major initials with interlaces and vegetal motifs, drawn in a typically French brown ink, also used for writing the rest of the text: one is at the beginning of the excerpt from Gregory's *Moralia* (fol. 11v), and the other at the beginning of the first grammatical *breuiarium* (fol. 27v). The largest (80 x 60 mm) and most elaborated initial is the A (*Ars quid est ...*) on fol. 27v, which seems to mark the beginning not only of a distinct work, but of the entire series of the three grammatical texts at the end of V_3^b. There are also medium-size initials in brown ink with interlaces and vegetal motifs, measuring about 33 x 29 mm (fol. 38'r: the C from *Cuius cause littere ...*), which could, in fact, be considered major ones, as they mark the beginning of a new text (fols. 15v, 38'r, 53r); other medium-size initials appear at the beginning of important sections of the works (such as fol. 43v and fol. 48r). "Lombard" majuscules were used for the beginning of the works that seem to have been considered of lesser importance, as well as for the beginning of chapters and sections. There are also *litterae notabiliores* in *capitalis rustica* at the beginning of the paragraphs, verses, and replies. The *Cento Vergilianus* has marginal glosses written by the same scribe.

Other particularities of V_3^b worth mentioning include the signature of Angelo Mai on fols. 2r and 4v, followed by "Inter Alcuini carmina" and "Inter carmina Alcuini." In addition, on fols. 11r and 15r a different hand wrote: "Christe tua agmina iubilant uoce precelsa" – "Christ, your flocks shout joyfully with lofty voice," and another one wrote on fol. 11r: "Dum fueris felix semper tibi proximus esto – "As long as you are happy, always be the closest person to yourself." There are some *probationes pennae* on fol. 70r, and on the verso is copied (probably in the eleventh century) a grammatical text containing some definitions from Book 1 of Isidore's *Etymologiae*. At

---

[43] According to one of Denis Muzerelle's formulas that define possible layouts of Latin manuscripts. This formula can be used to recreate the layout of V_3^b automatically (see http://www.palaeographia.org/muzerelle/mastara.htm).

[44] See Wilmart, *Codices Reginenses Latini*, 2:1–2.

the bottom of this page one can see some other *probationes pennae* and, in black ink and *capitalis rustica*, the following ownership note: *Liber Sancti Benigni*. This could mean that **V₃ᵇ** belonged to the monastery of St. Benignus of Dijon, but we cannot postulate with certainty that it was copied there.

Structure and Sources of the Breuiarium

The structure of the *Breuiarium* broadly follows the one of *Ars grammatica*. Alcuin conceived his *Ars* as a discussion of basic grammar rules, which opens with a short presentation of the dialogue setting (Alcuin's school), of the speakers (two pupils, Franco and Saxo, and their master), and of their intention regarding grammar learning (854B–C).[45] The debate on grammar does not start with *littera*, as the pupils consider, but with *uox* ("utterance, sound"), for the sake of which *littera* was invented. The speakers further refer to the parts of a discussion (*modi disputationis*), with a closer look on *uox* (854C–D), then to *littera* and its division into vowels and consonants (854D–856B), to syllable (856C–857D), and to grammar and its species (857D–858D).[46] The rest of the discussion focuses on the presentation of the eight parts of speech (858D–859A): name (859A–870D),[47] pronoun (870D–873D), verb (874A–886A), adverb (886A–889A), participle (889A–894D), conjunction (895A–896B), preposition (896C–901B), and interjection (901B–902B).[48] The text is animated by puns, jokes, and the teasing of the two pupils who offer details regarding their feelings, expectations, and some of the school conditions.

The *Breuiarium Artis grammaticae Alcuini* lacks the pedagogical force given by the vivid dialogue of the *Ars grammatica*. The *breuiator* pruned Alcuin's text of its dramatic situation and specificity; thus, there is no presentation of the dialogue setting, no introduction of the speakers (who have no identity), no jokes, and no chatting outside strict grammatical information. There is almost no trace of some speakers' presence behind the questions and answers; the exceptions would be (all

---

[45] The references are to PL 101.

[46] Alcuin mentions twenty-six grammar species (or divisions, categories, forms): sounds, letters, syllables, parts of speech, words, sentences, definitions, metrical feet, accents, punctuation marks, critical signs, orthography, analogy, etymology, glosses, differentiations, barbarisms, solecisms, faults, metaplasm, schemes, tropes, prose, metres, tales, and histories.

[47] I translate *nomen* with "name," since this term is used to designate both the noun (*nomen substantiuum*) and adjective (*nomen adiectiuum*); see Law, *Grammar and Grammarians*, pp. 262, 264.

[48] See more on *Ars grammatica*'s structure in Pierre Swiggers, "Alcuin et les doctrines grammaticales," *Annales de Bretagne et des Pays de l'Ouest*, 111/3 (2004), 147–61, at pp. 158–59. However, Swiggers presents a schema which is not without error (for instance, the students and the teacher first speak about *uox* and then about *littera*, not vice versa as Swiggers has it; he might have made the error because the students initially thought that their discussion should begin with *littera* but were corrected by their teacher).

references are to chapters and line numbers in the edition below): "Expone, pater, hanc nobis difinitionem propriam" – "Show us, father, this specific definition" (4.223); or "Pleniorem tamen declinationem horum quatuor uerborum ut reddas mihi deposco" – "However, I demand that you give me a more complete conjugation of these four verbs" (4.320–321). From this point of view, the text recalls more the lifelessness that characterizes Donatus's *Grammar* than Alcuin's own work. Moreover, the *Breuiarium* is not presented in the dialogue layout adopted in this edition; instead, the copyist left some visible spaces for each speaker's intervention, presumably with the intention of marking the questions and answers and not of adding the interlocutors' initials (as in the manuscripts that transmit the full *Grammar*). Besides these spaces, the text is divided into eight paragraphs of different lengths, one for each part of speech: *nomen* (preceded by the discussion about *uox*, *littera*, *syllaba*, etc.), *pronomen*, *uerbum*, *aduerbium*, *participium*, *coniunctio*, *praepositio*, *interiectio*. The first line of each paragraph is written in *capitalis rustica*. In the edition, I have opted to leave a blank line between the eight sections of the text.[49]

A closer look into the internal structure of the *Breuiarium* reveals an interesting composition, at least for the first part of the text, due to the interpolated fragments from other authors. The text begins directly with a presentation of *uox* ("Cuius causa littere inuente sunt?" – "For what purpose were letters invented?" – 1.1) and its etymology. Then, it continues with the *modi disputationis* and the types of *uox*, which in the complete *Grammar* come before the discussion about utterance mentioned at the beginning of the *Breuiarium*. Moreover, the *breuiator* soon intercalates some lines about *ars* and *littera*, which do not exist in the complete *Grammar*, but seem to have been excerpted from Pompeius Maurus's *Commentum artis Donati*[50] and given a question-and-answer form (1.14–24):

> Ars quid est? Vnius cuiusque rei scientia. Ars unde habet ethimologiam? *Apo tes aretes*, id est a uirtute, quam Greci scientiam uocauerunt.[51] Quare dicta est ars? Eo quod artis

---

[49] However, the cross-references to this edition refer to nine main sections: a first one regarding the preliminary discussion on *uox* and the other elements, and eight others regarding the parts of speech.

[50] Pompeius, *Commentum artis Donati*, ed. Heinrich Keil, *Grammatici Latini* 5 (Leipzig, 1868), p. 95.4–8; p. 98.10–11 and 15–20; and p. 99.15–16 and 18–20. As the reader will observe, the examples of intertextuality from the *Breuiarium* often refer to Pompeius's grammatical work. I find it significant to point out that after the year 850, with just one negligible exception, Pompeius's *Commentum* was not copied again for about four centuries; see Louis Holtz, "Tradition et diffusion de l'œuvre grammaticale de Pompée, commentateur de Donat," *Revue de Philologie, de Littérature et d'Histoire Anciennes* 45 (1971), 48–83, at p. 57. Since the *Breuiarium* seems to have been copied after 850, its existence may prove meaningful for the study of the transmission of Pompeius's work, especially with respect to a period when it appears to have been no longer copied.

[51] The phrase "quam Greci scientiam uocauerunt" does not appear in Pompeius's text, but was most probably inspired by Isidore's *Etymologiae*; see Isidorus Hispalensis episcopus, *Etymologiarum sive*

preceptis cuncta concludat. Quis inuenit primum litteras Latinas? Carmentis nimpha, Euandri mater, que Nicostrata dicebatur. Littere quare dicte sunt? Quia legentibus iter prebeant uel ideo quod in legendo iterentur. Quare dicta est articulata uox? Eo quod potest articulis digitisque tenentibus conprehendi.[52] Littere ad quam uocem pertinent? Ad articulatam.

What is an art? The science of any particular thing. Where does art take its etymology from? *Apo tes aretes* (i.e. 'from virtue'), which the Greeks called 'science'. Why is it called 'art'? Because it includes all things through the rules of the art. Who first invented the Latin letters? The nymph Carmentis, Evander's mother, who was called Nicostrata. Why are they called 'letters'? Because they provide a road to those who read or because they are reiterated through reading. Why do we say 'articulated utterance'? Because it can be seized by the joints and fingers which hold it. To what utterance do letters belong? To the articulated one.

With the last question ("Littere ad quam ...") the *breuiator* returns to Alcuin's text, but just to interpolate two lines thereafter his own definition of *litterae*: "Quid sunt littere? Amare cortices et fructus dulces" – "What are letters? Bitter hulls and sweet fruits" (1.26). This is a famous maxim traditionally ascribed to Cato ("Litterarum radices amarae, fructus dulces" – "The roots of learning are bitter, the fruits are sweet"), but with a slightly different form and meaning. In the case of the replacement of *radices* with (what should have been) *cortices*, the *breuiator* might have had in mind the image of the almond-tree as presented by Jerome, *In Hieremiam libri VI* (CCSL 74, 1.7.4):[53]

Et quomodo nux siue amygdalum amarissimam habet corticem et testa durissima cingitur, ut detractis austerioribus et duris fructus dulcissimus repperiatur, sic omnis

---

originum libri XX, vol. I, ed. Wallace M. Lindsay (Oxford, 1911), 1.1.2 and 1.5.2. It could have also been inspired by Donatus Ortigraphus; see Donatus Ortigraphus, *Ars grammatica*, ed. John Chittenden, CCCM 40D (Turnhout, 1982), p. 3.14–17. However, this phrase appears verbatim in the grammatical work of Murethach: "ars dicitur apothes arethes, id est a uirtute, quam Greci scientiam uocauerunt" – "Art has its name *apo tes aretes* (i.e. 'from virtue'), which the Greeks called 'science'"; see Murethach, *In Donati artem maiorem* 2, ed. Louis Holtz, *Grammatici Hibernici Carolini aevi Pars I*, CCCM 40 (Turnhout, 1977), p. 49.82. If our *breuiator* indeed had knowledge of Murethach's *Commentary*, then the *Breuiarium Artis grammaticae Alcuini* could not have been composed *ante* 844, since Louis Holtz dates Murethach's grammatical text to between 844 and 855; see Louis Holtz, "Murethach et l'influence de la culture irlandaise à Auxerre," in *L'École carolingienne d'Auxerre de Murethach à Remi, 830–908. Entretiens d'Auxerre 1989*, ed. Dominique Iogna-Prat, Colette Jeudy, and Guy Lobrichon (Paris, 1991), pp. 147–56, at 149.

[52] This is a condensed version of Pompeius: "idcirco articulata vox dicta est, quod potest articulis conprehendi. digitis autem tenemus calamos" – "An utterance is called 'articulated' because it can be seized by the finger-joints. Indeed, we hold the pens with the fingers."

[53] S. Eusebius Hieronymus, *In Hieremiam libri VI*, ed. Siegfried Reiter, *S. Hieronymi presbyteri opera Pars I, Opera exegetica* 3, CCSL 74 (Turnhout, 1960). The image is also used by Bede, *In Cantica Canticorum libri VI*, 4.6.524–29, ed. David Hurst, *Opera exegetica Pars II*, CCSL 119B (Turnhout, 1983), p. 312.

correptio et labor continentiae amara quidem uidetur ad praesens, sed fructus parit dulcissimos. Vnde et uetus illa sententia est: 'litterarum radices amarae, fructus dulces.'

And just as the nut or the almond has a very bitter hull and is enveloped in a very hard covering, so that after the more bitter and harder parts are removed the very sweet fruit may be obtained, in the same way every reproof and effort towards moderation certainly seems bitter in the present, but it brings forth very sweet fruits. That is why we have that ancient saying: 'The roots of learning are bitter, the fruits are sweet'.

I believe that the replacement made by the *breuiator* was not due to a mere inaccurate quotation, but had the purpose of changing the meaning of the maxim: *litterae* does not mean here "education" or "literature" but "letter forms," which are a bitter labour for the copyist, but a sweet delight for the reader; the act of writing the shape of the letters was bitter, but the words formed by them give the sweet meaning of the text.

The *Breuiarium* continues following Alcuin's text and presents concisely (by omitting examples and details about classifications) the vowels and the consonants, the syllables, and the definition of grammar. Then the *breuiator* introduces another passage inspired by Pompeius Maurus's *Commentum artis Donati* (*Grammatici Latini* 5, ed. Keil, p. 96.9–12): "Quare non incohat gramatica a uoce aut a littera, sed ab octo partibus orationis? Quia hoc proprium est gramaticorum; multi dicunt a uoce, sed hoc philosophorum est; multi dicunt a littera, sed hoc omnium est" – "Why does grammar not start from the utterance or from the letter, but from the eight parts of speech? Because this is specific to grammarians. Many say it starts from the utterance, but this is specific to philosophers. Many others say it starts from the letter, but this is specific to everybody else" (1.45–47).

Afterwards, the text continues with the grammar species and their definitions, as well as with short descriptions of each of the eight parts of speech. Here the *breuiator* preserves most of Alcuin's text, but he also interpolates two additional fragments. The first one is inspired by Pompeius Maurus's work (*Grammatici Latini* 5, ed. Keil, p. 134.21–23 and 28–29) and comes as an introduction to the presentation of the parts of speech: "Quare dicte sunt principales partes orationis nomen et uerbum? Quoniam ipsa faciunt eloquutionem et alia eloquutio sine ipsis nulla est uel sine ipsis nulla potest stare loquutio" – "Why are the name and the verb called 'main parts of speech'? Because they form the speech and there is no speech without them or no discourse can stand without them" (1.79–81). The second one is an addition of the interjection, omitted by Alcuin in the brief enumeration of the parts of speech from the beginning of his *Grammar*: "Proprium interiectionis quid est? Interiacere alias partes et mentis affectum significare" – "What is specific to the interjection? To lie between other parts of speech and to indicate the emotion of the heart" (1.94–95). The source for this second fragment has not been indentified, but the expression "mentis affectum significare" is most certainly also inspired by Pompeius's commentary on Donatus (*Grammatici Latini* 5, ed. Keil, p. 281.5).

The text continues with the definition of *nomen*, immediately followed by another interpolation from *Commentum artis Donati* (*Grammatici Latini* 5, ed. Keil, p. 137.3–6): "Sine quot rebus non potest ullum nomen inueniri? Sine tribus: ut casu careat, aut non sit corporale aut incorporale, aut non sit proprium aut appellatiuum" – "A name cannot be identified without how many aspects? Without three: when it does not have a case or it is not material or immaterial or it is not proper or common" (2.101–103). Following that, the *breuiator* skips the enumeration of name properties according to Donatus and Priscian, as well as the presentation of the first property from Priscian's classification.[54] He follows again Alcuin's text with reflections on comparison (superlatives are mentioned, but without examples, and diminutives with examples), and on gender. In the discussion about gender, the *breuiator* introduces a consistent fragment on names which can become adverbs and vice versa, also inspired by Pompeius's work (*Grammatici Latini* 5, ed. Keil, pp. 135.38–136.1–4; 136.6–10 and 20–25):

> Possunt nomina pro aduerbiis poni? Possunt, ut est *toruum clamat* pro eo quod est *torue clamat*. Possunt aduerbia pro nominibus poni? Possunt, utputa si dicas *cras, mane*; dicit Virgilius: *dum mane nouum*, iam *mane* non uult esse aduerbium, sed nomen. Item Terrentius: *propterea ipso meridiae*. Item Persius: *aliud cras*; et *aliud cras*, si habet genus, sine dubio nomen est. Nam nomina, quando pro aduerbiis ponuntur, tenent casus; aduerbium uero quando transit in nomen nequaquam potest accipere casus. Ne dicas mihi *hoc mane*, non potest sequi ut declinetur. Tamen legimus apud Plautum declinationem ipsam: *a primo mane*. (2.141–150)

> Can names be used instead of adverbs? They can, such is *toruum clamat* for what is *torue clamat*. Can adverbs be used instead of names? They can, as for example if you say *cras, mane*; when Vergil says *dum mane nouum*, he does not want *mane* to be an adverb, but a name. The same with Terence: *propterea ipso meridiae*. The same with Persius: *aliud cras*; and *aliud cras*, if it has gender, is doubtless a name. Indeed names, when used instead of adverbs, maintain the cases; as for the adverb, when it changes into a name, it can by no means receive cases. Do not tell me *hoc mane*: it cannot follow that it is declined. However, we read in Plautus the very declension *a primo mane*.

The *breuiator* further omits the presentation of declensions and continues with concise information on number, form, and case, by pruning the text of detailed classifications and examples. Moreover, when speaking about name forms, the *breuiator* mentions some definitions not occurring in Alcuin's *Grammar*. First of all, he gives a definition of *figura* that seems to be his own or, in any case, has an unknown source: "Figura unde dicitur? A figmento, id est exemplo; et figura est tecta imago ueritatis" – "Why is figure called thus? From figment, that is to say, from illustration; and the figure is the hidden image of truth" (2.173–174); then he continues with two

---

[54] The property called *species* and equivalent to *qualitas* and *comparatio* in Donatus's system; the other properties are *comparatio, genus, numerus, figura*, and *casus*.

phrases that seem to be taken – but this would be a very curious source – from (Pseudo) Boethius's *Geometria*,[55] or most probably from a work attributed to Cassiodorus (p. 169, 13–14):[56] "Et est iterum figura dicta uel quod aliquo uel aliquibus terminis continetur. Terminus uero est quod cuiusque est finis" – "And again it is called 'figure' because it is confined by some limit or limits. As for limit, it is that which is the end of a certain thing" (2.174–175). Moreover, the *breuiator* adds two more definitions of *figura*, one from Isidore's *Etymologiae* (1.7.30): "Et est iterum figura dicta, quia uel simplicia sunt uel composita sunt" – "And again it is called 'figure' because they are either simple or compound" (2.175–176); the other one from Priscian's *Institutiones* (*Grammatici Latini* 2, ed. Keil, p. 177.10):[57] "Et figura quoque dictionis in quantitate conprehenditur" – "And the figure is also contained in the size of the word" (2.176–177).

The last major differences between the *Breuiarium* and the complete *Grammar* appear in the discussion about cases, which is slightly different from what we read in Alcuin's *Ars*. All case exemplifications must have been invented by the *breuiator*, who seems to like Virgil very much, because he uses the poet's name to illustrate each case (2.184–194). Furthermore, the case forms are mentioned, but the lengthy presentation of their endings is omitted.

With respect to the other parts of speech, the *breuiator* does not interpolate data from any other sources (with only one exception) and just excerpts the passages that interest him from Alcuin's text. Regarding the pronoun, only its definition and the enumeration of its types are provided, with the presentation of its properties totally foregone. Concerning the verb, the *breuiator* keeps the definitions of the verb and the details regarding the voices. However, from the seven verb properties, that is, meaning, tense, mood, aspect, form, person, number (*significatio*, *tempus*, *modus*, *species*, *figura*, *persona*, *numerus*), he mentions only two: the tense (definition and short reference to present tense) and the mood (definition, enumeration and examples of the five verbal moods), which he immediately links to the discussion about verb conjugation; here he gives the definition, but omits mentioning the four types of conjugation and the verb paradigms that illustrate each of them. On the contrary, the *breuiator* finds it more important to mention how one can distinguish the conjugation of verbs that have identical forms in the first person singular, and how

---

[55] *"Boethius" Geometrie II: Ein mathematisches Lehrbuch des Mittelalters*, ed. Menso Folkerts (Wiesbaden, 1970), p. 114. If this was the source of our copyist, it would mean that the text edited by Folkerts is older than the eleventh century, but I have no other arguments to sustain this hypothesis.

[56] Cassiodorus Senator (dubium), *Principia geometricae disciplinae* (*appendix*), ed. Roger A.B. Mynors, *Cassiodori Senatoris Institutiones* (Oxford, 1961), pp. 169–72.

[57] Priscianus Caesariensis, *Institutionum grammaticarum libri I–XII*, ed. Heinrich Keil and Martin Hertz, *Grammatici Latini* 2 (Leipzig, 1855).

verbs with different conjugations can have the same meaning. Moreover, he preserves the list of defective verbs and the full paradigm of *sum*, but he does not include the conjugation of *fero*, *edo*, and *uolo*.[58]

With respect to the adverb, the *breuiator* is not interested in its definition or classification; instead, he mentions the main characteristic of an adverb (the fact that it has meaning only in relation to a verb or a participle) and includes the list of instances when other parts of speech may replace an adverb as well as the three *figurae aduerbiorum*. Following Alcuin's text, the *breuiator* continues with the discussion on the different meanings of the adverb, but only to present the temporal adverbs and to omit all the other types. Moreover, he chooses to mention the fact that adverbs deriving from other parts of speech preserve their original meaning. The last aspect included here concerns *synonyma* and *polyonyma* adverbs, while the discussion on the placement of the adverb with respect to its regent-term is omitted.

The *breuiator* drastically reduces the lengthy presentation of the participle found in Alcuin's text by completely omitting the discussion about its properties and the numerous examples of verbs with their participle and supine. However, he preserves almost entirely the introductory part containing the definition of the participle and its functions. When the *breuiator* excludes something, he usually does it in an intelligent manner, so as not to spoil the logical unfolding of ideas. There is one exception: the explanation of how one can distinguish a participle from a *nomen* and the remark that participles indicate time are omitted. Thus, the paragraph introduced by "Numquid non quedam nomina quoque tempus significant" – "Do not also some names express time?" (6.391) follows awkwardly after "Participia autem semper ab uerbis deriuantur et conparationem non possunt habere" – "But participles are always derived from verbs and they cannot have comparison" (6.389–390).

For the conjunction, the *breuiator* keeps the definition, the classification (though, most of the examples are excluded), and the discussion about the placement of the conjunction. Details about properties of the conjunction and the possibility of changing its value (*potestas*) are omitted. Furthermore, it is curious to observe that the *breuiator* has a special interest in the preposition. In contrast to the other parts of speech, he keeps almost all the details offered by Alcuin. He omits only some aspects regarding words compounded with prepositions, preposition placement, and some preposition lists mentioned before exemplifying them. In contrast, the last section of the *Breuiarium*, dedicated to the interjection, consists of only two lines that were not extracted from Alcuin's work, but again from Pompeius's Commentary (*Grammatici Latini* 5, ed. Keil, p. 97.33–34): "Interiectio quare dicta est? Eo quod interponitur ad

---

[58] In spite of previously mentioning Franco's request: "Pleniorem tamen declinationem horum quatuor uerborum ut reddas mihi deposco, id est *sum, fero, edo, uolo*" – "However, I demand that you give me a more complete conjugation of these four verbs, that is to say, of *sum, fero, edo, uolo*" (4.320–321).

exprimendos animi adfectus" – "Why is interjection called thus? Because it is interposed in order to express the emotions of the heart" (9.548–549). There are a few other minor differences and variants in the rest of the text, which are signalled in the *apparatus criticus*.

Punctuation and Orthography

The punctuation mark used most often by the copyist of the *Breuiarium* is the *punctus* (·), employed as modern comma, semicolon, full stop, and question mark, as well as a general orthographic sign when writing numbers, suffixes, and examples of letters. On fol. 52v the copyist twice used the *punctus interrogatiuus*. In this edition I have introduced modern punctuation, while at the same time attempting to maintain the structure of the medieval text; thus, some compromises had to be made in this respect. In addition, I have added hyphens to indicate the question-and-answer form, and the examples of suffixes and word endings.

I have used upper case for the proper nouns (including here the names of languages), otherwise commonly written in lower case. However, the copyist usually employed majuscules at the beginning of the sentences, as well as when giving examples of letters. Furthermore, while minuscule *u* was used all over the text, when noting the majuscule, the copyist oscillated between *U* (used more often) and *V* without any clear rationale. I have chosen to edit the text using *u* for the minuscule and *V* for the majuscule. As for the numbers, there is no consistency in the way they are expressed and abridged; for instance we find: *quatuor* and *IIIIor* (*-or* seems to be superscript), *xxetvi*, *xxti*, *C*. I have chosen to expand all the numbers, in order to prevent confusion. For clarity's sake I have put examples of any kind in italics.

I have kept as much of the orthography found in the codex as possible, unless it would have corrupted the meaning of the text or the consistency of an example, in which cases I have corrected the form and mentioned it in the apparatus. Furthermore, with just two exceptions: "Formae neutrorum quot sunt?" (2.122) and "Quid tamen quot [*sic*] prepositio …" (compare to 8.441–442), the copyist always wrote *quod* instead of *quot*; because of the frequency of this practice, I have not mentioned it in the apparatus but corrected it tacitly. Moreover, due to his strong tendency for dissimilation, the copyist often wrote the words *more suo*, even when they were given as examples of assimilation: "Et sciendum est quod *con* et *non* tunc mutant *N* in *M*, quando B, M uel P sequitur, ut *conburo, inbuo, comminus, inmunis, compello, inpello*" [*sic*] (compare to 8.511–512); or: "Et in sequentem mutat B consonantem s C uel F, G, M uel P sequitur, ut *succumbo, suffero, suggero, summito, subpono*" [*sic*] (compare to 8.526–528). In these cases I corrected the dissimilation without mentioning it in the apparatus.

One can also notice a general hesitation between the use of *ae*, *ę*, and *e*, which I have kept in the text. Still, *e* seems to be preferred, even though there are some cases of hypercorrection, such as *arma uirumquae cano*[59] or *piaetas, meridiae, indaeclinabilia, generę*. There are also variants such as *Aeneas* and *Enea[e]*.

There is a general tendency of confusing similar sounds: *d* and *t* (such as *faciad, capud*); *g* and *c* (*conclutinate*); *b* and *p* (*optinet, pubpim*); *b* and *u* consonant (*habe* instead of *aue*; *obat, iubabit*); *f* and *u* consonant (*defitando*); very frequently *e* and *i* (*diffinitio, diriuatiua, iuuenales*; *o, moris* instead of *o, mores*); *o* and *u* (*uarius* instead of *uarios*); *h* omitted or added (*hab* instead of *ab*, *habete* instead of *auete*, *omine* instead of *homine*; *detrao* instead of *detraho*; *actenus, autquaquam, exaptota*); *sci* and *si* (*persitus* and *situs* instead of *perscitus* and *scitus*). There are also orthographic confusions: *c* and *qu* (*loquutio* and *locutio*); *ci* and *ti* (*offitium, dictio* and *diccio, homuntio, sotiari*); *i* and *y* (*epicenon* and *epycenon*; *sinonima, polionima*).

The text has many errors, some probably due to the *breuiator*, some to the *copista*, and some coming from the model used by the *breuiator*. The number and variety of phonetic and orthographic confusions and errors suggest that the person who abridged Alcuin's *Grammar* and/or the one who copied the abridged text did not know the classical Latin orthography well.[60] Some types of phonetic confusions (such as the confusion of *b* and *u* consonant, *d* and *t*, the *gi* pronounced *i* – see *Serio* and *Seriolus* instead of *Sergio* and *Sergiolus*) could be a hint that either the *breuiator* or, most probably, the *copista* was of Spanish origin.[61]

In the cases where I considered a word form to be strange or of inconsistent usage, and that it would be difficult for a modern reader to grasp the right meaning of the text, I have corrected that form and specified it in the apparatus. However, I have preserved some of the particularities of the text, such as the use of an unnecessary *e* in the words *pen*e*ultimis, pen*e*ultima, antepen*e*ultima*. Due to the fact that this usage is consistent, it is possible that this is how the copyist knew the word, and since this spelling is still easy to understand, I have not changed it. Likewise, I have kept the consonant duplication in the name *Terrentius*, but I have corrected other occasional incorrect gemination. I have, however, preserved the haplography in such words as *gramatica, glosa, milies, cete*, as it can be remarked that the copyist has a regular tendency towards degemination for these words, which could still be easily

---

[59] The copyist actually wrote "arma uirum quae." Here one should account for the possibility that the copyist might have understood the renowned beginning of *Aeneid* otherwise than traditionally. However, there are many other situations where the word separation is wrong.

[60] The scribes who copied V_3^b clearly did not know Greek either, since, for the first grammatical text, either the Greek words are very corrupted (fol. 27v), or they are not copied at all and blank spaces are left instead (fol. 30v).

[61] See Peter Stotz, *Handbuch zur lateinischen Sprache des Mittelalters*, 5 vols. (Munich, 1996–2004), 3:223–24, 226 (§184.2, §184.7. § 184.9 – for the confusion of *d* and *t*), 269 (§ 227.4, § 227.5 – for the confusion of *b* and *v*).

understood. I have also kept the form *subiunctatiuus*, which is attested in other medieval grammars;[62] still, the form of this word could be based on a simple syllabic repetition, such as in the case of the word *coniuncti[ti]o*.

Final Observations

Most of the emendations, insertions, and suppressions that I have made in this edition follow the textual variants of S_1 and/or the text of the PL. However, I have taken into account that the text of V_3 is unique, and thus it cannot be compared in all its aspects with any other version of the complete *Ars grammatica*. As has been shown, there are also important fragments interpolated into this *Breuiarium*, which are not found in Alcuin's work. Therefore, as V_3 is a *codex unicus*, I have mentioned in the apparatus the variants of S_1 and the PL only when I found them of particular importance or when I could not emend the text by conjecture (where S_1 or PL contained a mistake, I have not mentioned it). Finally, whenever the two versions in S_1 and the PL differed, I have emended the text by choosing the one that I considered more correct and/or closer to V_3.

This edition also contains an *apparatus fontium*, in which I have mentioned the direct or indirect quotations, including the external sources of the text – the passages that are not part of Alcuin's *Ars grammatica* – which have already been discussed in this introduction.

Breuiarium Artis grammaticae Alcuini

Sigla

S_1 St. Gall, Stiftsbibliothek, MS 268 (saec. IX*in.*, Tours), pp. 19–165.
V_3 Vatican City, Biblioteca Apostolica Vaticana, MS Reg. lat. 251 (saec. IX$^{3/3}$, Reims?), fols. 38'r–52v.
ed. PL 101:849C–902B.

Fontes

Afran., *Comp.* = Lucius Afranius, *Compitalia*, ed. Otto Ribbeck, *Scaenicae Romanorum poesis fragmenta Volumen II. Comicorum fragmenta*, 2nd ed. (Leipzig, 1873, repr. Hildesheim, 1962).

Cassiod., *Inst. app.* = Cassiodorus Senator (dubium), *Principia geometricae disciplinae (appendix)*, ed. Roger A.B. Mynors, *Cassiodori Senatoris Institutiones* (Oxford, 1961).

---

[62] In the anonymous grammars *Ars Ambrosiana, Ars Bernensis, Anonymus ad Cuimnanum*, in Donatus Ortigraphus's and in Tatuinus's *Ars grammatica*, etc.

Cato, *Orig.* = Marcus Porcius Cato, *Originum reliquiae*, ed. Henri Jordan, *M. Catonis praeter librum de re rustica quae extant* (Leipzig, 1860).

Cic., *Catil.* = Marcus Tullius Cicero, *Orationes in L. Catilinam quattuor*, ed. Tadeusz Maslowski, *M. Tullius Cicero scripta quae mansuerunt omnia* 17 (Munich – Leipzig, 2003).

Cic., *Lig.* = Marcus Tullius Cicero, *Pro Q. Ligario oratio*, ed. Alfred Klotz, *M. Tulli Ciceronis scripta quae manserunt omnia* 8 (Leipzig, 1918).

Colum., *Rust.* = Lucius Iunius Moderatus Columella, *Res rustica*, ed. Robert H. Rodgers (Oxford, 2010).

Hier., *In Ier.* = S. Eusebius Hieronymus, *In Hieremiam libri VI*, ed. Siegfried Reiter, *S. Hieronymi presbyteri opera Pars I, Opera exegetica* 3, CCSL 74 (Turnhout, 1960).

Hor., *Sat.* = Quintus Horatius Flaccus, *Satirae*, ed. David Roy Shackleton Bailey, *Q. Horati Flacci Opera*, 3rd ed. (Stuttgart, 1995).

Isid., *Etym.* = Isidorus Hispalensis episcopus, *Etymologiarum sive originum libri XX Tomus I*, ed. Wallace M. Lindsay (Oxford, 1911).

Iuv., *Sat.* = Decimus Iunius Iuvenalis, *Saturae sedecim*, ed. Jacob Willis (Stuttgart, 1997).

Lucan., *Phar.* = Marcus Annaeus Lucanus, *De Bello Civili libri X* (*Pharsalia*), ed. David Roy Shackleton Bailey (Stuttgart, 1988).

Pers., *Sat.* = Aulus Persius Flaccus, *Saturae*, ed. Wendell V. Clausen (Oxford, 1959).

Plaut., *frg.* = Titus Maccius Plautus, *fragmenta*, ed. Wallace M. Lindsay, *T. Macci Plauti Comoediae Tomus II* (Oxford, 1963).

Pomp., *gramm.* = Pompeius, *Commentum artis Donati*, ed. Heinrich Keil, *Grammatici Latini* 5 (Leipzig, 1868).

Prisc., *Gramm.* = Priscianus Caesariensis, *Institutionum grammaticarum libri I–XII*, ed. Heinrich Keil and Martin Hertz, *Grammatici Latini* 2 (Leipzig, 1855).

Ter., *Andr., Ad., Eun.* = Publius Terentius Afer, *Andria, Adelphoe, Eunuchus*, ed. Robert Kauer and Wallace M. Lindsay, *P. Terenti Afri Comoediae*, 2nd ed. (Oxford, 1963).

Verg., *Aen.* = Publius Vergilius Maro, *Aeneis*, ed. Gian Biagio Conte (Leipzig, 2005).

Verg., *Eclog., Georg.* = Publius Vergilius Maro, *Eclogae, Georgica*, ed. Roger A.B. Mynors, *P. Vergili Maronis Opera* (Oxford, 1969).

<Breuiarium Artis grammaticae Alcuini>: *Edition*

1. [fol. 38'r] Cuius causa littere inuente sunt? – Vox.

Vnde dicta est? – A uocando.

Quibus modis constat disputatio? – Tribus.

Quibus? – Re, intellectu et uoce.

Quomodo? – Res sunt quae animi ratione percipimus; intellectus, quibus res ipsas addiscimus; uoces, quibus res intellectas ore proferimus.

Quot differentiae sunt uocis? – Principaliter duae: articulata, inarticulata. Sed cum his, que his subiciuntur, quatuor sunt: articulata, inarticulata, litterata, inlitterata.

Quomodo diuiduntur ille diuisiones? – Articulata est quae copulata atque coartata cum sensu profertur, ut: *arma uirumquae cano*. Inarticulata est que a nullo sensu proficiscitur, ut crepitus, mugitus. Litterata est quae scribi potest; [fol. 38'v] inlitterata est quae scribi non potest.

Ars quid est? – Vniuscuiusque rei scientia.

Ars unde habet ethimologiam? – *Apo tes aretes*, id est a uirtute, quam Greci scientiam uocauerunt.

Quare dicta est ars? – Eo quod artis preceptis cuncta concludat.

Quis inuenit primum litteras Latinas? – Carmentis nimpha, Euandri mater, que Nicostrata dicebatur.

Littere quare dicte sunt? – Quia legentibus iter prebeant uel ideo quod in legendo iterentur.

Quare dicta est articulata uox? – Eo quod potest articulis digitisque tenentibus conprehendi.

Littere ad quam uocem pertinent? – Ad articulatam.

Quid est littera? – Pars indiuidua.

Quid sunt littere? – Amare cortices et fructus dulces.

Ob quam rem littere elementa dicuntur? – Quia sicut elementa coeuntia corpus perficiunt, sic he conclutinate litteralem uocem exprimunt.

11 arma uirumque cano] Verg., Aen. 1.1 ‖ **14–17** ars quid est ... concludat] cf. Pomp., *gramm.*, p. 95.4–8 ‖ **15–16** apo tes ... uocauerunt] cf. Isid., *Etym.* 1.1.2, 1.5.2 ‖ **18–19** quis inuenit ... dicebatur] cf. Pomp., *gramm.*, p. 98.10–11 ‖ **20–21** littere ... iterentur] cf. Pomp., *gramm.*, p. 98.15–17, 19–20 ‖ **22–23** quare dicta ... conprehendi] cf. Pomp., *gramm.*, p. 99.15–16 ‖ **24** littere ad ... articulatam] cf. Pomp., *gramm.*, p. 99.18–20

1 causa] cause V_3 ‖ **6** intellectas] intellectu V_3 ‖ **11** coartata] coortata V_3 ‖ **17** artis] V_3 *sup.l. eadem manu* ‖ **22** eo quod] equod V_3 *a.c.* ‖ **26** cortices] corticeps V_3; fructus dulces] V_3 *in rasura*

Quid est inter uocales et consonantes? – Vocales sunt sicut animę, consonantes sicuti corpora. Anima uero et se mouet et corpus, corpus uero per se immobile est; sic sunt consonantes sine uocalibus.

Vnde dictae sunt uocales et consonantes? – Vocales dictae sunt eo quod per se uocem implent, nulla adherente consonante. Consonantes sunt, quia per se non sonant, sed cum uocalibus [fol. 39r] consonant.

Quae est differentia inter semiuocales et mutas? – Semiuocales a uocalibus incipiunt et in se desinunt, mute a se incipiunt et in uocales desinunt.

Syllaba quid est? – Vox litteralis sub uno accentu et uno spiritu prolata.

Quot litteris fiunt syllabae? – Ab una incipiens usque ad sex: *a, ab, abs, Mars, stans, styrps*.

Habet syllaba sensum per se? – Non habet, nisi plena dictio per unam syllabam constat, ut *ars, do, dic*.

Syllabae quot accidunt? – Quatuor: tenor, spiritus, tempus, numerus.

Gramatica quid est uel quod eius offitium? – Gramatica est litteralis scientia et est custos recte loquendi et scribendi.

Quare non incohat gramatica a uoce aut a littera, sed ab octo partibus orationis? – Quia hoc proprium est gramaticorum; multi dicunt a uoce, sed hoc philosophorum est; multi dicunt a littera, sed hoc omnium est.

Vnde constat gramatica? – Natura, ratione, auctoritate, consuetudine.

In quot species diuiditur gramatica? – In uiginti et sex: in uocem, litteras, syllabas, partes, dictiones, orationes, diffinitiones, pedes, accentus, posituras, notas, ortographiam, analogiam, ethimologiam, glosas, differentias, barbarismos, solecismos, uitia, metaplasmos, scemata, tropos, prosam, metra, fabulas, [fol. 39v] historias.

<Da> diffinitionem harum specierum. – Diccio est pars minima uocis constructe plenumque sensum habentis. Oratio est ordinatio dictionum, congruam sententiam perfectamque demonstrans; et est oratio dicta quasi *oris ratio*. Diffinitio est breuis oratio, unamquamque rem propria significatione concludens, ut: *homo animal mortale, rationale, risu capax*. Scire igitur debemus

---

45–47 quare non ... omnium est] cf. Pomp., *gramm.*, p. 96.9–12 ‖ **58** homo ... capax] cf. Isid., *Etym.* 2.25.2

---

29 uocales] uocale V_3 ‖ **33** adherente] adhorente V_3 *a.c.* ‖ **35** semiuocales] semiuocalibus V_3 ‖ **36** incipiunt] *scripsi cum* S_1 **ed.**, *om.* V_3 ‖ **48** auctoritate] autoritate V_3 *a.c.* ‖ **49** in[1]] i V_3 ‖ **51** ethimologiam] etimoliyam V_3 ‖ **51–52** barbarismos] barbarismus V_3 ‖ **52** solecismos] solacismus V_3; metaplasmos] metaplasmus V_3; tropos] tropus V_3; metra] metram V_3 ‖ **58** animal] animalem V_3; igitur] V_3 *in rasura*

quod diffinitio ad omnes disciplinas et res pertinet. Pes est conpositio syllabarum et temporum certa dimensio. Pedes dicti eo quod per ipsos metra ambulent. Accentus est certa lex et regula ad leuandam et conprimendam syllabam; positure sunt puncti ad distinguendos sensus. Note sunt figure quedam uel ad breuiendam uerba inuenta uel sensus exprimendos uel ob diuersas causas constitute, ut in Scriptura sacra obelus uel asteriscus. Ortographia est recta scriptura, utpote *ad* prepositio *d* accepit, *at* coniunctio *t*. Analogia est similium conparatio ut incerta certis probentur. Ethimologia est origo et ratio uocabulorum, ut a *regendo rex* et ab *humo homo* dicitur. Glosa est unius uerbi uel nominis interpretatio, ut: *catus, id est doctus*. Differentia est distinctio duarum [fol. 40r] rerum cum interpretatione, ut: *rex dicitur quia modestus, tyrannus quia crudelis est*. Barbarismus est una pars orationis uiciose dicta. Solecismus est oratio uitiose conposita. Vitia sunt que in eloquiis cauere debemus et sunt duodecim. Metaplasmus est metrica licentia uel necessitate inmutata regula locutionis. Scemata sunt ornamenta eloquii et habitus quibus sententiae uestiuntur. Tropus est dictio translata a propria significatione ad non propriam similitudinem, ornatus necessitatisue causa. Prosa est recta locutio absque metro uel uersu conposita. Metra uocata sunt, quia certis pedum mensuris terminantur. Fabula est res ficta ludendi causa uel cuiuslibet significationis. Historia est narratio rei geste.

Quare dicte sunt principales partes orationis nomen et uerbum? – Quoniam ipsa faciunt eloquutionem et alia eloquutio sine ipsis nulla est uel sine ipsis nulla potest stare loquutio.

Proprium nominis quid est? – Substantiam uel quantitatem significare.

Proprium pronominis quid est? – Pro nomine poni et certas significare personas.

Verbi uero proprium quid est? – Accionem uel passionem siue utrumque cum modis et temporibus significare. [fol. 40v]

69–70 rex ... crudelis est] cf. Isid., *Etym.* 1.31.1

59 disciplinas] dissiplinas **V₃** ‖ **61** leuandam] leuandum **V₃** *a.c.* ‖ **63** exprimendos] exprimedos **V₃** *a.c.* ‖ **65** d] **V₃** *alia manu ut uidetur*; t] **V₃** *alia manu ut uidetur* ‖ **66** analogia] anologia **V₃** ‖ **67** ab] hab **V₃** ‖ **69** distinctio] distinotio **V₃** ‖ **70** uiciose] uiciosa **V₃** ‖ **71** solecismus] solacismus **V₃**; uitiose] uitiosa **V₃** ‖ **73** scemata] scemetra **V₃** ‖ **77** ludendi] **V₃** *bis scripsit* ‖ **78** rei] re **V₃** ‖ **79** orationis] orationes **V₃** ‖ **80** ipsa] ipse **V₃**; eloquutionem] eloquutium **V₃** *a.c.* ‖ **83** pronominis] nominis **V₃** *a.c.*; nomine] nomini **V₃** ‖ **86** cum modis et] cumodis set **V₃**; temporibus] tem *add.* **V₃** *a.c.*

Proprium aduerbii quid est? – Cum uerbo poni et sine eo perfectam significationem non habere, ut *bene lego*.

Participii proprium quid est? – Tempus habere et casus; ideo a quibusdam uerbum casuale dicitur.

Proprium coniunctionis quid est? – Cum omnibus partibus modo preposita, modo postposita iungi et coniungere partes.

Proprium prepositionis quid est? – Anteponi casibus semper separatim.

Proprium interiectionis quid est? – Interiacere alias partes et mentis affectum significare.

2. Nomen quid est? – Vox significatiua secundum placitum, sine tempore, diffinitum aliquid significans in nominatiuo cum est uel non est, ut *homo est, homo non est*. In casibus licet addas *est* uel *non est*, nihil tamen certum significat si non adponas quid sit uel quod non sit, ut *hominis est, hominis non est*. Secundum placidum, id est singularum gentium.

Sine quot rebus non potest ullum nomen inueniri? – Sine tribus: ut casu careat, aut non sit corporale aut incorporale, aut non sit proprium aut appellatiuum.

Conparationes nominum unde ueniunt? – A nominibus adiectiuis et accedentibus alicuius substantiae, qualitatem uel quantitatem significantibus animi uel corporis, quae possunt incrementa uel detrimenta sumere.

Superla [fol. 41r] tiuorum species quot sunt? – Octo in quas plerumque desinunt superlatiua: *-rimus, -simus, -limus, -ximus, -timus, -tremus, -nimus, -fimus*; *pulcherrimus, doctissimus, simillimus, maximus, optimus, extremus, minimus, infimus*.

Possunt a propriis nominibus fieri diminutiua? – Possunt, ut a *Serio Seriolus*.

Quot modis fiu<nt> diminutiua? – Tribus modis: aut necessitatis causa, ut a *rege regulus*, hoc est *paruus rex*; aut urbanitatis causa, Iuuenalis: *malim esse fraterculus gigantis*; aut adolationis causa, ut in pueris *Seriolus*.

94–95 mentis affectum significare] cf. Pomp., *gramm.*, p. 281.5 ‖ **101–103** sine quot ... appellatiuum] cf. Pomp., *gramm.*, p. 137.3–6 ‖ **114–115** malim ... gigantis] Iuv., *Sat.* 4.98

---

87 aduerbii] aduerbi **V₃** *a.c.* ‖ **89** proprium] proprii **V₃** *a.c.* ‖ **99** si non adponas] **V₃** *in rasura* ‖ **100** singularum] sigularum **V₃** *a.c.* ‖ **102** incorporale] incorpora **V₃** *a.c.* ‖ **111** a²] as **V₃** ‖ **111–113** possunt ut ... diminutiua] **V₃** *in marg.* ‖ **114** a rege] agere **V₃**; malim] malis **V₃** *a.c.* ‖ **115** adolationis] adolantis **S₁**, adolentis **V₃**, adulationis **ed.**

Forme igitur diminutiuorum masculini generis quot sunt? – Vndecim: *-culus, -ulus, -olus, -ellus, -xillus, -illus, -ullus, -cio, -aster, -leus, -tulus*, ut: *agniculus, tantulus, capriolus, agnellus, pauxillus, codicillus, homullus, homuntio, parasitaster, aculeus, nepotulus.*

120   Feminini generis quot sunt? – Septem: *-cula, -ula, -ola, -ella, -xilla, - illa, -ulla*, ut: *agnicula, siluula, untiola, capella, maxilla, anguilla, ulla.*

Formae neutrorum quot sunt? – Septem: *-culum, -ulum, -olum, -ellum, -illum, -xillum, -ullum*; *corpusculum, capitulum, lauriolum, lacellum, uillum, uexillum, ullum.* Fiunt et diminutiua tertio uel quarto gradu, ut: *Paulus,*
125   *Paululus; pauxillus, pauxilulus; homo, homuntio, homunculus, homullus, homullulus.*

Genera unde dicta sunt? – A generando, quapropter genera sunt quae [fol. 41v] generare possunt, id est masculinum et femininum, nam neutrum et commune magis uocis qualitate quam natura dinoscuntur. Epicena promiscua
130   sunt et sub una uoce masculinum proferunt et femininum.

Quid est inter commune et epicenon? – Quod commune modo masculino, modo feminino articulo, prout constructio orationis eget, iungitur. Epycenon semper uno articulo profertur utriusque naturae animalia, sed una uoce et uno articulo significat, ut *passer, aquila*.

135   Num omnia nomina certi sunt generis? – Nequaquam, quia multa sunt dubii generis.

Vnde sit dubium genus? Forte differentia an aliqua necessitatis causa? – Non differentia an aliqua necessitatis causa, sed sola auctoritate ueterum, ut hic et hec *finis, cortex, radix, silex*; hic et hęc *sal*; Cato: *ex sale qui apud*
140   *Cartaginenses fit.* Afranius: *quid loquitur, sal merum est.*

Possunt nomina pro aduerbiis poni? – Possunt, ut est *toruum clamat* pro eo quod est *torue clamat.*

Possunt aduerbia pro nominibus poni? – Possunt, utputa si dicas *cras, mane*; dicit Virgilius: *dum mane nouum,* iam *mane* non uult esse aduerbium,
145   sed nomen. Item Terrentius: *propterea ipso meridiae*. Item Persius: *aliud cras*;

139–140 ex sale ... fit] Cato, *Orig.* 2, frg. 32, 9 ‖ **140** quid ... est] cf. Afran., *Comp.* 3 (1), p. 169 ‖ **141–142** possunt nomina ... clamat] cf. Pomp., *gramm.*, pp. 135.38–136.1 ‖ **143–145** possunt aduerbia ... sed nomen] cf. Pomp., *gramm.*, p. 136.2–4 ‖ **144** dum mane nouum] Verg., *Georg.* 3.325 ‖ **145** propterea ipso meridiae] cf. Ter. *Ad.* 847–48; aliud cras] Pers., *Sat.* 5.68 ‖ **145–147** item Terrentius ... casus] cf. Pomp., *gramm.*, p. 136.6–10

121 -ulla] a *add.*V$_3$ *a.c.* ‖ **124** gradu] gradui V$_3$; ut] aut V$_3$ ‖ **132** epycenon] epycena non V$_3$ ‖ **133** naturae] natura V$_3$ ‖ **140** Afranius] Affricanus V$_3$ ‖ **141** toruum] toruuum V$_3$ ‖ **144** uult] ult V$_3$

et *aliud cras*, si habet genus, sine [fol. 42r] dubio nomen est. Nam nomina, quando pro aduerbiis ponuntur, tenent casus; aduerbium uero, quando transit in nomen, nequaquam potest accipere casus. Ne dicas mihi *hoc mane*, non potest sequi ut declinetur. Tamen legimus apud Plautum declinationem ipsam: *a primo mane*.

Que sunt fixa nomina? – Que in alterum genus transire non possunt, ut *pater, mater*.

Que sunt mobilia? – Que moueri possunt et in aliud transire genus.

Quot litteris masculini generis finiuntur nomina? – Septem: -a, -o, -l, -n, -r, -s, -x; ut: *scriba, Cicero, sol, flamen, Cesar, bonus, rex*.

Femini generis quot sunt? – Eisdem, ut hec: *Roma, uirgo, Tanaquil, Siren, mater, ciuitas, capax*.

Neutra quot sunt? – Duodecim: -a, -e, -i, -u, -l, -m, -n, -r, -s, -c, -t, -d, ut: *poema, mare, gummi, cornu, mel, regnum, numen, tuber, sidus, lac, caput, aliquid*.

Numerus quid est? – Diccionis forma, discrecio quantitatis.

Quid est inter numerum singularem et pluralem? – Singularis finitus est, ut *homo* certum est unum significasse. Pluralem infinitus est, ut *homines* incertum est de quod dico, nisi addam decem aut centum uel quodlibet.

Quę dictiones habent numeros? – Que personas habent, id est nomina, pronomina, uerba, participia, ut: *uir, uiri; ego lego*, [fol. 42v] *nos legimus; hic legens, hi legentes*. Ideo infinita uerba et inpersonalia carent numeros, quia non habent personas.

Numquid aduerbia non habent numeros? – Habent.

Quid tum interest inter numerorum nomina indaeclinabilia et inter aduerbia? – Quod aduerbia et singularibus et pluralibus similiter iunguntur, ut *milies dixi* et *milies diximus*. Nomina uero non, nisi pluralibus, ut *mille homines diximus*.

Figura unde dicitur? – A figmento, id est exemplo; et figura est tecta imago ueritatis. Et est iterum figura dicta uel quod aliquo uel aliquibus terminis

---

147–150 aduerbium uero … mane] cf. Pomp., *gramm.*, p. 136.20–25; cf. Colum., *Rust.*, 11.1, p. 423.6 ‖ **174–175** et est … finis] cf. Cassiod., *Inst. app.*, p. 169.13–14.

---

153 in] **V₃** *sup.l.* ‖ **156** Siren] sirem **V₃** ‖ **158** duodecim] XI **V₃** ‖ **159** tuber] turber **V₃** *a.c.*; caput] capud **V₃** ‖ **165** pronomina] pronomi **V₃**; nos] **V₃** *bis scripsit* ‖ **170** aduerbia] et uerbia **V₃** ‖ **174** aliquo] aliquod **V₃** ; uel quod aliquod] **V₃** *in rasura*

175 continetur. Terminus uero est quod cuiusque est finis. Et est iterum figura dicta, quia uel simplicia sunt uel composita sunt. Et figura quoque dictionis in quantitate conprehenditur.

Quid est inter figuratas dictiones et diriuatiuas? – Quod figurate dictionęs aut simplices sunt, ut *magnus*, aut conposita, ut *magnanimus*; diriuatiua aut a
180 symplici nomine diriuantur, ut a *pio piaetas*, aut a conposito, ut a *magnanimo magnanimitas*.

Casus unde dicti sunt? – A cadendo.

Quot sunt casus? – Sex.

Illi casus unde acceperunt nomen? – Nominatiuus a nominando, utputa si
185 ais: *Quis fecit hanc domum?* Respondeo: *Virgilius*. Genitiuus a generę querendo, si ais: *Cuius generis est iste et bonus et formosus puer?* Respon [fol. 43r] deo: *Nobilis generis Virgilii*. Post hunc datiuus, quia dando dicitur, significans aliquid dare, ut: *Do illam rem Virgilio*. Qui et mandatiuus dicitur, ut: *Commendo Virgilio indoli omnia mea*. Quarto loco est accusatius qui et
190 causatiuus dicitur, ut: *Accuso inimicum Virgilium*. Tunc uocatiuus qui et salutarius uocatur, ut: *Ō Virgili, ueni cito*; et: *Salue, care mi Virgili*. Nouissime ablatiuus ponitur qui et conparatiuus dicitur, significans aliquid absumi uel conparari, ut: *Aufero ab homine gladium inimici*; *doctior et nobilior Enea Virgilius*.

195 Quot sunt forme casuales? – Sex: monoptota, diptota, triptota, tetraptota, pentaptota, exaptota.

Monoptota que sunt? – Quę in unam formationem cadunt, ut *gummi*, *nequam*. Sub qua regula etiam sunt nomina litterarum et numerorum a quatuor usque ad centum.

200 Diptota que sunt? – Que duos casus diuersos habent, ut *fors, a forte*; uel omnes casus diuersos, ut *cornu* omnes casus habet, tres in breuem *u*, tres in longam *u*.

175–176 et est … composita sunt] cf. Isid., *Etym.* 1.7.30 ‖ **176–177** et figura … conprehenditur] Prisc., *Gramm.*, 5, p. 177.10

---

175 continetur] continentur **V**₃ ‖ **176** composita] compositi **V**₃; figura] figure **V**₃; dictionis] dictiones **V**₃ ‖ **180** a²] **V**₃ *sup.l.* ‖ **186** et¹] est **V**₃ ‖ **187** generis] genere **V**₃; dicitur] datur **V**₃ ‖ **190** accuso] acuso **V**₃ ‖ **193** homine] omine **V**₃; Enea] eneae **V**₃ ‖ **194** Virgilius] uergilius **V**₃ *p.c.* ‖ **195** tetraptota] traptota *add.* **V**₃ *a.c.* ‖ **198** nomina] nomena **V**₃ ‖ **200** diuersos] diuersus **V**₃ ‖ **201** diuersos] diuersus **V**₃; u] *scripsi cum* **S**₁, *om.***V**₃ ‖ **202** u] *scripsi cum* **S**₁, *om.***V**₃

Triptota que sunt? – Que tres diuersos casus habent, ut est *templum, templi, templo*.

Tetraptota que sunt? – Que quatuor casus habent dissimiles, ut est *puer, pueri, puero, puerum*.

Pentaptota quae sunt? – Quae quinque casus diuersos habent, ut est *doctus, docti, docto, doctum, docte*. [fol. 43v]

Exaptota quę sunt? – Quae sex diuersos casus habent, ut est *unus, unius, uni, unum, une, ab uno*.

3. Pronomen quid est? – Pars orationis cum casu positum uice nominis, ne sepius iteratum nomen fastidium faciat audiendi uel legendi, et finitas recipit personas.

Species pronominum quot sunt? – Duae, quia sunt pronomina primitiua et diriuatiua.

Primitiua quot sunt? – Octo: *ego, tu, sui, ille, ipse, iste, hic, is*.

Diriuatiua quot sunt? – Septem: *meus, tuus, suus, noster, uester, nostras, uestras*.

4. Verbum, iuxta philosophiae rationem, haec tam principalis pars, habet subtilem difinitionem et nobilem et est huiusmodi: uerbum est uox significatiua secundum placitum, cum tempore, definitum aliquid significans et accidens.

Expone, pater, hanc nobis difinitionem propriam. – Dum dico *lego*, actum significo legentis; quem actum Grecus alia significat uoce et ideo uerbum secundum placitum est tempusque adtrahit. Difinitum, id est certum aliquid significans et accidens; accidit etiam accio uel passio homini.

Si uerba actum uel passionem significant, unde dicuntur neutra? – Non ideo quod actum uel passionem non significent, sed ideo [fol. 44r] quia unum horum significant. Nam actiua in nostro actu alterius passionem significant, sicut passiua in nostra passione alterius actum significant. Nam dum dico *amo te*, patiaris actum meum, id est quod amo te. Et dum dico *amor a te*, patiar ego actum tuum, id est quod tu me amas. Neutra uero uniformiter significant uel agentem, ut *ambulo, curro, prandeo*, uel patientem, ut *ardeo, ueneo, uapulo*. Sed et casus non egent, quibus actiua uel passiua egent. Nam actiua accusatiuo casu iunguntur, ut *amo te*. Sepe genetiuo et datiuo, ut *dico tibi*. Passiua ablatiuo

---

203 triptota] troptota V₃ *a.c.*; diuersos] diuersus V₃ ‖ **207** pentaptota] pentuptota V₃ *a.c.*; diuersos] diuersus V₃ ‖ **210** ab uno] ab unae V₃ ‖ **212** faciat] faciad V₃; audiendi] audiendum V₃ ‖ **217** diriuatiua] diriuitiua V₃; uester] uerter V₃; nostras] ab his *add.* V₃ ‖ **219** philosophiae] philosophiam V₃ ‖ **219-220** habet subtilem] *scripsi cum* S₁ **ed.**, *om.* V₃ ‖ **225** secundum] secucundum V₃ *a.c.*; adtrahit] adtrahitur V₃ ‖ **227** uerba] uerbum V₃ ‖ **235** ut²] at V₃

iunguntur, ut *amor a te*. Neutra uero absoluta sunt et per se plenum sensum significant, ut *uiuo*, *spiro*, *pergo*.

Vnde dictum est tempus? – A temperamento, quia omnia mortalia tempus habent.

Cur optinet primum locum praesens tempus in temporibus? – Quia in illo sumus, dum loquimur.

Modi uerborum qui sunt? – Modi sunt diuerse declinationes animi, uarios eius affectus demonstrantes, et sunt quinque: indicatiuus, qui et difinitiuus dicitur, quo indicamus uel difinimus quid uideatur uel patiatur a nobis. Qui ideo primus, quia perfectus personis et temporibus et alii ex eo modo regulam sumunt; uel quod ex eo participia uel nomina uel uerba deriuantur, ut a *duco*, *ducens*; a *duxi*, *ductus* et *dux*; a *ferueo*, *feruens*, *feruesco* et *feruor*. [fol. 44v] Imperatiuus est quo imperamus aliis ut faciant uel patiantur; et est per se absolutus nec alterius indiget partis ad significandum. Et ideo secundum tenet locum in modis. Et huic orantes sepissime utimur, ut: *Musa, memora mihi causas*. Deinde optatiuus per quem optamus. Qui ideo tertius in ordine ponitur, quia inferior est qui optat quam qui imperat et aduerbio optandi indiget ad conplendum sensum, ut *utinam legerem*. Quarto loco subiunctatiuus ponitur et iure. Eget enim modo non aduerbio uel coniunctione, uerum etiam altero uerbo ut perfectum significet sensum, unde et subiunctiuus dicitur; Virgilius: *cum faciam uitulam pro frugibus ipse uenito*. Et omnibus aliis modis sotiari potest, ut: *dum legerem scripsi* et *dum legam scribe* et *dum legerem utinam scriberem*. Infinitiuus, qui et personis et numeris deficit et eget uno ex supradictis quatuor modis, ut plenum sensum significet, ut: *legere propero, legere propera, utinam legere properarem, cum legere properem*.

Vnde dicta est coniugatio? – Coniugatio dicta est quod in unam declinationis rationem plurima coniungit uerba.

Num singula uerba certas habent coniugationes? – Sunt uerba in prima persona confusa, in secunda uero sensu et coniugatione discernuntur, ut: *dico, dicis* et *dico, dicas*; *uolo, uolas, uolo, uis*; *fundo, fundas, fundo, fundis*; *mando*,

---

250–251 musa … causas] Verg., *Aen.* 1.8 ‖ **256** cum … uenito] Verg., *Eclog.* 3.77

---

242 uarios] uarius **V₃** ‖ **243** demonstrantes] demonstruntes **V₃** *a.c.* ‖ **244** uel difinimus] **V₃** *in marg.*; uideatur] agatur **S₁ ed**. ‖ **246** ex eo] ex ea **V₃** *a.c.* ‖ **247** a¹] ad **V₃**; feruor] feuor **V₃** *a.c.* ‖ **250** memora] memera **V₃** *a.c.* ‖ **253** conplendum] conplendo **V₃** ‖ **254** coniunctione] coniuncttione **V₃** ‖ **255** subiunctiuus] subiunctiuum **V₃** ‖ **258** et²] in **V₃** ‖ **259** ut²] u **V₃** *a.c.* ‖ **260** propera] properare **V₃**; legere²] legerem **V₃**

[fol. 45r] *mandas, mando, mandis.* Sunt quedam e contrario unius significationis, sed diuerse coniugationis, ut: *denso, densas, denseo, denses; strideo, strides, strido, stridis; ferueo, ferues, feruo, feruis; cieo, cies, cio, cis; dureo, dures,* unde *duresco* et *duro, duras; tueor, tueris, tuor, tueris.* Correpta penultima: *fulgeo, fulges, fulgo, fulgis; excello, excelles, excello, excellis; sono, sonas, sono, sonis; uno, unas, unio, unis.*

Quot modis uerba uel aliae partes fiunt defectiua? – Tribus modis: aut naturae necessitate, aut fortune casu uel differentiae causa. Naturae necessitate, ut si uelimus masculinum ab eo dicere quod est *nupta, nuptus* uel a *puerpera, puerperus,* obpugnat ipsa rerum natura; uel inconsonantiae causa, ut si uelimus a *cursor curtrix* facere femininum, sicut a *uictor uictrix,* inconsonum. In fortune casu inusitata et turpia uitantur et quibus auctores non utuntur; quomodo a *do dor* secundum regulam dici potuit, sed quia in auctoribus non inueniuntur, recusamus dicere. Differentiae quoque causa plurima uitantur, ut *fero, fers, fert* per syncopam sine *i* littera in secunda et tertia persona profertur, ne si *feris, ferit* dicas, a *ferio* putetur uenire. Sic *edo, es, est* et *uolo, uis, uult.* Differentiae causa anomalam habent litteraturam. Et *uolo* naturaliter imperatiuo modo caret, quia [fol. 45v] imperata necessitatis sunt non uoluntatis. Sic *fac, duc, dic, fer* placuit auctoribus per apocopam proferri differentiae causa, ne si *face, duce, dice, fere* diceremus, aliud significare putaremur. Item multa non dicuntur, quia in auctoribus non inueniuntur, de quibus per singula accidentia aliqua tue pandam auiditati. Nam *queso* non habet alios modos, nisi indicatiuum, personam primam in utroque numero, et *quesere* infinitiuum. Item *ouat* et *infit* non habet, nisi tertiam personam et *ouans* participium. Item *ausim,* id est auctoritatem habeam, et *inquam* contra morem in prima persona proferuntur. Vt *salue* et *saluete* imperatiuo tantum secundam personam habet. Item *cede* pro *dic, cete* pro *date;* Terrentius: *cete patri meo,* id est pro *date*; et *aue* pro *gaude* et *auete* pro *gaudete* secunde persone sunt. Item *faxo* pro *faciam* futuri est tantum indicatiui modi; et *facit*: *faxo*, *faxis*, *faxit*, *faximus*, *faxitis*, *faxunt*, id est *facient*. Item *facesso* et *capesso* et *uiso* desideratiua sunt, non frequentatiua, quia primę non sunt coniugationis; *facesso*, id est desidero facere; *capesso*, desidero capere; *uiso*, desidero uidere. Item *sis*, id est si uis, et *sodes*, id est si audes, secunde persone sunt. Item *foret* pro *esset* et *forent* pro *essent* et *fore* pro *esse* inuenitur. Item *aio* et *meio* in mul [fol. 46r] tis deficiunt, nam *aio*, *ais*, *ait* et *aitis*, *aiunt* facit. In prima plurali deficit et *ait* preteritum perfectum. Sicut presens *meio* infinitiuum *meiere* facit. Sunt quę idem habent presens et preteritum perfectum, haec sola: *odi*, *noui*, *memini*, *coepi*, *pepigi*; haec imperatiuo deficiunt, preter *memini* quod *memento* et *mementote* facit; et in futuro et infinitiuo modo et in suppinis, nec non in participiis, utriusque temporibus deficiunt, preter *odi* quod in figura conposita duo participia preteriti temporis facit: *exosus* et *perosus*. Sunt passiua quoque et deponentia que in preterito deficiunt, nisi aliunde ad suplementum declinationis sumatur preteritum, ut: *feror*, *ferior*, *tollor*, *poscor*, *arguor*; faciunt enim preteritum: *latus sum*, *ictus sum*, *sublatus sum*, *postulatus sum*, *conuictus sum*. Item deponentia: *uescor*, *fruor*, *medeor*, *liquor*, *reminiscor* faciunt *pastus sum*, *potitus sum*, *medicatus sum*, *liquefactus sum*, *recordatus sum*. *Sum* uerbum, quod inequalem habet declinationem, siue in simplici participio, siue in conpositis presentis temporis deficit, nisi in duobus ab eo conpositis, id est *absum* et *presum* quod facit *absens* et *presens*. *Possum*, *potes*, *potest* mutat eufonie causa. Et facit *prosum prodes*, *prodest*; adsumit *d*, hiatus causa deuitandi. *Volo* uero, *malo* et ex eo conposita, id est *magis uolo*, naturali necessitate carent inperati [fol. 46v] uo modo, quia imperata necessitatis sunt non uoluntatis, quod tamen in alio suo conposito habet, id est *nolo* facit enim *noli* et *nolite*.

293 aue] habe **V₃**; auete] habete **V₃** ‖ **294** faciam] fatiem **V₃** ‖ **296** coniugationis] coniugationes **V₃** ‖ **297** uidere] **V₃** *bis scripsit a.c.* ‖ **302** et] *scripsi cum* **S₁ ed.**, *om.* **V₃** ‖ **303** preter] propter **V₃**; et] in **V₃** ‖ **306** preteriti] preterita **V₃** *a.c.* ‖ **307** preterito] preterita **V₃** ‖ **308** declinationis sumatur] *scripsi cum* **S₁**, declinationem sumatur **V₃**, declinationis assumatur **ed.**; preteritum] preteriter **V₃**; feror] ferer **V₃** *a.c.*; arguor] *scripsi cum* **S₁**, arcor **V₃**, urgeor **ed.** ‖ **309** sum¹] **V₃** *bis scripsit*; conuictus] *scripsi cum* **ed.**, coniunctus **V₃** ‖ **310** deponentia] deponentiae **V₃** ‖ **314** presum] prosum **V₃** ‖ **316** deuitandi] defitando **V₃**; naturali] *scripsi cum* **S₁ ed.**, natura **V₃** ‖ **317** quia imperata necessitatis] *scripsi cum* **S₁ ed.**, qua imperatam necessitate **V₃** ‖ **318** conposito] conpostia **V₃**

Pleniorem tamen declinationem horum quatuor uerborum ut reddas mihi deposco, id est *sum, fero, edo, uolo.* – Inusitata est multis in locis illorum declinatio. Adtamen ut in magistrorum libris eorum reperitur ratio, pandam. *Sum* uerbum neutrale est quod declinabitur sic: *sum, es, est*; et pluraliter: *sumus, estis, sunt*. Imperfectum: *eram, eras, erat*; et pluraliter: *eramus, eratis, erant*. Perfectum: *fui, fuisti, fuit*; et pluraliter: *fuimus, fuistis, fuerunt* uel *fuere*. Plusquamperfectum: *fueram, -ras, -rat*; et pluraliter: *fueramus, -tis, fuerant*. Futurum: *ero, eris, -rit*; et pluraliter: *erimus, -tis, -runt*. Imperatiuo modo tempore presenti ad secundam et tertiam personam: *sis* uel *es, sit*; et pluraliter: *simus, estote* uel *sitis, sint*. Futuro: *esto, sis, sit*; et pluraliter: *simus, estote* uel *sitis, sint* et *sunto* et *suntote*. Optatiuo modo: *essem, -ses, <-set>*; et pluraliter: *essemus, -tis, -sent*. Preteritum perfectum et plusquamperfectum: *fuissem, -ses, -set*; et pluraliter: *fuissemus, -tis, -sent*. Futurum: *sim, sis, sit*; et pluraliter: *simus, -tis, sint*. Coniuntiuo modo: *cum sim, sis, sit*; et pluraliter: *simus, sitis, sint*. Inperfectum: *essem, esses, -set*; et pluraliter: *essemus, -tis, -sent*. Perfectum: *fuerim, -ris -rit*; et pluraliter: *-mus, -tis, -rint*. Plusquamperfecto: *fuissem, -ses, -set*; et pluraliter: *-[e]ssemus,* [fol. 47r] *-tis, -sent*. Futuro: *fuero, -ris, -rit*; et pluraliter: *-mus, -tis, -rint*. Infinitiuo modo, numero et personis, tempore presenti: *esse*. Preterito: *fuisse*. Futuro: *esse* et *ire*. Cuius presens participium ueteres proferebant *-ens*, unde conponitur *potens*. *Fero* uerbum, discrecionis causa, per sincopam abiecit *i* in secunda et tertia persona propter *ferio* uerbum quod facit *ferio, ferit*. *Edo*, uerbum inaequale, cuius secunda et tertia persona, causa differentiae, per concisionem profertur. *Volo* quoque, uerbum neutrale, per sincopam prolatum in secunda et tertia persona et inperatiuo deficit.

5. Numquid aduerbium per se positum plenum potest habere sensum? – Non potest nisi uerbo uel participio iungatur, ut *bene lego, bene legens*.

Possunt aliae partes pro aduerbiis poni? – Possunt, nam nomina pro aduerbiis ponuntur.

320 reddas] redas V₃ ‖ **321** inusitata est] inustitate e V₃ ‖ **322** libris] exemplis S₁ ed.; pandam] *scripsi cum* S₁ ed., *om.* V₃ ‖ **323** uerbum] eorum *add.* V₃ *a.c.* ‖ **328** tempore] temporem V₃ ‖ **329** estote uel sitis sint] *scripsi cum* ed., estote uel *om.* S₁, uel este tis sent V₃; sis] esi V₃ ‖ **330** sunto] sunt V₃; -ses] -sis V₃ ‖ **331** preteritum perfectum] propter perfecit V₃; plusquamperfectum] plusquamperfectus V₃ ‖ **332** -tis²] -ti V₃ *a.c.* ‖ **333** sint¹] sunt V₃; coniuntiuo] V₃ *p.c.*; sitis] tis V₃ *a.c.* ‖ **337** infinitiuo] infinitiuum V₃; numero] numeri V₃; tempore] temporis V₃ ‖ **338** preterito] propter V₃; ire] iri V₃ ‖ **339** ueteres] ūr V₃; proferebant] preferebant V₃ ‖ **340** causa] cause V₃; i] *scripsi cum* S₁ ed., *om.* V₃; tertia persona] tertiae persone V₃ ‖ **341** persona] persone V₃ ‖ **343** inperatiuo] inperatiua V₃ ‖ **345** iungatur] iungantur V₃ *a.c.*

Breuiarium Artis grammaticae Alcuini 217

Da exempla. – Genitiuus pro aduerbio ponitur, ut *Rome*; Cicero: *Romene sit?* Datiuus: *uesperi, sorti*; Virgilius: *sunt quibus ad portam cecidit custodia sorti.*
350 Accusatiuus: *Romam pergo, Athenas*; Terrentius: *quid tu, indocte, Athenas?* Ablatiuus: Virgilius: *forte sub arguta consederat illice Dafnis.*

Quomodo discerni potest utrum nomina sint an aduerbia sic posita? – Cum nomina loco aduerbiorum accipiuntur manent indeclinabilia, licet diuersis iungantur casibus, [fol. 47v] ut *sublime uolans, sublime uolantis, sublime uolanti*
355 et cetera. Si uero nomina sunt, declinantur, ut *hoc sublime uolans, huius sublime uolantis, huic sublime uolanti* et cetera.

Num aliae partes pro aduerbiis ponuntur? – Ponuntur. Nam *uel* coniunctio et *per* et *ex* prepositio pro *ualde* accipiuntur: *uel magnum bellum* pro *ualde magnum*; *excelsus*, id est pro *ualde celsus*.

360 Figure aduerbiorum quot sunt? – Tres: symplex, ut *diu*; conposita, ut *interdiu*; deconposita, id est que a conpositis diriuantur, ut ab *indocto indocte*, a *misericorde misericorditer*.

Significatio aduerbiorum quae est? – Significatio aduerbiorum diuersas species habet. Sunt autem temporalia, ut *pridem, nuper, nudiustertius*. Sunt que
365 presens tempus tantum significant, ut *nunc, presto*. Sunt que preteritum, ut *heri, hesterno*. Sunt que futurum, ut *cras, perendiae*. Sunt alia communia diuersorum temporum, ut *olim, dudum, quondam*. Preteriti: *olim truncus eram ficulnus, inutile lignum*. Presentis uerum: *ac iam olim seras posuit cum uinea frondes*. Idem: *forsan et hec olim meminisse iuuabit*. Preteritum: *ego dudum nihil*
370 *ueritus sum*. Presentis uerum: *iam dudum sumite penas*. Preteritum: *quondam*

348–349 Romene sit] Cic., *Lig.* 11.10 ‖ **349** sunt ... sorti] Verg., *Georg.* 4.165 ‖ **350** quid ... Athenas] cf. Ter., *Andr.* 907 ‖ **351** forte ... Dafnis] Verg., *Eclog.*, 7.1 ‖ **367–368** olim ... lignum] Hor., *Sat.*, 1.8.1 ‖ **368–369** ac ... frondes] Verg., *Georg.*, 2.403 ‖ **369** forsan ... iuuabit] Verg., *Aen.* 1.203 ‖ **369–370** ego ... sum] Ter., *Andr.* 582 ‖ **370** iam ... penas] Verg., *Aen.* 2.103 ‖ **370–371** quondam fuit ... uirtus] Cic., *Catil.* 1.1.24

---

350 indocte] indote **V**₃ *a.c.*; Athenas²] adthenas **V**₃ ‖ **351** forte] magno **V**₃; Dafnis] dasnis **V**₃ ‖ **352** an] **V**₃ *sup.l.* ‖ **354** uolantis] uolatis **V**₃; uolanti] uolati **V**₃ ‖ **357** coniunctio] coniugatio **V**₃ ‖ **359** est] **V**₃ *bis scripsit* ‖ **361** indocto indocte] *scripsi cum* **S**₁ **ed.**, indocte docte **V**₃ ‖ **362** misericorde] misericordiae **V**₃ *a.c.* ‖ **363** quae est] *scripsi cum* **S**₁ **ed.**, in quo sunt **V**₃ ‖ **364** species] specias **V**₃ ‖ **365** ut²] t **V**₃ ‖ **367** preteriti] preter **V**₃ ‖ **369** hec] heo **V**₃; iuuabit] iubabit **V**₃ ‖ **370–371** presentis ... uirtus] **V**₃ *in marg. inferiore* ‖ **370** sumite] sumte **V**₃

fuit ista in hac republica uirtus. Presentis uerum: *quondam etiam redit uictis in precordia uirtus*. Futurum: *tempus erit quondam*. Similiter et ex eo conposita: *aliquando, nequando*, que in peneultimis accentum habent, ne due partes putentur. Sed *quando* [fol. 48r] et *commodo, ubi, unde, quo, qua* interrogatiua acuuntur, relatiua grauantur per omnes syllabas.

Numquid que ab aliis partibus diriuantur primitiuorum significationes uel qualitates seruant aduerbia? – Seruant utique, ut a *Tullio Tulliane*, a *corpore corporaliter*, ab *alio aliter*, <a> *Greco Grece*, a *uiro uiriliter*.

Numquid aduerbia sinonima uel polionima possunt esse? – Possunt. Sinonima, id est dum multe uoces unam rem significant, ut *en, ecce*. Et paene in omnibus significationibus inuenies polionima, ut *ubi, quo, qua, quomodo*. Ō quoque diuersas habet significationes. Est aduerbium uocandi; Vergilius: *ō regina, nouam cui condere Iupiter urbem*. Est admirandi; Iuuenalis: *o qualis facies!* Est indignandi, ut: *o tempora, o mores!* Est et optandi: *adsis o tantum!*

6. Participium unde dictum est? – Participium dictum est, quia partem nominis partemque uerbi tenet et medium inter ea locum habet et semper in diriuatione est. Quod nulla alia pars orationis habet, dum aliae partes primitiuas habent species, unde diriuantur, ut a *rege regalis*, a *mei meus*, a *ferueo feruesco*, a *prope proprius*, ab *ex extra*. Participia autem semper ab uerbis deriuantur et conparationem non possunt habere.

Numquid non quedam [fol. 48v] nomina quoque tempus significant, ut *annus, menses, dies, hora* et talia multa? – Significant. Sed interest quod nomina illa nihil aliud significant, nisi ipsum tempus per se; participia itaque actionem uel passionem in quolibet fieri tempore demonstrant, non ipsum tempus; et quod participium exsequitur casus quos et uerba ex quibus nascuntur; et quod

---

371–372 quondam etiam ... uirtus] Verg., *Aen.* 2.367 ‖ 382–383 o ... urbem] Verg., *Aen.* 1.522 ‖ 383–384 o qualis facies] Iuv., *Sat.* 10.157 ‖ 384 o tempora, o mores] Cic., *Catil.* 1.1.10–11; adsis o tantum] Verg., *Aen.* 8.78

---

371 uictis] uictus **V₃** ‖ **372** uirtus] uictus **V₃** ‖ **373** peneultimis] -ltimis **V₃** *in rasura alia manu* ‖ **374** unde] uinde **V₃** ‖ **375** acuuntur] *scripsi cum* **S₁ ed.**, acciuntur **V₃** ‖ **377** Tullio] tuilio **V₃** *a.c.* ‖ **379** sinonima] sinomina **V₃** ‖ **380** sinonima] sinomina **V₃**; ut en] unem **V₃** ‖ **381** polionima] polienima **V₃**; qua] que **V₃** *a.c.* ‖ **383** Iuuenalis] iuuenales **V₃** ‖ **384** mores] moris **V₃** ‖ **387** diriuatione] diriuationem **V₃**; partes] pates **V₃** ‖ **388** regalis] regales **V₃** ‖ **389** ab²] **V₃** *in rasura alia manu*; uerbis] aduerbis **V₃** ‖ **391** non] num **V₃**; significant] significat **V₃** ‖ **393** actionem] auctionem **V₃** ‖ **394** tempore] tempote **V₃** *a.c.*; demonstrant non] *scripsi cum* **S₁ ed.**, demonstrantur **V₃**

uerborum significationes habent; et quod pro uerbo ponuntur. Vnde quidem participium uerbum casuale nominatur. Quia quod uerbo per se deest, id est casus, possidet in participio. Ideo in constructione per obliquos casus, ubi uerbum iungi non potest, participium loco uerbi subit, ut: *bonus homo*
400 *loquebatur; boni hominis loquentis orationem audiui; bono homini loquenti respondi; bonum hominem loquentem audiui; tu, bone homo, loquere; a bono homine loquente didici.* Et ex eo nominatiuus et uocatiuus recti casus nominantur, quia per se uerbis iungi possunt. Nam diuersa uerba sine coniunctione recte iungi non possunt, ut *lego scribo, doceo discis* non est dicendum, sed *lego* <et>
405 *scribo, doceo et discis.* Si participium loco prioris uerbi ponas, bene sine coniuntione proferatur, ut *legens scribo* et *docens discis.* Igitur participium inuentum, ut in nominatiuo et uocatiuo sine coniunctione proferatur cum alio uerbo, ut *legens doceo* pro *lego et doceo*, et *legens fac* pro *lege et fac*, que positio intransitiua est, hoc est ipsam in se ostendit manere personam. Obliqui uero
410 [fol. 49r] casus participiorum ad hec sunt utiles, quod non solum sine coniunctione proferantur, sed etiam ad alias transeant personas, ut *docentis potior, docenti respondeo, docentem audio, illo docente didici.*

7. Coniunctio quid est? – Pars orationis indeclinabilis, coniunctiua aliarum partium et consignificatiua, uim uel ordinationem demonstrans.
415 Quomodo uim uel ordinationem demonstrans? – Vim quando aliquas res simul esse significat, ut: *pius et fortis fuit Aeneas.* Ordinationem quando consequentiam aliquarum demonstrat rerum, ut: *si ambulat, mouetur.* Sequitur enim ambulationem motus.

Copulatiue que sunt? – Que copulant tam uerba quam sensum, ut *et, que,*
420 *at, atque, ac, ast.*

396 pro] *scripsi cum* **S₁ ed.**, *om.* **V₃** ‖ **397** uerbum] uerborum **V₃**; nominatur] nominant **V₃**; quia] quot **V₃** ‖ **398** possidet] posidet **V₃** *a.c.*; per obliquos] *scripsi cum* **S₁ ed.**, publiquos **V₃** ‖ **400–401** orationem … respondi] *scripsi cum* **ed.**, *om.* **V₃** ‖ **401** loquentem] loquente **V₃** ‖ **405** scribo] scribeo **V₃** ‖ **406** discis] *scripsi cum* **S₁ ed.**, dicens **V₃** ‖ **407** in] *scripsi cum* **S₁ ed.**, com̄ **V₃**; coniunctione] coniuntione **V₃** *a.c.* ‖ **410** solum] sola **V₃** ‖ **411** proferantur] proferatur **V₃**; transeant] transe ut **V₃** ‖ **412** docentem] *scripsi cum* **S₁ ed.**, *om.* **V₃** ‖ **414** consignificatiua] consignificatiuam **V₃**; uim] **V₃** *sup.l. alia manu*; ordinationem] ordinatione **V₃**; demonstrans] demonstrant **V₃** *a.c.* ‖ **417** ambulat] ambulet **V₃** ‖ **419** copulatiue] copulatiua **V₃** ‖ **420** ast] est **V₃**

Disiunctiue que sunt? – Que quamuis dictiones iungant, sensus tamen disiungunt et unum e duobus esse significant, ut *uel, ue, ne, nec, neque*.

Expletiue que sunt? – Que bonum uel malum explent sensum.

Causales que sunt? – Que causam antecedentem significant, ut: *doctus sum, nam legi; si sol est, iam lucet*, causa enim luminis sol est.

Rationales quae sunt? – Que rationem reddunt.

Ordo coniuntionum in quo est? – Quia alie quae semper preponuntur, ut *at, ast, aut, ac, uel, nec, neque, si, quin, quatenus, sint, seu, siue, ni*; [fol. 49v] alie subponuntur: *quidem, quoque, autem*; alie pene omnes indiferenter et preponi et subponi possunt, ut *ergo, igitur*.

8. Quod habent prepositiones offitii? – Vt aliis preponantur partibus apositione uel conpositione.

Aposicione quomodo? – Quando foris aponitur diccioni, et hoc nomine uel pronomine, casu accusatiuo uel ablatiuo, ut *ad hominem* uel *ab homine*, *ad illum* uel *ab illo*.

Quomodo per conpositionem? – Quando aliis partibus conponitur in unam dictionem, ut nomine per omnes casus, ut *indoctus, indocti, indocto, indoctum, indocte, ab indocto*. Pronomini non conponitur. Verbo conponitur, ut *induco, expleo*.

Habent prepositiones accentus per se? – Habent acutum accentum in fine, tam apud Grecos, quam apud Latinos. Qui tamen in grauem semper uertitur, quod prepositio ubique sequenti dictioni seu <per> apositionem, seu per conpositionem adnectitur et quasi una pars cum ea profertur. Inueniuntur quoque prepositiones in media poni diccioni, ut *qua de re, quam ob rem, qua in parte*.

Possunt prepositiones in alias transire partes? – Possunt.

---

422 ne] uel V_3; neque] que V_3 a.c. ‖ **423** sensum] sensunt V_3 ‖ **425** sol est^1] solem V_3; sol est^2] solem V_3 ‖ **426** rationem] rationum V_3 ‖ **428** ni] V_3 *alia manu ut uidetur* ‖ **429** quidem] quid est V_3; indiferenter] indiferentes V_3 a.c. ‖ **434** pronomine] pronomin V_3 ‖ **437** unam] unum V_3 ‖ **438** ab indocto] ad indocte V_3 ‖ **441** qui] quid V_3; in grauem semper uertitur] *scripsi cum* S_1 **ed.**, *om.* V_3 ‖ **442** ubique] *scripsi cum* S_1 **ed.**, inulique V_3; dictioni] dictione V_3; apositionem] apositione V_3 ‖ **443** conpositionem] conpossitionem V_3 ‖ **444** diccioni] dicioni V_3; qua^2] quam V_3

Da exempla. – *Post* prepositio, Virgilius: *post montem oppositum*, transit in aduerbium. Idem: *post mihi non simili pena commissa luetis*. *Ante* prepositio, Virgilius: *ante Iouem nulli subigebant arua coloni*, transit in aduerbium: [fol. 50r] *ante et Trinacria lentandus remus in unda*. Sic *supra*, *contra*, *prope* transeunt in aduerbia.

Si aliae partes in prepositiones possunt transire? – Possunt, nam aduerbia sepe transeunt in prepositiones, ut *pridie Kalendas*. *Pridie* hoc loco prepositio est. Subtracte quoque nominibus quibusdam loco aduerbiorum faciunt nomina accipi, ut *domu uenio* pro *a domu*; et *domum eo* pro *ad domum*. *Ad iuxta* significat in conpositione uel apositione, ut *ad currum* pro *iuxta currum*, *ad Troiam* pro *iuxta Troiam*. Significat quoque *contra*: *ad illum mihi pugna est*, hoc est *contra illum*. Accipitur et pro *usque*: *ad bellum Persicum*, hoc est, *usque bellum*. *Ob* et *pro* et *contra* et *circum* significat, ut: *haudquaquam ob meritum*, id est *pro merito*; *ob unius*, *contra unius*; *obambulo*, *circumambulo*. *Per* est et localis, ut *per medium forum*, est et temporalis, ut *per medium diem*, est et iurandi: *per te, per qui te talem genuere parentes*; aduerbii ualde uim obtinet, Terrentius: *persitus puer*, id est *ualde situs*; abnegationem quoque significat in conpositione, ut *perfidus*. *Post* conponitur et separatur et locum significat, Virgilius: *post montem oppositum*; significat et tempus, ut *post multum tempus*. *Cis* localem habet significationem, ut *cis Alpinam Galliam*; et pro *ultra* accipitur, ut *cis difinitum tempus*, hoc est *ultra*; et ex eo, *citra*. *Trans* conponitur et separatur, ut *transfero*, *trans Padum*; et in [fol. 50v] conpositione sepae N et S amittit, ut *traduco*, *trado*, *trano*; et pro *super* ponitur, ut *transgressus*, id est *supergressus*. *Apud* locum significat, ut *apud Numantiam*. *Ante* locum et tempus, ut *ante ianuam*, *ante annum*; diriuantur ex eo *antiquus*, *antiquarius* nomina. *Citra* pene eandem significationem habet quam *cis*, nisi quod propriis nominibus *cis*, *citra* appellatiuis saepius preponi solet: *cis Renum, cis Alpes, citra*

---

447 post montem oppositum] Verg., *Georg.* 3.213 ‖ **448** post ... luetis] Verg., *Aen.*, 1.136 ‖ **449** ante ... coloni] Verg., *Georg.* 1.125 ‖ **450** ante ... unda] Verg., *Aen.* 3.384 ‖ **461–462** per te ... parentes] Verg., *Aen.* 10.597 ‖ **463** persitus puer] cf. Ter., *Andr.* 486 ‖ **465** post montem oppositum] Verg., *Georg.* 3.213

---

447 oppositum] appositum V₃ ‖ **448** luetis] luctis V₃ ‖ **449** Virgilius] ueni V₃; subigebant] subiecebant V₃; coloni] colon V₃ ‖ **450** ante et Trinacria lentandus remus] ante crinacria letandus renus V₃ ‖ **453** prepositiones] prepossitiones V₃; pridie¹] pride V₃ ‖ **455** domu¹] domo V₃ *a.c.*; a] *scripsi cum* S₁ **ed.**, *om.* V₃ ‖ **456** apositione] apossitione V₃ ‖ **458** contra] tra V₃ *a.c.*; ad] *scripsi cum* S₁ **ed.**, *om.* V₃ ‖ **459** pro] per V₃; significat] significant V₃; haudquaquam] autquaquam V₃ ‖ **460** obambulo] oambulo V₃ *a.c. alia manu* ‖ **464** post] pos V₃; separatur] seperatur V₃ ‖ **470** Numantiam] numantium V₃ ‖ **471** diriuantur] diriuante et V₃ ‖ **472** quam] *scripsi cum* **ed.**, quod S₁ V₃

forum; et a *cis citra* diriuatur, *a citra citer, citerior, citissimus*. *Circa* loci et temporis pro *iuxta* positum inuenitur, ut *circa templum, circa uiginti annos*. *Circum* conponitur et apponitur, ut *circumfero, circum mare*. *Circiter* ad tempus solum pertinet, ut *circiter Kalendas Ianuarias*. *Erga* non conponitur et affectum significat, ut *bonus est erga propinquos*. *Contra* separatur et conponitur: *contra adulteram* et *contradico*. *Extra* apponitur, ut *extra me*. *Inter* utramque, ut *inter amicos, interuallum, interpres*, cuius symplex in usu non est. Et ab *in inter* et *intra* nascuntur; a *sub, subter*; a *pro, propter*; a *cis, citra*; ab *ex, extra*. *Iuxta* pro *prope* ponitur, ut *iuxta te*, id est *prope te*. *Secundum* duas habet significationes, proximitatem et emulationem: *secundum eam sedeo* et *secundum mores eius uiuo*.

Potestatem singularum expone. – *A* et *ab* et *abs* et *e* et *ex* eandem fere significationis uim habent. Nam et locales, [fol. 51r] et temporales, et ordinales similiter inueniuntur, ut est *a domu, a die, a te*; sic et cetera. Sed *a* et *e* saepius consonantibus preponuntur, ut *a templo, e culmine*. Alia utrumque et uocalibus, et consonantibus apositione uel conpositione iunguntur, ut *abito, ab illo, abduco, ab hora*. Et sepe *B* eufoniae causa in aliam mutabitur litteram *R*: *arripio*, in *U*: *aufero*, in *S*: *asporto*. *Ex* quoque pro *extra* inuenitur poni, ut *excludo, extracludo*; *exsul, extra solum*; modo pro *ualde*, ut *excelsus*, id est pro *ualde celsus*; modo priuatiuum uel intentiuum uel perfectiuum: *extirpo, extendo, expleo*. *E* in conpositione priuatiuum uel intentiuum et pro *extra* accipitur, ut *enodes trunci, enarro, educo*. Diriuatur a *ab absque*, nam *que*, quando uim et significationem coniunctionis non habet, syllaba est, non pars orationis, quomodo in *ubique, utique, denique, itaque, uterque, plerumque*, et ideo accentum non mutant de prima syllaba; aditio syllabica est, non

---

495 enodes trunci] Verg., *Georg.* 2.78

---

473 appellatiuis] appellatiuus V₃; citra²] contra V₃ ‖ **474** citra²] *scripsi cum* S₁ **ed.**, *om.* V₃ ‖ **475** circa²] circum V₃ ‖ **476** circumfero] *scripsi cum* **ed.**, circumiero S₁ V₃; circiter] V₃ *p.c.*; ad] V₃ *p.c.* ‖ **480** interuallum] interualles V₃; in usu] musu V₃ ‖ **481** pro²] *scripsi cum* S₁ **ed.**, *om.* V₃ ‖ **483** emulationem] aemulationem V₃ *a.c.* ‖ **485** singularum] singularem V₃; et e] *scripsi cum* S₁ **ed.**, *om.* V₃; eandem] eudem V₃ ‖ **487** est a domu] *scripsi cum* S₁ *p.c.*, eam domum V₃, est a domo **ed.**; a et e] a e et V₃ ‖ **489** apositione] uides poscione V₃ ‖ **490** sepe] sape V₃ ‖ **491** asporto] asperto V₃ ‖ **492** exsul] exul V₃ *a.c.* ‖ **493** priuatiuum] primitiuum V₃ ‖ **494** priuatiuum] primitiuum V₃; intentiuum] intentatiuum V₃ ‖ **495** trunci] terrantia V₃ ‖ **496** coniunctionis] conuictionis V₃; syllaba est] syllabẹm V₃; non²] nem V₃ ‖ **497** ubique] V₃ *sup.l.*; uterque] utemquem V₃ *a.c.*

coniuntio, ut in pronomine *ce* et *met* et *te*. De memoratiuum et intentiuum et priuatiuum: *de homine, detrao, desum*. *Pro* in apositione uel conpositione localis et temporalis: *pro templo, prouideo*. Et loco *e* et *super* uel *ante* uel *ad* uel *in* accipitur, ut *prominet*, id est *supereminet*; *pro curia signa sotiis dare*, id est *ante curiam*; Virgilius: *summis incuruant uiribus arcus pro se quisque uiri*, [fol. 51v] id est *ad suas uires*; *pro testimonio*, hoc est *in testimonio*. *Pro* interiectione accipitur, ut *pro dolor*, et circumflectitur. *Pre* in apositione uel conpositione inuenitur et *ad* uel *ob* uel *super* uel *ualde* uel *ante* significat; Terrentius: *contempsi illum hic pre me*, hoc est *ad conparationem mei*. Item: *fit misera pre amore*, id est *ob amorem*; *presideo, supersideo; preualidus, ualde ualidus; predico, ante dico*. *Cum* prepositio est copulatiua, ut: *cum duabus uado*, et numquam conponitur, quia *con* in eius loco in conpositione ponitur, ut *concurro, contraho*. Et sciendum est quod *con* et *in* tunc mutant *N* in *M*, quando *B*, *M* uel *P* sequitur, ut *comburo, imbuo, comminus, immunis, compello, impello*. Tunc *N* conuertunt in sequentes consonantes, quando *L* uel *R* sequitur, ut *collido, illido, corripio, irruo*. *Cum* quoque postponitur quibusdam pronominibus euphoniae causa, ut *mecum, tecum, secum, nobiscum, uobiscum*; et antepeneultima in his eleuatur. Aliis postposita acuitur, ut *quocum, quacum, quicum, quibuscum*. *Coram me, te, se*. *Palam* ad omnia accipitur, ut *palam omnibus*. *Sine* et *absque* negatiua sunt: *sine homine, absque homine*. Et *sine* anteposita grauatur, ut *sine timore*, postposita acuitur; Virgilius: *si sine pace tua*. *Tenus* postponitur, ut *actenus*, et genitiuo quoque iungitur, [fol. 52r] ut: *crurum tenus a mento palearia pendent*. Nam *in*, si pro *contra* uel *ad* ponitur, accusatiuo iungitur, ut: *in hostem*, id est *contra hostem*; et *in pubpim rediere rates*

503 summis ... uiri] cf. Verg., *Aen.* 5.500–1 ∥ **507** contempsi ... me] cf. Ter., *Eun.* 239 ∥ **507–508** fit ... amore] Ter., *Eun.* 98 ∥ **519** si sine pace tua] Verg., *Aen.* 10.31 ∥ **521** crurum ... pendent] Verg., *Georg.* 3.53 ∥ **522** in pubpim rediere rates] Lucan., *Phar.* 3.545

499 coniuntio] iuntio **V₃** *a.c.*; ce] c **V₃**; met] *scripsi cum* **S₁ ed.**, in e **V₃** ∥ **500** priuatiuum] priuitiuum **V₃** ∥ **502** prominet] preminet **V₃** ∥ **503** summis] sum s **V₃** ∥ **505** pre] per **V₃** ∥ **506** et] ut **V₃** ∥ **508** ob amorem] ab amore **V₃** ∥ **509** cum prepositio] conpositio **V₃** ∥ **510** in conpositione ponitur] *scripsi cum* **ed.**, in positione ponitur **S₁**, positi inponitur **V₃** ∥ **511** in¹] non **V₃** ∥ **515** causa] causam **V₃**; ut mecum tecum] tecum ut mecum **V₃** ∥ **516** ut] u **V₃** ∥ **517** se] re **V₃** ∥ **518** sine²] siue **V₃** ∥ **519** si sine pace] si sine te pace nus **V₃** ∥ **520** tenus] *scripsi cum* **S₁ ed.**, *om.* **V₃**; genitiuo] genus **V₃** ∥ **521** palearia] palliaria **V₃** ∥ **522** accusatiuo] accussatiuo **V₃**

pro *ad pubpim*; et *sub lucem exornant calatis* pro *ante lucem*; et *sub noctem cura recursat* pro *per noctem*. *In* modo in conpositione priuatiuum est, ut *iniustus,* 525 *inprobus*, modo intentiuum: *inprimo, incuso. Sub* est et localis: *subeo, subpono*, est et diminutiuum: *subrideo*, id est *paululum rideo, subtristis.* Et in sequentem mutat *B* consonantem si *C* uel *F, G, M* uel *P* sequitur, ut *succumbo, suffero, suggero, summito, suppono. Super*, si pro *supra* ponitur, accusatiuum est, ut: *seua sedens super arma*, id est *supra*. Si *de* uel *in* significat, ablatiuum, ut: *multa super* 530 *Priamo rogitans*, hoc est, *de Priamo*. Item: *fronde super uiridi*, id est *in uiridi*. Item *subter* accusatiuum est, ut *subter terram*. Item ablatiuum, ut *subter densa testudine*.

Vnde dicuntur quedam prepositiones loquelares? – Quia semper in conpositione loquelis, id est diccionibus, conponuntur et sunt sex: *di-, dis-, re-,* 535 *se-, am-, con-*; ut *diduco, distraho, recurro, secubo, amplector, congero. Di* quidem et *dis* separatiua sunt et eandem significatio [fol. 52v] nem habent quomodo *a* et *abs*, ut *diuido, distraho*. Et *dis* ponitur quando sequitur *C, F, P, S, T* et *I* loco consonantis posita, ut *discutio, differo, diffundo* – *S* in *F* mutat euphoniae causa –, *disputo, dissero, distraho, disiungo*. In aliis consonantibus *di* preponitur, ut 540 *diduco, digero, diluo, dimitto, diruo* et ubique *di* producitur, preter *dirimo, disertus. Re* uidetur a *retro* per apocopam factum sicut ipse sensus probat. Quid est *respicio*, nisi *retro spicio*? *Reuertor, retro uertor*? *Se* separatiua est, ut *separo, seiungo*; est et abnegatiuum, ut *securus*. Et a *se seorsum*, sicut a *de deorsum*, et a *super sursum* aduerbium uenit. *Am circum* uel *circa* significat, ut *amplector,* 545 *amputo, ambio* in quo aditio *B* consonantis fit propter *M. Com* pariter significat, ut *coneo*, et loco *cum* prepositione ponitur, ut *concurro, coniungo*. Ecce habes de prepositione quantum breuitas disputationis sinebat.

9. Interiectio quare dicta est? – Eo quod interponitur ad exprimendos animi adfectus.

523 sub lucem ... calatis] cf. Verg., *Georg.* 3.402 ‖ **523–524** sub noctem ... recursat] Verg., *Aen.* 1.662 ‖ **528–529** seua sedens ... arma] Verg., *Aen.* 1.295 ‖ **529–530** multa ... rogitans] Verg., *Aen.* 1.750 ‖ **530** fronde super uiridi] Verg., *Eclog.* 1.80 ‖ **531–532** subter densa testudine] Verg., *Aen.* 9.514 ‖ **548–549** interiectio ... adfectus] cf. Pomp., *gramm.*, p. 97.33–34

523 noctem] nocte V_3 ‖ **524** in¹] *scripsi cum* S_1 **ed.**, *om.* V_3 ‖ **525** inprobus] improbo V_3; intentiuum] *scripsi cum* S_1, *om.* V_3, intensiuum **ed.**; subeo] sabeo V_3 ‖ **527** si] s V_3 ‖ **529** in] *scripsi cum* S_1 **ed.**, *om.* V_3; significat] significant V_3 ‖ **531** subter¹] super V_3 ‖ **536** sunt] ut separato seiungo *add.* V_3 ‖ **540** preter] propter V_3 ‖ **541** apocopam] apocopa V_3 ‖ **542** separatiua] separatiuatiua V_3 ‖ **543** a de] ad V_3 ‖ **544** aduerbium] *scripsi cum* S_1 **ed.**, ab aduerbio V_3 ‖ **545** fit] fuit V_3 ‖ **548** eo] e V_3

Abstract

Alcuin's *Ars grammatica* is preserved in twenty-four manuscripts, either completely or partially. Only one ninth century manuscript from Biblioteca Apostolica Vaticana, MS Reg. lat. 251, transmits an abridged version of it. This study presents a critical edition of the *Breviarium Artis grammaticae Alcuini*, preceded by a presentation of the context in which the text was written and a description of the Vatican manuscript. Furthermore, it offers an analysis of the structure of the *Breviarium* compared to that of the *Ars grammatica* and also a discussion of the interpolations from other texts. The purpose of this edition is, on the one hand, to bring to light a *textus unicus* from the textual tradition of the *Ars grammatica*, and, on the other, to present the work of an early medieval abbreviator by preserving, as much as possible, its phonetic and orthographic peculiarities.

Résumé

L'*Ars grammatica* d'Alcuin est conservée, complètement ou partiellement, dans vingt-quatre manuscrits. Un seul manuscrit du neuvième siècle siècle de la Biblioteca Apostolica Vaticana, MS Reg. lat. 251, en transmet une version abrégée. Cette étude présente une édition critique du *Breviarium Artis grammaticae Alcuini*, précédée d'une présentation du contexte dans lequel le texte a été composé et d'une description du manuscrit du Vatican. En outre, cette étude offre une analyse de la structure du *Breviarium* par rapport à l'*Ars grammatica* et des interpolations d'autres textes. Le but de cette édition est, d'une part, de mettre en lumière un *textus unicus* issu de la tradition textuelle de l'*Ars grammatica* et, d'autre part, de présenter le travail d'un abréviateur du haut Moyen Âge, en préservant, autant que possible, ses particularités phonétiques et orthographiques.

Isabela Grigoraș
University of Fribourg / University of Bucharest
isabela.stoian@gmail.com

A New Manuscript Source
for the Legend of Saint Clement in Denmark[*]

ÅSLAUG OMMUNDSEN
University of Bergen

Introduction

The Nordic collections of medieval book fragments contain numerous items warranting far more attention than they have received until now. Fragments from a volume with texts about St. Clement from ca. 1200 is a case in point. Thus far, six fragments have been identified in Copenhagen and Oslo from a large volume containing two works of Leo of Ostia: the *De origine beati Clementis* (BHL 1851ab) and the *De translatione sancti Clementis* (also known as *Legenda Italica*) (BHL 2073), as well as the anonymous *Passio sancti Clementis* (BHL 1848).

The works on Clement of Leo of Ostia (ca. 1046–ca. 1115), a monk in Monte Cassino and later appointed cardinal bishop of Ostia and Velletri, are known from only a very few manuscripts. In 1955 Paul Meyvaert and Paul Devos revealed the discovery of a manuscript in Prague containing texts by Leo of Ostia, the first known medieval witness of the *De origine beati Clementis* and the second of the *De translatione sancti Clementis*.[1] To my knowledge, no further manuscript witnesses of either have been

---

[*] I would like to thank Jonas Wellendorf and Astrid Marner for their help with this article. I am also grateful to the staff at the Danish National Archives, not least to Michael H. Gelting for invaluable assistance during my visit there in 2012, and to Abelone Alstrup for supplying additional photographs in 2016. I also thank the staff at the National Archives of Norway, especially Gunnar Pettersen and Tor Weidling for their patient assistance, including providing good conditions for photographs. As always, the work on these particular fragments has benefited greatly from the insights of Michael Gullick. Finally, I would like to thank the two anonymous reviewers of *The Journal of Medieval Latin* for their careful reading of an earlier draft of this article and for their valuable suggestions for improvements.

[1] Paul Meyvaert and Paul Devos announced their discovery of the manuscript Prague, Castle Archives, Library of the Metropolitan Chapter of St. Vitus, MS XXIII (1547) in 1955, and edited the *Translatio sancti Clementis* (BHL 2073) collated with the Vatican City, Biblioteca Apostolica Vaticana, MS Vat. lat. 9668; see Paul Meyvaert and Paul Devos, "Trois énigmes Cyrillo-Méthodiennes de la "Légende Italique" résolues grace à un document inédit," *Analecta Bollandiana* 73 (1955), 375–461, at pp. 455–61. Two seventeenth-century copies of the *Translatio* have been shown by Meyvaert and Devos to be independent copies of Vat. lat. 9668. See Meyvaert and Devos, "Trois énigmes," p. 449; and Paul Meyvaert and Paul Devos, "Autour de Léon d'Ostie et de sa *Translatio S. Clementis* (Légende Italique des SS. Cyrille et Méthode)," *Analecta Bollandiana* 74 (1956), 189–240, at pp. 190–96. In 1968, the *De origine beati Clementis* (BHL 1851 ab [Nov. Suppl.]), from the same Prague manuscript, was edited by

discovered since then, making the Danish and Norwegian fragments the second medieval witness of the *De origine* and the third of the *De translatione* (see Table 1). Their fragmentary state does not detract from their overall significance: not only do they place Leo of Ostia's works in Scandinavia for the first time, but they also represent the first identified Latin manuscript witness to Clement's legend in Denmark. Furthermore, the surviving sections of Leo's texts in the Scandinavian fragments contain readings that appear superior to those found in the Prague manuscript, thus contributing to the transmission and current state of Leo of Ostia's compositions.

The first-century pope and saint Clement I enjoyed immense popularity both in the Eastern and Western Church, and his cult seems to have played a significant role in the Nordic countries in the early phases of their Christianization. A number of modern studies are devoted to Clement's cult, the churches dedicated to him, and the vernacular versions of his legend.[2] The mention of his relics in Aarhus could account for some of his popularity in Denmark.[3] Nonetheless, the study of Clement in the North is challenged by the poor survival of manuscript sources in the Nordic countries, particularly Latin ones.

Dietrich Hofmann's thorough investigation of the literary witnesses of Clement's legend in Scandinavia found no surviving Latin sources from medieval Denmark. He could only point to a fragment (a bifolium) of a late medieval vernacular translation of the *Legenda Aurea*, and a Danish translation of a Swedish text on Clement (the

---

Giovanni Orlandi together with Gauderic of Velletri's *Vita sancti Clementis* (from the Monte Cassino manuscript Codex Casinensis 234); see Ioannes Orlandi, *Iohannis Hymmonidis et Gauderici Veliterni, Leonis Ostiensis, Excerpta ex Clementinis recognitionibus a tyranno Rufino translatis* (Milano, 1968).

[2] Erik Cinthio, "The Churches of St. Clemens in Scandinavia," in *Res mediaevales: Ragnar Blomqvist kal. Mai. MCMLXVIII oblata*, ed. Anders W. Mårtensson, Archaeologica Lundensia 3 (Karlshamn, 1968), pp. 103–16; Barbara Crawford, "The Churches Dedicated to St. Clement in Norway: A Discussion of their Origin and Function," *Collegium Medievale* 17 (2004), 100–31; Barbara Crawford, *The Churches Dedicated to St. Clement in Medieval England: A Hagio-Geography of of the Seafarer's Saint in 11th Century North Europe* (St. Petersburg, 2008). For the vernacular legend, see for instance Helen Carron, *Clemens Saga: The Life of St Clement of Rome* (London, 2005) (available online at: http://www.vsnrweb-publications.org.uk/Text%20Series/Clemens_saga.pdf); Dietrich Hofmann, *Die Legende von Sankt Clemens in den skandinavischen Ländern im Mittelalter* (Frankfurt am Main, 1997); Ole Widding, Hans Bekker-Nielsen, and Laurence Shook, "The Lives of the Saints in Old Norse Prose: A Handlist," *Medieval Studies* 25 (1963), 294–337. See also Kirsten Wolf, *The Legends of the Saints in Old Norse-Icelandic Prose* (Toronto, Buffalo, London, 2013).

[3] Cinthio, "The Churches," p. 107, with reference to Helge Søgaard, *Det Ældste Århus* (Århus, 1961), p. 46. Cinthio indicates that the relics, which may have been a gift received by Canute the Great during his visit to Rome after the battle of Helgeå in 1026, may actually have caused the "wave" of Danish-founded Clement churches, including one in London (where Canute came on his return journey from Rome to Denmark); see Cinthio, "The Churches," p. 113.

Siælinna trøst).[4] He did, however, assume that a Latin version of Clement's legend must have existed in Århus, at least after 1200 when Clement became the patron saint of the cathedral. In this light, he understandably concludes: "Aus dem Mittelalter ist aber offenbar nichts erhalten geblieben."[5]

While the majority of the Latin manuscripts in Scandinavia are lost, at least some parts of the medieval book corpus have survived in the form of fragments (roughly 50,000 fragments for the Nordic countries combined).[6] Most of these fragments are transmitted as parchment covers or binding material in sixteenth- or seventeenth-century archival protocols, either for the royal Swedish administration in Stockholm or the royal Danish administration in Copenhagen. Since one medieval manuscript could supply the administration with binding material for several protocols or account books, it is to some extent possible to "reassemble" once existing books based on the bindings. For this reason twentieth-century scholars of the Scandinavian fragments have established the practice of assigning a codex signature or research *signum* to "reconstructed" manuscripts, although these most often remain incomplete and highly fragmentary.

This is the context for the survival and identification of the above mentioned fragments from the Clement volume. Five fragments from two (now incomplete) leaves with Clement texts were used in the bindings of account books from two regions in Western Norway under the governor of Bergenhus (Bergen Castle) for the years 1624 and 1650. These fragments were studied and registered by the great Norwegian liturgist Lilli Gjerløw (1910–1998), although they were registered under two different codex signatures, Lec Br 22 and Vita 4.[7] Gjerløw's private notes show that she had actually identified the content of Lec Br 22 as part of Leo of Ostia's *De translatione*. She

---

[4] Hofmann, *Die Legende von Sankt Clemens*, p. 54.

[5] Hofmann, *Die Legende von Sankt Clemens*, p. 55.

[6] For an overview on Nordic fragments and fragment research, see *Nordic Latin Manuscript Fragments: The Destruction and Reconstruction of Medieval Books*, ed. Åslaug Ommundsen and Tuomas Heikkilä (London and New York, 2017). The Swedish National Archives and the University Library in Helsinki, Finland, already have searchable and illustrated databases of their medieval manuscript fragments (22,500 and 11,000 fragments respectively). See https://sok.riksarkivet.se/mpo (for Sweden) and http://fragmenta.kansalliskirjasto.fi/ (for Finland).

[7] One fragment, Oslo, The National Archives of Norway (NRA), Unnumbered Box III [25] (from Statholderarkivet D IX 15 regarding church incomes from the bishopric of Bergen, Nordhordland 1624, detached by Sandaaker) was registered as Lec Br 22 (*Lectionarium breviarii* number 22); Oslo, NRA, Lat. fragm. 23,1–4 (1: Voss 1624; 2: Nordhordland 1624; 3: Nordfjord 1650, 4: no place or year, formerly registered as 46.50.51 [7]) were registered as *Vita sanctorum* 4.

had, however, not connected it to the other fragments, and it is doubtful if her discovery was ever communicated to anyone.[8]

Michael Gullick took the reconstruction work one step further about a decade ago by identifying the scribe of Lec Br 22 and Vita 4 as one and the same, connecting the five fragments into one group. The fragment registered as Lec Br 22 can be shown to come from the same leaf as three of the fragments registered as Vita 4 (see Fig. 4), leaving no doubt about Gullick's scribal identification. I here suggest that the same scribe wrote the leaf registered as DRA, fragm. 8535 in the Danish National Archives and that the Danish fragment was once part of the same book as the five Norwegian fragments. The Danish leaf, containing parts of the *De origine beati Clementis*, was used as a parchment cover of an account book for building materials in Copenhagen for the years 1622–1628 (see Fig. 2).[9]

Although leaves from the Clement volume were used to bind account books from both Denmark and Norway in early modern times, the book was probably in Danish ownership in the Middle Ages. Fragments in Norwegian bindings can only rarely be joined with Danish ones, even though Norway was under Danish rule and administration between 1536–1814.[10] The Norwegian account books were most often bound before they were shipped off to Copenhagen, and the parchment for the bindings was as a rule procured locally.[11] In the cases where Norwegian fragments can be linked to Danish ones, it is apparently because leaves or quires were brought from Copenhagen

---

[8] Cf. Lilli Gjerløw's files in the National Archives under Lec Br 22 (five sheets), including a facsimile of the fragment Oslo, NRA, Unnumbered Box III, [25]. Here she gave references to Paul Meyvaert and Paul Devos. Regarding the fragments registered as Vita sanctorum 4, Gjerløw's notes state that "the text immediately preceding Clement [i.e. Leo's *De origine*] is not identified" (my translation). The third fragment in the envelope (NRA, Lat. fragm. 23,3), containing another part of *De translatione*, is also unidentified. I am very grateful to Tor Weidling for sending me scans of Lilli Gjerløw's notes for Lec Br 22 and Vita sanctorum 4.

[9] Copenhagen, The Danish National Archives (DRA), fragm. 8535 (Regnskaber 1559–1660, Udgiftsbilag til rentemesterregnskabet, Pk 379: K Bygningsskriverens regnskaber for bygningsmaterialer 1622–1628). The identification of the Clement text was made at the beginning of 2012 using one of the early online initiatives to present fragments in the Nordic countries, namely Knud Ottosen's database of Danish liturgical fragments (now available at https://web.archive.org/web/20190424213614/http://www.liturgy.dk/), which happened to include the Clement fragment.

[10] The Norwegian body of government was dissolved in 1536 and Norway came to be ruled directly by the Danish king, and was no longer considered a kingdom in union with Denmark as it had been since the fourteenth century; see Sverre Bagge and Knut Mykland, *Norge i dansketiden 1380–1814* (Oslo, 1987–1996), p. 78. Norway gained independence from Denmark in 1814, and a few years later the Norwegian account books were returned to Oslo.

[11] Gunnar Pettersen, "From Parchment Books to Fragments: Norwegian Medieval *Codices* before and after the Reformation," in *Latin Manuscripts of Medieval Norway*, ed. Espen Karlsen (Oslo, 2013), pp. 41–65.

to supply the local administration with binding material (rather than the accounts being bound in Copenhagen).[12] It is therefore most likely that the Clement volume was dismembered in Copenhagen and its parchment distributed from there to various parts of the Danish realm.

The fragments identified from the Clement volume and their content are presented in more detail below, after a brief introduction to Leo of Ostia's text. Finally, a short discussion of the historical context and possible clues to the manuscript's origin and intended use is offered. The text from the fragments is presented in an Appendix.

Leo of Ostia's Texts on St. Clement and Their History

Thanks to the discoveries of Paul Meyvaert and Paul Devos in the middle of the twentieth century we now know much about Leo of Ostia's writings on Clement, his motivation, and the context in which the texts were composed. According to Leo's Prologue to the *De translatione*, his work started with a text on Clement's background and early life, the *De origine beati Clementis*.[13] His purpose, says Leo in the preface, was to provide a text for a more ample and devout celebration of the vigils of Clement's feast day (23 November).[14] Then, there was an account of Clement's rise to the papal see – the *De ordinatione seu cathedra S. Clementis* – to be used for readings of the feast of his ordination (23 January). And finally, Leo wrote a text, at the request of Anastasius, Cardinal of San Clemente, on Clement's passion and miracles and the discovery of his body. This text was written between 1099 and Leo's death in 1115.[15] Leo's texts are substantial, but not extensive: for example, in Prague, Castle Archives, Library of the Metropolitan Chapter of St. Vitus, MS XXIII (1547), the *De origine* and the *De*

---

[12] So far, only fifteen identifications have been made from codices split between the National Archives of Norway and Denmark; see Åslaug Ommundsen, "Danish Fragments in Norway and Their Connections to Twelfth-Century Lund," in *Nordic Latin Manuscript Fragments*, ed. Ommundsen and Heikkilä, pp. 184–220, at 213–14. Although manuscripts may also have been collected in Norway for use in Denmark, the governor of Bergenhus in 1624 used fragments from three different manuscripts probably sectioned up in Denmark, which is unusual and may indicate that he had stocked up on parchment from Copenhagen; see Åslaug Ommundsen, "A Norwegian – and European – Jigsaw Puzzle of Manuscript Fragments," in *Nordic Latin Manuscript Fragments*, ed. Ommundsen and Heikkilä, pp. 135–62, at 150–51.

[13] For the prologue, see Meyvaert and Devos, "Trois énigmes," pp. 412–13.

[14] For the preface, see Orlandi, *Excerpta ex Clementinis Recognitionibus*, pp. 1–3.

[15] See Meyvaert and Devos, "Trois énigmes," pp. 410–16. Anastasius became Cardinal of San Clemente between 1099–1102; he is the same Anastasius who was responsible for covering the fourth-century church of San Clemente, and for building the present church above it. See Leonard Boyle, "The Fate of the Remains of St Cyril," in *Cirillo e Metodio. I santi Apostoli degli Slavi. Conferenze tenute nel Pontificio Istituto Orientale nei giorni 9–11 Maggio 1963* (Rome, 1964), pp. 159–194 (repr. in *San Clemente Miscellany* II, *Art and Archaeology*, ed. Luke Dempsey (Rome, 1978), pp. 13–35.

translatione, including the prologue, cover nineteen leaves altogether (fols. 132–150).[16]

Leo of Ostia's twelfth-century texts are essentially one stage in a long line of related Clement narratives, reaching back to late antiquity. The Greek original from the second or third century is now lost, but its contents survive in the form of a Greek reworking, the *Homiliai*, and a Latin translation, Tyrannius Rufinus's *Recognitiones* from ca. 400.[17] These oldest narratives are often referred to as the Pseudo-Clementines, as they were long believed to have been written by Clement himself, since the story is told in the first person. The Pseudo-Clementines build on the drama typical for the ancient novel, with motifs of love, lust, shipwrecks, pirates, long separations, and emotional reunions, and have accordingly been referred to as the first Christian novel.[18] In this particular case, the novelistic *topoi* merely form a framework for a philosophical defence of Christianity, as shown in the disputations of Peter.[19] The well-known ingredients present the Christian message in a way that would appeal to the pagan audience at the time of their composition. The Pseudo-Clementines, the *Homiliae*, and the *Recognitiones*, have been the focus of a long and substantial research tradition.[20]

The fourth-century descriptions of St. Clement as a martyr inspired Cyril and Methodius, the "Apostles of the Slavs," to seek his relics in the Black Sea, where they "miraculously" found his body together with the anchor used to weigh it down, on a small island in January 861. Following an invitation from Pope Nicholas (858–867), Clement's relics were brought to Rome in 867, although by the time they arrived Pope Nicholas had already died and been succeeded by Pope Hadrian II (867–872). The new pontiff was equally excited about Clement's relics and had them placed in

---

[16] Cf. Meyvaert and Devos, "Trois énigmes," pp. 410–11.

[17] Bernhard Rehm, *Die Pseudoklementinen I: Homilien* (Berlin, 1953); and Bernhard Rehm, *Die Pseudoklementinen II: Rekognitionen in Rufins Übersetzung* (Berlin, 1965). A long strand of the research tradition has been committed to a reconstruction of the Grundschrift; see for example, Werner Heintze, *Der Clemensroman und seine griechischen Quellen* (Leipzig, 1914).

[18] Thomas Hägg, *The Novel in Antiquity* (Berkeley and Los Angeles, 1983–1991), pp. 162–63. See further discussion and references in István Czachesz, "The Clement Romance: Is it a Novel?," in *The Pseudo-Clementines*, ed. Jan N. Bremmer (Leuven, 2010), pp. 24–35.

[19] See Hägg, *The Novel in Antiquity*, pp. 163–64, and Hofmann, *Die Legende von Sankt Clemens*, pp. 12–13. The philosophical perspective in *Recognitiones* is the subject matter for several studies; see for example Christoph Jedan, "Philosophy Superseded? The Doctrine of Free Will in the Pseudo-Clementine Recognitions," in *The Pseudo-Clementines*, ed. Jan Bremmer (Leuven, 2010), pp. 200–16.

[20] For a survey of the research status of several questions related to the Pseudo-Clementines and further references to a full *Forschungsgeschichte*, see Jan N. Bremmer, "Pseudo-Clementines: Texts, Dates, Places, Authors and Magic," in *The Pseudo-Clementines*, ed. Jan N. Bremmer (Leuven, 2010), pp. 1–23.

the church of San Clemente.[21] A year later Cyril himself died and was also buried in San Clemente.[22]

This is the background story for the *Vita Sancti Clementis* (ca. 880), commissioned by Gauderic, bishop of Velletri, and dedicated to Pope John VIII (872–882). In the preface, Gauderic explains that the *Vita* was begun by the deacon Johannes Hymonides at his request, but that Johannes died as he was approaching the final stages of the work. Gauderic completed the *Vita* and organized it in three books.[23] A manuscript from Montecassino transmits the preface, the first book, and parts of the second,[24] but the third book of Gauderic's work is lost. Gauderic's point of departure for his *Vita Sancti Clementis* was Tyrannius Rufinus's *Recognitiones*, but the narrative was abbreviated and changed from the first person to the third. For the third (now lost) book of the *Vita*, which included the discovery and translation of the relics, Gauderic used as his source a letter from Anastasius Bibliotecarius, containing a translation from Greek into Latin of Cyril's own account of the events.[25]

For the section of Leo of Ostia's work that can be compared to Gauderic's *Vita*, namely the *De origine beati Clementis*, it is clear that Leo based his work directly on Gauderic's *Vita* and reworked it into a more abbreviated version. Leo claims, however, that this first part of his text is a condensed version of Tyrannius Rufinus's *Recognitiones*.[26] Curiously, he does not acknowledge any dependence on or knowledge of

---

[21] For a brief description of San Clemente, the illustrations of the frescos, and the Vatican manuscript containing the *Translatio Sancti Clementis* by Leo of Ostia, see Leonard Boyle, *A Short Guide to St. Clement's, Rome* (Rome, 1989).

[22] See for example, Boyle, "The Fate of the Remains of St Cyril."

[23] Gauderic describes the first book as containing Clement's background, life, conversion, and "the nature of his recognition", i.e. the reunification of Clement with his family through the agency of Peter. The second book was dedicated to doctrinal matters, while the third was an account of miraculous signs, the exile, martyrdom, and miraculous return of Clement to Rome. For Gauderic's preface, see Meyvaert and Devos, "Trois énigmes," pp. 383–85.

[24] The manuscript is Montecassino, Archivio dell'Abbazia, MS 234, dated to the first half of the eleventh century; see Meyvaert and Devos, "Trois énigmes," p. 384.

[25] Anastasius's letter was published for the first time in 1892 by Johann Friedrich, "Ein Brief des Anastasius Bibliothecarius an den Bischof Gaudericus von Velletri, über die Abfassung der Vita cum Translatione s. Clementis Papae," *Bayerische Akademie der Wissenschaften. Philosophisch(-philologisch)-historische Klasse. Sitzungsberichte* 3 (Munich, 1892), pp. 393–442. The letter was later printed in MGH Epp. 7 (Berlin, 1928), pp. 435–38. For further discussions about Anastasius's text and the significance of Clemens in the power struggle of the ninth-century papacy, see Bronwen Neil, "The Cult of Pope Clement in Ninth-Century Rome," *Ephemerides Liturgicae* 117 (2003), 103–13.

[26] This has been clear from 1955 when Meyvaert and Devos compared Leo of Ostia's *De origine* to Gauderic's *Vita* and Rufinus's *Recognitiones*; see Meyvaert and Devos, "Trois énigmes," pp. 421–23. The relationship was made even more clear in Orlandi's synoptic edition of both texts; see Orlandi, *Excerpta ex Clementis recognitionibus*.

Gauderic's work in either the preface to the *De origine* or the prologue to the *De translatione*. This is all the more remarkable, since Leo was bishop of Ostia and Velletri, and Gauderic had been bishop of Velletri a few centuries earlier.[27] In the prologue to the *De translatione* Leo claims as his sources Slavonic writings and a description of the discovery of Clement's body translated from Greek, probably referring to the above mentioned letter from Anastasius Bibliothecarius to Gauderic.[28] While the lost third part of Gauderic's text on the translation cannot be compared with Leo's text, on the basis of Leo's approach observed in *De origine* (i.e. using Gauderic's text without crediting him), it is nonetheless likely that Leo also modeled his *De translatione* on Gauderic's now lost text. Whatever Leo's motives for wanting to "hide" his debt to Gauderic's text, Meyvaert and Devos suggested that Gauderic's *Vita Sancti Clementis* was so little disseminated that Leo could be virtually certain that no one else had access to it.[29]

The afterlife of Leo's *De translatione* is mainly represented through its inclusion, albeit in abbreviated form, in the Dominican archetypal lectionary from ca. 1260.[30] Jacobus de Voragine also included an abbreviated version in his *Legenda aurea* (from the 1260s) with a reference to Leo of Ostia. However, as shown by Leonard Boyle, the text in the *Legenda aurea* is dependent on the Dominican lectionary, and not on Leo's original text.[31] The Icelandic hagiographical text known as the *Clemens saga* from around the end of the twelfth century is apparently based on a combination of the *Recognitiones*, Gauderic's *Vita sancti Clementis*, the *Passio*, and the account of miracles associated with the saint, and not on the work of Leo of Ostia.[32]

The identification of Leo of Ostia as the text's author has a long and convoluted history starting with the edition of the *De translatione sancti Clementis* in 1668 as an anonymous text for the common feast day of Cyril and Methodius (9 March).[33] The scholarly debates concerning the authorship of the *De translatione sancti Clementis*

---

[27] For the combination of the bishoprics of Ostia and Velletri, see Meyvaert and Devos, "Trois énigmes," pp. 414–15.

[28] See the discussion in Meyvaert and Devos, "Trois énigmes," pp. 433–35.

[29] Meyvaert and Devos, "Trois énigmes," p. 427.

[30] Leonard Boyle, "Dominican Lectionaries and Leo of Ostia's *Translatio Sancti Clementis*," *Archivum Fratrum Praedicatorum* 28 (1958), pp. 362–94 (repr. in *San Clemente Miscellany* II, *Art and Archaeology*, ed. Luke Dempsey (Rome, 1978), pp. 195–214, at 204.

[31] Boyle, "Dominican Lectionaries and Leo of Ostia's *Translatio*," p. 207.

[32] Hofmann, *Die Legende von Sankt Clemens*, pp. 102–3. See also Carron, *Clemens saga*, pp. vii–xxv.

[33] "Vita [SS. Cyrilli et Methodii] cum translatione S. Clementis, in *Acta sanctorum Martii tomus secundus, IX Martii* (Paris and Rome, 1865), cols. 19–21. The manuscript used is referred to as MS Francisci Duchesne V.CL. and is according to Meyvaert and Devos the current Paris, Bibliothèque nationale de France, no. 84 de la Collection Duchesne, fols. 166–168. See Meyvaert and Devos, "Trois énigmes," p. 449; and Meyvaert and Devos, "Autour de Léon d'Ostie," pp. 190–96.

(also referred to as *Legenda italica*) have been thoroughly treated by Meyvaert and Devos.[34] Their extraordinary discovery in the Prague Metropolitan Library was significant enough to solve the mystery and put an end to the debate: the manuscript contained the *De translatione sancti Clementis* with a prologue written by Leo of Ostia describing himself and his work (written in three parts), and his motivation for writing it.[35] The manuscript also contained the *De origine beati Clementis*, a text not previously known, completed with a prologue confirming Leo of Ostia's authorship. Moreover, it revealed the existence of a third text, the *De ordinatione seu cathedra S. Clementis*, of which only a fragment of the beginning survives, in a single leaf written in the Italian monastery of Fossanova.[36]

The transmission of Leo of Ostia's three books on St. Clement as we have them today, can be displayed as follows:

Leo of Ostia	*De origine beati Clementis*	*De ordinatione seu cathedra S. Clementis*	*De translatione sancti Clementis* (*Legenda italica*)
MS	Prague, Met. Lib., MS XXIII (1547) (saec. XIV), fols. 132–147	Brussels, Royal Library, MS 8953–8954, fol. 40	Vatican City, BAV, MS Vat. lat. 9668 (saec. XII), fols. 10–11v
MS	Copenhagen, DRA, fragm. 8535; Oslo, NRA, Lat. fragm. 23,3 (saec. XII/XIII)		Paris, BnF, Coll. Duchesne 84 (saec. XVII), fols. 166–68. (André Duchesne's copy of Vat. lat. 9668)
MS			Berlin, Staatsbibl., MS Phillipps 1717 (saec. XVII). (Jacques Sirmond's copy of BAV, Vat. lat. 9668)
MS			Prague, Met. Lib., MS XXIII (1547) (saec. XIV), fols. 147–150.
MS			Oslo, NRA, Lat. fragm. 23,1–2 and 4; Unnumbered Box III [25] (saec. XII/XIII)

Table 1: The Transmission of Leo of Ostia's Clement Trilogy.

---

[34] For a detailed account of the debates concerning the relationship between the Eastern and Western *vitae* of Cyril and Methodius and the significance of the discovery of Anastasius Bibliothecarius's letter to Gauderic, see Meyvaert and Devos, "Trois énigmes," pp. 379–409.

[35] Meyvaert and Devos printed the prologue in full in "Trois énigmes," pp. 412–13.

[36] See Meyvaert and Devos, "Trois énigmes," p. 432; and Meyvaert and Devos, "Autour de Léon d'Ostie," pp. 224–25. The Rubric reads: "Sermo Domni Leonis Ostiensis episcopi De Ordinatione seu Cathedra S. Clementis Papae, quae colitur X. Kal. Febr." (now fol. 40 in Brussels, Royal Library of Belgium, MS 8953–8954).

The Remains of the Danish Clement Volume

As outlined above, the collection of the six fragments from the Clement volume has been a gradual process, with the identification of the Danish fragment 8535, first published here, as the last addition. Not only the scribal connection, but also the size, layout, and other codicological features of the fragments support the conclusion that all pieces come from the same manuscript.

Because of the hand's recognizable aspect and distinctive features, the identification of the scribe does not seem particularly problematic or controversial (compare Fig. 1a and Fig. 1b). Worth noticing with regard to the execution of single graphemes distinguishing the scribe are the letter "g" (see Fig. 1a last line, "signa" and Fig. 1b third line, "digno"), the Tironian note for "et" (see Fig. 1a second last line and Fig. 1b third line), and the shape of the *punctus elevatus* (see second last line in Fig. 1a and second line in Fig. 1b). The scribe writes an easy to read medium formal hand that can be dated to about 1200 on palaeographical grounds. There is biting between round "d" and "o," but biting is not consistently used. The Tironian note for "et" is uncrossed. Small capital "R" occurs relatively frequently.

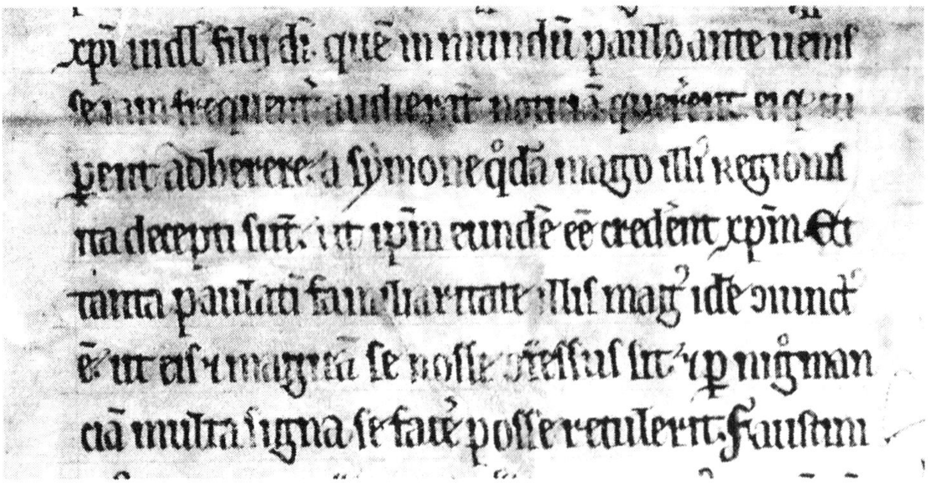

Fig. 1a: The scribe of the Copenhagen fragment (Leo of Ostia's *De origine*, BHL 1851 ab). Copenhagen, The Danish National Archives, fragm. 8535. Photo: Abelone Alstrup.

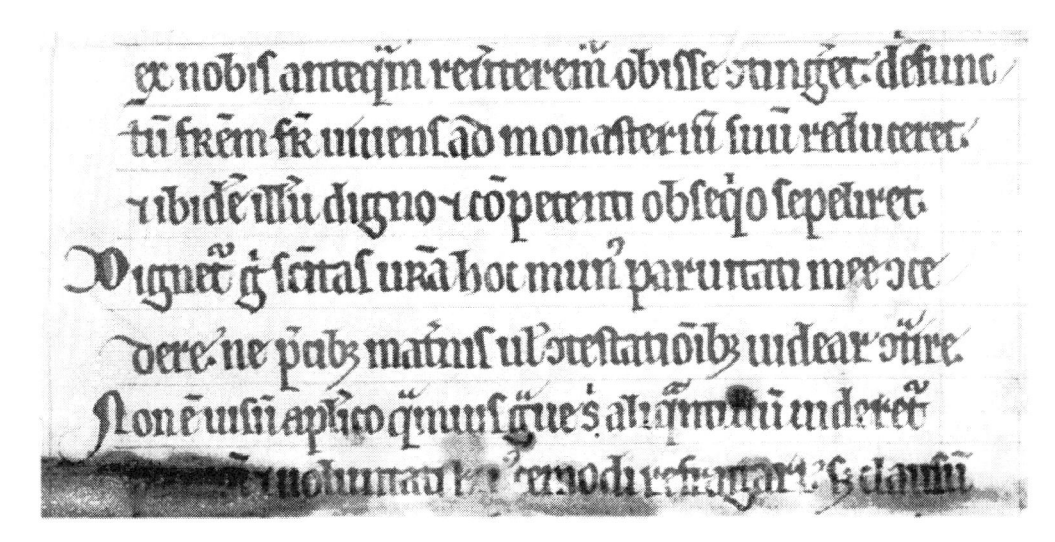

Fig. 1b: The Scribe of the Oslo Fragment (Leo of Ostia's *De translatione*, BHL 2073). Oslo, The National Archives of Norway, Lat. fragm. 23, 1–2. Photo: Åslaug Ommundsen.

Of the three leaves represented by the six identified fragments, only the Copenhagen fragment (DRA, fragm. 8535) is almost complete (see Fig. 2). Since its text is devoted to Clement's life before his pontificate, it is presumably the first of our three leaves. It preserves fragments of Leo of Ostia's *De origine*, chapters 2–13 (out of 87 chapters in Orlandi's organization).[37]

The leaf is ca. 44 x 33 cm, although cropped in the inner margin, and reveals that the original codex must have been a grand manuscript, nearly half a meter in height.[38] The page is laid out in two columns (11–11.5 cm wide) with 41 (or 42) lines per column.[39] The ruling appears as thin grey lines with two vertical lines framing the outer edges of the columns, and three vertical lines in the centre separating them. The initial, a green "C," has purple pen decoration. Smaller capitals are pen drawn in brown ink, and touched with red. The running title in red reads "[Clem]entis pape et martyris."

---

[37] Orlandi, *Excerpta ex Clementinis recognitionibus*, pp. 6–24.

[38] Ottosen provides the measurements 43.7 x 32.7 cm; see https://web.archive.org/web/20190424213614/http://www.liturgy.dk/

[39] Ten lines cover ca. 8.8 cm.

Fig. 2: Top half of an almost complete leaf, still *in situ*, containing parts of Leo of Ostia's *De origine beati Clementis* (BHL 1851 ab). Copenhagen, The Danish National Archives, fragm. 8535. Photo: Abelone Alstrup.

A small fragment from another leaf (Oslo, NRA, Lat. fragm. 23,3) also contains parts of the *De origine*, although mere snippets, corresponding to Orlandi's chapters 60–61 and 70.[40] This Norwegian fragment is much smaller than the Danish one, possibly as a result of further reuse (Fig. 3).[41]

---

[40] Orlandi, *Excerpta ex Clementinis recognitionibus*, pp. 104 and 130.

[41] Multiple reuse of fragments seems to have been common practice in Norway, and the evidence is quite commonly found in the National Archives in Oslo: sometimes parchment was removed from one account book, cut into smaller pieces and used again, as shown by remnants of older inscriptions. The late date of the archival binding in question (1650) could support this hypothesis. For the reuse of fragments, see Ommundsen, "A Norwegian – and European – Jigsaw Puzzle," pp. 152–53.

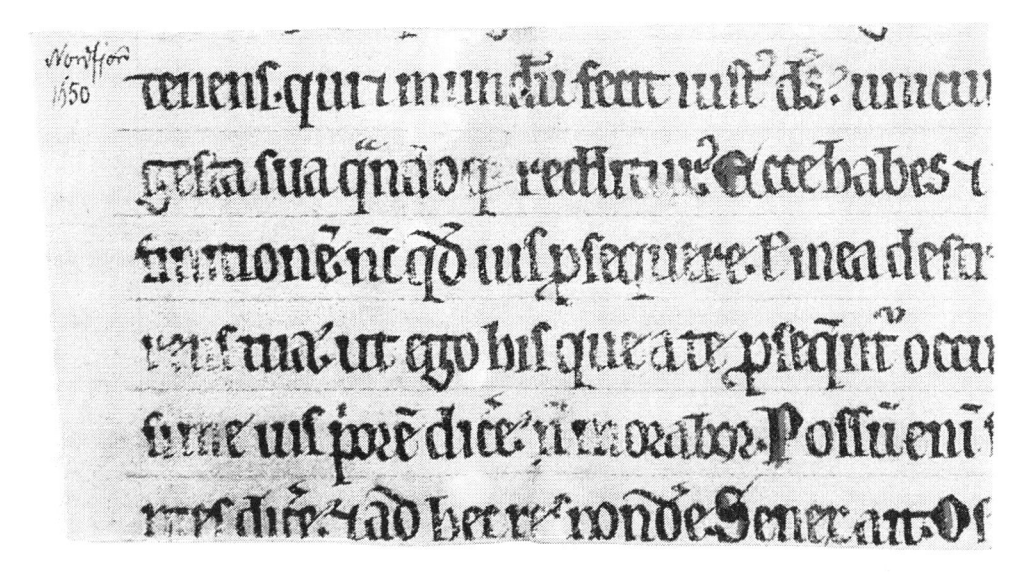

Fig. 3: The single survivor from a leaf containing Leo of Ostia's *De origine* (BHL 1851 ab), removed from an account book from Nordfjord 1650. Oslo, The National Archives of Norway, Lat. fragm. 23,3. Photo: Michael Gullick.

The third and last leaf can be "reconstructed" on the basis of the four remaining fragments (see Fig. 4). One of the remaining fragments contains a rubric, which states: "[Hic expli]cit de inventione corporis beati [Clementis. Incipit] pa[ssio eiusdem]." The rubric is followed by a red initial "T" with purple pen decoration which introduces: "Tercius romane ecclesie prefuit episcopus Clemens," the incipit of the *Passio sancti Clementis papae et martyris* (BHL 1848), a very common narrative.[42]

---

[42] The *Passio* was edited by Boninus Mombritius in his fifteenth-century printed edition and re-edited at Solesmes in 1910; see Bonino Mombritius, *Sanctuarium seu Vitae Sanctorum* I (Paris, 1910–1978), pp. 341–44. A critical edition was prepared in 1913 by Franciscus Xaverius Funk and Franciscus Diekamp in *Patres Apostolici*, 2 vols. (Tübingen, 1913), 2:50–81.

Fig. 4: One partially reconstructed leaf containing Leo of Ostia's *De translatione sancti Clementis* (*Legenda italica*) (BHL 2073) and *Passio sancti Clementis* (BHL 1848). Oslo, The National Archives of Norway, Lat. fragm. 23,1–2 + 4, Unnumbered Box III, [25].
Photo: Åslaug Ommundsen.

The text preceding the *Passio*, referred to as the *De inventione corporis beati [Clementis]*, is Leo of Ostia's *De translatione sancti Clementis* (or *Legenda italica*). The status of the "reconstruction" of the Clement volume in its present state is shown in Table 2.

Inst.	Signature	Number of Fragments	Archival provenance	Content	Signum
DRA	fragm. 8535	1	Copenhagen 1620–28	*De origine beati Clementis* (Leo 2–13*)	–
NRA	Lat. fragm. 23,3	1	Nordfjord 1650	*De origine beati Clementis* (Leo 60*; 70*)	Vita 4
NRA	Lat. fragm. 23,1–2 + 4 and Unnumbered Box III [25]	4	Nordhordlen og Voss 1624	*De translatione sancti Clementis Passio sancti Clementis*	Vita 4 and Lec Br 22
		6			

Table 2: Fragments containing Leo of Ostia's
De origine beati Clementis and *De translatione sancti Clementis*.

The origin of the manuscript should currently be categorized as uncertain. Although the scribe may well be of Scandinavian origin.

Regarding a possible owner of the manuscript, its size points away from a parish church and towards a larger institution. The Danish fragment also shows that the codex was probably not used as an office lectionary, since there are no rubrics for lessons. However, it could have been used for chapter readings or readings during mealtimes. Unfortunately, none of the preserved fragments contains foliation or pagination, so it is difficult to say how many leaves the Clement material would have filled, or how thick the volume might have been. As mentioned above, the first and third part of Leo of Ostia's text covered about 19 leaves in the fourteenth-century Prague manuscript.[43] The large leaves of the Danish volume hold more text than the leaves in the Prague manuscript, so in this volume the present section of Leo's trilogy would have filled even fewer leaves.[44] It seems unlikely that a large volume like this would have been filled only with Clement material. In comparison, the Prague manuscript contains a number of texts, the most extensive of which is Conrad of Hirsau's

---

[43] See above, p. 232 and n. 16.

[44] The one Danish leaf holds text which in the Prague manuscripts starts halfway down fol. 133r and ends on fol. 135r.

Speculum virginum (fols. 1–127),[45] two homilies, a text on the translation of St. Stephen, a text on the image of the Virgin Mary, and sermons on St. Stephen.[46] The large Danish volume could have been a similar collection of texts of particular interest to a person or an institution, or it could have been a hagiographical volume with Clement holding a special place. If the other parts of the codex were written by the same scribe, it should in time be possible to identify more fragments in the Danish National Archives and obtain more answers.

The *De origine beati Clementis* (BHL 1851 ab)

The Copenhagen fragment (DRA, fragm. 8535) tells the story of Clement's mother Mathidia: she is incessantly pursued "romantically" by her husband's brother and, to get away, departs from Rome with her two eldest sons on a sea voyage to Athens, leaving the five year old Clement at home with his father. After a shipwreck, Mathidia is washed up on a rock near the island of Rhodes.[47] The two boys, Faustinus and Faustus, are rescued from the waves by pirates and sold to an honest woman who ensures that they get an education in Greek philosophy. After a time, the father, Faustinianus, hearing nothing about his wife and sons, goes out searching, leaving Clement, now twelve, in Rome. After almost twenty years of searching, Faustinianus falls into utmost poverty, and settles as a farmer in Laodicia. Meanwhile, Clement is leading a chaste life in Rome, engaged in the study of deep philosophical and theological questions. In the schools of the philosophers, however, he finds only empty rhetoric.

On the following pages (going beyond fragm. 8535) Clement goes to Palestine and is introduced to Peter, among whose followers are Clement's two brothers, renamed Niceta and Aquila. Upon learning of the sad fate of Clement's family, Peter talks to a woman outside a temple and after hearing her story recognizes her as Mathidia, Clement's mother. Some very moving chapters follow: Peter takes Mathidia to meet her son Clement, who is first quite confused about the emotional embraces of the strange woman, but all is revealed. Afterwards they meet Niceta and Aquila, and Clement explains: "Mater mea est, quam redonavit michi Deus per dominum meum Petrum" – "That is my mother, who God gave back to me through my master Peter." Now Peter tells the whole story from the beginning, and all becomes clear to Niceta and Aquila: "Si hec – inquiunt –, doctor amabilis, vera sunt, nos procul dubio sumus infelices illi gemini fratres Faustus et Faustinus" – "If these things are true, beloved

---

[45] Snippets from the *Speculum virginum* are also preserved in a fragment in the National Archives of Norway (NRA, Lat. fragm. 31) from about the same date as the fragments treated here, but in a different hand.

[46] See Meyvaert and Devos, "Trois énigmes," pp. 410–11.

[47] For the name of the island, see below, p. 244.

teacher, we are beyond a doubt the unfortunate twin brothers Faustus and Faustinus." The brothers then reveal their identity to Mathidia through tears and kisses, and we hear the story – yet again – from their point of view. The following day Mathidia is baptized in the sea, and there is a natural ending of the narrative. At this point, the same story has been presented from all perspectives: a "neutral" narrative followed by the story of Clement, then of Mathidia, then Peter's retelling of the same events, and finally the account given by Niceta and Aquila.

In chapter 56, Peter, Clement, Niceta, and Aquila go down to the beach where they meet an elderly pauper, with whom they have a long philosophical dispute about (among other things) the governing force of the universe (a part of which is found in Oslo, NRA, Lat. fragm. 23,3). For three days the men debate about God's providence, the creation, and scientific matters. In defence of astrology (or predestination, *genesis*), the old man uses his wife as an example. From the arguments that follow, Clement understands that the old man is his father and starts crying. When the father recognizes his three sons, new scenes of embraces, tears, and emotion follow. Now Peter begins recounting the story yet again to all present, with its different elements. The father is, of course, converted and baptized, and Peter can go back to Rome to continue his mission. The story ends here.

The general outline of the text preserved in the Danish fragment corresponds relatively well with Leo's *De origine* as transmitted in the Prague manuscript, although with a number of variants. In the limited amount of text seen in the fragment, there are more than seventy discrepancies between it and the Prague text. In some cases, the differences merely concern word order such as: "inter dilectos fratres discordiam" in the Danish fragment vs. "discordiam inter fratres dilectos" in the Prague manuscript (see Appendix, Leo 2). In several other cases, however, the fragment offers a better reading. For example, when the text describes Mathidia's meeting with female "comforters," the Danish fragment provides two superior readings in one sentence. Where the Prague manuscript reads "Viri nobilis ac pii pectoris femina," the fragment gives: "Verum nobilis ac pii pectoris femina," with "verum," unlike "viri," being a natural opening of the sentence (see Appendix, Leo 4). In addition, "gratia compassionis" (which also agrees with Gauderic) makes better sense than "gratia passionis" in the Prague text (see Appendix, Leo 4). Thus, the text from the Danish fragment would translate: "*But* the woman of noble and pious disposition did not merely abstain from considering the suffering of others for her own consolation, but was, rather, saddened out of *compassion*."

Another example is seen in the scene where Faustinianus goes to the harbour to ask if anyone has seen or heard anything regarding his wife and sons – the Prague manuscript merely reads "aut vidisset," conjectured by Orlandi to read "audisset aut vidisset." The Danish fragment reads "aut vidisset aut audisset," which is probably the authorial reading (see Appendix, Leo 9).

In some cases, however, the Prague manuscript offers a better reading. One example concerns the island where Mathidia is washed up, which in the Danish fragment is called "Rodus," indicating modern Rhodes. In the Prague text, in contrast, the island is referred to as "Anterodum." Since the island is described as being located "inter Tripolim Fenicis urbem et Laodiciam," with Tripoli being in modern Lebanon and Latakia in modern Syria, this probably refers to the island of Aradus (modern Arwad, Syria). "Anteradus," strictly speaking, refers to the town facing the Aradus island (modern Tartus, Syria), but a certain confusion regarding the use of Aradus and Anteradus is also found elsewhere in the Clement tradition.[48]

The *De translatione corporis sancti Clementis* (*Legenda italica*) (BHL 2073)

The four Norwegian fragments forming one fragmentary leaf (see Fig. 4) fortunately show the transition from one Clement text to another, clarifying at least something of the character of this particular codex. The first part of the recto contains the discovery of Clement's martyred body by Cyril and Methodius (corresponding to lessons 10–12 as numbered in the *Acta sanctorum* and in Meyvaert and Devos).[49] It ends with the rubric: "[Hic expli]cit de inventione corporis beati [Clementis. Incipit] pa[ssio eiusdem]."

The narrative is situated in the time of Emperor Michael of Byzantium (856–867), when there was a man in Thessaloniki named Constantinus, called Philosophus for his wisdom. While in a town called Cersona (on the Crimean Peninsula), where Clement spent the last days of his life, the Philosophus heard that the saint's final resting place had fallen victim to the waves through time and neglect. Putting his faith in God's guidance, the Philosophus convinced the bishop, some clergy, and other followers to sail out in search of Clement's body. They reached an island surrounded by a splendid light, and recovered what was left of the saint, along with the anchor with which he had been drowned. With song and praise they brought the saint's relics back to Cersona and laid them to rest in the church of St. Leontius.

When the prince of Moravia needed help to instruct his people in the true faith, the emperor sent the Philosophus to the Slavic people along with his brother Methodius. After four and a half years the brothers were invited to Rome by Pope Nicholas, who died soon afterwards. When his successor Hadrian heard that the brothers were carrying the relics of St. Clement, he went out to meet them. At this time, the relics were performing miracles, and to ensure that they would continue to shine, not only on the

---

[48] For the confusion regarding the use of Aradus and Antaradus, see Daron Burrows, *The Life of Saint Clement: A Translation of La Vie de seint Clement* (Tempe, 2016), p. 63. I thank the anonymous reviewer of the journal for drawing my attention to the issue of the name of the island.

[49] *Acta sanctorum, Martii tomus secundus*, cols. 19–21; and Meyvaert and Devos, "Trois énigmes," pp. 455–61.

holy city, but also on the world, the pope made Methodius bishop and the followers of the brothers deacons and priests. When the Philosophus – or Constantinus – felt that the end of his life was approaching, he took the name "Cyrillus." The text of the Oslo fragments starts at this point (see Fig. 4), with Cyril's funeral, when the Greek as well as the Roman clergy gather with psalms and songs, candles and incense, giving him the same honour in death as they would a pope. Methodius wanted to bring Cyril's body home, but the Roman clergy and people prevailed to have him buried in Rome, in St. Peter's basilica. He was, however, upon Methodius's request, laid to rest in San Clemente.

Since the transition between the *De origine* and the *De translatione*, the first and third book in Leo's trilogy, is lost, we do not know whether the second book mentioned in Leo's prologue, the *De ordinatione*, originally preceded the *De translatione* in the Danish manuscript.

The *Passio sancti Clementis* (BHL 1848)

After the rubric and decorated initials on the Norwegian fragmentary leaf, the text which is perhaps the most common or widely known legend of Clement, starts, opening with his rise to the papal see (see also Fig. 4):[50]

> Tercius Romane ecclesie prefuit episcopus Clemens qui <disciplinam apostoli Pe>tri secutus: ita morum orna<mentis pollebat, ut et> Iudeis, et gentilibus et omnibus Christian<is populis placeret>.

> Clement was the third bishop of the Roman Church, who followed the teachings of Peter. He exercised his powers with such dignity that he pleased Jews and pagans as well as all Christians.

It is doubtful that Clement was actually martyred, but the popularity of the fourth-century legend firmly established his status as a martyr saint. The fragmentary Norwegian leaf contains the *Passio* from the beginning to about the halfway point, with lacunae. It starts with the description of Sisinius who follows his wife Theodora to church, where Clement is celebrating mass, to find out what she is doing there. During the service, which he witnesses in secret, he becomes both blind and deaf. After his servants help him home in his helpless state, Theodora begs Clement to help her husband, and through his prayers Sisinius is cured. Following this miracle both Sisinius and several other noblemen are converted to Christianity. Out of jealousy a riot is arranged for which the Christian faith in general and Clement in particular are blamed. The prefect of Rome orders that Clement should be sent into exile to a desert by the town of Cersona.

---

[50] Oslo, NRA, Lat. fragm. 23,1–2 + 4, Unnumbered Box III, [25].

When the ship arrives at Cersona, Clement finds two thousand Christians condemned to a life in a quarry with no water. He prays to God for a spring, and then sees a lamb scraping the ground with its foot. He understands that the lamb is Jesus Christ showing him the right place and, as he hits the ground in that very spot, water springs from it. After this miracle the people from the area are all converted and baptized, and within one year seventy five churches are erected and all the temples and idols are crushed. These events do not go unnoticed in Rome, and Clement is severely punished: an anchor is tied to his neck and he is thrown into the sea and martyred. After much lamenting and prayers from his followers, the ocean recedes, and they can walk on dry ground to a resting place prepared by God in the shape of a marble temple. There lies Clement's body, and next to him the anchor. It was then revealed to his followers that every year on the day of his passion the ocean would part for seven days to offer a dry path for the visitors, which happens "until this day."

The *Passio* was probably followed by an account of the miracles associated with Clement (also edited by Mombritius),[51] especially since this volume seems to have given much room to Clement narratives.

Conclusion

As mentioned at the beginning of this article, Dietrich Hofmann was puzzled to find no surviving Latin sources containing Clement's legend from medieval Denmark.[52] Now it seems that we are able to provide at least one: a large volume containing Leo of Ostia's *De origine beati Clementis* and *De translatione sancti Clementis* followed by the far more common *Passio sancti Clementis*. The fragments discussed here represent the second manuscript witness to Leo's *De origine* (although fragmentary) and the third medieval manuscript witness to his *De translatione* (even more fragmentary). As far as I can tell, it is the first manuscript where it is known that Leo of Ostia's work is placed immediately before the *Passio sancti Clementis*, although it may not have been uncommon that reworkings of the *Recognitiones* were placed alongside the *Passio*, as the Old Norse *Clemens saga* indicates.

We may assume that miracle narratives were present in the volume, but the other content is impossible to outline at present. Where the book was made or used is unknown, although its size indicates a cathedral or larger institution rather than a parish church. It is likely that the manuscript's medieval provenance was Denmark rather than Norway. The Norwegian fragments were in this particular case probably brought from Copenhagen to Bergen as post-medieval binding material.

---

[51] See above, n. 42.

[52] Hofmann, *Die Legende von Sankt Clemens*, p. 55.

The thousands of Scandinavian manuscript fragments are valuable, but not easily accessible source material, as medieval and post medieval use and reuse of parchment has left a confusing jigsaw puzzle. An additional challenge is posed by the fact that the fragments "produced" by the Danish administration are today spread over multiple collections, of which the Norwegian and the Danish National Archives are the most significant. There may very well be other fragments from this manuscript yet undiscovered, most likely in Copenhagen.

The reason or reasons contributing to the assembly of the Clement volume in about 1200 cannot yet be determined, but fortuitously some of it has survived after the unfortunate encounter with the knives of Danish royal officials.

ABSTRACT

Among the manuscript fragments in the Norwegian and Danish National Archives in Oslo and Copenhagen, six fragments have been identified from a large manuscript from about 1200 containing texts on St. Clement. These fragments constitute rare medieval witnesses to the work on St. Clement written by Leo of Ostia at the beginning of the twelfth century, transmitting parts of the first and third book: *De origine beati Clementis* (BHL 1851ab) and *De translatione sancti Clementis* (also known as *Legenda italica*) (BHL 2073). Although five fragments are found in Oslo and one in Copenhagen, the manuscript was probably dismembered in Copenhagen in the early seventeenth century, making a Danish medieval ownership more likely than a Norwegian one in this particular case.

St. Clement played a significant role in Denmark and the rest of Scandinavia, and the lack of surviving Latin texts on Clement has previously been puzzling to scholars. Not only do these fragments testify to the dissemination of Leo of Ostia's work to the northernmost parts of Europe, they also in several cases offer a better transmission of the author's texts than the manuscripts known up to now. A transcription of the transmitted texts is presented in an Appendix.

RÉSUMÉ

Parmi les fragments de manuscrits des Archives nationales d'Oslo et de Copenhague, six fragments ont été identifiés comme provenant d'un manuscrit de grande taille, datant d'environ l'an 1200 et contenant des textes sur saint Clément. Ces fragments constituent de rares témoins médiévaux de l'œuvre sur saint Clément rédigée par Léon d'Ostie au commencement du XIIe siècle et ils transmettent des sections du premier et du troisième livre de cette œuvre: *De origine beati Clementis* (BHL 1851ab) et *De translatione sancti Clementis* (aussi connue sous le titre de la *Legenda italica*) (BHL 2073). Bien que cinq fragments puissent être trouvés à Oslo et un seul à Copenhague, le manuscrit d'origine a probablement été démembré à Copenhague au début du XVIIe siècle. Ceci rend plus plausible la possibilité que ce manuscrit soit d'appartenance danoise plutôt que norvégienne.

Saint Clément a joué un rôle important au Danemark ainsi que dans le reste de la Scandinavie. Pourtant, on y a retrouvé peu de textes latins sur Clément au grand étonnement des chercheurs. Ces fragments témoignent non seulement de la dissémination de l'œuvre de Léon d'Ostie jusqu'aux régions les plus septentrionales d'Europe, elles offrent de surcroît dans plusieurs cas une meilleure transmission des textes de l'œuvre que les manuscrits connus des chercheurs jusqu'à aujourd'hui. Une transcription des textes transmis est présentée dans l'appendice.

Åslaug Ommundsen
University of Bergen
aslaug.ommundsen@uib.no

Appendix

Transcriptions of the Fragments

Following the practice of the other publications of Leo of Ostia's works, I will also supply a transcription of the text material found in Copenhagen, DRA, fragm. 8535 and Oslo, NRA, Lat. fragm. 23,3 (*De origine beati Clementis*, BHL 1851ab) as well as Oslo, NRA, Lat. fragm. 23,1–3 + 4 and Unnumbered Box III [25], 1 (*De translatione sancti Clementis*, BHL 2073). The transcriptions are made on the basis of reproductions, which means that some letters hidden in folds or creases that one might perhaps be able to make out *in situ* are left missing. I have not supplied a translation but merely a gist of the content before each transcription.

For the *De origine* I have compared the text in the Danish/Norwegian fragments with the Prague manuscript (**P**) in the form of Orlandi's edition from 1968. I have also inserted the chapter divisions in brackets. For the *De translatione* I have compared the text preserved in the Norwegian fragments with the *Acta sanctorum* and Meyvaert and Devos, "Trois énigmes," and have used this edition to indicate missing words. I have followed the orthography of the fragments, with minor differences in orthography between the text and the editions not indicated (for example variation between the use of "ti" and "ci.") The abbreviations are expanded silently. Words or letters supplied (mainly from other sources) are placed in angle brackets <...>. If sections of text larger than a few lines are missing, they are not filled in, but left as *lacunae*. *Lacunae* are indicated through points inside square brackets [...]. The punctuation found in the fragments has been followed in most cases, although both medial pause *punctus* and *punctus elevatus* are transcribed using modern commas. Proper names are capitalized.

I. *The* De origine beati Clementis (*BHL 1851 ab*)

1. *Copenhagen, DRA, fragm. 8535*

The brother in law makes his romantic advances in vain, and Mathidia leaves for Athens with her two older sons. The five-year-old Clement remains in Rome with his father, Faustinianus. After the ship suffers a shipwreck, Mathidia is helped by locals, while her two sons are sold by pirates. Faustinianus goes searching for his wife and sons. Clement is losing hope that his parents will return and ponders philosophical questions. For the text and the passages printed in angle brackets, compare Orlandi, *Excerpta ex Clementis Recognitionibus*, pp. 6–24 (Leo, chapters 2–13).

[**DRA, fragm. 8535ra**] (**Leo 2**) [...]cia motus, cepit eam nunc blandimentis, nunc pollicitationibus ad nefandissimi amoris illecebras prouocare, et ut sibi in opere nefario consensum preberet uehementer ac frequenter instare. Verum matrona nobilis appellationes impudicas pudice mentis intentione contempnens, tantique sceleris negocium, ne uidelicet inter dilectos fratres discordiam generare uideretur coniugi reuelare pauescens, quid super hoc ageret quoue se uerteret, intra semetipsam diutissime queritabat. Sompnium tandem huiusmodi se uidisse coniugi simulat, quod sibi a quodam numine denunciatum dicebat, ut nisi mox cum duobus geminis filiis ciuitatem exiens, extra prouinciam quoad ipsi placuisset numini exularet, ipsa pariter cum tribus liberis maturato discrimine sine aliqua dubitatione periret. Quo Faustinianus qui tenere filios diligebat audito, et uerbis uxoris nimium credulus merens extimuit, ac protinus deliberato consilio, et Clemente solo quinquenne sibi retento, Faustinum et Faustum geminos fratres coniugi tradidit, seruos quoque et ancillas ei cum sufficientia deputans, Athenas illam ubi filios Grecorum studiis erudiret, nauigare permisit.

(**Leo 3**) Mathidia igitur pudicicia comite cum suis omnibus nauim conscendens, totius tandem fines reliquit Italie. Cumque per uastum pelagus Athenas tendens, ad Rodum insulam que inter Tripolim Fenicis urbem et Laodiciam sita est, nocturno nauigio pertransiret <uiolencia subite tempestatis dirum et ualde miserandum occulto Dei iudicio naufragium pertulit, quo, et filiis et facultatibus uniuersis> amissis, ipsa multis ac ualidis iactata fluctibus, in saxum quoddam sola proiecta est. Vbi cum tota nocte lugens ac nuda nobilis femina resideret, ea dumtaxat spe qua dulcia sibi natorum corpora posse repperire se confidebat, precipitare se distulit in profundum.

(**Leo 4**) At ubi dies illuxit, turbe incolarum hinc inde conueniunt, uestem illi ad tegendum proiciunt, sicque merentem ac lamentantem feminam ad litus perducunt. Illa uero clamoribus et eiulatibus indesinentibus dolori proprio satisfaciens, manuumque suarum pulchritudinem diris morsibus lanians, cepit contigua maris ora lustrare, si forte alicubi posset proiecta natorum corpora

---

1–2 blandimentis ... pollicitiationibus] pollicitiationibus ... blandimentis P ‖ **2** et] *om.* P, *suppl.* Orlandi ‖ **5** dilectos fratres] fratres dilectos P ‖ **6** coniugi] hoc *add.* P, *del.* Orlandi ‖ **7** quoue] quo P ‖ **8** quod] quo *scripsit* Orlandi ‖ **9** mox cum duobus] cum duobus mox P; ciuitatem] ciuitate *scripsit* Orlandi ‖ **10** quoad] quoadusque P ‖ **13** quinquenne] quinquennium agente P ‖ **15** sufficientia] sufficienti pecunia P ‖ **18** Italie] Ytalie P ‖ **19** Athenas tendens] tendens Anterodum P ‖ **24** dulcia sibi natorum] dulcium natorum sibi P ‖ **27** illi] sibi P ‖ **28** indesinentibus] *om.* P ‖ **30–31** corpora suorum] suorum corpora P

suorum prouidere. Plerosque etiam incolarum tanta miseratione commouit ut per diuersa littora ad geminorum [**DRA, fragm. 8535rb**] <corpora requirenda curiosissime partirentur. Sed cum nullius eorum aliquod posset> repperiri uestigium, mulieres indigene Mathidiam consolari ceperunt, referentes singule suas quasque miserias, quatinus ex calamitatum similitudine orbata liberis quodlibet infortunii sui solatium capere potuisset. Verum nobilis ac pii pectoris femina aliarum erumpnas non solum sua solatia non reputabat, sed gratia compassionis potius contristabat. Quam cum nonnulle nobiles matrone certatim ad sua hospicia inuitarent, illa uero pre nimia orbitatis tristicia totius gaudii, totiusque se consolationis exortem manere decerneret, una tandem quedam paupercula inibi mansitans uix extorsit ab ea ut tuguriolo suo succederet asserens fuisse sibi uirum nautam, eumque adolescentem marino perisse naufragio, atque cum multi ex illis se in matrimonium sumere cuperent, amore uiri castitatem potius delegisse. Cum hac igitur Mathidia labore manuum suarum uictum queritans, eo libentius habitauit, quo fidelius eam defuncto coniugi fidem seruasse cognouit.

(**Leo 5**) Cum non multo post illa que Mathidiam susceperat paralitico languore correpta est, Mathidie quoque manus quas quondam pro geminorum naufragio morsibus laniauerat, penitus dissolui ceperunt. Quibus operari solito non ualentibus, et mulierum que primo Mathidie compasse fuerant affectibus refrigentibus, compulsa est nobilissimi generis femina in eadem Rodo insula pro templi foribus residere, stipemque ab ingredientibus mendicando exigere, atque ex ipsa cum predicta paralitica per uiginti circiter annorum curriculam pariter uiuere, ne<minem prorsus filiorum commune naufragium euasisse existimans.

(**Leo 6**) Qui uidelicet, eiusdem naufragii> tempore diuina prouisione seruante cum innitentes fragmento cuiusdam tabule per incertos procellarum uertices iactarentur, pirate quidam repertos illos in suam nauiculam sustulerunt, fortique remigio undarum cumulos superantes, Cesaream stratonis urbem Palestine maxime perduxerunt. Ibi eos terroribus nimiis affligentes, ne

---

31 prouidere] peruidere *scripsit Orlandi*; tanta] tota **P** ‖ **36** liberis] mulier *add.* **P**; uerum] uiri **P** ‖ **38** compassionis] passionis **P** ‖ **39** inuitarent] *scripsit Orlandi*, inuitarunt **P**; pre nimia] *scripsit Orlandi*, pmia **P** ‖ **42** eumque] eundemque **P** ‖ **43** illis] eo **P** ‖ **44** castitatem potius] pocius castitatem **P** ‖ **45** libentius] lubentius **P** ‖ **47** illa] *scripsit Orlandi*, illa illa **P** ‖ **51** refrigentibus] refugentibus **P**; nobilissimi] nobilis **P**; Rodo insula] insula Antherodo **P** ‖ **52** pro] pre **P**; foribus] cottidie *add.* **P**; ingredientibus] introeuntibus **P** ‖ **57** per] in *add.* **P**, *del. Orlandi* ‖ **58** suam] eos *add.* **P**, *del. Orlandi* ‖ **60** maxime] maximam **P**

uel genus uel patriam proderent, conuersis nominibus eorum, Faustinum quidem Nicetam, Faustum uero Aquilam nuncupauerunt, demum uero iudee cuidam ad modum honeste femine Iuste nomine uendiderunt. Hec illos filiorum uice complexa, quoniam prudentis ualde et docilis ingenii cernebantur, Grecis eos litteris et liberalibus studiis tradidit informandos. Qui, cum adoleuissent ceperunt in philosophorum etiam studiis operam propensius dare, quo pos [**DRA fragm. 8535va**] sent <religionis diuine> dogmata philosophicis disputationibus ac rationibus repperire.

(**Leo 7**) Ergo dum ueri prophete Christi uidelicet filii Dei, quem in mundum paulo ante uenisse iam frequenter audierant noticiam quererent eique cuperent adherere, a Symone quodam mago illius regionis ita decepti sunt, ut ipsum eundem esse crederent Christum. Et tanta paulatim familiaritate illis magus idem coniunctus est, ut eis et magicam se nosse confessus sit, et per nigromanciam multa signa se facere posse retulerit.

(**Leo 8**) Faustinianus interea postquam, ut supra diximus, coniugem cum filiis Athenas direxerat, mox ut unius anni circulus transiit, homines suos illuc sumptusque necessarios uisitationis gratia affatim destinauit, addiscere paterna sollicitudine cupiens, quid erga filios, quid erga coniugem ageretur. Quorum cum ne minimum quidem quemlibet recepisset tercio rursum anno alios illuc simili tenore transmisit. Qui uidelicet post aliquantum temporis remeantes, retulerunt neque matrem se neque filios uspiam repperisse, sed neque Athenas eos aliquando peruenisse, neque usquam se alicuius eorum qui cum ipsis fuerant uestigium aliquo modo inuenire potuisse.

(**Leo 9**) His Faustinianus auditis merens ualde et quod erat in re uerissime suspicans una cum Clemente descendit ad portum, et sollicite requirere cepit a diuersarum gentium nautis sicubi aliquis eorum aut uidisset aut audisset ante illos quatuor annos corpus mulieris duorumque paruulorum proiec<tum>. Vnde cum multi multa referrent, non inde aliquid certi indicii elucesceret, pascebatur quidem <miser uanis spebus, a luctibus tamen nullomodo temperare ualebat, uxoris ac filiorum nomina inter ipsas lacrimas indesinenter inclamitans.

62–63 uero iudee cuidam ad modum] uero cuidam **P** ‖ **64** docilis] docibilis **P** ‖ **67** quo] *scripsit Orlandi*, quod **P**; religionis diuine] *scripsit Orlandi*, in religionis diuine **P** ‖ **69** ueri] dum **P** ‖ **72** esse] *om.* **P** ‖ **73** magicam] magiam **P** ‖ **74** signa] *om.* **P** ‖ **76** mox ut unius anni circulus transiit] cum filiis transmisit **P**; suos illuc] illuc suos **P** ‖ **79** minimum] nuncium **P**; rursum] rursus **P** ‖ **81** retulerunt] *om.* **P** ‖ **82** se alicuius] alicuius saltem **P** ‖ **83** inuenire potuisse] potuisse dixerunt **P** ‖ **86** aut uidisset aut audisset] audisset aut uidisset *scripsit Orlandi*, aut uidisset **P** ‖ **88** non inde aliquid] nec aliquid tamen **P**

(**Leo 10**) Quem supradictus frater suus tam atro>citer angustiari conspiciens, uir super omnes nequissimus seorsum illum assumens, cepit quasi ad consolationem ipsius asserere, quod Mathidia quam isdem pudicissimam eatenus estimaret, se primo turpiter adamasset, sed dum ipse prorsus abnuisset fraternum thorum maculam incestus polluere illam cum seruis fornicationis sue incentiua nequiter expleuisse, ac maritum proinde metuens et turpitudinis sue infamiam muliebri dicacitate preueniens sompnium tale finxisse, quo uideretur et uirum honeste relinquere, et suis amoribus tota decetero securitate seruire. Que si uel Athenas ut iussa fuerat expetisset, uel naufragium quod putabatur aliquod pertulisset, tam longo tempore celari mi [**DRA, fragm. 8535vb**] nime potuisset.

(**Leo 11**) His Faustinianus auditis, affectum erga se germani esse sincerissimum credens, licet ab amore coniugis tanquam reuera adultere deceptus a fratre des[...]ceret, de filiorum tamen amissione quos cum ea direxerat omnino consolari non poterat. Communicato itaque cum amicis consilio uisum est ei ut Clementem iam duodennem sub curatoribus ordinatum Rome relinqueret, et ipse quaquauersum ad Faustinum et Faustum geminos filios pergeret requirendos. Ita descendens ad portum, et nauim multis onustam diuiciis flendo conscendens, fatis inanibus fidens profectus est, ac per uiginti ferme annos, urbes, castella, uicos, littora, portus, promunctoria, insulasque diuersas circuiens post dampna rerum, et desperationem ultimam filiorum in tantam tandem perductus est paupertatem, ut prorsus erubescens ad sua reuerti, penes Laodiciam alienas terras fodiendo ac si agricola rusticanus excoleret, et labore manuum suarum diurni sibi stipendia uictus acquireret, non modo filios quos cum matre transmiserat nusquam repperiens, uerum etiam neque si Clemens, quem Rome reliquerat, uiueret nosse certius preualens.

(**Leo 12**) Clemens igitur super parentum reuersione a quibus uidelicet per tot annos, neque litteras aliquas neque nuntium qualemcumque receperat, funditus desperatus, inuiolabilis pudicitie studium quod a primeuo conceperat totis uisibus conseruare certabat. Sed cum eum animi sui intentio uelut

---

95 eatenus] actenus **P**; ipse] *om.* **P** ‖ **96** incestus] incesti **P**; cum] suis *add.* **P** ‖ **97** ac] at **P**; proinde] perinde **P** ‖ **98** infamiam] famam **P** ‖ **99** et¹] *om.* **P**; amoribus] amatoribus **P** ‖ **101** quod] ut **P** ‖ **103** auditis] et *add.* **P**; esse] tunc **P** ‖ **105** des[...]ceret] desisteret **P** ‖ **108** quaquauersum] quaquauersus *scripsit Orlandi*, quamquamuersus **P**; geminos] suos *add.* **P** ‖ **110** fatis] fratris **P** ‖ **114** fodiendo] *om.* **P** ‖ **120** desperatus] desperans **P**; conceperat] ceperat **P** ‖ **121** totis] *om.* **P**; uisibus] **P**, uiribus *scripsit Orlandi*

uinculis quibusdam <multe sollicitudinis a puero innexum teneret, illud incessanter curioso uersabat in pectore, utrum foret sibi aliqua uita post mortem, an nichilum omnino postmodum foret futurus; et utrum fuerit an non antequam nasceretur, uel si erit aliqua uite huius post obitum recordatio; illud quoque, quando factus sit mundus, uel antequam fieret quid esset an uero semper> fuerit. Certum etenim uidebatur quod si esset factus, esset procul dubio resoluendus, et si fuerit resolutus quid iterum erit, nisi forte obliuio et silentium omnia teget, aut forte aliquid aliud erit quod nunc mortalium sentire sensus non possit.

(**Leo 13**) Ista et horum similia sollerti animo Clemens reuoluens nimietate tedii tabescebat, et si quando a se huiusmodi curas reicere, ac si minus utile cogitabat, ualidiores nichilominus in eum fluctus sollicitudinum insurgebant. Cum a primeua igitur etate in huiusmodi curis seu intencionibus estuaret, cupiens certe super immortalitate aliquid certitudinis capere, philosophorum frequentab[...] [**End of text in Copenhagen, DRA, fragm. 8535.**]

2. *Oslo, NRA, Lat. fragm. 23,3*

Clement and his brothers debate with the old man (the father) for three days, covering various topics. For the text and the passages printed in angle brackets, compare Orlandi, *Excerpta ex Clementis Recognitionibus*, pp. 104–30 (Leo, chapters 60–70).

[**NRA, Lat. fragm. 23,3 recto**] (**Leo 60**) tenens, qui et mundum fecit iustus Deus, unicui<que secundum> gesta sua quandoque redditurus. Ecce habes et <nostram de>finitionem, nunc quod uis prosequere, uel mea destr<uens uel asse>rens tua, ut ego his que a te prosequantur occu<rram. Aut> si me uis priorem dicere, non morabor. Possum enim <tuas pa>rtes dicere, et ad hec respondere. [**Leo 61**] Senex ait. Os[...]

[**NRA, Lat. fragm. 23,3 verso**] (**Leo 70**) egresse terminos, finitime gentis uiris miscen<tur solem>pnitatem quandam ex hoc obseruantes, ex quibus <cum conceperint redeunt> et si quidem mares peperer<int> abiiciunt, feminas <uero nutriunt>. Cumque unius temporis sit omnium partus, absur<dum est, ut in> maribus quidem putetur Mars cum Saturno in <tempore equis> esse portionibus, in feminarum uero genesi numquam. [**End of text in Oslo, NRA Lat. fragm. 23,3.**]

129 omnia] semper P ‖ **129–130** sentire sensus] sensus sentire P

5 possum] possumus P ‖ **7** gentis] *scripsit* Orlandi, *om.* P ‖ **8** miscentur] commiscentur P ‖ **9** pepererint] *scripsit* Orlandi, peperint P ‖ **12** uero] *om.* P

II. *The* De inventione corporis beati Clementis (*BHL* 2073)

1. *Oslo, NRA, Lat. fragm. 23,1–2 + 4 + Unnumbered Box III, [25]*

After Cyril's funeral, his brother Methodius asks the pope for permission to bring his body back to Greece in accordance with his mother's wish. The Roman clergy objects, and eventually they all agree that Cyril should be placed in San Clemente. For the text and the passages printed in angle brackets, compare *Acta sanctorum, Martii tomus secundus*, col. 21 (lect. 10–12); or Meyvaert and Devos, "Trois énigmes," pp. 460–61, where the Prague manuscript (**P**) is collated with Vatican City, Biblioteca Apostolica Vaticana, MS Vat. lat. 9668 (**V**).

[**NRA Lat. fragm. 23,1–2 + 4 + Un. III, (25), recto**] [...] exequias eius occurrerent cum psalmis et canticis cum cereis et thimiamatibus, et non aliter ei quam ipsi quoque apostolico funeris honorem impenderent. Tunc supradictus frater eius Methodius accedens ad sanctum pontificem, et procidens ad uestigia illius ait: Dignum ac necessarium duxi sugg<er>ere
5   beatitudini tue apostolice pater, quoniam quando ex domo nostra ad seruitium quod auxiliante Domino fecimus sumus egressi, mater cum multis lacrimis nos obtestata est, ut si aliquem ex nobis antequam reuerteremur obisse contingeret, defunctum fratrem frater uiuens ad monasterium suum reduceret, et ibidem illum digno et competenti obsequio sepeliret. Dignetur igitur sanctitas
10 uestra hoc munus paruitati mee concedere, ne precibus maternis uel contestationibus uidear contraire. Non est uisum apostolico quamuis graue sibi aliquantulum uideretur petitioni et uoluntati huiuscemodi refragari, sed clausum diligenter defuncti corpus in locello marmoreo et proprio insuper sigillo signatum, post septem dies dat ei licenciam recedendi. Tunc romanus
15 clerus simul cum episcopis ac cardinalibus atque nobilibus urbis, consilio habito conuenientes ad apostolicum ceperunt dicere: Indignum nobis ualde [...] <monume>nto. Cernens Methodius ita su<um defecisse propositum> orauit iterum dicens: Obsecro u<os, domini mei, quandoqui>dem non est placitum uobis meam peti<tiunculam adimplere> ut in ecclesia beati
20 Clementis, cuius <corpus multo suo la>bore ac studio repertum huc de<tulit, recondatur. Ann>uit huiusmodi petitioni presul s<anctissimus, et concurrent>e maxima cleri ac populi frequ<entia, cum ingenti laetitia et reuerentia multa, simul cum locello marmoreo in quo pridem illum predictus

4 illius] eius **PV** ‖ 10 paruitati mee] mee paruitati **PV**; maternis] matris **V** ‖ 10–11 contestationibus uidear] uidear aliquatenus **PV** ‖ 12 uoluntati] uoluptati **V** ‖ 14 signatum] signatur **P** ‖ 15 atque] ac **V** ‖ 21 huiusmodi] huiuscemodi **P** ‖ 22 cleri] dei **V**

papa condiderat, posuerunt in monumento ad id preparato in basilica beati Clementis ad dexteram partem altaris ip>sius cum ymnis et laudibus maxim<is gratias agentes Deo> qui in loco eodem multa et mira<nda opera operatur, ad lau>dem et gloriam nominis sui per mer<ita et orationes ipsorum sanctorum> suorum qui est benedictus et gloriosus in s<ecula seculorum. Amen>.

<Expli>cit de inuentione corporis beati <Clementis. Incipit > pa<ssio eiusdem.>

Tercius Romane ecclesie prefuit episcopus Clemens; qui <disciplinam apostoli Pe>tri secutus: ita morum orna<mentis pollebat, ut et> iudeis, et gentilibus et omnibus Christian<is populis placeret.> etc. [**The rest of the very commonly found *Passio* is not included.**]

27 ipsorum] *om.* **V**

The Manuscript Tradition of Burchard of Mount Sion's *Descriptio Terre Sancte**

JONATHAN RUBIN
Bar Ilan University

Introduction

For historians studying the medieval Holy Land, Burchard of Mount Sion's *Descriptio Terre Sancte* hardly needs an introduction. Burchard's detailed and systematic description of a great number of sites, as well as his treatment of additional themes such as the populations inhabiting this territory or even its agriculture, makes it extremely useful for scholars working on a wide range of fields, and, indeed, recent years have seen a growing interest in Burchard and his work. And yet, as surprising as it may seem, the *Descriptio*'s precise content, and even scope, are unclear, because until quite recently our actual knowledge of Burchard's composition was completely dependent on Johann C.M. Laurent's 1864 edition which is based on a very limited and accidental selection of manuscripts. While, as we shall soon see, several recent publications shed light on manuscripts which offer a more complete text than that found in Laurent's edition, these studies nevertheless do not provide a full survey of the various extant versions of the *Descriptio* and the relationships between them. The aim of this study is to present, for the first time, a full survey of the manuscripts providing the so-called long version (a term that will be clarified below) of the *Descriptio*, and to reveal their division into families, as well as the relationships between them. This work is meant to shed light on both the text, as Burchard actually authored it, and on the ways in which it was constantly re-edited by later generations of scribes and editors. It is hoped that this analysis will bring us much closer to Burchard's original version and, at the same time, facilitate future studies on specific problems related to the *Descriptio*'s tradition and reception, such as the motives behind the various changes inserted into the text by different agents.

---

* I would have never been able to achieve the results presented here without the immense work of Eva Ferro and Michael Schonhardt who have done a tremendous job as assistants in this project. I am also most grateful to Paolo Trovato for his kindness in providing me, once and again, so much priceless advice. Finally, I would like to thank the anonymous reviewers of *The Journal of Medieval Latin* for their valuable comments. This research was supported by the Israel Science Foundation (grant no. 1443/17).

Johann C.M. Laurent's Edition and Some Recent Developments

In 1864 Johann C.M. Laurent published an edition of Burchard of Mount Sion's *Descriptio Terre Sancte*. In the introduction to the edition, Laurent provided his readers with as much information as he could concerning Burchard and the date of his work. He also included a list of manuscripts, earlier printed editions, and translations. Laurent's main contribution to the discussion of the textual tradition of the *Descriptio* is his identification of two recensions of the text: a longer and a shorter one which differ, *inter alia*, in their incipits. The manuscripts of the long version begin with the words "cum in veteribus" and the short version witnesses begin with "dilectissimo in Christo."[1] Notably, Laurent chose to edit the long version.

The text Laurent provided and the distinction between the two textual versions of the *Descriptio* form the basis for the later critical study of Burchard's work. While, up to the present, no complete survey of the manuscripts of the *Descriptio* had been undertaken, and no analysis of the relationships between them was published, one can talk of an advancement in the study of the text in several directions. First, several manuscript lists were published with the result that we are now aware of a far greater number of witnesses of the *Descriptio* than were known to Laurent.[2] Second, the question of the relationship between the short and long versions has been discussed by several scholars. While over the years different opinions have been expressed, it now seems accepted that the longer version is closer to the original than the shorter one.[3]

As already noted, there has also been a significant advancement with regard to the use, by several scholars, of manuscripts which were not utilized by Laurent. In order to appreciate this, one should first return to Laurent's selection of manuscripts. In the introduction he states that he had used two manuscripts from Hamburg, three manuscripts from Wrocław, and one manuscript from Bern. In fact, when one looks at the apparatus, it becomes clear that Laurent systematically used only the two Hamburg

---

[1] *Peregrinatores medii aevi quatuor*, ed. Johann C.M. Laurent (Leipzig, 1864), pp. 3–18.

[2] Reinhold Röhricht, *Bibliotheca Geographica Palaestinae* (Berlin, 1890), pp. 56–58; Thomas Kaeppeli, *Scriptores Ordinis Praedicatorum Medii Aevi*, 4 vols. (Rome, 1970–1993), 1:257–60; Ekkehart Rotter, "Windrose statt Landkarte. Die geografische Systematisierung des Heiligen Landes und ihre Visualisierung durch Burchardus de Monte Sion um 1285," *Deutsches Archiv für Erforschung des Mittelalters* 69.1 (2013), 45–106, at pp. 103–6 (note that Rotter says that his list is incomplete).

[3] John R. Bartlett, "Burchard's *Descriptio Terrae Sanctae*: The Early Revision," *Palestine Exploration Quarterly* 145.1 (2013), 61–71, at pp. 70–71; Paul D.A. Harvey, *Medieval Maps of the Holy Land* (London, 2012), pp. 98–99; Denys Pringle, *Pilgrimage to Jerusalem and the Holy Land, 1187–1291* (Farnham, 2012), p. 48.

manuscripts and occasionally the one from Bern.[4] The three Wrocław manuscripts could not have been very relevant for his edition, since, as he notes in the introduction, they all provide the short version of the *Descriptio* rather than the long one which, as noted above, is the one Laurent chose for his published text. In an appendix Laurent also provided some variants from a Basel manuscript, which can be identified as **Ba1**. As will become evident, except for the Bern manuscript – which, while Laurent noted as significant, he only partially utilized – the rest of the manuscripts he used all belong to just one of the five families identified below (referred to as *c*), which is not the closest to the archetype. For this reason, Laurent's edition is of limited value only, if one wishes to get as close as possible to Burchard's original or to follow the development of his text over time.

As already mentioned, in the years that have passed since the publication of Laurent's edition, scholars did occasionally make use of additional manuscripts. As early as 1903, Henri Omont published the final passage of a version of the *Descriptio* which he found in one Paris manuscript,[5] but he did not examine other manuscripts and was thus unable to place this passage within the work's textual history. Consequently, it remained uncertain whether this section was actually authored by Burchard.[6] Much more recently, considerable manuscript evidence has been used by Ingrid Baumgärtner in her discussions of the text and Ekkehart Rotter has made use of various manuscripts in his discussion of the maps associated with Burchard's *Descriptio*.[7] Still more recently I have published an article focusing on a manuscript held in London (**Lo2**) which includes significant phrases and passages missing from Laurent's edition. Most notably, the text provided by this manuscript does not end, as does Laurent's text, at the point where Burchard enters Egypt, but rather includes an elaborate account of Egypt and then follows Burchard's journey through Sicily and Italy and then back to

---

[4] These three manuscripts are included in our list as: **Ha1**, **Ha2**, and **Be4**. The signature of the Bern manuscript was provided by Laurent. The two other codices are easily identifiable through details provided by Laurent in their descriptions. Here and throughout the article I use *sigla* as references to the manuscripts mentioned. For their complete signatures, see the Appendix.

[5] Henri Omont, "Manuscrits de la bibliothèque de sir Thomas Phillipps récemment acquis pour la Bibliothèque nationale," *Bibliothèque de l'École des Chartes* 64 (1903), 490–553, at pp. 498–503. This manuscript is our **Pa4**.

[6] For a skeptical view, see for example, Ingrid Baumgärtner, "Burchard of Mount Sion and the Holy Land," *Peregrinations: Journal of Medieval Art & Architecture* 4.1 (Spring, 2013), 5–41, at pp. 14–15. Baumgärtner did, however, identify another manuscript which includes this section (see n. 31 in her article).

[7] Baumgärtner, "Burchard," pp. 5–41; Ingrid Baumgärtner, "Reiseberichte, Karten und Diagramme. Burchard von Monte Sion und das Heilige Land," in *Geschichtsvorstellungen: Bilder, Texte und Begriffe aus dem Mittelalter: Festschrift für Hans-Werner Goetz zum 65. Geburtstag*, ed. Steffen Patzold, Anja Rathmann-Lutz, and Volker Scior (Cologne, 2012), pp. 460–507; Rotter, "Windrose."

the Holy Land.[8] In another publication, I have studied and edited the account of Egypt, as provided by **Lo2** and by an additional manuscript from Zwickau (**Zw3**). In this study some preliminary comments were also made concerning the relationship between several versions of the *Descriptio*.[9]

Most recently, while this study was in preparation, a new work on the *Descriptio* appeared. This is a considerable volume by John R. Bartlett which includes new editions and English translations of both the short and long versions of the *Descriptio* along with elaborate introductory discussions and a rich commentary.[10] While Bartlett should definitely be praised for his immense undertaking, this project contributes very little to our understanding of the manuscript tradition of the long version of the *Descriptio*. Firstly, Bartlett used for his edition only six manuscripts, and while he adds comments on some additional witnesses, he clearly did not examine all (or even the majority) of the extant manuscripts. Furthermore, the list of manuscripts he provides is based, as he notes, on that of Kaeppeli (he clearly was unaware of the more recent one by Rotter) and, among other problems, he mistook the Oviedo and Wolfenbüttel 391 manuscripts for proper witnesses of the *Descriptio* and, much more crucially, missed the very important **Zw3**.[11]

Even more significantly, Bartlett does not systematically employ any method in order to understand the relationship between the manuscripts he used. Indeed, while in several cases he speaks of similarities between various witnesses, he does not divide them into families (except making a problematic distinction between those that have and those that lack the account of Egypt), does not use the notion of common errors, and makes no attempt to provide a stemma.[12] Instead, he uses expressions such as "standard text" or "main tradition" and alternatively refers, for example, to a scribe that felt free to create "his own hybrid version" (this is **Le1**, which, as we shall see, actually belongs to an important branch in the transmission).[13] Needless to say, with-

---

[8] Jonathan Rubin, "Burchard of Mount Sion's *Descriptio Terrae Sanctae*: A Newly Discovered Extended Version," *Crusades* 13 (2014), 173–90.

[9] Jonathan Rubin, "A Missing Link in European Travel Literature: Burchard of Mount Sion's Description of Egypt," *Mediterranea: International Journal on the Transfer of Knowledge* 3 (2018), 55–90.

[10] *Burchard of Mount Sion, OP, Descriptio Terrae Sanctae*, ed. and trans. John R. Bartlett (Oxford, 2019).

[11] For the Oviedo and Wolfenbüttel 391 manuscripts, see below, n. 16.

[12] While Bartlett only distinguishes between manuscripts that include an account of Egypt and others that do not, the picture is in reality more complex. Cf. Burchard, *Descriptio*, ed. Bartlett, pp. cxxxviii–cxxxix, and Rubin, "A Missing Link," pp. 69–75.

[13] For the expressions "standard text" and "main tradition," see Burchard, *Descriptio*, ed. Bartlett, pp. xxxiii, xxxiv, cxlix, clviii. For the reference to the hybrid version see Burchard, *Descriptio*, ed. Bartlett, p. cxl.

out a survey of the complete (or at least nearly complete) corpus of manuscripts, and an analysis of the relationships between them, such observations mean very little. Indeed, this procedure led Bartlett to choose for the text of his edition a particular manuscript (**Pa3**) which, as we shall see, is in all likelihood quite far removed from the archetype.

In conclusion, despite some recent advancements in the study of this important text, the relationships between all witnesses of the *Descriptio* have never been fully explored. As a result, it has been impossible thus far to determine which of the extant manuscripts provides the text closest to Burchard's original, or to follow the ways in which his text was reshaped in subsequent decades and centuries. It is this lacuna that the present study intends to fill. Since, as noted above, it is now generally accepted that the longer version is closer to the original text of the *Descriptio* than the short version, the focus is on this recension.[14] Based on a new, updated list of manuscripts (see the Appendix), a painstaking process of collation of dozens of lines across the entire corpus of complete manuscripts, and of hundreds of lines across representative witnesses, was undertaken. This procedure enabled us both to divide the witnesses of the long version into five families and to reconstruct the relationships between them.

It is noteworthy that for the analysis of the families and the relationship between them I rely only on what can be considered "more or less complete" witnesses, since excerpts and abbreviated witnesses naturally do not provide sufficient evidence in terms of common errors and significant variants. Abbreviated witnesses and excerpts are, however, included in the manuscript list in the Appendix, and each of the former is also tentatively placed in one of the families.[15] Compilations, that is, texts in which Burchard's *Descriptio* was used along with other texts in order to produce a new work, are also not useful for our analysis, and are thus excluded from the present study.[16]

---

[14] This does not mean, of course, that the manuscripts of the short version and their relationship to the longer one should be neglected. I intend to treat these subjects in a future study.

[15] In order to make clear that their connection to each of the families is tentative, they appear, in the lists included in the discussion of each of the families, in square brackets (see below, n. 44). In the appendix a question mark is adjoined to their family *sigla*.

[16] Three compilations which make use of the *Descriptio* are currently known. The first, included in only one manuscript (Versailles, Bibliothèque municipale, MS Lebaudy 8° 52), was studied in Régine Pernoud, *Un guide du pèlerin de Terre-Sainte au XVe siècle* (Mantes, 1940). For the second compilation, extant in four manuscripts (Naples, Biblioteca nazionale, MS Vindob. lat. 49, olim Vienna, Österreichische Nationalbibliothek, MS 440; Pisa, Archivio capitolare, C.89 inserto 3, Miscellanea Zucchelli XXXIII; Vienna, Österreichische Nationalbibliothek, MS 3468; Wolfenbüttel, Herzog August Bibliothek, MS 391 Helmst.), see Michele Campopiano, "Note sulla presenza francescana in Terrasanta: Le descrizioni dei luoghi santi tra XIV e XVI secolo e il ruolo della Custodia di Terrasanta," in *Gli Italiani e la Terrasanta*, ed. Antonio Musarra (Firenze, 2014), pp. 49–69, at 56–63 (note, however, that Campopiano was unaware of the Naples manuscript). The third compilation, extant in two manuscripts (Oviedo, Biblioteca Capitular de la Catedral de Oviedo, MS 18; Salamanca,

The Division of the Manuscripts into Families

As noted, the *Descriptio*'s tradition can be divided into five families, which will be referred to as ***a***, ***b***, ***c***, ***d***, and ***e***.[17]

1. The ***a*** Family. To this family belong four witnesses:

> Bern, Burgerbibliothek, MS 46 [**Be4**].
> Leiden, Bibliotheek der Rijksuniversiteit, MS B.P.L. 69 [**Le1**].
> Wolfenbüttel, Herzog August Bibliothek, MS Weissenb. 41 [**Wo2**].
> Zwickau, Ratsschulbibliothek, MS I XII 5 [**Zw3**].

As noted in a previous article, **Zw3** is of great importance, as it is one of only two manuscripts that contain, in addition to Burchard's account of the Holy Land, a complete description of Egypt as well as an account of Sicily and Italy. Moreover, this manuscript includes significant information about Burchard himself which most of the *Descriptio* witnesses omit.[18] The other manuscripts of this branch are not of similar scope, but rather are abbreviated in different ways. Most notably, **Le1** omits Burchard's introductory comments on the terms Arabia and Syria,[19] ending abruptly with Burchard's notes concerning the Bedouins, just at the end of a folio, clearly showing that at least one more folio became lost at some stage.[20] **Be4** and **Wo2** omit much of the preface, starting only with "Quia vidi quosdam devocione," and then skip the discussion of the terms Arabia and Syria.[21] Both end with Burchard's comments on the size of sheep in the East (which, however, are significantly different from those included in Laurent's edition).[22] All three manuscripts also omit various other comments and paragraphs.[23] Still, despite the differences between them, common innova-

---

Biblioteca Universitaria, MS 2761) combines the *Descriptio* with Marino Sanudo's *Liber secretorum fidelium crucis*. It is studied in Cecilia Blanco Pascual, "Los manuscritos del Tractatus de Terra Sancta compilatus a fratre Marino et a fratre Brocardo (anónimo): Algunas notas críticas," *Exemplaria Classica. Journal of Classical Philology. Revista de Filologia Clásica* 12 (2008), 181–93.

[17] The discussion of each family begins with a list of the manuscripts which belong to it. For complete details of all of the manuscripts mentioned, as well as for their *sigla*, see the Appendix.

[18] For more on the **Zw3** manuscript, see Rubin, "A Missing Link."

[19] Cf. Laurent, *Peregrinatores*, pp. 21–23.

[20] "… cum tabernaculis suis transfe" [*sic*], fol. 115v. Cf. Laurent, *Peregrinatores*, p. 89.

[21] Cf. Laurent, *Peregrinatores*, p. 20.

[22] **Be4**: "que sit oneri arieti ad portandum;" **Wo2**: "quod sit oneri ad portandum arieti." Cf. Laurent, *Peregrinatores*, p. 90.

[23] Indeed, one could have excluded them from this discussion and treated them as abbreviated witnesses. However, since they belong to a small and crucially important family, I prefer to include them in the present analysis.

tions shared by these four manuscripts make it clear that they belong to the same family. Here are several examples:[24]

> *a*: vidi ... Iordanem insuper usque Sarthan ... et v civitates Philistinorum usque Gazarim[25]
>
> *bcde*: vidi ... Iordanem insuper usque Sethim ... totum litus maris magni ab Ioppe usque Gazam[26]

Clearly, the *a* family provides a different phrase structure and all of its witnesses include the incorrect Sarthan for Sethim or Setim (Joshua 2.1). Except for **Le1**, the manuscripts included in this family also provide Gazarim for Gazam.

Another interesting case occurs in the description of Megido. In the four manuscripts belonging to the *a* family we read the following: "De isto loco sex leucis contra austrum est Magedo quod nunc Sybule dicitur."[27] Sybule is a unique form which appears only in these manuscripts, while families *bcde* include Suburbe or closely related forms. Thus, all but *a* provide readings which can easily be identified with the name of a village still known today as Zububa, located ten km northwest of Jenin.[28]

A third example has to do with the description of Dothan. As can be seen from this comparison, the word *habundans* is missing in the *a* family witnesses:

> *a*: opidum valde bonum amenum vineis et olivetis et ficetis et pascuis.[29]
>
> *b*: opidum valde amenum vineis olivetis et ficubus habundans et pascuis pinguibus.
>
> *ce*: opidum valde amenum in vineis olivetis et ficubus habundans et pascuis pinguibus.[30]
>
> *d*: opidum valde amenum vineis olivetis et ficetis habundans et pascuis pinguibus.[31]

---

[24] Here, as elsewhere, slight orthographical variants are ignored.

[25] **Le1**: usque Gazam; **Wo2**: usque ad Sarchan.

[26] Variants for the *b* family: **Le2**, **Pr2**: Sychem. For *c*: **Ba2**: litum, ad Gazam; **Ha1**: totus; **Vi3**: igitur insuper, Sethey, ad Ioppe; **Zw1**: in ab Ioppe. For *d*: **Br1**: Iordanemque usque, et Ioppe; **Es1**, **Fl1**, **Lo1**, **Ox1**: insuper *om.*, et Ioppe; **Fl3**, **Fl2**, **Pa1**: Iordanem vero usque; **Tu1**: insuper *om.* For *e*: **Be1**, **Ol1**: et Ioppe; **Be2**: ad Ioppe; **Mi3**: et usque Sethim; **Mi1**, **Sa3**: Sichem; **Ve1**: usque ad Sethim. The words "Iordanem insuper" are very difficult to read in **Va5**.

[27] **Le1**: est *om.*; **Zw3**: que for quod.

[28] **Be2** omits this place name from this phrase, providing it a little later.

[29] **Le1**: bonum *om.*, vinetis olivetis.

[30] There are some variants here with the regard to the placing of the word *et*; **Vi2**: oliveti; **Be1** (*e* family) provides here a reading much closer to *d*: "opidum valde amenum habundans vineis olivetis et ficetis habundans [*sic*] etiam pascuis pinguibus." Additional evidence presented below also raises the possibility that it is contaminated. See below, nn. 67, 77, 114.

[31] **Na1**: "oppidum valde amenum in vineis olivetis et ficubus habundans pascuis pinguibus." This manuscript is possibly contaminated. See below, nn. 57, 58, 59, 61, 63.

Given that *habundans* is so frequent in this construction in the *Descriptio* across its manuscript tradition, this is in all likelihood a common omission in this family.[32] To this may be added that *a* appears to omit *pinguibus* which indeed appears in the other families.

Further support for the connection between these four manuscripts is found in the following variant taken from the discussion of Thecua: *a*: "in qua fuit Amos propheta" *vs. bcde*: "de qua fuit Amos propheta."[33]

2. The *b* Family. This family includes the following three manuscripts:

Leipzig, Universitätsbibliothek, MS 525 [**Le2**].
London, British Library, MS Add. 18929 [**Lo2**].
Prague, Archiv Pražského hradu, Knihovna metropolitní kapituly, MS A CVI 2 [**Pr2**].

Of these three witnesses, **Lo2** is the most significant, providing the most complete text of the *Descriptio* in terms of scope. Thus, the text includes, in addition to the description of the Holy Land, a full account of Egypt followed by that of Burchard's journey to Bologna and then back to the East.[34] The two other manuscripts belonging to this family follow quite closely the text of **Lo2** up to the discussion of the Bedouins. Both manuscripts end with the words: "que sunt oneri arieti ad portandum (**Pr2**: onera)," and are then followed by a short, unknown, text beginning with the words: "Montes Bethel sunt in Iudea vicini Ierusalem." This suggests that these two manuscripts are closely related, as can also be seen by at least two common errors which they share against all of the other witnesses.[35] It is also noteworthy that they both end at precisely the same point at which the above-mentioned **Be4** and **Wo2** of the *a* family also do (while **Le1** lacks its end due to the loss of at least one folio).[36] This does not seem to be a coincidence but rather the result of contamination. In other words, it seems that for the last part of the text **Le2** and **Pr2** or **Be4**, **Le1**, and **Wo2** rely on an exemplar different from the one on which their previous sections are based, and which is closely related to the other group. Significant evidence for this comes from a lacuna

---

[32] For the construction of *habundans* with ablative in the *Descriptio*, see for example, Laurent, *Peregrinatores*, pp. 23, 26, 34; and **Zw3**, fols. 115v, 116v, 117r.

[33] **Be1**: fuerat(?); **Mi2**: propheta(?); **Ri1**: de quo.

[34] Rubin, "Burchard."

[35] They are the only ones to speak of "vellestes botri" (**Pr2**: botris) where all others refer to *Neelescol* (or, as we shall see in the *d* family: *Nemphecor*) and "torrens botri." Both also skip from the midst of the section on the fruits and animals of the Holy Land right into the section about its inhabitants: "porci silvestres capreoli lepores et vulpes et similes fere multum habundant ibi. Caldei, Persi Medi, Ethyepes ..." (**Le2**, fol. 74v; **Pr2**, fol. 349v, is almost completely identical. Cf. Laurent, *Peregrinatores*, pp. 88–89).

[36] See above, p. 262.

which all of these manuscripts share in the subsection discussing the Latins of Outremer.[37] Given the popularity of the *Descriptio*, such an occurrence is not surprising. While the three manuscripts belonging to ***b*** are very different in terms of the scope of text they provide, they include common errors which makes it clear that they are closely related. Here are several examples:

> ***b***: unde Aretha regio Arabie dicitur[38]
> **Zw3**, ***cde***: unde Aretha rex Arabie dicitur[39]

An incorrect insertion of the word *mare* only in the ***b*** family points in the same direction:

> ***b***: montes ... sunt ... contra locum istum ultra mare Iordanis.
> ***a***: montes ... sunt ... super locum istum ultra Iordanem.[40]
> ***ce***: montes ... sunt ... contra locum istum ultra Iordanem.[41]
> ***d***: montes ... sunt ... contra istum locum ultra Iordanem.[42]

The connection between the ***b*** family manuscripts can be further demonstrated using Burchard's discussion of Bethel, in which he describes what he perceives as the corrupted Arabic pronunciation of this toponym. He is therefore likely to have written: "Sarraceni corrupte appellant locum istum ..." And, indeed, in almost all of the witnesses, we find the form *corrupte*. On the other hand, the ***b*** family manuscripts provide *corrupti*.[43]

3. The ***c*** family. To this family belong the following manuscripts:[44]

> Basel, Universitätsbibliothek, MS A.I.28 [**Ba2**].
> Basel, Universitätsbibliothek, MS A.V.17 [**Ba1**].
> Berlin, Deutsche Staatsbibl. zu Berlin – Preussischer Kulturbesitz, MS Lat. oct. 293 [**Be3**].
> Hamburg, Staats- und Universitätsbibliothek, MS Cod. Petri 30b [**Ha1**].

---

[37] Cf. Laurent, *Peregrinatores*, pp. 88–89.

[38] **Pr2** has *rex*, but given its very strong connection to **Le2**, this is probably the result of a correction.

[39] **Le1**, **Be4**, and **Wo2** omit the discussion that includes this phrase. **Zw3** has a slightly different reading: Unde et Arocha rex Arabie dicitur; **Ha2**: rex de Arabia; **Ve1**: rex in lingua Arabica dicitur; **Vi1**: Arabia dicitur.

[40] **Le1**: contra locum; **Wo2**: super Iordanem.

[41] **Ba1**, **Be3**, **Ha1**, **Up1**: et ultra Iordanem; **Li1**: istum *om*.; **Ri1**, **Sa3**, and **Va6**: contra Iordanem; **Vi3**: illum for istum.

[42] **Be1**: locum istum; **Br1**: usque Iordanem; **Na1**: contra locum istum usque Iordanem.

[43] The ***a*** family does not include this line. **Es1**: corrupe [*sic*]; **Ri1**, **Va6**: corruptum; **Up1**: corrupti.

[44] Manuscripts which appear in brackets provide a partial text of the *Descriptio* and lack a significant part of the innovations and errors upon which our analysis is based. Consequently, they are not included in the present discussion. However, on the basis of the partial evidence that they do provide, it seems possible to connect them tentatively to the different groups. See also above, p. 261.

Hamburg, Staats- und Universitätsbibliothek, MS Cod. Geogr. 59 [**Ha2**].
Klagenfurt, Universitätsbibliothek, MS Pap.-Hs. 152 [**Kl1**].
[Klagenfurt, Archiv der Diözese Gurk, MS Maria Saal 15 [**Kl2**]].
Lilienfeld, Stiftsbibliothek, MS 145 [**Li1**].
[Melk, Stiftsbibliothek, MS 952 [**Me1**]].
Prague, Národní knihovna České republiky, MS XIV C 16 [**Pr1**].
Rimini, Biblioteca Civica Gambalunga, MS SC-71 [**Ri1**].
Uppsala, Universitetsbiblioteket, MS C 78 [**Up1**].
[Vatican City, Biblioteca Apostolica Vaticana, MS Pal. lat. 1358 [**Va3**]].
Vatican City, Biblioteca Apostolica Vaticana, MS Vat. lat. 3759 [**Va7**].
Vatican City, Biblioteca Apostolica Vaticana, MS Vat. lat. 4360 [**Va6**].
Vienna, Österreichische Nationalbibliothek, MS 1628 [**Vi3**].
Vienna, Österreichische Nationalbibliothek, MS 3341 [**Vi2**].
Zwettl, Stiftsbibliothek, MS 76 [**Zw1**].
Zwettl, Stiftsbibliothek, MS 315 [**Zw2**].

This is a very significant family not only because of the considerable number of manuscripts belonging to it, but also because, as noted above, the edition produced by Laurent is based on several of its representatives. The clearest characteristic of this family is its closing line, "In hac eciam lapidatus est Jeremias," followed in some of the manuscripts by a more or less corrupted form of what should probably have read: "De Taphnis [Tinnis] venimus in Memphis et inde."[45] Since this cannot possibly have been the way in which Burchard would have ended his well-organized treatise, one must assume that all of the manuscripts belonging to this family depend on a witness which underwent some kind of corruption at this point. That these witnesses lacked a proper ending was evident to at least one scribe whose comment following this phrase, "non inveni plus," appears in several manuscripts.[46]

This family is further characterized by common errors in comparison to the rest of the tradition. For example, having mentioned the site of Kabul, the text goes on to say:

    c: terra illa terra Kabul est appellata[47]
    a: a quo terra illa est cognominata[48]
    b: a quo terra illa Cabul est appellata
    d: a quo terra illa Gabul est appellata[49]
    e: a quo terra illa terra Zabul est appellata[50]

---

[45] Rubin, "A Missing Link," p. 70.

[46] **Li1** (non plus inveni), **Va7**, **Vi2**, **Zw2**.

[47] **Kl1**(?), **Li1**: Rabul; **Ri1**: est nominata; **Vi3**: est *om.*; **Zw2**: appellata est; **Vi2**: terra terra Kabul appellata est.

[48] **Be4**: cognominata est; **Wo2**: a qua.

[49] **Br1**: Gabi; **Br1**, **Es1**, **Fl3**, **Ox1**, **Tu1**: est vocata; **Fl1**, **Lo1**: terra Cabul; **Na1**: Kabul.

[50] **Sa3**: a quo terra ista; the second *terra* is omitted in numerous manuscripts: **Be2**, **Mi2**, **Mi3**, **Mi1**, **Pa3**, **Pa4**, **Sp1**, **Va1**, **Vi1**, **Wo1**.

Another common error typical to this family has to do with the account of the Assassins.[51] According to Burchard, several years before he wrote his text, they decided to become obedient to the Catholic Church and, for that reason, sent an envoy to Acre. On the way back to their territory, Burchard recounts, the envoy was killed by those who were to escort him.[52] Of all the manuscripts which include this passage, the *c* family witnesses are the only ones which do not state that the perpetrators belonged to the order of the Temple.[53]

These errors can be further supported by an interesting reading unique to the *c* family. Describing the Hebron region, the *Descriptio* refers to Neelescol (Num. 13.25), and **Lo2** provides the Latin equivalent, "torrens botri," as does the Vulgate.[54] At this point, the *c* family adds "vel vallis lacrimarum." Families *d* and *e* include here only the words "vel vallis."[55]

4. The *d* Family. This family includes the following manuscripts:[56]

Brussels, Bibliothèque Royale, MS 9176–9177 [**Br1**].
El Escorial, Real Biblioteca del Monasterio de San Lorenzo, MS O.III.34 [**Es1**].
Florence, Biblioteca nazionale centrale, MS Conv. Soppr. C.VIII.2861 [**Fl2**].
Florence, Biblioteca nazionale centrale, MS Conv. Soppr. F.IV.733 [**Fl1**].
Florence, Biblioteca Medicea Laurenziana, MS Plut. 76.56 [**Fl3**].
[Lindau, Stadtarchiv, MS E.R.B. P I 1 [**Li2**]].
London, British Library, MS Harley 3995 [**Lo1**].
Nancy, Bibliothèque municipale, MS 1082 [**Na1**].[57]

---

[51] For this group, whose members are referred to in modern scholarship as Nizarite Isma'ilis, see: Farhad Daftary, *The Assassin Legends: Myths of the Isma'ilis* (London, 1995).

[52] Cf. Laurent, *Peregrinatores*, p. 90. This murder took place in 1173 and is recounted by William of Tyre, who attributes the crime to the Templars. Willelmus Tyrensis, *Chronicon*, ed. R.B.C. Huygens, CCCM 63–63a, 2 vols. (Turnhout, 1986), 2:954.

[53] As was already noted (see above, pp. 262, 264), several manuscripts do not include this passage: **Be4**, **Le1**, **Wo2**, **Le2**, **Pr2**. Of the *c* family only one manuscript, which abbreviates the section on the Holy Land's inhabitants, does not include this passage: **Vi3**.

[54] As we have seen, the two other witnesses of *b* seem to share a common innovation here: "vellestes botri." The *a* family refers to "vallis Neellescol" with no further elaboration with regard to this toponym.

[55] There is only one exception in the *c* family: **Ba2** has "vallis." The *e* family has two exceptions here: **Sp1**: Neellescol idest torrens vel vallis botri; **Va1**: vel vallis lacrimarum.

[56] For manuscripts in brackets, see above, n. 44.

[57] This manuscript (**Na1**) is very difficult to classify. It was clearly made by a very able scribe who was both interested in and capable of correcting the text he had before him. To mention just one example, he produced the only witness which gives the full name of the biblical conqueror of Cariath Sepher properly: "Othoniel filius Cenez." The colophon provided by this manuscript also suggests that the scribe had access to information about Burchard which is reminiscent of that included by **Lo2** and **Zw3**. On the other hand, this manuscript does not share common errors with families *a* and *b*, and

Oxford, Magdalen College, MS 43 [**Ox1**].
Padua, Biblioteca Universitaria, MS 1027 [**Pa1**].
Turin, Biblioteca Nazionale e Universitaria, MS D.IV.21 [**Tu1**].
[Warsaw, Biblioteka Narodowa, MS 8052 [**Wa1**]].

The manuscripts belonging to this family are characterized by the ending of the text they provide, "Istud sine dubio videre et audire devotissimum est," relating to the account of the Armenian prayer. All of these, except **Na1**, share several unique readings.[58] For example, for the above-mentioned Neelescol, all manuscripts belonging to this family have "Nemphecor" or slightly different versions of this corrupted form.[59]

Another error common to this family concerns the description of Dothan, or Dothaym, as it appears in Laurent's edition.[60] All manuscripts except those of the *d* family state that it is situated three, or in some manuscripts, four, *leuce* to the south of the previous site noted in the text. The *d* manuscripts mention the distance but omit the direction.[61] As Burchard's habit was indeed to include the direction, this is in all likelihood an error.

An additional common error which is typical for this family appears in the context of the production of sugar to which Burchard devotes a lengthy account. Speaking about sugar canes, Burchard says that they are not hollow but rather filled with a certain substance. In the manuscripts belonging to families *abce*, that substance is described, with some exceptions, as *porosa*.[62] In *d* on the other hand, it is described as *ponderosa*.[63]

The *d* family can further be characterized by another variant. Discussing a certain road which passes through the city of Kedar, **Lo2** (fol. 10v) provides the following explanation:

> In Ysaia autem via ista vocatur *via maris transiordanem Galilee gentium*. Via enim maris dicitur, quia omnino precedit in litore maris, *trans Iordanem* additur, quia ducit ultra Iordanem in regionem que dicitur Aran, *Galilee gentium* additur, quia in rei veritate Galilea gentium ibidem in Iordane terminatur.
>
> In Isaiah, however, this road is called "the way of the sea beyond the Jordan of the Galilee of the nations." It is called "the way of the sea" because it leads entirely along the

---

indeed, as we shall see later, it does show innovations common, for example, to *d* and *e* and, on another occasion, to *c*, *d*, and *e*. It is likely that it is contaminated. See above, n. 31.

[58] See previous note.

[59] Exceptional is the above-mentioned **Na1**, which has the proper Neelescol.

[60] Laurent, *Peregrinatores*, p. 39.

[61] Except **Na1** which does provide the direction.

[62] **Le2** and **Pr2** do not include this discussion. **Be1**: ?; **Be3**: perosa; **Kl1**: parosa; **Mi3**, **Pa4**: prosa; **Va6**: rosa; **Be2**, **Br2**, **Mi1**, **Ol1**, **Pa2**, **Ph1**, **Va1**, **Va5**, **Ve1**: preciosa.

[63] Except for **Na1**: porosa.

shore, "beyond the Jordan" is added, because it leads across the Jordan to the region called Aran, "Galilee of the nations" is added, because truly the Galilee of the nations ends at that point in the Jordan.

Clearly, what we have here is an explanation of the verse in Is. 9.1: "Primo tempore adleviata est terra Zabulon et terra Nephthalim: et novissimo adgravata est via maris trans Jordanem Galileae gentium." While the various manuscripts include some variations in comparison to **Lo2**, they all, except those belonging to families *a* and *d*, keep the general form of discussion: "In Ysaya … via enim maris dicitur quia … trans Iordanem additur quia … Galilee gentium additur quia …"[64] The *d* family manuscripts include at this point a clearly flawed text:[65] "Via maris dicitur, quia omnino procedit transiordanem Galilee gentium."

5. The *e* Family[66]

> Berlin, Deutsche Staatsbibl. zu Berlin – Preussischer Kulturbesitz, MS Lat. fol. 464 [**Be1**].[67]
> Berlin, Deutsche Staatsbibl. zu Berlin – Preussischer Kulturbesitz, MS Lat. qu. 466 [**Be2**].
> Brussels, Bibliothèque Royale, MS 733–741 [**Br2**].
> Klosterneuburg, Stiftsbibliothek, MS 722 A [**Kl3**].
> Milan, Biblioteca Ambrosiana, MS Trotti 500 [**Mi1**].
> Milan, Biblioteca Ambrosiana, MS A 219 inf. [**Mi2**].
> Milan, Biblioteca Ambrosiana, MS A 223 inf. [**Mi3**].
> [Naples, Biblioteca nazionale, MS VIII D 10 [**Na2**]].
> Olomouc, Státni vědecká knihovna, MS M II 128 [**Ol1**].
> Oxford, Bodleian Library, MS Lat. Hist. e. 1 [**Ox2**].
> Padua, Biblioteca del Seminario Vescovile, MS 74 [**Pa2**].
> Paris, Bibliothèque nationale de France, MS nouv. acq. lat. 288 [**Pa3**].
> Paris, Bibliothèque nationale de France, MS nouv. acq. lat. 781 [**Pa4**].
> Philadelphia, University of Pennsylvania, Rare Book & Manuscript Lib., Ms 60 [**Ph1**].
> Salzburg, Erzabtei Sankt Peter, MS b.IX.22 [**Sa1**].
> Salzburg, Erzabtei Sankt Peter, MS b.III.31 [**Sa2**].
> Salzburg, Erzabtei Sankt Peter, MS b.X.30 [**Sa3**].
> Sankt Paul in Lavanttal, Stiftsbibliothek, MS Hosp. Chart. 145/4 [**Sp1**].

---

[64] **Pr2** (*b*) has a somewhat corrupt text, but still refers to the three basic elements: via maris … trans Iordanem … Galilee gentium. **Mi2**, **Mi3**, **Pa3**, **Pa4**, **Va4** (all belonging to *e*): Galilee gencium ibidem in Iordane terminatur; **Vi2** (*c*): quia omnino precedit in litore maris *om*.

[65] The *a* family includes a completely different reading: "In Ysa. vero dicitur via maris transiordanem Galilee gencium quia in litore maris procedit ab uno fine usque ad alium finem eius." **Na1** has the structure that appears in the *bce* families. **Fl2**, **Pa1**: dicitur *om*.

[66] For manuscripts in brackets, see above, n. 44.

[67] I include this manuscript (**Be1**) in this family since it includes the abbreviated account of Egypt (see below), but it should be noted that it is difficult to classify, not always sharing the errors common to the other manuscripts of this family (see above, n. 30). Furthermore, it is a problematic witness, where the *Descriptio* appears in two separate sections and the order of the folios is not completely correct.

Vatican City, Biblioteca Apostolica Vaticana, MS Reg. lat. 462 [**Va1**].
[Vatican City, Biblioteca Apostolica Vaticana, MS Pal. lat. 832 [**Va2**]].
Vatican City, Biblioteca Apostolica Vaticana, MS Urb. lat. 393 [**Va4**].
Vatican City, Biblioteca Apostolica Vaticana, MS Barb. lat. 1952 [**Va5**].
Venice, Biblioteca nazionale Marciana, MS lat. X 24 [**Ve1**].
Vienna, Österreichische Nationalbibliothek, MS 9530 [**Vi1**].
Wolfenbüttel, Herzog August Bibliothek, MS 354 Helmst. [**Wo1**].

Like the *d* family, this family too can be characterized by its closing words: "Istud retulerunt omnes Egiptii et Christiani et Saraceni bona fide." This phrase ends what we have described in a previous study as an abbreviated description of Egypt.[68] In other words, this family includes, following the text of the *Descriptio* more or less as transmitted by the *c* family and therefore also by Laurent's edition, an account of Egypt which is a re-edited version of what is included in **Zw3** and **Lo2**. This family is of great importance for our understanding of the reception, and particularly the early modern reception, of the *Descriptio*, since it dominated the early printed editions of the text.[69]

Here, too, one can note several variants common to the witnesses belonging to this family. For example, the great majority of manuscripts included in *e* omit the verb *faciunt* in the following phrase:

e: similiter peregrini et alii Christiani visitantes loca ista[70]
a: similiter faciunt omnes Christiani et Sarraceni[71]
bc: similiter faciunt peregrini alii et Christiani visitantes loca ista[72]
d: sicut faciunt peregrini et alii visitantes loca ista[73]

Another unique reading typical to this family has to do with the account of Shunem, and, more specifically, to the distance between this city and Mount Carmel.[74] **Lo2** (fol. 16v) provides the following:

De ipsa etiam civitate eadem mulier mortuo filio suo venit ad eum [Eliseum] in monte Carmeli qui distat per 4 leucas de loco illo.

From that same city, on the death of her son, that woman came to him [Elisha] in Mount Carmel which is four leagues away from there.

---

[68] Rubin, "A Missing Link," pp. 70–75, 88–90.

[69] Rubin, "A Missing Link," pp. 75–77.

[70] I ignore here differences in the placing of *alii* as well as the doubling of this word. **Be1**, **Be2**, **Ol1**, **Pa2**, **Va1**, **Va5**, **Ph1**: loca sancta. Several manuscripts belonging to this family do provide the verb *faciunt*: **Mi2**, **Mi3**, **Pa3**, **Pa4**, **Va4**.

[71] **Wo2**: similiter et fciunt [*sic*].

[72] **Ba2**: loca illa; **Kl1**: faciunt *om.*; **Va7**: sicut faciunt.

[73] **Na1**: similiter faciunt Christiani et peregrini visitantes loca ista.

[74] Cf. Laurent, *Peregrinatores*, p. 50.

Only the *e* family manuscripts add after the words "de loco illo" (or in some manuscripts "de loco isto"), the expression "contra citerium" or closely related forms such as "cucium," which appear to be corrupted versions of a term meant to report the geographic relationship between the two sites.[75] **Va1** and **Br2** seem to reflect attempts of scribes to improve the text at this point by providing "contra vulturnum" and "contra illud castrum" respectively.

This family is also characterized by a notable omission: Burchard devotes a paragraph to several towns in the Holy Land named Rama. This ends with the following comment:[76]

> Rama autem excelsum interpretatur et revera omnes iste ville in collibus excelsis sunt site.
>
> Rama, however, is understood as meaning elevated and in fact all of these villages are located on high hills.

While the various families provide some variations here, only the *e* manuscripts completely omit the words "Rama excelsum interpretatur," without which the next phrase loses much of its sense.[77]

A *Proposed* stemma codicum

Having characterized the different families, it is now possible to look at the relationships between them. These can best be visualized as follows:

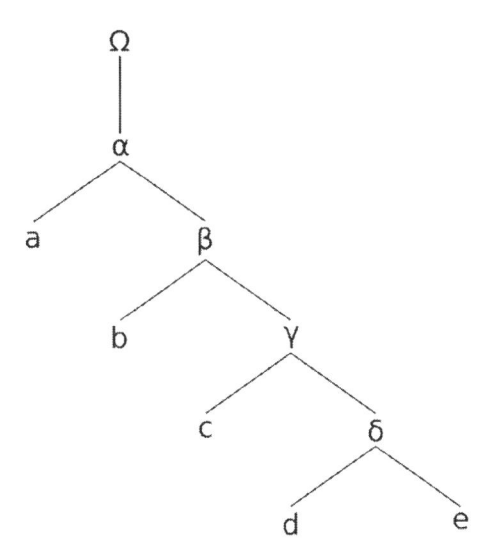

[75] Of the *a* family manuscripts only **Zw3** includes the phrase "de loco illo." Several other manuscripts also omit this phrase: **Be1**, **Fl1**, **Lo1**. **Pa2**: circa citerium.

[76] **Lo2**, fol. 19v.

[77] **Be1** does include this phrase.

The following comments are intended to provide support to the stemma:

1. Common Innovations for **bcde**

Several variants reveal that **bcde** have a common ancestor (β). A particularly significant and interesting innovation common to all of the witnesses included in these families has to do with a village in the Bethlehem area. In the **a** family we read:[78] "De Bethleem ad ½ leucam contra occidentem est Bezeel villa" – "Half a league to the West of Bethlehem is the village of Bezeel." This phrase almost certainly refers to the village of Beit Jala which still exists today.[79] All of the other witnesses of the *Descriptio* provide other forms of the village's name: Bezek, Boreth (which is unique to the **b** family), Berech, and so on. But what makes this a clear case of a common innovation is the fact that almost all witnesses belonging to **bcde** add, several phrases later, at the end of the discussion of this village, the following phrase, which is not in **a**: "In hac villa captus est Adonibezech cesis summitatibus manuum eius et pedum"[80] – "In this village Adonibezek was captured, his thumbs and great toes having been cut off." This phrase is a clear reference to Judges 1.5–6, where we read: "Inveneruntque Adonibezec in Bezec, et pugnaverunt contra eum, ac percusserunt Chananeum et Ferezeum. Fugit autem Adonibezec: quem secuti conprehenderunt, caesis summitatibus manuum eius ac pedum."

The additional phrase that appears in **bcde** thus refers to the biblical Bezek and cannot in any manner be tied to the site Burchard had in mind: Bezek, as the biblical context makes clear, should be sought to the north of Jerusalem, and is identified today to the north of Nablus, while the *Descriptio* refers here to a site near Bethlehem. Consequently, the addition of this phrase should be explained in the following manner: the original toponym, which was Bezeel, or a closely related form of that name, was substituted, in some manuscripts, with Bezek, probably because the latter was better known in the West on account of its biblical background. This quite naturally led a certain scribe to add a biblical quote related to Bezek to his text. Later scribes generally saw no reason to omit this comment.

Further support for the existence of a common ancestor for **bcde** (β) comes from the *Descriptio*'s discussion of the place where John was beheaded. This is the phrase as provided by **a**:[81] "… concordant in hoc quod in Macheruta que hodie Haylem dicitur

---

[78] **Le1**, **Wo2**: orientem.

[79] Pringle, *Pilgrimage*, p. 304, n. 413.

[80] In the variations of this phrase I ignore variants of the name "Adonibezec" and changes in the placing of *eius* and *et*, as well as the insertion of an additional *et* (e.g. "et manuum"). **Ba1**, **Be3**, **Ha1**, **Pr1**, and **Up1**, all belonging to **c**, omit the phrase altogether; **Br1**, **Va1**: fuit (for "est"); **Es1**: cisis; **Kl1**: eius *om.*; **Le2**, **Pr2**: fuit (for "est"), eius *om.*

[81] This is the text as it appears in **Zw3**, fol. 125r. **Be4**: Babylon, fuit; **Le1**: in [Macheronta] *om.*, Hayson, et vidi, fuerat; **Wo2**: etiam vidi, fuit.

quam et vidi fuerit decollatus" – "… agree in this matter that he was beheaded in Macheruta, which is today called Haylem, which I also saw." And this is its parallel in **Lo2** (***b***):[82]

> … communiter ac concorditer dicunt eum in Macherunta que hodie Haylon dicitur et est ultra Iordanem, quam et vidi, eum fuisse decollatum.

> … they say in common agreement and unanimously that he was beheaded in Macherunta, which is today called Haylon, and is across the Jordan [and] which I also saw.

Clearly, the second *eum* is redundant. Indeed, this was also noted by Laurent who found the same doubling of *eum* in the manuscripts he used.[83] Notably, this error is shared by the great majority of manuscripts belonging to the ***bcde*** families, which suggests that it first appeared in their common ancestor.[84] Here are a few examples, from the different families:

> **Ba2** (***c***): … communiter dicunt et concorditer eum in Macherunta que hodie Haylon dicitur et est ultra Iordanem quam et vidi eum fuisse decollatum (fol. 210r).
> **Fl1** (***d***): … communiter et concorditer dicunt eum in Macherotha que hodie Babylon dicitur et est ultra Iordanem quam et vidi eum fuisse decollatum (fol. 6r).
> **Sa2** (***e***): … communiter et concorditer dicunt eum in Macheruta que hodie Hailon dicitur et est ultra Iordanem quam et vidi eum fuisse decollatum (fol. 200v).

Burchard's comments on Miʿiliya, or Castellum regium, as it is referred to by the *Descriptio*, also provide useful evidence in this context:

> ***a***: Inde castrum regium ad tres leucas.[85]
> ***b***: Inde 3 leucis est castellum regium in valle …[86]
> ***c***: Inde 3 leucis est castellum regium in valle …[87]
> ***d***: Inde ad tres leucas est castrum regium in valle …[88]
> ***e***: Inde una leuca est castellum regium in valle …[89]

---

[82] Fol. 18r.

[83] Laurent, *Peregrinatores*, p. 53.

[84] Among the exceptions are: **Br1**: communiter et concorditer dicunt Macerontam ductum que hodie Haylon dicitur et est ultra Iordanem quam et ego vidi eum decollatum fuisse; **Li1**: communiter dicunt et concordant eum in Macherunta fuisse sepultum que hodie Babylon dicitur et est ultra Iordanem quam vidi et eum ibi fuisse decollatum; **Na1**: communiter dicunt eum in Macheronta que hodie Samaria dicitur et est ultra Iordanem quam et vidi.

[85] Variations between *regum* and *regium* are ignored. **Le1**: castellum, ad *om*.

[86] **Le2**, **Pr2**: per tres leucas, castrum.

[87] **Pr1**: in valle *om*.

[88] **Br1**, **Es1**, **Ox1**, **Tu1**: quatuor leucas, castellum; **Fl3**: inde ad 4 leucas contra aquas Maron est castrum regium in valle; **Na1**: et ab hoc quatuor leucis ab Accon est enim castrum regium in valle.

[89] **Be1**, **Va5**: castrum; **Be1**, **Ox2**, **Sa2**, **Sa1**, **Sa3**, **Sp1**, **Vi1**, **Wo1**: ad unam leucam; **Va1**: castellum nigrum.

That "in valle" was omitted from ***a*** seems far less likely than that it was inserted into **β**, because *inter alia* the site described here is actually on a hill.

Another error in ***bcde*** appears in a comment concerning the relative direction between Gilgal and Jericho: while the ***a*** family witnesses say that Jericho is located to the south-east of Gilgal, all others say that it is located to its east. Here are some representative examples:[90]

> **Zw3** (***a***): De Galgalis ad 1 leucam inter austrum et orientem Iericho est sita civitas quondam gloriosa (fol. 127r).
> **Lo2** (***b***): De Galgalis contra orientem i leuca Iericho civitas sita est quondam gloriosa (fol. 20r).
> **Ba1** (***c***): De Galgala contra orientem ad 1 leucam Ierico sita est quondam gloriosa (fol. 10r).
> **Fl1** (***d***): De Galgala contra orientem 1 leuca Ierico civitas sita est quondam gloriosa (fol. 6v).
> **Be2** (***e***): De Galgalis contra orientem una leuca est Iericho civitas sita quondam gloriosa (fol. 48r).

At a first glance, one could have argued that this is an innovation in ***a*** rather than in ***bcde***. That, however, is very unlikely since several paragraphs earlier the *Descriptio* includes a statement which makes it clear that Burchard did not place Gilgal to the west of Jericho:

> **Zw3** (***a***): Inde [de Galgalis] ad ½ leucam eundo in Iericho ad dexteram est mons Quarentena … (fol. 127r).
> **Pa3** (***e***): De Galgalis ad dimidiam leucam eundo in Iericho ad dexteram iuxta viam est mons Quarentena dictus … (fol. 18r).

Since we know that "mons Quarentena"/Jabal Quruntul is located to the north-west of Jericho, Burchard could not have possibly located Gilgal directly to the west of the city, since in that case, Jabal Quruntal would have been on the left of the way leading from it to Jericho. Thus, the reading provided by the ***a*** family is in all likelihood closer to the original.

To such evidence concerning the opposition between ***a*** on the one hand and ***bcde*** on the other, one may add numerous cases in which there is no evident error in the latter, but there is a clear division between ***a*** and the rest of the families. Here, for example, is the discussion of the name of the town of Beth Shean, as it appears in the different families. That ***bcde*** are in common opposition to ***a*** is evident:[91]

---

[90] The variations within ***a*** and within ***bcde*** are very slight and are irrelevant to the geographical relation between Gilgal and Jericho.

[91] Variations in the orthography of the toponyms, as well as slight differences in word order, are ignored.

a: Hec postea dicta fuit Scitopolis sed nunc iterum Bethsan appellatur.[92]

bce: Dicebatur aliquando Scitopolis, ut dicit Iosephus, sed nunc ab omnibus Bethsan appellatur.[93]

d: Dicebatur aliquando Scitopolis, ut dicit Iosephus, sed nunc ab omnibus dicitur Bethsan.[94]

2. Common Innovations for *cde*

One of the better-known sections in the *Descriptio* includes an account of the various religious groups found in the Holy Land. Following Laurent's edition, the opening words of this chapter are known to scholars in the manner presented by *cde*:

ce: Sunt in ea habitatores ex omni natione que sub celo est et vivit quilibet secundum ritum suum et ut veritatem dicam peiores sunt nostri Latini …[95]

d: Sunt in ea habitatores de omni natione que sub celo est et vivit quilibet secundum ritum suum et ut veritatem dicam peiores sunt nostri Latini …[96]

Notably, however, the text which the two remaining families provide is completely different:

ab: Sunt in ea habitatores ex omni natione que sub celo est et vivit quilibet secundum ritum suum. Sarraceni Mahumetem predicant …[97]

That the text as provided by *cde* is an innovation is made clear by the structure of the phrases preceding this one. Burchard's previous section describes the fruits and animals of the Holy Land. Ending this discussion, he writes:

Zw3 (*a*): Breviter ibi habundant omnia bona mundi ita quod possim dicere quod revera fluit rivis lactis et mellis ut ex hiis omnibus probari potest, sed cultores non dico fortissimos sed pessimos habet peccatores … (fol. 137r).

Lo2 (*b*): Breviter ibi habundant omnia bona mundi ita ut possim dicere quod revera fluit rivis lactis et mellis ut ex hiis omnibus probari potest. Cultores non dico fortissimos sed habet pessimos peccatores … (fol. 37r).

---

[92] **Be4**: nominatur; **Le1**: vocatur; **Wo2**: nunc *om*.

[93] Variants for *c*: **Ba2**: et Bethsan; **Ri1**, **Va6**: autem for aliquando. Variants for *e*: **Mi1**: ab omnibus dicitur Bethsan; **Ol1**, **Ph1**: dicebatur autem aliquando; **Ox2**: vocatur.

[94] **Br1**: ut dicitur Iosephus; **Fl1**, **Lo1**, **Na1**: ab omnibus Bethsan appellatur; **Pa1**: Scitopolis *om*.

[95] Variants for the *c* family witnesses: **Ba2**: dico; **Ha2**, **Kl1**, **Ri1**, **Va6**, **Va7**, **Vi2**, **Zw1**, **Zw2**: omni *om*. **Ha2**: quelibet; **Li1**: nostri Latini *om*.; **Pr1**: viri Latini; **Vi3**: viri nostri Latini sunt; **Vi2**: sunt in ea peccatores. Variants for the *e* family witnesses: **Be1**: sunt autem, quisque (for quilibet); **Mi2**, **Mi3**, **Mi1**, **Pa3**, **Pa4**: in veritate; **Mi1**: *quilibet* moved to follow *suum*; **Ox2**, **Sa1**, **Sa3**, **Vi1**, **Wo1**: sed vivit; **Pa3**: quilibet vivit; **Ve1**: ut *om*., *sunt* moved to the end of the sentence.

[96] **Br1**: vivunt; **Es1**: est *om*., vunt [*sic*], Latini nostri; **Fl1**, **Lo1**: habitantes; **Fl2**, **Pa1**: ut *om*.; **Na1**: ex omni; **Ox1**: quelibet.

[97] **Le2** and **Pr2** do not include this phrase. The *a* family manuscripts add "ut credo" in different places in the first phrase; **Wo2**: et vivit *om*.

> **Li1** (*c*): Et breviter ibi habundant omnia bona mundi et terra ista fluit omnino lacte et mellis rivis. Sed cultores non dico fortissimos sed pessimos et turpissimos habet peccatores ... (fol. 190r).
> **Lo1** (*d*): Et ibi habitant [*sic*] omnia bona mundi et fluit terra illa omnino rivis lactis et mellis sed cultures non fortissimos sed turpissimos habet et peccatores ... (fol. 156r).
> **Mi1** (*e*): Breviter ibi habundant omnia bona mundi et terra fluit omnino rivos lactis et mellis sed cultores non dico fortissimos sed pessimos et turpissimos habet et peccatores ... (fol. 122r–v).

This phrase is clearly based on Num. 13.27–28: "… et narraverunt dicentes venimus in terram ad quam misisti nos quae re vera fluit lacte et melle ut ex his fructibus cognosci potest sed cultores fortissimos habet."

Considering that Burchard was writing in the 1280s, when almost all of the Holy Land was already in Mamluk hands, and that he is most likely to have structured this part of the text with the analogy between the Franks and Joshua's Hebrews in mind, it makes much more sense that he originally started this discussion with the Kingdom's greatest enemies, the Muslim Mamluks, than with a condemnation of Frankish society. That in the following decades there took place a process, in which the tone towards the Franks of Outremer became harsher, is easy to explain: such a discourse would make the destruction of the Kingdom of Jerusalem more comprehensible.

Further evidence for the connection of *cde* seems to come from the discussion of sugar cane to which we already referred earlier:

> ***ab***: Canne mellis similiter ibi crescunt in locis oportunis que sunt similes cannis communibus exterius, sed maiores multo. Interius vero non …[98]
> ***cde***: Canne mellis similiter crescunt ibi que sunt similes cannis communibus, sed maiores. Interius non …[99]

We see here that all manuscripts other than those belonging to ***ab*** omit the expression "in locis oportunis" as well as the word *exterius*, which, given the use of the word *interius* later, is most likely to have originally been used by the author. It is therefore plausible that this phrase includes additional evidence for the existence of a common ancestor for ***cde*** (**γ**).

---

[98] **Le2** and **Pr2** do not include this phrase. Variations related to the movement of *ibi* are ignored. **Be4**: interius enim; **Le1**: locis optimis, que sunt *om.*, vero *om.*; **Lo2**: vero *om.*; **Wo2**: mellis *om.*

[99] Variations in the form of the words *canne mellis* as well as in the location of *similes* are ignored. Variations for *c*: **Be3**, **Pr1**: non *om.*; **Ha1**, **Up1**: similes *om.*, non *om.*; **Kl1**: commilis (for "canne mellis"); **Li1**: maioribus; **Vi2**: plures (for "similes"). Variations for *d*: **Fl1**: cannis communibus *om.*, non *om.*; **Lo1**: gais(?) communibus, non *om.*; **Na1**: interius vero non; **Ox1**: interius vero sunt. Variations for *e*: **Be1**: interius vero non; **Ol1**: tarminalibus [?]; **Ph1**: *similiter* placed after *ibi*; **Ve1**: ibi que sunt ibi similes; **Va1**: ibi *om.*; **Va5**: que maiores.

Additional evidence for the existence of this common ancestor comes from the *Descriptio*'s reference to the tomb of Chariton and his followers in the region of Tekoa. Here, we read the following:

ab: et ostenditur ibidem usque hodie sepultura ...[100]
cde: et fuit quondam concursus magnus ad locum ipsum ...[101]

It seems likely that, while Burchard phrased this remark in the present tense, a later scribe/editor thought that it would make more sense in the past tense.

3. Common Innovations for *de*

Several readings suggest that families *d* and *e* are based on a common ancestor (δ). Speaking about the view seen from a vantage point to the south of Hebron, we read the following in **Lo2** (fol. 33r):

> In colle quodam sublimi, stans cum aliis multis, vidi totam terram Arabie usque ad montem Seyr, et omnia loca circa Mare Mortuum et loca latibulorum David, Iordanem insuper usque Sechim et usque ad montem Abarim. Contra occidentem vero vidi in eodem loco totum litus maris magni ab Ioppe usque Gazam ...

> Standing, with many others, on a certain high hill, I saw all of the land of Arabia as far as mount Seir, and all of the places around the Dead Sea and David's hiding places, moreover the Jordan as far as Sechim and as far as Mount Abarim. Toward the west I saw in that same place the whole coast of the great sea from Jaffa as far as Gaza ...

The relevant variant has to do with the words "in eodem loco," which, in the great majority of manuscripts belonging to the *d* and *e* families, were substituted by the words "in Hebron loco" or simply "in Hebron," the word *loco* having been omitted as it seemed to have made little sense within the new phrase.[102]

Another common innovation which appears in both of these families occurs in the description of the Calvary. The walls there are described as decorated "opere musivo" in the *b* and *c* families but "opere mosaico" by the great majority of manuscripts

---

[100] **Le2** and **Pr2** omit this phrase; **Be4**: eorum sepultura; **Le1**: ibi; **Wo2**: sepultura eorum.

[101] Variants for *c*: **Ba2**: conversus; **Ha2**: istum; **Kl1**: fuit *om.*, ipsum *om.*; **Pr1**: ipsum locum; **Zw1**: quondam(?). Variations for *d*: **Br1**: magnus excursus, istum; **Es1, Fl3, Ox1, Pa1, Tu1**: istum; **Fl1, Fl2, Lo1, Ox1, Pa1**: quidam; **Na1**: eundem locum. Variants for *e*: **Be1**: et sit concursus magnus ad locum istum; **Be2, Pa2, Ph1, Va5, Ve1**: quondam *om.*, istum; **Mi2, Pa3**: illum; **Mi3, Pa4**: vir conversus, illum; **Ol1**: istum; **Va1**: magnus concursus populorum ad locum istum.

[102] The *a* family does not include the expression "in eodem loco" in the parallel form of this phrase. Five witnesses from the *c* family omit this expression: **Ba1, Be3, Ha1, Pr1, Up1**. The variants for *d* and *e* are: **Pa1** omits the relevant words; **Br1, Es1, Fl2, Fl3, Na1, Ox1, Sa3, Tu1**: loco *om.* (in **Fl2** the words "in Ebron" appear to have been deleted); **Mi2, Mi3, Pa4**: in *om.*

belonging to the ***d*** and ***e*** families.[103] The hypothesis for a strong connection between these families can be further supported by a variant we have already explored while discussing the ***c*** family. We have noted there that in the discussion of *Neelescol*, the ***c*** family adds "vel vallis lacrimarum," while families ***d*** and ***e*** include here only the words "vel vallis."[104]

4. All Families (***abcde***) Depend on One Archetype

It has proved quite difficult to find common errors appearing in all of the extant witnesses. This is not surprising, of course, given the extent of engagement with the text by numerous scribes, some of whom clearly tried to improve it. Nonetheless, there are some errors, shared by numerous witnesses from all families, which do suggest that all of the extant witnesses ultimately depend on one archetype (***a***). Here is one such error as it appears in a variety of manuscripts coming from different families:

> **Zw3** (***a***): Est autem munita valde milicia et castris fortissimis scilicet hospitalis templi et arcis civitatis (fol. 115v).
> **Lo2** (***b***): Est etiam munita multa militia hospitalis templi et domus teutonice et castris eorum et arcis civitatis (fol. 4r).
> **Ba1** (***c***): Est munita multa milicia hospitalis templi et theutonie et castris eorum et arcis civitatis (fol. 3r–v).
> **Fl2** (***d***): est etiam munita multa militia templi et hospitalis et domus theotonice et castris eorum et arcis civitatis (fol. 2v).
> **Pa3** (***e***): Est eciam munita multa militia hospitalis templi et domus teothonice et castris eorum et arcis civitatis (fol. 3v).

The word *arcis* is likely an error for *arce*, which was indeed noted by Laurent who corrected this phrase.[105] While some witnesses, mainly in the ***e*** family, include other readings (such as *arcibus*), the fact that this error appears in numerous witnesses across all families of the tradition makes it probable that it originated in a common archetype.

Another error which appears across the manuscript tradition and seems to originate in the archetype (***a***) is the appearance of the form "Barach filius Achynoe" instead of "Barac filius Abinoem" as in the Vulgate (Judges 4.6).[106] Out of all of the extant witnesses, only three include the proper form, probably as a result of the work of scribes who were able to identify the error.[107]

---

[103] The ***a*** family does not include this phrase. The exceptions in ***bc*** are: **Pr2**: opere musaico; **Ri1**: opere subtilissimo; **Up1**: opere finissimo. Variations in ***d*** and ***e***: **Es1, Ox1, Tu1**: opere masayco; **Mi2, Mi3, Pa3, Pa4, Va4**: opere musyno. **Na1** is clearly trying to face a difficulty in his model: opere musicio vel musivo.

[104] See above, p. 267.

[105] Laurent, *Peregrinatores*, p. 23.

[106] Some manuscripts include very corrupted forms of that name, such as Ethinee.

[107] These are **Ha2** (where this results from a later correction), **Sa1, Vi1**.

Another interesting case has to do with the discussion of Sarona:[108]

> ***ab***: est mons Saron et Sarone cuius oppidi mentio fit in Actibus apostolorum.[109]
>
> ***cde***: est mons Saron et oppidum Sarona cuius mentio fit in Actibus apostolorum.[110]

As can be seen, ***ab*** provide a reading which is difficult to understand, perhaps the result of the substitution of *vel* with *et*. My suggestion is that the reading in ***cde*** reflects an attempt in their common ancestor (γ) to face this textual problem. That this was not the text as Burchard composed it can perhaps be supported by the fact that there is no evidence for the existence of a settlement known as Saron.[111]

Another error in the text of the *Descriptio* which in all likelihood goes back to the archetype (α) concerns Burchard's discussion of the Decapolis. The text is provided by Laurent as follows:[112]

> Et dicitur Decapolis a X civitatibus principalibus in ea sitis. Que sunt: Tiberias, Sephet, Cedes Neptalim, Asor, Cesarea Philippi, Capharnaum [quam Iosephus Iuliam appellat], Iotapata, Bethsayda, Corrozaym, Bethsan, que eciam Scythopolis dicebatur.
>
> And this region is called Decapolis after the ten major cities located in it. They are: Tiberias, Sephet, Cedes Neptalim, Asor, Cesarea Philippi, Capharnaum [to which Josephus refers as Iulia], Iotapata, Bethsayda, Corrozaym, Bethsan, which is also called Scythopolis.

Both Laurent and Pringle note that the words in brackets are a wrongly placed gloss since they should refer to Bethsaida rather than to Capernaum.[113] Given Burchard's familiarity with Josephus' work, it is unlikely that this was his own error. Rather, as Laurent had already suggested, it is much more probable that it was a scribe who incorrectly placed this comment. As this gloss appears following the toponym Capernaum in all of the long version witnesses of the *Descriptio* which include this phrase, one must assume that this error was already included in the archetype (α).[114]

---

[108] Note that there is a considerable degree of variation in the order in which sites are presented in this part of the *Descriptio*. In the variants of this phrase I ignore differences in the orthography of the toponyms as well as changes between *sit/fit* and *mentio/mensio*.

[109] **Le1**: mons Zaron et Zarone opidum cuius mensio fit in Actibus apostolorum; **Wo2**: et Sarone *om*.; **Zw3**: fit mentio; **Le2** and **Pr2** omit this phrase.

[110] **Be1**: de quo fit mentio; **Kl1**: mons Saron et opidum est Sarona cuius mencio fit in actibus apostolorum; **Mi2**: mentio(?); **Pr1**: cuius(?).

[111] Pringle, *Pilgrimage*, p. 308, n. 450. The biblical text (Acts 9.35) reads: "Et viderunt eum omnes qui habitabant Lyddae et Saronae: qui conversi sunt ad Dominum."

[112] Laurent, *Peregrinatores*, p. 46.

[113] Laurent, *Peregrinatores*, p. 46, n. 283; Pringle, *Pilgrimage*, p. 269, n. 202.

[114] The whole phrase is not included in **Be4**, **Le1**, and **Wo2**. This section is also omitted from **Va6**. The ***d*** family manuscripts, except for **Na1**, have *vocat* for *appellat* and so does also **Be1**. In several manuscripts the gloss is slightly corrupted.

Evidence from the discussion of Jerusalem's size as provided by **Lo2** and **Zw3** seems to show that **a** included marginalia. To begin with **Lo2**, this discussion appears here, as it also does in Laurent's edition, between the city's description and an account of its gates. It includes, following an account of Jerusalem's size based on Josephus,[115] a long citation from Jacques de Vitry's *Historia orientalis* beginning with the words: "dicit enim venerabilis pater dominus Iacobus de Vitriaco" and ending with "hucusque verba domini Iacobi patriarche."[116] However, just before these closing words, we read the following:

> Ego mensuravi ipsam sanctam secundum magnitudinem quam habuit tempore Salomonis vel etiam passionis et inveni per dyametrum a porta vallis usque ad portam veterem 380 passus et ista fuit <ambitus> latitudo civitatis que est hodie plurimum ampliata quia locus dominice passionis nunc est intra qui fuit antiquitus extra civitatem.

> I measured that same holy [city] according to its size in the time of Salomon or even of the Passion and I found 380 paces in diameter from the gate of the valley to the old gate, and this was the width of the city which is much larger today because the place of the Passion of the Lord now is inside the city while anciently it was outside of it.

Since this comment, which does not appear in Jacques' work, is placed between the opening and closing comments enclosing a citation from his *Historia orientalis*, it should in all likelihood be understood as a marginal note wrongly inserted into Burchard's text.[117] A comparison with manuscript **Zw3** is instructive. Here, the whole discussion of Jerusalem's size is placed differently, at the beginning of the city's description. Following a comment on the city's small population in comparison to its size,[118] we read, in slight changes, the above-noted comment beginning with "ego mensuravi."[119] This is followed by the phrase "de magnitudine civitatis sancte sciendum quod secundum Iosephum ...," which is followed in turn by the above-noted citations from Josephus and Jacques de Vitry. This structure makes it likely that the scribe whose work formed the basis for **Zw3** also saw this comment, and perhaps all of the discussion of the city's size, on the margins and decided to place it differently.

---

[115] Josephus, *The Jewish War, Books IV–VII*, trans. Henry S.J. Thackeray, Loeb Classical Library 242 (Cambridge, Mass., 1979), 5.4.3, p. 247.

[116] **Lo2**, fol. 28r–v.

[117] For Jacques' parallel text, see Jacques de Vitry, *Histoire orientale*, ed. and trans. Jean Donnadieu (Turnhout, 2008), pp. 240–42.

[118] Cf. Laurent, *Peregrinatores*, p. 63.

[119] **Zw3**, fol. 129r–v.

That the "ego mensuravi" note was in the archetype is supported by the fact that it is also found in *e*.[120]

The evidence presented above suggests that all the extant witnesses of the long version depend on a common archetype (**a**). With the necessary caution, it is possible to make a few hypothetical suggestions concerning the nature of that manuscript. It seems likely that **a** was a copy that a scribe prepared from an earlier manuscript which had marginal comments on it (**Ω**). This would explain, for example, the incorrect placing, across the tradition, of the above-noted comment "quam Iosephus ... ." After this copy, our archetype (**a**), was produced, it seems that additional glosses were added to it, some at least by Burchard himself. This would explain why a comment such as "ego mensuravi" is not uniformly located. Further support for this hypothesis comes from Burchard's dated comments concerning his visit to Mount Gilboa, which appear in **Lo2** in the context of the route between Mount Gilead and Jezreel but in **Zw3** following his account of Shunem.[121] That a comparison between **Zw3** and **Lo2** reveals a considerable number of additional, differently located, passages gives further weight to this hypothesis. While, of course, such a manuscript of the *Descriptio* is not known to us, a near contemporary and fellow friar of Burchard did leave a comparable manuscript behind. **Be2**, which includes the *Descriptio*, also provides a unique witness of Riccoldo of Monte Croce's *Liber peregrinationis*. Its detailed study revealed that while it was produced by an unknown scribe, it also includes annotations and revisions by Riccoldo himself, who, however, did not completely remove errors from the copied text.[122] The evidence provided above suggests that Burchard may have worked in a similar manner, and that **a** may have resembled the *Liber peregrinationis* section of **Be2**.

Preliminary Conclusions

The present examination enables us to reach some conclusions with regard to several main themes or questions. The first of these is, of course, the reconstruction of a text as close as possible to Burchard's original. In that context, our analysis shows that such a reconstruction should be based on the agreement between families *a* and *b* and specifically on **Zw3** and **Lo2** which provide a far more complete text than the other

---

[120] See, for example, **Be2**, fol. 52v, **Br2**, fols. 162v–163r, and **Kl3**, fol. 25r–v (where this comment appears between the citation from Josephus and that from the *Historia orientalis*), **Pa3**, fol. 27r, and **Pa4**, fol. 35v (where the comment follows Jacques de Vitry's citation).

[121] For the text of these comments as they appear in **Lo2**, see Rubin, "Burchard," p. 180. **Zw3**, fol. 124v, provides a very similar, but not identical, text. Cf. Laurent, *Peregrinatores*, p. 52, where only a partial version of these comments appears in the same location in which **Lo2** has them.

[122] Pringle, *Pilgrimage*, pp. 55–57; Riccold de Monte Croce, *Pérégrination en Terre Sainte et au Proche Orient, Lettres sur la chute de Saint-Jean d'Acre*, ed. and trans. René Kappler (Paris, 1997), pp. 11, 22–27.

witnesses belonging to these families. When they present erroneous readings, the other manuscripts belonging to their families can be used to correct the text. Our stemma also supports the authenticity of the sections concerning Burchard's journeys to Egypt and the West which appear in both of these manuscripts. It should be noted, however, that the archetype upon which *a* and *b* are based (**α**) included both errors and marginalia. Thus, one should be careful in any attempt to reconstruct the *Descriptio*, even when there is a consensus between these two families.

The results of this study make it possible not only to get closer to Burchard's original, but also to learn about the innovations inserted into the *Descriptio* by various scribes/editors. Thus, for example, we have seen that while Burchard was thought to have begun his discussion of the religions of the Holy Land with the Franks, he in fact opened this section of his work with a narrative about the Muslims, and it was a later editor who decided that this discussion should begin with the Franks. Another example may be added in this context: Laurent's edition includes a passage in which the author describes comments which he had heard from the Greek patriarch concerning the Greek attitude toward the Catholic Church.[123] But these comments do not appear in *a* and *b* and are thus, in all likelihood, an innovation of **γ**. Further editorial interventions have also meant that for centuries most of what Burchard wrote about himself remained hidden in neglected manuscripts, most notably **Lo2** and **Zw3**. From the point of view of cultural history, it is also noteworthy that the omission of sections of the *Descriptio*, which are not devoted to the Holy Land, took place on more than one occasion, as can be attested from the fact that they occurred in both of the tradition's main branches. Finally, the available evidence shows that the *Descriptio* was intensively reworked in the decades immediately following its composition. This is attested by the likely dating of a witness from the *d* family to before 1322 (**Fl1**),[124] as well as by the fact that Marino Sanudo (who died ca. 1334) used a manuscript of the *Descriptio* which included the abbreviated account of Egypt, typical to *e*.[125] These are, obviously, only some preliminary findings. Following the results of this study, they will hopefully contribute to the advancement of our understanding of Burchard's *Descriptio Terre Sancte* and its later development.

---

[123] Cf. Laurent, *Peregrinatores*, p. 89.

[124] Gabriella Pomaro, "Censimento dei manoscritti della Biblioteca di S. Maria Novella. Parte I: Origini e Trecento," *Memorie Domenicane, Nuova serie* 11 (1980), pp. 389–402, 418.

[125] Rubin, "A Missing Link," pp. 75–76; *Marino Sanudo Torsello, The Book of the Secrets of the Faithful of the Cross*, trans. Peter Lock (Farnham, 2011), p. 3.

Abstract

Burchard of Mount Sion's *Descriptio Terre Sancte* is well known to scholars of the medieval Holy Land as a systematic account of that territory composed in the 1280s. It was also extremely popular in late medieval and early modern times, as is made clear by the considerable number of extant manuscripts and printed editions which provide it. And yet, very little is known about the text as Burchard actually composed it and about the way it evolved over time. The aim of this paper is to propose, for the first time, a full survey of the manuscripts providing the so-called long version of the *Descriptio*, revealing their division into families as well as the relations between them. It is hoped that this analysis will bring us much closer to Burchard's original text and, at the same time, facilitate future studies on specific problems related to the *Descriptio*'s tradition and reception.

Résumé

La *Descriptio Terre Sancte* de Burchard de Mont Sion, rédigée vers 1280, est une œuvre familière aux spécialistes de la Terre Sainte médiévale, qui la considèrent comme un compte-rendu systématique de cette région. Ce texte connut également une grande popularité au cours du bas Moyen Âge ainsi qu'au début de l'époque moderne, comme le démontre le vaste nombre de manuscrits et d'éditions imprimées de cette œuvre qui nous sont parvenus. Pourtant, nous savons très peu de choses sur le texte tel qu'il fut rédigé par Burchard ainsi que sur la façon dont il a évolué au fil du temps. Le but de cet article est d'offrir, pour la première fois, une étude exhaustive de tous les manuscrits de ce qu'on appelle la "longue version" de la *Descriptio*. Nous analyserons les différentes familles de manuscrits ainsi que les rapports entre celles-ci. Nous espérons que cette étude permettra nous rapprocher du texte original de Burchard, et en même temps facilitera la recherche concernant la tradition et la réception de la *Descriptio Terre Sancte*.

Jonathan Rubin
Bar Ilan University
jonathan.rubin5775@gmail.com

Appendix

Part I: Manuscripts of the Descriptio: *Long Redaction*

*   Witnesses missing folia.
** Abbreviated witnesses.
[…] Family.[126]

Ba1   Basel, Universitätsbibliothek, MS A.V.17 (saec. XIV–XV, Basel, Library of the Dominican Order), fols. 2r–20v [**c**].

Ba2   Basel, Universitätsbibliothek, MS A.I.28 (saec. XV, Basel, Library of the Dominican Order), fols. 195r–232r [**c**].

---

[126] For question marks adjoined to the family *sigla*, see above, p. 261 and n. 15.

Be1	Berlin, Deutsche Staatsbibliothek zu Berlin – Preussischer Kulturbesitz, MS Lat. fol. 464, fols. 46r–53v, 88r–99v [**e**, probably contaminated].
Be2	Berlin, Deutsche Staatsbibliothek zu Berlin – Preussischer Kulturbesitz, MS Lat. qu. 466 (saec. XIV); online description [http://resolver.staatsbibliothek-berlin.de/SBB000168EA00000000], fols. 36v–62v [**e**].
Be3	Berlin, Deutsche Staatsbibliothek zu Berlin – Preussischer Kulturbesitz, MS Lat. oct. 293 (olim Hildesheim Gymnasialbibliothek MS 17; saec. XIV), fols. 3r–110v [**c**].
Be4	Bern, Burgerbibliothek, MS 46 (saec. XIV), fols. 1r–18r [**a**].
Br1	Brussels, Bibliothèque Royale, MS 9176–9177 (saec. XV), fols. 25r–43r [**d**].
Br2	Brussels, Bibliothèque Royale, MS 733–741 (saec. XV, Leuven, St. Martin), fols. 143r–175r [**e**].
Es1	El Escorial, Real Biblioteca del Monasterio de San Lorenzo, MS O.III.34 (saec. XIV), fols. 32v–60v [**d**].
Fl1	Florence, Biblioteca nazionale centrale, MS Conv. Soppr. F.IV.733 (saec. XIII–XIV), fols. 29r–43r [**d**].
Fl2	Florence, Biblioteca nazionale centrale, MS Conv. Soppr. C.VIII.2861, fols. 1r–27r [**d**].
Fl3	Florence, Biblioteca Medicea Laurenziana, MS Plut. 76.56, fols. 94r–101v [**d**].
Ha1	Hamburg, Staats- und Universitätsbibliothek, MS Cod. Petri 30b (saec. XIV), fols. 249r–275v [**c**].
Ha2	Hamburg, Staats- und Universitätsbibliothek, MS Cod. Geogr. 59, pp. 10–64 [**c**].
Kl1	Klagenfurt, Universitätsbibliothek, MS Pap.-Hs. 152 (saec. XIV–XV); online description [https://permalink.obvsg.at/UKL/AC05989352]), fols. 15r–46v [**c**].
**Kl2	Klagenfurt, Archiv der Diözese Gurk, MS Maria Saal 15 (saec. XIV–XV), fols. 134r–155r [**c**(?)].
Kl3	Klosterneuburg, Stiftsbibliothek, MS 722 A (saec. XV, Klosterneuburg), fols. 1r–40v [**e**].
*Le1	Leiden, Bibliotheek Rijksuniversiteit, MS B.P.L. 69 (saec. XV), fols. 99r–115v [**a**].
Le2	Leipzig, Universitätsbibliothek, MS 525 (saec. XIV), fols. 58v–74v [**b**].
Li1	Lilienfeld, Stiftsbibliothek, MS 145 (saec. XIV, Lilienfeld); online description [http://manuscripta.at/?ID=31317], fols. 174r–192r [**c**].
**Li2	Lindau, Stadtarchiv, MS ERB P I 1 (saec. XV), fols. 129r–161r [**d**(?)].
Lo1	London, British Library, MS Harley 3995 (saec. XIV–XV, Florence, Santa Croce), fols. 141r–158r [**d**].
Lo2	London, British Library, MS Add. 18929 (saec. XIV, Erfurt, S. Peter), fols. 1r–50v [**b**].
**Me1	Melk, Stiftsbibliothek, MS 952 (saec. XIV, Melk), pp. 73–94 [**c**(?)].
Mi1	Milan, Biblioteca Ambrosiana, MS Trotti 500 (saec. XIV), fols. 89r–129r [**e**].
Mi2	Milan, Biblioteca Ambrosiana, MS A 219 inf. (saec. XV, Milan, Schola dom. Hieronymi Calchi), fols. 1r–34v [**e**].
Mi3	Milan, Biblioteca Ambrosiana, MS A 223 inf. (saec. XIV, Brugora, Monastero dei Santi Pietro e Paolo), fols. 83r–108v [**e**].
Na1	Nancy, Bibliothèque municipale, MS 1082, 250, fols. 89r–178r [**d**, probably contaminated].
*Na2	Naples, Biblioteca nazionale, MS VIII D 10 (saec. XIV–XV), fols. 6r–30v [**e**(?)].
Ol1	Olomouc, Státni vědecká knihovna, MS M II 128 (saec. XV, Königsfeld Charterhouse), fols. 288r–315v [**e**].
Ox1	Oxford, Magdalen College, MS 43 (saec. XIV–XV, London, Carmelite convent [?]), fols. 24r–43r [**d**].

Ox2	Oxford, Bodleian Library, MS Lat. Hist. e. 1 (olim Admont, Benediktinerstift, MS 401; saec. XIII, Admont); online description [https://medieval.bodleian.ox.ac.uk/catalog/manuscript_6433]), fols. 1v–31v [e].
*Pa1	Padua, Biblioteca Universitaria, MS 1027 (saec. XV, Padua, Santa Giustina), fols. 63r–134v [d].
Pa2	Padua, Biblioteca del Seminario Vescovile, MS 74 (saec. XIV–XV, Venice), fols. 1r–27v [e].
Pa3	Paris, Bibliothèque nationale de France, MS nouv. acq. lat. 288 (Milan), fols. 1r–45r [e].
Pa4	Paris, Bibliothèque nationale de France, MS nouv. acq. lat. 781 (olim Cheltenham 7498), fols. 5r–54r [e].
Ph1	Philadelphia, University of Pennsylvania, Rare Book & Manuscript Library, MS 60 (olim MS Lea 4; saec. XIV–XV, Bologna (?); online description [http://dla.library.upenn.edu/dla/medren/record.html?id=MEDREN_9914739373503681]), fols. 1r–42v [e].
Pr1	Prague, Národní knihovna České republiky, MS XIV C 16 (saec. XIV–XV, Ostrov), fols. 31r–56v [c].
Pr2	Prague, Archiv Pražského hradu, Knihovna metropolitní kapituly u sv. Víta, MS A CVI 2 (olim Knihovna pražské metropolitní kapituly), fols. 324r–350v [b].
Ri1	Rimini, Biblioteca Civica Gambalunga, MS SC-71 (olim D. IV 116; saec. XV), fols. 269r–320r [c].
Sa1	Salzburg, Erzabtei Sankt Peter, Stiftsbibliothek, MS b.IX.22 (saec. XV, Salzburg, St. Peter), fols. 99r–132r [e].
Sa2	Salzburg, Erzabtei Sankt Peter, Stiftsbibliothek, MS b.III.31 (saec. XV, Salzburg, St. Peter), fols. 168v–256r [e].
Sa3	Salzburg, Erzabtei Sankt Peter, Stiftsbibliothek, MS b.X.30 (saec. XV, Salzburg, Nonnenberg), fols. 46r–86v [e].
Sp1	Sankt Paul in Lavanttal, Stiftsbibliothek, MS Hosp. Chart. 145/4 (saec. XV, Spital am Pyhrn), fols. 146r–180r [e].
Tu1	Turin, Biblioteca Nazionale Universitaria, MS D.IV.21, fols. 235r–262r [d].
Up1	Uppsala, Universitetsbiblioteket, MS C 78 (saec. XIV, Vadstena Abbey), fols. 2v–58r [c].
Va1	Vatican City, Biblioteca Apostolica Vaticana, MS Reg. lat. 462, fols. 1r–106r [e].
**Va2	Vatican City, Biblioteca Apostolica Vaticana, MS Pal. lat. 832 (saec. XIV), fols. 71r–80r [e(?)].
**Va3	Vatican City, Biblioteca Apostolica Vaticana, MS Pal. lat. 1358 (saec. XV), fols. 1r–36v [c(?)].
Va4	Vatican City, Biblioteca Apostolica Vaticana, MS Urb. lat. 393, fols. 1r–16r [e].
Va5	Vatican City, Biblioteca Apostolica Vaticana, MS Barb. lat. 1952, fols. 146r–169v [e].
Va6	Vatican City, Biblioteca Apostolica Vaticana, MS Vat. lat. 4360, fols. 21r–72v [c].
Va7	Vatican City, Biblioteca Apostolica Vaticana, MS Vat. lat. 3759, fols. 37r–62v [c].
Ve1	Venice, Biblioteca nazionale Marciana, MS lat. X 24 (olim 3296; saec. XV), fols. 1r–58v [e].
Vi1	Vienna, Österreichische Nationalbibliothek, MS 9530, fols. 2r–61r [e].
Vi2	Vienna, Österreichische Nationalbibliothek, MS 3341, fols. 1r–14v [c].
Vi3	Vienna, Österreichische Nationalbibliothek, MS 1628 (saec. Unknown, Aggsbach Charterhouse), fols. 1r–21v [c].
**Wa1	Warsaw, Biblioteka Narodowa, MS 8052 (saec. XV, Święty Krzyż), fols. 280r–293v [d(?)].

Wo1 Wolfenbüttel, Herzog August Bibliothek, MS 354 Helmst. (saec. XV), fols. 132r–167r [e].
Wo2 Wolfenbüttel, Herzog August Bibliothek, MS Weissenb. 41 (saec. XV), fols. 179v–197r [a].
Zw1 Zwettl, Stiftsbibliothek, MS 76 (saec. XIV, Zwettl), fols. 221v–256r [c].
Zw2 Zwettl, Stiftsbibliothek, MS 315 (saec. XIV, Zwettl), fols. 121v–154r [c].
Zw3 Zwickau, Ratsschulbibliothek, MS I XII 5 (saec. XV, Zwickau, St. Marien), fols. 112v–144v [a].

Part II: Excerpts of the Descriptio, *Long Redaction*

Ko1 Copenhagen, Det Kongelige Biblioteket, MS Thott 580 4° (saec. XV, Brødentz), fols. 400r–404v.
Mu1 Munich, Universitätsbibliothek, MS 2° 672 (saec. XV, Regensburg(?)), fols. 102r–115v.
Mu2 Munich, Bayerische Staatsbibliothek, cgm 2928 (saec. XV Munich, Franciscans), fols. 125v–128v.
Mu3 Munich, Bayerische Staatsbibliothek, clm 14583 (saec. XV, Regensburg, St. Emmeram), fols. 457r–472v; 476v–485r.
Wo3 Wolfenbüttel, Herzog August Bibliothek, MS 643 Helmst. (saec. XIV), fols. 196r–211r.

English Hebraism and Hermeneutic History:
The Psalter Prologues and Epilogue of Henry Cossey, OFM

ANDREW KRAEBEL
Trinity University, San Antonio

"Although this man was literate, and he probably knew Hebrew, he is nevertheless unworthy of such authority and should not be believed. Instead, return to the Hebrew about which he spoke, and if he spoke the truth, then it is the Hebrew that should be believed, not him."[1] Though Roger Bacon, OFM (d. ca. 1292) is unusually disdainful of those of his fellow scholastics who depend upon Latin intermediaries – in this case, the twelfth-century canon Andrew of St. Victor – for their knowledge of Hebrew, his belief that the interpretation of Scripture should be grounded in a familiarity with the text's original languages was much more widespread, reflected in the interpretive priorities of exegetes active in the decades following his death. The most influential proponent of such scholastic Hebraism was undoubtedly Nicholas of Lyre, OFM (d. 1349), who makes his facility with the language evident throughout his literal postils on the Old Testament, offering corrections to the Vulgate and drawing on medieval Jewish sources to establish the text's *sensus litteralis*.[2] The success of these postils was rapid, and within a decade of his death Lyre had become a standard authority, a "commentator of first resort, based in large part on his perceived mastery of the

---

[1] Roger Bacon, *Compendium Studii Philosophiae*, VIII, in *Fr. Rogeri Bacon opera quaedam hactenus inedita*, ed. J. S. Brewer (London, 1859), p. 482: "Quamvis igitur fuerat literatus homo, et probabiliter sciverit Hebraeum, tamen quia non est dignus auctoritate tanta, non est ei credendum, sed recurrendum est ad Hebraeum de quo loquitur, et si verum dicat, credendum est Hebraeo, sed non ipsi."

[2] On Lyre, see Deeana Copeland Klepper, *The Insight of Unbelievers: Nicholas of Lyra and Christian Reading of Jewish Texts in the Later Middle Ages* (Philadelphia, 2007), as well as the essays collected in *Nicholas of Lyra: The Senses of Scripture*, ed. Philip D.W. Krey and Lesley Smith (Leiden, 2000); and *Nicholas de Lyre, Franciscain du XIV{e} siècle: Exégète et théologien*, ed. Gilbert Dahan (Paris, 2011). For an overview of recent work on scholastic literalism, see Alastair Minnis, "Figuring the Letter: Making Sense of *Sensus Litteralis* in Late-Medieval Christian Exegesis," in *Interpreting Scriptures in Judaism, Christianity and Islam: Overlapping Inquiries*, ed. Mordechai Z. Cohen and Adele Berlin (Cambridge, 2016), pp. 159–82. On the topic of medieval Christian Hebraism more generally, the recent study by C. Philipp E. Nothaft, *Medieval Latin Christian Texts on the Jewish Calendar: A Study with Five Editions and Translations* (Leiden, 2014), is exceptionally useful; see especially chapters 3 and 4 on English material.

Hebrew Bible."[3] Even as Lyre's unrivaled influence ensured that later commentators would value readings based on the Hebrew text, however, his authority seems to have discouraged other exegetes from learning the language for themselves. In a way that Bacon would surely have condemned, Lyre's "perceived mastery" of Hebrew led his postils to be used as a convenient intermediary. Likewise, and just as problematically, the dominance of his postils quickly overshadowed similar efforts to bring knowledge of Hebrew to bear on the interpretation of the Old Testament, evident in a host of commentaries that now survive in very few manuscripts and have received little if any scholarly attention.[4] More than simply attesting to the wide influence of Bacon's interpretive ideals, these works illustrate the variety of ways in which those ideals could be realized, and at least some of their authors were openly critical of Lyre's approach.

English writers figure prominently among the neglected scholastic Hebraists contemporary to Lyre, and arguably none engaged more fully with recent trends in biblical interpretation than Henry Cossey (or "de Costesey"), OFM, regent master at Cambridge, ca. 1325–1326.[5] Little is now known of Cossey's life.[6] His surname suggests his origin in the town of Costessey, outside of Norwich, and in all likelihood he made his profession in that city and was educated at its Franciscan *studium*, then going up to Cambridge to continue his theological training.[7] His presence in Cambridge after his regency is indicated by his inclusion among a group of Franciscans who, in 1329 and 1330, were accused of heresy and ordered to be "kept in close custody" at the university, "in the charge of the vice-guardian and of Friar Thomas Canynge, then master of the school, till they could be sent to the papal court at Avignon for further examination."[8] Whether Cossey and his fellow Franciscans ever made

---

[3] Klepper, *Insight of Unbelievers*, p. 5.

[4] Klepper, "Nicholas of Lyra and Franciscan Interest in Hebrew Scholarship," in *Senses of Scripture*, ed. Krey and Smith, pp. 289–311, usefully presents Lyre as reflecting an established interest, especially among Franciscans, in the study of Hebrew, but she does not fully account for comparable contemporary efforts, including the texts discussed here.

[5] The dating is based on his position in the list of Franciscan masters at Cambridge in London, British Library, MS Cotton Nero A.ix., fol. 78r, on which see Andrew G. Little, *Franciscan Papers, Lists, and Documents* (Manchester, 1943), pp. 132–34.

[6] For relevant sources, see Alfred B. Emden, *A Biographical Register of the University of Cambridge to 1500* (Cambridge, 1963), p. 161.

[7] The shift in practice, from sending English Franciscans to Paris for their theological training, to sending them to either Oxford or Cambridge, seems to have taken place in Cossey's lifetime; see William J. Courtenay, *Schools and Scholars in Fourteenth-Century England* (Princeton, 1987), p. 68.

[8] Little, *Franciscan Papers*, pp. 139–40, where he suggests the unnamed heresy involved the Franciscan theory of poverty opposed by John XXII. Less plausibly, Kathryn Kerby-Fulton, *Books Under Suspicion: Censorship and Tolerance of Revelatory Writing in Late Medieval England* (Notre Dame, 2006), p. 2,

the trip to the curia is unknown. Bale reports that he died at Babwell Friary (Suffolk) in 1336 and, without giving any indication of his source, claims that he studied at Oxford – a suggestion that becomes all the more intriguing in light of the material discussed below.[9] Though certainly not as prolific as Lyre, Cossey was nevertheless an accomplished exegete, writing commentaries on Luke and Wisdom which no longer survive, as well a commentary on the Apocalypse, drawing on Joachimite sources and enjoying fairly wide circulation among English Franciscans.[10] His most ambitious and innovative work, however, was almost certainly his commentary on the Psalms, now preserved uniquely in Cambridge, Christ's College, MS 11 [= **Ch**].[11] The prologues

suggests that Cossey was "arrest[ed] for revelatory authorship," apparently referring to the Joachimite content of his Apocalypse commentary. Later in the same study, however, Kerby-Fulton endorses Little's conclusion (*Books Under Suspicion*, p. 82).

[9] *Scriptorum illustrium maioris Bryttanie quam nunc Angliam & Scotiam uocant catalogus* (Basel: Oporinus, 1557), sig. ff1r. On the strength of Bale's comment, Cossey is also included in Alfred B. Emden, *A Biographical Register of the University of Oxford to A.D. 1500*, 3 vols. (Oxford, 1957), 1:495. Arduin Kleinhans's unsupported claim, in "Heinrich Cossey, OFM, ein Psalmen-Erklärer des 14. Jahrhunderts," in *Miscellanea Biblica et Orientalia R.P. Athanasio Miller OSB, Secretario Pontificae Commissionis Biblicae, Completis LXX Annis Oblata*, ed. Adalbertus Metzinger (Rome, 1951), pp. 339–53, that, before studying in Cambridge, "seine Studien machte er in Oxford, wo er auch in den Orden eintrat" (at p. 240), appears to be an attempt to reconcile Bale's comment with the fact of Cossey's regency in the other university.

[10] See Richard Sharpe, *A Handlist of the Latin Writers of Great Britain and Ireland before 1540* (Turnhout, 2001), pp. 165–66. Sharpe includes Oxford, Bodleian Library, MS Rawl. C. 16 among the manuscripts of Cossey on the Apocalypse, though, as Little, *Franciscan Papers*, pp. 140–41, demonstrates, the commentary in this manuscript is distinct from the text preserved in the other witnesses, and the attribution in Rawl. C. 16 therefore appears to be mistaken. Confusingly, without offering any evidence, Kerby-Fulton, *Books Under Suspicion*, p. 83, claims that the work in Rawl. C. 16 is actually Cossey's second commentary on the same biblical book, with its more conservative contents reflecting his timidity after the arrest of 1329–1330. For discussion of the authentic commentary's Joachimite contents, see David Burr, *Olivi's Peaceable Kingdom: A Reading of the Apocalypse Commentary* (Philadelphia, 1993), pp. 255–63.

[11] For a description of this manuscript, see M.R. James, *Descriptive Catalogue of the Western Manuscripts in the Library of Christ's College, Cambridge* (Cambridge, 1905), pp. 28–36, supplemented below. It is attributed to Cossey in its opening (fol. 1r, reproduced below in Fig. 2): "Opus fratris Henrici Costeseye magistri de Ordine Fratrum Minorum." Based on its provenance and dating, discussed below, there is no reason to doubt this attribution. Two potential further copies are attested but do not survive, one in the library of the Friars Minor in London (seen by Leland, a partial copy, ending after Psalm 61, and lacking any note of its incipit) and another in Norwich (seen by Bale, though the incipit recorded does not match the surviving text); see *The Friar's Libraries*, ed. Kenneth Wood Humphreys, Corpus of British Medieval Library Catalogues 1 (London, 1990), p. 219; and *Index Britanniae Scriptorum: John Bale's Index of British and Other Writers*, ed. Reginald Poole with Mary Bateson (Oxford, 1902), p. 160. Cossey's Psalter commentary is quoted to begin a sermon in Oxford, Bodleian

and epilogue to this commentary are edited and translated here for the first time. These texts show Cossey to have been among the earliest and most attentive readers of Lyre's literal postils on the Psalter, as well as the recent commentary on Jerome's Hebraicum translation by Nicholas Trevet, OP (d. ca. 1334), and Cossey uses his knowledge of Hebrew, in addition to his scouring of patristic writings and several more obscure sources, to offer a thorough critique of his contemporaries' interpretive efforts.

After identifying the commentary's major sources and assessing the evidence for its composition in distinct stages, indicative of its author's prolonged care and attention, this study focuses on Cossey's hermeneutic commitments, the ideas of proper interpretation which were supported by his work with the Hebrew text, and which informed his criticisms of Trevet and Lyre. Though Cossey was devoted to the general notion of scholastic literalism, his prologues reveal an understanding of the Psalter's literal sense that is more capacious and flexible than these other exegetes allowed, and he is therefore willing to interpret portions of the text as prophetic and Christological, offering the kind of readings that his contemporaries had consigned to the Psalter's spiritual or mystical senses. At the same time, Cossey is especially vigorous in his attempts to "demystify" the biblical text and to see the Psalter as a collection of songs composed by a range of different authors, and he therefore maintains that the Psalter is, in many respects, comparable to the Church's hymnary. These seemingly contradictory moves, arguing for a text that is at once more rarefied and more mundane, derive from Cossey's rigorous commitment to his authoritative sources: the Hebrew text of the Psalms, other biblical and para-biblical writings, and the works of the Fathers. In his overriding adherence to these sources, and his excoriation of scholastics who would go beyond them and present their conjectures as though they were fact, Cossey's work is arguably the fullest realization of Bacon's ideals for biblical commentary, at the same time as it captures some of his Franciscan predecessor's prickly, even rebarbative attitudes.[12]

Sources and Setting

As the notes to the edition indicate, Cossey's careful citations make it relatively easy to identify almost all of the major and minor sources of his commentary, and many of the patristic works to which he refers – the letters of Jerome, for example, and Augustine's *De ciuitate Dei* and *De doctrina christiana* – are so commonly attested as to make

---

Library, MS Laud. misc. 213, fol. 192r; see Henry O. Coxe, *Quarto Catalogues, II: Laudian Manuscripts*, rev. by Richard W. Hunt (Oxford, 1973), col. 185.

[12] Immediately before the passage quoted above, Bacon expresses his belief that "post Bedam non fuit aliquis cui ecclesia dederit auctoritatem in expositione Scripturae" – "after Bede there has not been anyone to whom the Church has given authority in the exposition of Scripture" (ed. Brewer, p. 482).

his use of them unremarkable.[13] Likewise, his recourse to twelfth-century works, including Peter Comestor's *Historia scholastica* and Peter Lombard's *Magna glosatura in Psalmos*, is standard among scholastic exegetes.[14] At least some of Cossey's sources, however, are more noteworthy, including the text of the Psalter on which his work was based, and his use of this material can allow the composition of his commentary to be dated and localized with perhaps surprising precision.

Throughout his text, as noted above, Cossey responds to the Psalter commentaries of two contemporary Christian Hebraists, Nicholas of Lyre and Nicholas Trevet, both of whom are named, and their writings quoted and paraphrased, in his prologues.[15] Though Cossey seems to be familiar with Lyre only through his writings, his references to Trevet are suggestive of a more personal acquaintance, seen in the prologues when he describes the Oxford-trained Dominican as "hic senex" – "this old man."[16] Trevet's work can be dated ca. 1317–1320, at which point he would have been in his early sixties, while a note commonly found in manuscripts of Lyre's literal postil on the Psalter dates that portion of his larger project to 1326.[17] Cossey therefore must have prepared his commentary after his Cambridge regency, in 1326 or 1327 at the earliest, supporting William J. Courtenay's suggestion that such commentaries, especially by mendicants, "were not the result of magisterial lectures, as has often been assumed, but the fruit of several years of study, reflection, and writing," benefitting

---

[13] See for example, Prol. 1.21, 73; and Prol. 3.11, 34, 37, 46–53, 66–75, etc. (Throughout the following, my edition of Cossey's text will be cited by prologue and line number.) For the wide attestation of the *De ciuitate* and the *De doctrina*, as well as Jerome's letters, in English libraries, see, e.g., *Registrum Anglie de Libris doctorum et auctorum ueterum*, ed. Richard H. Rouse and Mary A. Rouse, with Roger A.B. Mynors, Corpus of British Medieval Library Catalogues 2 (London, 1991), pp. 13, 19, and 90; Henry of Kirkestede, *Catalogus de libris autenticis et apocrifis*, ed. Richard H. Rouse and Mary A. Rouse, Corpus of British Medieval Library Catalogues 11 (London, 2004), pp. 27, 34, and 284–300.

[14] See for example, Prol. 3.19, 174–175, 220, 225 note, 523, etc. For the treatment of the Lombard as a standard exegetical reference work throughout the fourteenth century, see the examples discussed by Andrew Kraebel, *Biblical Commentary and Translation in Later Medieval England: Experiments in Interpretation* (Cambridge, 2020), chapters 1–3. The comparable status of the *Historia scholastica* is discussed more briefly in the same study, chapter 2, and see further Mark Clark, *The Making of the Historia Scholastica, 1150–1200* (Toronto, 2015), esp. pp. 214–53.

[15] For Lyre, see Prol. 3.77, 115, 195, 207, 234. For Trevet, see Prol. 3.11, 66, 77, 121, 425.

[16] Prol. 3.16.

[17] For the note dating Lyre's work, see Charles-Victor Langlois, "Nicolas de Lyre, Frère Mineur," in *Histoire littéraire de la France*, 46 vols. as of 2018 (Paris, 1733–), 36:373. Trevet's commentary was apparently written at the request of John of Bristol, then Prior Provincial of the English Dominicans (cf. Oxford, Bodleian Library, MS Bodley 738, fol. 1ra), whose tenure began in 1317 and extended to 1327. Trevet's retirement from Oxford to London ca. 1320, however, provides a more likely *terminus ante quem* for the commentary's composition. See Emden, *Biographical Register of Oxford*, 3:1902, as well as James Clark's more recent *ODNB* entry.

from "the freedom from lecturing and administrative duties that the end of the regency entailed."[18]

Following his regency, then, Cossey appears to have returned to his studies, learning enough Hebrew to parse the text of the Psalms and assess the merit of its different Latin translations and glosses. Indeed, though he begins his third prologue by announcing that he will follow the "common" translation – i.e., the widely used Gallican version, Jerome's second attempt to revise a preexisting Latin translation of the Greek Septuagint, as opposed to his final rendering, based on the Hebrew text and therefore called the Hebraicum – in practice this version serves as a simple starting-point for his glosses, and he constantly compares it to other Latin renderings, as well as to his own transliteration of the Hebrew.[19] This continuously comparative method appears to reflect the material copy of the Psalms on which Cossey based his work, a volume he associates with Robert Grosseteste (d. 1253), bishop of Lincoln and formerly lecturer to the Oxford Franciscans. (The precise nature of this attribution will be discussed below.) Cossey describes this book as "psalterium domini Lincolniensis, ubi tria uel quattuor simul coniunctim psalteria continentur" – "the lord of Lincoln's psalter, containing three or four psalters together," and he further indicates that one of these "three or four" texts is in Hebrew, while another is a Latin translation interlineated in the Hebrew.[20] As Beryl Smalley observed, this account of Grosseteste's psalter precisely matches the presentation of texts in Oxford, Corpus Christi College, MS 10 and Cambridge, Trinity College, MS R.8.6, where Jerome's Gallican and Hebraicum versions are presented in parallel columns, with a third column taken up by the Hebrew text with interlineated Latin (see Fig. 1).[21] Elsewhere in his commentary,

---

[18] William J. Courtenay, "Franciscan Learning: University Education and Biblical Exegesis," in *Defenders and Critics of Franciscan Life: Essays in Honor of John V. Fleming*, ed. Michael F. Cusato and Guy Geltner (Leiden, 2009), pp. 55–64, at 62.

[19] Prol. 3.1–5, 87–102. For examples of this comparative approach, see below.

[20] For the quotation, see **Ch**, fol. 14r, lower margin. In addition to the next passage on the interlinear rendering, see the examples from Psalms 105, 118, and 126 quoted by James, *Descriptive Catalogue*, pp. 33–34.

[21] Beryl Smalley, *Hebrew Scholarship among Christians in XIIIth Century England, as Illustrated by Some Hebrew-Latin Psalters* (London, 1939), pp. 4–5; repeated in her *Study of the Bible in the Middle Ages*, 3rd rev. ed. (Oxford, 1983), p. 344. For more recent discussions of these manuscripts, see Judith Olszowy-Schlanger, *Les manuscrits Hébreux dans l'Angleterre médiévale: Étude historique et paléographique* (Paris, 2003), pp. 52–58, 157–61, and 170–76, as well as her essays, "The Knowledge and Practice of Hebrew Grammar among Christian Scholars in Pre-Expulsion England: The Evidence of 'Bilingual' Hebrew-Latin Manuscripts," in *Hebrew Scholarship and the Medieval World*, ed. Nicholas de Lange (Cambridge, 2001), pp. 107–28, at 115; and "Christian Hebraism in Thirteenth-Century England: The Evidence of Hebrew-Latin Manuscripts," in *Crossing Borders: Hebrew Manuscripts as a Meeting-Place of Cultures*, ed. Piet van Boxel and Sabine Arndt (Oxford, 2009), pp. 115–22, at 117–18.

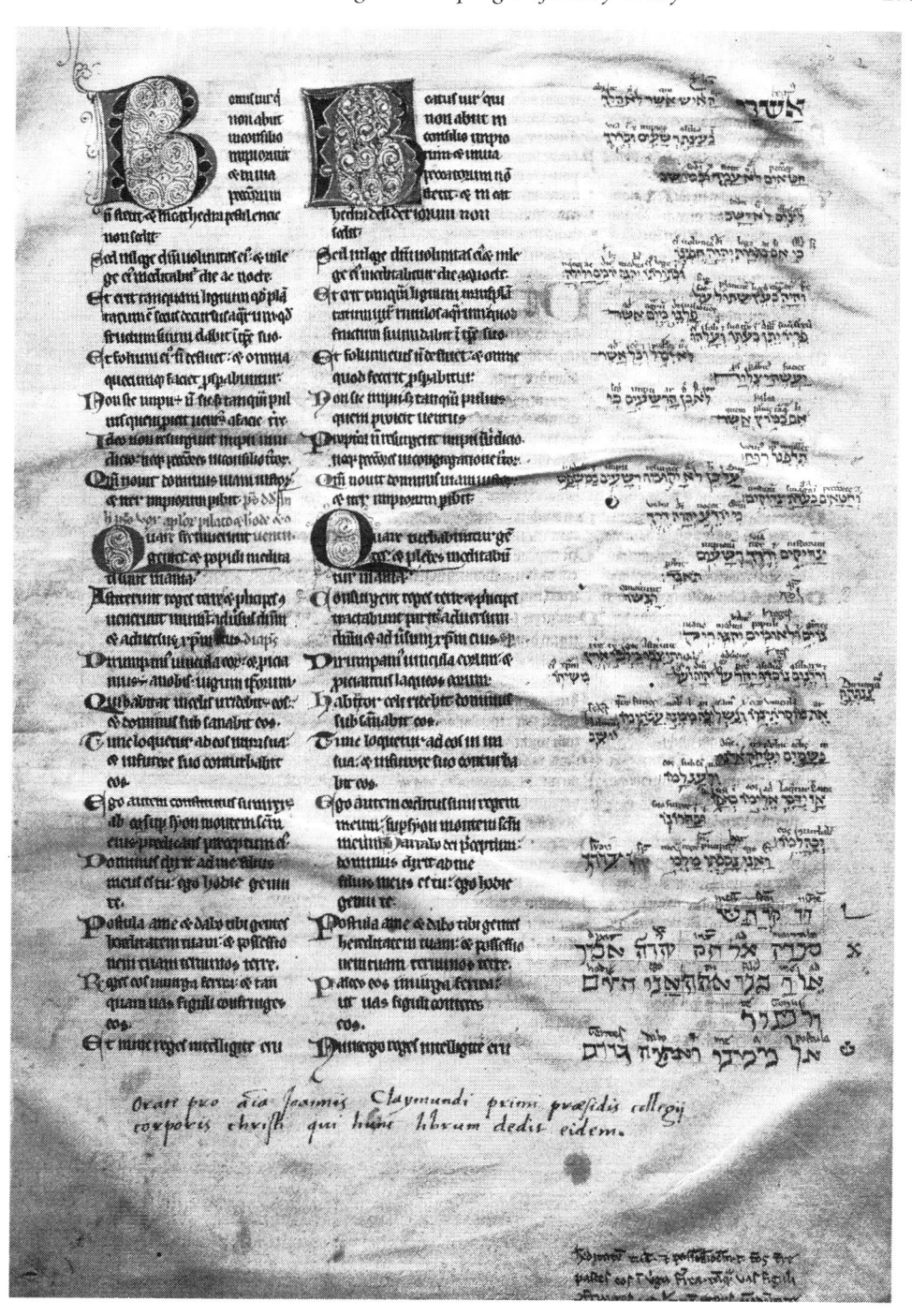

Fig. 1. Oxford, Corpus Christi College, MS 10, fol. 2r: Quadruple Hebrew-Latin psalter. Reproduced by permission of the President and Fellows of Corpus Christi College, Oxford.

Cossey notes the uncertain status of the interlinear rendering, writing that "Ecclesia uero non adhuc autentizauerit superscriptionem quam superscribi fecit dominus Lincolniensis in psalterio suo Hebraico de uerbo ad uerbum sicut in Hebreo" – "the Church has not yet authorized the superscription which the lord of Lincoln made to be interlineated in his Hebrew psalter, following the Hebrew word for word."[22] Still, he finds it convenient to quote this version throughout his commentary, referring to it as the "superscriptio Lincolniensis," and, on the basis of these quotations, Smalley was able to establish that he did indeed consult a manuscript closely related to Oxford, Corpus Christi College, MS 10, one that likely shared an exemplar with that copy or was itself Corpus's exemplar.[23]

The high regard in which Cossey appears to have held Grosseteste's quadruple psalter helps to account for several details in his prologues. It is in this volume, for example, that Cossey almost certainly found the anonymous preface ("in quadam prefacione, ... nescio cuius sit") which he discusses and quotes in full as part of his larger consideration of the Psalter's authorship.[24] This early medieval text is rarely attested in English manuscripts, but it does appear in Oxford, Corpus Christi College, MS 10, fol. 1r, and its presence in Grosseteste's psalter could therefore explain why, though he disagrees with many of its claims, Cossey devotes so much space to it in his own prologue.[25] Even more substantially, his work with Grosseteste's psalter can account for one of the most significant mistakes in Cossey's prologues, one with repercussions for his commentary as a whole. As part of his detailed account of the Psalter's translation history, Cossey attempts to identify the versions of the Latin Psalter currently in use in Rome, on the one hand, and in the wider Church, on the other, with two of the three texts prepared by Jerome. Throughout this discussion, Cossey appears to be working with the Latin texts of the Psalms copied in the first two columns of Grosseteste's psalter, and, since he recognizes one of them as the version in common use, he mistakenly assumes that the other must reflect the use of Rome. (He apparently does not know that these are the Gallican and Hebraicum versions, respectively.) Likely reflecting the distinction between common and Roman use presented in the Franciscan rule and repeated at the start of his third prologue, this assumption leads Cossey to conclude, incorrectly, that the text in common use (the Gallican) was Jerome's first version, since it matches the translation of the Greek Septuagint of Psalm 89 provided in Jerome's letter to Cyprian, while the text he takes to represent

---

[22] **Ch**, fol. 18v. This uncertainty may account for his hedging, "three or four," in the earlier quotation.

[23] Smalley, *Hebrew Scholarship*, p. 13.

[24] Prol. 3.130–172.

[25] For early examples, see St. Gall, Stiftsbibliothek, MS Sang. 22, pp. 4–7 (saec. IX, last quarter); London, British Library, MS Cotton Vespasian A.i, fols. 4v–5r (part of a ninth-century addition to the eighth-century psalter). For the text, see Donatien De Bruyne, *Préfaces de la bible latine* (Namur, 1920), pp. 43–44.

Roman use (the Hebraicum) is either Jerome's second version, emending the earlier rendering in light of the Greek and Hebrew of Origen's Hexapla, or his third version, prepared directly from the Hebrew, since it comes close to the Hebrew original translated in the same letter.[26] Throughout his commentary, then, Cossey believes that by grounding his readings in the common (Gallican) text, he is glossing a straightforward translation of the Septuagint, and, when he compares it to other versions, he refers to the Hebraicum translation as being found "in psalterio Romano" or simply as "Ieronimus," reflecting his belief that, in contrast to his earlier revisions, this is the only version that can properly be called Jerome's translation.[27] Though unfortunate, this mistake reflects Cossey's effort to scrutinize the underpinnings of an exegetical commonplace, his insistence on working from the evidence of his patristic sources, and, again, his valuing of a volume he associated with the bishop of Lincoln.

This psalter was not Cossey's only source for the Hebrew text of the Psalms. Throughout his commentary, though with less frequency than his references to Grosseteste's book and its *superscriptio*, he also cites a volume variously described as "psalterium I. dudum conuersi, "psalterium Hebraicum illius iam conuersi magistri," and "psalterium Hebraicum magistri Iohannis."[28] Cossey turns to this volume to compare its readings of specific Hebrew words to what he found in his other psalter, and to challenge some of Trevet's claims about the Hebrew text, especially its presentation in contemporary manuscripts.[29] Though it is possible that Cossey simply acquired this

---

[26] *Regula Bullata*, III, in *Opuscula Sancti Patris Francisci Assisiensis*, ed. Kajetan Esser (Grottaferrata, 1978), p. 229: "Clerici faciant divinum officium secundum ordinem sanctae Romanae Ecclesiae excepto psalterio, ex quo habere poterunt breviaria" – "Clerics should perform the Divine Office according to the order of the Roman Church, with the exception of the psalter, for which they may have their breviaries," cf. Prol. 3.1–2 (and note) and 53–55. For the comparisons with the translations in Jerome's letter, see Prol. 3.85–114. Here, and throughout the following, references to the Psalter follow the Septuagint numbering unless otherwise indicated.

[27] See the examples of Psalm 5.10, discussed below. On the status of Jerome's earlier versions as revisions rather than translations, see Prol. 3.56–77. James, *Descriptive Catalogue*, p. 35, is therefore misleading in his account of the different Latin versions of the Psalms used by Cossey, believing him to have access to all three of Jerome's renderings.

[28] **Ch**, fols. 168r, 14r, and 155r, respectively.

[29] For comparison of Hebrew texts, see the example from Psalm 82 quoted by James, *Descriptive Catalogue*, p. 33. For criticism of Trevet, see the discussion of Psalm 2, quoted by James, *Descriptive Catalogue*, p. 35: though without naming him, Cossey is here quoting and rebutting Trevet's claims (cf. Oxford, Bodleian Library, MS Bodley 738, fol. 6rb). He likewise draws on both Grosseteste's and master John's psalters to dismiss what Trevet says about the title of Psalm 76: "Et dicit Triuet quod istud, *Asaph Psalmus*, in ueris exemplaribus non habetur: sed istud est mirabile, cum in utroque psalterio, quorum unum erat diligentius scriptum et quo correctum, planissime scribatur" – "And Trevet says that this, *A Psalm of Asaph*, is not to be found in true exemplars: but this is strange, since it is written very clearly in both psalters, one of which was very diligently written and therefore correct" (**Ch**, fols. 122v–123r).

book from John, perhaps even at second-hand, his description of its owner as a "master" holds out the possibility that this John could have been responsible for teaching Cossey how to read Hebrew, and, indeed, Cossey's ongoing engagement with someone familiar with Jewish interpretive traditions is suggested elsewhere in his text. Commenting on the title (*titulus*) or superscription to Psalm 5, for example, he reports, "Dicunt Hebrei quod Ieronimus fuit deceptus" – "The Hebrews say that Jerome was mistaken" with regard to the meaning of נחילות, which the saint had rendered *hereditatem* (Gallican) or *hereditatibus* (Hebraicum), but which his source (or sources) claims to be "nomen cuiusdam instrumenti uel cantilene in templo que cantabatur ad instrumentum" – "the name of a certain instrument or of a song which is sung with an instrument in the temple."[30] This opinion can be found in Rashi's exposition of the Psalms, but, though Cossey cites Rashi elsewhere in his commentary, these references are consistently borrowed from Lyre, and it therefore seems likely that such vaguer accounts of what "the Hebrews say" derive instead from his conversations with a Jewish convert.[31] The most likely candidate is surely the "master John" whose psalter he consulted.

Taken together with his use of Grosseteste's psalter, these references to a Jewish convert and teacher named John suggest that, though he is otherwise associated with Cambridge, Cossey studied Hebrew and composed his commentary on the Psalms at Oxford. In response to the decree from the Council of Vienne (1312) that major universities should make provision for the teaching of Hebrew, Syriac, Arabic, and Greek, in 1320 the Archbishop of Canterbury, Walter Reynolds (d. 1327), worked to secure the funding needed for Hebrew instruction at Oxford, and for much of the following decade, perhaps through 1327, that post appears to have been filled by a Jewish convert named John of Bristol.[32] Since the council's decree did not include

---

[30] **Ch**, fol. 20r.

[31] See Mayer I. Gruber, *Rashi's Commentary on Psalms* (Leiden, 2004), p. 188. The single citation of Rashi in Cossey's prologues is, as noted below, borrowed from Lyre; see Prol. 1.140–41. Later in his discussion of the title of Psalm 5, Cossey cites Rashi on the performance of this psalm in the temple: "Et hic dicit Rabi Salomon quod iste psalmus factus est a Dauid ad hoc quod sacerdotes et Leuite decantarent ipsum ad impetrandum diuinum auxilium contra hostes irruentes in terram Israel, que erat hereditas Domini diuisa per duodecim tribus" – "Rashi says that this psalm was made by David for priests and Levites to sing to obtain divine aid against enemies invading the land of Israel, which was the inheritance of the Lord divided among the twelve tribes" (**Ch**, fol. 20v). This claim, considerably expanded from Rashi's original (cf. Gruber, *Commentary*, p. 188), is borrowed verbatim from Lyre's postil, for which see *Biblia sacra cum Glossa ordinaria nouisque additionibus*, ed. François Feruardent (Venice, 1603), III, sig. p7v, with Cossey simply adding a final dependent clause to gloss the passage. The notion that Cossey's "Hebrei" represent conversations with a contemporary interlocutor is supported by other references to this source, cited as "moderni Hebrei" at the start of his gloss, for example, of Psalm 47 (**Ch**, fol. 84v).

[32] This John of Bristol should not be confused with the Dominican prior provincial of the same name, mentioned above. On the decree and its implementation in England, see Robert Weiss, "England and

Cambridge, it is plausible that Cossey would have traveled to Oxford to study with this John, to confer with him about Jewish interpretations of the Psalms, and to consult his Hebrew psalter.[33] Further, working in the library of the Oxford Greyfriars, Cossey would have had access to Grosseteste's manuscripts, donated to the convent library after the bishop's death.[34] Evidence from Thomas Gascoigne's later use of the collection, between 1434/5 and 1456, indicates that at least some of these books were then identified with the bishop by their classmark, including what Gascoigne calls "psalterium suum quod non scribitur manu propria domini Lincolniensis registratur ibidem *Episcopus Lincoln. F*" – "his psalter, which is not copied in the hand of the lord of Lincoln, registered as *Bishop of Lincoln F*."[35] If this was indeed the quadruple psalter consulted by Cossey, its classmark alone could account for his association of it with Grosseteste. His use of the Greyfriars library would also help to account for one of the more obscure sources appearing in Cossey's prologues, namely, the *Institutes* of Junillus (or Junilius) Africanus (*fl*. 541–549).[36] This Antiochene text was rare in later medieval England, but it is also quoted by William Woodford, OFM in his *Quattuor Determinationes*, prepared at Oxford in 1389–1390, thus placing a copy of it, at least

---

the Decree of the Council of Vienne on the Teaching of Greek, Arabic, Hebrew, and Syriac," *Bibliothèque d'Humanisme et Renaissance* 14 (1952), 1–9. John of Bristol's name is recorded by Anthony Wood, *Historia et Antiquitates Universitatis Oxoniensis* (Oxford, 1674), I, sig. Ii4ra. See further Cecil Roth, "The Jews in the English Universities," *Jewish Historical Society of England, Miscellanies* 4 (1942), 102–15, at p. 104; and Cecil Roth, "Jews in Oxford after 1290," *Oxoniensia* 15 (1950), 63–80, at p. 63.

[33] Other English mendicants moved between universities, including Robert Holcot, OP (d. 1349), who may have taught at Cambridge after his Oxford regency; John Baconthorpe, OCarm (d. 1345/1352), who studied at Oxford and had his regency at Paris before teaching at Cambridge; and Richard Conington, OFM (d. 1330), who was regent master in theology in Oxford and then in Cambridge. See Beryl Smalley, "Robert Holcot, OP," *Archivum Fratrum Praedicatorum* 26 (1956), 5–97, at p. 9; Beryl Smalley, "John Baconthorpe's Postill on St Matthew," *Mediaeval and Renaissance Studies* 4 (1958), 91–145, at p. 93; and Victorin Doucet, "L'œuvre scolastique de Richard de Conington, OFM," *Archivum Franciscanum Historicum* 29 (1936), 396–442, at pp. 396–97.

[34] On Grosseteste's library and its donation, see Richard W. Hunt, "The Library of Robert Grosseteste," in *Robert Grosseteste, Scholar and Bishop*, ed. Daniel A. Callus (Oxford, 1955), pp. 121–45. See too Anne Hudson, "Wyclif and the Grosseteste Legacy at the Oxford Greyfriars," in *Robert Grosseteste: His Thought and Its Impact*, ed. Jack Cunningham (Toronto, 2012), pp. 201–16, who describes Wyclif's efforts to make use of the apparently ample resources of this collection.

[35] Oxford, Lincoln College, MS Lat. 118, p. 306. Robert M. Ball, "Robert Grosseteste on the Psalms," in *Grosseteste*, ed. Cunningham, pp. 79–108, at 81, suggests that Gascoigne is attempting to describe a second copy of Grosseteste's commentary on Psalms 1–100, though it seems significant that, in describing the autograph copy of the commentary, he specifies that this is a "psalterium expositum." Cf. *The Friars' Libraries*, ed. Humphreys, p. 228: "There seems to be no evidence that this contained a commentary."

[36] Prol. 1.46–47 and Prol. 3.175–177.

later in the century, in the Greyfriars library.[37] Likewise, if less remarkably, all of the patristic sources referenced in Cossey's prologue are almost certain to have been in Grosseteste's collection.[38] Finally, since his involvement in the arrests of 1329–1330 and his death in Babwell indicate that Cossey's relocation to Oxford was only temporary, his decision to quote at length from various texts – including, for example, all of the anonymous preface found in Oxford, Corpus Christi College, MS 10, mentioned above, and the *Testamenta duodecim patriarcharum*, discussed below – could be explained as an effort at preserving sources to which he knew he would only have temporary access.

And this brings us back to Smalley's claims about the role of Grosseteste in the creation of the interlinear translation, the "superscriptio Lincolniensis," preserved in Oxford, Corpus Christi College, MS 10 and Cambridge, Trinity College, MS R.8.6, and apparently consulted by Cossey in the Greyfriars library. Smalley took Cossey's various comments as an authorial attribution, a claim that Grosseteste prepared the *superscriptio*. She believed this attribution to be generally accurate, though she thought that it was more likely that the *superscriptio* had been made at Grosseteste's request than by the bishop himself, and she also suggested that Grosseteste composed a brief prologue, quoting from the *superscriptio*, that survives uniquely in Oxford, Corpus Christi College, MS 10.[39] Further, noting that the quotations in this prologue

---

[37] Oxford, Bodleian Library, MS Bodley 703, fol. 82r. On the *Determinationes*, see Kantik Ghosh, *The Wycliffite Heresy: Authority and the Interpretation of Texts* (Cambridge, 2002), pp. 67–85; Eric Doyle, "William Woodford on Scripture and Tradition," in *Studia Historico-Ecclesiastica: Festgabe für Prof. Luchesius G. Spätling* OFM, ed. Isaac Vázquez (Rome, 1977), pp. 481–504. Smalley, *Study of the Bible*, pp. 18–19, describes the rarity of Junillus's text after the ninth century. See further Marianne Pollheimer, "Divine Law and Imperial Rule: The Carolingian Reception of Junillus Africanus," in *The Resources of the Past in Early Medieval Europe*, ed. Clemens Gantner et al. (Cambridge, 2015), pp. 118–34. The only surviving English copy is a fragment preserved in London, British Library, MS Cotton Tiberius A.xv, fols. 175–180, a text associated with Malmesbury, apparently related to the copy used by Aldhelm, who quotes from the text in his *De metris*. For a useful introduction to the *Institutes*, see Michael Maas, *Exegesis and Empire in the Early Byzantine Mediterranean: Junillus Africanus and the Instituta regularia divinae legis* (Tübingen, 2003).

[38] See Hunt, "Library of Grosseteste," pp. 133, 136, and 141–42. Grosseteste's copy of Augustine's *De ciuitate Dei* is Oxford, Bodleian Library, MS Bodley 198, in the Greyfriars library until given to Gascoigne. Grosseteste's copy of the letters of Jerome is described by Gascoigne, Oxford, Lincoln College MS Lat. 117, p. 473, as bearing the classmark *Ieronimus L*. The remaining texts are included in the list of works indexed by Grosseteste in Lyon, Bibliothèque municipale, MS 414, fols. 17r–32r, suggesting their presence in his collection.

[39] Smalley, *Hebrew Scholarship*, pp. 5 and 7–8, where she says that "the problem of [the prologue's] authorship must be further examined." In *Study of the Bible*, p. 343, she simply states: "I think that the author of the prologue was Grosseteste." The prologue is edited in *A Descriptive Catalogue of the Hebrew Manuscripts of Corpus Christi College, Oxford*, ed. Peter E. Pormann (Cambridge, 2015), pp. 66–69 (see pp. 5–8 for translation), described as "presumably a copy of that written by Grosseteste" (p. 65).

correspond more closely to the interlinear text in Cambridge, Trinity College, MS R.8.6 than to that in Oxford, Corpus Christi College, MS 10, Smalley observed that the interlinear translation in Corpus (and in its twin, consulted by Cossey) reflects some effort at revision and correction, and that Trinity therefore contains the earlier version of the translation, originating (she believed) from Grosseteste's circle.[40] In this scenario, then, Cossey was working with a copy of the *superscriptio* derived, at some remove, from the original form of the "Grosseteste" text.

There are several problems with this account. If, for example, the *superscriptio* did originate with Grosseteste's circle, then the revision identified by Smalley must have been prepared very quickly, perhaps implausibly so, since the scripts used for the Gallican and Hebraicum translations and the Latin superscription in Corpus date the book to Grosseteste's lifetime, perhaps more likely before his departure from Oxford in 1235 than after.[41] Further, though Smalley focused in particular on Cossey's association of the *superscriptio* with Grosseteste, the description quoted above appears to refer to the physical book as a whole, reflecting not an attribution so much as a note on provenance, Cossey's belief that he was in possession of Grosseteste's manuscript ("psalterium domini Lincolniensis"), which contained ("ubi ... continentur") multiple texts of the Psalms. Likewise, while his account of Grosseteste having the *superscriptio* written in this psalter ("superscribi fecit ... in psalterio suo") may describe the commission of a text, as Smalley believed, it seems more likely (and straightforwardly) to refer to the physical act of having the interlinear version, whatever its origin, written in the volume that reached Cossey.[42]

---

[40] Smalley, *Hebrew Scholarship*, p. 8

[41] Smalley, *Hebrew Scholarship*, p. 6, dates this script to "about the second quarter of the thirteenth century, probably the 'thirties or 'forties,'" and subsequent descriptions date the volume on the authority of Smalley's assessment: see Raphael Loewe, "The Mediaeval Christian Hebraists of England: The *Superscriptio Lincolniensis*," *Hebrew Union College Annual* 28 (1957), 205–52, at p. 214: "assigned by Miss Smalley, on western palaeographical grounds, to ca. 1230–40"; Olszowy-Schlanger, *Les manuscrits Hébreux*, p. 157: "datée des années 1230–1240 par B. Smalley"; and *Hebrew Manuscripts*, ed. Pormann, pp. 65 and 69: "produced in the second quarter of the thirteenth century according to Smalley ... probably dating to the 1230s or 1240s." The script is, however, almost certainly earlier than Smalley allowed: in private correspondence, Ralph Hanna has suggested that it could be as early as 1210, while Elaine Treharne dates it between 1220 and 1240, and my own work with the catalogues of English dated and dateable manuscripts would favour the earlier side of their range. All of this – indeed, including Smalley's dating – renders problematic Loewe's contention that the creation of the *superscriptio* postdates Grosseteste's elevation to the episcopacy; "Medieval Christian Hebraists," p. 213.

[42] In her discussion of the prologue in Oxford, Corpus Christi College, MS 10, Smalley suggests that Grosseteste's role, as described in Cossey's "quam superscribi fecit," is reflected in the prologue-author's account of his own activities: "scripturam Ebreorum edisseram," on which she comments: "He does not claim to be [the *superscriptio*'s] author: he has 'edited' it" (*Hebrew Scholarship*, p. 7). Similarly, *Hebrew Manuscripts*, ed. Pormann, p. 8, translates "edisseram" as "publish." In medieval usage, however,

If Cossey was right to claim that he was working with a book once owned by the bishop of Lincoln, and if the version of the *superscriptio* in this manuscript and in Oxford, Corpus Christi College, MS 10 represents at least a partial revision of an earlier interlinear translation, then it would be unlikely that the *superscriptio* was, in the first instance, prepared "at the bishop's behest."[43] Instead, Grosseteste appears to have found this interlinear translation, either on its own or already as part of a multi-text psalter, and decided that it was a useful tool for biblical studies, and he therefore had a copy of it prepared for his own consultation. If Oxford, Corpus Christi College, MS 10 was copied from Grosseteste's manuscript, rather than sharing an exemplar with it, it could be that the bishop was responsible for the revisions Smalley observed, and it may also have been at his request that the preface quoted by Cossey, but omitted in Cambridge, Trinity College, MS R.8.6, was included at the head of this psalter – but this is now impossible to know with any certainty, just as it is hard to be certain of how long the *superscriptio* was in circulation before reaching Grosseteste.[44] Regardless, it was because of the bishop's decision to have this volume produced, as well as his donation of it to Greyfriars, that it was able to be consulted by Cossey in the creation of his commentary, serving as a foundational source for his study of the Hebrew text and its Latin translations.

Cambridge, Christ's College, MS 11 and the Making of Cossey's Autograph

More than a century stands between Cossey's work in Oxford and the production of **Ch**, dateable on the basis of its script to the middle of the fifteenth century. Apart from some material added on the flyleaves, this volume contains only Cossey's text, and a note added at the start of the commentary places it in the library of the Carthusians of Coventry (see Fig. 2).[45] The book was almost certainly a product of its original owner's time at university, prepared as he pursued his theological studies and, like many of the scholastic volumes identified in surviving Carthusian booklists,

---

edisserere means "to expound" or "to interpret" (cf. *DMLBS* s.v. edisserere), and the prologue-author, reflecting a common scholastic understanding of translation as a function of exposition, does therefore claim that he created the *superscriptio*.

[43] Smalley, *Hebrew Scholarship*, p. 5.

[44] Cf. Eva de Visscher, *Reading the Rabbis: Christian Hebraism in the Works of Herbert of Bosham* (Leiden, 2014), p. 66, who suggests that Herbert of Bosham, glossing the Hebraicum ca. 1190, used a psalter similar to Oxford, Corpus Christi College, MS 10.

[45] The St. Anne's Charterhouse *ex libris* seen in Fig. 2 is written in the same hand as that in London, British Library, MS Royal 5.A.v, fol. 134r, distinct from (and, of course, later than) the notice of that book's donation by Robert Odyham on the front flyleaf, discussed by Edward A. Jones, "A New Look into the *Speculum Inclusorum*," in *The Medieval Mystical Tradition: England, Ireland, and Wales*. Exeter Symposium VI, ed. Marion Glasscoe (Cambridge, 1999), pp. 123–45, at 136.

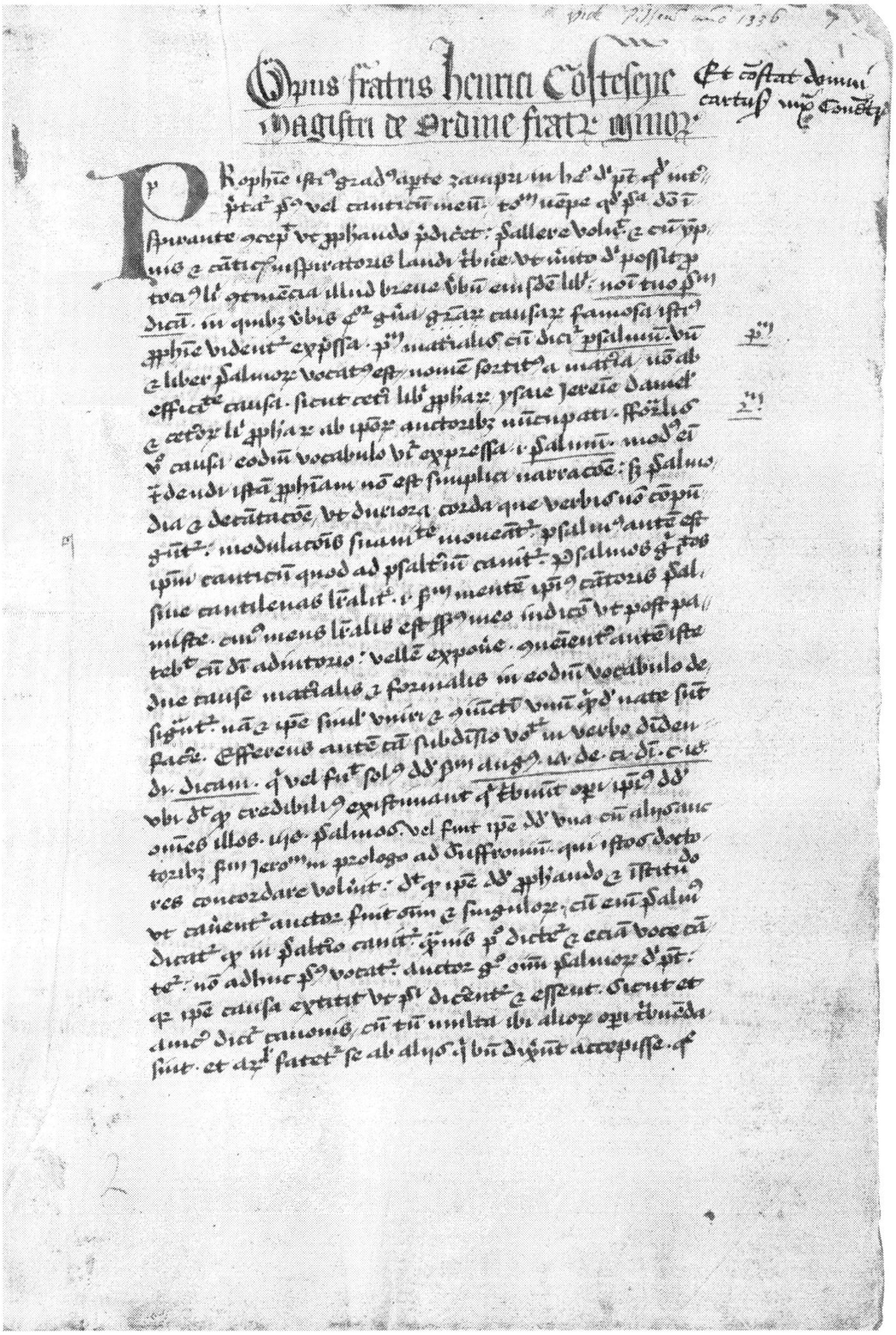

Fig. 2. Cambridge, Christ's College, MS 11, fol. 1r: The opening of Cossey's first prologue, including attribution and later ex-libris. Reproduced by kind permission of the Master and Fellows of Christ's College, Cambridge.

taken with him when he entered the charterhouse.[46] More specifically, **Ch** appears to have been prepared either directly or at one remove from Cossey's working copy, likely kept in the library of the Greyfriars at either Oxford or Cambridge, and, insofar as it at least partially preserves the material disposition of the text in its exemplar, this belated manuscript provides a valuable witness to the process by which Cossey composed his commentary.

Though unusually detailed and still generally reliable, M.R. James's description of **Ch** passes over one of the most striking details of the manuscript, that is, the numerous notes that are written in the hand of the main scribe and crowd its margins.[47] Admittedly, some of these notes are relatively commonplace, marking divisions or drawing attention to specific topics treated in the text, but others are more substantial, apparently reflecting further work with Cossey's sources after the initial drafting of his commentary.[48] Toward the end of his prologues, for example, Cossey claims that a "glosa sancti Ieronimi," by which he appears to mean a comment attributed to Jerome in the *Magna glosatura*, indicates that the Psalter should be divided into five books based on the appearance of the phrase "fiat fiat" (אמן אמן), while a nearby marginal note specifies that this comment originates in Jerome's *Ep.* 36, to Marcella.[49] That is, whoever was responsible for this annotation has traced the patristic source of a detail which, in preparing the commentary, Cossey had taken from an early scholastic intermediary. A similarly retrospective or supplementary effort appears in Cossey's account of the meaning of נחילות in the title or superscription of Psalm 5, already mentioned above. In the main text of the commentary, Cossey presents his Hebrew sources, on the one hand, and, on the other, Jerome as offering two potentially viable though mutually exclusive interpretive options. The writer responsible for the marginal note, however, finds reasons to doubt one of them:

> Quod autem male intelligant per *nehilot* instrumentum uel modulacionem instrumenti patet ex eo quod Dauid in fine libri huius, cum enumerat [enumert **Ch**] omnia instrumenta musica in quibus monet laudare Deum, non enumerat *nehilot* [ne **Ch**], quod tamen fecisset cum aliis, si in usu tunc fuisset. Item apparet quod fingunt ea que dicunt,

---

[46] Compare, for example, the books given to Witham by John Blacman, ca. 1463–1474, which, in addition to constituting "the largest and most comprehensive collection of devotional and mystical writings known to have been owned by any individual in late medieval England," as it is described by Roger Lovatt, "The Library of John Blacman and Contemporary Carthusian Spirituality," *Journal of Ecclesiastical History* 43 (1992), 195–230, at p. 195, include volumes of scholastic philosophy and theology almost certainly acquired during his studies; see *The Libraries of the Carthusians*, ed. A. Ian Doyle, published with *Syon Abbey*, ed. Vincent Gillespie, Corpus of British Medieval Library Catalogues 9 (London, 2001), pp. 639–51.

[47] James, *Descriptive Catalogue*, pp. 31 and 34, quotes from two of these notes without further comment.

[48] For examples of structural glosses, see the marginal "primum" and "secundum" in Fig. 2; for subject matter glosses, see Prol. 2.1 note; 2.21 note; and Prol. 3.19 note.

[49] Prol. 3.523–524 and note.

cum nesciant exprimere quale instrumentum uel qualis cantilena erat illa quam ipsi dicunt uocari *nehilot* (fol. 20v, outer margin).

> It is clear that those who understand *nehiloth* to refer to an instrument or the playing of an instrument are mistaken, since at the end of the book, when he enumerates all the musical instruments on which he teaches us to praise God, David does not list *nehiloth*, which he would have done, along with the others, if it was then in use. Likewise, it seems that these people are making up what they say, since they do not know how to explain what kind of instrument or song it was that they say is called *nehiloth*.

The work of the commentary evidently continues in its margins, with the note's author consulting the Hebrew text of Psalm 150.3–5 and, for his second counter-argument, either drawing attention to the vague generality of what "the Hebrews say" or, perhaps more likely, pursuing this point further by addressing more questions to a contemporary Jewish *conversus*. This continuity is even more apparent in other marginal glosses, which the scribe not only ties (as in this last example) to specific points in the text, but which he also attempts to integrate into the prose of the commentary itself, making the text and marginal gloss legible as an uninterrupted whole. After Cossey quotes the Gallican text of Psalm 5.10, for example, the scribe inserts a *signe-de-renvoi*, tied to a passage in the lower margin of fol. 21r:

> In Psalterio Romano: *Non est in ore eorum rectum* (ueritas est quedam rectitudo, secundum Anselmum, libro de ueritate) *interiora eorum insidie*. In Hebreo sic: *Non est in ore eorum apparatus, inter eos falsitas*. In Hebreo enim non habetur *riber* [sic], quod signat uanum et inane, sed *auote*, quod signat falsitatem, et datur etc.

> In the Roman Psalter: *There is nothing upright in their mouth* – truth is a kind of uprightness, according to Anselm, *On Truth* – *their thoughts are treachery*. In the Hebrew thus: *There is nothing fitting in their mouth, among them is falsity*. For the Hebrew does not have *riyq* [?], which means "vain" or "empty," but *hawwowt*, which means "falsity," and it is given etc.

The marginal note appears to end mid-sentence, but its final two words actually repeat the text that follows immediately after the *signe-de-renvoi* in the body of the commentary: "et datur intelligi quod non solum falsum locuntur, sed menciuntur, quia in corde eorum est falsitas" – "and it is given to understand that they do not just speak falsely but they lie, for falsity is in their hearts." This marginal gloss, in other words, has been designed to accommodate the pre-existing text of Cossey's commentary and to be inserted seamlessly into his interpretation of the psalm. The gloss's author appears to have found more material related to the general notion that this verse is about lying – a definition from Anselm's *De veritate* and the specification of the Hebrew word translated in the Gallican as "uanum" – and has added this to bolster his interpretive claim.[50] As with the apparent consultation of Jewish sources in

---

[50] Cf. Anselm, *De veritate*, II, in *S. Anselmi Cantuariensis Archiepiscopi Opera Omnia*, ed. Franciscus Salesius Schmitt, 6 vols. in 2 (Stuttgart, 1968), 1:178.

the previous example, here too the discussion of the Hebrew and, in this case, the reference to Jerome's Hebraicum translation as the "Roman Psalter," support the notion that these marginal notes were created by Cossey himself, continuing to refine his commentary after its initial composition.

All of these examples are relatively brief, but in several other instances, almost all contained in the manuscript's second quire, Cossey appears to have revisited and reconsidered his text at greater length. In the middle of his account of the superscription or title of Psalm 6, for example, a sign draws attention to a marginal note in which Cossey summarizes and dismisses Trevet's interpretation of שמינית as describing a kind of song associated in particular with Mattithiah and his companions (cf. 1 Par. 15.21), and the marginal material ends, again, with two words that match the text immediately after the sign.[51] This addition from one of his major sources seems gratuitous, and if Cossey meant to present it as a less compelling alternative, he could simply have included it when initially preparing his commentary. It makes better sense, however, when taken together with a much larger addition concerning the psalm's title, a note of over five hundred words that begins in the outer margin of fol. 21v, fills the lower margin, and continues into the lower margin of the facing recto (Fig. 3). In the main text of his commentary, immediately after the point at which Trevet's discussion of שמינית is to be inserted, Cossey reports that "the Hebrews say" this word describes an eight-stringed instrument, and, just as the ten-stringed psaltery evokes the Decalogue, so too is this instrument associated with the circumcision on the eighth day (cf. Gen. 17.12).[52] Another sign then directs attention to the longer addition, where Cossey expands on this point, first explaining that deprecatory songs were set to the accompaniment of this instrument,

---

[51] **Ch**, fol. 21v (outer marg.): "Dicit Triuet quod *seminith* nomen est cantici quod spectabat ad Mathathiam et socios eius, sicut habetur Paral. 15, ubi dicitur: *Porro Mathathias et Eliphalu* et ceteri *in citharis suis pro octaua canebant*. Vnde omnes psalmi qui habent in titulis *pro octaua* spectabant ad Mathathiam et socios eius. Sed melius uidetur, ut dicunt Hebrei" – "Trevet says that *sheminith* is the name of a song which pertained to Mattithiah and his companions, as in 1 Par. 15, where it is said: *And Mattithiah and Eliphelehu* and the rest *sang for the octave on their citharas*. And so it is that all the psalms which have *for the octave on their citharas*. And so it is that all the psalms which have *for the octave* in their titles pertain to Mattithiah and his companions. But it seems better, as the Hebrews say." For the main text of the commentary, following the *signe-de-renvoi*, see the next note.

[52] **Ch**, fol. 21v: "Dicunt Hebrei quod *seninith*, hoc est *octaua*, est nomen musici instrumenti eo quod octo cordas habeat sic nominati. Sicut infra testatur psalterium decacordum, id est decem cordarum, in memoriam Decalogi habebatur, ita et aliud psalterium ob memoriam circumcisionis, que octaua die fiebat, uel citharam octo cordarum habebant. Ergo hec uocabula *pro octaua* et *epinichion* sunt nomina cantilenarum in Hebreo" – "The Hebrews say that *sheminith*, i.e., *octave*, is the name of a musical instrument so named because it should have eight strings. Just as below it is attested that the psaltery is thought to be decacordal, i.e., ten-stringed, to commemorate the Decalogue, so too they held this other psaltery or cithara to have eight cords to commemorate the circumcision, which was done on the eighth day. Therefore, the words *for the octave* and *epinicion* are the names of songs in Hebrew."

Fig. 3. Cambridge, Christ's College, MS 11, fol. 21v: The end of Cossey's commentary on Psalm 5 and the start of Psalm 6, including substantial marginal additions in the hand of the main scribe, which continue onto the facing recto. Reproduced by kind permission of the Master and Fellows of Christ's College, Cambridge.

ut quasi significacione ipsius instrumenti Deum alloquerentur dicentes: Domine, noli uindicacionem sumere de peccatis nostris, sed respice ad patres nostros et ad pactum quod pepigisti cum eis, cuius pacti signum in carne nostra gerimus [gimus **Ch**] et in instrumenti modulacione designamus, et miserere ut non uincamur ab inimicis et confundamur (fol. 21v, outer marg.).

so that, as though by the signification of this instrument, they addressed God and said: Lord, do not exact vengeance for our sins, but consider our forefathers and the agreement you made with them, the sign of which we bear on our flesh and denote by playing this instrument, and have mercy, so that we are not conquered and confounded by our enemies.

The discussion in the marginal addition then shifts to the significance of למנצח, and especially its confusion with לנצח by the translators of the Septuagint, a mistake which explains (he says) the Gallican rendering "in finem," as opposed to "uictori" in the Hebraicum and "pro uictoria" in the "superscriptio Lincolniensis." While the Septuagint translators could simply have been confused, Cossey thinks it more likely that they intentionally disguised the word's proper meaning, since, he says, it identifies certain psalms as prayers for victory in battle, and the Hebrew translators working at the behest of an Egyptian king might not have wanted this foreign ruler to use these psalms to pray for his own military triumphs.[53] Then, still in this larger marginal note,

---

[53] **Ch**, fol. 21v (lower marg.): "*Lamenaseha*, quod interpretatur 'pro uictoria' uel 'ad uictoriam' uel 'uictori'. *Menaseha* enim signat 'uictoriam', sed littera *lameth* preposita signat genitiuum uel datiuum casum, uel preposicionem 'in', 'ad', uel 'pro'. Vbicumque igitur ponitur *lamenaseha* intendo quod psalmus ille est deprecatorius pro uictoria habenda de inimicis uel pro uictoria euadenda ab inimicis. Humilior enim est hec deprecacio et in tanto magis accepta Deo ubi rogatur non ut uincat, sed saltem ut non uincatur. Vel est psalmus regraciatorius pro uictoria habita. Est autem hec deprecacio pro euadenda uictoria cordis contriti et humiliati, ideo penitencialis oracio est. ... Videtur autem quod Septuaginta fuerunt decepti similitudine istorum uocabulorum *lanesah*, quod infra, Ps. 9, ubi nos habemus sicut Septuaginta transtulerunt, *Inimici defecerunt framee in finem*, habetur in Hebreo *lanesah*, putantes *lamenaseha* idem signari, uel (quod melius [meus **Ch**] puto) a proposito hoc fecerunt nolentes regi alienigene psalmos pro uictoria a Deo impetranda manifestare, sicut ubi in Veteri Testamento ad misterium Trinitatis aliquid pertinere uidetur gratis Septuaginta aliter transtulerunt, sicut dicit Ieronimus in prologo super Pentateucum: 'Vbicumque inquit sacrarum aliquid scripturarum testator ...'" – "*Lamenaseha*, translated 'for victory' or 'to victory' or 'to the victor'. For *menaseha* means 'victory', but the letter *lamed* as a prefix indicates the genitive or dative case, or the preposition 'in', 'to', or 'for'. Therefore, wherever *lamenaseha* appears I consider that psalm to be deprecatory, seeking victory over enemies or in evading enemies. For that petition is humbler and therefore more acceptable to God when one does not ask to conquer but that one not be conquered. Or the psalm [i.e., in which *lamenaseha* appears] is an expression of thanks for a victory won. But this [i.e., Ps. 6] is a contrite and humble heart's petition to evade [an enemy's] victory, and therefore it is a penitential prayer. ... But the Seventy seem to have been deceived by the similarity with the word *lanesah*, which below, Ps. 9, where we have what the Seventy translated as *The swords of the enemy have failed unto the end*, the Hebrew has *lanesah*, and [it seems that the Seventy] thought *lamenaseha* meant the same thing [as *lanesah*]. Or (and I think this the better option) they did this on purpose, not wishing to disclose to

he returns to Trevet, whose gloss on the title of Psalm 4 includes the claim that למנצח is a kind of song.[54] Cossey finds this inconsistent with Trevet's interpretation of שמינית, since the psalm would then seem to be identified, gratuitously, as two different types of song, and, noting the further complication introduced by the Septuagint's apparent mistranslation of לנצח as though it were למנצח in 1 Chron. 15.21, he concludes that it is best to follow his Hebrew sources on the meaning of all of these terms. Still, he holds open the possibility that, in some cases, שמינית could be transferred from the instrument to describe a song as well.[55]

Quite clearly, the work standing behind these two marginal notes represents an extension of Cossey's exegetical efforts more generally, his decision either to continue developing his commentary after its initial composition or to return and augment his work on earlier psalms while he glossed later ones. Since all of the sources on which these notes draw were available to Cossey when he initially composed his

---

a foreign-born king the psalms for asking victory from God, just as wherever in the Old Testament something seems to pertain to the mystery of the Trinity, the Seventy freely translated it otherwise, as Jerome says in his prologue to the Pentateuch: 'Wherever anything of sacred Scripture is witnessed … .'" For the full quotation of Jerome, see De Bruyne, *Préfaces*, p. 8; here and in the next few notes, it has seemed best to leave manuscript's transliteration of words related to למנצח uncorrected in my translation.

[54] **Ch**, fol. 21v (lower marg.): "Et dicit Triuet quod *lanesah*, id est *epinichion*, est nomen alicuius cantilene in templo, ut dicunt Hebrei, sed non unius solius, sed omnium que cantabantur ad uictoriam, sicut in quibusdam sequenciis solent aliqui uersus repeti ad uictoriam, uel altitudinis uocis uel uelocitatis uel suauitatis, sed istud non congrue stat cum eo quod supra dixit, quod *pro octaua* est nomen cantici" – "And Trevet says that, according to the Hebrews, *lanesah*, i.e., *epinicion*, is the name of a certain song in the temple, and not of one in particular but of all that are sung for victory, just as some verses are customarily repeated in certain sequences for victory, and this kind of song is characterized either by high voice or by rapidity or by sweetness – but this is inconsistent with what he said before, that *for the octave* is the name of a song."

[55] **Ch**, fol. 21v (lower marg.) and fol. 22r (lower marg.): "Et est aduertendum quod, Paral. 15, Septuaginta pro *lanesah* transtulerunt *epinichion*, id est *super uictoria*, ab *epi-*, quod est 'supra', et *nichos*, uictoria, sed forte codex Hebraicus ex defectu scriptorum habet ibi *lanesah* pro *lamenaseha* ... Vnde pocius adherendum est illis Hebreis qui dicunt quod *seminith* est nomen istrumentorum illorum que octo cordis tangebantur ob memoriam circumcisionis quam nomen cantilenarum, sicut infra, Ps. 32, *asor* pro quo Septuaginta dixerunt *decem cordarum*. Signat enim idem quod *decanum* nomen. Vel pocius denominatiuum est talis instrumenti et cantilene. Et dicit Lira etc." – "Note that, at 1 Par. 15.21, the Seventy translate *lanesah* as *epinicion*, i.e., *up to victory*, from *epi-* (meaning 'above') and *nicos* ('victory'), but perhaps their Hebrew codex there read *lanesah* instead of *lamenaseha* by scribal error. ... But instead one should follow the Hebrews, who say that *sheminith* is the name of those instruments which are played with eight strings to commemorate the circumcision, rather than the name of songs, just as below, Ps. 32.2, *asowr*, for which the Seventy read *of ten strings*. For it signifies also the noun *leader of ten*. Or perhaps it derives from such an instrument and a song. And Lyre says, etc." On transferring the name of an instrument to the song sung to its accompaniment, see Prol. 3.272–273.

commentary on Psalm 6 – they are cited in his prologue and in his work on earlier psalms – it seems most likely that he was aware from the outset of the discrepancy between the views of his Hebrew source and what he found in Trevet's commentary, and he decided to return to this complicated issue after further study of the Hebrew text of the Psalter (and 1 Par., adduced by Trevet), as well as additional work with his other sources, including, presumably, whoever had introduced him to what he presents as the standard Jewish interpretation of the text.[56] By the end of these additions, Cossey still arrives at the same conclusions as in the original version of his commentary, but the marginal notes elaborate considerably on those opinions, explaining the symbolic significance of an ancient instrument and its performance, and they lend further support, treating Trevet's reading as a potentially legitimate alternative and explaining why, after careful consideration, it should not be preferred. Altogether, these marginalia illustrate the ongoing and incremental process of the commentary's composition, suggesting that Cossey took note of various interpretive problems – uncertain sources, ambiguous Hebrew phrases, apparent contradictions in the glosses of his fellow Christian Hebraists – and he set about resolving them, entering the results in the margins of his working copy. At least some of this arrangement was preserved by the scribe of **Ch**.

As noted above, however, though shorter glosses persist throughout the volume, these longer marginal notes, ending with the resumption of the commentary's prose, are generally limited to the second of the manuscript's twenty-one quires. It could be that Cossey's more substantial revisionary work was limited to the beginning of the Psalter, not including the prologue, or that, after a certain point, a scribe taking Cossey's working copy as his exemplar simply decided that including both the main text and the longer marginalia was making his task too onerous. Other details, however, suggest another alternative, namely that, while Cossey's marginal additions have been preserved in this configuration in quire two, in the remainder of the volume they have been incorporated into the prose of the commentary itself. Indeed, the scribe may have begun with this integrative approach, indicated by a major error in the copying of Cossey's third prologue, edited below. In line with the opening division of its contents into ten sections, this prologue begins with an account of the Psalter's translation history, followed by a consideration of its authorship. This second section is interrupted, however, by further comments on the history of the book's translation,

---

[56] As in the examples from Psalms 5 and 47 (see above, notes 30–31), discussion with his teacher seems to be indicated by his references (in notes 51–52 and 54–55) to what "the Hebrews say." The interpretation of *sheminith* as an eight-stringed instrument may be found in Rashi (see Gruber, *Commentary*, p. 191), but the linking of that instrument to ritual circumcision must have come from another source, and it is also mentioned in passing by Trevet (Oxford, Bodleian Library, MS Bodley 738, fol. 13rb).

criticizing Lyre for repeating the commonplace of Jerome's three translations and their later use, referring to the earlier discussion of Trevet to dismiss this view as overly simple, and then noting that one of Lyre's dubious claims – that Jerome's first translation is used in Rome – derives from the *Chronicon pontificum et imperatorum* of Martin of Opava, OP (d. 1278).[57] This last detail is new, and, as with the additions discussed above, it seems likely to be the result of further research undertaken after Cossey's initial treatment of the topic. The passage, in other words, contains material plausibly added to the margins of Cossey's working copy, and, perhaps indicative of a missing or incorrectly positioned *signe-de-renvoi*, it appears to have been integrated into the main text of the prologue at the wrong point. Of course, had the scribe brought it into the text where it is positioned in the edition below, there would be no reason to identify it as a later addition, just as the more substantial marginal notes discussed above could have been incorporated into the prose of Cossey's commentary without trouble. It is, therefore, almost impossible to know how many similar additions have been correctly positioned in the main text.[58] Likewise, it is impossible to know if any material was included in the first version of the commentary but cancelled as part of the revision process, and therefore not included in **Ch**. Cossey may have focused his revisions on only some sections of the commentary, but the frequency and variety of the marginal additions attested in the second quire of **Ch** are just as likely to be representative of his practice across his working copy, indicating a sustained and careful effort at revision.

The preservation of so many of these authorial notes in **Ch** suggests that its scribe was either consulting Cossey's working copy directly or, at most, at one remove, i.e., following an exemplar made from Cossey's autograph.[59] This observation in itself does not make the volume particularly unusual: other manuscripts of scholastic commentaries bearing signs of direct consultation of an authorial working copy may

---

[57] Prol. 3.115–126 and notes.

[58] The persistence of more substantial marginal additions in the scribe's exemplar may be indicated by his decision to copy, in the lower margins of fols. 66v–67r, a series of parallel columns, tying lemmata from Psalms 33.12–34.3 to rhyming moral precepts, e.g. "Venite" (Psalm 33.12) tied to "Districtum iudicium formidare" and "Prohibeat linguam" (Psalm 33.14) tied to "Et fictum eloquium deuitare." The distinctive form of this addition, as well as its general applicability across a series of verses, would have made it impossible for the scribe to incorporate it into the prose of the commentary, perhaps explaining its preservation as the only long marginal note outside of the manuscript's second quire.

[59] Cf. Jane Griffiths, *Diverting Authorities: Experimental Glossing Practices in Manuscript and Print* (Oxford, 2014), p. 9: "The risk of non-preservation is especially pronounced when it comes to glosses, which – as physically separate from the body of the text – are particularly susceptible to loss and alteration."

readily be identified, especially in the case of texts with only limited circulation.[60] It does, however, indicate that the surviving text of Cossey's commentary is the product of at least some revision. In line with the dating of the text to the period following his regency, this work cannot be seen as a *reportatio* of his lectures or a straightforward illustration of his university teaching. The commentary is, instead, a scholarly tool that benefitted from its author's efforts to learn Hebrew and to trace recent interpretive claims to their ultimate sources, clearing the ground in order to establish an authoritative reading of the Psalter's literal sense and enabling later exegetes to continue the study of its original language. The marginalia in **Ch** illustrate, at least in part, the stages in which that work was done.

Psalmic Literalism: Cossey's Hermeneutic Commitments

Cossey's avowed interest in the literal sense of the biblical text is typical of scholastic exegetes, as is his broad definition of that sense as the *mens* ("mind" or "intention") of its human authors.[61] As the examples discussed above have already indicated, however, this general framework left ample room for disagreement, and throughout his commentary Cossey frequently queries, challenges, or simply rejects what he found in the work of his fellow Hebraists. While many of these disagreements arise from his reading of specific details in the Hebrew text, in general, and especially in the prologues, Cossey adopts an idiosyncratic approach to the Psalter's literal sense that necessarily sets him at odds with his recent scholastic sources. More thoroughly than any of these antecedents, Cossey considers the Psalter as an ancient Hebrew equivalent to the medieval Church's book of hymns, though distinct in both the specific ritual uses for which it was composed and, of course, its divine inspiration, seen especially in the prophetic foresight of one of its principal authors, David. Cossey is committed primarily to reading the Psalms in these terms, and he often has trouble reconciling these priorities with the purportedly literalistic glosses found in the commentaries of Lyre and Trevet.

Cossey's understanding of the Psalter as an ancient book of hymns is made clear at various points in his prologues, when he turns, for example, to familiar Latin hymns to illustrate the different meters in which, following Jerome, he believed the Psalms to have been composed, and in his briefer discussion of the Psalter's *divisio*, where he holds out the possibility that, though now unrecoverable by commentators, the

---

[60] See, for example, Woodford's commentary on Matt. 1–5, preserved uniquely in Cambridge, University Library, MS Add. 3571, discussed by Jeremy Catto, "William Woodford, OFM (ca. 1330–ca. 1397)," D.Phil. thesis, University of Oxford, 1969, p. 63.

[61] Prol. 1.16 and Prol. 3.465–466.

ordering of different psalms may reflect their use in the liturgies of ancient Israel.[62] It is also reflected in his discussion of the *finalis causa* of the Psalms, the heading under which exegetes addressed "the ultimate justification for the existence of a work, the end or objective (*finis*) aimed at by the writer."[63] Following an etymology of *psalterium* also found in Cossey's prologues, Trevet had identified the "final cause" of the Psalms as the praise of God, and Lyre likewise focused on "praise" as the single mode in which the Psalter is composed.[64] Cossey argues for a more nuanced approach. Certainly, he says, praise is one of the primary purposes of some psalms, but many more are written for other ends – some are complaints, some are meant to teach proper belief, some are expressive of repentance, etc. – and, in many cases, several of these ends can be found in one and the same psalm.[65] The unity of the Psalter as a whole, then, should be identified only with the formal consistency of its component parts, each of which is *hymnidicus* – "written as a hymn," as well as the ritual setting in which they were meant to be performed.

This approach to the Psalter as a collection of hymns may help to explain why Cossey readily accepts Jerome's claim that many different authors were responsible for their composition. These authors, he says, are named in the superscriptions or titles, and when psalms lack such references, their author or authors must remain unknown. By following Jerome, Cossey departs from a longstanding interpretive tradition, which, on the authority of Augustine, saw David as the sole author of the

---

[62] Prol. 1.101–132 and Prol. 3.526–529, and see too Prol. 3.270–271. Note that, in the first case, this work leads Cossey to conclude that the meters of the psalter must be different from Latin meters. Certainly, earlier commentators draw attention, in passing, to the meters supposedly present in the Hebrew text of the Psalms, noting that these meters are not preserved in the Latin translations, but Cossey's account is unusual for its length and detail. See, e.g., Andrew Kraebel, "Poetry and Prophecy in the Psalter Commentaries of St Bruno and the Pre-Scholastics," *Sacris Erudiri* 50 (2011), 413–59, at p. 448. Likewise, Cossey's understanding of the Psalter's meter does at times appear to influence his reading of specific verses, e.g., on Psalm 6.4: "*Et tu Domine usquequo*, suple 'differs remissionem.' Homo enim anxiatus et territus non profert frequenter completam sentenciam, et eciam propter metrum aliqua uocabula subintelligenda non scribebantur" – "*And thou, Lord, how long*, supply 'do you delay forgiveness.' For an anxious and frightened person often does not utter a complete sentence, and also on account of the meter certain words that should be inferred have not been written" (**Ch**, fol. 22r).

[63] Alastair Minnis, *Medieval Theory of Authorship: Scholastic Literary Attitudes in the Later Middle Ages*, reissued 2nd ed. (Philadelphia, 2010), p. 29.

[64] According to Trevet, "Causa uero finalis notatur in eo quod dicit *tibi*, scilicet Deo inquam laus omnis creature debet ordinari" – "The final cause is noted when he says *to you*, i.e., I say that all of a creature's praise ought to be directed to God" (Bodleian Library, MS Bodley 738, fol. 2rb). For Lyre, see *Biblia sacra*, III, sig. o2vbD. Most of Lyre's prologue is translated in *Medieval Literary Theory and Criticism, c. 1100–c. 1375: The Commentary-Tradition*, ed. Alastair Minnis and A. Brian Scott with David Wallace, rev. ed. (Oxford, 1991), pp. 271–74.

[65] Prol. 1.34–65.

Psalter: this view is dominant in early scholastic exegesis, including the *Magna glosatura*, and it can still be found in more recent works, such as the unfinished commentary of Thomas Aquinas, OP (d. 1274).[66] Trevet notes both opinions in his prologue, and, in his commentary, he sometimes raises the possibility that specific psalms could have been written by authors other than David.[67] In general, however, lacking other evidence, he tends to assume Davidic authorship. Though he acknowledges that Psalm 41 may have been composed by the sons of Korah, for example, when these figures are mentioned again in the superscription to Psalm 43, Trevet simply refers back to his earlier remarks and proceeds to discuss the psalm as composed by "the Prophet," the common antonomastic title given to David in scholastic exegesis.[68] It is for the same assumption of Davidic authorship that Cossey chastises Trevet in his account of Psalm 1, included in the prologues edited below, and, in this case, the Dominican's error is (for Cossey) compounded by discussing the psalm as though it had been positioned at the head of the collection by David rather than by its postexilic compiler, identified by Jerome as Ezra.[69] Lyre, in contrast, comes

---

[66] For the Lombard, see PL 191:59B. For Aquinas's views on the Psalter's authorship, see Thomas Ryan, *Thomas Aquinas as Reader of the Psalms* (Notre Dame, IN, 2000), pp. 15–16.

[67] Oxford, Bodleian Library, MS Bodley 738, fol. 2rb: "Causa efficiens notatur in hoc secundum quod dicitur *psallam*. Hoc enim ex persona Dauid dicitur, qui uel omnes psalmos secundum Augustinum uel saltem maiorem partem eorum eciam secundum Hebreos composuit" – "The efficient cause is indicated insofar as he says *I will sing psalms*. For this is said in the *persona* of David, who composed either (according to Augustine) all of the psalms or at least (according to the Hebrews) the greater part of them."

[68] Regarding the reference to the *filii Core* in the title to Psalm 41, Trevet writes that it "significat hunc psalmum pertinere ad filios Chore, uel quia fuerunt auctores psalmi uel quia ipsi fuerunt materia psalmi uel quia psalmus iste fuit eis deputatus ad cantandum uel secundum aliquem modum ad eos pertinebat" – "signifies that this psalm pertains to the sons of Korah, either because they were the psalm's author or because they were themselves the subject matter of the psalm or because this psalm was assigned to them to sing or reflecting some other way in which it pertained to them" (Oxford, Bodleian Library, MS Bodley 738, fol. 76rb). He then avoids the question of authorship by writing that this psalm "was composed" ("editus est") in the *persona* of one lamenting for the captivity in Babylon, and he proceeds to gloss the psalm as written in this voice (fol. 77ra). Glossing the title of Psalm 43, he notes that this is "secundus in quo ponitur *lebene Chore* pro quo habemus *filiorum Chore*, de quo in titulo [xli] dictum est" – "The second which includes the phrase *libne-qorah*, for which we have *of the sons of Korah*, discussed in the title to Ps. 41." When giving his *divisio* of the psalm, he then notes that, in the first portion, the psalmist "docet quomodo de Dei beneficiis fuit Propheta eruditus" – "teaches how the Prophet was learned concerning the gifts of God," and then, when he turns to gloss the psalm itself, he begins: "Docuit Propheta per quos Dei beneficia cognouit" – "The Prophet taught how he recognized the gifts of God" (fol. 79va–b). On the antonomastic reference to David as "the Prophet," see Prol. 3.277–278.

[69] Prol. 3.425–458. Compared to other scholastic exegetes, however, Cossey's discussion of the role of Ezra as compiler is relatively brief; see further Kraebel, *Biblical Commentary and Translation*, chapter 1.

closer to Cossey's view of mixed authorship, regularly identifying the authors of psalms with figures named in their superscriptions and, when such names are lacking, reporting attributions found in his Jewish sources.[70] In his prologue, Lyre reports both the single- and multiple-authorship theories, expressing his preference for the latter, but, unlike Cossey, he nevertheless maintains that it is proper to identify David as the book's "causa efficiens instrumentalis" (that is, its human author), simply because he was responsible for the "maior pars" – "greater part" of the text.[71]

Of course, many psalms are indeed attributed to David in their superscriptions, but even in these cases Cossey finds reason to disagree with his fellow Hebraists. Following recent trends in scholastic literalism, he sometimes ties psalms to specific events in David's life – such as Psalm 4, in which David is said to give thanks to God for his victory over Saul – but Cossey is generally more hesitant than Trevet or Lyre to read the biblical text so straightforwardly in terms of David's biography.[72] In part, this is simply because he often fails to find any mention of the events identified by his sources in these psalms, but his hesitancy also reflects Cossey's understanding of when David would have been able to find the time necessary to compose in verse. As he suggests in his first prologue, this was surely only possible at the end of the ruler's life, after his military campaigns had been successfully concluded, and so, though some psalms may have been composed spontaneously on the battlefield (as in the case of Psalm 4), Cossey typically sees David writing in considered retrospection, summing up his long experience of prayer and penitence.[73]

---

[70] E.g., on Psalm 91: "Secundum Hebraeos Moyses fecit hunc psalmum decantandum in die Sabbathi, quae celebris est apud Hebraeos, in memoriam beneficii creationis, secundum quod dicitur Gen. 2, *Et benedixit Deus diei septimo et sanctificauit illum*, etc." – "According to the Hebrews, Moses made this psalm to be sung on the Sabbath, which is celebrated among the Hebrews, to commemorate the gift of creation, in accordance with what is said in Gen. 2: *And God blessed the seventh day and sanctified it*, etc." (*Biblia sacra*, III, sig. O2ra). The reference is to Gen. 2.3.

[71] *Biblia sacra*, III, sig. o2vaB.

[72] "Iste ergo psalmus regratiatorius est pro uictoria, ... et specialiter pro illa quam Deus quasi miraculose fecit eum habere de Saul, sicut habemus 1 Reg. 23" – "Therefore, this psalm expresses thanks for victory ... and in particular for that [victory] which God caused him to have, as though miraculously, against Saul, as we find in 1 Reg. 23" (Kleinhans, "Cossey," p. 250). On this interpretive habit in scholastic Psalter commentaries, see Kraebel, *Biblical Commentary and Translation*, ch. 1.

[73] Prol. 1.132–137. On Psalm 4, he writes, "Et quamuis non scribatur quod orando tunc, certum tamen est quod orauit instanter" – "And while it what he prayed for may not be what is written here, it is nevertheless certain that he prayed immediately" (ed. Kleinhans, "Cossey," p. 251). For his dismissal of settings adduced by Lyre and Trevet, and his preference for more general readings, see his remarks on Psalm 6: "Et dicit Lira quod Dauid in hoc psalmo petit misericordiam super diuinam offensam, quia iactanter contra legem iussit populum numerari absque dacione argenti quod daretur in usum tabernaculi testimonii in tali numeracione, sicut precipitur Exod. 30, propter quod Gad propheta ex precepto Domini dixit ei: *Trium tibi datur opcio* etc., Reg. 24, et Dauid dixit: *Coartor nimis* etc., quia

Further, as part of this compositional process, Cossey insists that David inevitably included some of his prophetic knowledge in his psalms, and especially prophecy of the life and death of Christ.[74] As Theresa Gross-Diaz has noted, though he praises David's prophetic foresight in his prologue, Lyre generally distinguishes between the text's literal sense and its Christological prophecy, the major exceptions being those verses cited as prophetic in the New Testament.[75] Likewise, echoing Aquinas, Trevet begins his commentary by declaring that his interest in the "literal or historical" meaning of the text sets him apart from earlier exegetes, who have exclusively explored its "prophetic or spiritual understanding."[76] Cossey seems to take issue with

uidebat sequi penam horribilem super se et super populum occasione sui. Alii autem Hebrei et Triuet exponunt de Absalone filio suo, cuius persecucionem ut euaderet rogat in hoc psalmo Dei misericordiam, penitendo de peccato Bersabee, pro quo Deus sibi per Nathan dixerat quod semen suum surgeret contra eum. Sed quia non apparet magis in hoc psalmo mencio de penitencia quam fecit pro uno peccato istorum quam pro alio, et quia psalmos composuit quando altissima pace feriabatur et expeditus erat ab omnibus bellis, magis uidetur quod penitendo de omnibus peccatis suis et a Deo petendo ueniam ediderit hunc psalmum, et hoc pro uictoria generaliter omnium hostium imposterum euadenda uel de ipsis hostibus obtinenda si qui insurgerent" – "And Lyre says that in this psalm David asks for mercy for having offended God, for, arrogantly and contrary to the law, he ordered the people to be counted without giving the silver that was to be given for the use of the tabernacle of the testimony in such counting, as is commanded in Exod. 30.16, on account of which the prophet Gad, acting at the Lord's command, said to him: *The choice of three things is given to you*, 2 Reg. 24.12, and David said, *I am in great distress*, etc., for he saw that horrible punishment would follow for him and his people because of him. But other Hebrews and Trevet expound it as concerning Absalom his son, and in this psalm he asks for God's mercy in order to evade Absalom's persecution, repenting for the sin of Bathsheba, for which God had said to him through Nathan that his seed would rise against him. But since no mention appears in this psalm of the penance which he did for one or the other of these sins, and since he composed the psalms when he rested in most profound peace and was free from all wars, it seems more likely that he composed this psalm repenting for all his sins and seeking pardon from God, and this for victory generally in evading all enemies henceforth or obtaining [victory] over those same enemies if they rise up" (**Ch**, fols. 21v–22r; cf. Oxford, Bodleian Library, MS Bodley 738, fol. 13ra–b and *Biblia sacra*, III, sig. q1va–b).

[74] Prol. 1.50–55, including the quotation of 2 Reg. 23.1 invoked in the examples from Psalms 29 and 50 below; see too the lengthy discussion of Davidic prophecy, essentially analyzing a *quaestio* presented in Lyre's prologue, in Prol. 3.173–257.

[75] Theresa Gross-Diaz, "What's a Good Soldier to Do? Scholarship and Revelation in the Postills on the Psalms," in *Senses of Scripture*, ed. Krey and Smith, pp. 111–28; for Lyre's praise of Davidic prophecy, see *Biblia sacra*, III, sig. o2va.

[76] Oxford, Bodleian Library, MS Bodley 738, fol. 1rb: "Quia uero omnes prisci temporis doctores circa allegoriarum misteria profunda perscrutanda totis studiis occupati, aut neglexerunt aut perfunctorie tetigerunt uelut abiecta testa, nuclei dulcedinem consectantes, postulauit a me uestra paternitas, ut quo clarius pateret spiritualis propheticusque intellectus qui littere uelud basi innititur, Psalterium expositione litterali et hystorica illustrarem" – "Since all the doctors of former times devoted their efforts wholly to studying the profound mysteries of allegories and therefore either neglected or gave

this distinction, suggesting that, since the literal sense includes the whole of its human author's intended meaning, and since this author was a prophet, there is therefore every reason to think that at least some Davidic psalms could contain literal prophecy of Christ. At Psalm 50.8, for example, glossing the "incerta et occulta sapientiae Dei" revealed to David before his present spiritual blindness, Cossey echoes the definition of prophecy offered in his prologue, claiming that these things are "*incerta* hominibus et secundum naturam et humanum ingenium" – "*uncertain* to human beings with respect to nature and human intelligence," and he maintains that the knowledge described here is specifically Christological: "Sibi enim erat constitutum prophetare de Christo Deo Iacob, sicut patet Reg. 23" – "For to him it was appointed to prophesy of Christ, the God of Jacob, as is clear in 2 Reg. 23."[77] Lyre, in contrast, had suggested that this verse could refer either to Christological prophecy or to the succession of David's royal line, and Trevet insisted that it could only have to do with succession, which was an especially urgent concern, since the king's son and heir, Solomon, had not yet been born.[78] The limited sense of literalistic prophecy seen in Trevet's approach to this verse – restricting what is being predicted to events before the birth of Christ – recurs throughout his and Lyre's commentaries, for example, in their interpretation of Psalm 29 as prophesying the construction of the temple under Solomon (according to Lyre) or its restoration after the Babylonian captivity (according to Trevet). For Cossey, again drawing on the apparent reference to David's Christological insights in 2 Reg. 23.1, if this psalm is to be understood as prophetic, then it should be read, in its literal sense, as referring to Christ.[79]

---

only perfunctory treatment to it [i.e., the literal meaning] like a lowly covering, seeking instead the sweetness of the kernel, you, father, have asked me to elucidate the Psalter with a literal and historical exposition, thereby making clearer the spiritual and prophetic understanding which rests upon the letter as though on a foundation."

[77] **Ch**, fol. 89r; cf. Prol. 3.177–183 and 291–295. The reference is to 2 Reg. 23.1.

[78] *Biblia sacra*, III, sig. C1rb; Oxford, Bodlean Library, MS Bodley 738, fol. 93va.

[79] **Ch**, fol. 41v: "De materia psalmi dicit Triuet quod est regraciatorius pro reditu de captiuitate Babilonica, et cantabatur in templi dedicacione, et sic tractat totum psalmum, et quod infra dicitur, *Domine eduxisti ab inferno*, exponit de ergastulo Babiloniorum. Sed si iste psalmus sit propheticus, sicut oportet secundum istam exposicionem, et prophecia Dauid fuit de Christo maxime, sicut testatur 2 Regum 23, multo melius uidetur de Christo exponere ad literam" – "Concerning the subject matter of this psalm, Trevet says that it is an expression of thanks for the return from the Babylonian captivity, and it was sung in the dedication of the temple, and he treats the whole psalm accordingly, and what is said below (Ps 29.4), *Lord, you have brought from hell*, he expounds as concerning the prison of the Babylonians. But if this psalm is prophetic, as it must be according to this exposition, and David's prophecy chiefly concerned Christ, as witnessed in 2 Reg. 23, it seems much better to expound it literally as concerning Christ." Cf. Oxford, Bodleian Library, MS Bodley 738, fol. 23va–b; *Biblia sacra*, III, sig. v8va–b.

In this regard, Cossey could appear to be advocating a return to a way of reading the psalms more commonly attested in early scholastic commentaries, including the *Magna glosatura*, where Christological prophecy is identified as the apparent meaning of the book as a whole.[80] While these earlier sources consider the Psalter as principally prophetic, however, Cossey is insistent that this is only a secondary feature of the text. As he says in his prologues, the psalmists sometimes include prophetic content in their hymns of praise, but this is crucially different from claiming that they praise God in the course of writing prophecy.[81] Further, in a move without precedent in his sources, Cossey argues that not all of the psalms that appear to be prophetic are in fact indicative of their author's gift of prophecy. In many cases, these authors were likely repeating prophecies passed down in other sources, refashioning this received knowledge into verse. To support this point, he turns to the *Testamenta duodecim patriarcharum*, a pseudepigraphic text purporting to give the deathbed pronouncements of the sons of Jacob. As translated from its Greek version by Grosseteste, the Latin *Testamenta* enjoyed considerable popularity in the fourteenth century, but Cossey seems to be the first exegete to put it to substantial use in a biblical commentary.[82] Perhaps reflecting his familiarity with Bacon's similar discussion of the text, Cossey draws attention to the *Testamenta*'s various Christological prophecies, suggesting that, in its original form, this material would have been available to the different authors of the psalms, and that it could be the source of their apparently prophetic knowledge.[83] Indeed, he extends this line of thinking to explain the *Testamenta* itself, indicating that where the patriarchs describe what they have read in the book of Enoch, they are themselves acting as reporters of prophecy rather than

---

[80] For example, PL 191:57D: "Ea quippe quae alii prophetae obscure et quasi per aenigmata dixerunt de passione et resurrectione Christi, et aeterna genitura et de caeteris mysteriis, David prophetarum excellentissimus ita evidentissime aperuit, ut magis videatur evangelizare quam prophetare" – "Those things which other prophets said obscurely or as it were by means of enigmas concerning the passion and resurrection of Christ, and the eternal begetting and other mysteries, David, the most excellent of prophets, disclosed so plainly that he appears to write gospel more than prophecy."

[81] Prol. 3.258–260; cf. Prol. 1.38–41.

[82] For the Latin text, see PG 2:1025–1160; for the manuscripts, see S. Harrison Thomson, *The Writings of Robert Grosseteste, Bishop of Lincoln 1235–1253* (Cambridge, 1940), pp. 43–44. The translation is discussed by Marinus de Jonge, "Robert Grosseteste and the Testaments of the Twelve Patriarchs," *Journal of Theological Studies* 42 (1991), 115–25, and its influence is explored by Henk Jan de Jonge, "Die Patriarchentestamente von Roger Bacon bis Richard Simon," in *Studies on the Testaments of the Twelve Patriarchs: Text and Interpretation*, ed. Marinus de Jonge (Leiden, 1975), pp. 3–42 (though unfortunately skipping from Bacon to the sixteenth century), and, more recently, Ruth Nisse, *Jacob's Shipwreck: Diaspora, Translation, and Jewish-Christian Relations in Medieval England* (Ithaca, 2017), pp. 127–47.

[83] Prol. 3.299–422; cf. Bacon, *Opus Maius*, II.xiv, ed. John Henry Bridges, 3 vols. (Oxford, 1897), 1:58–59.

actually prophesying.[84] Cossey is careful, however, to specify that psalms attributed to David contain Christological details that cannot be explained with reference to the *Testamenta*, making it clear that at least those portions of the Psalter are indeed prophetic, and he is therefore able to maintain both the possibility of literalistic prophecy in some psalms and the book's composition by many different writers.[85]

Dwelling on the Psalter's mixed authorship, the avenues by which prophetic content came to be expressed in its verses, and the different ends for which the Psalms were written, Cossey's prologues articulate a set of literalistic hermeneutic priorities that, though clearly responding to recent trends in scholastic exegesis, are specific to this biblical book, understood as an ancient and inspired collection of hymns. In Cossey's view, other Christian Hebraists have not sufficiently recognized the unusual demands that the Psalter's status as a versified compilation places on its interpreter, and he clearly thinks that his contemporaries have been led astray, either through an insufficiently rigorous study of Hebrew or because they have adopted interpretive methods leading to conclusions not supported by the text itself. As he writes toward the beginning of his gloss on Psalm 5, the curiosity of commentators leads them to try to extract as much meaning as possible from Scripture, but it would seem that this interpretive eagerness has not always been properly directed.[86] Cossey thus presents an alternative to the scholastic commentator's typical pose, recently described by Gilbert Dahan, as a humble worker seeking to add to the interpretive edifice begun by his predecessors.[87] For Cossey, many of the bricks laid by recent exegetes need to be pulled up and cast away for the building to conform to its proper plan, and the terms used in his critique of Trevet in particular are startlingly harsh (e.g., "Que nugacio!").[88] Conjectures about compositional settings, doctrinaire readings that push prophecy off to the spiritual senses, vestigial attributions of anonymous psalms to David – all of these can only get in the way of an interpretation based on ancient and authoritative sources, the biblical text itself and the various para-biblical and patristic writings that cast light on its interpretation.

Clearing away these misleading glosses, Cossey offers his commentary as a new standard reference work of scholastic exegesis, providing as many details as possible of the Psalter's Latin translation history, its original language, and a basic account of its literal meaning. Indeed, in his frequent and lengthy definitions of significant Hebrew

---

[84] Prol. 3.335–336.

[85] Prol. 3.422–424.

[86] **Ch**, fol. 20v: "Ad curiositatem tamen expositorum pertinet elicere quantum possunt de litera" – "It pertains to the curiosity of expositors to draw as much as they can from the letter."

[87] Gilbert Dahan, *Lire la bible au moyen âge: Essais d'herméneutique médiévale* (Geneva, 2009), pp. 27–33.

[88] Prol. 3.434.

words, as in the introduction to Hebrew prepositions and articles appended as an epilogue to the commentary, Cossey apparently sought to enable further work with the original language of the Psalms. If his detailed discussions of the text and its translations sometimes dwarf his relatively brief and straightforward interpretive offerings, as several of the examples discussed above indicate, this could be because he hoped that subsequent commentators would draw on the resources he had provided and offer more elaborate readings in keeping with his general view of the text. His work, like Trevet's, was one of the many early fourteenth-century biblical commentaries overshadowed by the rapid and widespread success of Lyre's literal postils, and Lyre's more straightforward reporting of the Hebrew text and its Jewish interpretation – in contrast to Cossey's expectation that his readers learn some Hebrew for themselves – may have further discouraged the use of the English Franciscan's commentary. By holding potential readers to a standard which most seemed disinclined to attain, Cossey follows in the steps of Roger Bacon, and his ambitious and painstaking work is no less impressive for its lack of willing followers.

Edition and Translation

The four texts edited below are preserved uniquely in Cambridge, Christ's College, MS 11 [= **Ch**], fols. 1r–3v, 4v–5r, 5v–13v, and 252r, respectively. The first three are prologues, presenting Cossey's discussion of the Psalter's four Aristotelian causes, followed by a consideration of other issues germane to the book as a whole; his glosses on Jerome's preface to the Hebraicum translation; and finally a much longer discussion of ten introductory topics: the Psalter's translation history, its authors, their intention, the work's utility, its title, its proper student, its subject matter, the order and mode in which it should be read, the part of philosophy to which it pertains, and its division into parts. Jerome's Hebraicum preface is copied on fols. 3v–4v, and his shorter Gallican preface on fol. 5r, but neither of these has been included here.[89] Finally, by introducing the reader to different Hebrew prepositions and articles, the "epilogue" on fol. 252r supplements the discussions of Hebrew vocabulary and grammar found throughout the commentary.

The present edition generally preserves the orthography of **Ch**, with the exception of the lower case "v" which is rendered as "u" throughout. All abbreviations are expanded silently, while punctuation, capitalization, and the division of the text into paragraphs are editorially imposed. The text has required relatively little emendation, with most corrections being obvious from context. Emended readings are included in the text, with the manuscript's readings provided in the *apparatus criticus*; more conjectural emendations are explained in the notes to the edition. These are more

---

[89] For the text of these prefaces, see De Bruyne, *Préfaces*, pp. 46–47; *Biblia Sacra iuxta Vulgatam Versionem*, ed. Bonifatius Fischer et al., 2 vols. (Stuttgart, 1975), 1:767–69.

frequent in the epilogue than in the prologues, since the scribe seems to have been unfamiliar with the Hebrew characters encountered in his exemplar. Quotations of biblical *lemmata*, generally underlined in red ink in the manuscript, are given in italic, while other quotations are, where possible, set off in double quotation marks. However, Cossey's habit of integrating phrases drawn from his major sources into his own sentences, shifting frequently between paraphrase and quotation, has made it seem unnecessarily cumbersome to indicate every verbatim borrowing in this way. The notes indicate Cossey's sources, insofar as it has been possible to identify them, and they also preserve some marginalia that, as demonstrated above, are likely to be authorial. English translations of each text are given immediately after the Latin.

Prologue 1: On the Four Causes of the Psalms

Prophecie istius gradus aperte *zampri* in Hebreo dici potest, quod interpretatur "psalmus" uel "canticum meum." Totum nempe quod Psalmista Deo inspirante concepit ut prophetando prediceret psallere uoluit et cum ympnis et canticis inspiratoris laudi tribuere, ut merito dici possit pro tocius libri continencia illud breue uerbum eiusdem libri, *Nomini tuo psalmum dicam*,[1] in quibus uerbis quattuor genera causarum famosa istius prophecie uidentur expressa. Primum materialis cum dicitur *psalmum*. Vnde et "liber Psalmorum" uocatus est, nomen sortitus a materia, non ab efficiente causa sicut ceteri libri prophetarum, Ysaie, Ieremie, Danielis et ceterorum libri prophetarum ab ipsorum auctoribus nuncupati. Formalis uero causa eodem uocabulo uidetur expressa, id est *psalmum*. Modus enim tradendi istam propheciam non est simplici narracione, sed psalmodia et decantacione, ut duriora corda que uerbis non compunguntur modulacionis suauitate moueantur. Psalmus autem est ipsum canticum quod ad psalterium canitur. Psalmos igitur istos siue cantilenas litteraliter, id est secundum mentem ipsius cantoris Psalmiste, cuius mens litteralis est sensus meo iudicio, ut post patebit, cum Dei adiutorio uellem exponere.[2] Conuenienter autem iste due cause, materialis et formalis, in eodem uocabulo designantur; nam et ipse simul uniri et coniunctim unum quiddam nate sunt facere.

Efficiens autem causa subdiuisio uocatur in uerbo diuidendi *dicam*, qui uel fuit solus Dauid, secundum Augustinum, 17 *De ciuitate Dei* capitulum 14, ubi dicit quod credibilius existimant qui tribuunt operi ipsius Dauid omnes illos centum quinquaginta psalmos,[3] uel fuit ipse Dauid una cum aliis auctoribus, secundum Ieronimum in prologo ad Suffronium.[4] Qui istos doctores concor-

5–6 Ps. 17.50

6 genera] graciarum *add.* Ch *a.c.* ‖ 20 efficiens] efferens Ch ‖ 21 14] 10 Ch

[1] All citations of Psalms reflect the Gallican or LXX numbering, unless otherwise noted. According to *Biblia Sacra iuxta Vulgatam Versionem*, ed. Bonifatius Fischer et al., 2 vols. (Stuttgart, 1975), 1:788, Cossey's lemma is a variant of the verse, which more commonly appears as "Psalmum dicam nomini tuo." (This edition will subsequently be cited as *Vulgate*, ed. Fischer et al. Significantly, then, Cossey's lemma is favoured in the Hebrew-Latin Psalter manuscripts discussed above, e.g., Cambridge, Trinity College, MS R.8.6, fol. 9va.)

[2] Compare below, Prol. 3.465–466.

[3] See Aug., *De ciu.* 17.14, in *Aurelii Augustini De ciuitate Dei libri XI–XXII*, ed. Bernard Dombart and Alphons Kalb, CCSL 48 (Turnhout, 1955), p. 579.21–22.

[4] Donatien de Bruyne, *Préfaces de la bible latine* (Namur, 1920), pp. 46–47; *Vulgate*, ed. Fischer et al., 1:768.

dare uoluerit, dicit quod ipse Dauid prophetando et instituendo ut canerentur auctor fuit omnium et singulorum. Cum enim psalmus dicatur quod in psalterio canitur, quamuis primo dictetur et eciam uoce cantetur, non adhuc psalmus uocatur. Auctor ergo omnium psalmorum dici potest, quia ipse causa extitit ut psalmi dicerentur et essent, sicut et Auicena dicitur canonis, cum tamen multa ibi aliorum operi tribuenda sint, et Aristoteles fatetur se ab aliis qui bene dixerunt accepisse que [fol. 1v] tamen omnia eius operi tribuuntur. Si tamen aliquem istorum doctorum negare oporteat, senciendum est pocius cum Ieronimo in hiis que ad Hebraicam pertinent ueritatem.

Finalis uero causa designatur cum premittitur *nomini tuo*, id est ad honorem nominis tui Deus. Vnde in Hebreo uocatur liber iste *sephar talim*, quod interpretatur secundum Ieronimum "uolumen ympnorum."[5] Ympnus autem est carmen in laudem Dei editum. Vnde *ympnus* Grece "laus Dei" interpretatur. Hec est causa finalis, per quod patet quod totus iste liber non est propheticus, sed laudatorius (ut plurimi) et ympnidicus, sicut est ympnarium ecclesie iam catholice. Vnde mihi uidetur quod de omnibus istis centum quinquaginta psalmis quidam sunt simpliciter doctrinales, quidam prophetales, quidam querimoniales, quidam penitenciales, quidam deprecatorii et quidam increpatorii, quidam uero regraciatorii, quidam animatorii et quidam laudatorii. Quandoque enim in psalmo principaliter docere intendit et docet quid est humanum bonum, felicitas seu beatitudo, sicut psalmo primo describit beatum uirum et sibi oppositum, qui modus Scripture sacre uocatur a Iunilio in suis *Institutis* simpliciter doctrinalis.[6] Sicut enim Christus in sermone quem dixit in monte describit uiros beatos pluraliter, hic Psalmista in primo psalmo describit in singulari beatum uirum, per quod patet ista beatitudo que ultimus finis dicitur a philosophis et bene actuum humanorum. Quandoque psalmus est principaliter prophetalis et hoc de Christo, sicut sunt multi. Quod enim aliqui psalmi ad litteram sint prophetici patet per uerba Dauid nouissima, Reg. 23: *Dixit Dauid filius Ysai, dixit uir cui constitutum est de Christo Dei Iacob, egregius psaltes Israel, "Spiritus Domini locutus est per me et sermo eius per linguam meam."*[7] Quandoque enim de inimicis conqueritur dicens, *Domine quid multiplicati sunt*, etc. Quandoque de commissis conteritur: *Domine ne in furore, Beati quorum*, etc. Quandoque deprecatur pro se uel pro aliis, sicut pa-

53–55 2 Reg. 23.1–2 ∥ **55–56** Ps. 3.2 ∥ **56–57** Ps. 6.2/37.2, Ps. 31.1

[5] *Prol. ad Soph.*, in De Bruyne, *Préfaces*, p. 47; *Vulgate*, ed. Fischer et al., 1:768.

[6] See Junillus, *Inst.* 6, in *Theodor von Mopsuestia und Junilius Africanus als Exegeten*, ed. Heinrich Kihn (Freiburg im Breisgau, 1880), pp. 478–79.

[7] See the discussion above, pp. 312–13.

tet in diuersis psalmis. Quandoque imprecatur illis qui finaliter mali sunt penam et tormentum: *Deus laudem meam*.⁸ Quandoque uero eos increpat et obiurgat: *Quid gloriaris in malicia*. Quandoque uero regraciatur et beneficia recitat: *Diligam te*. Quandoque uero semetipsum in periculis animat et [fol. 2r] confortat: *Dominus illuminacio*. Et quandoque, ymmo frequenter, eius magnificenciam extollit et laudat, sicut patebit. Ista decem in omnibus hiis principaliter continentur meo iudicio, quamuis multa istorum in psalmo eodem frequenter exprimantur et mixtim.

   Habet iterum Psalmista in diuidendo hos psalmos decem loquendi modos, hinc inde permixtos. Modo enim loquitur Deo sed non de Deo, modo de Deo sed non Deo, modo Deo et de Deo. Item modo sibi ipsi loquitur, sed non de se, modo de se et non sibi, modo sibi et de se. Item quandoque loquitur homini alteri sed non de illo, modo de illo sed non illi, modo illi et de illo. Quandoque uero sic simpliciter loquitur et absolute, et in eodem psalmo hos modos hinc inde permiscet, sicut patet intuenti. Decem adhuc sunt nomina quibus apud Hebreos nominatur Deus secundum Ieronimum ad Marcellam, scilicet *El, Eloym, Eloe, Sabaoth, Elion, Eser eie, Adonay, Ya, Tetragramaton, Saday*.⁹ Quibus nominibus decem et decem nominum istos psalmos Psalmista depromsit, et hoc in instrumento musico psalterio decem cordarum, in quo placuit ipsi Dauid Deo psallere: *In psalterio*, inquit, *decem cordarum psallam tibi*, et hoc in memoriam decem preceptorum et ad internecionem decem bestiarum, sicut dicit Augustinus in libello de decem cordis.¹⁰ Et sunt ille decem bestie decem uicia seu decem demones qui ipsis uiciis presunt, scilicet demon supersticionis, erroris, amoris seculi, impietatis, libidinis, crudelitatis, rapacitatis, falsitatis, adulterine cogitacionis, cupiditatis, que contraria sunt ipsis decem preceptis. Ad quarum bestiarum seu demonum necem et fugam

---

59 Ps. 108.2 ‖ **60** Ps. 51.3 ‖ **61** Ps. 17.2 ‖ **62** Ps. 26.1 ‖ **77–78** Cf. Ps. 143.9

---

59 Deus laudem meam] *add.* **Ch** *in marg.* ‖ **60** Quid … malicia] *add.* **Ch** *in marg.* ‖ **61** Diligam te] *add.* **Ch** *in marg.* ‖ **61** et] et et **Ch** ‖ **62** Dominus illuminacio] *add.* **Ch** *in marg.*

---

⁸ This and the following three illustrative examples are written by the main scribe in the margin and tied to the relevant point in the text with hairlines.

⁹ Hier., *Ep.* 15, in *Eusebii Hieronymi Epistulae 1–70*, ed. Isidore Hilberg, CSEL 54/1 (Vienna – Leipzig, 1910), pp. 218–20.

¹⁰ The following (lines 79–84) summarizes Aug., *Serm. ad pop.* 9.13, in *Aurelii Augustini Sermones de Vetere Testamento*, ed. Cyrillus Lambot, CCSL 41 (Turnhout, 1959), pp. 132–34.

iste Psalmista psallebat. Sicut enim in antiquis fabulis poetarum legitur quod Orpheus uxorem suam Euridicem in talo a serpente uulneratam et mortuam et ad inferos iam deductam cum cithara est secutus ut eam ab inferis extraheret, et ibi ita dulciter citharizauit quod omnes dii infernales tanta dulcedine commoti ei Euridicem reddiderunt, ita [fol. 2v] fuit de isto citharedo animas a peccatorum inferis extrahente et psalmodie suauitate fugante demonia. Item in isto libro sunt decem penthadecades psalmorum, id est decies quindecim; nam centum quinquaginta sunt decies quindecim. Penthadecas[11] uero propter misterium ebdoadis et ogdoadis insinuat Noui Testamenti et Veteris continenciam. In quo tam Nouo quam Veteri Testamento mencio fit publica decem preceptorum, per quod patet quod quicquid in Scriptura sacra historialiter, doctrinaliter, prophetice et prouerbialiter traditur, in hoc libro metrice et ympnidice continetur. Adhuc cum quindecim sint condiciones caritatis quas enumerat Apostolus, Cor. 13: *Caritas paciens est, benigna est*, etc.,[12] et in caritate tota lex pendat et prophete, constat quod decem psalmorum penthadecades ipsum decalogum in caritate diffusum et quicquid latet uel patet in diuinis sermonibus prefigurat.

Omnes siquidem psalmi metrice in Hebreo compositi et scripti sunt, secundum Ieronimum et Ysidorum, libro 6 *Ethymologiarum*,[13] sed quo metro, utrum uidelicet iambico trimetro et tetrametro, sicut currunt communiter ympni nostri, "Primo dierum omnium quo mundus extat conditus,"[14] sicut pa-

97 Cf. 1 Cor. 13.4–7 ‖ **98** lex ... prophetae] Cf. Matt. 22.40

84 in] *om.* **Ch** ‖ **85** Euridicem] eruditem **Ch**; serpente] serpentem **Ch** ‖ **88** Euridicem] eruditem **Ch** ‖ **98** pendat] pendet **Ch**

---

[11] Note in margin: "De hoc in communi glosa" – "On this point, see the common gloss." This could refer to the *Glossa ordinaria*, for which see *Biblia sacra cum Glossa ordinaria nouisque additionibus*, ed. François Feruardent (Venice, 1603), III, sig. o5vbEF, but it more likely refers to the Lombard's *Magna glosatura*, which offers a similar discussion (PL 191:55C–56C).

[12] In his prologue, Trevet cites the same verse to justify his division of the Psalter into, not ten groups of fifteen, but fifteen groups of ten (Oxford, Bodleian Library, MS Bodley 738, fol. 2ra-b; Trevet may be following Aquinas, who divides each of the conventional quinquagenes into five groups of ten. On this structure, see Thomas Ryan, *Thomas Aquinas as Reader of the Psalms* (Notre Dame, 2000), pp. 20–28.

[13] Isid, *Etym.*, 6.2.17, in *Isidoro de Sevilla, Etimologías, Libro VI: De las Sagradas Escrituras*, ed. César Chaparro Gómez (Paris, 2012), pp. 21, 23. In addition to the discussion in *Ep.* 53, cited below, Jerome refers to iambic trimeter and tetrameter with regard to specific psalms in Hier., *Ep.* 30.3, ed. Hilberg, pp. 244–45.

[14] See *Analecta hymnica medii aevi* 51, ed. Clemens Blume (Leipzig, 1908), pp. 25–26, no. 23.

105 tet in commento Boecii, *De consolatione*, "O stelliferi conditor orbis,"[15] dubitari posset, sed patet per Ieronimum, in prologo ad Paulinum, qui uocat ipsum Dauid Simonidem, Flaccum et Pindarum propter similia metra que in psalmis cecinit.[16] Isti autem carmine lirico scripserunt. Liricum uocatur a uarietate secundum Papiam.[17] Vnde non uno et eodem metro currunt omnes psalmi,
110 sed sicut dicit Ysidorus, *Ethimologiarum*, libro 6, capitulo de scriptoribus et uocabulis sanctorum librorum, nunc alii iambico currunt, nunc alchaico personant, nunc saphico miscent trimetro uel tetrametro pede incedentes.[18] Scito quod pedes uarii sunt, quod si a dissillabis usque ad exsasillabos conputentur centum uiginti quattuor, sed dissillabi tantum quattuor, trissillabi
115 octo. Dissillabi ut pirichius qui ex duabus breuibus, cui contrarius est spondeus ex duabus longis, iambus ex breui et longa, cui contrarius est trocheus ex longa et breui. Iambicum ergo metrum est quod ex pedibus iambis constat dimetrum, trimetrum, [fol. 3r] uel tetrametrum, uel quia pes predominans in metro iambus est, exemplum in ympno illo "Primo dierum omnium," ubi est
120 metrum iambicum dimetrum continuum metrum. In hoc ergo metro ad minus duos habet pedes, dimetrum quattuor, trimetrum sex, tetrametrum octo. Alchaicum autem metrum uocatur quod Alcheus fecit et saphicum quod Sapho fecit. Saphicum autem metrum est quale est illud: "Vt queant laxis," etc.[19]

105 o stelliferi] constelliferi **Ch**

---

[15] This is a citation of an unidentified gloss on Boethius, *De consolatione*, I m. 5. The comparison to the meter of "Primo dierum" does not appear in any of the Boethius commentaries I have investigated, which tend (correctly) to identify this metrum as an example of anapestic dimeter: see, e.g., Trevet's influential gloss, ed. E.T. Silk, unpublished typescript, p. 199 (for which see my website: sites.trinity.edu/akraebel). Cossey's anonymous citation may indicate that the work did not include an attribution. Though the major commentaries present discussions of meter, many ultimately deriving from Lupus of Ferrières, the use of a Latin hymn as an illustrative analogue is unusual, and it may reflect the unidentified commentary's reliance on Bede, *De arte metrica*, I.21, ed. Calvin B. Kendall, CCSL 123A (Turnhout, 1975), pp. 135–36, who does adduce several hymns (though not "Primo dierum") as examples of what Bede calls iambic tetrameter (more commonly, as later in this paragraph, called iambic dimeter), and the indirect dependence on Bede for this point could also explain Cossey's apparent inconsistency in the labeling of this meter (dimeter vs. tetrameter).

[16] See Hier., *Ep.* 53.8, ed. Hilberg, p. 461, used as a prologue to the Pentateuch; see De Bruyne, *Préfaces*, p. 6.

[17] Papias, *Elementarium*, s.v. "lyrici poetae" (Venice: Andreas de Bonetis, 1485), sig. n8r.

[18] See Isid., *Etym.*, 6.2.17, ed. Chaparro Gómez, pp. 21, 23.

[19] See *Analecta hymnica medii aevi* 50, ed. Guido Maria Dreves (Leipzig, 1907), pp. 120–23, no. 96. The first line of this hymn, quoted further below, reads: "Vt queant laxis resonare fibris."

Habet enim heroicum coma, id est finem uersus heroici, id est uersus exametri, sicut dicit Ieronimus (et Ysidorus).[20] Saphicum est quando uersus precedentes tali fine concluduntur et est metrum pentametrum dactilicum: "pentametrum" quia quilibet uersus metricus habet quinque pedes, primo trocheum, "Vt queant," secundo spondeum, tercio dactilicum, quarto trocheum, quinto similiter trocheum, "fibris." "Dactilicum" dicitur a pede precedente in loco inpari, scilicet tercio. Ex hiis patet quod psalmi non currunt in Hebreo talibus uersibus qui dicuntur exametri et pentametri apud nos uersificantes, sed aliis metris et uersibus uariis. Sed mirum est quomodo ipse Dauid de post fetantes assumptus et postea per totam uitam suam in actibus bellicis occupatus sciuerit uersificare, sed in lingua materna eciam laici sciunt uersificare.[21] Verumptamen ipse Dauid litteratus fuit. Dicunt enim Hebrei et recitat Ysidorus, libro 6 *Ethimologiarum*, quod Dauid scripsit ultimam partem libri Samuelis usque ad calcem.[22]

Habuerunt autem psalmi decem auctores secundum Hebreos, scilicet Moysen, Dauid, Salomon, Asaph, Ethan, Idithun, Eman, filii Chore, Helcana, Abiathar. Sed Rabi Salomon numerat decem auctores, sed omittit Eman et Ethan et nominat Melchisedech et Abraham,[23] quod "quia de Scripturis non habet auctoritatem," etc.[24] Conuenienter ergo cum decem essent in psalterio decem cordarum psallere potuerunt, et hoc denario nominum Domini. Omnia siquidem dicta decem nomina in Psalterio inueniuntur expressa, excepto scilicet Tetragramaton, *Iehaue*, quod cum frequenter modo quasi psalmo scri-

---

132–133 ipse Dauid … assumptus] Cf. Ps. 77.70

---

124 heroicum] cum **Ch**; heroici] herorci **Ch** ∥ **126** pentametrum] pentat^m **Ch** ∥ **127** pentametrum] pentat^m **Ch** ∥ **143** Domini] dominorum **Ch** ∥ **145** Tetragramaton Iehaue] Tetraiehaue **Ch**

---

[20] See Hier., *Ep.* 30.3, ed. Hilberg, p. 245; Isid., *Etym.* 6.2.23, ed. Chaparro Gómez, pp. 25, 27.

[21] See the discussion above, pp. 311–12.

[22] See Isid., *Etym.*, 6.2.10, ed. Chaparro Gómez, p. 17.

[23] Nicholas of Lyre offers the same contrast between Jerome's list and Rashi's (*Biblia sacra*, III, sig. o7ra), and it seems more likely that Cossey is responding to this intermediary (and affirming his support for Jerome's position) than drawing on Rashi directly. Cf. Mayer Gruber, *Rashi's Commentary on Psalms* (Leiden, 2004), p. 165.

[24] See Hier., *In Matheum* 4 (3.35–36), in *S. Hieronymi presbyteri Commentariorum in Matheum libri IV*, ed. David Hurst and Marc Adriaen, CCSL 77 (Turnhout, 1969), p. 220. The phrase continues: "eadem facilitate contemnitur qua probatur."

batur, non tamen audent proferre illud Hebrei, nisi in sanctuario tantum in benediccione sacerdotali et a maiori sacerdote in die ieiunii, sicut dicit Rabi Mosse, *De duce dubiorum* seu in libro *Direccionis perplexorum*.²⁵ [fol. 3v] Sed hoc ex errore introductum est Iudeorum; nam secundum ueritatem non est illud nomen magis quam aliquod aliud subticendum, nec tempore Dauid uidetur quod illud subticebant, cum psalmi ipsi non possent metrice decantari nisi illud nomen ubi ponitur exprimeretur. *El* autem *Eloim*, *Eloe*: unumquidque istorum "Deus," et sparsim ponuntur in psalmis. *El*, psalmo 21, *Hely, Hely*, id est *Deus meus, Deus meus*. *Eloym*, psalmo 7 circa medium ubi dicitur, *Heloym saduk*, id est *Deus iustus*. *Eloe*, psalmo 4, *Eloe sadeki*, id est *Deus iusticie mee*. *Sabaoth* uero, quod interpretatur "exercituum," expresse ponitur psalmo 23, *Dominus uirtutum: ipse est rex glorie*. *Helion* uero, quod interpretatur "excelsus," psalmo 7, *Psallam nomini Domini altissimi*. *Eser eie* uero, quod interpretatur "qui est," quoad unam partem ponitur psalmo primo, *Beatus uir*.²⁶ *Adonay*, quod "Dominus" interpretatur, psalmo 8, *Domine Dominus noster*. *Ya* uero, quod et interpretatur "Dominus," in titulis et in ipsis psalmis ultimis frequenter ponitur, *Alleluia*. *Tetragramaton* uero non est nomen Dei, sed nomen huius nominis *Iehaue*, quod frequencius quam aliquod aliorum ponitur et est ineffabile, nec est eius interpretacio nota hominibus. Vltimum uero, *Saday*, quod interpretatur "omnipotens" et "robustus," psalmo 90, *Qui habitat in adiutorio altissimi*, ubi nos habemus *in proteccione Dei celi commorabitur*, habetur in Hebreo *in umbra Saday manebit habitans in abscondito Elyon*, id est altissimi, ubi nos habitare et manere concedat, qui uiuit et regnat, etc. Amen.

153–154 Cf. Ps. 21.2 ‖ **154–155** Cf. Ps. 7.12 ‖ **155** Cf. Ps. 4.2 ‖ **157** Ps. 23.10 ‖ **158** Ps. 7.18 ‖ **159** Ps. 1.1 ‖ **160** Ps. 8.2 ‖ **165–167** Ps. 90.1

---

148 perplexorum] perplexcup **Ch** ‖ **153** 21] *om.* **Ch** ‖ **154** meus²] Domine Deus *add.* **Ch** ‖ **155** Eloe²] cum monhilche **Ch** ‖ **156** interpretatur] Dominus *add.* **Ch** *a.c.*

English Translation

The degree of this prophecy can certainly be called *zamiri* in Hebrew, which is translated "my psalm" or "my song," for the divinely inspired Psalmist wished to sing whatever he thought to predict and prophesy, to offer it in hymns and songs to the praise of the inspirer. Rightly, then, can the contents of the whole book be conveyed

---

²⁵ See Maimonides, *Dux seu director dubitantium aut perplexorum*, I.60 (Paris: Josse Bade, 1520), sig. c8v, corresponding to I.61 in modern editions.

²⁶ This is an apparent confusion of *beatus* (*esher*) with *qui* (*asher*).

in this little phrase: *To your name will I say a psalm*. In these words, the well-known four categories of causes of this prophecy appear to be expressed. First, the material cause, when he says *psalm*. For this is called the "book of Psalms," its name deriving from its subject matter rather than its efficient cause, as is the case with the other books of the prophets, those of Isaiah, Jeremiah, Daniel, and the books of the other prophets named after their authors. The formal cause appears to be expressed in the same word, i.e., *psalm*. For the mode in which this prophecy is conveyed is not by means of a simple narrative but rather by psalmody and singing, so that harder hearts which are not pricked by the words may be moved by the sweetness of the melody. A psalm is a song which is sung to the accompaniment of a psaltery. It is these psalms or songs, therefore, that I have sought to expound, with God's help, after the intention of the singer or Psalmist, whose intention I judge to be their literal sense, as will later become clear. It is fitting for these two causes, the material and formal, to be denoted in the same word, for they themselves are likewise united and arise together to make a thing whole.

The efficient cause, however, may be picked out in the words *will I say*, and this was either David alone, according to Augustine, *City of God*, 17.14, where he says that the more credible opinion belongs to those who attribute all one hundred fifty psalms to the work of David himself, or it was David together with other authors, according to Jerome in the prologue to Sophronius. If someone wanted to reconcile these doctors, he could say that David was the author of each and every psalm insofar as he prophesied and commanded that they be sung. For since it is said that a psalm is what is sung on a psaltery, if it is first read aloud or even sung without accompaniment, it cannot be called a psalm. Therefore he can be called the author of all the psalms, since he caused the psalms to exist and be performed – just as Avicenna is called the author of the *Canon of Medicine*, even though many of the things in that text should be attributed to others, and Aristotle confesses that what, as a whole, is attributed to him was taken from others who had spoken well. Yet, if we must deny the claims of one of these doctors, we should come down on the side of Jerome in matters which pertain to the Hebrew language.

The final cause is denoted by the opening words, *to your name*, to the honour of your name, O God. So it is that in Hebrew this book is called *sefir tehillim*, which according to Jerome is translated "book of hymns." A hymn is a song written in praise of God, and the Greek word *hymn* is translated "praise of God." Insofar as this is the final cause, it is clear that this book as a whole is not prophetic but rather laudatory (as are many) and hymnidic, like the hymnal of the catholic Church. It seems to me, then, that of all of these one hundred and fifty psalms, some are straightforwardly didactic, some prophetic, some complaints, some penitential, some deprecatory and some reproving, some giving thanks, some rousing, and some laudatory. Sometimes in a psalm the primary intention is to teach, and it teaches human good, i.e., happiness or blessedness, just as the first psalm describes the blessed man and his opposite. In his *Institutes*, Junillus calls this mode of Scripture "straightforwardly didactic." For just as Christ describes blessed men in the plural in the sermon he delivered on the mountain, here the Psalmist describes the blessed man in the singular in the first psalm, clearly expressing that beatitude which philosophers call the final end and the well-being of human actions. Sometimes a psalm is principally prophetic, and in particular about Christ, as are many of them. Indeed, the last words of David, 2 Reg. 23, make it clear that many psalms are literally prophetic: *David the son of Jesse said, the man to whom it was appointed concerning the Christ of the God of Jacob, the preeminent Psalmist of Israel said, "The spirit of the Lord has spoken by me, and his word by my tongue."* Sometimes he complains about his enemies, saying, *Lord, why are they multiplied*, etc. Sometimes he expresses contrition for what he has done: *Do not, O Lord, in your wrath, Blessed are they whose*, etc. Sometimes he prays for himself or for others, as is apparent in various psalms. Sometimes he curses with punishment and torment those who are, finally, wicked: *My praise, O God*. Sometimes he rebukes and chides them: *Why do you boast of wickedness*. Sometimes he gives thanks and recalls what he has been given: *I will love you*. Sometimes he rouses and consoles himself amid dangers: *The Lord is my light*. Finally, sometimes – indeed, frequently – he extols and praises God's magnificence, as will become clear. These ten may be found across the Psalter, in my opinion, though frequently several of them are mixed together and expressed in one and the same psalm.

Similarly, with regard to the classification of these psalms, the Psalmist had ten modes of speaking, often likewise intermixed. Sometimes he speaks to God but not about God, sometimes about God but not to God, sometimes to God and about God. Again, sometimes he speaks to himself but not about himself, sometimes about himself but not to himself, sometimes to himself and about himself. Again, sometimes he speaks to another person but not about that person, sometimes about him but not to him, sometimes to him and about him. Sometimes, finally, he speaks both simply and absolutely – and in one and the same psalm he mixes these modes together here and there, as is apparent to anyone paying attention. Furthermore, according to Jerome in his letter to Marcella, there are ten names for God among the Hebrews, i.e., *El, Elohim, Eloah, Sabaoth, Elyon, Asher ehyeh, Adonai, Jah,* the Tetragrammaton, and *Shaddai*. To these ten names and about these ten names the Psalmist uttered the psalms, and this on a psaltery, a musical instrument of ten cords, on which David himself took pleasure in singing psalms to God: *On a psaltery of ten cords*, he says, *I will sing psalms to you* – thereby memorializing the ten commandments and massacring the ten beasts, as Augustine says in his little book about the ten cords. Those ten beasts are the ten vices or the ten demons in control of those vices, i.e., the demon of superstition, of error, of love of the world, of impiety, of lust, of cruelty, of rapacity, of falseness, of impure thought, and of cupidity, and these are opposed to the ten commandments. To kill these beasts or demons, or to put them to flight, the Psalmist sang his psalms. For in the ancient stories of the poets we read that, after Eurydice had been wounded on her ankle by a snake and died and already been led down to the underworld, Orpheus took up his harp and followed his wife to rescue her, and there in the underworld he played his harp so sweetly that all the infernal gods, moved by this uncommon sweetness, returned Eurydice to him. Likewise, by this harper, the Psalmist, souls were rescued from the underworld of their sins and demons were made to flee by the sweetness of his psalmody. Further, in this book there are ten "pentadecades" of psalms, i.e., ten groups of fifteen, for one hundred and fifty is ten times fifteen. A pentadecade, because of the mystery of the groupings of seven and eight, is suggestive of the contents of the New and Old Testament, and in both the New and Old Testament the ten commandments are openly proclaimed. And all of this makes it clear that whatever is conveyed in holy Scripture, whether historically, didactically, prophetically or proverbially, is also contained in this book, metrically and hymnidically. Furthermore, since the Apostle enumerates fifteen conditions of charity, 1 Cor. 13, *Charity is patient, it is kind*, etc., and since all the law and the prophets hang on charity, it follows that the ten pentadecades of the psalms prefigure the Decalogue diffused in charity, along with anything hidden or openly stated in the divine words.

All the psalms were composed and written metrically in Hebrew, according to Jerome and Isidore, *Etymologies*, Book 6, but it is unclear what that meter is, i.e., whether it could be iambic trimeter or tetrameter, the common meter of our hymns (e.g., "On this, the first of all the days, / When God the world's foundation laid"), as is made clear in a commentary on Boethius, *On the Consolation of Philosophy*, "O founder of the star-filled heavens." Still, in his prologue to Paulinus, Jerome makes it clear that they are indeed metrical, referring to David as Simonides, Horace, and Pindar on account of the similar meters which he sang in the psalms. All of these authors wrote lyric songs. According to Papias, "lyric" derives from a word meaning variety, and so it is that the psalms do not all run along in one and the same meter, but rather, as Isidore says, *Etymologies*, Book 6, in the chapter on the writers and names of holy books, now some of them run in iambic, now they resound in Alcaic, now they mix in a Sapphic, proceeding with a trimeter or tetrameter foot. Now, you should know that there are many different metrical feet – one hundred twenty four in total if you were to count from the disyllables to the hexasyllables – but there are only four disyllables and eight trisyllables. The disyllables include the pyrrhic (two short syllables) and its opposite the spondee (two long syllables), as well as the iamb (one short and one long syllable) and its opposite the trochee (one long and one short syllable). Iambic meter, therefore, whether dimeter, trimeter, or tetrameter, is either made up entirely of iambic feet or is a meter in which the iamb predominates, e.g., in the hymn "On this, the first of all the days," where the meter is a continuous iambic dimeter. In this meter, therefore, at the very least there are two feet, while dimeter has four, trimeter six, and tetrameter eight. Alcaic meter takes its name from Alchaeus, who made it, and Sapphic from its maker Sappho. An example of Sapphic meter is the hymn "Now may with loosened," which has a heroic period, i.e., the end of a heroic (or hexameter) verse, as Jerome and Isidore say. A meter is Sapphic when the preceding verses are concluded with this kind of ending and otherwise the meter is dactylic pentameter: "pentameter" because each verse has five feet, the first a trochee ("Now may"), the second a spondee, the third a dactyl, fourth a trochee, fifth another trochee ("fibers"), and it is called "dactylic" from the preceding foot in the unequal (i.e., third) position. From all this it is clear enough that the psalms do not run along in Hebrew in the verse-forms which our versifiers call hexameters or pentameters, but in various other meters and verse-forms. But is it not astonishing that the same David who was chosen from the sheepfolds and afterwards, throughout his life, was kept busy waging war, also knew how to compose in verse? Then again, even the laity know how to versify in their mother tongue. Still, David was literate, for (as Isidore reports in Book 6 of the *Etymologies*) the Hebrews say that David wrote the last part of the book of Samuel, up to the end.

According to the Hebrews, the psalms had ten authors, i.e., Moses, David, Solomon, Asaph, Ethan, Jeduthun, Heman, the sons of Korah, Elkanah, and Abiathar. Rabbi Solomon also enumerates ten authors, but he omits Heman and Ethan and instead names Melchizedek and Abraham, but "since this opinion does not have the authority of the Scriptures," etc. It is fitting, therefore, since there were ten of them, that they were able to sing psalms on a ten-stringed psaltery, and this to the ten names of the Lord. For all of the aforementioned ten names are found expressly stated in the Psalter, except, that is, for the Tetragrammaton, *Yahweh*, which, although it is now written frequently in almost every psalm, the Hebrews do not dare to say out loud, except in the sanctuary in the priestly benediction and by the High Priest on the day of fasting, as Rabbi Moses says in his *Guide for the Doubting* or *Direction for the Perplexed*. But this practice was introduced by the Jews in error, for in truth that name is not more worthy of silence than any other, and it does not appear to have been left unsaid in the time of David, for the psalms could not be recited metrically if that name were not pronounced where it is written. *El, Elohim, Eloah*: each one of these means "God," and they may be found throughout the psalms. *El* in Psalm 21, *Eli, Eli*, i.e., *My God, my God. Elohim*, Psalm 7, near the middle, where it is written, *Elohim saddiq*, i.e., *God is just. Eloah*, Psalm 4, *Elohe sidqi*, i.e., *O God of my justice. Sabaoth*, which is translated "of hosts," appears clearly in Psalm 23, *The Lord of hosts: he is the king of glory. Elyon*, translated "exalted," Psalm 7, *I will sing psalms to the name of the Lord most high.* At least one part of *Asher ehyeh*, translated "who is," appears in the first psalm, *Blessed is the man. Adonai*, translated "Lord," Psalm 8, *O Lord, our Lord. Jah*, also translated "Lord," frequently appears in the titles and in the last psalms, in the word

Alleluia. The Tetragrammaton is not a name of God but rather a name for the name *Yahweh*, which appears more frequently than any other and is ineffable, and no one knows its meaning. Finally, *Shaddai*, translated "almighty" and "powerful," Psalm 90, *He who dwells in the aid of the most high*, where we have *will abide in the protection of the God of heaven*, which in Hebrew is *will remain in the shadow of Shaddai, dwelling in the hiding place of Elyon*, i.e., *of the most high*. May he indeed grant that we dwell and remain there, who lives and reigns, etc. Amen.

Prologue 2: Glosses on Jerome's Hebraicum Preface

Nota[1] quod Ieronimus binomius fuit: uocabatur Eusebius. Vnde Valerius Maximus, libro 10,[2] dicit quod mos Romanorum erat aliorum nomina suis preponere quandoque amoris uel honoris alia uel alia de causa, sed pueris non antequam uirilem togam acciperent imponebantur, puellis non antequam
5 nuberent, uocaturque illud quod sic preponitur "prenomen" et illud quod sequitur, Ieronimus, "nomen," et tercium, si adhuc adderetur, diceretur "cognomen."

Prima decisio per *fiat fiat* est psalmo 40, *Beatus qui intelligit*, secunda psalmo 71, *Deus iudicium tuum*, tercia psalmo 88, *Misericordias Domini*, quarta psalmo
10 105, *Confitemini secundum*, et durat usque ad finem, sed finis non est per *fiat fiat*, sed *cal hanesama te halleluya*, id est *omnis anima laudet Dominum*.[3]

8 Ps. 40.2 ‖ 9 Ps. 71.2, Ps. 71.2, Ps. 88.2 ‖ 10 Ps. 105.2 ‖ 11 Ps. 150.6

---

9 71] 70 **Ch**

---

[1] Note in margin: "Ieronimus binomius erat" – "Jerome had two names."

[2] Valerius Maximus, *De factis dictisque*, 10.3 (i.e., the Julius Paris epitome), ed. Karl Kempf (Leipzig, 1888), p. 589.

[3] There is a note in the lower margin, not tied to this point in the text but clearly related to the foregoing discussion: "Nota tamen quod Ieronimus in epistola sua ad Marcellam etc., 99, dicit sic: Septuaginta *senocto* [*sic for* "genoito"], id est *fiat*. Vnde et in fine librorum (in quinque siquidem uolumina Psalterium apud Hebreos diuisum est) *fiat fiat* transtulerunt, quod in Hebreo legitur *amen amen*. Hic ibi. Item Ieronimus, epistola 119, et est ad Marcellam, dicit sic: Cum hora ferme tercia hodierne diei, septuagesimum secundum psalmum, id est tercii libri principium, legere cepissemus, et docere cogeremur tituli ipsius partem ad finem secundi libri partem ad principium tercii libri pertinere, etc." – "Note, however, that in his letter 99 [= 26] to Marcella, etc., Jerome says thus: 'The Septuagint reads *génoito*, i.e., *so be it*. For this reason at the end of books – and indeed among the Hebrews the Psalter is divided into five volumes – they write out *so be it, so be it*, which in Hebrew is *amen amen*.' This is what he says here. Likewise,

Potest[4] autem prologus iste diuidi in nouem partes, in quarum prima premittit consuetam salutacionis caritatem, *Eusebius*, etc., secundo ostendit huius uoluminis unitatem, *Scio quosdam*, tercio eiusdem auctoritatem, *Psalmos quoque*, quarto sue translacionis neccessitatem, *Quia ergo*, quinto ostendit sue translacionis ueritatem, *Certe confidenter*, sexto redarguit emulorum peruersitatem, *Nunc cum*, septimo ostendit sui laboris utilitatem, *Nec hoc dico*, ubi primo ostendit quod non facit hoc propter deprauacionem priorum, sed ad satisfaciendum calumpnie Iudeorum et respondendum, octauo ostendit quod in hiis sibi prestat solamen et iocunditatem, *Quod si opusculum*, ultimo conclusiue recommendacionis congruitatem, *Vale*. Et[5] nota hic, parte septima, quod Ieronimus innuit quod nollet quod translacio sua in ecclesiis Christianorum cantaretur, nec hoc intendebat sed dare uiam respondendi Iudeis.

Item nota secundum translacionem septuaginta interpretum, que facta fuit de Hebreo in Grecum, quos Augustinus putat [fol. 5r] in diuersis cellis fuisse et quasi miraculose in unum concordasse,[6] sed Ieronimus uult, sicut patet in prologo ad Desiderium,[7] quod in una basilica congregati contulerunt adinuicem et non prophetabant. Erant enim Iudei ex omni tribu sex electi et in summa septuaginta duo, sed dicit Magister Historiarum quod de paruo numero Scriptura non facit curam, et ideo illi duo cum septuaginta non nominantur,[8] uel forte illi duo aliis in percameno et incausto et in aliis necessariis seruiebant. Isti ad peticionem Philadelfi regis Egipti missi a summo sacerdote Iudeorum Eleazaro transtulerunt, fuitque translacio eorum lecta et approbata ab omnibus Iudeis qui Alexandrie erant utriusque lingue, Hebree scilicet et Grece, periti.

---

in his letter 119 [= 23], which is also to Marcella, Jerome says thus: 'Today, at about the third hour, when we were beginning to read Ps. 72, i.e., the first psalm of the third book, and when we were compelled to teach how in part its title pertained to the end of the second book and in part to the beginning of the third book,' etc." The two quotations come from Hier., *Ep.* 36.4 and *Ep.* 23.1, ed. Hilberg, pp. 222 and 211.

[4] Note in margin: "Diuisio istius prologi" – "This prologue's division."

[5] Note in margin: "Ieronimus nollet quod sua translatio in ecclesia legeretur" – "Jerome would not have wanted his translation to be read in church," i.e., in the liturgy.

[6] Aug., *De doctrina christiana* 2.15, ed. Joseph Martin, CCSL 32 (Turnhout, 1962), p. 47; cf. Aug., *De ciu.* 18.42, ed. Dombart and Kalb, p. 638.

[7] De Bruyne, *Préfaces*, p. 8; *Vulgate*, ed. Fischer et al., 1:3–4.

[8] No such remark appears in Peter Comestor's *Historia scholastica*, but compare below, Prol.3.19–20.

English Translation

Jerome had two names, the other being Eusebius. Valerius Maximus, 10.3, says that it was Roman custom for the names of others to be added before one's own, whether out of love or honour or some other cause, but they were not bestowed on boys before they received the toga of manhood or on girls before they were married, and this added name was called the "prename" and what followed, Jerome, the "name," and, if a third was added, it was called the "surname."

The first break caused by *so be it, so be it* occurs at the end of Psalm 40, *Blessed is he who understands*, the second Psalm 71, *Your judgment, O God*, the third Psalm 88, *The mercies of the Lord*, the fourth Psalm 105, the second psalm beginning, *Acknowledge*, and this section persists to the end, but the whole text does not end with *so be it, so be it*, but rather with *kol hannesamah te hallelujah*, i.e., *let every soul praise the Lord*.

This prologue can be divided into nine parts, the first of which begins with the customary expression of charity in the salutation, *Eusebius*, etc., secondly he demonstrates the unity of this volume, *I know some*, thirdly its authority, *The Psalms likewise*, fourthly the necessity of its translation, *Since therefore*, fifthly he demonstrates the trustworthiness of his translation, *Truly, confidently*, sixthly he refutes the perversity of the envious, *Now when*, seventhly he demonstrates the utility of his undertaking, *Neither do I say this*, first demonstrating that he does not do this on account of the corruption of earlier translations but to satisfy and respond to the false accusations of the Jews, eighthly he demonstrates that these efforts bring him comfort and joy, *But if this little work*, and finally, in conclusion, the appropriate commendation, *Farewell*. And note that, in the seventh part, Jerome indicates that he would not have wanted his translation to be sung in Christian churches, and that this was not his intention, but rather to provide a way to respond to the Jews.

Further, with respect to the version made by the seventy translators, which was rendered from Hebrew into Greek, note that Augustine thinks they were in different cells and, as though miraculously, they all agreed on one text, but, as is clear in the prologue to Desiderius, Jerome prefers to think that they were gathered together in a single hall and collaborated in their work, and that they did not prophesy. Six Jews were chosen from each tribe, adding up to seventy-two in total. The Master of Histories says that Scripture does not bother with small numbers, and therefore two of them are not named along with the other seventy. Alternatively, perhaps those two served the others, providing parchment, ink, and other necessities. These men prepared their translation at the request of Ptolemy Philadelphus, the King of Egypt, a petition he sent to Eleazar, High Priest of the Jews, and their translation was read and approved by all the Alexandrian Jews who were learned in both languages, i.e., Hebrew and Greek.

Prologue 3: Notes on the Psalter, Its Composition, and Interpretation

Beatus uir. Quia sanctus Franciscus in regula sua suis fratribus officium diuinum iniungens secundum usum curie Romane excepit Psalterium,[1] per hoc manifeste preponens commune Psalterium, ideo circa eius exposicionem insistam de capite meo nichil asserturus nisi quod sancti patres et catholice consonat ueritati. Sunt autem in psalmis decem inquirenda, scilicet quod nomen interpretis, quod nomen auctoris, intencio auctoris, utilitas operis, titulus operis, conueniens discipulus, que materia, quis ordo legendi et modus, ad quam (si ad aliquam) partem philosophie spectet, et tandem diuisio libri in partes, etc.

De primo uidendum est utrum translacio Septuaginta sit illa que "uulgata" uocatur, sicut Triuet dicit, et pro se allegat Augustinus, 18 *De ciuitate Dei*, quod ipse uelit translacionem Septuaginta ideo uocari "uulgatam," quia "tam communis fuerit eius usus, ut multi an aliqua alia esset penitus ignorarent."[2] Certum est quod, libro 16 capitulo 10.4, dicit uulgatam edicionem esse translacionem Septuaginta et eam sic exponit.[3] Sed miror uel de ignorancia uel non aduertencia huius senis, ut enim auctoritatem Ysidori, *Ethimologiarum*, libro 6, capitulo de interpretibus, taceam, et libro 5 de etatibus, ubi breuiter signat quibus temporibus interpretes fuerunt – et proprie qui eadem uerba dicit[4] – et Magistri Historiarum, cito post principium, qui omnes edicionem quintam "uulgatam" dicunt appellari, quia auctor eius ignoratur.[5] Probo[6] per ipsummet Augustinum, qui cum hiis concordat et non contradicit, libro 18 capitulo 43, qui c. 42 dicit quod septuaginta duo erant interpretes, de singulis tribubus seni utriusque lingue, Hebree scilicet et Grece, doctissimi, missi ab

---

8 philosophie] prophecie **Ch** ∥ **19** Historiarum] Sentenciarum **Ch** ∥ **21** Augustinum] Augustinus **Ch** ∥ **22** 43] 44 **Ch**; 42] 43 **Ch**; septuaginta duo] 72 72 **Ch** *a.c.* ∥ **23** Grece] Latine **Ch**

---

[1] *Regula Bullata*, III, p. 229, quoted in the Introduction, n. 26.

[2] Trevet, *In Pss.*, praef. ep. (Oxford, Bodleian Library, MS Bodley 738, fol. 1ra).

[3] Aug., *De ciu.* 16.10, ed. Dombart and Kalb, p. 512.

[4] Isid., *Etym.*, 6.4.3, ed. Chaparro Gómez, p. 47 (quoting Aug., *De ciu.* 18.43); and Isid., *Etym.*, 5.39.22 and 29, in *Isidoro de Sevilla, Etimologías, Libro V: De legibus – De temporibus*, ed. Valeriano Yarza Urquiola and Francisco Javier Andrés Santos, Auteurs latins du moyen âge (Paris, 2013), pp. 155, 161, 163.

[5] Peter Comestor, *Historia scholastica*, Gen. 16, ed. Agneta Sylwan, CCCM 191 (Turnhout, 2005), p. 33.

[6] Note in margin: "Quare dicitur edicio uulgata" – "Why it is called the common version."

Eleazaro summo sacerdote Iudeorum ad Phtolomeum regem Egipti, quorum interpretacio, ut Septuaginta uocetur, iam optinuit consuetudo. Et post: "Nam cum fuerint alii interpretes qui ex Hebrea lingua in Grecam sacra eloquia transtulerunt, sicut Aquila, Simachus, et Theodocion, sicut est eciam illa interpretacio cuius auctor non apparet et ob hoc sine nomine interpretis quarta uel quinta edicio" (quarta, inquam, post Christum, sed quinta post Septuaginta) "nuncupatur, hanc tamen que Septuaginta est tanquam sola est sic recipit Ecclesia, eaque utuntur [fol. 6r] Greci populi Christiani, quorum plurique utrum alia sit aliqua ignorant."[7] Patet quod non uocat translacionem Septuaginta "uulgatam," sed que dicatur "uulgata" non expressit. Sed alii omnes et ipse Ieronimus illam quintam edicionem, cuius auctor ignoratur, uocari "uulgatam" manifestant. Vlterius est aduertendum quod de Hebreo in Grecum sextam et septimam edicionem Origenes fecit et cum ceteris edicionibus comparauit. Octauam uero Ieronimus de Hebreo in Latinum, quam edicionem Suffronius de Latino uertit in Grecum. Latinorum autem interpretum, qui de Greco in nostrum eloquium transtulerunt, nomina et numerus ignorantur, sicut dicit Augustinus, libro 2 *De doctrina christiana*.[8] Quiscumque enim primis Ecclesie temporibus utriusque lingue, Grece scilicet et Latine, periciam habuit, ausus est transferre, propter quod nimia est littere confusio introducta. Verumptamen ipsius Psalterii Latinos interpretes enumerat beatus Ieronimus in epistola quadam ad beatum Augustinum,[9] ubi sic dicit:

Psalmos apud Grecos interpretati sunt multis uoluminibus primus Origenes, secundus Eusebius, tercius Theodorus Eracleotes, quartus Asterius Sticepolitanus, quintus Appolinarius Laodicensis, sextus Didimus Alexandrinus. Feruntur et diuersorum in paucos psalmos opuscula, sed nunc de integro Psalmorum corpore dicimus. Apud Latinos autem Hillarius Pictauensis et Eusebius Vercellensis episcopi, Origenem et Eusebium transtulerunt, quorum priorem et noster Ambrosius in quibusdam secutus est.[10]

31 populi] et *add.* **Ch** ‖ **42** est²] littera *add.* **Ch** a.c

---

[7] Aug., *De ciu.* 18, paraphrasing 42 and then quoting 43, ed. Dombart and Kalb, pp. 638–39.

[8] Cf. Aug., *De doctrina christiana* 2.11, ed. Martin, p. 42.

[9] Note in margin: "Et est epistola 24, sed nota quod ibi accipit interpretes, id est expositores, quod satis patet per antecedencia et illa que secuntur" – "And it is Letter 24 [= 112]: but note that he does not approve of these interpreters, i.e., expositors, which is clear enough from what comes before and what follows."

[10] Hier., *Ep.* 112.20, ed. Hilberg, p. 390.4–12.

Omnia ista dubitacionem augent que sit ista translacio super quam fuerit glosa, qua et singule fere Latinorum utuntur ecclesie, qua et sanctus Franciscus uti uoluit fratres suos et non Psalterio uso Romano.

Et dicit Triuet quod Ieronimus translacionem Septuaginta, ut pura erat, de Greco uertit in Latinum, sed postea, cum hec translacio esset uiciata, interpellantibus Paula et Eustochio iterum Psalterium de Greco transtulit in Latinum, sed Origenis imitatus est studium, scilicet asteriscos et obelos. Et circa litteram istarum duarum [fol. 6v] translacionum tota antiquorum desudauit intencio, inter quos Septuaginta simplicem translacionem, que prior erat, Senator Cassiodorus exponit, commixtam uero, que secunda erat, beatus Augustinus edisserit.[11] Sed miror quod iste "translacionem" uocat quam ipse Ieronimus non "translacionem," sed "correccionem" appellat. Ait enim in prefacione super Psalterium, a qua iste accepit:

> Psalterium Rome dudum positus emendaueram et iuxta Septuaginta interpretes magna illud ex parte correxeram, quod quia rursum uidetis, O Paula et Eustochium, scriptorum uicio deprauatum plusque antiquum errorem quam nouam emendacionem ualere, cogitis, etc.

Et post:

> Notet igitur unusquisque uel iacentem lineam uel signa radiancia, id est obelos uel asteriscos, et ubicumque uiderit uirgulam precedentem ab ea usque ad duo puncta que impressimus sciat in Septuaginta translatoribus plus haberi. Vbi autem similitudinem stelle perspexerit de Hebreis uoluminibus additum nouerit.[12]

Patet igitur quod non fuerunt nisi due emendaciones secundum eum, non translaciones. Et dicit Triuet (et Lira) quod Psalterium prime translacionis est in usu ecclesie Romane usque in presens, secunde uero translacionis Psalterium Damasus Papa in ecclesiis Gallicanis decantari instituit.[13] Sed hec secunda, ex quo continebat talia signa (quorum uno, obelis, superflua iugulabantur, et asteriscis que superflua ibidem scribebantur), non potuit

55 uso] suo **Ch** ‖ **59** Origenis] Origenes **Ch**; scilicet] *om.* **Ch**; asteriscos] astericos **Ch** ‖ **68** antiquum] antiquum **Ch** ‖ **72** asteriscos] astericos **Ch** ‖ **81** et asteriscis] ut asserit **Ch**

---

[11] Trevet, *In Pss.*, praef. ep. (Oxford, Bodleian Library, MS Bodley 738, fol. 1rb), omitting some material.

[12] De Bruyne, *Préfaces*, p. 46; *Vulgate*, ed. Fischer et al., 1:767.

[13] Trevet, *In Pss.*, praef. ep. (Oxford, Bodleian Library, MS Bodley 738, fol. 1rb); Nicholas of Lyre, *In Pss.*, praef. (*Biblia sacra*, III, sig. o3aC).

conuenienter nec debuit decantari, quin oporteret illa superflua decantare, nec fiebat illa emendacio nisi ad differenciam duarum translacionum Septuaginta et Origenis cognoscendam.

Item prior translacio est in usu ecclesie Gallicane et aliarum: ipsa enim est pure secundum translacionem Septuaginta, que ualde aliter habet quam habeat Psalterium Romanum. Verbi gracia: dicit Ieronimus in epistola ad Ciprianum presbiterum de psalmo 89 secundum quod habetur in Hebreo uel in antiqua alia translacione: *Imple nos matutina misericordia tua, laudabimus et letabimur pariter omnes in cunctis diebus nostris*,[14] et sic habetur in Psalterio Romano, excepto *et*.[15] Septuaginta uero, sicut dicit Ieronimus, habent sic: *Repleti sumus mane misericordia* [fol. 7r] *tua, et exultati et delectati sumus in omnibus diebus nostris*. (In omnibus pene locis hanc habent Septuaginta consuetudinem, ut quod apud Hebreos in futurum ostenditur hoc illi quasi iam factum referant.) Post: *Letifica nos pro diebus quibus afflixisti, annis quibus uidimus mala*, sic habetur eciam in Psalterio Romano, et Septuaginta sic dicit Ieronimus: *Letati sumus pro diebus quibus nos humiliasti*, etc., sicut nostrum habet Psalterium. *Et sit decor Domini Dei nostri super nos, et opus manuum nostrarum fac stabile super nos et opus manuum nostrarum confirma*. Et totaliter sic habetur in Romano Psalterio. Septuaginta sic: *Et sit splendor Domini Dei nostri super nos, et opera manuum nostrarum dirige super nos et opus manuum nostrarum dirige*. Hec Ieronimus. Ex hiis apparet quod Psalterium quo utimur est secundum translacionem Septuaginta, quod ipse Ieronimus Rome correxit. (Vtrum autem habeamus sicut ipse correxit, nescio.) Psalterium uero Romanum uidetur esse illud quod transtulit immediate de Hebreo in Latinum, quia tamen in aliquibus quamuis ualde paucis differt, sicut patebit in processu, putari potest fuisse secunda translacio que facta fuit de Greco in Latinum, non secundum Septuaginta. Omissis enim hiis que uirgulis iugulabantur et supplementis additis de Hebreo, proueniret Psalterium fere sicut in Hebreo habetur in Latinum translatum. Siue autem Psalterium Romanum sit immediate translatum de Hebreo siue (ut dictum est) eiusdem Ieronimi de Greco secunda facta translacio partim et correccio, nostrum teneamus, quod

88 89] dicit *add.* **Ch** ‖ **110** Latinum] Latino **Ch**

---

[14] Beginning here he quotes Ps. 89.14–15 and 17 from Jerome's *Ep.* 140.18–21, in *Sancti Hieronymi Epistolae 121–154*, ed. Isidor Hilberg, CSEL 56 (Vienna – Leipzig, 1918; 2nd ed. Vienna, 1996), pp. 287–89, with the texts alternately corresponding to the Hebraicum and Gallican translations. (On the source of Cossey's confusion, see above, pp. 293–94).

[15] Apparently referring to the "et" between "tua" and "laudabimus" in the Hebraicum.

constat de Greca translacione Septuaginta in Latinam linguam esse translatum et a Ieronimo emendatum.

Beatus Ieronimus, ut dicit Nicholaus de Lira, ter transtulit Psalterium, primo secundum Septuaginta interpretes, quod dicitur Psalterium Romanum eo quod ecclesia beati Petri illo utitur. Secundo fecit aliam translacionem non multum differentem a prima, sed plus appropinquantem Hebraico, et uocatur Psalterium Gallicanum eo quod Damasus Papa precepit in Gallia cantari, quo et Fratres Minores utuntur. Tercio ad preces Suffronii, etc.[16] Iste concordat cum Triuet, et contra eum sunt eadem argumenta, et scito quod isto Psalterio Gallicano, quod est pure secundum translacionem Septuaginta, utitur quasi totum residuum Ecclesie, excepta curia Romana et quibusdam abbathiis. Et istum errorem acceperunt a cronica Martini, qui de Damaso Papa dicit quod Romanum Psalterium est secundum translacionem Septuaginta, quod Ieronimus primo emendauit.[17]

Quid autem sit nomen auctoris uel auctorum Psalmorum? Quamuis secundum Ieronimum teneamus quod illi fuerunt auctores qui nominantur in titulis, sunt tamen psalmi uel carentes titulis uel saltem ubi nullius nomen exprimitur. Dubium est qui auctores eorum sunt. Et dicitur in quadam prefacione super Psalterium (nescio cuius sit) quod nouem psalmos fecit ipse Dauid, et triginta duo non sunt suprascripti, septuaginta duo in Dauid et in Asaph uiginti duo et duo in Ydithun, nouem filiis Chore, unus Moysi, duo in Salomonem, duo in Aggeum et Zachariam. Fuerunt itaque omnes Psalmi Dauid numero centum quinquaginta. Cui et ego dico quod hec mala sit calculacio. Nouem enim et triginta duo et septuaginta duo et uiginti duo et duo, [fol. 7v] nouem, unus, duo et duo faciunt centum quinquaginta unus. Item unde habet quod "nouem fecit ipse Dauid," cum multo plures sibi ascribantur in titulis hoc modo, *psalmus* seu *cantus* uel *canticum Dauid*, sicut patebit et patet intuenti? Item cum Ieronimus in epistola sua ad Suffronium dicat et nominet Eman unum de auctoribus,[18] da aliquem psalmum sibi et tunc plures erunt quam centum quinquaginta unus, uel aliquem de istis quem aliis dedisti auferes et sic sibi

---

118 appropinquantem] apropinquantem **Ch** ‖ **119** eo] *om.* **Ch**

---

[16] Nicholas of Lyre, *In Pss.*, praef. (*Biblia sacra*, III, sig. o3vaC).

[17] Martin of Opava, *Chronicon pontificum et imperatorum*, ed. Ludwig Weiland, MGH SS 22 (Hanover, 1877), p. 417.7–10. This paragraph (lines 115–126) is found after line 172 in **Ch**; for the rationale for moving it here, see above, pp. 306–7.

[18] De Bruyne, *Préfaces*, p. 46; *Vulgate*, ed. Fischer et al., 1:768.

assigna. Psalmus quippe 87, *Domine Deus salutis*, intitulatur *Eman Ezraite*, et 88 intitulatur *Intellectus Ethan Ezraite*, et in Hebreo sic: *Sapiens Ethan Ezraite*. Quare ergo ipsi Ethan nullum psalmum ascribitur? Illa autem prefacio talis est:

> Dauid filius Iesse, cum esset in regno suo, quattuor elegit qui psalmos facerent, id est Asaph, Eman, Ethan et Ydithun. Octaginta octo ergo dicebant psalmos, et ducenti super psalteria et citharam percuciebat Abiud. Cum Dauid reduxisset archam in Ierusalem post annos uiginti reuocatam ab Azotis et mansit in domo Aminadab, hanc inposuit in subiugali nouo et adduxit in Ierusalem electis uiris ex omni genere filiorum Israel septuaginta. De tribu autem Leui electi sunt ducenti octaginta octo uiri, ex quibus quattuor principes preesse cancionibus instituit Asaph, Eman, Ethan et Ydithun, unicuique eorum diuidens septuaginta duos uiros subclamantes laudem cancionum Domino. Et unus quidem eorum feriebat cimbalum, alius autem cinaram, alius citharam, alius autem tuba cornea exultans. In medio autem eorum stabat ipse Dauid tenens psalterium. Archa autem antecedebat septem choris et sacrificium uitulis; populus autem uniuersus sequebatur post archam. Sunt ergo psalmi Dauid omnes numero centum quinquaginta, quorum omnium quidem nouem fecit ipse Dauid, triginta duo non sunt suprascripti, septuaginta duo in Dauid, uiginti duo in Asaph, duo in Ydithun, nouem filiis Chore, unus Moysi, duo in Salomonem, duo in Aggeum et Zachariam. Fuerunt itaque omnes Psalmi Dauid numero centum quinquaginta, diapsalmata numero septuaginta quinque, cantica graduum numero quindecim. Psalmus primus nulli assignatus est quoniam omnium est. Deinde quis alius intelligitur in primo nisi primogenitus, ut merito inscripcio non fuerit neccessaria. Deinde, quia ipse psalmus Christi mencionem facit, aduersus Christum tuum exponendo personam, causam non habuit omnino. Ordinem historie immutatum legimus et in titulis psalmorum, sed psalmi non secundum historiam sed secundum propheciam leguuntur. Ita [fol. 8r] ordinem psalmorum turbare non potest ordo titulorum. Psalmi omnes qui inscribuntur ipsi Dauid ad Christi pertinent sacramentum, quia Dauid dictus est "christus."[19]

---

143 Ps. 87.2, Ps. 87.1 ‖ **144** Ps. 88.1

---

143 Psalmus] Psalmum **Ch** ‖ **144** intellectus] ipsi **Ch** ‖ **148** percuciebat] percuciebant **Ch** ‖ **154** subclamantes] suos clamantes **Ch** ‖ **158** uitulis] uituli **Ch** ‖ **160** suprascripti] scripti **Ch** ‖ **161** in Asaph duo] *om.* **Ch** ‖ **163** dia-psalmata] diaplasmo **Ch**

---

[19] De Bruyne, *Préfaces*, pp. 43a–44a. On this preface, and Cossey's decision to gloss and quote it, see above, pp. 293 and 297–299.

Et quia Dauid expressissime de Christo prophetat, dubitari potest utrum ipse fuerit maior et eximius omnium prophetarum, sicut uocatur in glosa Cassiodori.[20] Et quid sit prophecia declarat Iunilius dicens: "Prophecia est rerum latencium preteritarum, presentium, et futurarum ex diuina inspiracione manifestacio,"[21] et uide ibi septem genera propheciarum. Intelligenda est autem latencia ista illi cui fit reuelacio quantum ad humanam inuestigacionem, sicut inferius est dictum.[22] Cogitacio enim Simonis Magi bene erat sibi ipsi nota per naturalem experienciam, sed Petro per reuelacionem, Act. 8, *In felle amaritudinis uideo te esse*. Similiter quod Giezi puer Elisei accepit munera, Reg. 4 c. 5, notum erat sensibiliter ipsi Naaman et aliis qui circumstabant, sed ipsi Elizeo per inspiracionem. Prophecia autem de preterito sicut Moyses prophetauit creacionem mundi, sicut dicit Gregorius super Ezechielem.[23]

Est eciam sciendum quod proprie non est prophecia nisi intelligat illud quod prophetando dicit.[24] Vnde qui modo prophete dicuntur olim "uidentes" uocabantur, quia uidebant intelligendo ea que prophetabant. Verumptamen in Scriptura quandoque quamuis non intelligat prophetare dicitur dummodo ad instinctum Spiritus sancti uerba proferat, quorum alium intellectum habet quam Spiritus sanctus habeat, sicut Caiphas, Ioh. 11, *Expedit uobis*, etc. Intellexit enim quod expediens erat quod Christus quamuis innocens moreretur, ne occasione ipsius [fol. 8v] uenirent Romani, etc.[25] Ille igitur gradus prophecie est excellencior, cuius ceteris paribus est intelligencia clarior, dum tamen prophecie limites non excedat, sicut dicit Lira, quia semper prophecia debet esse enigmatica. Vnde uisio diuine essencie excludit actum

181 Act. 8.23 ‖ 191 Ioh. 11.50

---

175 Iunilius] Papa Damasus **Ch** ‖ 179 inferius est] superius fuit **Ch**

---

[20] Peter Lombard, *Magna glosatura*, prol., PL 191:55A.

[21] Junillus, *Inst.*, 1.4, ed. Kihn, p. 473.

[22] See below, Prol.3.291–295.

[23] Greg., *Hom. in Hiez.*, 1.1.2, in *Sancti Gregorii Magni Homiliae in Hiezechihelem Prophetam*, ed. Marc Adriaen, CCSL 142 (Turnhout, 1961), p. 6.

[24] A similar point is made by Nicholas of Lyre, *In Pss.*, praef. (*Biblia sacra*, III, sig. o3raA). Much of this discussion draws on and responds to the *quaestio* on prophecy that concludes Lyre's prologue.

[25] Nicholas of Lyre, *In Pss.*, praef. (*Biblia sacra*, III, sig. o3raA), who goes on to conclude that Caiaphas therefore "non fuit propheta proprie loquendo."

prophecie.[26] Contra: tunc Christus non fuisset uerus propheta, cuius oppositum tota Scriptura testatur. Item, Num. 12, Deus ipse uolens preferre propheciam Moysi dicit: *Siquis fuerit propheta in uisione apparebo ei uel per sompnium, at non talis seruus meus Moyses. Ore enim ad os loquor ei et palam non per enigmata et figuras Dominum uidet.*

Sunt autem quattuor gradus prophecie. Primus quando cum uisione alicuius signi datur uisionis intelligencia, sicut Ieremias uidit *ollam succensam a facie aquilonis*, per quod intellexit exercitum regis Babilonis uenturum ad conburendum ciuitatem. Secundus gradus est per auditum alicuius uocis absque figura, Reg. 3, de Samuele, et iste est excellencior quam primus secundum Liram.[27] Contra: uoces magis sunt faciles ad exprimendum ueritates quam alia signa, sed si per alia signa et uisiones reueletur sibi sine uoce ita clare uel clarius sicut per uoces, maioris excellencie uidetur esse. Quod enim prophete fallantur per uoces auditas in Iona et Niniue. Visus eciam nobilior est sensus et magis cognoscitiuus quam auditus, id est metafisice. Tercius gradus quando cum uoce apparet aliqua persona loquens, ut aliquis homo sanctus, Mach. 15, uel angelus, sicut frequenter in Scriptura, aut effigies representans ipsum Deum, sicut Ysa. 6. Et hoc uel in sompnis uel in uigiliis, et tunc est excellencior gradus illo qui fit in sompnis uel in raptu uel extasi, ubi protunc non est usus sensuum exteriorum.[28] Contra: tunc excellencior esset uisio Moysi quam uidit in rubo uisione Pauli quam habuit in raptu. Quartus gradus est, quando sine apparicione alicuius figure uel signi sensibilis capitur ueritas intelligibilis de occultis per diuinam reuelacionem, quo modo reuelacio facta est ipsi Dauid, sicut dicitur in principio glose communis.[29] Et iste ergo gradus est excellencior predictis, sicut ille diceretur melioris ingenii qui caperet scienciam conclusionum geometricalium sine descripcione figurarum quam ille qui sine talibus capere non posset.[30] [fol. 9r] Contra: illa anima magis perficitur cognicione que perficitur quoad intellectum equali cogitacione et quoad

199–201 Num. 12.6–8 ‖ **203–204** Ier. 1.13 ‖ **206** Cf. 1 Reg. 3 ‖ **213** Cf. 2 Mach. 15.12–16 ‖ **214** Cf. Is. 6.1 ‖ **216–217** Contra … in raptu] Cf. Ex. 3.2–4.17, 2 Cor. 12.1

223–224 perficitur] proficitur **Ch** *a.c.*

[26] Nicholas of Lyre, *In Pss.*, praef. (*Biblia sacra*, III, sig. o3rbF).

[27] Nicholas of Lyre, *In Pss.*, praef. (*Biblia sacra*, III, sig. o3raB).

[28] Cf. Nicholas of Lyre, *In Pss.*, praef. (*Biblia sacra*, III, sig. o3raC–o3rbD).

[29] Possibly *Glossa ordinaria in Pss.*, prol. (*Biblia Sacra*, III, sig. o5vaC), but more likely Peter Lombard, *Magna glosatura*, prol., PL 191:58CD.

[30] Nicholas of Lyre, *In Pss.*, praef. (*Biblia sacra*, III, sig. o3rbD).

sensum et ymaginem suis propris cogitacionibus, qua non perficitur alia anima. Hinc enim maius gaudium habebit anima in celo resumpto corpore quam modo habeat, quia tunc corporaliter sensibus corporalibus perficietur. Si ergo Moyses ostenso sibi rubo ardente cognosceret reuelacione Spiritus sancti Virginem parituram ita clare sicut unus alius sine tali ostensione, non propter hoc esset gradus cognicionis eius imperfeccior, sed perfeccior pocius, quia cognosceret rem et figuram eius, alius autem cognosceret rem tantum.

Vnde ualde difficile est homini cognoscere quis prophecie gradus perfeccior sit, et ualde difficilius quis prophetarum habuerit illum gradum post Christum. Et dicit Lira quod Dauid non fuit perfeccior propheta quam apostoli, quia ipsi plenius acceperunt graciam Spiritus sancti.[31] Sanctus Thomas de Alquino, secunda secunde, dicit quod Moyses eciam propheta fuit perfeccior, eo quod uidit diuinam essenciam in presenti uita, secundum quod dicit Augustinus, *De uidendo Deum*.[32] Maiora eciam signa et mirabilia fecit Moyses, et prophetauit communi populo Iudeorum. Sed si racio sua ualeret, sequitur quod Moyses fuit perfeccior propheta quam apostolus qui uiderat diuinam essenciam, quod tamen ipse negat ibidem.[33] Similiter Iohannes Baptista non fecit multa signa, sicut patet Ioh. 10, et tamen ipse concedit quod fuit maior propheta quam Moyses.[34] Item quamuis apostoli fuerunt uiri perfecciores, quia et uiderunt corporaliter Messiam et alia de quibus Dauid prophetauerat, non propter hoc sequitur quod fuerunt perfecciores prophete, nec quod habuerunt perfecciorem gradum prophecie, ymmo raro leguntur prophetasse, nisi Iohannes in Apocalipsi.

Dico ergo quod propheta excellit prophetam uel propter maiorem certitudinem et euidenciam rerum sibi reuelatarum, uel propter maiorem dignitatem rerum ipsarum, uel maiorem multitudinem reuelatorum, uel propter

238–239 Maiora ... Iudeorum] cf. Deut. 34.12 ‖ **242** Ioh. 10.41

244 quia] *add.* **Ch** *sup.l*

[31] Nicholas of Lyre, *In Pss.*, praef. (*Biblia sacra*, III, sig. o3rbF).

[32] Thomas Aquinas, *Summa theologiae* 2a2ae, 174, 4; Aug., *Ep.* 147.13, in *Sancti Aureli Augustini Epistulae*, ed. Alois Goldbacher, CSEL 44 (Vienna – Leipzig, 1904), p. 286. Cossey quotes Aquinas, including the citation of Augustine, by way of Nicholas of Lyre, *In Pss.*, praef. (*Biblia sacra*, III, sig. o3rbF).

[33] Thomas Aquinas, *Summa theologiae* 2a2ae, 174, 6, arg. 3, quoted by way of Nicholas of Lyre, *In Pss.*, praef. (*Biblia sacra*, III, o3vaA).

[34] Thomas Aquinas, *Summa theologiae* 2a2a, 174, 4, ad 3, quoted by way of Nicholas of Lyre, *In Pss.*, praef. (*Biblia sacra*, III, o3vaA).

concursum omnium istorum, et iste est perfectissimus gradus, qui excellit in omnibus istis. Sed quando unus propheta excellit in uno et alius in alio, quis est perfectissimus gradus difficile est dicere, nisi Deus reuelet, et quia omnes prophete in celo sunt unanimes de eorum excellenciis, non disputemus in terris. Tamen Dauid potest dici "prophetarum eximius"[35] qui suo tempore prophetabant secum, uel eciam quia rex erat, uel quia suam propheciam metrice et ympnidice concinebat, uel aliis de causis quas Deus nouit. [fol. 9v]

De intencione uero istorum auctorum michi uidetur quod principaliter intendunt laudare Deum, et ubi quidem ex intencione prophetant, finaliter magis intendunt prophetando laudare quam prophetare, quod et ipsum nomen ostendit, secundum Ieronimum de musicis instrumentis ad Dardanum: "Psalterium quoque *nablum* Hebraice, Grece autem *psalterium*, Latine dicitur *laudatorium*, de quo in 54 psalmo dicitur, *Consurge psalterium et cithara*."[36] Ista autem intencio magis declarabitur in processu.

Vtilitas uero huius operis quanta sit difficile est explicare. Habet enim utilitatem euangelice doctrine et uere ac manifeste de Christo prophecie, contricionis et penitencie, deuote oracionis et diuine laudis. Quam bonum quantus fructus est istarum operacionum.

Titulus autem operis est in Hebreo *sephar talim*, quod interpretatur "uolumen ympnorum." Ympnus autem est laus Dei cum cantico.[37] Est ergo istud ympnarium Sinagoge in Ecclesia iam crebrius frequentatum. Sunt et alii tituli multi. Vocatur enim "Psalterium" a nomine instrumenti translato ad ipsa cantica que in ipso canebantur, uocaturque apud Grecos "Monologium ipsius Dauid," id est soliloquium, "Liber Soliloquiorum." Sed quare pocius "monologium" quam "prosologium," id est alloquium, cum ut plurimi ipsum Deum alloquatur, non apparet.[38] "Incipit liber soliloquiorum prophete de Christo."[39] *Prophete* antonomastice, id est Dauid, ut cum dicitur "Apostolus" intelligitur Paulus.

Sed quid est prophecia? Dicit Cassiodorus quod est inspiracio uel reuelacio diuina rerum euentus immobili ueritate denuncians. Vnde prophecia "uisio,"

263 Ps. 56.9

262 quoque] quod **Ch** ‖ 277 antonomastice] antonomatice **Ch**

[35] Peter Lombard, *Magna glosatura*, PL 191:55A.
[36] Ps.-Jerome, *Ep.* 23.8, PL 30:215A, following the letter's citation of Ps. 56.9 as Ps. 54.
[37] Peter Lombard, *Magna glosatura*, PL 191:58B.
[38] Cf. the use of "alloqui" in the passage discussed above, p. 303.
[39] Cf. Peter Lombard, *Magna glosatura*, PL 191:58A.

propheta "uidens" interpretatur.[40] Sed tunc si inspirare uel reuelare proprie esset prophetare, non homini competeret, sed soli Deo inspiranti. Nec ipsa uisio proprie prophecia est, quamuis qui modo "prophete" olim dicerentur "uidentes," alioquin mutus et qui nec uerbis nec signis loqui potest, si uideret prophetaret, quod non conceditur. Et dicit Brito quod dicitur a *profor, -aris*, quod est "procul ab intencione exfari," scilicet aliud uerbo proferre aliud in corde habere.[41] Sed hec est mala nominis exposicio, cum secundum eam mentitores proprie prophete dicerentur, quia hoc modo procul ab intencione fantur. Plana eciam denunciacio alicuius futuri, qualis est illa Danielis, *Post ebdomades sexaginta duas occidetur Christus*, non esset prophecia, quia quod mente intellexit non procul a mente, sed planis uerbis expressit. Melius est ergo ut dicamus secundum Ysidorem, *Ethimologiarum*, libro 7, prophetas quasi "prefatores."[42] Videtur itaque prophecia esse denunciacio alicuius ueritatis a Deo ipsi prophete reuelate et non per humanam inuestigacionem cognite. Hinc enim prefatores eclipsium non prophetant, quamuis futura predicant.

Item oportet quod sit reuelacio [fol. 10r] facta sibi. Si enim reuelacionem Danieli factam ego denunciauero, numquid propheta ero? Absit. Vnde ualde dubium esse potest utrum Dauid et alii prophetauerint uel ab aliis prophetis prioribus acceperint que dixerunt. Non enim latuit ipsum Dauid prophecia patriarche Iacob et filiorum eius duodecim, de quibus habetur in illo libello qui dicitur *Testamenta duodecim patriarcharum*, quorum quilibet prophetauit de Christo. Nam Ruben cum preciperet filiis honorare et audire Leui adiecit:

Quoniam ipse noscit legem Domini et diuidet in iudicium et sacrificia pro omni Israel, usque ad consummacionem temporum principis sacerdotis Christi, quem dixit Dominus.[43]

Et Symeon:

Tunc, inquit, requiescet omnis terra a turbacione et omnis qui sub celo est a bello.

289–290 Dan. 9.26

---

290 ebdomades sexaginta duas] quinquaginta ebdomades etc. **Ch** ‖ **298** alii] lii **Ch** *a.c.*

---

[40] Peter Lombard, *Magna glosatura*, PL 191:58BC; cf. Cassiod., *Exp. Pss.*, praef.1, in *Magni Aurelii Cassiodori Exposition psalmorum 1–70*, ed. Marc Adriaen, CCSL 97 (Turnhout, 1958), p. 7.3–4.

[41] *Summa Britonis. Expositiones Vocabulorum Biblie*, s. v. "propheta," ed. Lloyd W. Daly and Bernadine A. Daly, 2 vols. (Padova, 1975), 2:603.

[42] Isid., *Etym.*, 7.8., in *Isidore de Séville, Étymologies, Livre VII: Dieu, les anges, les saints*, ed. Jean-Yves Guillaumin, Auteurs latins du moyen âge (Paris, 2012), pp. 103, 105.

[43] *Testamenta*, 1.6, PG 2:1046A. On this use of the *Testamenta*, see above, pp. 313–15.

Sem glorificabitur, quoniam Dominus Deus magnus Israel apparebit in terra ut homo et saluabit in ipso Adam. Tunc dabuntur omnes spiritus erroris in conculcacionem, et homines regnabunt super perniciosos spiritus. Tunc resurgam in leticia et benedicam Altissimum in mirabilibus ipsius, quoniam Deus corpus assumens et comedens cum hominibus saluabit homines. Et nunc, filioli mei, obedite Leui et in Iuda liberabimini, et non efferamini super duas tribus has, quoniam ex ipsis orietur salutare Dei. Suscitabit enim Dominus ex Leui ut principem sacerdotem et ex Iuda ut regem, Deum et hominem. Iste saluabit omnes gentes et genus Israel. Propter hec omnia mando uobis, ut et uos mandetis filiis uestris, ut custodiant hec in generaciones eorum.[44]

Leui autem sic dicit:

Rex ex Iuda exsurget et faciet sacerdotem nouum secundum tipum gencium in omnes gentes. Aduentus autem ipsius ineffabilis, ut prophete Altissimi ex semine Abraham patris nostri.[45]

Et post:

Innocens sum ab omni impietate uestra et transgressione quam facietis in consummacione seculorum, in Saluatorem mundi impie facientes et errare facientes Israel et suscitantes ei mala magna a Domino, et inique facientes cum Israel, ut non portet Ierusalem a facie malicie uestre, sed scindatur uelum templi, ut non uelet deformitatem uestram. Et dispergemini captiui in gentibus et eritis in opprobrium et malediccionem et conculcacionem.[46]

Et post:

Et pater noster Israel mundus erit ab impietate principum sacerdotum qui inponent manus suas in Saluatorem mundi. Et nunc, filii, cognoui Enoch, quoniam in fine [fol. 10v] impie agetis, in Dominum manus inponentes in omni malicia.[47]

Hoc quod Leui sic accepit ab Enoch, sibi non fuit prophetare, sed alterius referre propheciam. Post:

Quid facient omnes gentes, si uos tenebrescatis in impietate, inducentes malediccionem super genus uestrum, pro quibus lumen mundi datum est uobis

309 omnes] omes **Ch**

---

[44] *Testamenta*, 2.6–7, PG 2:1050C–1051B.

[45] *Testamenta*, 3.8, PG 2:1058D–1059A.

[46] *Testamenta*, 3.10, PG 2:1059CD.

[47] *Testamenta*, 3.14, PG 2:1063B.

ad illuminacionem omnis hominis, hunc uolentes occidere, contraria mandata docentes Dei iustificacionibus?[48]

Post:

Et nisi propter Abraham, Ysaac et Iacob, patres nostros, unus ex semine meo non relinqueretur in terra. Et nunc cognoui in libro Enoch quoniam septuaginta ebdomades errabitis et sacerdocium inquinabitis et sacrificia polluetis et legem exterminabitis et sermones prophetarum contempnetis. In peruersitate persequemini uiros iustos et pios odio habebitis. Veracium sermones abhominabimini et uirum renouantem legem in uirtute Altissimi erroneum appellabitis, et in fine, ut estimabitis, occidetis eum, nescientes ipsius resurreccionem, innocentem sanguinem in malicia super capita uestra recepturi, et eritis in dispersionem, donec rursus ipse uisitabit et miserens recipiet uos in fide et aqua.[49]

Post:

Et suscitabit Dominus sacerdotem nouum qui faciet ueritatem in terra. Et orietur astrum ipsius in celo et ipse resplendebit sicut sol, etc. Celi aperientur et ex templo glorie ueniet super ipsum sanctificacio cum uoce paterna, sicut ab Abraham patre Ysaac. Et gloria Altissimi super ipsum dicetur et spiritus intellectus et sanctificacionis requiescet super ipsum in aqua, etc. Et ipse aperiet portas paradisi et stare faciet minantem gladium aduersus Adam, et Belial ligabitur ab ipso, et dabit potestatem filiis suis ad calcandum super perniciosos spiritus. Tunc exultabit Abraham, Ysaac et Iacob, et ego gaudebo et omnes sancti induentur leticia.[50]

Et in testamento Iude sic:

Et nunc diligite Leui et non efferamini super ipsum, ut non dispereatis. Michi enim dedit Dominus regnum et illi sacerdocium, et subiecit regnum sacerdocio. Michi dedit que in terra, illi que sunt in celis, et ut supereminet celum terre, ita supereminet Dei sacerdocium regno quod est in terra.[51]

Et post prophetat de Christo:

Ipse inquit custodiet potestatem regni mei usque in seculum. [fol. 11r] Iuramento enim iurauit michi Dominus non deficere regnum meum et seminis mei omnibus diebus usque in seculum.[52]

355 ab] ad **Ch** ‖ **356** patre] ipse **Ch** ‖ **363** efferamini] effraini **Ch**

[48] *Testamenta*, 3.14, PG 2:1063C.
[49] *Testamenta*, 3.15–16, PG 2:1066AB.
[50] *Testamenta*, 3.18, with omissions, PG 2:1067AB.
[51] *Testamenta*, 4.21, PG 2:1082AB.
[52] *Testamenta*, 4.22, PG 2:1082C.

– et alia similia que dixit Leui. Ysachar uero non multum prophetauit. Zabulon uero plane prophetat sicut Leui et cetera:

> Videbitis, inquit, Deum in forma hominis, Ierusalem nomen ei, et rursus in malicia sermonum uestrorum ad iracundiam prouocabitis eum, et abiecti eritis usque ad tempus consummacionis.[53]

Et Dan:

> Et ducet uos Dominus in sanctificacionem clamans uobis pacem. Et orietur uobis ex tribu Iuda et Leui salutare Domini, et ipse faciet aduersus Belial prelium et uincet, etc. Et Dominus erit in medio Israel, cum hominibus conuersatus in humilitate et paupertate. Et est mediator Dei et hominum, et nouit quod in qua die credet Israel, consummabitur regnum inimici, etc.[54]

Neptalim et Gad similia de Christo dixerunt filiis. Et Aser dixit filiis:

> Eritis in dispersione dispersi usquequo Altissimus uisitabit terram, ipse ueniens ut homo cum hominibus manducans et bibens, et in silencio conterens caput draconis. Per aquam hic saluabit Israel et omnes gentes, Deus in uirum absconditus. Dicite igitur hec filiis uestris, ut non discredant ei. Legi enim in tabulis celorum quoniam discredentes discredetis ei et impie agetis in eum, non attendentes legem Dei, sed mandata hominum, etc.[55]

Et Ioseph:

> Audite, filii mei, que uidi sompnia, uidelicet quoniam ex Iuda nata est uirgo habens stolam bissinam, et ex ipsa prodiit agnus immaculatus et a sinistris eius ut leo. Et omnes bestie impetum fecerunt aduersus eum, et uicit eas agnus et perdidit in conculcacionem. Et gaudebant in eo angeli et homines et omnis terra. Hec autem fient tempore suo ultimis diebus. Vos igitur, filii mei, honorate Iudam et Leui, quoniam ex ipsis orietur uobis agnus Dei, gentes omnes et Israel gracia saluans. Regnum enim Israel eternum: uero meum in uobis consummatur ut pomorum custodia, quoniam post messem non apparebit.[56]

Et Beniamin filiis suis:

> Fornicabimini, inquit, fornicacione Sodomorum et renouabitis in mulieribus motus inordinatos, et regnum Dei non erit in uobis, etc., [fol. 11v] usquequo

373 Ierusalem] nullum **Ch** ‖ **382** Gad] Dan **Ch** ‖ **394** mei] mi **Ch** ‖ **400** fornicabimini] fornicabitur **Ch**

---

[53] *Testamenta*, 6.9, PG 2: 1098B.

[54] *Testamenta*, 7.5–6, with omissions, PG 2:1102D–1103B.

[55] *Testamenta*, 10.7, PG 2:1123C–1126A.

[56] *Testamenta*, 11.19, PG 2:1139AB.

Altissimus mittat salutare suum in uisitacione unigeniti, et ingredietur templum et illic Dominus iniuriam pacietur et contempnetur, in ligno exaltabitur. Et erit uelum templi scissum et descendet spiritus Dei super gentes ut ignis effusus. Et ascendens ex inferno erit ascendens a terra in celum, etc.[57] Et tunc omnes resurgent, hii quidem in gloriam, hii uero in ignominiam, et iudicabit Dominus inprimis Israel de eis que in ipsum iniusticia fecerunt, quoniam aduenientem Deum in carne liberatorem non crediderunt, et tunc iudicabit omnes gentes.

Post:

Et congregabitur omnis Israel, et non amplius uocabor lupus rapax propter rapinas uestras, sed operator Domini, tribuens cibum operantibus bonum. Et suscitabitur ex semine meo in extremis temporibus dilectus Domini, audiens in terra uocem eius, cognicione noua illuminans omnes gentes, lux cognicionis ascendens Israeli in salute, et rapiens ut lupus ab ipsis et dans Sinagoge gencium, et usque ad consummacionem seculorum erit in sinagogis gencium et in principibus eorum sicut musicum melos in ore omnium, et in libris sanctis et in scripturis erit opus et sermo eius. Et de ipso instruxit me Iacob pater meus.[58]

– et dormiuit sompnum secularem.[59] Cum igitur multa que ab aliis prophetis dicta sunt hic predicta fuerunt, non oportet eos dicere in omnibus prophetasse. Magis tamen in speciali prophetauit Dauid de Christo et ad eum pertinentibus, propheciaque sua in Scriptura sancta posita est, quomodo non fuit de istis duodecim patriarchis. Ideo antomastice propheta dici potest.

Sed mirum est quare iste psalmus primus titulum non habet. Et dicit Triuet quod, cum secundum Ieronimum titulus libri sit "uolumen ympnorum," superuacuum esset addere "ympnus Dauid." Titulum autem istum non uidit in Hebreo, sed supletur ubi dicit psalmus 39, *In uolumine libri scriptum est de me*,

428 Ps. 39.8 (Hebraicum)

---

407 eis] *om.* **Ch** ‖ **413** suscitabitur] scrutabitur **Ch** ‖ **414** cognicione] cognoui **Ch**; noua] nouam **Ch** ‖ **416** erit] et **Ch** ‖ **418** erit] et **Ch** ‖ **426** cum] *om.* **Ch** ‖ **428** 39] 79 **Ch**

---

[57] *Testamenta*, 12.9, PG 2:1146C–1147A, followed by a paraphrase of *Testamenta*, 12.10, PG 2:1147AC.

[58] *Testamenta*, 12.10–11, PG 2:1150AB.

[59] Not part of the foregoing quotation, but apparently adapting some of the phrasing commonly used to end chapters in the *Testamenta*, e.g., 11.20, PG 2:1139B: "dormivit somnum perpetuum."

quod autem de primo psalmo intelligat patet per aliam translacionem: *In capite libri scriptum est de me ut facerem placitum tibi*, etc., sed noluit hic titulum premittere, ne uideretur a laude propria incepisse.[60] Sed quomodo superuacuum foret exprimere cuius ympnus sit iste uel psalmus, sicut in aliis fit? Non enim est superuacuum genus sic specificare, "Incipit uolumen ympnorum," et postea diceretur "ympnus Dauid." Que nugacio! Item quomodo nosti [fol. 12r] quod ille psalmus erat caput libri credendum, uel ipse Dauid dictum titulum gratis omiserit, cum dicatur quod Esdras sic psalmos disposuisse et in unum redegisse uolumen et titulos prescripsisse?[61] Et iterum, si de se ipso loquitur quasi in tercia persona,[62] manifestum est eum a laude propria incepisse, et uideri posset quod mendaciter se diceret in consilio impiorum et in uia peccatorum non abisse. Illud autem quod dicitur infra, *In capite libri scriptum est de me ut facerem placitum tibi*, melius est referri ad librum legis Domini, scilicet ad Pentateuchum totum uel ad librum Exodi, qui specialiter liber legis dici potest. Et si ad caput tocius Pentateuci referatur, id est ad librum Genesis, manifeste patet ex peccato primorum parentum per inobedienciam et eorum iusta punicione scriptum super se, et de se Psalmista cognouit ut obediret diuine uoluntati et faceret placitum sibi. Si uero ad librum Exodi referatur, qui libri caput dici potest, quia antequam legem daret in monte Syna, dum erant filii Israel in Marath transito mari Rubro, Ex. 15, constituit Dominus populo precepta atque iudicia dicens: *Si audieris uocem Domini Dei tui et quod rectum est coram eo feceris et mandatis eius obedieris, cunctum languorem quem posui in Egipto non inducam super te*, ubi obediencia iniungitur quasi in capite libri. Verumptamen multo melius est sicut in Hebreo habetur, *In uolumine libri*, quam *In capite libri*, pro eo quod ubique per totam Scripturam docetur obediencia ut faciamus que Deo placent. Si autem primus psalmus fuerit ipsius Dauid et ad illum referatur quod dicit, *In capite libri*, oportet quod ipse Dauid librum Psalmorum instituisset et illum tanquam principium et caput libri posuisset, et tunc ipse se ipsum auctorem allegare uideretur, quod non conuenit.

429–430 Ps. 39.8–9 (Gallican) ‖ **440** in uia peccatorum non abisse] Cf. Ps. 1.1 ‖ **440–441** Ps. 39.8–9 (Gallican) ‖ **449–451** Ex. 15.26

---

[60] Trevet, *In Pss.*, in Ps. 1 (Oxford, Bodleian Library, MS Bodley 738, fols. 4vb–5ra), quoting the reference to the "uolumen hymnorum" from Jerome's Hebraicum prologue; see De Bruyne, *Préfaces*, p. 47; *Vulgate*, ed. Fischer et al., 1:768.

[61] Cf. De Bruyen, *Préfaces*, p. 47; *Vulgate*, ed. Fischer et al., 1:768, a passage glossed by Trevet in his commentary on this prologue (Oxford, Bodleian Library, MS Bodley 738, fols. 2vb–3ra).

[62] As claimed by Trevet, *In Pss.*, in Ps. 1 (Oxford, Bodleian Library, MS Bodley 738, fol. 5ra).

Quis autem sit huius libri conueniens discipulus? Certe quanto senior et sapiencior et Deo deuocior tanto conueniencior.

Materia enim libri deissima est et [fol. 12v] tocius theologie finem continere uidetur, qui in diuinis laudibus et contemplacione diuinorum existit. Hec est felicitas que est ultimum bonum actuum humanorum.

Ordo autem legendi esse debet, pro nunc, quo psalmi ipsi sunt scripti. Modus autem legendi erit ad mentem auctorum quantum possibile est declarandum, que sensus litteralis dicitur. Intelligi potest scilicet uel apparens et non existens, secundum quod dicit Apostolus, *Littera occidit*, et hic sensus recitandus est quandoque et reprobandus. Alius autem litteralis est sensus eorum qui scripserunt, et iste sensus meo iudicio quadrifarie est in Scriptura. Quandoque enim sensus litteralis historicus est, sicut cum docetur quid gestum sit uel non gestum. Quandoque est ethimologicus,[63] id est originis et cause interpretantis, sicut est illud quod Moyses precepit dari libellum repudii et recedendi licenciam. Hoc ethimologice intelligendum est, sicut Christus ostendit in Euangelio: *Hoc*, inquit, *Moyses fecit propter duriciam cordis uestri*, quasi diceret: Modo non est illud obseruandum, et ita de multis, que tempore Christi aduentus cessauerunt, consideranda est causa quare pro tempore concessa erant. Quidam autem sensus litteralis uerus est anologicus, id est irrationalis nec contradictorius sermo, quo ostenditur non sibi aduersari duo testamenta, Vetus et Nouum, sicut et ostendit Apostolus: *Lex igitur aduersus promissa Dei? Absit*, etc. Aliquis autem sensus litteralis est allegoricus, id est tropologicus et figuratiuus, sicut in Euangelio: *Sicut fuit Ionas in uentre ceti, sic erit filius hominis*, etc., et Apostolus, Cor.: *Nolo uos ignorare fratres quoniam patres nostri omnes sub nube fuerunt*, etc. Hec autem in figura contingebant illis. Et alibi: *Quoniam Abraham duos filios habuit*, etc. *Itaque non sumus ancille filii*, etc. Sensus litteralis uerborum istorum Christi et Apostoli allegoricus est et figuratiuus. Istos quattuor sensus quere in Augustino, *De utilitate credendi*, in

467 2 Cor. 3.6 ‖ **472–473** sicut est ... licenciam] Cf. Deut. 24.1–3 ‖ **474** Cf. Matt. 19.8 ‖ **479–480** Gal. 3.21 ‖ **481–482** Matt. 12.40 ‖ **482–483** 1 Cor. 10.1 ‖ **484** Gal. 4.22; Gal. 4.31

---

469 eorum] existens **Ch** ‖ **481** tropologicus] tropicus **Ch** ‖ **486** Augustino] Augustinus **Ch**

---

[63] In Augustine's text, cited below, this sense is called "aetiology," though "etymology" seems to have been substituted frequently in scholastic discussions; see *Medieval Literary Theory and Criticism*, ed. Minnis and Scott, pp. 241–43 (Thomas Aquinas) and 256–66 (Henry of Ghent), at p. 257.

principio.⁶⁴ Omnes isti sensus ad uaria Scripture loca referuntur. Conuenit tamen inuenire auctoritatem ad historiam pertinentem. Cuius quidem sensus ibi litteralis historicus est tantum, qui tamen exponi potest ethimologice, analogice, uel allegorice, et si illa [fol. 13r] exposicio alibi in Scripura ponatur, sensus litteralis illius loci Scripture est ethimologicus uel allegoricus etc., cuius tamen auctoritatis in priori loco Scripture, sensus litteralis erat tantum historicus. Non ergo idem est dictu sensus litteralis et historicus.

Sensus autem allegoricus continet sub se tam illum quem uocant anagogicum siue tropologicum, nisi quia tropologia et allegoria idem sonant, si tropologia dicatur a *tropus, -pi*, sed si a *tropos*, "conuersio," tunc continetur sub sensu allegorico. Quod enim anagogicus sensus continetur sub allegorico, ostendit Apostolus, Gal. 4, ubi dicit: *Qui de ancilla secundum carnem natus est: qui autem de libera*, etc., *que sunt per allegoriam dicta*. Et declarat hoc dicens de libera: *Illa autem que sursum est Ierusalem libera est*, etc. Vult igitur Apostolus quod Ierusalem signat allegorice Ecclesiam triumphantem, que sursum est, mater nostra. Ille autem est sensus anagogicus secundum modernos, quod eciam tropologicus sensus, id est conuersiuus ad nos instruens in moribus. Tropologicus sub allegoria contineatur patet per Apostolum qui dictam allegoriam conuertit ad nos ad nostram instruccionem. Ita ergo patet quod nullo sensu exponenda est Scriptura, nisi aliquo illorum quos Augustinus expressit. Illa enim pars Scripture que nos mores instruit quandoque figuratiue loquitur et ad allegoriam pertinet, quandoque uero simpliciter docet quid faciendum uel non, quid gerendum uel non, et hoc ad historiam pertinet. Historia enim non solum gestorum, sed gerendorum est: historia, id est gesticulacio.⁶⁵ Patet eciam quod non omne uerbum Scripture potest et debet sic quadriformiter exponi: *Diligite iusticiam, In principio erat uerbum*. Nam etsi quattuor sensus

498–499 Gal. 4.23–24 ‖ **500** Gal. 4.26 ‖ **512** Sap. 1.1, Ioh. 1.1

500 etc.] que sunt per allegoriam dicta *add.* Ch

⁶⁴ Aug., *De util. cred.* 3.5, in *Sancti Aureli Augustini De utilitate credendi*, ed. Joseph Zycha, CSEL 25/1 (Prague – Vienna – Leipzig, 1891), pp. 7–8. This text is quoted commonly in scholastic discussions of the senses of Scripture: see, e.g., *Medieval Literary Theory and Criticism*, ed. Minnis and Scott, pp. 220–21 and 222 (Alexander of Hales), 241–42 (Thomas Aquinas), and 257 and 261–62 (Henry of Ghent).

⁶⁵ Cf. Thomas Docking, OFM, *In Epp. Pauli*, on Gal. 6, quoted in Little, *Franciscan Papers*, p. 108.

ueros quis inuenerit, ad hos quattuor sensus uix concordia traheretur, ita sic in proposito sensui litterali est insistendum.

515 Ad moralem autem philosophiam, sicut et tota theologia, meo iudicio spectat, sicut alibi est probatum.[66] Nec enim ad aliam poterit pertinere, nec aliquam sanam doctrinam ad nullam partem philosophie pertinentem possibile est reperire.

520 Diuiditur autem liber [fol. 13v] iste in centum quinquaginta partes secundum numerum tot psalmorum, nec est alia diuisio immediacior ista secundum rem,[67] nisi quis uoluerit diuidere secundum quinque distincciones que fiunt per *fiat fiat* in fine psalmi. Secundum quas glosa beati Ieronimi inponit quod librum Psalmorum in quinque libros distinxerit,[68] cuius 525 oppositum uult ipsemet Ieronimus in epistola ad Sophronium.[69] Dicta eciam distinctio tantum uerbalis est. Non enim est aliquis ordo psalmorum racione subtilis materie, nisi forsitan aliqui eorum, "in prima Sabbati," etc., cantari instituti sunt uel secundum aliquem alium ordinem festiuitatum succe- dencium in Sinagoga temporis illius, sicut modo est in ympnario ecclesie.

530 Accedamus ergo singillatim ad psalmorum exposicionem singulorum.

English Translation

Blessed is the man. In his rule, St. Francis enjoined his brothers to perform the divine Office according to the use of the Roman curia, but he made an exception for the Psalter, thus clearly preferring its common version. I will therefore undertake the interpretation of this version, asserting nothing of my own devising, except insofar as it is consistent with the holy Fathers and catholic truth. Ten things about the psalms need to be investigated: the name of the translator, the name of the author, the au-

---

[66] Perhaps a reference to Cossey's lectures on the *Sentences*, which are lost. Little, *Franciscan Papers*, p. 141, records a reference to these lectures in the *Sentences* commentary of Adam Wodeham, OFM; see too Sharpe, *Handlist*, p. 166.

[67] This claim should indicate that Cossey's earlier discussion, dividing the Psalter into ten groups of fifteen, was focused on the possible spiritual or mystical meaning of the text's structure, and, indeed, he does not there suggest that the ten parts have any internal coherence based on their contents or any other criteria (see above, Prol.1.89–100).

[68] Note in margin: "Ieronimus, epistola 98 ad Marcellam de uerbis Hebreis, dicit quod aput Hebreos Psalterium in quinque uolumina diuisum est per *fiat fiat*" – "In letter 98 [=26] to Marcella concerning Hebrew words, Jerome says that according to the Hebrews the Psalter is to be divided into five volumes by the words *so be it, so be it*." This refers to Hier., *Ep.* 26.4, ed. Hilberg, p. 222, also marginally cited above, in Prol. 2, as "epistola 99." The reference in the text to a *glosa* may indicate that Cossey is working from the *Magna glosatura*, the prologue to which includes a discussion of Jerome on this point (PL 191:57D–58A), and the marginal reference could have been supplied belatedly.

[69] De Bruyne, *Préfaces*, p. 46; *Vulgate*, ed. Fischer et al., 1:768.

thor's intention, the utility of the work, the work's title, the appropriate student, the subject matter, the order and mode of reading, the part of philosophy (if any) to which it pertains, and finally the division of the book into parts, etc.

On the first point, we need to see whether the Septuagint translation is the one which is called the common version, as Trevet says, on this point citing Augustine, *City of God* 18, who (he says) prefers to call the Septuagint translation the common version because "its use was so widespread that many people were wholly unaware that there was any other." Now it is certainly true that at 16.10 Augustine says that the common version is the Septuagint translation, and he expounds it accordingly – but I am astonished by my elder's ignorance or carelessness, and so I will not say anything about the authority of Isidore, *Etymologies* 6, in the chapter on translators (where he quotes Augustine verbatim), and 5, on periodization, where he briefly indicates the times in which the translators lived, or, indeed, the authority of the Master of Histories, a little after the beginning, that everyone says the fifth version should be called the common one because they do not know who its author was. Instead, I base my argument on Augustine himself, who agrees with these men and does not contradict them, 18.43, and who in chapter 42 says that there were seventy-two translators – six from each of the tribes – who were learned in both languages (i.e., Hebrew and Greek), and they were sent by Eleazar the High Priest of the Jews to Ptolemy, King of Egypt. Their translation was called the Septuagint and was then in common use. Further: "For there were other translators who translated Holy Writ from Hebrew into Greek, including Aquila, Symmachus, and Theodotion, and there is also that translation whose author is unknown and therefore, lacking the translator's name, is called the fourth or fifth translation" – fourth, that is, after Christ and fifth after the Septuagint. "But it is the Septuagint that is, almost exclusively, received by the Church, and the Greek-speaking Christian people use it, many of them being unaware that there is any other." It is clear that he does not call the Septuagint translation the common version, and he does not expressly say which one is called common. But all the other authorities, even Jerome himself, are clear that the fifth version, whose author is unknown, is called the common translation. Further, it should be noted that Origen made the sixth and seventh translations, working from Hebrew to Greek, and he compared it to the other versions. The eighth was made by Jerome, working from Hebrew to Latin, and this translation was in turn translated by Sophronius from Latin into Greek. We do not know the names and numbers of the Latin translators who worked from Greek into our language, as Augustine says in *On Christian Teaching* 2. For, in the first age of the Church, whoever had knowledge of both languages, i.e., Greek and Latin, presumed to translate for themselves, and this led to considerable confusion concerning the text. Nevertheless, blessed Jerome enumerates the Latin interpreters of the Psalter in a letter to blessed Augustine, where he says:

> The Greek text of the Psalms has been interpreted in many different books, first by Origen, then Eusebius, third Theodorus of Heraclea, fourth Asterius of Scythopolis, fifth Apollinaris of Laodicea, sixth Didimus of Alexandria. Additionally, there are treatises on a few psalms by many different writers, but at present I am just speaking of the complete corpus of the Psalms. Among the Latins, Hilary, bishop of Poitiers, and Eusebius, bishop of Vercelli, translated Origen and Eusebius, and the first of them was followed in some respects by our Ambrose.

All of these things cast more doubt on the identity of the translation interpreted in the *Gloss*, used by almost all churches in the Latin world, and which St. Francis wished his brothers to use instead of the Roman Psalter.

Trevet says that, inasmuch as it was pure, Jerome rendered the Septuagint translation from Greek into Latin, but then, since this translation was corrupted, at the behest of Paula and Eustochium he again translated the Psalter from Greek into Latin, and he imitated Origen's efforts, i.e., with regard to asterisks and obeli. And it was to the text of these two translations that all the efforts of the ancients were devoted, among whom the straightforward translation of the Septuagint, which was earlier, was expounded by Cassiodorus Senator and the mixed version, which was second, by blessed Augustine. But I am astounded that he calls a "translation" what Jerome himself terms not a "translation" but a "correction." For in the preface to the Psalter, from which Trevet takes these points, Jerome says:

> A little while ago, when I was in Rome, I emended and, in accordance with the seventy translators, in large part corrected that Psalter, and since you see, O Paula and Eustochium, that it has again been corrupted by scribal mistakes, and that the ancient error is being favoured over the new emendation, you urge, etc.

And further on:

> Let everyone take heed, therefore, of either a horizontal line or a radiating sign, i.e., an obelus or an asterisk, and wherever the first of these marks is seen, from there until we have put a double point know that the Septuagint contains extra material. But where one sees the likeness of a star, know that there something has been added from the Hebrew volumes.

It is therefore clear that, according to Jerome, these were only two emendations, not translations. And Trevet (and Lyre too) says that the first translation of the Psalter is in use in the church of Rome up to the present, and that Pope Damasus established the singing of the second translation in the churches of Gaul. But this second version, insofar as it contained those symbols (the first, obeli, eliminating extra material and the second, asterisks, adding more material), could not suitably be sung (nor should it be), since then at those points it would be necessary to sing the extra material, and in any case Jerome only undertook that emendation so that the difference between the two translations – the Septuagint, that is, and Origen's – would be known.

Likewise, it is the earlier translation that is in use in the church of France and elsewhere: for this purely follows the Septuagint translation, which is quite different from what is found in the Roman Psalter. For example, in his letter to Cyprian the priest, Jerome discusses Ps. 89 according to what is found in the Hebrew or in another ancient translation: *Fill us in the morning with your mercy, we will all praise and rejoice together in all our days*, and this is what is found in the Roman Psalter, except it adds an *and*. The Septuagint, however, as Jerome says, has the following: *We are filled in the morning with your mercy, and we have rejoiced and delighted in all our days.* (At almost all points, as here, the Septuagint has this habit, that it reports as having already happened what is given in the future tense according to the Hebrews.) Further on: *Make us rejoice for the days in which you afflicted us, the years in which we saw evil* – this is also in the Roman Psalter, and Jerome says the Septuagint is as follows: *We have rejoiced for the days in which you humbled us*, etc., just as is contained in our Psalter. *And may the beauty of the Lord our God be upon us, and make the work of our hands steadfast upon us, and confirm the work of our hands* – all of this is in the Roman Psalter, while the Septuagint reads thus: *And may the splendour of the Lord our God be upon us, and direct the work of our hands upon us, and direct the work of our hands.* Thus Jerome. It is therefore apparent that our Psalter is the one that follows the Septuagint translation, and which Jerome himself corrected in Rome. (I do not know whether or not we have it just as he corrected it.) The Roman Psalter appears to be the one that he translated directly from Hebrew into Latin, but since in some (though very few) respects it seems to differ from the Hebrew, as will be clear in the course of my glosses, it could also be thought to have been the second translation which was made from Greek into Latin, not following the Septuagint. For having omitted the material eliminated by the virgules and adding in the new material from the Hebrew, the resulting Psalter could have the appearance of having been translated from Hebrew into Latin. But regardless of whether the Roman Psalter is the one translated directly from Hebrew or (as I just said) it was the second one that Jerome prepared, a correction and in part a translation, let us keep our attention fixed on our Psalter, which, it is evident, was translated from the Greek Septuagint version into the Latin language and then emended by Jerome.

Nicholas of Lyre says that blessed Jerome translated the Psalter three times, first following the Septuagint version, producing what is called the Roman Psalter, since it is used in the Church of blessed Peter. Second, he made another translation that is not very different from the first but is closer to the Hebrew, and this is called the Gallican Psalter, since Pope Damasus ordered it to be sung in France, and the Friars Minor use this translation. Third, at the request of Sophronius, etc. Lyre thus agrees with Trevet, and he is contradicted by the same arguments. And you should know that this Gallican Psalter, which purely follows the Septuagint translation, is used by very nearly the whole Church, with the exception of the Roman curia and certain abbeys. Trevet and Lyre derive their error from the *Chronicle* of Martin, who, concerning Pope Damasus, says that the Roman Psalter follows the Septuagint translation, which Jerome emended first.

But what is the name of the author or authors of the Psalms? Following Jerome, we hold to the idea that the authors are those who are named in the superscriptions, but some psalms lack superscriptions or have ones that do not include anyone's name, and it is therefore uncertain who their authors are. And in a certain preface, whose author is unknown to me, it is said that David composed nine psalms, thirty two lack a superscription, seventy two are said to be by David, twenty two by Asaph, two by Jedethun, nine by the sons of Korah, one by Moses, two by Solomon, and two by Haggai and Zachariah, and therefore all the Psalms of David total one hundred fifty. And to this I say: this is a faulty calculation. For nine and thirty two and seventy two and twenty two and two, nine, one, two and two make one hundred fifty one. Likewise, why does he think that "David made nine psalms," when many more are ascribed to him in the superscriptions thus: *psalm* or *song* or *canticle of David*, as will become clear, and as should already be clear to anyone who considers it? Likewise, since in his letter to Sophronius Jerome identifies Heman as one of the authors, give him a psalm and then there would be more than one hundred fifty one, or perhaps you could take back one of the ones you attributed to another author and give it to him instead. Indeed, Ps. 87, *Lord, God of my salvation*, is entitled, *Of Heman the Ezrahite*, and Ps. 88 is entitled, *The understanding of Ethan the Ezrahite*, and in Hebrew, *Wise Ethan the Ezrahite*. Why, therefore, is no psalm ascribed to this Ethan? Here is the preface in question:

> In the midst of his reign, David, son of Jesse, chose four people who made psalms, i.e., Asaph, Heman, Ethan, and Jedethun. They therefore recited eighty eight psalms, and two hundred played on psalteries while Abiud struck the harp. When he had recovered the ark from the Azotians after twenty years and led it back into Jerusalem, staying in the home of Aminidab, David set it on a new yoked animal and led it into Jerusalem with seventy men chosen from every lineage of the children of Israel. From the tribe of Levi two hundred eighty-eight men were chosen, four of whom were appointed as song-leaders, Asaph, Heman, Ethan, and Jedithun, each one of them allotted seventy-two men proclaiming praise to the Lord in songs. And one of these four played the cymbal, another the cinara, another the harp, and another the triumphant horned trumpet, and in their midst stood David, holding his psaltery. The ark went before the seven choirs and sacrificial calf, and all the people followed behind the ark. Altogether, then, there are one hundred fifty psalms of David, out of which David himself composed nine, thirty two are lacking superscriptions, seventy two are said to be by David, twenty two by Asaph, two by Jedithun, nine by the sons of Korah, one by Moses, two by Solomon, and two by Haggai and Zachariah. And so there were one hundred and fifty psalms of David in total, seventy-two diapsalms, fifteen gradual canticles. The first psalm is not assigned to anyone because it is everyone's. No one but the firstborn could be understood in the first psalm, and so, appropriately, an inscription

was unnecessary, and since this psalm makes mention of Christ, describing a person "against your Christ," it did not have any reason whatsoever [i.e., for adding a superscription]. We read the unchanged order of history in the psalms' superscriptions, but the psalms themselves are read not according to history but according to prophecy. So the order of the superscriptions cannot disrupt the order of the psalms. All the psalms which, by their inscriptions, are attributed to David himself pertain to the mystery of Christ, for David was called "anointed."

And since David prophesies very clearly about Christ, it can be doubted whether or not he was better, or indeed the best of the prophets, as he is called in Cassiodorus's gloss. Junillus sets out what prophecy is, saying, "Prophecy is the manifestation, by means of divine inspiration, of hidden things, past, present, and future," and see his work on the seven kinds of prophecy. These things are "hidden" from those to whom they are revealed with respect to their powers of human investigation, as is said below. For the thought of Simon Magus was of course well known to Simon himself by his natural experience, but it was made known to Peter by revelation, Acts 8, *I see you are in the gall of bitterness.* Similarly, Naaman and others who were standing around him knew by means of their senses that Elisha's servant Gehazi accepted his gifts, 4 Reg. 5, but Elisha knew it by inspiration. Prophecy about things past is exemplified by Moses, who prophesied about the creation of the world, as Gregory says in his work on Ezekiel.

Moreover, know that it is not truly prophecy if the person does not understand what he says in his prophecy. So it is that those who we now call prophets were once called "seers," since they saw and understood what they prophesied. Still, sometimes in Scripture someone is said to prophesy even though they do not understand, provided that they offer their words at the instigation of the Holy Spirit, though they have a different understanding of their words than the Holy Spirit has, e.g., Caiaphas, John 11, *It is expedient for you*, etc. For he thought it would be expedient for Christ to die even though he was innocent, so that he would not give the Romans a reason to come, etc. All things being equal, that degree of prophecy is more excellent when the prophet's understanding is clearer, as long as it does not exceed the limits of prophecy, as Lyre says, for prophecy should always be enigmatic. That is why the vision of divine being excludes the act of prophecy. On the other hand, then Christ was not a true prophet, the opposite of which is attested by all of Scripture. Likewise, in Num. 12, wishing to promote the prophecy of Moses, God himself says: *If anyone is a prophet, I will appear to him in a vision or in a dream, but it is not so with my servant Moses. For I speak to him face to face, and he sees the Lord plainly, not by means of enigmas and figures.*

There are four degrees of prophecy. The first is when, along with the vision of some sign, the prophet is given understanding of his vision, just as Jeremiah saw the boiling cauldron from the face of the north, by which he understood that the army of the King of Babylon would come to burn down the city. The second degree is when words are heard without a figure, e.g., in the case of Samuel, 1 Reg. 3, and Lyre maintains that this is more excellent than the first degree. On the other hand, it is much easier to express truths with words than with other signs, and if something is revealed to a person without words but by means of other signs and visions as clearly or more clearly than it would be by means of words, then it would seem to be of greater excellence. Prophets are deceived by words, as you hear in the case of Jonah and Nineveh, and, metaphysically, sight is a more noble sense than hearing, and more important to the cognitive faculties. The third degree is when, in addition to the prophet hearing words, a person appears and speaks to him, whether a holy man (e.g., 2 Mach. 15) or an angel (as frequently in Scripture) or an effigy representing God himself (e.g., Is. 6). This can take place when someone is asleep or awake, and the latter case is more excellent than if it happens to someone in their sleep or in a rapture or ecstasy, during which time they do not have the use of their exterior senses. On the other hand, then the vision Moses saw in the bush would have been more excellent than what Paul saw in his rapture. The fourth degree is when, without the apparition of any figure or perceivable sign, the intelligible truth of hidden things is grasped by divine revelation, and this is the kind of revelation made to David, as is said at the start of the common *Gloss*. Therefore, this degree is more excellent than the others, just as someone who can understand a geometry problem without drawing the figures could be said to be of greater intelligence than someone who cannot understand without them. On the other hand, that soul is more perfect in its cognition which is perfect with respect to its understanding, being equal to another soul's cogitation, and with respect to its sense and its idea, with its own particular cogitations, with which another soul is not perfected. And thus, a soul will have more joy in heaven when it is reunited with its body than it has now, for then it will be perfected bodily with its bodily senses. If, therefore, when he saw the burning bush, Moses by means of the Holy Spirit's revelation understood as clearly as someone else might have understood without the sight of the bush that the Virgin would give birth, it does not follow that the degree of Moses's cognition was less perfect, but rather, indeed, it was more perfect, since he understood both the thing and its figure, and this other person only understood the thing itself.

Consequently, it is quite difficult for a person to know which degree of prophecy is more perfect, and, after the Incarnation of Christ, it is much more difficult to know which of the prophets attained to which degree. Lyre says that David was not a more perfect prophet than the apostles, since they received the grace of the Holy Spirit more fully. St. Thomas Aquinas says in *Summa Theologiae* that Moses was more perfect, since he saw the divine being in the present life, according to what Augustine says in *On Seeing God*. Indeed, he performed greater signs and miracles, and he prophesied to the whole population of the Jews, but following this reasoning it would seem that Moses was a more perfect prophet than the Apostle, who saw the divine being – and St. Thomas himself denies that this is so. Likewise, John the Baptist did not perform many signs, as is clear in John 10, and yet St. Thomas concedes that he was a better prophet than Moses. Likewise, though the apostles were more perfect men, since they saw the Messiah in the flesh, as well as other things about which David had prophesied, it does not therefore follow that they were more perfect prophets, nor that they enjoyed a more perfect degree of prophecy – no, indeed, with the exception of John in the Apocalypse, they are only rarely said to have prophesied.

Therefore, I maintain that one prophet excels another either because of the greater certainty and evidence of what is revealed to him, or because of the greater dignity of the matters so revealed, or because of the greater number of his revelations, or because of some concurrence of all of these things – and this last, which excels in all these ways, is the most perfect degree. But when one prophet excels in one respect and another in another, it is difficult to say which degree is the most perfect – unless God reveals it! – and since all the prophets in heaven are in accord about their excellence, let us not dispute about it on earth. Still, David can be called "the best of the prophets" who prophesied in his time with him, or indeed because he was a king, or because he sung his prophecy metrically and in the form of hymns, or for some other reasons which God alone knows.

As regards the intention of these authors, it seems to me that they principally intend to praise God, and even when they intentionally prophesy, it is, finally, more correct to say that they intend to praise in their prophesying than simply that they intend to prophesy. The name of their text itself demonstrates this point, following what Jerome says about musical instruments in his letter to Dardanus: "The Psalter, called *nablum* in Hebrew and *psalter* in Greek, in Latin means 'praise-maker,' as expressed in Ps. 56, *Arise, psaltery and harp*." This intention will be set out at greater length in the commentary that follows.

It is difficult to explain how great the utility of this work is. It has the utility of Gospel teaching and of true and open prophecy about Christ, of contrition and penitence, of devout prayer and divine praise. How good and all-encompassing is the fruit of these actions!

In Hebrew, the title of this work is *sefer tehillim*, which is translated "book of hymns." A hymn is the praise of God with a song, and therefore this is the hymnal of the Synagogue, which is now used with great frequency in the Church. It has many other titles. It is called "Psalter," with the name of the musical instrument transferred to the songs which are sung to its accompaniment, and among the Greeks it is also called the "Monologion" (i.e., soliloquy) "of David" or the "Book of Soliloquies." But it is unclear why it should be called "monologion" rather than "proslogion" (i.e., address), when David, like many other people, addresses his words to God. *Here begins the Prophet's book of soliloquies about Christ*. David is called "the Prophet" by antonomasia, just as "the Apostle" is understood to refer to Paul.

But what is prophecy? Cassiodorus says that it is the inspiration or divine revelation of things, declaring what will happen with immovable truth, and, for this reason, prophecy is translated "sight," prophet "seer." But, then, if to inspire or to reveal were properly to prophesy, the term would not be fittingly applied to any person, but only to God the inspirer. Neither is sight properly prophecy, though those who are now called "prophets" were once called "seers," for then someone who is mute or who cannot speak with words or signs, as long as he can see, could prophesy, which I am unwilling to concede. William Brito says that "to prophesy" derives from "to speak out," i.e., to speak at some remove from one's intention, i.e., to proffer one thing with one's words and to have something else in one's heart. But this is a poor interpretation of the word, since it would suggest that liars should properly be called prophets, since they speak at a remove from their intentions. Indeed, then the plain declaration of something in the future – such as Daniel, *After sixty-two weeks, Christ will be slain* – would not be prophecy, since he did not say something far off from what he understood in his intention, but he expressed it with plain words. It is better, then, for us to follow Isidore, *Etymologies* 7, and say that prophets are, as it were, "foretellers." It would seem, then, that prophecy is the declaration of a certain truth revealed to the prophet by God and not known by any human investigation. Those who foretell an eclipse do not prophesy, therefore, though they predict the future.

Likewise, it is necessary for the revelation to be made to the prophet himself. For if I were to declare the revelation made to Daniel, would I then be a prophet? Certainly not! It is therefore very doubtful whether David and the others prophesied or whether they took what they said from earlier prophets. For the prophecy of the patriarch Jacob and his twelve sons was not unknown to David. This material is now contained in the little book called *The Testaments of the Twelve Patriarchs*, in which each of the patriarchs prophesied about Christ. For after Ruben had instructed his sons to honour and listen to Levi, he added:

> For he knows the law of the Lord, and he will allot judgment and offer sacrifices for all of Israel, until the completion of the ages of the chief priest Christ, whom he has called the Lord.

And Simeon says:

> Then will all the earth rest from trouble, and all that is beneath heaven from war. Then will Shem be glorified, for the Lord, the great God of Israel, will appear on the earth as a man, and in himself he will save Adam. Then all the spirits of error will be trampled underfoot, and human beings will rule over the pernicious spirits. Then I will arise in joy and bless the Most High in his wonders, for God will take on a body and eat among

the people, and thus he will save them. And now, my little sons, obey Levi and in Judah you will be free: do not rise up against these two tribes, for from them the salvation of God will arise. For the Lord will raise up a chief priest from Levi and from Judah a king, God and man. He will save all the nations and the people of Israel. Therefore, I entrust you with all of these things, so that you also entrust your sons with them, to keep them in all their generations.

Levi speaks thus:

A king will arise from Judah and establish a new priest after the model of the nations in all the nations. His advent will be ineffable, as that of a prophet of the Most High from the seed of Abraham our father.

And further on:

I am innocent of all your impiety and the transgression which you will carry out in the completion of the ages, acting impiously toward the Saviour of the world and making Israel go astray and raising up great evils from the Lord against it, behaving wickedly with Israel so that it cannot save Jerusalem from the face of your wickedness, but the veil of the temple will be split so that it does not cover your deformity. And you will be scattered as captives among the nations, and you will be disgraced and accursed and tread underfoot.

And further on:

And our father Israel will be clean from the impiety of the chief priests who lay their hands on the Saviour of the world. And now, my sons, I have learned from Enoch that in the end you will act impiously, laying your hands on the Lord in all wickedness.

What Levi took from Enoch was not prophesied by him, but rather it was his report of someone else's prophecy. Further on:

What will all the nations do if you are darkened in impiety, bringing wickedness upon your people, for whose sake the light of the world has been given to you, to enlighten every human being, and you wish to kill this man, teaching commandments contrary to God's justice?

Further on:

But for Abraham, Isaac, and Jacob, your fathers, not one of my descendants would be left on the earth. And now I have learned in the book of Enoch that for seventy weeks you will go astray, staining the priesthood and polluting the sacrifices and dismissing the law and despising the words of the prophets. In your perversity you will persecute just men and hate the pious. You will abhor the words of the truthful and you will label as erroneous the man renewing the law in the strength of the Most High, and, in the end, you will think that you have killed him, not knowing of his resurrection. In wickedness you will take his innocent blood upon your heads, and you will be dispersed until he visits a second time and mercifully receives you in faith and water.

Further on:

And the Lord will raise up a new priest who will enact truth on the earth, and his star will rise in heaven and he himself will shine forth like the sun, etc. The heavens will be opened and from the temple of glory sanctification will come upon him with the voice of the Father, as from Abraham, father of Isaac, and the glory of the Most High will be spoken over him and the spirit of understanding and sanctification will rest upon him on the water, etc. And he himself will open the gates of paradise and make the sword stand threatening against Adam, and Belial will be bound by him, and he will give power to his sons to trample upon the pernicious spirits. Then will Abraham, Isaac, and Jacob rejoice, and I will be joyful, and all the saints will be clothed in joy.

And in the testament of Judah:

And now, love Levi and do not rise up against him, lest you perish. For the Lord has given the royal power to me and the priesthood to him, and he has made the royal power subject to the priesthood. He gave me what is on the earth, and he gave him what is in the heavens, and just as heaven is above the earth, so too is the priesthood of God above royal power on the earth.

And further on, he prophesies concerning Christ:

He will guard the power of my kingdom forever. For the Lord has sworn an oath to me, that my kingdom and that of my descendants will not fail for all days and forever.

– as well as other things, similar to what Levi said. Issachar did not prophesy very much, but Zebulun clearly prophesies like Levi and the rest, saying:

You will see God in the form of a human being, and the name "Jerusalem" will be given to him, and a second time the wickedness of your words will provoke his wrath, and you will be cast down until the end of time.

And Dan:

And the Lord will lead you to sanctification, proclaiming peace to you. And the salvation of the Lord will rise for you from the tribe of Judah and Levi, and he will wage war against Belial and be triumphant, etc. And the Lord will be in the midst of Israel, dwelling with men in humility and poverty. And he is a mediator between God and men, and he knows that on the day on which Israel will believe, the kingdom of the enemy will come to an end, etc.

Naphtali and Gad said similar things about Christ to their sons. And to his sons Asher said:

In the dispersion, you will be dispersed until the Most High visits the earth, coming as a man and eating and drinking with men, and in silence crushing the dragon's head. Through water will this one, God hidden in man, save Israel and all the nations. Tell your sons these things, so that they do not fail to believe in him. For I have read in the tablets of the heavens that, unbelieving, you will not believe him, and you will act impiously toward him, not heeding the law of God but rather the commands of men, etc.

And Joseph:

My sons, hear what I saw in a dream: from Judah a virgin wearing a linen stole was born, and from her the immaculate lamb came forth, and one as a lion on his left. And all the beasts attacked him, and the lamb conquered them and destroyed them underfoot. And angels and men and the whole earth rejoiced in him. These things will take place at their appointed time, on the last days. Therefore, my sons, honour Judah and Levi, for from them the Lamb of God will arise for you, by grace saving all the nations and Israel. For the kingdom of Israel is eternal, but mine among you will come to an end like a place to keep fruit, for after the harvest it will not appear.

And Benjamin said to his sons:

You will fornicate in the fornication of Sodom, and you will revive disordered stirrings in women, and the kingdom of God will not be among you, etc., until the Most High sends his salvation in the visitation of the only begotten. He will enter the temple, and there the Lord will suffer injury and be despised, and he will be lifted up on a tree, and the veil of the temple will be split, and the spirit of God will descend upon the nations like a fire poured out. And ascending from hell he will ascend from earth to heaven, etc. And then all will arise, some to glory, some to disgrace, and the Lord will first pass judgment on Israel for the injustices they carried out against him, for they did not believe in God, coming in the flesh as a liberator, and then he will judge all the nations.

Further on:

And all Israel will be gathered together, and I will no longer be called a rapacious wolf on account of your rapacity, but instead a worker of the Lord, allotting food to those who do good work. And the beloved of the Lord will be raised up from among my descendants in the last days, hearing his voice on the earth, enlightening all the nations with new understanding, the light of understanding ascending for the salvation of Israel, and taking it away from them like a wolf and granting it to the Synagogue of the nations, and until the end of the age it will be among the synagogues of the nations and among their princes like a tuneful melody on all their mouths, and his work and his word will be in their holy books and writings. My father Jacob has instructed me about him.

– and he slept the long sleep. Since, therefore, many things said by other prophets were predicted here, it is not necessary to say in every case that those others were prophesying. Still, David prophesied more about Christ and things pertaining to him, and his prophecy is included in sacred Scripture, while that was not the case with these twelve patriarchs. Therefore, he can rightly be called "the Prophet" by antonomasia.

But it is remarkable that this first psalm does not have a title. Trevet says that this is because the title of this book is, according to Jerome, "book of hymns," and so it would be redundant to add "a hymn of David." Trevet did not see this title in the Hebrew, but he says it is supplied in Ps. 39, where the Hebrew says: *In the volume of the book it is written of me*, which in the other translation is clearly meant to be understood (according to Trevet) as referring to the first psalm: *In the head of the book it is written of me, that I should do your will*, etc., and he says that David did not wish for this title to be put at the opening of the text, lest he appear to begin by praising himself. In reply, I ask: In what way would it be redundant to provide an attribution for this hymn or psalm, as is done with the others? Indeed, it would not at all be redundant to specify the genre, thus: "Here begins the book of hymns," and then to say "a hymn of David." What a joke! Likewise, how can we believe that you knew that this psalm was the head of the book, or that David deliberately omitted the aforementioned title himself, when Ezra is said to have arranged the psalms, reassembled them into a single volume, and affixed the titles? Further, if David speaks of himself as though in the third person in this psalm, it is apparent that he began it by praising himself, and he could seem to be lying when he claimed that he had not dwelt in the counsel of the wicked or in the way of sinners. What is said further on, *In the head of the book it is written of me, that I should do your will*, is better understood as referring to the book of the law of the Lord, i.e., to the whole Pentateuch or the book of Exodus, which in particular can be said to be the book of the law. If it refers to "the head" of the whole Pentateuch, i.e., to the book of Genesis, then based on the sin of our first parents by their disobedience and their just punishment, it is clearly demonstrated that this is written about him, and, in regard to himself, the Psalmist recognized that he should obey the divine will and do as he pleased. But if it refers to the book of Exodus, this can be called "the head of the book" because before the Lord gave the law on Mount Sinai, when the children of Israel were in Mara after crossing the Red Sea, he established precepts and judgments for the people, saying, Ex. 15: *If you will hear the voice of the Lord your God and do what is right before him and obey his commandments, I will not bring upon you all the sorrow which I imposed upon Egypt*, and here obedience is enjoined as though at the head of the book. Still, it is much better as the Hebrew has it, *In the volume of the book*, than *In the head of the book*, since obedience is taught throughout all of Scripture, so that we might do what is pleasing to God. If, however, the first psalm was in fact by David himself and what he later says, *In the head of the book*, refers to this psalm, it would be necessary for David himself to have established the book of Psalms and to have positioned that psalm at the beginning and head of the book, and then he would have appeared to allege that he was himself the author, which is not consistent with what we have said.

Who is the appropriate student of this book? Certainly, the older and wiser and more devoted he is to God, the better suited he is to study it.

The subject matter of this book is very godly, and it would appear to contain the ends of all theology, consisting in divine praise and contemplation. This is the happiness which is the greatest good of human actions.

The order of reading should be, at present, the order in which the psalms are now written. The mode of reading will be set forth, as much as is possible, according to the intention of the authors, which is called the literal sense. This can be understood as being only apparent and not existent, following what the Apostle says, *The letter kills* – and this meaning must sometimes be recited and rejected. But another "literal" is the meaning of those who wrote the text, and, in my opinion, this sense is fourfold in Scripture. Sometimes the literal sense is historical, when it teaches what did or did not happen. Sometimes it is etymological, i.e., dealing with the interpretation of origins and causes, as when Moses ordered that a libel of repudiation and license of divorce be given, which is to be understood etymologically, as Christ demonstrates in the Gospel: *Moses did this on account of the hardness of your hearts*, as though he said: Nowadays this should not be observed. We should thus consider the reasons why many things which ceased in the time of Christ were formerly permitted. Sometimes the literal sense is analogical, i.e., an irrational but not contradictory saying, demonstrating that the two testaments, the Old and the New, are not incompatible, as the Apostle illustrates: *Was the law, then, contrary to the promises of God? Hardly*, etc. Sometimes the literal sense is allegorical, i.e., it contains tropes and figures, as in the Gospel: *Just as Jonah was in the belly of the whale, so too will be the son of man*, etc., and the Apostle, 1 Cor.: *I would not have you ignorant, brothers, that all your fathers were under a cloud*, etc. These things are said to have happened to them figuratively. And elsewhere: *For Abraham had two sons*, etc. *And so, brothers, we are not sons of the handmaid*, etc. The literal sense of these words of Christ and the Apostle is allegorical and figurative. You will find more about these four senses in Augustine, *On the Utility of Belief*, toward the beginning. All of these senses can be found at various points in Scripture, but it is appropriate to locate authority as pertaining in particular to history. Indeed, when the literal sense of a phrase is historical, and the same phrase, located elsewhere in Scripture, can be expounded etymologically, analogically, or allegorically, then the literal sense of that second instance is etymological or allegorical, etc., but its authority rests on the prior instance, the literal sense of which is only historical. The literal sense is therefore not identical to the historical sense.

The allegorical sense contains under itself what is called the anagogical or tropological, though, if "tropology" derives from the word *tropus*, meaning a rhetorical trope, then tropology and allegory would seem to denote the same thing. If, however, it derives from *tropos*, meaning "turn," then it is contained distinctly under the allegorical sense. The Apostle demonstrates that the anagogical sense is contained under the allegorical when he says, Gal. 4: *He who was born of the handmaid after the flesh, but he who was of the freewoman*, etc., *which are said by allegory*. And he makes this clear, saying of the freewoman: *But that Jerusalem which is above is free*, etc. The Apostle therefore wishes Jerusalem to signify, allegorically, the Church triumphant, our mother, which is above. According to modern usage, this is the anagogical sense, which is also a tropological sense, i.e., turned so as to instruct us in behaviour. The positioning of tropology under allegory is made clear by the Apostle, who turns the aforementioned allegory to us for our instruction. It is therefore clear that Scripture should only be expounded according to those senses set forth by Augustine. For that part of Scripture which instructs us in behaviour sometimes speaks figuratively and pertains to allegory, sometimes it simply teaches us what should or should not be done, how we should or should not behave, and this pertains to history. Indeed, history does not only have to do with things that were done but also with what should be done: "history," i.e., gesture. It is also apparent that not every word of Scripture can or should be expounded in four ways, e.g., *Love justice*, *In the beginning was the word*. For even if someone finds four true senses, only rarely will there be harmony among them, and thus it is my intention to focus on the literal sense.

Like all theology, in my opinion, this book pertains to moral philosophy, as is proven elsewhere. For it cannot pertain to any other, nor it is possible to find any sound teaching pertaining to another part of philosophy.

This book is divided into one hundred fifty parts, following the number of as many psalms, and there is not any intermediate division according to its content, unless one were to want to divide it according to the five breaks which are made by the use of *so be it, so be it* at the end of a psalm. The gloss of St. Jerome indicates that the book of Psalms should be divided into five books following these breaks, but Jerome himself argues to the contrary in his letter to Sophronius, and, indeed, this division is really only nominal. Likewise, there is not any order to the psalms by reason of their detailed subject matter, unless perhaps some of them – the ones beginning "on the first day of the week," etc. – were instituted to be sung in their present order or in some other order on successive feast days in the Synagogue in the time of David, just as now is the case with the hymnal of the Church.

Let us turn, therefore, to the interpretation of individual psalms, one by one.

Epilogue: Hebrew Prepositions

Nota quod *mem* cum duobus punctis iacentibus quos uocamus *sceri*, isto modo מֵ, semper signat hanc preposicionem, *de*. Similiter *sin* Hebraice cum eisdem punctis signat hanc coniunccionem, *quod*, isto modo שֵׁ. Similiter cum tractu sub, quem uocant *patha*, hec littera, *he*, הַ, signat articulum in uulgari, sicut in Gallico *le*, uerbi gracia: הָאדם signat Gallice *le homme*, Anglice þe man. Sed in Latino talis articulus non habet locum. Item nota quod hec tria littere, *mem, sin, he*, integrant nomen Mosse, id est Moyses. Item nota quod tria littere integrantes nomen Caleb in Hebreo, scilicet *caf, lamed, beth*, signant alia tria que frequenter sunt in usu. Nam *caf* cum *patha* et duobus punctis a dextris, sic כַּ׃, signat hanc coniunccionem, *sicut* et *quasi* et consimiles, et eodem modo est si idem puncti stantes quos uocant *seua* ponantur per se sine *patha*, sic כְּ. Similiter *lameth* cum duobus punctis eisdem, sic לְ, signat hanc preposicionem, *ad*. Similiter *beth*, בְּ, uel cum eisdem punctis signat hanc preposicionem, *in*, בְּ. Et semper articulus sine preposicione sic preponitur diccioni, הָרְשָׁעִים.[1] Item eedem cum punctis in medio litterarum faciunt sonum asperum, sine autem tali puncto et cum linea superius posita, que uocatur *rafa*, facit sonum mollem, uerbi gracia: *phe* in hac diccione, *Caleph*, liquescit. Si eciam scribatur per *beth* in fine, sic כָלֵב, et cum *rafa* superius liquescit, quamuis non sit linea superius, dummodo non sit punctus adhuc mollescit, sed cum puncto aspere sonat.

4 הַ] דַ **Ch** ‖ 5 האדם] דדאדם **Ch** ‖ 6 hec] het **Ch** ‖ 13 בְּ] בְּ **Ch** ‖ 14 preposicione] preposicio **Ch**; הָרְשָׁעִים] כַּל|חֹטַשֶׁה **Ch** ‖ 16 rafa] rosa **Ch**

English Translation

Note that *mem* with two points underneath, which we call *tzere*, thus מֵ, always signifies the preposition *of*. Likewise, in Hebrew *shin* with the same points signifies the conjunction *that*, thus שֵׁ. Likewise, with a line underneath, which they call *patach*, this letter, *he*, הַ, signifies the article in the vernacular, just as *le* in French, e.g., האדם signifies *l'homme* in French, *the man* in English. But this kind of article is not used in Latin. Further, note that these three letters, *mem, shin, he*, constitute the name "Moshe," i.e., Moses. Further, note that the three letters making up the name Caleb in Hebrew, i.e., *kaf, lamed, beth*, signify three other things that are in common use. For *kaf* with *patach* and two points to the right, thus כַּ׃, signifies the conjunction *like* and *as*, etc., and the same holds true if upright points which they call *shva* are used without

---

[1] Here the scribe seems to have written nonsense across the line break and my emendation is conjectural, though the prose makes clear that the word must begin with an article.

patach, thus כָ. Likewise, *lamed* with the same two points, thus לְ, signifies the preposition *to*. Likewise, *beth*, written thus בַ or with the same points signifies the preposition *in*, בְ. And without a preposition, an article is always put before a word, thus: הָרְשָׁעִים. Further, the same letters with points in the middle make an aspirated sound, but without such a point and with a line above, which is called *rafe*, they make a soft sound, e.g., the *b* in the word *Caleb* is liquid. For if a word is written with a *beth* in the end and with *rafe* above, thus כָלֵב, it is liquid. If there is not a line above, provided that there is not a point, it is still soft, but with a point it is aspirated.

Abstract

This article presents the first edition and English translation of substantial selections from the Psalter commentary of Henry Cossey, OFM (d. ca. 1336). Though largely absent from recent discussions of medieval Christian Hebraism, Cossey evidently learned some Hebrew, and he used this knowledge to critique other recent literalistic exegetes, most prominently Nicholas Trevet and Nicholas of Lyre. An introductory essay places Cossey's work at Oxford ca. 1330, discusses the complex program of marginal notes in the single surviving manuscript (Cambridge, Christ's College, MS 11), and explores some of his critical disagreements with Trevet and Lyre. The edition and translation include his prologues and an epilogue on Hebrew prepositions.

Résumé

Cet article présente la première édition et traduction anglaise de sélections majeures du commentaire du Psautier d'Henri Cossey, OFM (mort vers 1336). Bien qu'il soit largement absent des récentes discussions autour de l'hébraïsme chrétien médiéval, il semble clair que Cossey ait acquis quelques connaissances de l'hébreu et qu'il s'en servît pour critiquer d'autres exégètes littéralistes contemporains, en particulier Nicolas Trevet et Nicolas de Lyre. Un essai introductif situe les activités de Cossey à Oxford vers 1330, aborde le programme complexe d'annotations marginales qu'on retrouve dans le seul manuscrit nous étant parvenu (Cambridge, Christ's College, MS 11) et se penche sur certains des désaccords critiques de Cossey avec Trevet et Lyre. L'édition et la traduction comportent les prologues de Cossey et son épilogue qui traite des prépositions en hébreu.

Andrew Kraebel
Trinity University, San Antonio
akraebel@trinity.edu

Latin Poetic Stories About Muhammad and Their Stylistic Network[1]

FRANCESCO STELLA
University of Siena

The Earliest Biographical Information

The metrical lives of Muhammad, or better – Mahomet, his legendary and literary double, all appear suddenly during the eleventh and the twelfth centuries, but the origins of the information on which they are based remain unclear. The first short references to biographical data about the Prophet are found in writings of the Byzantine authors from the Arab-conquered territories during the first decades of their expansion after 632,[2] as seen for example in the so-called *Doctrina Iacobi nuper baptizati*[3]

---

[1] I first addressed this topic in Italian many years ago, after having taught a university course on the medieval Latin sources of Islam, for a conference in Zürich on medieval versifications published as "Le versificazioni latine della vita di Maometto. Dall'antiagiografia al romanzo picaresco," in *Dichten als Stoff-Vermittlung. Formen, Ziele, Wirkungen. Beiträge zur prazis der Versifikation lateinischer Texte im Mittelalter*, ed. Peter Stotz (Zürich, 2008), pp. 119–49. I am now revisiting the subject after the kind invitations of Princeton University and the University of Toronto where I presented this paper as the 2020 annual O'Donnell lecture. This version presents both new content and new results in addition to incorporating revisions of the material discussed in my contribution of 2008, after which the literature on the Latin reception of Mohammed has grown exponentially. Only the most important contributions in the field will be mentiond here for the reader's convenience: John V. Tolan, *Faces of Muhammad. Western Perceptions of the Prophet of Islam from the Middle Ages to Today* (Princeton, 2019); *Medieval Latin Lives of Muhammad*, ed. and trans. Julian Yolles and Jessica Weiss (Cambridge, Mass., 2018); *Mahometrica: Ficciones poéticas latinas del siglo XII sobre Mahoma*, ed. Fernando González Muñoz (Madrid, 2015), which gathers only the poetic rewritings, with Spanish translations and a thorough introduction containing updated information. New data and insights can be found in the proceedings of the Barcelona conference *Vitae Mahometi. Reescritura e invención en la literatura cristiana de controversia*, ed. Cándida Ferrero Hernández and Óscar de la Cruz Palma (Madrid, 2014), which collects Latin, French, and Arabic sources, taking the discussion into modern times. The rich collection by Michelina Di Cesare, entitled *The Pseudo-Historical Image of the Prophet Muḥammad in Medieval Latin Literature: A Repertory* (Berlin – Boston, 2012), analyzes 53 Latin sources on Muhammad between the eighth and fifteenth centuries, but does not dedicate any chapter to the poetic texts. On the twelfth-century poems, and on Walter of Compiègne in particular, the literature remains scarce.

[2] Some major guides on the topic are: Alessandro D'Ancona, "La leggenda di Maometto in occidente," *Giornale storico della letteratura italiana* 13 (1889), 199–281 (repr. Rome, 1994); *L'Occidente e l'Islam nell'alto medioevo*. Settimane di Studio del Centro Italiano di Studi sull'Alto Medioevo 12, 2–8 aprile 1964 (Spoleto, 1965); Norman Daniel, *Islam and the West. The Making of an Image* (Edinburgh, 1960);

and above all in the Christian theologian Yuhanna ben Mansur ben Sarjun,[4] known in the West as John of Damascus, grandson of the officer Mansur ben Sarjun who surrendered to the Arabs in 635. Especially telling is John's *Liber de haeresibus* within his larger work *Source of Knowledge* (*Fons cognitionis,* Πηγὴ Γνώσεως), where in chapter 100, *sive de Sarracenis* (which some scholars consider to be an interpolation),[5] Muhammad is presented as a false prophet who, having come to know about the Bible and having met an Arian monk, had created his own heresy on the basis of divine revelations after winning the favor of the people through devotion and *pietatis larva*.[6]

3rd ed. 2019); Norman Daniel, *The Arabs and Medieval Europe* (London, 1975; Italian trans. *Gli arabi e l'Europa nel Medio Evo*, Bologna, 1981); Richard William Southern, *Western Views of Islam in the Middle Ages* (Cambridge, Mass., 1962); Philippe Sénac, *L'image de l'autre. Histoire de l'Occident médiéval face à l'Islam* (Paris, 1983); John V. Tolan, *Saracens. Islam in the Medieval European Imagination* (New York, 2002); Stephan Hotz, *Mohammed und seine Lehre in der Darstellung abendländischer Autoren vom späten 11. bis zur Mitte des 12. Jahrhunderts. Aspekte, Quellen und Tendenzen im Kontinuität und Wandel* (Frankfurt am Main – Berlin – Bern – Bruxelles, 2002); Suzanne Conklin Akbari, *Idols in the East. European Representations of Islam and the Orient, 1100–1450* (Ithaca, 2004); Luís A. García Moreno, "Literatura antimusulmana de tradición Bizantina entre los Mozárabes," *Hispania Sacra* 115 (2005), 7–46; *Christian-Muslim Relations. A Bibliographical History*, 5 vols., ed. David Thomas and Alexander Mallett (Leiden, 2011), esp. vol. 3 for the years 1050–1200; Avinoam Shalem et al., *Constructing the Image of Mohammad in Europe* (Berlin – Boston, 2013); Christiane J. Gruber and Avinoam Shalem, *The Image of the Prophet between Ideal and Ideology: A Scholarly Investigation* (Berlin – Boston, 2014). The website Islamolatina (http://grupsderecerca.uab.cat/islamolatina/content/fuentes) comprises a collection of sources.

[3] See *Juifs et chrétiens dans l'Orient du VIIe siècle*, ed. Gilbert Dagron and Vincent Déroche (Paris, 1991), pp. 47–229 (edition by Vincent Déroche) and pp. 230–73 (commentary by Gilbert Dagron).

[4] Before becoming a monk in Palestine, John had been one of the administrators of the Umayyad caliphs Abd al-Malik and Walid I, and had therefore a thorough knowledge of Islamic doctrine and beliefs, which he put to good use in two works: first, in the *Short Dispute between a Saracen and a Christian* on free will, creation, christology, and baptism, in which a Saracen character sets dialectical traps, which the Christian interlocutor evades skilfully; and second, in the last part of the treatise *The Source of Knowledge*, which examines Islam as the last of a hundred heresies.

[5] The text seems to have become known in the West only after the translation of Cerbano is cited by Gerhoh of Reichersberg in 1147 and by Burgundio of Pisa in 1153–1154. Armand Abel (see below, n. 19), however, has argued for its inauthenticity; see Alain Ducellier, *Chrétiens d'Orient et Islam au Moyen Age: VIIe – XVe siècle* (Paris, 1996; *Cristiani d'Oriente e Islam nel Medioevo. Secoli VII–XV*, Torino, 2001); and *Le Roman de Mahomet de Alexandre Du Pont* (1258), ed. Yvan G. Lepage avec le texte des *Otia de Machomete* de Gautièr de Compiègne établi par Robert B.C. Huygens (Paris, 1977), pp. 19–20.

[6] After John of Damascus there are numerous Byzantine texts that contain information, more or less deformed, on Muhammad. Among them are: Bartolomaeus of Edessa, *Confutatio Agareni*, PG 104:1428–1448; the anonymous *Contra Muhammed*, PG 104:1447–1458; Constantinus Porfirogenita (saec. X), *De administrando imperio*, cap. 14: *De genealogia Mahometis*, PG 113:189–193; Niceta the Philosopher (saec. IX), *Confutatio Falsi libri quem scripsit Mohamedes Arabs*, PG 105:669–806 (see below, n. 13; at cols. 841–842 he quotes a Greek version of the Qu'ran); Georgius Cedrenus (saec. XI),

In the French territories, chronicles such as that of Fredegarius in pre-Carolingian times mention the victories of the Muslim army without dwelling on the Prophet.[7] In Spain, the *Chronicle of 741* simply indicates that the leader of the Saracens was "called Muhammad, born of the noblest tribe of his people, a very wise man who could foresee future events,"[8] whom the Arabs revered with such honor as to maintain in all their sacraments that he was an apostle and prophet of God. There is also a *Continuatio* of Isidore of Seville's *Chronica*, wrongly attributed by Luca of Pontevedra's *Chronicon Mundi* (1249) to Ildefonsus of Toledo (d. 667), which includes a long story about the Prophet that has so far been neglected by scholars.[9] This short life of Muhammad has no relationship with the story found in the *Chronica Adephonsi Imperatoris* (composed after 1146),[10] and is the one included in Hugh of Fleury's *Historia ecclesiastica* (1109–1010).[11]

In general, the modern accounts of Arab expansion record attitudes of relative tolerance that led Muslim regimes not to impose conversion of the *dhimmi* or the

---

Compendium Historiarum, PG 121:807–816; Eutimius Zigabenus (saec. XIex.), *Panoplia Dogmatica*, PG 130:1331–1360; and Iohannes Zonara (saec. XII² ²), *Annales*, PG 134:1285 BD).

[7] The Chronicle of Fredegarius (658) is in fact the first historiographic work in the West to mention the Arab victories over the Byzantine emperor Heraclius, then describing the invasions in semi-apocalyptic terms. In the Franco-gallic territory, the topic remains obscure, and even in the Carolingian age the only work expressly dedicated to it seems to be Alcuin's *Disputatio Felicis cum Sarraceno*, which unfortunately has not survived. The Carolingian era experienced several conflicts with the Emir of Cordova and the Saracen pirates who ravaged the French and Italian coasts. We also learn of diplomatic relations with Harun al-Rashid, the Abbasid Caliph of Baghdad, who sent to Charlemagne an elephant as a gift, but these stories remain isolated episodes, and the image of Islam does not seem to have a particular importance in Carolingian writings.

[8] See *Chronica Byzantia-Arabica* 13, ed. Juan Gil, in *Corpus scriptorum Muzarabicorum*, 2 vols. (Madrid, 1973), 1:7–14, at p. 9: "Mahmet nomine, de tribu illius gentis nobilissima natus, prudens admodum uir et aliquantorum futurorum prouisor gestorum."

[9] PL 96:320–321; see the introduction of Emma Falque to Lucas Tudensis, *Chronicon mundi* (Turnhout, 2003), p. lii. The *Vida de Mahoma* is found on pp. 166–69 of Falque's book. In Falque's opinion, the sources go back to Eulogius, *Apol.* 16 and Albarus *Epist.* 6.9, but this is not evident from the provided references. See Manuel C. Díaz y Díaz, "Los textos antimahometanos más antiguos en códices españoles," *Archives d'histoire doctrinale et littéraire du Moyen Âge* 37 (1970), 149–68; and Peter A. Linehan, "The Toledo Forgeries c.1150–c.1300," in *Fälschungen in Mittelalter* I (Hannover, 1988), pp. 663–74.

[10] See *Chronica Hispana saeculi XII,* ed. Antonio Maya Sánchez, CCCM 71 (Turnhout, 1990), pp. 109–248.

[11] See *Hugonis Floriacensis Historia Ecclesiastica*, ed. Georg Waitz, MGH: Scriptores 9 (Hannover, 1851), pp. 337–64; repr. in PL 163:805–854. See also Leendert Martin de Ruiter, *Hugo van Fleury: Historia Ecclesiastica, editio altera*: Kritische teksteditie (Diss., Rijksuniversiteit Groningen, 2016).

"peoples of the book" (that is, Christians and Jews), but limited themselves to collecting taxes and prohibiting the construction of new churches, proselytism, and blasphemy against Muhammad. We have no documentation about the Christian point of view during and after the Muslim conquest of North Africa, because the Latin and Greek languages were completely uprooted in the region. In contrast, in Spain a group resistance arose in Cordoba in the middle of the ninth century, which was destined to leave a deep wound in the consciousness of the two communities. Here, fifty "voluntary" martyrs faced death, provoking the Islamic authorities with offensive and blasphemous opinions regarding Muhammad's religious status. He was presented as one of the false prophets announced in the Gospel of Matthew (24.24), who seduced other devotees to sacrilegious magical practices that would lead many souls to eternal perdition, in particular through the sexual permissiveness granted to the faithful.

The First Life of Muhammad Discovered by Eulogius of Cordoba

Eulogius composed his *Apologeticus Martyrum* in 857. Chapter 16 of this work includes a brief life of Muhammad, allegedly found by Eulogius in the monastery of Leyra, near Pamplona, during the journey that had taken him to Navarre seven years earlier. This life, transmitted autonomously in three additional manuscripts, including the famous Codex Rodensis,[12] reveals some knowledge of Islam,[13] containing descriptions (albeit always negative in tone) of the marriage between Muhammad and the rich widow whose servant he was; the role of Gabriel, who presented himself in the form of a vulture in the revelation of the Koran; the marriage between Muhammad and Zaynab, the ex-wife of his disciple Zayd; and the power Muhammad won by killing the emperor's brother. Even the Prophet's death is narrated according to exclu-

---

[12] Madrid, Real Academia de la Historia, MS 78 (saec. X–XI, Roda) contains patristic extracts, Orosius, Isidore, and *Chronica Adephonsi III*, also including the *Storia de Mahomet* on fols. 187r–188v (within the so-called *Chronica prophetica*) as well as the mysterious *Tultuscepru de libro domini Metobii*. Some scholars believe that this text is an expanded version of the life copied by Eulogius. See Elisa Ruíz García, *Catalogo de la Sección de Códices de la Real Academia de la Historia* (Madrid, 1997), pp. 395–405; and *Chronica Adefonsi Imperatoris*, ed. Maya Sanchez. The incipit of the text in the manuscript reads: "Exortum erat Mahomet eresiarches tempore Eraclii imperatoris anni Imperii ipsius septimo" [*sic*].

[13] *Corpus scriptorum Muzarabicorum*, ed. Gil, 1:483–86 (plus the Mohammedan law explicated on pp. 398–99) is based on an Oviedo codex used in the 1574 *editio princeps* of Alcalá de Henares (Compluti) and now lost. Pedro Herrera Roldán's new translation (San Eulogio, *Obras*, Madrid, 2005) is based on Gil's text. The only critical edition of this life is the *Notitia de Mahmet pseudo Propheta*, in Díaz y Díaz, "Los textos antimahometanos," pp. 153–56 (title given by the editor); English translation with some annotations is found in Kenneth Baxter Wolf, "The Earliest Lives of Muhammad," in *Conversion and Continuity. Indigenous Christian Communities in Islamic Lands. Eight to Eighteenth Centuries*, ed. Michael Gervers and Ramzi Jibran Bikhazi (Toronto, 1990), pp. 89–101.

sively Christian legends and is based on an anti-Christological model, which attempts to shape the highlights of Muhammad's existence on those of Christ but in reverse. According to Eulogius, Muhammad,

> feeling that his end was imminent and knowing that in no way would he be resurrected for his merits, ... predicted that he would return to life on the third day by the intervention of the angel Gabriel, who usually appeared to him in the form of a vulture. When he delivered his soul to hell, he ordered his corpse to be watched over by an attentive guard, because he was worried about the miracle he had announced. When the third day arrived and the corpse was decomposing, confirming that it would in fact not rise, he then said that the angels had not come because they were intimidated by their presence. Convinced by the warning, the sentries left the corpse unguarded and immediately, instead of angels, the stench attracted dogs that devoured its flanks.[14] This fact warned them that they should leave the rest of the body on the ground, and to avenge this outrage they ordered that every year dogs be slaughtered so that those, who deserved a worthy martyrdom in the Prophet's name here, could share his merits there. It was right for a prophet of this kind to fill the stomachs of dogs, a prophet who entrusted to hell not only his own soul but the souls of many.[15]

Obviously, in the authentic texts of the Islamic tradition,[16] such as the collection of biographical materials by Ibn Isḥāq (lost, edited by Ibn Hishām), whose authoritativeness is difficult to establish, the death of the Prophet is narrated differently.[17] In the life reported by Eulogius the polemical deformation of Muslim traditions reaches the point of the author's denouncing Muhammad's intention to deflower the Virgin Mary in the afterlife, an idea obviously blasphemous for the Islamic faith also, which is never found again in the anti-Islamic literature. In general, the tone of this text is strongly derogatory, although it is acknowledged that in preaching to the men of his tribe

---

[14] The dogs that pounce on the corpse recall the death of Jezebel, queen of Baal, described in II Kings 9.22 and 9.33–37.

[15] See *Corpus scriptorum Muzarabicorum*, ed. Gil, 1:486. In a similar way, the *Chanson de Roland* 157, 2589–2590 recounts that an idol of Muhammad preserved in the mosque of Zaragoza was thrown into a ditch and "e porc e chen le mordent e defulent." Cf. *Ysengrimus* 7.295–298, ed. and trans. Jill Mann (Leiden – New York, 1987), pp. 532–33.

[16] See *Vite antiche di Maometto*, ed. Michael Lecker, trans. Roberto Tottoli (Milan, 2007), which however does not publish the translations of individual ancient texts, but a sort of unitary reconstruction based on a dozen different sources.

[17] A new perspective has been outlined by Michelina Di Cesare in her essay about the pseudo-prophet Musaylima ibn Habib, leader of the community of Yamama, located east of Medina and Mecca, who rose as an ambitious anti-Muhammad by pretending to have received angelical inspiration under the advice of an apostate; see Michelina Di Cesare, *Un gioco di specchi: Interazioni e influenze tra l'immagine di Musaylima nella letteratura islamica e l'immagine di Muhammad nella letteratura latina medievale*, in *Las Vitae Mahometi*, ed. Óscar de la Cruz Palma and Cándida Ferrero Hernández (Madrid, 2015), pp. 41–54.

Muhammad had invited them to abandon the worship of idols and to adore an incorporeal God who dwells in the heavens. There is also a reference to the Qu'ran, which is alluded to by recalling the "psalms" composed by Muhammad and the songs for Joseph, Zachariah, and the Virgin Mary. Thus, it is evident that in Eulogius as well as in many other Christian texts[18] there is a strong need to frame or adapt the historical facts into a perspective that would make the role of the new "sect" comprehensible within the Christian history of salvation.

The Crusades and the Texts of Guibert of Nogent and Peter Alfonsi

At the end of the eleventh century, close to the start of the first Crusades, Europe developed a stronger interest in acquiring information about the culture of the enemy as well as about the other populations cohabiting with the crusaders who settled in Palestine after 1099. An example is offered by Guibert of Nogent (1052–1124) who dedicates a few pages to the story of Muhammad in Book 4, chapter 1.3–4 of his *Gesta Dei per Francos* (completed in 1108, revised in 1121). Guibert's account is based on what he defines as a *plebeia opinio*, which already contains almost all the narrative ingredients that we will find in subsequent lives of the Prophet. Thus, we read about the hermit, who here is styled as a Christian expelled from the Alexandrian church and who, bent on revenge against the Catholic hierarchies, helps Muhammad to marry a rich widow, convincing her with several pragmatic and psychological arguments. Muhammad's epileptic attacks frighten his wife, but the hermit explains that these are in fact visions from which Muhammad derives his reputation as a prophet. The text of the new law appears between the horns of a cow hidden in Muhammad's tent, a detail coming from the *Apocalypse of Bahira*, a ninth-century Arabic legend about the influence of the monk Bahira on Mohammed, later partially translated into Latin.[19] This revelation is welcomed with great favour by the population, since it endorses dissolute sexual freedom, and thus spreads quickly throughout North Africa and Spain. But a final epileptic attack leaves Muhammad at the mercy of a drove of pigs, which devour him. This is clearly a version that follows a slanderous narrative strand "from overseas," namely, legendary texts of Byzantine derivation which circulated in the Crusaders' era, in contrast to a Hispanic tradition whose characteristics include deeper

---

[18] Tolan, *Saracens*, p. 93.

[19] Armand Abel, "L'Apocalypse de Baḥīra et la notion islamique de Mahdī," *Annuaire de l'Institut de philologie et d'histoire orientales et Slaves* 3 (1935), 1–12, at p. 9. A date after the ninth century is suggested by Jeanne Bignami-Odier and Giorgio Levi Della Vida, "Une versione latine de l'Apocalypse de Serge-Baḥīra," *Mélanges d'École Française de Rome* 62 (1950), 125–48, at p. 132, n. 3. Barbara Roggema, *The Legend of Sergius Bahira: Eastern Christian Apologetics and Apocalyptic in Response to Islam* (Leiden, 2009), confirms that the earliest Latin manuscripts date to the thirteenth century, but sees influences of this legend on the "Spanish" pseudo-Eulogian *Istoria de Mahomet*.

knowledge of the Arabic texts, greater theological interest, and a stronger polemical undertone.

An exmple of the latter is the work of Peter Alfonsi, a Jewish convert and connoisseur of Arabic who died in ca. 1140. In his *Dialogus adversus Iudaeos* Peter devotes a chapter to the exposition of Islamic doctrines, based on Christian-Arabic sources. These include *Risālat*, a dialogue between a Muslim and a Nestorian Christian – Abd al-Masih al-Kindi – set in a ninth-century Abbasid court and translated into Latin after 1142 in the *Collectio Toletana* inspired by Peter the Venerable.[20] Alfonsi describes Muslim rituals and customs with knowledge of the facts and attempts a thorough refutation of the theological objections of Islam to the Christian faith (especially on questions such as the Trinity, the incarnation, and some interpretations of the Old Testament). Thus, Alfonsi's discussion reveals a new stage of the confrontation between the two faiths which has moved from legend to theology. In Peter's reply to Moses there is a brief biography of Mohammad,[21] based in part on quotations from the Qu'ran, which presents him as an orphan raised by his uncle Panefo – his real name is actually Abū Ṭalīb – at the service of the noble widow Khadija, whom he later married. The great wealth he now possessed made him politically ambitious. To win the trust of his people, he pretended to be a prophet, relying on the ignorance of the majority and following the advice of a Jacobite archdeacon from the region of Antioch[22] and of two Jews who helped him compile a set of religious laws that would reconcile these diverging doctrines. Peter then raises the issue of the miracles that Mohammad did not in fact perform in comparison with Moses, the other great legislative prophet. Peter Alfonsi's discussion, although filled with legendary details, is the best informed and probably the most widespread medieval text on the subject of Islam. Once again, however, Muhammad's biography here is still only a chapter in a larger work on a broader topic.

The First Autonomous Biography of Muhamad: Embrico of Mainz

The first extensive history of Muhammad with its own textual autonomy and the first European work specifically dedicated to him is the *Machumeti Vita* attributed to Em-

---

[20] For the Latin text with English translation, see *Medieval Latin Lives of Muhammad*, ed. and trans. Yolles and Weiss, pp. 215–515. For an Italian translation, see Laura Bottini, *Al-Kindī: Apologia del cristianesimo* (Milan, 1998), pp. 47–49.

[21] PL 157:559D–601A.

[22] The Jacobites are a monophysite sect of Syria founded in the seventh century by the monk Jacob Baradeo, bishop of Edessa. Peter describe the heresy as follows: "circumcisionem praedicantes, Christumque non Deum sed hominem tantum iustum de Spiritu sancto conceptum, ac de virgine natum, non crucifixum tamen neque mortuum credentes" (PL 157:600A).

brico of Mainz. This verse life met with considerable success, as is seen by its transmission in sixteen manuscripts.[23]

Some codices attribute this work to Hildebert of Le Mans,[24] and many modern historians still mention it with this attribution, following the *Patrologia Latina*. However, an important manuscript from St. Arnoul in Metz, now Berlin, Deutsche Staatsbibliothek zu Berlin – Preussischer Kulturbesitz, MS Phillipps 1694,[25] and another in Reims, Bibliothèque municipale, MS 1073, provide after the text of the poem a verse life of its author Embrico Moguntinus who supposedly composed it "dum studuit," that is, at a young age. Thanks to the information found in the *Vita auctoris*, this otherwise unknown Embrico was identified by Guy Cambier (the latest editor of the text) as a canon of Mainz who lived between 1010 and 1077. In contrast, Max Manitius believed that the author was Embrico, Bishop of Augsburg from 1064 to 1072.[26] Objections to these identifications were first raised by Wolfram von den Steinen, mainly on stylistic grounds,[27] after which other scholars also preferred a later date for the work and identified its author with a certain Embrico, Chancellor of Mainz between 1090 and 1112.[28]

However, in 2017 Fernando González Muñoz brought to light new documentation supporting Valentin Rose's forgotten hypothesis that the Embrico in question was Embrico, Bishop of Würzburg from 1127 to 1146, who was born in Mainz and was active at the court of Emperor Lothair III of Supplinburg. Moreover, this Embrico was a friend of the poet Hugh Metel, whose work is transmitted in the same Berlin

---

[23] The most complete critical edition of the poem is *Embricon de Mayence. La Vie de Mahomet*, ed. Guy Cambier (Bruxelles – Berchem, 1961). Revised editions are produced in *Mahometrica*, ed. González Muñoz, pp. 97–167 (with Spanish translation) and in *Medieval Latin Lives of Muhammad*, ed. and trans. Yolles and Weiss, pp. 23–101 (with English translation).

[24] The text is printed among Hildebert's works in PL 171:1343–1366. The attribution is found in Paris, Bibliothèque nationale de France, MS lat. 5129, fol. 127r: "Historia Hildeberti Cinomannensis Episcopi de Mahumedi."

[25] On the dating of the manuscript, see Christopher J. McDonough, "Hugh Metel and the *Floridus aspectus* of Peter Riga (Staatsbibliothek zu Berlin Preussischer Kulturbesitz, Philipps 1694)," *Mediaeval Studies* 67 (2005), 27–74. Embrico's poem is copied on fols. 105r–111v of the Berlin manuscript.

[26] Max Manitius, *Geschichte der lateinischen Literatur des Mittelalters*, 3 vols. (München, 1923), 2:582–87.

[27] Wolfram von den Steten, "Literarische Anfänge in Basel" (Warnerius Basiliensis), *Basler Zeitschrift für Geschichte und Altertumskunde* 32 (1933), 239–88, at p. 283, reprinted in *Menschen im Mittelalter. Gesammelte Forschungen, Betrachtungen, Bilder*, ed. Peter von Moos (Bern, 1967), pp. 157–95, at 191.

[28] See Southern, *Western Views*, pp. 29–30; François Chatillon, "Embricon de Mayence, 'Iste catus,'" *Revue du Moyen Âge latin* 19 (1963), 171–76; and Lieven Van Acker, "Embricho von Mainz," in *Verfasserlexikon*, 14 vols. (Berlin, 1980), 2:515–17.

manuscript (MS Phillipps 1694) as the *Machumeti Vita*.[29] Embrico of Mainz's *confessio*, published by Wattenbach in 1877,[30] offers striking stylistic similarities with verses from the *Vita Mahumeti*. Godebold, to whom the work is dedicated, could then be identified as the count of Henneberg who was the lord of the castle of Würzburg and who died in 1144. In conclusion, the poem, which was written during Embrico's studies and thus before his episcopate, must have been composed prior to 1127 or, even better, before 1118, during Embrico's student years in Toul. It is, therefore, written after the First Crusade.

The *Vita* Mahumeti, consisting of 1148 lines of Leonine couplets, opens with a long rhetorical sermon against the detractors of Christ, at the end of which the poet announces that he wants to speak of the pagans who adore Muhammad, both because his addressee Godebold, "speculum summorum virorum," has asked him to do so and because he considers it necessary: "conveniens esse quoniam reor, immo necesse" (v. 77). After warning that the internal enemy is the most dangerous of all, the poet goes on to describe a Christian Magician, the real protagonist of the text, who in the entire poem is never given a proper name. After the death of the Patriarch of Jerusalem, this holy man aspires to his succession,[31] but King Theodosius – probably a confusion with the sixth-century Patriarch Theodosius, a contemporary of the monk Sergius who taught Muhammad – blocks his aspirations, thus provoking the Magician to react by threatening to ruin the Church, as indeed happens later. In fact, he moves to the kingdom of Libya in northern Africa, where he meets *Mammutius*, a servant of the rich local consul, with whom he forms an alliance. He achieves his plan when Muhammad's master falls ill: secretly they speed up his death, after which the Magician convinces the widow to grant Muhammad his freedom and marry him. Muhammad then becomes consul and after the death of the king manages to succeed as king thanks to eloquent public speeches and a fake prophecy. In this prophecy a bull, covertly raised by Muhammad, is unleashed into the crowd, creating havoc until the Magician declares that the one who manages to subdue the bull will be chosen as king. This episode seems to have classical parallels in the oxen of Vulcan tamed by Jason through

---

[29] Fernando González Muñoz, "La datación y la autoría del poema 'Vita Mahumeti' atribuido a Embrico de Mainz," *Anuario de Estudios Medievales* 47/2 (2017), 589–605.

[30] Wilhelm Wattenbach, "Bericht über eine Reise durch Steiermark im August 1876," *Neues Archiv der Gesellschaft für ältere deutsche Geschichtskunde* 2 (1877), 385–425, at pp. 404–7, discussed in González Muñoz, "La datación," pp. 598–99.

[31] This figure, whose historical foothold is perhaps found in Sures 16 and 103 of the Koran, where Muhammad alludes to the insinuations of his detractors about him serving a foreign master, is perhaps the man mentioned in the *Apocalypse of Bahira* as the "teacher monk" whom *Risālat al-Kindī* and Peter Alfonsi call "Sergius," while another biography, written by a certain Adelfus in the twelfth century, identifies him with the heresiarch Nestorius and others (*Liber Nicolay*) with the deacon Nicolas, founder of the Nicolaite sect.

the magic of Medea as well as in many folk tales.[32] This passage is accompanied by the only poetic account about tauromachy in that time. Men, both young and old, attempt the feat, and some even die doing so, but of course only Muhammad knows how to tame the bull and succeeds, finding on its horns an inscription that validates his nomination.[33]

The two accomplices then start their anti-Christian reform, abolishing sexual prohibitions to the point of authorizing not only polygamy and polyandry but also homosexuality and incest, thereby obtaining great popular support, except for the resistance of some few who are martyred. As divine punishment Muhammad suffers epileptic attacks, but the Magician takes advantage of them by presenting them as abductions into heaven, which the Prophet describes in a long and detailed speech, also regretting having to come back to earth. Other laws are enacted by speeches to angels and humans, of which only the rule to wash oneself after committing sinful acts is described. During his final epileptic seizure, Muhammad ends up being eaten by a drove of pigs, but the Magician knows how to profit even from the Prophet's death – he takes the opportunity to implement the ban on eating pork and to deify Muhammad, and finally builds his famous tomb suspended in air thanks to huge magnets placed around the room.[34]

As can be seen, the narrative structure isolates certain elements in the legend of Muhammad-Mahomet that are destined to become permanent in the various rewritings that follow: the failed clergyman becomes a Magician; Muhammad allies with

---

[32] John V. Tolan, "Anti-Hagiography: Embrico of Mainz's 'Vita Mahumeti,'" *Journal of Medieval History* 22/1 (1996), 25–41, discusses some rather forced hagiographical comparisons with saints who master wild beasts (but not bulls).

[33] Several possible classical sources have been proposed as inspiration for this episode: Pliny, Ausonius, Claudian, and especially Augustine, *De ciuitate Dei* 21.6, followed by Rufinus, *Hist. eccl.* 2.23; see Alexandre Eckhardt, "Le cercueil flottant de Mahomet," in *Mélanges de philologie romane et de littérature médiévale offerts à E. Hoepffner* (Paris, 1949), pp. 77–88. Many texts after Embrico and Walter mention the story (see Lepage, *Le Roman de Mahomet*, pp. 43–46), and in my opinion its most likely source is again the *Apocalypse of Bahira*, through some unknown oral or written mediations; see Richard Gottheil, "A Christian Bahira Legend," *Zeitschrift für Assyriologie* 13 (1898), 189–242; 14 (1899), 203–68; 15 (1900), 56–102; 17 (1903), 125–66.

[34] Cf. *Chanson d'Antioche* 5.24–25, 708–11: "Mahomes fu en l'air par l'aïmant vertus, | Et Paiens, l'aourèrent et rendent lor salus | Or et argent li offrent et pailes de boffus | Nis les bous de lor bras, et le avir desus." The author hopes that with this "Musa manum teneat et Mahumet pereat!" – "the Muse stays his hand and Muhammad goes to ruin," v. 1148. About the follow-up of this image even in late medieval maps, see Folker E. Reichert, "Der eiserne Sarg des Propheten. Doppelte Grenzen im Islambild des Mittelalters," in *Grenze und Grenzüberschreitung im Mittelalter. 11. Symposium des Mediävistenverbandes vom 14. bis 17. März 2005 in Frankfurt an der Oder* (Berlin, 2007), pp. 453–69, now reprinted in Folker E. Reichert, *Asien und Europa im Mittelalter. Studien zur Geschichte des Reisens* (Göttingen, 2014), pp. 181–95.

him to acquire power; he succeeds thanks to speeches and tricks such as the training of a bull; and he issues a legislative reform based on sexual freedom. The epileptic attacks are presented as revelations, but in the last one Muhammad remains alone and is torn to pieces by a herd of animals.

The poem neither has nor pretends to have real historical value, since it places the events in the time of Theodosius and Ambrose;[35] however, it needs to be recognized that this biography of Muhammad attests for the first time to the need for narratives, albeit deformed, about the founder of Islam, and in this it is of great consequence. The importance of the text was acknowledged by John Tolan and Marieke Van Acker, who both interpret the *Vita Machometi* as an example of an "anti-hagiographic" model of a heresiarch, composed in response to concerns that were taking hold in twelfth-century Europe.[36] Still, despite the attractiveness of this hypothesis, the intertexts of Emrico's poem do not suggest hagiographic models, except for some references to Hrotsvitha's compositions. In fact, the textual parallels of the poem have not been properly explored, and in his 2018 article Josep Escolà only managed to identify some predictable commonplaces from Virgil and Ovid.[37] I have tried to contribute a more extensive analysis by surveying the available digital archives (such as the CD-ROM *Poetria Nova*, published by SISMEL in 2001), and the results have confirmed my impression of the poem's originality. Where the poet's models are recognizable, they lead back to, first – classical[38] or late antique poets;[39] second – authors of the tenth and

---

[35] See *Vita auctoris*, vv. 3–8: "Ergo sciant noti cuncti pariterque remoti | Hec quod composuit carmina dum studuit | Embrico, quem mores, genus exaltant et honores. | Forsitan et, natus unde sit iste catus | Queritur; hoc mente describam non metuente: | Moguntinus erat, mater ut eius erat." See Guy Cambier, "Embricon de Mayence (1010? –1077) est-il l'auteur de la 'Vita Mahumeti'?," *Latomus* 16/3 (1957), 468–79. According to this attribution, Cambier dates the poem to 1040–1041. The same position was supported by Wilhelm Wattenbach, "Lateinische Gedichte aus Frankreich im elften Jahrhundert," *Sitzungsberichte der Berliner Akademie der Wissenschaften, Philosophisch-historische Klasse* 27 (1891), 97–114, at pp. 113–14. Christine Ratkowitsch in her "Das Grab des Propheten: Die Mohammed-Dichtungen des Embricho von Mainz und Walter von Compiègne," *Wiener Studien* 106 (1993), 223–56, prefers a later dating.

[36] See Tolan, "Anti-Hagiography"; and Marieke Van Acker, "Mahomet dans ses biographies occidentales du Moyen Age: Entre anti-saint et Antéchrist" (Diss., Universiteit Gent, a.a. 1998–1999).

[37] Josep M. Escolà, "Comentari estilístic de la 'Vita Mahumeti' d'Embricó de Mainz," in *'Vitae Mahometi'. Reescritura e invención*, ed. Ferrero Hernández and de la Cruz Palma, pp. 85–99.

[38] See for example, v. 131 "latet hostis in urbe": cf. Verg., *Ecl.* 3.93; and v. 230 "voce superba": cf. Verg., *Aen.* 7.544. Classical parallels to vv. 1115–1148 are listed in Ratkowitsch, "Das Grab des Propheten," pp. 254–55.

[39] Compare v. 4: "Quem Dominum sōlum iam tremit omne sòlum" with Dracontius, *Satisfactio*, v. 2: "Quem tremit omne solum, qui regis igne polum (unique comparison); v. 59: "Vivere dicentes sicut fenum comedentes" with *Anthologia latina* 791.23: "Tam comedens fenum, quam panem et cetera edebat"; v. 271: "obstruit ora" with Corippus, *Ioh.* 6.177–178: "spiritus ora/obstruit"; v. 379: "vertex

eleventh century such as Otloh of St. Emmeram,[40] Fulcoius of Beauvais,[41] and the *Ecbasis captivi*;[42] and third – to epic poems of the Crusader era such as Gilo Parisiensis's *Historia gestorum vie nostri temporis Ierosolymitane*, written between 1118 and 1121.[43] Afterwards, the widespread diffusion of the text is confirmed not only by possible imitations found in Gutolf of Heiligenkreuz[44] and Hugh of Mâcon,[45] but also by Walter of Compiègne's continuation and by the fourteenth-century prose re-writing transmitted in one Pisa manuscript.[46]

Embrico's Latin is not elegant, his style is marked by frequent redundancies and the woodenness of an immature, mediocre writer; yet, the poem demonstrates the author's ability to draw characters, like the Magician who is portrayed in every facial expression, colour, and attitude, as well as that of creating scenes and describing events, while occasionally commenting on the moral of the story with brief gnomic

---

cristatus" with *Anthologia latina* 198.39: "cristatus ... vertex"; and v. 415: "vita patroni" in clausula only in Venantius Fortunatus, *Mart.* 4.17.

[40] Cf. v. 117: "Sed Deus inspector cordis, iustus quoque rector" with Otloh, *Doctr. spirit.* 1007: "cum Deus, inspector cordis, rerumque probator."

[41] Cf. v. 419: "rege sepulto" in clausula only in Fulcoius, *De nupt.* 4.538 and 5.229.

[42] Cf. v. 85: "domesticus hostis" in clausula found for the first time in *Ecbasis* 1178, then in William of Apulia's *Gesta Roberti Wiscardi* 4.487, Nigel Wireker's *Miracula sancte Dei genetricis* 2419, Gunther's *Ligurinus* 10.292, and Walter of Châtillon's *Alexandreis* 7.24.

[43] Cf. v. 43: "Sed sunt pagani qui spe ludfuntur inani" with Gilo, *Historia gestorum* 2.177: "instant pagani, iactu frustrantur inani"; v. 281: "sua pectora tundit" (from Ovid, *Met.* 8.536) with Gilo, *Historia gestorum* 1.333 and ps. Ovid, *De Pyramo e Tisbe* 1.1165.

[44] On this Cistercian poet of the mid-thirteenth century, see Carmen Cardelle de Hartmann, "Der Dyalogus Agnetis des Gutolf von Heiligenkreuz," in *Poesía latina medieval (siglos V–XV)*, ed. Manuel Cecilio Díaz y Díaz and José Manuel Díaz de Bustamante (Florence, 2005), pp. 425–35. Embrico's v. 69: "cessit cultura deorum" is comparable only with Gutolf, *Dialogus Agnetis* 438; v. 341: "vox vitulina" has poetic precedents only in Plautus, *Aulularia* 375, the *Cena Cypriani* 2.119, and the *Ecbasis captivi* 1216. Cf. also Gutolf, *Opus de accentibus* 457, ed. Anton Schönbach, in *Studien zur Geschichte der altdeutschen Predigt*, 8 vols. (Vienna, 1896–1907), in vol. 4 (1906); and *Regimen sanitatis ad regem Aragonum* 130, ed. Luis Garcia Ballester and Michael R.M. Vaugh (Barcelona, 1996). It is worth mentioning that one of Embrico's manuscripts is preserved in Heiligenkreuz – i.e. Heiligenkreuz, Stiftsbibliothek, MS 115 (saec. XII) – where Gutolf could have read it.

[45] Cf. v. 515: "transvolat arva" in clausula with Hugo Matisconensis, *Gesta militum* 9.26 (mid-thirteenth century).

[46] Augusto Mancini, "Per lo studio della leggenda di Maometto in Occidente," *Rendiconti della Reale Accademia Nazionale dei Lincei* (Classe di scienze morali ser. 6) 10 (1934), 325–49; and Fernando González Muñoz, "Dos versiones tardías de la leyenda de Mahoma: La *Vita Mahometi* del ms. Pisa, Biblioteca del Seminario 50 y el tratado 'Sobre la seta mahometana' de Pedro de Jaén," in *Actas do IV Congreso Internacional de Latim Medieval Hispánico. Lisboa, 12–15 de outubro de 2005* (Lisbon, 2006), pp. 591–98.

explanations or longer invectives and apostrophes. But above all the poem has the merit of showcasing the figure of Muhammad as a self-standing character through detailed narratives that are independent of the profile of Islam and therefore from any ideological pressure, thus providing a strong literary counterpart to the figure of the Magician.

The reasons that Embrico offers for the intent of the work are clear, though generic. The address to Godebold presents the work as an attempt to explain "quod fuerit principium sceleris | primaque tantorum fuerit quae causa malorum" – "what was the beginning of this sin and what was the first cause of such great evils" (vv. 74–75; trans. Weiss, in Yolles and Weiss, p. 29). It is, therefore, a polemically fictionalized history of the origins of Islam, presented as a phenomenon which is currently creating troubles in the poet's own times. In the introduction Embrico talks of the Muslim peoples as being capable of conversion to the true faith, if only they could realize their errors. Later he declares that he wants to fight against an internal enemy ("domesticus hostis," v. 85), as if Islam were a form of Christian or Abrahamic heresy that might spread among the Christians themselves. Thus, an alleged apostolic and missionary intent emerges, along with that of providing further information about the heresy, which outside of the Iberian Peninsula can be explained as necessary only during the period of the Crusades.

Apart from the long introductory protasis, true meta-narrative references are rare; one example is found in v. 560, where the poet says that in order to explain the meaning of the figure of the bull as a symbol of the people, "he will hasten not only briefly but lightly" – "absolvam leviter, si placet, et breviter"; and another is seen in v. 611, where the author announces that he does not want to pass by an important detail in silence: "hic – quod dicendum reor et minime reticendum." The ending is announced abruptly as "musa manum teneat et Mahumet pereat," confirming that the intent of the poem is twofold: on the one hand, it is moral, as the text is meant to engage with and ward off heretical danger that is immediate and ongoing; on the other hand, the intent is literary, with attention to narrative structures that go well beyond educational necessities and thus evince the poetic abilities of the author, who is even able to construct virtuoso ten-word hexameters.

There are also declarations of the ineffability of a subject too vast for the poet's talent and a recommendation not to transcribe or diffuse the work for fear of public criticism ("Ne transcribantur aut a multis videantur! | Nostra timent vicia publica iudicia," vv. 81–82), which seems to limit the purpose of the work to private or community entertainment. Among the most probable sources of the poem are the early Latin versions of the Arabic letter of Al-Kindi and the above-mentioned *Apocalypse of*

Bahira.[47] If the new dating of the composition to about 1120 is taken into account, other sources, such as the ones also used by Guibert of Nogent, who declares that he has based his work on oral narratives, have to be taken into consideration. However, even though Guibert's text is closest to Embrico's in narrative development, there are some striking differences between the two authors. In fact, Guibert makes no mention of the magician (he speaks about an Alexandrian heresiarch) or the suspended tomb. Therefore, Embrico is the first author to describe Muhammad's tomb, which can be considered an autonomous development of the basic story, accompanied by elements that are at times largely inaccurate, although this inaccuracy can be justified by the still very nebulous aura surrounding the historical events.

Walter of Compiègne, Otia de Machomete

A further step in creating a narrative for the wider public is the entertaining poem attributed to a certain monk Walter, identified with Walter of Compiègne, abbot of St. Martin in Chartres. During his formative years at Marmoutier, between 1131 and 1137, Walter was told the story of Muhammad by a certain brother Guarnierus, himself later an abbot, who in turn had heard it from one Paganus of Sens, who in turn had heard it from a converted Muslim, in a narrative chain typical of Oriental tales. Walter put the story into verse in a poem entitled *Otia de Machomete*, transmitted in two Latin manuscripts,[48] to which was later added the manuscript Vaticanus

---

[47] Both the letter of Al-Kindi and the *Apocalypse of Bahira*, composed in Arabic in the ninth century, were translated into Latin only in the twelfth and fourteenth centuries, but according to Guy Cambier they were known before, also to Guibert of Nogent and Walter of Châtillon. Ibn Isham's *Sīrat Rasūl Allāh*, based on the biography of Ibn Ishaq (d. 773), speaks about Bahira, presenting him as a monk from Bosra (Syria) versed in the Christian doctrine, who prophesies the future greatness of Muhammad, a legend taken from the *Chronicle* of Al-Tabari (d. 922/3). The Byzantine texts that cite the legend are Bartholomew of Edessa's *Confutatio Agareni* (PG 104:1381–1448), where the protagonist is a Nestorian monk called Pachura, who assimilates Bahira to the figure of Waraqa b. Naufal, a scriptural expert and Kadigia's cousin, who reassures her when she was shaken by her husband's epileptic fits. The name Sergius appears in Peter Alfonsi and in *Risālat Al-Kīndi* (see above, n. 31), while Peter the Venerable confuses the man with Nicolas, founder of the Nicolaism. See *Liber Nicholay* in Paris, Bibliothèque nationale de France, MS lat. 14503 (now to be read in the Yolles–Weiss collection) and Pisa, Biblioteca del Seminario, MS 50.

[48] Paris, Bibliothèque nationale de France, MSS lat. 8501A and lat. 11332. For an edition, see Robert B.C. Huygens, "Otia de Machomete. Gedicht von Walter von Compiègne," *Sacris Erudiri* 8 (1956), 287–328. Previous editions include: Édélestand du Méril, *Poésies populaires latines du Moyen Âge* (Paris, 1847), pp. 369–415 (based on the first Paris manuscript) and Hans Prutz, "Über des Gautier von Compiègne *Otia de Machomete*. Ein Beitrag zur Geschichte der Mohammedfabeln im Mittelalter und zur Kulturgeschichte der Kreuzzüge," *Münchener Sitzungsberichte* (1903), pp. 65–115 (from the second Paris manuscript).

Reginensis 620,[49] which gave rise to a new and final edition of the text by Huygens in 1977,[50] lastly reproduced, with corrections, by Yolles and Weiss in 2018.[51]

After explaining that these *Otia* are not in fact frivolous because they are based on reliable sources, Walter reports that Muhammad was an Idumean with Christian education, a servant of a rich nobleman and a successful merchant. A Christian hermit predicts his demonic delusions and subsequent subversion of law, faith, family, and social structures. After a meditation on the inscrutability of history, the poem reports that when Muhammad's master dies he becomes a servant of the widow, who after asking him for advice is told of the disadvantages of marrying nobles or in fact any other man, at the end of which Muhammad proposes himself as her new husband. The woman discusses the proposal with the nobles, one of whom exposes unexpected arguments against class disparity based on the interpretation of Genesis.[52] A sumptuous wedding follows, but Muhammad is struck by an epileptic seizure, which he presents as the effect of Gabriel's angelic inspiration. Then he explains his vision as a new revelation meant to replace the Christian one. It imposes lighter rules, requires no baptism, and allows polygamy and polyandry, that is, a return to pre-biblical times.

The woman does not believe him, and Muhammad plots with the hermit to simulate a testimony, and the hermit agrees to support him as long as he does not subvert Christianity.[53] The new law is presented to the people with the expedient of the calf and with the discovery, carefully prepared, of milk and honey as a celestial sign. Faced with an attack by the Persians, Muhammad advises caution, but the young men want to fight and are consequently slaughtered.[54] Muhammad immediately implements the new law to repopulate the earth, dies soon afterwards, and is buried in the magic tomb suspended in Mecca.

The Transformation of the Magician into Mohammed

It is evident that Walter of Compiègne is carried away by narrative creativity even more than Embrico; he takes up the by then traditional themes to compose sketches

---

[49] Vatican City, Biblioteca Apostolica Vaticana, MS Reg. lat. 620 (saec. XII*ex.*, Ambert (Loiret), Monastery of Notre Dame), fols. 33r–48v; online reproduction: https://digi.vatlib.it/view/MSS_Reg.lat.620.

[50] *Le Roman de Mahomet*, ed. Lepage (see above, n. 5).

[51] See *Medieval Latin Lives of Muhammad*, ed. and trans. Yolles and Weiss, pp. 103–77.

[52] Qu'ran 16.71, as well as many biblical passages, seems very clear on the duty to leave social differences unchanged.

[53] González Muñoz, "La leyenda," p. 1095 underlines that some passages of the Qu'ran (16.103, 25.4-5 and 44.14) mention some Christians aknowledging Muhammad as a new prophet.

[54] This is a reference to the battle of Uhud, 21 March 625, in which Muhammed was indeed obliged to fight by his young followers and was defeated by the "pagans" of Mecca; see Alfred Guillaume, *The Life of Muhammad. A Translation of Isḥāq's Sīrat Rasūl Allāh* (Oxford, 1996), pp. 371–72.

and characters of amusing legibility. For example, after the death of his master, Muhammad, who was a learned Christian born in Idumea,[55] introduces himself to the widow in the guise of a wise man and gives her advice about her future husband, particularly that he should not be a young nobleman, because that would endanger her family inheritance; nor should he be an old man, because his physical incompatibilities with a young woman would be embarrassing (vv. 181–200):

> Sed iam de senibus tecum, puto, mente reuolues:
> ille uel ille senex est bonus, est sapiens;
> congruit ille mihi, bene me reget et sapienter
> omnia disponet; nubere quaero seni.
> Sed non hoc quaeras, quia non sibi conuenienter
> iunguntur iuuenis femina uirque senex.
> Illa calore uiget, nitida cute, corpore recto:
> pallidus, incuruus, sordidus ille tremit.
> Illa iuuentutis amplexus factaque quaerit.
> [*a pentameter is missing here*]
> Ille dolet, tussit, emungitur, excreat; illa
> sanior et iuuenis paene nihil patitur.
> Auditus, gustus, olfactus, uisio, tactus,
> integritas mentis in sene deficient;
> sed, nisi turbetur casu natura, iuuentus
> sensibus his sanis, laeta uigere solet.
> Cum sibi dissimiles ita sint iuuenesque senesque,
> cum sene quo pacto copula stet iuuenis?
> Non igitur iuueni, qualem praediximus ante,
> nec cuiquam uetulo conueniat domina.

But now you are thinking about old men, I imagine: 'This old man or the other, is good, wise; he is suited to me, and he will rule me well and administer everything wisely. I want to marry an old man!' But you should not desire this, since it is not suitable for a young woman and an old man to be joined in marriage. She possesses healthy coloring, glowing skin, an upright body; he trembles, is pale, hunched, dirty. She seeks the embraces and deeds of youth; … he has pains, coughs, wipes his nose, spits. She is healthier and young and has almost no complaints. An old man lacks hearing, taste, smell, vision, touch and soundness of mind, while, unless nature is disturbed by an accident, youth is usually happily endowed with healthy senses. And since the young and the old are so different from each other, how can a young woman and an old man

---

[55] As in Marcus of Toledo, *Alchoranus latinus, quem transtulit Marcus canonicus toletanus: Estudio y edición crítica*, ed. Nàdia Petrus Pons (Madrid, 2007), p. 4; Fernando González Muñoz, "Liber Nycholay. La leyenda de Mahoma y el cardinal Nicolas," *Al-Qanṭara* 25 (2004), 8–19, at p. 8, and others. Some comparative remarks about the highlighting of "Christian" features of Islam in the works about the first crusade are found in Armelle Leclercq, *Portraits croisés. L'image des Francs et des Musulmans dans les textes sur la Première Croisade. Chroniques latines et arabes, chansons de geste françaises des XIIe et XIIIe siècles* (Paris, 2010).

couple? Therefore, neither the young man of the sort I have already described nor just any miserable old man is appropriate for my lady (trans. Weiss, in Yolles and Weiss, p. 117).

In conclusion, Muhammad designs a character which matches himself perfectly as the ideal solution to the matrimonial problem. This is what happens every time Muhammad has to convince someone of the reliability of his theses – he resorts to well-articulated speeches, brief encounters conducted with taste and irony, refined biblical references,[56] historico-social frameworks, concrete arguments as well as economic and political strategies. When, persuaded by Muhammad, a nobleman tries to present the same arguments to his own community, the defense of the marriage candidate becomes in Walter's pen a praise of freedom and man's original equality, presented not as a subversion of social norms but as a fulfilment of biblical law. The epileptic fits, which frighten the wife to death, are described as moments of inscrutable communication with the supernatural, and the explanation is expressed with so much stylistic balance that it is likely to convince even the modern reader. Obviously, the episodes of the calf hidden by the Prophet to make it bellow miraculously and the finding of milk and honey in a plot of land where they had previously been buried are described as cheating, but overall Muhammad's character is not sketched in negative terms, but rather with a kind of amused sympathy (I would say, with the same involvement and affinity that we feel for the skilled trickster in Boccaccio's novellas). Moreover, when Muhammad advises the young Arabs not to engage in armed conflict against the Persians because the auspices are negative, fate proves him right and the young people's desire to fight leads to disaster.

In the wake of a light-hearted and even ironic inspiration that is perhaps influenced by the climate created in France by the elegiac comedies and later by the fabliaux, Walter leaves a great deal of room for "matrimonial" details, both when it comes to choosing Khadija's new husband and when he describes the new Qu'ranic law, which introduces a revolutionary innovation with respect to Christian conjugality, namely polygamy. In Walter's description this aspect of Islam also extends to female polygamy, or polyandry, in a dream of sexual liberation and gender equality that has nothing to do with the authentic Islam, but obviously derives, though disrespectfully, from Sura 4 of the Qu'ran, called "Women." Thus, in the *Otia*, women are granted up to ten husbands and men up to ten wives, while in Qu'ran 4.3 up to four are recommended and only for men. This dream had a strong influence on the image of Muhammad in

---

[56] For some preliminary suggestions about the biblical influence on the *Otia*, see Johannes Baptist Bauer, "Walter von Compiègne: Bibelverse in metrischer Schmiede," *Mittellateinisches Jahrbuch* 42 (2007), 397–99.

Boccaccio,[57] who like Luca from Pontevedra called him a "seducer" (*De casibus* IX.1),[58] and who transcribed in his Zibaldone, with some modifications, a biography drawn on Paolinus Venetus's *Chronologia magna* or *Historia satyrica*[59] that I would interpret as a sign of interest for the narrative character, completely outside religious contexts. This revolutionary sexual custom finds a pseudo-sociological explanation: Muhammad decides to implement mass polygamy and polyandry in order to restore the male population that was decimated by the war against the Persians, thus justifying it with demographic reasons that are presented through explicit agricultural metaphors (vv. 1011–1024):

> Ergo Deus uobis parcet, uestraeque puellae
> et pueri thalami foedere conuenient;
> taliter, ut denas sibi copulet unus, et una,
> si libeat, denos copulet ipsa sibi;
> nec tamen ille Deo mandante putetur adulter,
> nec reputetur ob hoc criminis illa rea:
> cultor enim terrae si multos seminet agros,
> messibus e multis horrea multa replet,
> sic et ager quando multis uersatur aratris,
> sic fuerat sterilis, fertilis efficitur.
> Sic gignet multos multis e matribus ille,
> illa uel ex uno semine concipiet.
> Nam si de tot erit natura frigidus unus,
> alter erit calidus et sobolem faciet.

> Therefore God will spare you, and your girls and boys will come together in the marriage bond thus: one man will couple with ten women, and one woman, if she wishes, will couple with ten men. And yet the man will not be considered an adulterer, since God commands it, nor will the woman be guilty of an offense: for if a farmer sows many fields, from his many harvests he fills many granaries, and if the field had been barren then, when it is turned over by many plows, it will thus be made fertile. Thus the man will engender many from many mothers, and the woman will conceive perhaps

---

[57] See Roberta Morosini, *Dante, il Profeta e il Libro. La leggenda del toro dalla "Commedia" a Filippino Lippi, tra sussurri di colomba ed echi di Bisanzio* (Roma, 2018); and Roberta Morosini, "Venere alla Mecca: Il viaggio nel Mediterraneo dei *Dialogi contra Iudaeos* di Pietro Alfonso dal *De regno Saracenorum* di Paolino Veneto al *De Mahumeth* di Boccaccio," in *Boccaccio Veneto. Settecento anni di incroci mediterranei a Venezia*. Atti del Convegno internazionale (Venezia, 20–22 giugno 2013), ed. Roberta Morosini and Luciano Formisano (Roma, 2015), pp. 155–89. While waiting for the forthcoming critical edition of the whole *Zibaldone* by Raul Mordenti, the text can be read in Roberta Morosini, "De Mahumeth propheta," *Studi Boccacciani* 40 (2012), 273–314.

[58] "Seductor ille cuius artes quam libentissime audissem novit Deus, et qualiter post prophete nomen assumptum legesque letiferas datas in suam luxuriam, deperisset"; see Giovanni Boccaccio, *De casibus virorum illustrium* (Milan, 1983), p. 748.

[59] This in its turn derives from Vincent of Beauvais.

from one seed. For if of so many men one should by nature be cold, another will be warm and will produce offspring, and thus, by God's will, no woman will remain without fruit, and no woman will fear being thrown on the pyre like a sterile tree (trans. Weiss, in Yolles and Weiss, pp. 171, 173).

Finally, it will be from this sexual freedom, which the poet calls Mechia ("adultery," from the Greek μοιχεία) that the city of devout pilgrimage, Mecca, will take its name.

Thus, in the *Otia* Muhammad absorbs the religious and prestidigitatory characteristics of Embrico's magician, who plays a far more marginal role and is even eventually subdued to the will of the astute Prophet thanks to a proper *suasoria* (vv. 579–596). The shifting of narrative functions, which in Genette's terms is a case of transvaluation of the hypotext,[60] is therefore the mechanism that allows the creation of the Muhammad character, but the stylistic tool through which this mechanism finds expression is the change of the poetic climate and the system of genres.

In fact, the *Otia* offer more opportunities than does Embrico's *Life* for observations on style and models. The general tone achieves the lightness that Embrico had also aimed at in vain, because it minimizes ideological conflict and downplays religious rhetoric. Fernando González Muñoz rightly underlines that Walter abandons the anti-hagiographic typology attributed by Van Acker and Tolan to Embrico, and explains this new direction by the changed conditions of the period following the translation of Arabic texts and by the new humanistic culture that dominated the twelfth century, or, as the final verse suggests, by a softer attitude toward Islam after the defeat of Conrad III and Louis VII in the second crusade, around 1150–1155: "Sic igitur Machomem divo venerantur honore, | Et venerabuntur dum deus ista sinet" (vv. 1075–1076) – "Thus they venerate Muhammad with divine honor, and they will continue to venerate him as long as God will allow it" (trans. Weiss, in Yolles and Weiss, p. 175). Yet, this date is certainly later than the composition of the *Otia*, and in my opinion the change of mood is due not so much to historical as to cultural and specifically literary reasons. Indeed, the author's insistence on marginal sexual themes (like the love between an old man and a young woman), the complacency to parodic sketches like the "holy face" that the magician manages to put on in public as well as the ability to reduce theological problems to virtuosic displays of learned examples about non-trivial themes could be related to the influence of the poetic schools of the Loire and the climate of the elegiac comedies (see below).

---

[60] See Gérard Genette, *Palimpsestes: La littérature au second degré* (Paris, 1982), p. 183: the aim is to accentuate or mitigate some traits of the characters, to operate "recentrages axiologiques" (diegetic modifications). Genette also calls it "revalorisation" on p. 190.

Medieval Intertexts

This point of view seems to be confirmed by a first, partial sample analysis of Walter's poetic models: the most frequent intertexts in the *Otia* are almost never hagiographic poems (except maybe Hrotsvitha[61]), nor are they late antique Christian poetry. Rather, we find a few borrowings from Virgil and Ovid,[62] from Carolingian poetry (especially Theodulf),[63] and above all, for whole scenes, from the poets of the circle of Angers. For instance, the epistle of Marbod of Rennes to Countess Ermengarda (daughter of Fulco Richinus and wife of Aladus, known as Fergent, Duke of Burgundy)[64] is imitated twice in two verses of the speech to the widow (vv. 137–146):

> Postquam post domini decessum transiit annus,
> disponit iuuenis nubere iam domina
> secretoque uocans Machometem tempore dicit:
> "Sum iuuenis, sexu femina, res fragilis;[65]
> possideo *seruos, ancillas, praedia, uillas*;[66]
> sunt castella mihi, sunt etiam proceres;
> sum uiduata uiro, natis et utroque parente:
> ignoro prorsus qualiter ista regam.
> Ergo tu, qui *consilio callere* probaris,[67]

---

[61] Cf. v. 37: "conversans solus inter montana rogansque" with Hrotswitha, *Maria* 163: "angelus apparens inter montana refulgens" and Walter of Châtillon, *Alexandreis* 2.265: "Hec pocior ducibus inter montana iugosis"; v. 411: "flatuque resumpto solo" is found in Hrotswitha, *Agnes* 305.

[62] Many classical comparisons are listed in Ratkowitsch, "Das Grab des Propheten" (Appendix). I would add the following: v. 201: "Ut vulgare loquar" finds a comparison only in Statius, *Sylvae* 5.3.214: "non vulgare loqui" (compare later Aegidius of Paris, *Karolinus* 2.214: "iuxta vulgare loquamur"); and v. 287: "quemque ligatum" can be compared with Statius, *Theb.* 10.280: "quemque ligatus"; Silius 7.105 is the only possible comparison for the clausula "inutile bello" (v. 989), which Walter repeats in v. 995; v. 1064: "membra sepulta iacent" can be found in epigraphic models such as Venantius Fortunatus, *Appendix* 8.2, *Anthologia Latina* 613.6, and *Carmina Salisburgensia* 5.6. For vv. 594–595 the opposition "modico de semine ... magna seges" remounts to Venantius's *Appendix* 28.2: "ut tibi sit modico semine magna seges"; finally, v. 963: "des modo consilium" can be compared with Ausonius, *Epigr.* 103.2: "da modo consilium."

[63] v. 766: "caelica verba sonent" is exactly the same in Theodulf, *Carmina* 47.47, which is also adopted in Bernard of Morlaix's *De contemptu mundi* 1.1022: "dicta prophetica verbaque coelica perficiuntur." Compare v. 948: "pagina sancta docet" with Theodulf 17.54: "signatur, docet hoc pagina sancta dei." Comapre v. 455: "scripta Dei digito" and v. 834: "que fertur digito scripta fuisse dei" with Alcuin, *Carmina* 69.70 (Biblical preface): "in tabulis sancto scripta dei digito." Some other coincidences are weaker. Suprising is v. 53: "intima cordis" which is only present in *Gesta Apollonii* 29.

[64] For Marbod's text, see PL 171:1659–1660 (English at: https://epistolae.ctl.columbia.edu/letter/240.html).

[65] See Marbod, *De tribus inimicis* 2.3: "femina, res fragilis," also found in Hildebert, *De sancto Vincentio* 304 and *Carmina miscellanea* 96.6; Petrus Pictor, *Carmina* 14.73; and Hugo Matisconensis, *Gesta militum* 9.245.

[66] See Marbod's letter to to Ermengarda, v. 29: "Seruos, ancillas, cum turribus, oppida, uillas."

praemeditare mihi quae facienda probes."

When the first year after his master's death had passed, Muhammad's young mistress was already planning to wed. And at a private moment she called Muhammad to her and said: "I am a young woman, a frail thing; I own slaves, maidservants, estates, villas, I have castles, and I even have nobles. I am a childless widow, and both my parents are dead. I am completely ignorant of the administration of all these assets. So since you have been proven to give clever advice, consider what you think that I should do (trans. Weiss, in Yolles and Weiss, p. 113).

A further parallel to Marbod, *Carmina* 1.28.4 is found in *Otia*, v. 500: "Thome palpandum prebuit ipse latus" which can be compared to Marbod's "palpandumque dedit latus, bibit atque comedit," concerning the same biblical scene from John 20.26–29.

Baldricus of Bourgueil, author of one of the most brilliant collections of poems of the twelfth century, is in his turn the model for the wedding scene; compare *Otia*, v. 760: "pransores, cytharas cinbala sistra liras" with Baldricus's famous description of Countess Adele's bedchamber: "quae sibi dextra sedet quasi cimbala percutiebat, | Tangebat citharas, organa, sistra, liras" (134.975–76).[68]

A closer examination also revealed some formulae typical of the elegiac comedy diffused in twelfth-century France,[69] here used to create a lighter and more ironic tone in the narrative. A few esamples will suffice: the expression "quemque silere iubet" in *Otia*, v. 784, is the same as *De tribus puellis*, v. 88 et alibi;[70] the form "prescissem" in v. 1006, which can be compared to "praescisse" of Terentius, *Andria* 239, can be found only in Embrico, *Vita* 41 ("prescisset"), *De nuntio sagaci* 208,[71] *Ysengrimus* 1.995,[72] and Johannes de Hauvilla, *Architrenius* 6.342.[73] In the same group can also be placed the ps. Ovidian *De vetula* (mid-thirteenth century),[74] which adopts from Walter the opposition "frigidus/calidus" in a sexual sense: see *Otia*, vv. 1023–1024 and *De vetula* 2.36, (together with Petrus de Eboli, *De baneis puteolanis* 18.12 and *Carmina Burana*, amatoria 60.3.1 and 4.) as well as *Otia*, v. 835: "deferbuit ira" which can be compared with *De vetula* 1.576: "defervesceret ira."

---

[67] See Marbod's letter to Ermengarda, v. 18: "Pollens eloquio, callida consilio."

[68] Baudri de Bourgueil, *Poèmes*, 2 vols., ed. and trans. Jean-Yves Tilliette (Paris, 1998–2002), 2:1–43, at p. 32.

[69] See *Commedie latine del XII e XIII secolo*, 6 vols. (Genova, 1976–1998).

[70] *De tribus puellis*, ed. Stefano Pittaluga, in *Commedie latine* 1:279–333, at p. 312.

[71] *De nuntio sagaci*, ed. Gabriella Rossetti, in *Commedie latine* 2:11–125, at p. 100.

[72] *Ysengrimus*, ed. and trans. Mann, p. 256.

[73] Johannes de Hauvilla, *Architrenius*, ed. Paul Gerhard Schmidt (Munich, 1974), p. 226.

[74] *Pseudo Ovidius "De vetula,"* ed. Paul Klopsch (Leiden – Köln, 1967), where Ovid is presented as a philosopher who discovers the Christian truth.

As Fortleben, possible imitations are noticed in Nigel Wireker (d. ca. 1200),[75] Alexander Neckham (1157–1217),[76] the *Ysengrimus* (1148–1149), and Bernard or Morlaix.[77] What is more, beyond the poetic formulae shared with the "circle of the Loire" (in the wider sense of the label), many connections with previous poems or later imitators frequently lead to authors and texts from the Breton and Norman (*lato sensu*) area: Peter Riga, Anonymous of Jumièges, William of Armorica, Henry of Avranches, Bernard of Morlaix, Stephen of Rouen, and authors possibly related to that area such as Alexander Neckham, Aegidius of Paris, Nigel Wireker, and others. Among these, the biblical versification of Peter Riga, the *Aurora*,[78] is one of the most widespread poems of the entire Middle Ages, which, according to our survey, draws extensively on Walter's text. This intruiguing relationship will be examined in depth in further investgations. At present, only a few examples will be presented:

- v. 78: "permissuque Dei" cf. Riga, *Liber Iob* 209: "Dei permissu."
- v. 112: "cuius lingebat ulcera lingua canum" cf. Riga, *Euang.* 2062: "cuius curabat uulnera lingua canum."
- v. 378: "quisque fidelis homo" cf. Riga, *Num.* 338: "quisque fidelis homo."
- v. 455: "scripta Dei digito" cf. Riga, *Ex.* 1170: "scripta Dei digito" (beginning of line), also Henry of Avranches, *Franc.* 1.1.244.
- v. 747: "longinquas igitur abiit doctrina per orbes" cf. Riga, *Euang.* 2101: "longinquas abiit huius doctrina per urbes."
- v. 792: "ad astra uolant" cf. Riga, *Ex.* 674: "ad astra uolant."
- v. 820: "gustant." This verb is only employed in Hildeber, Peter Riga, and Matthew of Vendôme.
- v. 829: "flesse" is found only in Riga, *I Reg.* 575, Baldricus, and Abaelard.
- v. 847: "plebs et proceres" cf. Riga, *Hester* 143 (also Stephen of Ripon and Geoffrey of Vinsauf, both "Normans").

---

[75] For example, v. 528: "dum novus ordo fuit": "novus ordo" is found in poetry only in Nigel Wireker, *Speculum stultorum* 889, 2385, and 3198; v. 825: "quanta dulcedine mundum" can be compared with Nigel Wireker, *Passio Laurentii* 1842 (and ps. Ovid, *De vetula* 1.46); v. 837: "tanto clamore replevit" can be read in Nigel's *Passio Laurentii* 2284: "moriens clamore replevit" and again ps. Ovid, *De vetula* 1.186: "clamore repleverit aures."

[76] The clausula of v. 430: "taliter alloquitur" is found only in Alexander Neckham, *Aesopus* 31.4, and William of Apulia, *Gesta Roberti Wiscardi* 1.351. The clausula of v. 910: "subdita colla iugo" is found only in Paulinus of Nola, *Carmina* 25.4: "et moderare levi subdita colla iugo" and Alexander Neckam, *Vita monachorum* 458: "quemque premat duro subdita colla iugo."

[77] Cf. v. 487: "homo deus idem" with Bernard of Cluny, *De Trinitate* 842: "est et natus homo deus idem virgine matre"; and v. 428: "defervuit ira" is comparable with Bernard, *Liber Regum* 263: "deferveat ira," *Quid suum virtutis* 415: "regis defervere feceris iram," and ps. Ovid, *De vetula* 1.576: "quin mox sua defervesceret ira."

[78] See Paul Beichner, *Aurora: Petri Rigae Biblia Versificata: A Verse Commentary on the Bible*, 2 vols. (Notre Dame, 1965).

v. 879: "ab ore sonabat" cf. Martialis, *Epigrammata* 8.50.14 and Riga, *Euang.* 2506: "ab ore sonat" (in addition to *Rapularius* 1.338).

v. 949: "peccauerunt grauiter" cf. Riga, *Euang.* 2541: "grauiter peccasse" (the same also in Guillelmus Apulus, *Gesta* 1.215).

v. 962: "cum pueris sedeas" cf. Riga, *Macc.* 50: "cum pueris sedit."

v. 1008: "destruet ira Dei" cf. Riga, *III Reg.* 280: "destruet ira Dei" (later also Quilichinus, *Alex.* 450).

Also influenced by the *Otia* is the so-called Anonymous of Jumièges, a versification of the *Dialogues* of Gregory the Great,[79] which is dated to the thirteenth century because of an allegedly autograph thirteenth-century manuscript; however, the close parallels of the Anonymous with the *Otia* not only in the poetic "langue," but also in the detail of the "parole," compel us to reconsider the authorship issues, or at least to explain the connection between the two works. The following examples will suffice for the time being:

v. 40: "carne retentus humo" cf. Anon. 3.1024: "qui carne retentus" and 4.1243: "adhuc in carne retentus."

v. 335: "conuenientem" in clausula is found only in Hrotsvitha, *Passio Dionysii* 171; Ruodlieb 10.128; and Anon. 2.153.

v. 375: "apostolus ille" cf. Anon. 2.665, 3.1268: "apostolus idem"; Anon. 2.649, 4.237, 4.1682: "apostolus inquit"; and Anon 3.1283: "apostolus ipse" (with precedents in Arator and Florus).

v. 381: "atque fidelis" in clausula cf. Anon. 4.321 (and Bernard of Morlaix, *De contemptu mundi* 1.422, and William the Breton, *Philippide* 2.513).

v. 451: "per eundem" in clausula only in Anon. 3.1779, 4.34, 4.1963.

v. 501: "cernentibus illis" in clausula only Anon. 4.366 after Victor, *Vita Domini* 75 and Arator, *De actibus apostolorum* 1.22.

v. 811: "prece finita" in Ovid, *Met.* 1.548, and only three authors, among them Anon.

As is seen in these examples, the issue here is not so much a direct imitation (which nonetheless is evident for Peter Riga), but the sharing of a common formulaic and stylistic heritage. A confirmation of this conclusion also comes from the "Norman" and Northern French provenance of many of Embrico's manuscripts which are linked to St. Amand, Clairmarais, Douai, and Anchin.

Stylistic Features of the Otia and Vernacular Versions

Both Embrico's and Walter's versifications share an underlying narrative structure, a fable with the same characters and a similar plot. Embrico's poem declares itself to be an edifying text for an individual reader, and is therefore informative and ideologically polemical refelecting a climate of religious anxiety; in contrast, Walter's composition

---

[79] See *I "Dialogi" di Gregorio Magno: Parafrasi in versi latini (sec. XIII)*, ed. Mauro Donnini (Roma, 1988).

appears to be a literary game that from the beginning plays on the Wortspiel *otia/negotia*, as it will then also do on the double meaning of the word *verum*, noun and conjunction. It confesses that it runs the risk of adding and omitting elements of the original version which slips further away with each verse: an abbot told him that a certain cleric bearing the antiphrastic and paradoxical name of Paganus had collected the stories of an Arab man who had converted to Catholicism. Thus, Walter's text becomes a rewrite four levels removed from the original.

Walter's real sources are difficult to reconstruct; he certainly read Embrico, because his version roughly follows Embrico's narrative structure and clearly imitates a couple of passages,[80] though not explicitly quoting him. In Walter's time, the compositions of Guibert of Nogent and Peter Alfonsi were in circulation, yet the *Otia* includes details, such as the discovery of the milk and honey, which are not found in these two writers but which will reappear, for example, in later narrations such as that in Book 23, chap. 39–67 of Vincent of Beauvais's *Speculum historiale*.[81] Thus, for Walter as for Embrico further sources beyond Guibert and Alfonsi have to be conjectured.

Even in its light-heartedness, Walter's poem does not shy away from moral comments and theological digressions. In fact, Walter seems a more accomplished poet than Embrico, in that he resorts to thematic meditations that demonstrate his mastery of both the techniques of amplification and of a real theological method. This is above all evident in the four long passages in which Walter discusses divine justice, the historical origin of slavery, the problem of repentance, and the married status, in the context of re-evocation of evangelical history. This cultural background is expounded with aplomb and nuance and inserted into a story that is continually supported by meta-narrative references. These include apostrophes to the reader (v. 123), the returning to the main theme after a digression (vv. 129–130), direct speech reported

---

[80] See *Otia*, v. 1000: "debilitas senum" (= v. 406 in Embrico) and v. 248: "succubuisse tibi" (= v. 646 in Embrico). See Guy Cambier, "Quand Gauthier de Compiègne composait les Otia de Machomete," *Latomus* 17 (1958), 533–55, now surpassed by González Muñoz, "La datación." A summary of the current scholarship on Walter's relationship with Peter Alfonsi is found in in Franz Hasenhütl, *Die Muhammad-Vita bei Petrus Alfonsi und bei Walter von Compiègne. Petrus Alfonsi and his "Dialogus". Background, Context, Reception*, ed. Carmen Cardelle de Hartmann and Philipp Roelli (Florence, 2014), pp. 93–110.

[81] In those same years another life of Muhammad, discovered by Bischoff in a Trier manuscript, is the one signed by a certain Adelphus, who claims to have obtained his information from a Greek man during a journey. According to this Greek, the Arabs worshipped as a god a *monstrum* called Muhammad, presented in the text as a shrewd man who wins credit and popularity thanks to the teachings of a learned heretic named Nestor and to his own ability to learn. But the differences are so great as to lead us to believe that the two authors have never read each other. In fact, in *Adelphus* he assassinates his master out of jealousy, and the companion who convinces the queen to marry him is therefore not the same one which Muhammad had instructed. The text is now to be read in *Medieval Latin Lives of Muhammad*, ed. and trans. Yolles and Weiss, pp. 179–213.

inside direct speech, new accounts of events already described, and internal references (v. 707: "que supra diximus aut que | sunt retegenda sua tempore sive loco" – "many more things that we have mentioned above or that must be revealed at the proper place or time"; v. 756: "dixit que supra ima me scripsisse recordor" – "He said those things I remember having written already above"; and v. 860: "que scio sepe suis me meminisse locis" – "since I know I have often mentioned them in the appropriate places"). This greater attention to narrative structure makes the *Otia* more similar to a romance, with all its apparatus of the fake manuscript or the more or less fake oral report, than an edifying versification. The presence of direct speeches that constitute more than half of the text brings us closer to the literary context of the elegiac comedy, with which it also shares an interest in sexual matters and the use of rhetorical devices such as drawing portraits of characters (old, young, holy) or including typical scenes (like weddings or seizure attacks). Similar aspects are also common, for example, in the vulgarization of hagiographic legends.[82]

A confirmation of the reception of the *Otia* as a narrative of wide appeal is seen in the vernacular reworking of Walter's text, the *Roman de Mahomet*, composed in 1258 by Alexandre du Pont in Laon and transmitted in Paris, Bibliothèque nationale de France, MS fr. 1553, fols. 367v–379r.[83] The *Roman* is 1997 octosyllabic verses long, and it represents an approximation of the contents of the *Otia*, including the story developed in the subsequent oral versions. While strongly suppressing the stylistic qualities and colour of the Latin text, it respects the purely narrative elements, with some slight amplifications: the poet defines his working method as follows (vv. 20–24):

> Li moignes lués en versefie:
> .I. livret en latin en fist,
> U Alixandres dou Pont prist
> La matere dont il fait
> Cest petit romanch et estrait.

> The monk then put it in verses,
> He made of it a Latin booklet
> from where Alexandre Du Pont took
> the matter with which he extracted
> and composed this little romance.

---

[82] See Françoise Laurent, *Plaire et édifier. Les récits hagiographiques composés en Angleterre aux XIIe et XIIIe siècles* (Paris, 1998), chap. 9: "Dramatisation du récit," pp. 347–404; and Monique Goullet, *Écriture et réécriture hagiographiques. Essai sur les réécritures de Vies de saints dans l'Occident latin médiéval (VIIIe–XIIIe s.)* (Turnhout, 2005), p. 190.

[83] See *Le Roman de Mahomet*, ed. Lepage.

This is a *romance*, then, which is the definition of a linguistic choice, and an *estrait*, which is the definition of a type of reworking. However, it is not an abbreviation in the absolute sense because, as Yvan Lepage observed when analyzing the poem, Du Pont adds a series of examples to the source,[84] and its paraphrase amplifies the original text in sixteen passages.

After Walter we have no real Latin biographies or narratives about Muhammad in verse, even though there are some unedited poems which still need to be examined.[85] Nevertheless, the information about the Prophet grows in Latin and in the Romance languages through works on more general arguments based on the fusion of different sources reworked during the Crusades. The most important of these works is the "historical" part of the Latin version of Al-Kindi.[86] The tradition is continued by Godfrey of Viterbo, chronicler at the Swabian court, in the *particula* 28 of the final draft of his *Pantheon*,[87] Jacques of Vitry in the *Historia Hierosolymitana*,[88] and Vincent of Beauvais.[89] A manuscript of Santa Maria de Uncastillo from the same period contains another life of Muhammad, which the editor Vitalino Valcárcel dates to the thirteenth century without giving specific reasons[90] and in which miraculous elements absent in the other texts prevail.

---

[84] For example, the episods of the knight and the squire, vv. 227–284, and the legend of the three candles and the magic lamp (1916–1951).

[85] Some other poetical texts referring to Muhammad are quoted in Hans Walther, *Initia carminum ac versuum medii aevi posterioris Latinorum* (Göttingen, 1969), nos. 7770a (epitaph for Muhammad); 10636 ("Mamutii gesta, qui scire velit, legat ista"; see *Historische Vierteljahrschrift für Literaturwissenschaft und Geistesgeschichte* 29 (1955), 446, probably a excerpt from Embrico's poem); 15730a (another epitaph, transmitted in Pavia, Biblioteca Universitaria, MS 435, saec. XV, fol. 133r); and 20577 ("Viri tres sub arbore quadam quieuerunt," a dialogue between a Christian, a Jew, and a Saracen transmitted in Berlin, Deutsche Staatsbibliothek zu Berlin – Preussischer Kulturbesitz, MS germ. oct. 138, saec. XIII–XIV, fols. 26r–27v, published by Hans Walther, *Das Streitgedicht in der lateinischen Gedichten des Mittelalters* (Munich, 1920), pp. 227–29.

[86] *Recriptum christiani* § 38–43, to be read in the *Islamolatina* site from the edition of Fernando González Muñoz, *Exposición y refutación del Islam. La versión latina de las epístolas de al-Hasimi y al-Kindi* (Coruña, 2005). As it is known, these are two letters that would have been composed in the ninth century under the caliphate of al-Ma'mun (813–833) by Al-Hasimi and Al-Kindi to defend Islam and Christianity respectively.

[87] Now republished in Di Cesare, *Pseudo-Historical Image*, pp. 173–80, no. 22.

[88] Di Cesare, *Pseudo-Historical Image*, pp. 220–35, no. 31.

[89] Di Cesare, *Pseudo-Historical Image*, pp. 316–36, no. 40.

[90] Vitalino Valcárcel, "La 'Vita Mahometi' del códice 10 de Uncastillo (s. XIII): Estudio y edición," in *Actas III Congreso Hispánico de Latín medieval (Léon, 26–29 de septiembre de 2001)*, 2 vols., ed. Maurilio Pérez González (Léon, 2002), 1:211–45.

In his life of Saint Pelagius, Pope (555–561), Jacobus de Voragine also provides a long digression on Muhammad and Islam. Alain Boureau traces this back to Eulogius and in part to Peter Alfonsi,[91] from whose work the text clearly reproduces extensive extracts, even though some differences in the particulars are to be noted.[92] The awareness of a historical tradition that is by now perceptible surfaces decidedly in both Jacobus de Voragine and Vincent of Beauvais. The latter is the first to name his genuine sources, which, he writes, are Al-Kindi and a certain *Libellus in partibus transmarinis de Machometi fallaciis*,[93] where the name of Corazania (Korashan) also makes it seems likely that he had some knowledge of Hugh of Fleury's *Historia ecclesiastica*. Still, Vincent's mention of this *libellus* suggests that the legend of Muhammad developed gradually and prior to the earliest texts now known to us. This source, independent of Hispanic polemics but probably influenced by Byzantine historiography, is quite likely the basis of Embrico's account. It belongs to the vein of the legend that we have called the overseas tradition, spreading in Europe immediately after the first Crusade and deriving from the Latin translations of Byzantine tales.

Essentially, with Guibert of Nogent and the verse versions discussed above, a "Mahumeti fabula" is finally constructed that will continue to be the foundation of the late-medieval stories;[94] thus, tenth-century poetic hagiography, Arab tales such as those told by Peter Alfonsi, and eleventh- and twelfth-century short stories come together to form a relatively homogeneous narrative, which in the period of the Crusades is accompanied by more or less imaginary elements and subsequent rewriting of the basic episodes.

Yet, only versification, which especially in the "Norman" and Rheinland area reflects the pleasure for telling stories and the influence of both the satirical style and naturalistic and erotic lexicon in vogue in the twelfth century, allows the European imagination of the earlier Middle Ages to transform the Western literary Muhammad into a brilliant and lucky picaro and Islam into a republic of sexual liberation born to relieve the hardness of Christian morality. Later narratives, reworkings, and sequels, especially those in the vernacular langages, will not be unaware of these experiments

---

[91] See Alain Boureau, *Jacques de Voragine. La Legénde dorée* (Paris, 2004), pp. 1477–78.

[92] Other attestations of the legend of Muhammad are listed in González Muñoz, "Dos versiones tardías." Further sources are included in Di Cesare, *Pseudo-Historical Image*, pp. 63–70, no. 10.

[93] In *Speculum historiale* 40.2 Vincent cites a *Libellus disputationis cuiusdam Saraceni et cuiusdam Christiani de Arabia super lege Saracenorum et fide Christianorum inter se*, which coincides with the *Apologia* or *Risālat al-Kindi*, which probably has a connection to the Latin translation commissioned by Peter the Venerable (see above, n. 31).

[94] Among the texts that confirm this trend are the *Liber Nicholay*, composed in Rome or in the south of Italy around the second half of the thirteenth century, the Pisa *Vita Machometi* (see above, nn. 46–47), and the treaty of Pedro Pascual (late 13th century); see Tolan, *The Faces of Muhammad*, pp. 82–85.

or their sources, thus giving a boost to the diffusion of the "European" character of Muhammad in underground or mainstream theater dramas[95] and epics.[96] Such a process created a set of mythologems resulting in Voltaire's *Mahomet ou le fanatisme*, which was the subject of a discussion between no less than Napoleon and Goethe when they met in Erfurt on October 2, 1808. In modern times, the Hungarian proverb "Lebeg mint Mohammed koporsojá ég és föld között" – "It hovers between heaven and hearth like the tomb of Mohammed" recalls the early and still mysterious literary invention of Embrico from Mainz.

Abstract

The Latin verse lives of Mohammed appear suddenly between the eleventh and twelfth centuries, developing in a novelistic direction the scant information found in the prose biographies of the Prophet written between the eight and tenth centuries. The poems of Embrico of Mainz (saec. XI/XII) and Walter of Compiègne (saec. XII) go beyond the educational and apologetic needs raised by the crusader culture and show a special attention to the structure of the narrative. The literary climate of the twelfth century combines tenth-century poetic hagiography, the Arab tales of Peter Alfonsi, and eleventh-century novels to develop a relatively homogeneous narrative about Mohammed, which in the period of the Crusades is accompanied by more or less imaginary elements and subsequent rewriting of the main episodes in the story. Still, only versification, which reflects the influence of both the satirical style in vogue from the twelfth century onwards and its expressive naturalistic and erotic lexicon, allows the European literature of the earlier Middle Ages to transform the figure of Muhammad into a brilliant and lucky picaro, and Islam into an imaginary republic of sexual liberation.

Résumé

Les vies latines en vers de Mahomet font soudainement leur apparition entre le XIe et le XIIe siècle, élaborant de façon romanesque le peu d'information qu'on trouve dans les biographies en prose du Prophète, rédigées entre le VIIIe et le Xe siècle. Les poèmes hagiographiques d'Embrico de Mayence et de Gauthier de Compiègne font bien plus que seulement subvenir aux besoins éducatifs et apologétiques issus de la culture croisée et démontrent plutôt une attention particulière à la structure du récit. Le climat littéraire du XIIe siècle se conjugue alors

---

[95] For example, the *Vida y muerte del falso profeta Mahoma*, 1642 and many more; see Cándida Ferrero Hernández, "Mahoma como personaje teatral de una comedia prohibuida del siglo de oro, 'Vida y muerte del falso profeta Mahoma,'" in *Vitae Mahometi*, ed. Ferrero Hernández and de la Cruz Palma, pp. 237–54; and Tolan, *Faces of Muhammad*, passim.

[96] See Stefano Resconi, *Maometto-personaggio nel contesto. Forme della rappresentazione dell'Islam e del suo profeta in Dante e nella coeva letteratura italiana volgare*, online (DOI: https://doi.org/10.13130/2035-7362/3437).

à l'hagiographie en vers du XIIe siècle, aux contes arabes traduits par Pierre Alfonsi et aux romans et aux comédies élégiaques du XIIe siècle pour constituer un récit relativement homogène à propos de Mahomet, un récit qui, à l'époque des croisades, s'accompagne d'éléments plus ou moins imaginaires et de réécritures postérieures des épisodes principaux de la trame narrative. Pourtant, seule la versification, influencée à la fois par le style satirique en vogue à partir du XIIe siècle et par un lexique naturaliste et érotique, permet à la littérature européenne du haut Moyen Âge de transformer le Prophète en une figure picaresque, brillante et recevant les faveurs de la fortune, et l'Islam en une république imaginaire marquée par la libération sexuelle.

Francesco Stella
University of Siena
francesco.stella@unisi.it

Review Essay

Editions of Texts for Teaching Medieval Latin

TRISTAN MAJOR

Reading Medieval Latin with the Legend of Barlaam and Josaphat, ed. Donka D. Markus. Michigan Classical Commentaries. Ann Arbor: University of Michigan Press, 2018. Pp. xviii, 146.

Fifteen Medieval Latin Parodies, ed. Martha Bayless. Toronto Medieval Latin Texts 35. Toronto: Published for the Centre for Medieval Studies by the Pontifical Institute of Mediaeval Studies, 2018. Pp. vi, 122.

The Disputatio puerorum: *A Ninth-Century Monastic Instructional Text*, ed. Andrew Rabin and Liam Felsen. Toronto Medieval Latin Texts 34. Toronto: Published for the Centre for Medieval Studies by the Pontifical Institute of Mediaeval Studies, 2017. Pp. iv, 102.

The institutional divide between Classics and Medieval Studies has well-known ramifications for the teaching of medieval Latin. While medieval Latin often is allotted some space in a Classics program, it is all too often relegated to a single course. And certainly, there are important differences between the various forms of Latin written before 500 CE and after, though in many instances the difference between the Latin of Ennius and Virgil is probably greater than that between Virgil and Walter of Châtillon. Although some medieval Latin literature has been made available in student friendly editions, the kinds of resources available to students of canonical classical Latin authors in general do not exist for students of medieval Latin. Most students who eventually focus on medieval Latin literature must certainly struggle without access to the in-depth commentaries familiar to readers of Virgil, Horace, Cicero, etc.

1. *Reading Medieval Latin with the Legend of Barlaam and Josaphat*, ed. Markus

Donka D. Markus's student edition of the *Legend of Barlaam and Josaphat,* taken from Giovanni Paolo Maggioni's edition of the *Legenda aurea* (Florence, 2007), is a welcome endeavour. The book's strength falls squarely within its stated aim: to provide an accessible medieval Latin text for students who have completed their first year of Latin. Markus's commentary is extremely thorough and facilitates full understanding of the Latin text. The grammatical comments are occasionally accompanied with further contextualization of salient historical or comparative details.

The text is also well chosen. The *Legend of Barlaam and Josaphat* is of a suitable level for second-year Latin students. Its Latin is fairly easy, but it exhibits an adequate number of deviations from classical Latin grammar and spelling to showcase these differences. Markus provides a handy summary of medieval Latin grammar at the end of the volume, whose layout borrows much from Alison Goddard Elliott's grammatical introduction to K.P Harrington's *Medieval Latin* (Chicago, 1997). By following Markus's commentary and tracing the references to her grammar, students only familiar with classical Latin grammar will soon realize some of the commoner ways that medieval Latin differs from classical Latin (e.g. the use of the pronoun *se* when not referring to the subject of the main verb, greater use of pleonastic auxiliary verbs).

Markus's edition is, however, not without its own oddities. The Latin text, for example, appears twice; once without interruption and with the spelling as it appears in Maggioni's edition; and again, in smaller units broken up and followed by relevant commentary; this second version also gives the text according to conventions of classical spelling, with the altered words underlined. But the repetition seems like a waste of space that serves no practical purpose. In the fifty sections that make up the texts of the commentary, 169 words have been changed from their medieval to classical spellings (averaging only three words per section), not one of which would have caused much trouble for a second-year student of classical Latin. For example, the switch from *hystoriam* to *historiam*, *precepit* to *praecepit*, or *Vnicornis* to *Unicornis* certainly does not justify a second printing of the text in the commentary. Similarly, the short wordlists that appear after each section will only be of use to students without access to (or will for using) a dictionary. Some glosses, such as *diligens* as "diligent"; or *fides* as "faith, Christian faith (LL); trust (CL)" (p. 54), have little to no benefit, even for a beginning student. And despite the commentary's laudatory thoroughness, some of the information in it does seem too simple for the target readership.

In a similar vein, Markus's introduction strikes an odd note. Much of her interest is actually not on the Latin text but rather on the older, Eastern versions and their transformations across time and geographical region. A comparative study of this text is no doubt fascinating, but not exactly appropriate for the purposes of a student edition aimed to teach Latin. More focus on the text's own specific deviations, its historical contexts and ideological goals, its reception in the Middle Ages, and especially its language and rhetorical strategies would have been much more useful. The lengthy summary of the tale (pp. 22–31) is also of questionable value if the goal after all is for students to read the Latin itself. Besides these objections, the book provides an excellent model for future student editions of medieval literature, imitating the great student editions and commentaries of classical Latin and Greek literature. Markus's edition is a worthy effort that serves to teach and pique interest in the Latin literature of the Middle Ages.

2. Two Volumes of the Toronto Medieval Latin Texts Series

Similar to Markus's aims at presenting a text that would be suitable for teaching students medieval Latin, the TMLT series has a longstanding tradition of publishing affordable editions of medieval Latin literature that facilitate accessibility to medieval texts for both teaching and scholarship. Although the editions of this series tend to have little commentary and are aimed at more advanced students, they fulfil the important role of presenting unique manuscript witnesses that showcase actual medieval Latin language and orthography. For this reason, some of the editions in the series have rightly become standard editions and important contributions to scholarship outside of the classroom, remaining important tools for students of medieval Latin. In the two latest volumes of the series, Martha Bayless edits fifteen short parodies from various relevant manuscripts, and Andrew Rabin and Liam Felsen edit a medieval pedagogical text, the *Disputatio puerorum* from Vienna, Österreichische Nationalbibliothek, MS 458 (henceforth ÖNB 458).

2.1. *Fifteen Medieval Latin Parodies*, ed. Bayless

In *Fifteen Medieval Latin Parodies,* Bayless exhibits wide knowledge not only of the genre of medieval parody, but also the manuscript contexts in which these parodies are transmitted. The result is a compilation of different texts from different manuscripts that comes together in a compact edition useful for displaying the heterogeneity of medieval literature. With Bayless's edition in hand, it is difficult to uphold caricatures of pious medieval priests revering the Bible with utmost seriousness. Instead, students using this edition will be shown how complex (and fun) medieval literature can be. It should be stressed, however, that the texts selected all appear in manuscripts produced in the fifteenth and sixteenth centuries. While some of these fifteen parodies were evidently composed earlier, much more could be said of the very late dates of their manuscript contexts. In fact, by presenting a sample of parodies unified by their later manuscript dates, this edition could act nicely as an appendix to Bayless's *Parody in the Middle Ages: The Latin Tradition* (Ann Arbor, 1996).[1]

While most of the texts are entertaining and will work well in a classroom, I myself found some too tedious to be worthwhile. In particular, section 4, "Biblical Hijinks" is a collection of biblical characters who become associated with specific objects, actions or characteristics in a feast put on by Ab[b]atheos and his son Theos. This text may

---

[1] Reviewed Chrstopher J. McDonough in *The Journal of Medieval Latin* 8 (1998), 219–21.

have been a helpful mnemonic tool for its medieval readership but will be found somewhat boring for its modern readership, far less familiar with the numerous arcane biblical characters who appear. While this text will have the benefit of building unusual vocabulary, I suspect this section will frequently be passed over in the classroom. Likewise, two nonsense-centos (sections 5–6) could be useful for displaying unfamiliar types of medieval humour. It might be cautioned, however, that modern students, with very different senses of humour, might have a difficult time getting the joke or, worse, appreciating the point of reading close to ten pages of jumbled up biblical passages.[2] On the contrary, section 3, "A Philosophers' Debate," is only 9 lines (56 words) of fairly simple Latin. To make it more worthwhile, this parody could have been accompanied by other relevant texts from the same manuscript. With these quibbles aside, the edition will have much value as an introduction to a marginalized, and little known aspect of Latin literature.

Finally, the presentation of Bayless's edition is for the most part of excellent quality. She provides copious notes to the various biblical allusions parodied and the text is mostly free from error.[3] When the manuscripts do not follow usual grammatical conventions, she is sure to note so. My own preference would have been to emend in some of these instances. The simple emendation of *illi* to *illo* at 2.5 would correct the grammar by turning the phrase into an ablative absolute. 4.152–53 reads "Volo omnino ut adhuc diem nuptiarum coniunctis et leti celebrate festum," but the sentence could make sense if emended to: "Volo omnino ut adhuc diem nuptiarum coniuncti et leti celebretis festum" – "I utterly desire that you, married and joyful, continue to celebrate the festive day of the wedding."[4] On the contrary, when the scribe leaves out a finite verb at 4.211–13, the text cannot be rescued by reasonable editorial emendation and Bayless does right to leave it stand with a note. A few instances require emendation that have not been noted by Bayless. The word *aquas* at 4.59 should read *aqua*. Lines 6.16–17, "Venit *enim malibus* princeps ... et uni eorum dedit alapam," almost certainly should be emended to 'Venit *animalibus* [or *enim animalibus*] princeps ...," which would then correspond loosely to Revelation 15.7: "Et unum de quatuor animalibus dedit septem angelis septem phialas aureas." Occasionally, Bayless's punctuation could also be improved. Examples include: the comma after *Supplicamus* at 1.9, which should be removed; the colon after *turbine* at 2.3, which should be removed or replaced with a comma; the period ending a dependent clause at 5.79, which should be a comma. The phrase at 5.80 erroneously

---

[2] With that said, these texts are reminiscent of certain playful sections of Joyce's *Ulysses* or *Finnegans Wake*, which could be cleverly exploited by a student of comparative literature.

[3] For example, "Mt 12:2" should read "Mt. 12:27" (p. 59, n. 28.2), and "*Parody*, 97–91" should read "*Parody*, 87–91" (p. 76).

[4] Retaining the imperative *celebrate* is also possible, though straying from the rules of classical Latin.

closes a quotation early (it closes properly at 5.82). And the clause "collo capitique pendentibus et pedibus sursum se erigentibus" at 7.13.6–7 is an ablative absolute that begins a new sentence and should be punctuated accordingly (in the edition, it follows immediately the previous sentence with no punctuation). Less seriously, an accompanying note, clarifying "Ipse" as "ipsae", would have been helpful.

2.2. *The* Disputatio puerorum, *ed. Rabin and Felsen*

From the same series, the *Disputatio puerorum* is a colloquy outlining the important aspects of scientific and theological knowledge produced from a Christian Carolingian worldview. The text, for this reason, is very well chosen since it presents an introduction to both straightforward medieval Latin language and the foundations of Carolingian (perhaps monastic) intellectual discourse. As the editors state, the text was first edited by Frobenius Forster in 1777 who attributed it to Alcuin; J.P. Migne then used Forster's edition for his works of Alcuin in the *Patrologia Latina* (vol. 101). Rabin and Felsen convincingly argue that this attribution should be questioned and likely abandoned (elsewhere they state that it is "erroneous" [p. 2]). They argue that it is never attributed to Alcuin in the manuscripts, does not have a preface typical of Alcuin's genuine works, and (I think most convincingly) makes statements on reading a work by Alcuin that would not be appropriate if Alcuin was the author.

Rabin and Felsen also attempt to supersede the editions of Forster and Migne by making forays into textual comparison and the establishment of a stemma. Based on collation of four manuscripts, they argue that ÖNB 458 (**A**) "appears to approximate most closely" an original manuscript of the textual tradition [a], "the *Urtext*." This is a problematic claim. Just because **A** takes the highest position on the stemma does not necessarily mean that it is the most direct witness to [a], but only that it is a representative of the textual descendants that differ from those of [b]. An unknown number of manuscripts may separate **A** from [a], and **C** may be a very faithful witness to [b], which may in turn be a faithful witness to [a]. In fact, an examination of the edition in Felsen's doctoral dissertation shows both **B** and **C** to have better readings than **A** (see below). Unfortunately, in the current edition, it is impossible for the reader to assess the veracity of the arguments presented, since a full list of variants is not given and not all manuscripts (or indirect witnesses) have been consulted.[5] Only four variants are given in the introduction and only four others are noted in the apparatus, but solely for the purpose of giving a better reading when the base text

---

[5] Liam Felsen, "*Disputatio puerorum*: Analysis and Critical Edition," PhD diss. (University of Oregon, 2004), more thoroughly collates the manuscripts in the apparatus, provides more examples of shared readings among the manuscripts to determine their relationships, and is much more cautious with the establishment of the stemma. Inexplicably, the edition in Felsen's dissertation handles punctuation better and does not introduce errors by emending incorrectly. In my opinion, it remains the best edition of the text.

needs emendation (205, 473–75, 1689–90, 2061); sigla **E** and **F** never appear in the apparatus. Finally, Munich, Bayerische Staatsbibliothek, clm 6385, a witness to the *Disputatio puerorum*, whose images are freely accessible online, is not collated (or even mentioned).

Despite this discussion on the conjectural origins of the manuscripts, the editors are not much concerned with constructing a text that resembles the *Urtext*, and their edition is for the most part a fairly faithful transcription of ÖNB 458. The text produced, however, is plagued with serious problems stemming from general errors, unclear or erroneous punctuation, erroneous editorial emendations or failure to emend when necessary, and loose, inconsistent editorial principles including the content of the footnotes. The result is a very sloppy edition that will not well serve either students or scholars.

General errors can be found throughout the edition, ranging from minor to serious. For only a few examples, the phrase "'pro ualde celsus'" should read "pro 'ualde certus'" (507); "passiont" should read "passiones ut" (584); eight lines of the manuscript are missing (675); "ἠώς" should read "ἠώς" (920n); "legitu" should read "legitur" (923n); the phrase "'ab inuocatione, renouatur enim semper'" should read "'ab inuocatione'; renouatur enim semper" (1084–85); the phrase "υἱὸς Nauê" should appear entirely in Greek font as "υἱὸς Ναυῆ" (1171n); and "above" should read "below" (1587–99n).

Such errors are unfortunate, but per se they do not necessarily determine the quality of a work, especially one meant ultimately for teaching Latin. The punctuation of such an edition, on the contrary, which often differs greatly from that of the manuscript, is one of the fundamental tasks for any editor aiming to make his or her text comprehensible to students of medieval Latin. In this edition, Rabin and Felsen never state their principles for punctuating; they are not always consistent; and their punctuation choices sometimes obscure the meaning of the text, occasionally introducing grammatical solecisms. Since punctuation choices can be matters of subjective preference, I refrain from listing all the problems I myself found and give the most egregious cases. There are a number of examples where the editors have placed a full stop separating a dependent clause from the main clause. For example, the very first *Responsio* is punctuated thus: "quoniam ... nec possumus nec audemus altius initium nostrae protrahere disputationis. Si tibi uidetur incipiamus ..." (11–13). The period between *disputationis* and *Si* should be replaced by a comma or semicolon to connect the dependent clause set up by *quoniam* with the independent clause of the main verb, *incipiamus*. At 869–70 the punctuation also makes the Latin nonsensical. The *ne*-clause goes with the previous clause and should not start the sentence. The words *et ut*, as in Isidore, should also likely be added by editorial emendation before the word *consolarentur* for the sentence to make sense. At 1870, the period before *Quia* should be a comma since *quia* sets up a clause dependent on the previous sentence; likewise, at 2048 the period before *Seu* should be a comma, since the clause set up by *seu* is dependent on the previous sentence. And at 2225 the period before *Et* should probably be a comma since the subjunctive verb that follows is better understood as falling within the *ut*-clause of the previous sentence than as a jussive. Alongside these examples also appears misleading and inexplicable puntuation. The comma between *faenum* and *species* in line 658 should be removed as it breaks up the noun clause "plaustri portantis faenum species": *faenum* is the object of *portantis*, which modifies *plaustri*, which is a genitive modifying *species*. At 515–16, the punctuation is very confusing and, if a note is not to be provided, could be clarified as: "ea, quae commutabilia, facta sunt quasi non sint." Similarly, at 912 clearer punctuation would have a comma after *praenuntios* to show that it is in apposition to *gallos* and not *gallicinium*. The punctuation of section V.19 (1215–19) does not help the reader make sense of an already difficult paragraph. The opening accusative noun *occultationem* finds its resolution with the participle *denuntians*. But this is confused by the punctuation of the phrase as "diuersitatem uitae mala, quae eis uentura essent, denuntians." The word *mala*, as in the source, is actually in the nominative case and belongs in the relative clause; the comma should precede it to avoid confusing it as a second object of *denuntians*. And at 1844 the punctuation is particularly vexed: "quod ut sit ex fructibus terrae sanctificatum, et fit sacramentum" would be better punctuated as "quod, ut sit ex fructibus terrae, sanctificatum et fit sacramentum."[6] In ten instances, question marks should be replaced by periods since the sentences are not questions (21, 379, 392, 633, 711, 721, 1214, 1359, 1607, 1798).

More so than punctuation, editors must sometimes make difficult decisions to change the readings of a manuscript, especially when the manuscript reading seems to be erroneous. Clear editorial principles should be stated and rigorously followed. The present edition gives two statements of editorial principles. The first is in the general preface to the series which states that the "base manuscript is emended only to restore sense" and that "manuscript orthography and syntax are carefully preserved" (p. v); the second is by the editors themselves, who state that "minor emendations following the sources ... have been incorporated to clarify the text for student readers"; and that they have "reproduced the spellings which appear in MS A without regularization" (p. 14). The editors, however, make emendations that do not appear in the source and thereby either emend unnecessarily or, worse, introduce errors into the text; they also fail to emend when the manuscript does not make sense.

At 19 the very rare word *adseruisti* does not make sense and should be emended to something like *adseuerauisti*. At 54 *conceditur* makes no sense and should be emended to *conditur*. At 68–69, the phrase "ne hoc solum ei consessit quod..." should be emended to "non solum ei consessit quod..." (which then parallels "sed etiam quod"

---

[6] See also Lindsay's punctuation (*Etym*. 6.19.38).

in line 70). This emendation is also the reading in **C** (see Felsen, "Disputatio puerorum," p. 66). At 145 since "honor" is masculine, "Quae" should be emended accordingly. At 313 "uiuendum" should be emended to "uidendum." At 345 "noti" is nonsensical and should be emended to "non," as understood in the translation provided. At 772 "mesonictios" should be emended to "mesonictius," or at the very least explained as taking a Greek nominative form. At 1039 "dicitur" should be emended to the subjunctive "dicatur." Although at 1042 the editors note "variations" in the ultimate source (Virgil, *Georg.* 1.340), the reading "hiemps" is not one of these; it should be emended to the genitive "hiemis" for the verse to make any sense. At 1115 "annis" should be emended to "annus." At 1131 the phrase "haec ita se aguntur" is problematic and should be emended. I suggest that "se aguntur" read "sequuntur." At 1348 "Ecclesiastes" should read "Ecclesiasticus" (as in **C**; see Felsen, "Disputatio puerorum," p. 138). At 1405 "calcem" should be emended to "ad calcem" (as in **B** and **C**; see Felsen, "Disputatio puerorum," p. 141). At 1592 the dependent *si*-clause with a subjunctive demands that the independent clause also be in the subjunctive; "erat" should therefore be emended to "esset," which is how the verb appears when the sentence is repeated at lines 1800–2. Finally, at 2357 "ut ne" should probably be emended to "et ne," which better reflects the pericope, "et ne nos inducas in temptationem" (Mt 6.13).

Whereas the decision to not emend may reflect an editorial preference to retain the manuscript reading, it is particularly bad practice to emend unnecessarily or incorrectly. This edition does both. At 193–94 the emendation of the manuscript reading "uentris oboedientia" to "uentribus oboedientia" is not necessary since "oboedientia" often takes a genitive (unlike with English). The two lines are also an unrecognized quote from the opening of Sallust, *De coniuratione Catilinae* 1.1, who happens to use the dative singular: "uentri oboedientia." At 206 the editors recognize the need to emend "quae," but their suggestion of "quia" misses the mark; "qui" would be better as a relative pronoun clarifying earlier "quidam." At 576–77 the emendation of "eandemque" to "eiusdemque" makes little sense, even if this is the suggestion in the PL. The word should be emended to the adverb (with enclitic) "eademque." At 674 the abbreviation *ī* (which is how it appears in the manuscript) means 1000 (see Cappelli, *Dizionario delle abbreviazioni* [Milan, 2001], p. 414); the decision to emend *ī* and *īī* to *M* and *MM* is therefore not needed, although a note to clarify the matter would have been appropriate. The apparatus also contains an error here: the manuscript does not read *IDCLCVI* but gives the correct number as *ĪDCLVI*. At 829–30 the editors claim that they have emended these lines based on Isidore, *Etym.* 5.30.11, but inexplicably they follow the edition in the PL:216–17, instead of that in Lindsay, which is much closer to ÖNB, 458. Moreover, even if Migne is preferred, the emendation of *his* to *iis* is not needed and the word *institute* should read *instituti*. At 1093 the emendation of "ea" to "eum" is an error; it should be emended to "eam" since "aera" is feminine. At 1569 and 1765 the conjectural addition "rerum" to clarify "gestarum" is not necessary since *gesta* very frequently functions as a substantive noun. At 2142 emendation of the manuscript reading "propriae diuinitatis" is needed, but not as the editors would have it, to the dative "diuinitati," which is difficult to make sense of. Emendation to "propia diuinitate," as suggested in the PL, makes far better sense.

Despite the editorial principles stated in the general preface and the introduction, a number of emendations are unnecessary. At 1583 the emendation of "promiserat" to "promiserit" (future perfect) is based on Isidore, *Etym.* 6.2.41, but it is not needed since the pluperfect also makes sense. At 1629 emendation of "religatus" to "relegatus" is not needed since "religatus" is a valid medieval variant (see DMLBS, s.v "relegare"). At 1676 emendation of "persteterunt" to "perstiterunt" is not needed since "persteterunt" appears in DMLBS (although there marked by *sic*). At 140 and 349 the emendations of "deuortia" to "diuortia" and "tundere" to "tondere" are not needed to keep the sense of the Latin (they both appear as orthographical variants in DMLBS) and the manuscript spelling should be retained. Emending them is also not consistent with editorial practice elsewhere (see 510: "*tinet*: viz. tenet" and 2082: "postolabant"). Likewise, at 880 emendation from "eodem" to "eadem" is sound, but breaks editorial principles, since retaining "eodem" as an adverb is possible and does not destroy the sense of the passage. And at 1842 the emendation of "quia" to "quod" (the relative pronoun) may be sound, but it is not necessary since the manuscript reading is still comprehensible. A less serious editorial matter is the handling of *ae*, *oe* and its collapsed form *e*, for which the editors are not consistent. For example, if the editors are expanding *e* to *ae* (as they do at 356 where *leuaque* is emended to *laeuaque*), at 340 and 345, the words *cedendo* and *cessi* should read *caedendo* and *caessi*, especially to avoid confusion with the verb *cedere*. At the very least, a note should be provided such as the one at 914 which indicates an *e* should be read as *ae*.

While much of the information in the footnotes is helpful and informative, there remain problems. At 1348 the note is incorrect; the *Liber Sapientiae* is not Ecclesiasticus or Sirach, but the "Book of Wisdom" or "Wisdom of Solomon"; and in the note for 1963–2043, the claim that Bruno of Würzburg is using the *Disputatio* as his "primary source" seems very unlikely. Both are probably using a shared unidentified source. Particularly problematic and inconsistent is the editors' handling of Greek (some examples have already been given above). At 348 if declined forms are taken into consideration, *caimos* is better understood as a Latinization of the accusative plural κόμας instead of the accusative singular κόμην. At 487 and 741, if Greek words (and spelling) are given for Latinized forms (as is common throughout), a note should be added to explain *Chyros* as derived from ἐχυρός and *Hora* from ὥρα. At 1084 the editors give ἀνανεοῦσθαι for the manuscript's garbled *apotilnanystai*, but miss the initial *apotil-*. Lindsay gives the answer as ἀπὸ τοῦ (*Etym*. 5.36.2). At 1367 πέντα is not a Greek word; the correct form is either πέντε or πεντα-.

Similarly, the occasional translations provided in the footnotes are often either not helpful for a student edition or inaccurate. At 281–84 the editors' translation of this complex passage, which compares to the English translation of its source, Isidore, *Etym.*, 11.1.18 (*The Etymologies of Isidore of Seville*, trans. Stephen A. Barney et al. [Cambridge, 2006], p. 232), is not quite accurate. Both Rabin and Felsen (and Barney et al.) seem to take *uenientes* as modifying *spiritu* (R/F: "a radiant inner spirit that travels through slender passages from the brain"; B et al.: "a luminous inner spirit that proceeds from the brain through thin passages"). The participle *uenientes*, however, is modifying *uias* and the passage could be translated more accurately as: "some claim that vision is created by ... a radiant inner spirit, through slender passages that travel from the brain and enter the air ... ." The translation of *tunicis* as "outer membranes" is also slightly misleading as the *tunicae* are layers of tissue lining the eye specifically (see *DMLBS* s.v. "tunica" 5; and *OED* s.v. "tunic," 4a). Similarly, for the phrase "'Hiems' est ratio emisferii nuncupata" (1053), a note leads the reader to understand *ratio* as "principle" or "condition," apparently implying that the verse should be translated: "'Winter' was so named as the principle/condition of the hemisphere." But here the word *ratio* has nothing do to with the nature (principle or condition) of the hemisphere, but rather the etymological relationship between two words. The point is that the word *hiems* derives from the word *(h)emisferium*, and the word *ratio* means something along the lines of "[linguistic] relationship": "Winter (*hiems*) was so named as linguistically related to the word hemisphere (*[h]emisferium*)." At 1439–40 the translation in the note renders *Eszrahelitae* as genitive plural ("of the Israelites"). Either this is an error for the singular ("of the Israelite psalmist") or, more likely, the noun is in the nominative. And at 1512–14 the editors rightly attempt to translate a difficult passage but, seemingly over-reliant on Barney et al., render it awkwardly and, I believe, incorrectly. The Latin sentence, "Dictus autem Ecclesiasticus, eo quod totius Ecclesiae disciplinae religiosae conuersationis magna cura et ratione sit edictus," is translated as "It is called Ecclesiasticus because it has been proclaimed with great care and reason about the teaching of the holy way of life of the entire Church" (Barney et al. have: "with great care and orderliness, it has been published about the teaching of the religious way of life of the whole Church" [p. 137]). But the handling of the genitives as such would be rare, and *cura* and *ratione* are odd if taken as ablatives of manner. Instead, it is more likely that the genitives are modifying *cura* and *ratione* which do not explain how the book was proclaimed but which relate to the content of Ecclesiasticus; furthermore, *cura* does not exactly mean "care" (i.e. "diligence") as the translations have it, but probably something along the lines of "pastoral care" (i.e. "management" or "administration" of the body of believers). The verb *sit edictus* is problematic; although I can find no other example of such use, I suggest that it is here best understood in the middle voice taking an ablative object. The whole sentence may thus be rendered loosely: "Ecclesiasticus was so titled because it made known the great administration and method of the way of life of the holy teaching of the entire Church [*Ecclesiae*]."

Especially due to the large number of problems with the Latin text, this reviewer has the unfortunate obligation of concluding that this edition, despite its potential, has little scholarly value. Besides identifying some of the major sources, it does not contribute much to knowledge of the text and presents a far inferior version.

3. Concluding Remarks

The teaching of medieval Latin continues to be particularly challenging for its lack of student-friendly resources. The three books under review are all laudable for aiming to provide poorly recognized, but important and useful, texts of medieval Latin in affordable, compact editions. While Markus' *Legend of Barlaam and Josaphat* will add little to scholarship on the text itself, it does function very well as a textbook for second-year students of medieval Latin. Other textbooks of this kind are rare but certainly in demand. Since standard scholarly editions of most medieval Latin literature have now been printed, it is a fitting time to begin to produce student editions, with copious notes to facilitate understanding of the language. Though Markus' edition works well as a shorter text from a larger collection, I am certain that the same treatment to lengthier works of interest to modern undergraduate and graduate students would be very welcome. Most often students must rely on translations of varying quality to access some of the fundamental literary works of the Middle Ages. But there really should exist editions of, say, Andreas Capellanus' *De amore*, Alain de Lille's *De planctu naturae*, or the *Carmina burana*, with thorough linguistic commentary, for intermediate students, who wish to tackle these texts with or without the guidance of a teacher. The more students who have better access to learning the language through such resources, the richer future scholarship on medieval Latin literature will be.

Similar sentiment applies to the editions of the Toronto Medieval Latin Texts, which take on a different but equally important approach. Each volume aims, first of all, to provide appropriate texts to students of medieval Latin, and only secondly to disseminate works of scholarly value. And despite the importance of this second objective, the series should not lose sight of its primary, pedagogical purpose. Bayless' edition must owe part of its success to her actual experience with the texts in the classroom, whose students she acknowledges in the role of its production. On the contrary, Rabin and Felsen's edition would probably have been much improved if there already existed a proper critical edition that had collated variants, determined the best base text, examined sources, etc. A student edition of the *Disputatio puerorum* could then have focused on functioning as an affordable introduction to the salient features of the Latin encyclopedic tradition, as presented in a question-and-answer format of relatively simple medieval Latin. As long as the aim of providing accurate, helpful editions for the learning of Latin is kept as the foremost objective of the series, future volumes will remain valuable resources for sustaining and encouraging wider reading in the field.

Tristan Major
Qatar University
tmajor@qu.edu.qa

Reviews

V. ALICE TYRRELL. *Merovingian Letters and Letter Writers*. Publications of the Journal of Medieval Latin 12. Turnhout: Brepols, 2019. Pp. xxxi, 386.

This is a fine piece of scholarship on a little-known source for a well-known period: the letters of the Merovingian era (ca. 500–750). A revised PhD thesis, the comprehensive book compiles over six hundred letters from many different Latin sources. It unifies otherwise disparate source material by loosely focusing on the role of friendship and networking in Merovingian letter writing, and sheds light on the significance of Merovingian epistolography through comparisons with the epistolary practices of the Anglo-Saxons and earlier Gallo-Romans.

Tyrrell defines a letter as "personal communication" with a named addressee (p. xiv). This is a rather narrow classification: episcopal and royal letters in particular were usually intended to be read by others for their edification. Reference to Roy Gibson and Andrew Morrison's introductory chapter "What is a Letter?" would have been helpful here.[1] Another question of definition arises when the author judges which letters, of the more than 2000 that survive from the Roman west in this period, should be categorised as 'Merovingian'. Tyrrell's solution is a sensible one: "the sender and/or the recipient of the letter was resident in the Frankish kingdom during the Merovingian era, even if that residency was temporary" (p. xiii).

Following an informative introduction, Tyrrell briefly provides useful information about the fourteen different letter collections that form the basis of her study, including their manuscript and translation history. A large timeline of the collections ranging from 417 to 786 is a valuable addition to the introduction. The first three chapters deal with the male friendship networks of various Merovingian elites. Most of these are bishops. Tyrrell defines friendship (*amicitia*) between writer and recipient as a relationship where each enjoys approximately equal status. This definition may be open to question, as it excludes kings and women from *amicitia* networks, kings being too lofty in the hierarchy and non-royal women presumably too lowly, although women of all ranks could enjoy friendship networks with each other. This methodological problem is intractable. Tyrrell's solution, to devote a single chapter to the correspondence of female royals, abbesses and other elite women, is perfectly adequate.

Chapter One ("Amicitia Networks Part 1") deals with the male networks of the "hyper-Roman" Sidonius Apollinaris (430–ca. 485), Nicetius of Trier and other friends, bishops and aristocrats of the fifth and early sixth centuries (p. 3). Tyrrell

---

[1] In *Ancient Letters: Classical and Late Antique Epistolography*, ed. Ruth Morello and A.D. Morrison (Oxford: Oxford University Press, 2007), pp. 1–16.

shows that Sidonius' epistolary practice, more Roman than the Romans in its many literary allusions to Greek and Roman philosophers, bucked the general trend of Gallo-Roman aristocrats. Sidonius' episcopal successors of the late fifth and early sixth centuries, who appear to have been more ascetically minded and theologically knowledgeable than Sidonius, began to look closer to home for their social and political networks after the "barbarian invasions." Chapter Two ("Amicitia Networks Part 2") addresses the epistolary evidence for the friendship networks of poet-cum-bishop Venantius Fortunatus and other figures of the later sixth century, including Felix of Nantes, Martin Braga, Gregory of Tours, and Syagrius of Autun. Tyrrell notes the continuity of the *amicitia* tradition in this period, despite the paucity of surviving source material. Chapter Three ("Amicitia Networks Part 3") treats the letters of the Irish missionary bishop, Columbanus (540-615), who spent twenty years in Gaul, and wrote to popes Gregory I and Boniface IV (among others), and concludes with the correspondence of Anglo-Saxon bishops Boniface and Lull during their time in Gaul in the early to mid 700s. Tyrrell observes that epistolary networks in the seventh century are far more local: "only rarely do we catch a glimpse of anything resembling a connection with the Roman past" (p. 90).

The subsequent two chapters treat letters not part of the *amicitia* networks. Chapter Four concerns kings and popes and their "vertical" correspondence with bishops of Rome, who include the seventh-century Pope Martin I and eighth-century popes Zacharias and Stephen II. Chapter Five considers letters written by and to women. Tyrrell points out that, although no female epistolary voices survive from fifth-century Gaul, in the Merovingian era twenty letters were (ostensibly) authored by women, including Brunhild, Radegund and Caesaria the Younger. She categorises their letters as either "emotional" or "non-emotional". The author also considers the small number of Merovingian letters addressed to women and discusses in detail Fortunatus writing letters about food to Poitiers and the correspondence between Pope Gregory the Great and his powerful Gallic liaison Brunhild.

The final chapters look at what letters can reveal about little-known aspects of Merovingian culture. Chapter Six ("Bearers and Gifts") examines the important role of the letter bearer in imparting oral as well as written messages and observes that while 15% of Merovingian letters refer to bearers, these important historical figures "remain in the shadows" (p. 195). The chapter's second section concerns the ritual of gift exchange and shows that, overall, Merovingian letters were very rarely accompanied by gifts other than the letter itself. Chapter Seven ("Letter Writers and the Bible"), treats biblical tropes and allusions in Merovingian correspondence. Tyrrell finds that while scriptural references were employed by letter writers for various purposes, including to express emotion and establish authority, they tended not to prompt exegetical discussions. This chapter is amplified by Appendix 1, an index of all the biblical quotations cited in Merovingian letters as noted by the editors of the *Monumenta Germaniae Historica*.

The second appendix is designed to be read in conjunction with the main body of the text. It is a very useful overview of over six hundred Merovingian letters, including those not mentioned in preceding chapters. Each letter is divided according to the collections, hagiography (*vitae*) or other literature in which it is preserved and accompanied by its probable date of composition, sender, and recipient. Tyrrell additionally supplies a brief English summary of every letter's contents. Many of the letters included have not yet received translation into any modern language.

The bibliography is a comprehensive list of secondary works up to the date when the author completed her thesis, but with only about twenty works from the last decade. A second edition might offer some updates on the secondary sources, since scholarship on late-antique letter writing and collections in this period has increased exponentially since 2010. Relevant additions could include the following volumes: *Medieval Letters: Between Fiction and Document*, ed. Christian Høgel and Elisabetta Bartoli (Turnhout: Brepols, 2015); Hailey K. LaVoy, "'Why Have You Been Silent for So Long?': Women and Letter Writing in the Early Middle Ages, 700–900" (Ph.D. diss., University of Notre Dame, 2015); and *Late Antique Letter Collections: A Critical Introduction and Reference Guide*, ed. Cristiana Sogno, Bradley K. Storin, and Edward J. Watts (Oakland, CA: University of California Press, 2017).

Tyrrell's engaging language, combined with her comprehensive approach and inclusion of detailed appendices, renders this paperback volume an essential reference work for scholars and students of Merovingian history, late-antique Gaul, and epistolography.

Bronwen Neil and Catherine Rosbrook, Macquarie University

JOSHUA BYRON SMITH. *Walter Map and the Matter of Britain*. The Middle Ages Series. Philadelphia: University of Pennsylvania Press, 2017. Pp. 272 (1 plate).

Walter Map is known in modern times for *De nugis curialium* (*Courtiers' Trifles*), a wild and shambolic collection of Latin prose stories treating many subjects and genres including religious satire, saints and miracles, romance, ghost stories, and British history. A churchman, courtier to Henry II, and eventual archdeacon of Oxford, Walter was born sometime around 1130 and died in the first decade of the thirteenth century. One of the enduring curiosities surrounding Walter is that, shortly after his death, authorship of the expansive *Lancelot-Grail Cycle* of French Arthurian romances was spuriously attributed to him. Despite the fact that Walter's genuine surviving writings are all in Latin and contain no Arthurian material, this misattribution held fast until its disentanglement by scholars in the nineteenth century.

Joshua Byron Smith has two main aims in his monograph: first, he challenges the popular characterisation of Walter as an "untidy" thinker by arguing that the apparent disorganization of *De nugis curialium* is the result of scribal error and interference rather than authorial incompetence. Smith argues that the single surviving manuscript of *De nugis* was copied from an exemplar containing at least five disparate works haphazardly cobbled together, frozen in various stages of revision, and interpolated with glosses. Careful examination of *De nugis* reveals that Walter was a thorough reviser of his writings and a "sober" thinker. Smith's second aim is to emphasise the role played by Latinate networks of "inventive" clerks in the dissemination of Arthurian and Welsh-historical material in Europe during the twelfth century, as opposed to the itinerant Brittonic minstrels imagined by earlier scholars such as Roger Sherman Loomis. An author of French Arthurian romance writing in the thirteenth century wishing to attach a plausible and recognisable name to his work "could have done no better than Walter Map," Smith argues (p. 172).

The first chapter, "Wales and Romance," reconstructs Walter's medieval literary reputation. Smith situates Walter in the multicultural landscape of the Welsh-English marches of the twelfth century. Walter, therefore, occupied an apt position to transmit Welsh material to an English audience, and his writings demonstrate familiarity with Welsh lore, culture, and legal customs, even if they often do so in order to satirise the Welsh for English readers. Smith analyses the four mini-romances contained within *Distinctio* 3 of *De nugis curialium*, arguing that they reveal familiarity with the conventions of the romance genre. Smith concludes the chapter by associating Walter with the court of Henry II and its reputation for literary production and patronage: "Thus, for an early thirteenth-century reader, invoking Walter Map could call to mind at least three elements strongly linked to Arthurian literature: Henry II's court, romance, and Wales" (p. 36).

The second chapter, "Works Frozen in Revision," challenges the popular perception of *De nugis curialium* as the disorganised work of an absent-minded courtier. The work survives in one manuscript, Oxford, Bodleian Library, MS Bodley 851, and the condition of this manuscript has shaped the modern reception of the text and its author. Entering a long scholarly debate about the composition and arrangement of *De nugis*, Smith argues that Bodley 851 contains multiple versions of the same stories "frozen" in the process of revision. *Distinctiones* 1 and 2, according to Smith, are more developed reworkings of 4 and 5. Close reading reveals that Walter removed unnecessary digressions and implemented organised stylistic strategies in the process of altering his material.

Chapter 3, "Glosses and a Contrived Book," argues that Walter was not responsible for the puzzling rubrics accompanying the text in Bodley 851, and offers orthographic and palaeographic evidence in support. Smith then discusses a number of explanatory statements imbedded within the main text, introduced "*id est* ...," which he believes were once glosses later interpolated during scribal transmission. These can have the effect of confusing the sense of the surrounding passage (Smith offers an appendix cataloguing these gloss-interpolations on pp. 175–76). Smith believes that the *De nugis* was never intended to be a single, unified work and that the *Distinctiones* were originally separate texts in various stages of completion. Most of the scholarly discourse surrounding the work (sloppy rubrics, repetition of material, disordered narrative structure, etc.) arose from problems related to the compilation of the manuscript and scribal transmission, not the "untidy" mind of Walter.

Chapter 4, "From Herlething to Herla," analyses Walter's use of Brittonic motifs during the process of revising one of his stories. Recasting a story into an ancient British setting can do important literary work; in the case of the tale of King Herla, it allowed Walter to write a satire of Henry II's court and the Welsh, and to evoke the *translatio imperii* trope. Henry II not only inherited Herla's kingdom but also his *errores*: a penchant for wandering hunts and revelry lasting deep into the night. Rather than scouring texts for folklore analogues and sources, Smith believes that we ought to parse the historical and political factors which animated "Celtic" motifs in their medieval contexts.

Chapter 5, "The Welsh Latin Sources of the *De nugis curialium*," investigates Latin sources of Welsh hagiographic and historical material in circulation during the twelfth century. As the Anglo-Norman aristocracy expanded its influence into Wales, monastic and clerical institutions gathered and reworked Welsh Latin texts related to their new holdings; this process explains the appearance within the *De nugis curialium* of tales with Welsh Latin sources. Walter may have had access to these materials at St. Peter's Abbey in Gloucester, a monastery straddling the border between England and Wales. There is reason to speculate that Walter attended the school at St. Peter's, where his main patron, Gilbert Foliot, was once abbot. The legend of St. Cadog contained in *Distinctio* 2 seems to be derived from a Latin *vita* possibly held at St. Peter's, for example. Smith also offers orthographic evidence of written, as opposed to oral, transmission of Welsh place and personal names.

Chapter 6, "Walter Map in the Archives and the Transmission of the Matter of Britain," returns to the association between Walter and the *Lancelot-Grail Cycle*. *Queste del Saint Graal* was the earliest text within the *Cycle* to invoke Walter, claiming that he assembled for Henry II ancient Latin texts held in an archive at Salisbury recording the feats of Arthur, and that these texts were translated into French. Smith argues that later depictions of Walter as the author or translator of the *Cycle* were imaginative extensions of this first attribution. Smith argues that there is some truth, nevertheless, in this fictive origin story; Latinate clerics and monks did rummage through monastic archives during the twelfth century, and this was a more likely avenue for Arthurian and ancient British historical material to leave Wales and circulate throughout Europe than the wandering Breton minstrels or Anglo-Welsh translators proposed elsewhere.

Smith concludes by discussing disciplinary problems: Celticists rarely investigate networks of cultural exchange outside of vernacular literary cultures; Arthurian scholars often define the Matter of Britain narrowly and neglect Welsh Latin texts lacking Arthurian material; "Celtic" culture is prejudicially conceived of as oral and primitive as opposed to written and Latinate; folklorist approaches ignore the possibility that texts were only superficially cast with ancient Brittonic motifs by authors in later contexts and are not survivals of ancient ur-myths. Smith advocates a "minimalist approach": there was a sudden interest in Welsh-Latin hagiographic and historical materials during the twelfth century which provided authors like Walter with Brittonic material, and it was these inventive authors who transmitted the Matter of Britain to the rest of Europe.

Walter Map and the Matter of Britain is an erudite, interdisciplinary work that offers a wide range of philological, palaeographic, text critical, and historical information to support its arguments. One objection could be made to Smith's frequent reliance on orthographic evidence as medieval practices of spelling are notoriously varied and unsystematised. Nevertheless, this astute study reminds us to constantly reassess and reinvestigate basic questions surrounding medieval literature and not to shy away from challenging entrenched assumptions about medieval authors and their texts.

Dylan Wilkerson, University of Toronto

VENETIA BRIDGES. *Medieval Narratives of Alexander the Great: Transnational Texts in England and France.* Studies in Medieval Romance. Woodbridge, Suffolk: D.S. Brewer, 2018. Pp. 319.

In this study, Venetia Bridges aims to fill a gap in Alexander scholarship, most of which is organized by language and/or region. By contrast, her "transnational" discussion examines Latin, French, Anglo-Norman, and Middle English versions of the Alexander legend, specifically Walter of Châtillon's *Alexandreis*, the *Roman d'Alexandre*, Thomas of Kent's *Roman de Toute Chevalerie*, and *Kyng Alisaunder*. She not only compares these quite different works, but also attempts to set them into both a literary and socio-political context. To do the latter she has chosen one or two contemporaneous works composed in a similar context to discuss more briefly. These non-Alexander comparisons generally underscore the observations that she makes about the principal work she examines.

Two main threads run through her treatment of the various works. The first is that, as retellings of classical material, the Alexander works exemplify the notion of *translatio studii*, which involves the transfer of learning from the ancient to the medieval world. Bridges, however, broadens this definition considerably to encompass "stylistic and hermeneutic perspectives as well as language difference" (p. 21). In addition, she argues that the various authors' approaches to the past are quite divergent, so that *translatio* takes a different form in each of the examined works. Her arguments might have been clearer if she had explained her use of the term, rather than simply repeating the Latin word. The second theme of the book is that Alexander himself was, even in antiquity, subject to conflicting evaluations, and that this ambivalence continued in the medieval works that are the focus of the present study.

The first chapter treats a broad range of early Alexander narratives in Greek and Latin (not all of which were known in the medieval period), in order to illustrate the varying interpretations available to later writers. Among these are the classical *Alexander Romance*, accounts of Alexander by Diodorus Siculus, Valerius Maximus, Plutarch, Quintus Curtius Rufus, Arrian, Justin, and Orosius. While many of these accounts adopt an ethical approach, the figure of Alexander was used by some authors as a model to be emulated (Diodorus, Valerius) but by others as an example of either moral degeneration (Curtius) or pagan depravity (Orosius).

Walter of Châtillon's *Alexandreis* is treated in the second chapter. Walter shared the ambivalence of classical writers towards the figure of Alexander and expressed this attitude through a *sic et non* technique. Bridges gives a close reading of an important passage of the work in order to examine whether Walter uses his hero as a "mirror for princes," but instead concludes that he exploited "the poetics of exemplarity to undermine that very practice" (p. 79). She extends that observation also to other parts of the poem. Since Walter worked for the Bishop of Reims, Bridges uses the city's intellectual tradition (particularly its twelfth-century interest in Ovid) as the poet's political and literary context even though she admits (p. 99) that there is no evidence for direct Ovidian influence on the poem. In the remainder of the chapter, Bridges turns to Joseph of Exeter's *Ylias* as a point of comparison and finds that despite a similar classicizing subject and political context, this poet does not adopt the *sic et non* technique. From these differing approaches, she asserts that there is an "implicit debate about the practice of *translatio studii*" (p. 105).

In Chapter 3 presents Alexander of Paris's *Roman d'Alexandre* as an "anxious romance" (p. 110). Bridges notes that although the hero is offered as an ethical model, the narrative often contradicts such a reading. Particularly fascinating is her interpretation (pp. 118–19) of the passage that describes Alexander's tomb, where she finds not only commentary but "meta-commentary" in the text. The comparison texts in this chapter are Benoît de Sainte-Maure's *Roman de Troie* and Chrétien de Troyes' *Cligès*, but these are not closely connected to the *Alexandre*. The *Roman de Troie* (as Bridges observes) was produced for the court of Henry II of England. Since the patron and the place of composition of Chrétien's remain uncertain, she asserts, rather unconvincingly, that its "engagement with *translatio studii* is both local and on a broader scale" and that it confirms "the idea that debates about the performance of *translatio* are played out across a transnational context" (p. 143).

Chapter 4 treats the Anglo-Norman *Roman de toute chevalerie* and its manuscript transmission. Although this work is dated to the twelfth century, Bridges chooses to examine a mid-thirteenth-century version which includes portions of the *Roman d'Alexandre*, on the grounds that "it is at its most defined textually and geographically" (p. 155). She argues that the author's approach to *translatio* is a learned one that includes examples of dialectical process, and that he was less interested in Alexander than in his story's potential to promote different kinds of learning. For literary comparison, she has chosen the *Romance of Horn* because of the similarity of date, context and verse form to the *Roman de toute chevalerie* (p. 172). Given that *Horn* was composed in 1162–1172 and she has focussed on a a mid-thirteenth-century version of the *Toute chevalerie*, this statement is somewhat misleading. In other respects, as she acknowledges, the two works are very different. The attempt to demonstrate the Abbey of Saint Albans as a context would have been stronger had there been more discussion of the two manuscripts associated with it, and had she mentioned the *Saint Albans Compilation* (a redaction of the *Philippic Histories*) earlier in her argument.

The final chapter is devoted to *Kyng Alisaunder*, whose fragmentary state requires a fairly detailed description of the manuscript evidence, although such evidence is not a major element of the other chapters. The *Roman de toute chevalerie* was one of the *Alisaunder*'s sources, and Bridges finds that the two works share a similarly learned *translatio* but argues further that the Middle English author "consciously invokes a multilingual literary-cultural world ... beyond political and geographical boundaries" (p. 213). The comparison texts in this chapter are the *Of Arthour and Merlin* and *The Seege or Batayle of Troie*, both of which are found with the *Alisaunder* in one of its manuscripts. Despite this shared transmission, these works do not share the *Alisaunder*'s *translatio*, and both are less intellectual in their approach, and more Insular in their focus.

In addition to a brief conclusion, Bridges provides a chronology of works discussed, an extensive bibliography, and a helpful index. One error must be corrected: on p. 9, n. 24, the manuscript of the *Chanson de Roland* is Digby 23 (not 32).

This book will be of interest to literary scholars and advanced students in many different fields: medieval Latin, medieval French and Anglo-Norman, and Middle English. Given Venetia Bridges's preoccupation with interpretive questions, it should have broad appeal. Although I found some parts of this book more convincing than others, it has many strengths. Not the least of these it its scope; it is rare to see a scholar discuss such a wide range of works, composed in so many languages over such a long period of time. Moreover, Bridges did not simply produce chapters devoted to individual works or groups of works but made interesting and useful comparisons among them from one chapter to the next. She has made her treatment of these numerous texts manageable by presenting close readings of selected passages to illustrate her points. (This selectivity is complemented by the inclusion of detailed plot summaries in Appendix 2). The only weakness of her method is that the treatment of the comparison pieces can seem somewhat perfunctory. Her attempt to situate these works in a literary and political context is also admirable, and the discussion of Reims as an intellectual centre in the second chapter is excellent.

Maureen Boulton, University of Notre Dame (emerita)
Pontifical Institute of Mediaeval Studies, Toronto

SARAH B. LYNCH. *Elementary and Grammar Education in Late Medieval France. Lyon, 1285–1530.* Knowledge Communities. Amsterdam: Amsterdam University Press, 2017. Pp. 192.

Studies on elementary and grammar education in Western European countries in the Middle Ages and the early modern period have attracted the interest of only few historians and historical linguists. This book, focusing as it does on elementary and grammar education both institutionalized and informal in the French city of Lyon, is of particular interest, not only because of the richness of its documentary sources, but also because it concerns a topic in a location which promises deeper insights into late medieval schooling and education. In the fourteenth and fifteenth centuries two authorities in Lyon, the Church and the city, i.e. the cathedral and the municipal government, vied with each other in trying to control pedagogical activities. In this respect the city of Lyon, which had no university, serves as a representative example to illustrate the rising interest and influence in the provision of education by the municipal council, which competed with and gradually eroded the control over schooling of the Church, the institution which played the main role in education in the Middle Ages. The rise of the mercantile class, the significant influence of cultural and political developments in the nearby northern Italian cities, and the lack of a powerful local magnate, contributed to this development. The author indicates these tensions over formal education which arose between the two authorities, the Church and the municipal schools, and a third party, the new class of independent schools and teachers.

Lynch first explores the institutional side of elementary education provided by the leading ecclesiastical authority in Lyon as represented by the chapter of the cathedral of Saint-Jean. She then goes on to concentrate on the position of teachers, and finally on the pupils, circumstances, conditions, and some teaching materials from which the concept of elementary and grammar education emerged in this city at this particular period. The study is based on a wealth of archival documents from late medieval Lyon church and municipal records as well as medieval pedagogical literature devoted to the question of education. All of them contribute to create a picture of the educational landscape of fourteenth and fifteenth century Lyon, and its principles of instruction and common concepts. The ecclesiastical and municipal documents yield precise information, for example, about the existence of schools, their organization and administration, locations, classrooms, and the conditions under which teaching took place, together with details of the internal life of the schools in this period. They further inform us about the role of teachers in charge of or related to formal education: some of these teachers are only known by name from documentary sources and tax rolls, or from their ownership of property. There were also teachers in the city outside the support of the cathedral and the municipal council, a fact that sheds interesting light on the role of education in the city. We also learn some details about the pupils and their parents and their social and economic situation. Apart from information on the different backgrounds of the teachers, the kinds of positions they held, and the hierarchy of those who worked in the choir school attached to Saint-Jean, the archival documents provide insight into how medieval elementary and grammar teachers were perceived by their contemporaries. The scale ranged from those teaching beginners the alphabet, the syllables, the most important prayers, and elementary Latin, to *maistres d'escole* or *magistri scolarum*, who were well educated, university trained, and taught Latin to an advanced level of students. On the other hand, the archives of the city of Lyon attest to the lower esteem of those teaching the practical skill of writing, the *maistres d'escripture*, which indicates that medieval society was aware of the differences between teachers and what they taught.

In this context Lynch's book draws our attention to one notable person who was teaching at a grammar school in Lyon, but whose name is generally connected with printing in early sixteenth century Paris. As the prefaces to books edited by him during his stay in Lyon attest, Josse (Jodocus) Badius Ascensius (1462–1535) also worked as a teacher in Lyon from 1492 to 1499, instructing the children of the city's elite. The textbook entitled *Silvae morales*, with commentaries and prefaces by him, and printed by the German publisher Johann Trechsel on 14 November 1492, provides evidence that Badius must have settled in Lyon by that date, and attests to his role as a teacher. This teaching manual includes popular texts by Latin authors used for the instruction of more advanced students in late medieval grammar schools and reflects instruction on humanist terms. Apart from teaching, Badius worked as a proofreader and editor in Trechsel's printing shop.

At the same time the documents in question illustrate a tendency that for the majority of the students it was no longer necessary to be fluent in Latin, and that the rudiments of the language were often considered sufficient as the vernacular gained in importance. Nevertheless, the desire and need for literacy rose and was considered an effective tool for social advancement, especially for children lower down the social scale, which, in turn, must also have encouraged poorer teachers to offer elementary education. Considering the conditions and circumstances of both elementary and grammar-school education, Lynch's research reflects a tendency in the documentation of elementary education, that is, the lower we look down the scale of school education, the less documentary evidence we have about pupils (apart from individual cases, and some of aristocratic background), their learning, and their teaching notes. In this respect the author makes an important point that archival sources in most cases reflect the factual information that was available and considered relevant to be recorded. We learn that in grammar schools, texts based on the classic grammar for beginners of Latin, Donatus's *Ars minor*, were used. However, the records do not appear to provide further evidence. This also applies to the *Janua*, framed as a parsing grammar with a sample word representing the part of speech and further questions asked about it, deriving from the tradition ultimately based on Priscian, which usually travelled under the generic name of "Donatus," and which was used in Western Europe at this stage of learning in the late Middle Ages. Elementary grammar teaching took place orally, and teaching materials in written form from masters and notes made by pupils, were usually not preserved. Some handwritten treatises, illustrating more advanced stages of learning, may have been considered worth documenting, and printed items have survived in singular cases. This is attested by the *Silvae morales*, a collection which includes some of the most popular texts of classical and medieval authors used in late medieval grammar schools, for example, Horace's *Odes* and excerpts from Virgil, Cicero, Baptista Mantuanus, Joannes Sulpicius Verulanus, and others. The collection may have been intended as a textbook to be read by students at the later stages of their education.

The rich information provided by Lynch's book allows us partially to reconstruct schooling in Lyon in the context of urban development, its institutions, the status of teachers and pupils, and some of the teaching materials. It introduces a picture of a city where high priority was placed on secular literacy and education, to some extent encouraged by the example set by Italian cities, and which must therefore have attracted highly educated instructors teaching humanist texts that could be multiplied in this city by the new invention of printing. At the same time Lynch's book sheds light on the work and circumstances of many dedicated but nameless teachers and their work, who responded to the growing interest in learning and literacy and provided the city's children with their knowledge. The author has produced a work of considerable originality, taking us significantly further in our understanding of elementary and grammar education in France than we have travelled hitherto.

Hedwig Gwosdek, Tübingen

PAULINA TARASKIN. *Reading Horace's Lyric: A Late Tenth-Century Annotated Manuscript from Bavaria (British Library, Harley 2724)*. King's College London Medieval Studies 27. London: King's College London School of Humanities, 2019. Pp. 178.

Revising the misapprehension of glossing as a technical sideshow to mainstream intellectual history, Taraskin's investigation of medieval Horace annotations demonstrates that avowedly pagan works enjoyed a vigorous afterlife in the Christian Latin West. Though the conventional diatribe against secular learning persisted and debate sometimes oscillated between apologetics and condemnation, the evidence of heavily glossed medieval manuscripts on classical authors shows that the inherited patristic bias against pagan learning was regularly ignored by medieval Christian commentators. This book furnishes the first detailed study of medieval Horace scholia in pre-twelfth-century Europe. The research can be situated within the following fields: the medieval reception of Horace and the history of glosses and commentaries on classical texts. To date our understanding of the role of the pagan canon in medieval culture has been hampered by the fact that a substantial body of evidence lies in anonymous notes in the margins and between the lines of texts in medieval manuscripts. Taraskin contributes to the growing body of scholarship that examines glosses on classical and late antique authors (e.g. on Virgil, Persius, Lucan, Boethius, Martianus Capella, and Priscian).

Taraskin's work fills a gap. Though occasional forays have been undertaken into the early medieval reception of Horace, as illustrated by David Daintree's conclusions about the influence of Horatian prosody on the poetry of a number of prominent Carolingian writers, studies of the medieval reading of Horace have largely concentrated on the later Middle Ages, as embodied by the oeuvre of Karsten Friis-Jensen. Taraskin also widens the chronological reach of our understanding of the medieval reading of Horace in a specific region, namely Bavaria. While we have ample evidence for the influence of Horatian lyric in Bavaria for the twelfth century, as illustrated by the poems of the monk Metellus of Tegernsee, Taraskin garners the evidence for the tenth and eleventh centuries, demonstrating an interest in Horace in the ecclesiastical networks of Bavaria, for instance, in places such as Tegernsee, which witnessed a cultural upsurge after its re-establishment by Otto II in 978.

This book furnishes a detailed study of the annotations on Horace's lyric poetry in a single heavily-glossed manuscript copied in Bavaria in the late tenth or early eleventh century (British Library, MS Harley 2724). The work of compiling the glosses is ascribed to a scholiast, who may stand for a group of annotators. The focus of the study is not on ancient Horace scholia (e.g. on glosses drawn from the work of Pomponius Porphyrio and "Pseudo-Acro"), but on the numerous annotations excerpted verbatim from an array of ancient, late antique and medieval sources. To this end, the introduction and first chapter reach beyond the immediate reception of

Horace. For the sources of the glosses Taraskin identifies many classical, late antique and medieval writers (e.g. Virgil, Cicero, Ovid, Statius, Sallust, Hyginus, Solinus, Eutropius, Orosius, Dares Phrygius, Dictys Cretensis, Macrobius, Martianus Capella, Isidore, Bede, and Paul the Deacon). She notes the importance of commentaries on Virgil, Statius, and Martianus, as reflected in the use of Servius and Remigius, as well as the *Thebaid* scholia. Taraskin shows that the sources deployed by the Harley scholiast were available in south Germany by the end of the tenth century. She observes that, in at least some cases, sources were gleaned via an intermediary work. Taraskin notes, in particular, that some of the sources used by the scholiast are tralatitious by nature.

The second chapter brings us into the heart of the study, providing detailed examination of the techniques of the scholiast. Significant conclusions are reached. Taraskin underscores the practice of collecting and combining materials from the same, different, and contrasting sources, an endeavour not delimited by relevance to the Horace lemma and one that, at times, resulted in distortions and errors, as in the case of a note on Manius Curius Dentatus. For this gloss, the scholiast blends different sources reporting on various republican heroes such as Fabricius and Atilius Serranus. The achievements of these heroes were silently attributed to Curius by the Harley scholiast.

The third chapter focuses on the scholiast's attitudes to specific aspects of pagan culture, noting the prominence accorded to myth and history, and highlighting the interest in rationalising myth, an interest found in the sources deployed by the scholiast. A few minor typos aside, this is a fluently formulated piece of work providing detailed and insightful discussion ("Holz," p. xi; "consistutes," p. 27; "heros," p. 40; "her," p. 92).

Notable strengths of the book are as follows. Firstly, Taraskin signals the importance of encyclopaedic gathering, especially in the fields of myth, history, geography, ethnography, natural history, and etymology. She demonstrates that extensive narrative and systematic collection of information on a wide variety of topics were the driving forces behind the Harley glosses, not provision of grammatical, syntactical, and literal meaning. She notes the efforts of the scholiast to cross-reference and interconnect materials and demonstrates a marked difference with the later medieval commentaries on Horace. The practices of the Harley scholiast cohere with the evidence of glosses on other writers. For instance, in glosses on Virgil considerable effort was often expended on accumulating materials from all the major available commentaries on Virgil, as well as on adding new material. In addition, compilers not only assembled material from a wide variety of sources but also collated, abbreviated, and stockpiled information. For early medieval glossators, then, a crucial context underpinning their endeavours was the encyclopaedic tradition, which had deep roots in the Graeco-Roman world and significant manifestations in Visigothic Spain,

Carolingian Europe, and medieval Byzantium. Glosses exhibit the vitality of the encyclopaedic tradition, with its age-old antiquarian priorities of excerpting, summarising, synthesising, and citing authorities.

Secondly, Taraskin notes that the Harley scholiast was not driven by Christian sensitivities, exhibiting no qualms about the pagan content of Horace. Far from it, the scholiast displays a keen interest in Trojan and Roman history. Important figures from the Trojan war and from the late Republic and early Empire such as Nestor, Antilochus, Caesar, and Octavian are the protagonists of some of the glosses. One such gloss transmits the tale of Caesar's catasterism, excising unflattering details from its sources in order to chime with Horace's glorification of Augustus, Caesar's heir. Crucially, Taraskin makes a highly suggestive remark, namely that the mythical and historical figures elucidated in the glosses functioned as "beacons in the navigation of Roman and Trojan history." This predilection for the Trojan and Roman pasts was no mere affection. The medieval understanding of the past was shaped, to a significant degree, by alignment with these foundational pasts. The Franks, for example, endeavoured to establish a direct link with Troy, capitalising on this momentous marker. The interest of the Harley scholiast in Trojan and Roman history accords with the prominence of these pasts in late antique and medieval historiographical culture. It coheres with the endeavours of medieval scholars to connect their worlds with the classical past. Above all, Taraskin's book contributes substantially to our understanding of the foundational status of Troy and Rome, as well as to the specific importance of Horace and other pagan works in the book culture of the early medieval West.

Sinéad O'Sullivan, Queen's University, Belfast

Hugonis de Sancto Victore De Oratione Dominica; De Septem Donis Spiritus Sancti, ed. Francesco Siri, CCCM 276. Turnhout: Brepols, 2017. Pp. 228.

Since Beryl Smalley's foundational *Study of the Bible in the Middle Ages* was first published nearly eighty years ago (Oxford, 1941), an exuberance of scholarly activity has been steadily concentrated on the School of St. Victor. Among the large number of Victorine editions issued during this time, Francesco Siri's critical edition of Hugh of St. Victor's opuscula stands as a model of medieval Latin philology. Due to the fact that Hugh's commentaries on the Lord's Prayer and the seven gifts of the Holy Spirit often enjoyed a common circulation in the manuscript tradition and may even, as the editor suggests, have originally been understood as constituents of a single work (p. 37), Siri has creditably presented these two short commentaries together as medieval readers might have encountered them.

Despite the brevity of the foreword to this edition, Siri makes good use of these pages to introduce several decisive problems faced by editors of the twelfth-century masters in general, and of Hugh of St. Victor in particular. Most significant is Siri's suggestion that philologists should make a restrained application of the Lachmannian method to medieval school texts, which frequently frustrate the theory of authorship and of the *ipsissima verba* presupposed by the method of "common errors." While Siri is cautious to classify variants in the manuscript tradition according to the Lachmannian notion of "error," he nevertheless argues for the essential use of this theory to establish the stemmatic relations between manuscript witnesses.

After laying out these principles, the editor describes the exceptional care taken by scribes to preserve accurately the writings of Hugh, observed consistently among the large number of manuscript witnesses from the mid-twelfth to late-fifteenth century. Siri associates the relative stability in the textual tradition with the medieval edition commissioned by Gilduin († 1155). In respect to the writings originating with Hugh's activity as a Master of the Sacred Page, I am also inclined to associate this stability with the unique supervision that Hugh enjoyed over the transcription and dissemination of his oral teaching thanks to the official student-reporter whom he appointed for this purpose.[1] Following Siri's elegant description of the contents of the two treatises, the editor expresses his reluctance to date the opuscula due to a lack of specific references which would help to situate them within Hugh's Victorine career. Admittedly, the reader is disappointed to find that this section concludes without any discussion of how these texts feature more broadly into Hugh's thought or into the scholastic milieu to which they belong. Nevertheless, a volume of essays previously edited by Siri on the *Pater noster* in the twelfth century serves as a helpful supplement to the present edition.[2]

Perhaps the most notable feature of this volume is the meticulous attention that Siri has paid to the manuscript tradition. It should first be mentioned that Siri's edition of the opuscula represents a complete recension, comprising altogether some thirty-three manuscripts following his elimination of defective witnesses. Indeed, the bulk of this volume (over 150 pages) is devoted to a professional, though necessarily economical, description of each of the manuscripts together with the early printed editions, and to tracing their stemmatic relations according to the "common errors" or variants that they bear. Needless to say, Siri's philological analysis is exhaustive, and I could detect no mistakes in the intricate *stemmata codicum* that he has constructed for both texts. Little surprisingly, an extant archetype could be identified for neither of these works, so the editor was bound to reconstitute the Hugonian text according to the stemmatic weight of each variant reading.

---

[1] For Lawrence of Westminster's famous account of his activities as Hugh's *reportator*, see: *Epistola Laurentii*, in Ambrogio Maria Piazzoni, "Ugo di San Vittore 'auctor' delle 'Sententiae de divinitate,'" *Studi Medievali* 23/2 (1982), 861–955, at p. 912.

[2] *Le Pater noster au XIIe siècle: Lectures et usages*, ed. Francesco Siri (Turnhout, 2005).

Turning to the edition proper, Siri's presentation of these opuscula conforms to the high standards of philological scholarship enforced by the *Corpus Christianorum*. By adopting the patterns of orthography represented by the preponderance of the oldest manuscript witnesses and punctuating his editions strictly to restore the syntactical structure and rhythm of Hugh's prose, Siri presents these texts with the character of medieval Latinity while facilitating a modern reader's comprehension. While he includes four apparatus in each edition, Siri's greatest care appears to have gone into the critical apparatus, which makes a thorough report of significant variants in the text including certain *lectiones singulares* which he considered noteworthy. Additionally, the editor has provided a satisfactory biblical apparatus, and, perhaps most usefully, a third reserved for parallel passages in Hugh's theological corpus. Finally, the reader may be disappointed to discover how seldom the *apparatus fontium* appears (Siri has reported only two patristic sources altogether), but this sparsity can be accounted for by the short, contemplative character of these works, and the medieval master's proclivity to digest his sources and to re-present them spontaneously in an original form.

While both editions are presented virtually without fault, I have encountered one passage in the second opuscule, *De septem donis*, where Siri seems to have adopted an error into the text. His edition reads: "Medicina prodesse uult, morbus ledere intendit. Propterea solus morbus *pacem* habet, non salutem; sola medicina salutem habet, penam non habet" (p. 216, ll. 66–69, *emphasis mine*). Due to the parallel construction that Hugh is here employing and the sense demanded by the text, the variant "penam" which has been relegated to the critical apparatus must be the correct reading in place of "pacem."

Finally, some brief discussion of these two lesser-known of Hugh's opuscula is warranted. Although intellectual historians have at times drawn a sharper distinction than is justified between the theological products of the cloisters and those of the schools in the twelfth century, it has well been observed that the Victorine masters, as canons regular, held a unique position between the active and contemplative aspects of this intellectual culture.[3] Characteristically, Hugh's treatises presented here display a "scholastic" concern for logical precision while recalling the devotional movement of the monastic *lectio divina*. The *De oratione dominica* (spanning just over thirty pages) is moral in structure, beginning with Hugh's extended reflection upon the seven deadly sins (*uicia principalia*) which he then opposes to the seven petitions of the Lord's prayer. As literal-historical interpretation (*historia*) is the foundation of Hugh's

---

[3] For a perceptive account of this characteristic of St. Victor's theological programme, see Giraud, Cedric, "L'école de St. Victor dans la première moitié du XIIe siécle, entre école monastique et école cathédrale," in *L'École de St. Victor de Paris: Influence et rayonnement du moyen âge à l'époque moderne*, ed. Dominique Poirel (Turnhout, 2011), pp. 101–19.

theological programme,[4] the master proceeds from definitions and distinctions to a dialectical reflection upon the spiritual sense of the *Pater noster*. Although the six-page text that follows, *De septem donis*, is read most profitably in light of Hugh's foregoing discussion of the seven vices, this short work represents a discrete meditation upon the spiritual life. Characterizing the vices as a septiform disease (*morbus*) and a darkness (*tenebrae*), Hugh exhorts his audience to take recourse to the seven gifts of the Holy Spirit which alone provide the soul with a remedy (*medicina*) and a light (*illuminatio*). By virtue of their devotional and psychologically rich character, Siri maintains that both of the opuscula may have originated as meditations proposed for the benefit of Hugh's Victorine confrères.

Despite the relatively minor importance of these works, Francesco Siri's meticulously-executed critical edition makes a significant contribution to our understanding of Hugh's character as a theologian. Indeed, the most effective means for modern historians to arrive at a deeper understanding of the twelfth-century theological enterprise is to make available the vast corpus of unedited manuscript materials from this period. Although Hugh of St. Victor has been regarded as a seminal figure in the twelfth-century renaissance, his influence cannot be fully measured until scholars have wider access to the emerging genres of theological literature – *glossae, sententiae, postillae*, and *summae* – which represent various degrees of separation from the oral culture of the twelfth-century classroom.

David M. Foley, University of Toronto

---

[4] Hugh articulates this principle of biblical scholarship most succinctly in *Didascalicon de studio legendi*, 6.3, ed. Charles H. Buttimer, Studies in Medieval and Renaissance Latin 10 (Washington, D.C., 1939), p. 116. For the seminal discussion of *historia* as it figures into the theological programme of Hugh of Saint-Victor, see: Grover A. Zinn, "'Historia fundamentum est': The Role of History in the Contemplative Life according to Hugh of St. Victor," in *Contemporary Reflections on the Medieval Christian Tradition: Essays in Honor of Ray C. Petry*, ed. George H. Shriver (Durham, NC: Duke University Press, 1974), pp. 135–58.

Index of Manuscripts

Angers
    Bibliothèque municipale
        477: 77 n. 44

Basel
    Universitätsbibliothek
        A.I.28: 265, 283
        A.V.17: 265, 283

Berlin
    Deutsche Staatsbibliothek zu Berlin – Preussischer Kulturbesitz
        germ. oct. 138: 394 n. 85
        Lat. fol. 464: 269, 284
        Lat. oct. 293: 265, 284
        Lat. qu. 466: 269, 284
        Phillipps 1694: 376, 377
        Phillipps 1717: 235

Bern
    Burgerbibliothek
        46: 162, 284
        123: 184 n. 2

Brussels
    Royal Library of Belgium
        733–741: 269, 284
        8953–8954: 235
        9176–9177: 267, 284

Cambridge
    Christ's College
        11: 289, 292 n. 20, 294 n. 22, 295 nn. 27–28, 296 nn. 30–31, 300, 301, 302, 304 nn. 51–52, 305, 306, 307 nn. 54–55, 308, 309, 310, 311 n. 62, 314 n. 73, 315 nn. 77 and 79, 317 n. 86, 318, 368
    Trinity College
        O.2.45: 98
        R.8.6: 292, 298, 299, 300, 320 n. 1

Copenhagen
    Det Kongelige Biblioteket
        Thott 580 4°: 286

The Danish National Archives [DRA]
    fragm. 8535: 230, 235, 236, 237, 238, 241, 242, 249, 250, 251, 252, 253, 254

Einsiedeln
    Stiftsbibliothek
        321: 77 n. 44

El Escorial
    Real Biblioteca del Monasterio de San Lorenzo
        O.III.34: 237, 284

Florence
    Biblioteca Medicea Laurenziana
        Ashburnham 876: 184 n. 2
        Plut. 76.56: 267, 284
    Biblioteca nazionale centrale
        Conv. Soppr. C.VIII.2861: 267, 284
        Conv. Soppr. F.IV.733: 267, 284

Hamburg
    Staats- und Universitätsbibliothek
        Cod. Geogr. 59: 266, 284
        Cod. Petri 30b: 265, 284

Heiligenkreuz
    Stiftsbibliothek
        155: 380 n. 44

Karlsruhe
    Badische Landesbibliothek
        Aug. CCLIII: 12 n. 48

Klagenfurt
    Universitätsbibliothek
        Maria Saal 15: 266, 284
        Pap.-Hs. 152: 266, 284

Klosterneuburg
    Stiftsbibliothek
        722 A: 269, 284

Laon
    Bibliothèque municipale
        422: 77 n. 44

Leiden
  Bibliotheek der Rijksuniversiteit
    B.P.L. 69: 262, 284

Leipzig
  Universitätsbibliothek
    525: 264, 284

Lilienfeld
  Stiftsbibliothek
    145: 266, 284

Lindau
  Stadtarchiv
    E.R.B. P I 1: 267, 284

London
  British Library
    Additional 18929: 264, 284
    Cotton Nero A.ix: 288 n. 5
    Cotton Tiberius A.xv: 298 n. 37
    Cotton Titus A.XX: 98
    Cotton Vespasian A.i: 294 n. 25
    Cotton Vitellius A.X: 98
    Harley 200: 118
    Harley 2724: 422
    Harley 3724: 118
    Harley 3995: 267, 284
    Royal 5.A.v: 300 n. 45

Lyon
  Bibliothèque municipale
    414: 298 n. 38

Madrid
  Real Academia de la Historia
    78: 372 n. 12

Melk
  Stiftsbibliothek
    952: 266, 284

Milan
  Biblioteca Ambrosiana
    A 219 inf.: 269, 284
    A 223 inf.: 269, 284
    D 14 inf.: 192 n. 40
    G 111 inf.: 192 n. 40
    L 22 sup.: 67, 69 n. 12, 83
    Trotti 500: 269, 284

Montecassino
  Archivio dell'Abbazia
    234: 233 n. 24

Munich
  Bayerische Staatsbibliothek
    2° 672: 286
    cgm 2928: 286
    clm 6404: 188
    clm 6385 : 404
    clm 14583: 286
    clm 14823 : 184 n. 2, 187 n. 21, 188

Nancy
  Bibliothèque municipale
    1082: 267, 284

Naples
  Biblioteca nazionale
    VIII D 10: 269, 284
    Vindob. lat. 49 (olim Vienna, Österreichische Nationalbibliothek, 440): 261 n. 16

Olomouc
  Státni vědecká knihovna
    M II 128: 269, 284

Oslo
  The National Archives of Norway [NRA]
    Lat. fragm. 23,1–2: 229 n. 7, 235, 237, 240, 241, 245 n. 50, 249, 255
    Lat. fragm. 23,3: 229 n. 7, 230 n. 8, 235, 238, 239, 241, 243, 249, 254
    Lat. fragm. 23,4: 229 n. 7, 235, 240, 241, 245 n. 50, 249, 255
    Lat. fragm. 31: 242
    Unnumbered Box III [25]: 229 n. 7, 230 n. 8, 235, 240, 241, 245 n. 50, 255

Oviedo
   Biblioteca Capitular de la Catedral de Oviedo
      18: 261 n. 16

Oxford
   Bodleian Library
      Bodley 198: 298 n. 38
      Bodley 703: 298 n. 37
      Bodley 738: 291 n. 17, 295 n. 29, 323 n. 12, 334 n. 2, 336 nn. 11 and 13, 348 nn. 60, 61 and 62
      Bodley 851: 98, 414
      Digby 166: 118
      Lat. Hist. e. 1 (olim Admont, Benediktinerstift, MS 401): 269, 285
      Laud. misc. 213: 290 n. 11
      Rawl. C. 16: 289 n. 10
   Corpus Christi College
      10: 292, 293, 294, 298, 299, 300
   Lincoln College
      Lat. 117: 298 n. 38
      Lat. 118: 297 n. 35
   Magdalen College
      43: 268, 284

Padua
   Biblioteca del Seminario Vescovile
      74: 269, 285
   Biblioteca Universitaria
      1027: 268, 285

Paris
   Bibliothèque nationale de France
      Collection Duchesne 84: 234 n. 33, 235
      fr. 1553: 393
      lat. 5129: 376 n. 24
      lat. 8319: 184 n. 2, 188 n. 25
      lat. 8433: 148 n. 4, 149, 159
      lat. 8501A: 382 n. 48
      lat. 11332: 382 n. 48
      lat. 13246: 11 n. 48
      lat. 14503: 382 n. 47
      lat. 17656: 43 n. 8
      nouv. acq. lat. 288: 269, 285
      nouv. acq. lat. 781: 269, 285

Pavia
    Biblioteca Universitaria
        435: 394 n. 85

Philadelphia
    University of Pennsylvania, Rare Book & Manuscript Library
        60: 269, 285

Pisa
    Archivio capitolare
        C.89 inserto 3: 261 n. 16
    Biblioteca del Seminario
        50: 380 n. 46, 382 n. 47

Prague
    Castle Archives, Library of the Metropolitan Chapter of St. Vitus
        A CVI 2: 264, 284
        XXIII (1547): 227 n. 1, 231, 235
    Národní knihovna České republiky
        XIV C 16: 266, 285

Reims
    Bibliothèque municipale
        1073: 376

Rimini
    Biblioteca Civica Gambalunga
        MS SC-71: 266, 285

St. Andrews
    University of St. Andrews Library
        38904: 184 n. 2, 187 n. 19

St. Gall
    Stiftsbibliothek
        22: 294 n. 25
        268: 183, 203

Salamanca
    Biblioteca Universitaria
        2761: 261 n. 16

Salzburg
   Erzabtei Sankt Peter
      b.III.31: 269, 285
      b.IX.22: 269, 285
      b.X.30: 269, 285

Sankt Paul in Lavanttal
   Stiftsbibliothek
      Hosp. Chart. 145/4: 269, 285

Turin
   Biblioteca Nazionale e Universitaria
      D.IV.21: 268, 285

Uncastillo
   Santa Maria de Uncastillo
      10: 394

Uppsala
   Universitetsbiblioteket
      C 78: 266, 285

Vatican City
   Biblioteca Apostolica Vaticana
      Barb. lat. 1952: 270, 285
      Pal. lat. 832: 270, 285
      Pal. lat. 1358: 266, 285
      Reg. lat. 251: 183, 188, 189, 192, 203
      Reg. lat. 462: 270, 285
      Reg. lat. 620: 382–83
      Urb. lat. 308: 184 n. 2
      Urb. lat. 393: 270, 285
      Vat. lat. 3759: 266, 285
      Vat. lat. 4360: 266, 285
      Vat. lat. 9668: 227 n. 1, 235, 255

Venice
   Biblioteca nazionale Marciana
      lat. X 24 (olim 3296): 270, 285

Versailles
   Bibliothèque municipale
      Lebaudy 8° 52: 261 n. 16

Vienna
　Österreichische Nationalbibliothek
　　458: 401, 403, 404, 406
　　1628: 266, 285
　　3341: 266, 285
　　3468: 261 n. 16
　　9530: 270, 285

Warsaw
　Biblioteka Narodowa
　　8052: 268, 285

Washington
　Hay-Adams House
　　1054: 187 n. 20

Wolfenbüttel
　Herzog August Bibliothek
　　354 Helmst.: 270, 286
　　391 Helmst.: 261 n. 16
　　643 Helmst.: 286
　　Weissenb. 41: 262, 286

Zwettl
　Stiftsbibliothek
　　76: 266, 286
　　315: 266, 286

Zwickau
　Ratsschulbibliothek
　　I XII 5: 262, 286

Submissions to *The Journal of Medieval Latin*

The Journal of Medieval Latin is produced in Canada and published yearly in the autumn by Brepols in Turnhout, Belgium.

Articles should be submitted electronically, in Word format, not PDF, to the General Editor, Greti Dinkova-Bruun <greti.dinkova.bruun@utoronto.ca>. The editor may request a PDF file for articles that have special formatting, tables, or figures. If the article contains an edition of a previously unpublished text, images of the manuscript/s on which the edition is based need to be supplied together with the submission. In case the manuscripts are digitized online, it is sufficient to provide the links to these reproductions. Submissions will undergo a double blind peer review. If an accepted article includes illustrations, the author is responsible for supplying high-resolution files as well as permissions to reproduce them in the *JMLat* both in print and online.

Books for review should be sent to Cillian O'Hogan, Centre for Medieval Studies, 125 Queen's Park, 3rd floor, Toronto, ON, M5S 2C7, Canada. He can be contacted at <cillian.ohogan@utoronto.ca>. Unsolicited reviews will not be accepted.

For queries and submissions to the *Publications of The Journal of Medieval Latin* contact Michael W. Herren <aethicus@yorku.ca>.

Complete updated information about the Journal, its Publications series, and style sheet is available on our website <medievallatin.utoronto.ca>. Queries regarding the website should be directed to Greti Dinkova-Bruun <greti.dinkova.bruun@utoronto.ca>.

Subscriptions are available to both institutions and individuals, and are offered in print and online. Access to the journal's archive (1991–2011) may also be purchased. Volumes 1–24 of the Journal can be consulted on JSTOR. For further information and all inquires relating to subscriptions, contact Brepols Publishers <info@brepols.net>.